Lecture Notes in Computer S

Edited by G. Goos, J. Hartmanis, and J.

Springer
*Berlin*
*Heidelberg*
*New York*
*Barcelona*
*Hong Kong*
*London*
*Milan*
*Paris*
*Tokyo*

Gilles Barthe Peter Dybjer
Luís Pinto João Saraiva (Eds.)

# Applied Semantics

International Summer School, APPSEM 2000
Caminha, Portugal, September 9-15, 2000
Advanced Lectures

Volume Editors

Gilles Barthe
INRIA Sophia-Antipolis, Projet Lemme
2004 Route des Lucioles
BP 93, 06902 Sophia Antipolis Cedex, France
E-mail: gilles.barthe@inria.fr

Peter Dybjer
Chalmers University of Technology, Department of Computing Science
412 96 Göteborg, Sweden
E-mail: peterd@cs.chalmers.se

Luís Pinto
Universidade do Minho, Departamento de Matemática
Campus de Gualtar, 4710-057 Braga, Portugal
E-Mail: luis@math.uminho.pt

João Saraiva
Universidade do Minho, Departamento de Informática
Campus de Gualtar, 4710-057 Braga, Portugal
E-mail: jas@di.uminho.pt

Cataloging-in-Publication Data applied for

Die Deutsche Bibliothek - CIP-Einheitsaufnahme

Applied semantics : advanced lectures / Gilles Barthe ... (ed.). - Berlin ; Heidelberg ; New York ; Barcelona ; Hong Kong ; London ; Milan ; Paris ; Tokyo : Springer, 2002
(Lecture notes in computer science ; 2395)
ISBN 3-540-44044-5

CR Subject Classification (1998): D.3, F.3, D

ISSN 0302-9743
ISBN 3-540-44044-5 Springer-Verlag Berlin Heidelberg New York



Springer-Verlag Berlin Heidelberg New York,
a member of BertelsmannSpringer Science+Business Media GmbH

http://www.springer.de


Printed in Germany

Typesetting: Camera-ready by author, data conversion by Olgun Computergrafik
Printed on acid-free paper SPIN: 10873544 06/3142 5 4 3 2 1 0

# Preface

This book is based on material presented at the international summer school on Applied Semantics that took place in Caminha, Portugal, in September 2000. We aim to present some recent developments in programming language research, both in semantic theory and in implementation, in a series of graduate-level lectures.

The school was sponsored by the ESPRIT Working Group 26142 on Applied Semantics (APPSEM), which operated between April 1998 and March 2002. The purpose of this working group was to bring together leading reseachers, both in semantic theory and in implementation, with the specific aim of improving the communication between theoreticians and practitioners.

The activities of APPSEM were structured into nine interdisciplinary themes:

**A:** Semantics for object-oriented programming
**B:** Program structuring
**C:** Integration of functional languages and proof assistants
**D:** Verification methods
**E:** Automatic program transformation
**F:** Games, sequentiality, and abstract machines
**G:** Types and type inference in programming
**H:** Semantics-based optimization
**I:** Domain theory and real number computation

These themes were identified as promising for profitable interaction between semantic theory and practice, and were chosen to contribute to the following general topics:

- description of existing programming language features;
- design of new programming language features;
- implementation and analysis of programming languages;
- transformation and generation of programs;
- verification of programs.

The chapters in this volume give examples of recent developments covering a broad range of topics of interest to APPSEM.

We wish to thank the European Union for the funding which made the school possible. Generous additional support was also provided by Adega Cooperativa de Monção, Câmara Municipal de Caminha, Centre International de Mathématiques Pures et Appliquées (CIMPA), Fundação para a Ciência e Tecnologia, Instituto de Inovação Educacional, Project FACS- PraxisXXI/EEI/ 14172/1998, Microsoft Research, Região de Turismo do Alto Minho, and Sociedade Interbancária de Serviços (SIBS).

We are also very grateful to the members of the organizing committee for their excellent organization of the school and their choice of a beautiful venue; to the scientific committee for planning the scientific programme; to the second readers for their helpful reviews of the chapters of this volume; and to the lecturers and participants who made the summer school such a stimulating event.

May 2002

Gilles Barthe
Peter Dybjer
Luís Pinto
João Saraiva

# Organization

The summer school was organized by INRIA (Institut National de Recherche en Informatique et en Automatique), France and the University of Minho, Portugal.

## Scientific Committee

Gilles Barthe, INRIA Sophia Antipolis
Peter Dybjer, Chalmers University
John Hughes, Chalmers University
Eugenio Moggi, Genova University
Simon Peyton-Jones, Microsoft Research
José Manuel Valença, Minho University
Glynn Winskel, BRICS

## Organizing Committee

José Bacelar Almeida, Minho University
Gilles Barthe, INRIA Sophia Antipolis
Maria João Frade, Minho University
Luís Pinto, Minho University
Carla Oliveira, Minho University
João Saraiva, Minho University
Simão Sousa, INRIA Sophia Antipolis

## Second Readers

Thorsten Altenkirch, Nottingham University
Gilles Barthe, INRIA Sophia Antipolis
Gérard Boudol, INRIA Sophia Antipolis
Peter Dybjer, Chalmers University
Martin Escardo, Birmingham University
Jörgen Gustavsson, Chalmers University
Daniel Hirschkoff, ENS Lyon
Achim Jung, Birmingham University
Luigi Liquori, LORIA - INRIA Lorraine
Eugenio Moggi, Genoa University
Jorge Sousa Pinto, Minho University
Thomas Streicher, Darmstadt Technical University
Peter Thiemann, Freiburg University
Tarmo Uustalu, Tallinn Technical University

# Table of Contents

# An Introduction to Dependent Type Theory

Gilles Barthe[1] and Thierry Coquand[2]

[1] INRIA Sophia-Antipolis, France
Gilles.Barthe@inria.fr
[2] Institutionen för Datavetenskap, Chalmers Tekniska Högskola, Göteborg, Sweden
coquand@cs.chalmers.se

**Abstract.** Functional programming languages often feature mechanisms that involve complex computations at the level of types. These mechanisms can be analyzed uniformly in the framework of dependent types, in which types may depend on values. The purpose of this chapter is to give some background for such an analysis.
We present here precise theorems, that should hopefully help the reader to understand to which extent statements like "introducing dependent types in a programming language implies that type checking is undecidable", are justified.

## Table of Contents



## 1 Introduction

Type systems were originally introduced in programming languages to predict run-time errors at compile-time, that is before actually running the program. A

G. Barthe et al. (Eds.): Applied Semantics, LNCS 2395, pp. 1–41, 2002.

well-known result of R. Milner [98] formalizes this idea by showing that "well-typed programs cannot go wrong". Hence it is sufficient to check that a program is well-typed to ensure that it will not produce some forms of run-time errors. Well-typedness itself is ensured by a type inference algorithm which computes the possible types of a program. It should be quite intuitive, and we shall actually formulate precisely this intuition in this chapter, that the possibility of deciding if a program is well-typed or not relies on the possibility of deciding the equality of types.

A dependent type is a type that may depend on a value, typically like an array type, which depends on its length [18, 85, 92, 109, 120, 133]. Hence deciding equality of dependent types, and hence deciding the well-typedness of a dependently typed program, requires to perform computations. If arbitrary values are allowed in types, then deciding type equality may involve deciding whether two arbitrary programs produce the same result; hence type equality and type checking become undecidable. We come in this way to the fundamental tension between the original use of type systems in programming languages, and the introduction of dependent types.

Yet widely used functional languages like Haskell [29, 138], SML [99, 100, 114] or Objective Caml [49, 126] rely on increasingly advanced type systems. On the one hand, computations at the level of types are becoming increasingly complex, as illustrated for example by the introduction of functional dependencies in the Haskell class system [78, 95, 107]. On the other hand, type systems are integrating increasingly complex extensions that lack apparent structure. One can argue that it would be clearer to recognize the source of these complexities in the unifying idea that types can be computational objects, i.e. depend on values, and to present systematically these different extensions in the framework of dependent types. This is a strong motivation for working with dependent types, which appears for instance in [81, 34].

In this chapter, we present precise theorems, that should hopefully help the reader to understand to which extent statements like "introducing dependent types in a programming language implies that type checking is undecidable", are justified. Our theorems are expressed in the framework of *Pure Type Systems* (PTSs) [16, 17, 58], which provide a uniform way to represent type systems, and thus account for predicative type theories such as Martin-Löf's type theory [91], impredicative type theories such as the Calculus of Constructions [45], as well as less standard type systems that could be used as the basis of a functional programming language [116, 127]. Most of these systems feature complex computations at the level of types, but retain decidable type checking. However, adding unbounded recursion leads to undecidable type checking.

*Contents.* The first part of this chapter is concerned with presenting Pure Type Systems and their properties that are relevant in programming. We particularly focus on two prerequisites for the decidability of type checking: convertibility checking, for which we provide an algorithm inspired from [40, 42], and normalization, for which we provide a method based on a realizability interpretation inspired from [91, 38] and which follows the operational interpretation of types.

Pure Type Systems are too minimalist for practical programming and do not support mechanisms to represent basic constructions such as structures and datatypes. The second part of this chapter thus sketches an extension of Pure Type Systems with structures and datatypes. We conclude with a brief presentation of Cayenne and DML, two dependently typed programming languages.

*Acknowledgments.* Thanks to Venanzio Capretta, Pierre Courtieu, Peter Dybjer and Tarmo Uustalu for commenting on an earlier version of the paper.

## 2 Pure Type Systems

Pure Type Systems (PTSs) [17, 58] provide a framework to specify typed $\lambda$-calculi. PTSs were originally introduced (albeit in a slightly different form) by S. Berardi and J. Terlouw as a generalization of Barendregt's $\lambda$-cube [16, 17], which itself provides a fine-grained analysis of the Calculus of Constructions [45].

### 2.1 Syntax

Unlike traditional type theories which distinguish between objects, constructors and kinds, PTSs have a single category of expressions, which are called *pseudo-terms*. The definition of pseudo-terms is parameterized by a set $V$ of *variables* and a set $\mathcal{S}$ of *sorts*. The latter are constants that denote the universes of the type system.

**Definition 1 (Pseudo-terms).** *The set $\mathcal{T}$ of* pseudo-terms *is defined by the abstract syntax*

$$\mathcal{T} = V \mid \mathcal{S} \mid \mathcal{T}\,\mathcal{T} \mid \lambda V{:}\mathcal{T}.\,\mathcal{T} \mid \Pi V{:}\mathcal{T}.\,\mathcal{T}$$

*Pseudo-terms inherit much of the standard definitions and notations of pure $\lambda$-calculus. E.g.*

1. *The set of* free variables *of a pseudo-term $M \in \mathcal{T}$ is defined as usual and written* $\mathrm{FV}(M)$. *Further, we write $A \to B$ instead of $\Pi x{:}\,A.\,B$ whenever $x \notin \mathrm{FV}(B)$.*
2. *The* substitution *of $N$ for all occurrences of $x$ in $M$ is defined as usual and written $M\{x := N\}$. We may write $M(N)$ for $M\{x := N\}$ if $x$ is clear from the context.*
3. *The notion of* $\beta$-reduction *is defined by the contraction rule*

$$(\lambda x{:}A.\,M)\,N \quad \to_\beta M\{x := N\}$$

*The reflexive-transitive and reflexive-symmetric-transitive closures of $\to_\beta$ are denoted by $\twoheadrightarrow_\beta$ and $=_\beta$ respectively. We also write $P \downarrow_\beta Q$ iff there exists $R \in \mathcal{T}$ such that $P \twoheadrightarrow_\beta R$ and $Q \twoheadrightarrow_\beta R$.*

*We also adopt the usual* association *and* binding conventions *thus application associates to the left, abstraction associates to the right and application binds more tightly than abstraction. Further, we write* $\lambda \boldsymbol{x} : \boldsymbol{A}.\ M$ *for* $\lambda x_1 : A_1.\ \lambda x_2 : A_2.\ \ldots\ \lambda x_n : A_n . M$ *and* $M\ \boldsymbol{P}$ *for* $M\ P_1\ \ldots\ P_n$*. Finally, we adopt some naming conventions: we use* $x, y, z$*, etc. to denote elements of* $V$*; and* $s, s'$*, etc. to denote elements of* $\mathcal{S}$*.*

This first definition reveals three salient features of PTSs.

1. Pure Type Systems describe $\lambda$-calculi *à la* Church in which $\lambda$-abstractions carry the domain of the bound variables. As a result, many PTSs of interest enjoy decidable type checking, see Subsection 3.3. This is in contrast with type theories whose $\lambda$-abstractions are not explicitly typed, see Subsection 2.2.
2. Pure Type Systems are *minimal.* The minimality of PTSs is useful for their conceptual clarity but imposes strict limitations on their applicability, see Section 4 for a description of some constructs that escape the realm of PTSs.
3. Pure Type Systems model *dependent types.* Indeed, the type constructor $\Pi$ captures in type theory the set-theoretic notion of generalized or dependent function space. Recall that in set theory, one can define for every set $A$ and $A$-indexed family of sets $(B_x)_{x \in A}$ a new set $\prod_{x \in A} B_x$, called generalized or dependent function space, whose elements are functions with domain $A$ and such that $f\,(a) \in B_a$ for every $a \in A$. We say that $\prod_{x \in A} B_x$ is a dependent function space because the set $B_a$ in which $f(a)$ lives depends on $a$. The $\Pi$-construction of PTSs works in the same way: informally, let $A$ be a type and let $B(x)$ be a type containing a variable $x$ of type $A$. Then the type $\Pi x{:}\,A.\ B(x)$ is the type of terms $f$ such that, for every $a : A$, $f\ a : B(a)$.

The typing system of Pure Type Systems is parameterized in such a way that different type theories may be captured by a suitable choice of three parameters: the set $\mathcal{S}$ of sorts, which are the universes of the type system, the set of axioms, which introduce a typing relation between universes, and the set of rules, which determine which dependent function types may be formed and where they live.

**Definition 2 (Specifications).** *A* PTS-specification *is a triple* $\mathbf{S} = (\mathcal{S}, \mathcal{A}, \mathcal{R})$ *where*

*1.* $\mathcal{S}$ *is a set of* sorts*;*
*2.* $\mathcal{A} \subseteq \mathcal{S} \times \mathcal{S}$ *is a set of* axioms*;*
*3.* $\mathcal{R} \subseteq \mathcal{S} \times \mathcal{S} \times \mathcal{S}$ *is a set of* rules.

*Following standard practice, we use* $(s_1, s_2)$ *to denote rules of the form* $(s_1, s_2, s_2)$*.*

Every specification $\mathbf{S}$ induces a Pure Type System $\lambda\mathbf{S}$ as described below, see Subsection 2.3 for examples of specifications.

| | | |
|---|---|---|
| (axiom) | $\langle\rangle \vdash s_1 : s_2$ | if $(s_1, s_2) \in \mathcal{A}$ |
| (start) | $\dfrac{\Gamma \vdash A : s}{\Gamma, x{:}A \vdash x : A}$ | if $x \notin \mathrm{dom}(\Gamma)$ |
| (weakening) | $\dfrac{\Gamma \vdash A : B \quad \Gamma \vdash C : s}{\Gamma, x{:}C \vdash A : B}$ | if $x \notin \mathrm{dom}(\Gamma)$ |
| (product) | $\dfrac{\Gamma \vdash A : s_1 \quad \Gamma, x{:}A \vdash B : s_2}{\Gamma \vdash (\Pi x{:}\, A.\, B) : s_3}$ | if $(s_1, s_2, s_3) \in \mathcal{R}$ |
| (application) | $\dfrac{\Gamma \vdash F : (\Pi x{:}\, A.\, B) \quad \Gamma \vdash a : A}{\Gamma \vdash F\, a : B\{x := a\}}$ | |
| (abstraction) | $\dfrac{\Gamma, x{:}A \vdash b : B \quad \Gamma \vdash (\Pi x{:}\, A.\, B) : s}{\Gamma \vdash \lambda x{:}A.\, b : \Pi x{:}\, A.\, B}$ | |
| (conversion) | $\dfrac{\Gamma \vdash A : B \quad \Gamma \vdash B' : s}{\Gamma \vdash A : B'}$ | if $B =_\beta B'$ |

**Fig. 1.** Rules for Pure Type Systems

**Definition 3 (Typing rules).**

1. *The set $\mathcal{G}$ of* contexts *is given by the abstract syntax*

$$\mathcal{G} = \langle\rangle \mid \mathcal{G},\ V : \mathcal{T}$$

   *Substitution (and any other map) is extended from expressions to contexts in the usual way. Also, we let $\subseteq$ denote context inclusion, and define the* domain *of a context by the clause $dom(x_1{:}A_1, \ldots, x_n{:}A_n) = \{x_1, \ldots, x_n\}$. Finally we let $\Gamma, \Delta \ldots$ denote elements of $\mathcal{G}$.*
2. *A* judgment *is a triple of the form $\Gamma \vdash A : B$ where $\Gamma \in \mathcal{G}$ and $A, B \in \mathcal{T}$. $\Gamma$, $A$ and $B$ are the context, the subject and the predicate of the judgment.*
3. *The* derivability *relation $\vdash$ is defined on judgments by the rules of Figure 1. If $\Gamma \vdash A : B$ then $\Gamma$, $A$, and $B$ are* legal. *If moreover $B \in \mathcal{S}$, then $A$ is a* type.

There are some important differences between judgments, say in simply typed $\lambda$-calculus, and judgments in PTSs. First, contexts may introduce type variables, typically with assertions of the form $A : s$ with $s \in \mathcal{S}$. Second, contexts are *ordered lists* so as to handle possible dependencies. For example, the context $A : s,\ a : A$ (read $A$ is a type of sort $s$ and $a$ is of type $A$) introduces a "type variable" and an "object variable" and is meaningful, whereas $a : A,\ A : s$ ($a$ is of type $A$ and $A$ is a type of sort $s$) is not.

The typing system for PTSs is concise and consists of seven rules: (axiom) embeds the relation $\mathcal{A}$ into the type system. (start) and (weakening) allow the introduction of variables in a context. (product) allows for dependent function types to be formed, provided they match a rule in $\mathcal{R}$. (abstraction) allows to build $\lambda$-abstractions; note that the rule has a side condition requiring that the dependent function type is well-formed. (application) allows to form applications; note that, in order to accommodate type dependencies, the type of an application is obtained by substituting the second argument into the codomain of the type of the first argument of the application. The last rule (conversion) ensures that convertible types, i.e. types that are $\beta$-equal, have the same inhabitants. The (conversion) rule is crucial for higher-order type theories, because types are $\lambda$-terms and can be reduced, and for dependent type theories, because terms may occur in types.

### 2.2 Variations on Pure Type Systems

Pure Type Systems feature typed $\lambda$-abstractions of the form $\lambda x : A.\, M$ and therefore only cover typed $\lambda$-calculi *à la* Church. However, there have been a number of proposals to adapt PTSs to typed $\lambda$-calculi *à la* Curry, that feature untyped, or domain-free, $\lambda$-abstractions of the form $\lambda x \,.\, M$:

- Type Assignment Systems: in [15], S. van Bakel, L. Liquori, S. Ronchi della Rocca and P. Urzyczyn introduce a cube of Type Assignment Systems which feature (1) a stratification of expressions into objects, constructors (of which types are a special case) and kinds; (2) an implicit type abstraction and implicit type application *à la* ML for objects. Hence objects are untyped $\lambda$-terms and do not carry any type information.
- Domain-Free Type Systems: [23] introduces a variant of Pure Type Systems, coined Domain-Free Pure Type Systems, which only differs from PTSs by the use of untyped $\lambda$-abstractions. Domain-Free Pure Type Systems are tightly related to PTSs via an erasure function $|.|$ which removes domains from $\lambda$-abstractions, and can be used to represent standard logics exactly as PTSs. However, Domain-Free Pure Type Systems and Pure Type Systems exhibit slightly different behaviors, in particular w.r.t. type checking and w.r.t. the equational theory of inconsistent type theories, see [21] and Exercise 11.
- Implicit Type Systems: in [101], A. Miquel introduces an Implicit Calculus of Constructions, which extends the Domain-Free Calculus of Constructions with the implicit operations of Type Assignment Systems. Unlike [15] which features implicit type abstraction/application for objects and explicit type abstraction/application for kinds, the Implicit Calculus of Constructions features explicit and implicit type abstraction/application, both for objects and constructors. Formally, this is achieved by the introduction of two type formers: the $\forall$-type former for implicit dependent function type and the $\Pi$-type former for the usual, explicit, dependent function type.

The use of untyped $\lambda$-abstractions leads to undecidable type checking even for non-dependent type systems. In fact, even the domain-free variant of $\lambda 2$ has undecidable type checking. However, a limited form of decidability is still possible, see Exercise 14.

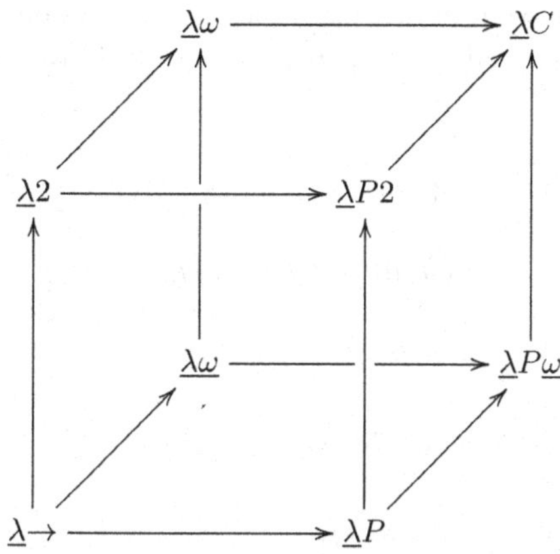


**Fig. 2.** The λ-cube

## 2.3 Instances

In this subsection, we recast some existing type theories in the framework of Pure Type Systems.

**Non-dependent Type Systems.** In [16, 17], H. Barendregt proposes a fine-grained analysis of the Calculus of Constructions based on the so-called λ-cube. The cube, depicted in Figure 2, consists of eight Pure Type Systems, most of which correspond to type systems that occur in the literature; arrows represent inclusion between systems. Systems on the left-hand side of the cube are non-dependent, because an expression $M : A$ with $A : *$ (such an expression corresponds to a program) cannot appear as a subexpression of $B : *$ (such an expression corresponds to a type); in logical terms, non-dependent systems of the λ-cube correspond to propositional logics. Among these systems one finds the simply typed λ-calculus $\lambda \rightarrow$, the polymorphic λ-calculus $\lambda 2$, that corresponds to Girard's system $F$, and the higher-order λ-calculus $\lambda\omega$ that corresponds to Girard's $F_\omega$ [64].

**Definition 4.** *Let $\mathcal{S} = \{*, \Box\}$ and $\mathcal{A} = \{(* : \Box)\}$.*

1. *The system $\lambda \rightarrow$ is obtained by setting*

$$\mathcal{R} = \{(*, *)\}$$

2. *The system $\lambda 2$ is obtained by setting*

$$\mathcal{R} = \{(*, *), (\Box, *)\}$$

3. *The system $\lambda\omega$ is obtained by setting*

$$\mathcal{R} = \{(*, *), (\Box, *), (\Box, \Box)\}$$

There are further well-known examples of non-dependent Pure Type Systems, for example $\lambda U$ and $\lambda U^-$, that correspond to Girard's System $U$ and System $U^-$ respectively [64].

**Definition 5.** *Let $\mathcal{S} = \{*, \Box, \triangle\}$ and $\mathcal{A} = \{(*, \Box), (\Box, \triangle)\}$.*

1. *The system $\lambda U^-$ is obtained by setting*

$$\mathcal{R} = \{(*, *), (\Box, *), (\Box, \Box), (\triangle, \Box)\}$$

2. *The system $\lambda U$ is obtained by setting*

$$\mathcal{R} = \{(*, *), (\Box, *), (\Box, \Box), (\triangle, *), (\triangle, \Box)\}$$

These systems are inconsistent in the sense that one can find a pseudo-term $M$ such that the judgment $A : * \vdash M : A$ is derivable. An interesting open question concerns the existence of fixpoint combinators in inconsistent Pure Type Systems, see Exercise 11.

Our last examples of non-dependent PTSs correspond to systems with predicative polymorphism. Recall that polymorphism in $\lambda 2$ is impredicative in the sense that one may form a type, i.e. an element of $*$, by quantifying over $*$. There are weaker PTSs that allow the quantification to be formed but have it live in a different universe.

**Definition 6.**

1. *The system $\lambda 2_{\mathrm{ml}}$ is obtained by setting*

$$\begin{aligned} \mathcal{S} &= \{*, \Box, \triangle\} \\ \mathcal{A} &= \{(* : \Box)\} \\ \mathcal{R} &= \{(*, *), (\Box, *, \triangle), (\Box, \triangle)\} \end{aligned}$$

2. *The system $\lambda 2_{\mathrm{x}}$ is obtained by setting*

$$\begin{aligned} \mathcal{S} &= \{*, \Box\} \\ \mathcal{A} &= \{(* : \Box)\} \\ \mathcal{R} &= \{(*, *), (\Box, *, \Box), (\Box, \Box)\} \end{aligned}$$

The system $\lambda 2_{\mathrm{ml}}$ distinguishes between types, i.e. pseudo-terms of type $*$, and polytypes, i.e. pseudo-terms of type $\triangle$ which contain a universal quantification over $*$. If we identify polytypes and kinds, i.e. pseudo-terms of type $\Box$, we obtain the system $\lambda 2_{\mathrm{x}}$, which is higher-order thanks to the rule $(\Box, \Box)$. In contrast to $\lambda 2$, $\lambda 2_{\mathrm{x}}$ admits set-theoretical models, see Exercise 2, and can be given a realizability interpretation, see Subsection 3.4.

**Dependent Types.** PTSs on the right-hand side of the $\lambda$-cube feature the rule $(*, \Box)$ which allows dependent types to be formed. Indeed, these systems allow to type expressions $B : *$ which contain as subexpressions $M : A : *$. In logical terms, these systems correspond to predicate logics.

**Definition 7.** *Let $\mathcal{S} = \{*, \Box\}$ and $\mathcal{A} = \{(* : \Box)\}$.*

1. *The system $\lambda P$ is obtained by setting*

$$\mathcal{R} = \{(*, *), (*, \Box)\}$$

2. *The system $\lambda P2$ is obtained by setting*

$$\mathcal{R} = \{(*, *), (\Box, *), (*, \Box)\}$$

3. *The system $\lambda C$ is obtained by setting*

$$\mathcal{R} = \{(*, *), (\Box, *), (*, \Box), (\Box, \Box)\}$$

The system $\lambda P$ captures the essence of Logical Frameworks [24, 69, 106, 120]. Variants of $\lambda P$ are implemented by Automath [106], Elf [119] and Alf [88]. Exercise 3 illustrates how formal theories can be encoded in such systems. The system $\lambda P2$, which is the PTS counterpart of the type system of [84], is powerful enough to encode the usual connectives and quantifiers, with their standard natural deduction rules, see Exercise 4. Finally, $\lambda C$, which is the most complex system of the $\lambda$-cube, is the PTS counterpart of the Calculus of Constructions [45]; its connections with higher-order logic are analyzed in [56].

Next we turn to an extension of the Calculus of Constructions with universes.

**Definition 8.** *The system $\lambda C^\omega$ is obtained by setting*

$$\begin{aligned}
\mathcal{S} &= \{*, \Box_i \quad (i \in \mathbb{N})\} \\
\mathcal{A} &= \{(* : \Box_0), (\Box_i : \Box_{i+1}) \quad (i \in \mathbb{N})\} \\
\mathcal{R} &= \{(*, *), (\Box_i, *), (*, \Box_i), (\Box_i, \Box_j, \Box_{\mathsf{max}(i,j)}) \qquad (i, j \in \mathbb{N})\}
\end{aligned}$$

A. Miquel [102] has recently given an elegant translation of intuitionistic Zermelo set theory with the Anti-Foundation Axiom in $\lambda C^\omega$—actually, Miquel's encoding only uses universes up to $\Box_2$.

The next PTS combines dependent types and predicative polymorphism. It is inspired by R. Harper and J. Mitchell's work on the ML type system [71] and by the type system of Cayenne [12].

**Definition 9.** *The system $\lambda C_{\mathrm{x}}$ is obtained by setting*

$$\begin{aligned}
\mathcal{S} &= \{*, \Box\} \\
\mathcal{A} &= \{(* : \Box)\} \\
\mathcal{R} &= \{(*, *), (\Box, *, \Box), (*, \Box), (\Box, \Box)\}
\end{aligned}$$

It can be shown that $\lambda C_{\mathrm{x}}$ has set-theoretical models as $\lambda 2_{\mathrm{x}}$, see e.g. [71]. In Subsection 3.4, we give a realizability interpretation of $\lambda C_{\mathrm{x}}$.

Our final example of PTS is exactly the original impredicative (and inconsistent) version of Martin-Löf's type theory [90].

**Definition 10.** *The system* $\lambda *$ *is obtained by setting*

$$\begin{aligned}\mathcal{S} &= \{*\}\\ \mathcal{A} &= \{(* : *)\}\\ \mathcal{R} &= \{(*, *)\}\end{aligned}$$

As for $\lambda U$ and $\lambda U^{-}$, there exists a pseudo-term $M$ such that $A : * \vdash M : A$.

## 3 Properties of Pure Type Systems

Pure Type Systems have an extensive theory which covers different aspects of type theory, including computational properties, decidability questions or representability questions. The purpose of this section is to summarize some of the most significant results in this theory and to emphasize their relevance in a general theory of type systems. Most proofs are omitted, since they can be found elsewhere, see [17, 56, 58].

### 3.1 Definitions

Some properties of PTSs rely on the erasure of legal terms being weakly normalizing.

**Definition 11.**

1. *The set* $\underline{T}$ *of (domain-free) pseudo-terms is defined by the abstract syntax*

$$\underline{T} = V \mid S \mid \underline{T}\,\underline{T} \mid \lambda V . \underline{T} \mid \Pi V{:}\underline{T}.\underline{T}$$

*Substitution is defined as usual and denoted by* $.\{. := .\}$. *As for domain-full pseudo-terms, we may write* $M(N)$ *for* $M\{x := N\}$ *if* $x$ *is clear from the context and* $M(N_1, \ldots, N_k)$ *for* $M\{x_1 := N_1\}\ldots\{x_k := N_k\}$ *whenever* $x_1, \ldots, x_k$ *are clear from the context.*

2. $\underline{\beta}$-reduction *is defined by the contraction rule*

$$(\lambda x . M)\, N \quad \to_{\underline{\beta}} M\{x := N\}$$

*The reflexive-transitive and reflexive-symmetric-transitive closure of* $\to_{\underline{\beta}}$ *are denoted by* $\twoheadrightarrow_{\underline{\beta}}$ *and* $=_{\underline{\beta}}$ *respectively.*

3. *Weak head reduction* $\to_{\underline{wh}}$ *is the relation*

$$(\lambda x.\ P)\ Q\ \boldsymbol{R} \quad \to_{\underline{wh}} \quad P\{x := Q\}\ \boldsymbol{R}$$

*(Weak-head reduction differs from* $\underline{\beta}$*-reduction by applying only at the top-level.)*

Note that $\to_{\underline{\beta}}$ is confluent and that there is an obvious erasure function $|.| : \mathcal{T} \to \underline{\mathcal{T}}$ which removes tags from $\lambda$-abstractions.

**Definition 12.**

1. *A domain-free pseudo-term $M$ is in* weak head normal form *if there is no $N \in \underline{\mathcal{T}}$ such that $M \to_{\underline{wh}} N$. We let* WHNF *denote the set of weak head normal forms.*
2. *A domain-free pseudo-term $M$ is* weakly head normalizing *if there exists $N \in$ WHNF such that $M \twoheadrightarrow_{\underline{wh}} N$. We let* WHN *denote the set of weakly head normalizing terms.*
3. *A domain-free pseudo-term $M$ is in $\underline{\beta}$-*normal form *if there is no $N \in \underline{\mathcal{T}}$ such that $M \to_{\underline{\beta}} N$. We let* $\mathrm{NF}_{\underline{\beta}}$ *denote the set of $\underline{\beta}$-normal forms.*
4. *A domain-free pseudo-term $M$ is $\underline{\beta}$-*weakly normalizing *if there exists $N \in \mathrm{NF}_{\underline{\beta}}$ such that $M \twoheadrightarrow_{\underline{\beta}} N$. We let* $\mathrm{WN}_{\underline{\beta}}$ *denote the set of $\underline{\beta}$-weakly normalizing terms.*
5. *A domain-free pseudo-term $M$ is $\underline{\beta}$-*strongly normalizing *iff all reduction paths starting from $M$ are finite, i.e. there is no infinite reduction sequence*

$$M \to_{\underline{\beta}} M_1 \to_{\underline{\beta}} M_2 \to_{\underline{\beta}} \dots$$

*We let* $\mathrm{SN}_{\underline{\beta}}$ *denote the set of $\underline{\beta}$-strongly normalizing terms.*
6. *By abuse of notation, we say that a (domain-full) pseudo-term $M$ belongs to* WHNF *(resp.* WHN, $\mathrm{NF}_{\underline{\beta}}$, $\mathrm{WN}_{\underline{\beta}}$, $\mathrm{SN}_{\underline{\beta}}$*) if $|M|$ does.*

Finally, for any set $X \subseteq \mathcal{T}$, we write $\lambda\mathbf{S} \models X$ iff $M \in X$ for every judgment $\Gamma \vdash M : A$ derivable in the system $\lambda\mathbf{S}$.

### 3.2 Basic Properties

The first lemma collects some closure properties of typing judgments.

**Lemma 1.**

1. Substitution. *If $\Gamma, x{:}A, \Delta \vdash B : C$ and $\Gamma \vdash a : A$, then $\Gamma, \Delta(a) \vdash B(a) : C(a)$.*
2. Correctness of Types. *If $\Gamma \vdash A : B$ then either $B \in \mathcal{S}$ or $\exists s \in \mathcal{S}.\ \Gamma \vdash B : s$.*
3. Thinning. *If $\Gamma \vdash A : B$, $\Delta$ is legal and $\Gamma \subseteq \Delta$, then $\Delta \vdash A : B$.*
4. Strengthening. *If $\Gamma_1, x : A, \Gamma_2 \vdash b : B$ and $x \notin \mathrm{FV}(\Gamma_2) \cup \mathrm{FV}(b) \cup \mathrm{FV}(B)$ then $\Gamma_1, \Gamma_2 \vdash b : B$.*

The proof of strengthening is rather involved [25].

**Proposition 1.**

1. *Confluence. Let $M, N \in \mathcal{T}$. If $M =_\beta N$ then $M, N \twoheadrightarrow_\beta P$ for some $P \in \mathcal{T}$.*
2. *Subject Reduction. If $\Gamma \vdash M : A$ and $M \to_\beta N$ then $\Gamma \vdash N : A$.*

The proof of Subject Reduction relies on confluence being a property of arbitrary pseudo-terms, not only of legal terms. Furthermore, Subject Reduction and Confluence ensure that the type system of PTSs is sound in the sense that any two convertible legal terms are convertible through legal terms [60] and that weak head normalization implies logical consistency.

**Proposition 2 (Consistency).**

1. *For every $s \in \mathcal{S}$, there is no $M \in$ WHNF such that $A : s \vdash M : A$.*
2. *If $\lambda\mathbf{S} \models$ WHN then there is no $s \in \mathcal{S}$ and $M \in \mathcal{T}$ such that $A : s \vdash M : A$.*

*Proof.* 2 follows from 1 by Subject Reduction, so we focus on 1. We prove 1 by contradiction, using confluence of $\beta$-reduction. Assume that such an $M$ exists. We analyze the possible shapes of $M$:

- if $M$ were a dependent function type, then $A$ would be convertible to a sort, which is impossible by confluence of $\beta$-reduction;
- if $M$ were a $\lambda$-abstraction, then $A$ would be convertible to an expression of the form $\Pi x{:}B.\,C$, which is impossible by confluence of $\beta$-reduction;
- if $M$ were a sort, then $A$ would be convertible to a sort, which is impossible by confluence of $\beta$-reduction.

Hence $M$ must be an application. Since $M$ is legal and $M \in$ WHNF, we must have $M \in \mathcal{B}$ where $\mathcal{B}$ is defined by the syntax

$$\mathcal{B} = V \mid \mathcal{B}\ \mathcal{T}$$

Furthermore, $M$ should be of the form $A\ P_1\ \ldots\ P_k$ since $A$ is the only variable declared in the context. But then $A$ would be of dependent function type $\Pi x{:}B.\,C$, which is impossible by confluence of $\beta$-reduction.

We conclude this subsection with properties related to specific classes of PTSs.

**Definition 13.** *Let $\mathbf{S} = (\mathcal{S}, \mathcal{A}, \mathcal{R})$ be a specification.*

1. $\mathbf{S}$ *is* functional *if for every $s_1, s_2, s_2', s_3, s_3' \in \mathcal{S}$,*

$$\begin{array}{ll}(s_1, s_2) \in \mathcal{A} \quad \wedge (s_1, s_2') \in \mathcal{A} & \Rightarrow s_2 \equiv s_2' \\ (s_1, s_2, s_3) \in \mathcal{R} \wedge (s_1, s_2, s_3') \in \mathcal{R} & \Rightarrow s_3 \equiv s_3'\end{array}$$

2. $\mathbf{S}$ *is* injective *if it is functional and for every $s_1, s_1', s_2, s_2', s_3 \in \mathcal{S}$,*

$$\begin{array}{ll}(s_1, s_2) \in \mathcal{A} \quad \wedge (s_1', s_2) \in \mathcal{A} & \Rightarrow s_1 \equiv s_1' \\ (s_1, s_2, s_3) \in \mathcal{R} \wedge (s_1, s_2', s_3) \in \mathcal{R} & \Rightarrow s_2 \equiv s_2'\end{array}$$

Functional PTSs enjoy Uniqueness of Types, and Injective PTSs enjoy a Classification Lemma. Both properties are useful for type checking [20].

**Lemma 2.**

1. *Uniqueness of Types. If $\mathbf{S}$ is functional, then*

$$\Gamma \vdash M : A \quad \wedge \quad \Gamma \vdash M : B \quad \Rightarrow \quad A =_\beta B$$

2. *Classification. If $\mathbf{S}$ is injective, then*

$$\begin{array}{ll}\Gamma \vdash M : A \wedge \Gamma \vdash A : s & \Rightarrow \mathsf{elmt}(\Gamma|M) = s \\ \Gamma \vdash M : A \wedge A \in \mathcal{S} & \Rightarrow \mathsf{sort}(\Gamma|M) = A\end{array}$$

*where* $\mathsf{elmt}(.|.) : \mathcal{G} \times \mathcal{T} \rightharpoonup \mathcal{S}$ *and* $\mathsf{sort}(.|.) : \mathcal{G} \times \mathcal{T} \rightharpoonup \mathcal{S}$ *are defined by simultaneous recursion in Figure 3.*

Note that the functions $\mathsf{elmt}(.|.)$ and $\mathsf{sort}(.|.)$ are non-deterministic when their first argument is a pseudo-context in which a variable occurs twice. However, such pseudo-contexts are not legal.

$$
\begin{aligned}
\mathsf{elmt}(\Gamma_0, x : A, \Gamma_1 | x) &= \mathsf{sort}(\Gamma_0 | A) \\
\mathsf{sort}(\Gamma_0, x : A, \Gamma_1 | x) &= \mathsf{elmt}(\Gamma_0, x : A, \Gamma_1 | x)^- \\
\mathsf{elmt}(\Gamma | s) &= (\mathsf{sort}(\Gamma | s))^+ \\
\mathsf{sort}(\Gamma | s) &= s^+ \\
\mathsf{elmt}(\Gamma | M\ N) &= \mu(\mathsf{elmt}(\Gamma | N), \mathsf{elmt}(\Gamma | M)) \\
\mathsf{sort}(\Gamma | M\ N) &= (\mathsf{elmt}(\Gamma | M\ N))^- \\
\mathsf{elmt}(\Gamma | \lambda x{:}A.\ M) &= \rho(\mathsf{sort}(\Gamma | A), \mathsf{elmt}(\Gamma, x : A | M)) \\
\mathsf{sort}(\Gamma | \lambda x{:}A.\ M) &= (\mathsf{elmt}(\Gamma | \lambda x{:}A.\ M))^- \\
\mathsf{elmt}(\Gamma | \Pi x{:}\ A.\ B) &= (\mathsf{sort}(\Gamma | \Pi x{:}\ A.\ B))^+ \\
\mathsf{sort}(\Gamma | \Pi x{:}\ A.\ B) &= \rho(\mathsf{sort}(\Gamma | A), \mathsf{sort}(\Gamma, x : A | B))
\end{aligned}
$$

where

$$
\begin{aligned}
s^- &= s' \text{ if } (s', s) \in \mathcal{A} \\
s^+ &= s' \text{ if } (s, s') \in \mathcal{A} \\
\rho(s_1, s_2) &= s_3 \text{ if } (s_1, s_2, s_3) \in \mathcal{R} \\
\mu(s_1, s_2) &= s_3 \text{ if } (s_1, s_3, s_2) \in \mathcal{R}
\end{aligned}
$$

**Fig. 3.** Classification

### 3.3 Type Checking and Type Inference

Some applications of PTSs require the decidability of type checking. In practice, type checking is often reduced to type inference, which aims at inferring the possible types of a given expression in a fixed context.

**Definition 14.** *Let $\lambda\mathbf{S}$ be a Pure Type System.*

1. *The type checking problem for $\lambda\mathbf{S}$ consists in deciding, given $\Gamma$, $M$ and $A$, whether the judgment $\Gamma \vdash M : A$ is derivable according to the rules of Pure Type Systems.*
2. *The type inference problem for $\lambda\mathbf{S}$ consists in deciding, given $\Gamma$ and $M$, whether there exists $A \in \mathcal{T}$ such that the judgment $\Gamma \vdash M : A$ is derivable according to the rules of Pure Type Systems.*

The typing rules of PTSs do not yield a type inference algorithm, in particular because the typing rules are not syntax-directed. Indeed, one cannot determine from the shape of $M$ what the last rule to derive $\Gamma \vdash M : A$ must be; this is partly caused by the rules of (weakening) and (conversion), which can be applied at any point in a derivation. The standard strategy to recover syntax-directedness is as follows:

1. first, specify a strategy to check convertibility of legal terms;
2. second, push applications of (weakening) as high as possible in the derivation tree, by using a restricted weakening rule

$$\frac{\Gamma \vdash A : B \quad \Gamma \vdash C : s}{\Gamma,\ x : C \vdash A : B} \quad \text{if } A \in \mathcal{S} \cup V \setminus \mathrm{dom}(\Gamma)$$

   and distribute applications of (conversion) over the remaining rules.

Convertibility is undecidable in general, see Exercise 13, but for $\beta$-weakly normalizing terms one can decide convertibility simply by reducing the expressions to their normal form and checking whether these normal forms coincide. Below we present an alternative, inspired from [40], where convertibility is checked by reducing expressions to weak-head normal form and proceeding recursively on subexpressions of these weak-head normal forms.

**Definition 15.**

1. Weak-head reduction $\rightarrow_{wh}$ *is the smallest relation such that*

$$(\lambda x : A.\ P)\ Q\ \boldsymbol{R} \quad \rightarrow_{wh} \quad P\{x := Q\}\ \boldsymbol{R}$$

*(Weak-head reduction differs from $\beta$-reduction by applying only at the top-level.)*

2. *The relation $M \Leftrightarrow N$ is defined by the rules of Figure 4.*

$$\frac{}{s \Leftrightarrow s}$$

$$\frac{M_1 \Leftrightarrow N_1 \quad \ldots \quad M_s \Leftrightarrow N_s}{x\ M_1\ \ldots\ M_s \Leftrightarrow x\ N_1\ \ldots\ N_s}$$

$$\frac{A \Leftrightarrow A' \qquad B \Leftrightarrow B'}{\Pi x{:}\,A.\ B \Leftrightarrow \Pi x{:}\,A'.\ B'}$$

$$\frac{M \Leftrightarrow M'}{\lambda x{:}A.\ M \Leftrightarrow \lambda x{:}A'.\ M'}$$

$$\frac{M \twoheadrightarrow_{wh} M' \qquad M' \Leftrightarrow N' \qquad N \twoheadrightarrow_{wh} N'}{M \Leftrightarrow N}\ M \neq M' \text{ or } N \neq N'$$

**Fig. 4.** Checking convertibility

**Lemma 3.**

1. *The relation $\Leftrightarrow$ is symmetric and transitive.*
2. *If $M \in \mathrm{WN}_{\underline{\beta}}$ and $M =_\beta N$ then $M \Leftrightarrow N$.*

The following lemma is an adaptation of [23].

**Lemma 4.** *Assume $\Gamma \vdash M : A$, $\Gamma \vdash M' : A'$ and $M \Leftrightarrow M'$ and $M, M' \in \mathrm{NF}_{\underline{\beta}}$.*

1. *If $A =_\beta A'$ then $M =_\beta M'$.*
2. *If $A, A' \in \mathcal{S}$ then $M =_\beta M'$.*

Soundness follows.

**Corollary 1 (Soundness).** *Suppose* $\lambda\mathbf{S} \models \mathrm{WN}_{\underline{\beta}}$. *Assume* $\Gamma \vdash M : A$, $\Gamma \vdash M' : A'$ *and* $M \Leftrightarrow M'$.

1. *If* $A =_\beta A'$ *then* $M =_\beta M'$.
2. *If* $A, A' \in \mathcal{S}$ *then* $M =_\beta M'$.

*Proof.* By hypothesis, $M \twoheadrightarrow_\beta N$ and $M' \twoheadrightarrow_\beta N'$ with $N, N' \in \mathrm{NF}_{\underline{\beta}}$. By Subject Reduction $\Gamma \vdash N : A$ and $\Gamma \vdash N' : A'$. By Lemma 3.2, $M \Leftrightarrow N$ and $M' \Leftrightarrow N'$, and by Lemma 3.1, $N \Leftrightarrow N'$. Hence by Lemma 4.1, $N =_\beta N'$. It follows that $M =_\beta M'$.

**Corollary 2 (Completeness).** *Assume* $\lambda\mathbf{S} \models \mathrm{WN}_{\underline{\beta}}$. *If* $\Gamma \vdash M : A$ *and* $M =_\beta N$ *then* $M \Leftrightarrow N$.

*Proof.* Immediate from Lemma 3.2.

Decidability of $\Leftrightarrow$ follows.

**Proposition 3 (Decidability of convertibility).** *Assume* $\lambda\mathbf{S} \models \mathrm{WN}_{\underline{\beta}}$. *Furthermore, suppose that* $\Gamma \vdash M : A$ *and* $\Gamma' \vdash M' : A'$ *are derivable, and that* $A =_\beta A'$ *or* $A, A' \in \mathcal{S}$. *Then* $M \Leftrightarrow M'$ *and* $M =_\beta M'$ *are equivalent and decidable. More precisely, the algorithm of Figure 4 terminates for the inputs* $M$ *and* $M'$.

Proposition 3 together with [25] yield a general decidability result for decidable PTSs, where a PTS $\lambda\mathbf{S}$ is decidable if $\mathbf{S} = (\mathcal{S}, \mathcal{A}, \mathcal{R})$ and $\mathcal{A}$, $\mathcal{R}$, $\exists s' \in \mathcal{S}.\ (s, s') \in \mathcal{A}$, $\exists s_3 \in \mathcal{S}.\ (s_1, s_2, s_3) \in \mathcal{R}$ and equality on $\mathcal{S}$ are decidable.

**Theorem 1.** *Let* $\lambda\mathbf{S}$ *be a decidable* PTS *with* $\mathbf{S} = (\mathcal{S}, \mathcal{A}, \mathcal{R})$. *Assume that* $\lambda\mathbf{S} \models \mathrm{WN}_{\underline{\beta}}$. *Then type checking and type inference for* $\lambda\mathbf{S}$ *are decidable.*

The question remains to define efficient, sound and complete type inference algorithms for decidable and normalizing PTSs. Unfortunately, defining such algorithms is problematic because of the second premise of the (abstraction) rule [123]. Hence several authors have proposed type inference algorithms that use a modified (abstraction) rule, and shown that these algorithms are sound and complete for interesting classes of PTSs. Typically, these modified (abstraction) rules replace the second premise by a syntactic condition [20, 122], or check the second premise using another system [26, 123, 131]. Below we provide an example of a type inference algorithm that uses such a modified (abstraction) rule and that is sound and complete for full PTSs.

Recall that $\lambda\mathbf{S}$ is full if $\mathbf{S} = (\mathcal{S}, \mathcal{A}, \mathcal{R})$ and for every $s_1, s_2 \in \mathcal{S}$ there exists $s_3 \in \mathcal{S}$ such that $(s_1, s_2, s_3) \in \mathcal{R}$. Such systems have "enough" rules and do not require to check the second premise of the (abstraction) rule; instead it is enough to check that if $b : B$ then $B$ is not a topsort.

**Definition 16.**

1. *Let* $\twoheadrightarrow_\rho$ *be a relation on* $\mathcal{T}$. *We write* $\Gamma \vdash_{\mathsf{sd}} M :\twoheadrightarrow_\rho A$ *for*

$$\exists A' \in \mathcal{T}.\ \Gamma \vdash_{\mathsf{sd}} M : A' \ \wedge\ A \twoheadrightarrow_\rho A'$$

| | | |
|---|---|---|
| (axiom) | $\langle\rangle \vdash_{\mathsf{sd}} s_1 : s_2$ | if $(s_1, s_2) \in \mathcal{A}$ |
| (start) | $\dfrac{\Gamma \vdash_{\mathsf{sd}} A :\twoheadrightarrow_{wh} s}{\Gamma, x : A \vdash_{\mathsf{sd}} x : A}$ | if $x \in V \setminus \mathrm{dom}(\Gamma)$ |
| (weakening) | $\dfrac{\Gamma \vdash_{\mathsf{sd}} A : B \quad \Gamma \vdash_{\mathsf{sd}} C :\twoheadrightarrow_{wh} s}{\Gamma, x : C \vdash_{\mathsf{sd}} A : B}$ | if $x \in V \setminus \mathrm{dom}(\Gamma)$ and $A \in V \cup \mathcal{S}$ |
| (product) | $\dfrac{\Gamma \vdash_{\mathsf{sd}} A :\twoheadrightarrow_{wh} s_1 \quad \Gamma, x : A \vdash_{\mathsf{sd}} B :\twoheadrightarrow_{wh} s_2}{\Gamma \vdash_{\mathsf{sd}} (\Pi x{:}\, A.\, B) : s_3}$ | if $(s_1, s_2, s_3) \in \mathcal{R}$ |
| (application) | $\dfrac{\Gamma \vdash_{\mathsf{sd}} F :\twoheadrightarrow_{wh} (\Pi x{:}\, A'.\, B) \quad \Gamma \vdash_{\mathsf{sd}} a : A}{\Gamma \vdash_{\mathsf{sd}} F\, a : B\{x := a\}}$ | if $A \Leftrightarrow A'$ |
| (abstraction) | $\dfrac{\Gamma, x : A \vdash_{\mathsf{sd}} b : B \quad B \in \mathcal{S} \Rightarrow \exists s' \in \mathcal{S}.\, (B, s') \in \mathcal{A}}{\Gamma \vdash_{\mathsf{sd}} \lambda x{:}A.\, b : \Pi x{:}\, A.\, B}$ | |

**Fig. 5.** Syntax-directed rules for Full Pure Type Systems

2. *The derivability relation* $\Gamma \vdash_{\mathsf{sd}} M : A$ *is given by the rules of Figure 5.*

The type checking algorithm is sound and complete for full PTSs.

**Proposition 4.** *For full* PTS*s* $\lambda\mathbf{S}$ *such that* $\lambda\mathbf{S} \models \mathrm{WN}_{\underline{\beta}}$*:*

1. *Soundness:* $\Gamma \vdash_{\mathsf{sd}} M : A \quad \Rightarrow \quad \Gamma \vdash M : A$
2. *Completeness:* $\Gamma \vdash M : A \quad \Rightarrow \quad \exists A' \in \mathcal{T}.\, \Gamma \vdash_{\mathsf{sd}} M : A' \wedge A \Leftrightarrow A'$
3. *Decidability: if* $\lambda\mathbf{S}$ *is decidable, then type inference and type checking for* $\lambda\mathbf{S}$ *are decidable.*

We refer to [19, 20, 123, 131] for type inference algorithms that are sound and complete for larger classes of PTSs.

### 3.4 Normalization

In this subsection, we present a (weak) normalization proof for the domain-free variant of $\lambda C_{\mathrm{x}}$ that was introduced in Definition 9. The normalization argument, which comes from [91, 38], has a simple and intuitive structure, based on a realizability interpretation, and is modular, so that it extends in a uniform way if we add further constructs ($\Sigma$-types, data types...).

Note however that the simple structure of the proof relies strongly on the language being *predicative*. Indeed, the proof proceeds by giving an interpretation of each type in an inductive way, which follows the structure of the type. This is not possible for impredicative calculi; we return to this point at the end of this section.

**Realizability Interpretation.** The interpretation is defined only using $\underline{T}$, with its reduction and conversion relations. Remarkably, the definition of the interpretation does not need to refer to the typing system. All terms are considered up to $\underline{\beta}$-conversion.

**Definition 17.** *The set $\underline{B}$ of neutral terms is defined to be the set of terms of the form $x\ a_1\ \ldots\ a_k$ where $x$ is a variable and $a_1, \ldots, a_k$ are normalizing terms.*

*Small Types and Types.* We define when a term $A \in \underline{T}$ is a *small type*, and in this case, what is the set $\phi_A$ of terms *realizing* $A$.

- if $A$ is neutral then $A$ is a small type and $\phi_A = \underline{B}$;
- if $A$ is $\Pi x : B.C$ and $B$ is a small type and $C(u)$ is a small type whenever $u \in \phi_C$ then $A$ is a small type; furthermore, in this case, $\phi_A$ is the set of all terms $t$ such that $t\ u \in \phi_{C(u)}$ whenever $u \in \phi_C$.

Notice that in the first clause, we take *all* neutral terms to be small types. This is crucial in order to get a simple realizability model, which does not refer to any typing system.

Next we define the set of all *types* and if $A$ is a type we define $\psi_A$ the set of terms *realizing* $A$. The term $*$ will be a type, but is not a small type:

- if $A$ is neutral then $A$ is a type and $\psi_A = \underline{B}$;
- if $A$ is $\Pi x : B.C$ and $B$ is a type and $C(u)$ is a type whenever $u \in \psi_C$ then $A$ is a type; furthermore, in this case, $\psi_A$ is the set of all terms $t$ such that $t\ u \in \psi_{C(u)}$ whenever $u \in \psi_C$;
- if $A$ is $*$ then $A$ is a type and $\psi_A$ is the set of all small types.

If $A$ is a type we shall write also $t \Vdash A$ for $t \in \psi_A$. Hence, $A \Vdash *$ iff $A$ is a small type. See below for a justification of the inductive definition of $\psi_A$ and $\phi_A$.

We now turn to proving properties of the interpretation. Our first lemma establishes that the interpretations $\phi_A$ and $\psi_A$ coincide on small types and that $\psi_A$ is a set of normalizing terms for every type $A$.

**Proposition 5.**

1. *If $A$ is a small type then $A$ is a type and $\phi_A = \psi_A$.*
2. *If $A$ is a type and $t \in \psi_A$ then $t \in \mathrm{WN}_{\underline{\beta}}$.*

*Proof.* By induction on the proof that $A$ is a small type (resp. a type). One needs to prove at the same time, also by induction, that if $A$ is a small type (resp. a type) then $\phi_A$ (resp. $\psi_A$) contains all neutral terms, and hence all variables.

**Soundness.** At this point, we can connect our "semantical" interpretation of terms with the typing relation of (Domain-Free) Pure Type Systems. In order to express the soundness of the typing relation w.r.t. our realizability interpretation, we say that $\gamma = u_1, \ldots, u_n$ fits $\Gamma = x_1 : A_1, \ldots, x_n : A_n$ iff $A_1$ is a type and $u_1 \Vdash A_1, \ldots$ and $A_n(u_1, \ldots, u_{n-1})$ is a type and $u_n \Vdash A_n(u_1, \ldots, u_{n-1})$.

**Proposition 6.** *If $\Gamma \vdash A : *$ and $\gamma$ fits $\Gamma$ then $A\gamma$ is a small type. If $\Gamma \vdash A : \Box$ and $\gamma$ fits $\Gamma$ then $A\gamma$ is a type. If $\Gamma \vdash t : A$ and $\gamma$ fits $\Gamma$ then $A\gamma$ is a type and $t\gamma \Vdash A\gamma$.*

*Proof.* By induction on the derivation of $\Gamma \vdash A : *$.

It follows that every legal term is normalizing.

**Corollary 3 (Weak Normalization).** *If $\Gamma \vdash M : A$ then $M \in \mathrm{WN}_{\underline{\beta}}$.*

Hence the system is consistent and has decidable type checking.

**Corollary 4.** *There is no term $M$ such that $A : * \vdash M : A$.*

The result follows immediately from Proposition 2.

**Corollary 5.** *Type checking is decidable.*

Again the result follows immediately from Proposition 4.

**Comment on This Proof.** What is crucial in this proof is the mutual inductive and recursive definition of first both the set $\mathsf{type}$ of *small types* and for each $A \in \mathsf{type}$ the subset $\phi_A \subseteq \underline{\mathcal{T}}$ and then both the set $\mathsf{TYPE}$ of *types* and for each $A \in \mathsf{TYPE}$ the subset $\psi_A \subseteq \underline{\mathcal{T}}$. Though these definitions have a definite inductive flavor (and are used as such without further comments in [91]), it seems interesting to explain such definitions in set theory. We only justify the definition of $\mathsf{type}$ and $\phi$, because the definition of $\mathsf{TYPE}$ and $\psi$ has a similar justification. Note that this justification of the definition of the set $\mathsf{TYPE}$ and the function $\psi$ is extracted from P. Aczel's work on Frege structures [5].

We consider the poset of pairs of the form $X, f$ with $X \subseteq \underline{\mathcal{T}}$ and $f : X \to \mathcal{P}(\underline{\mathcal{T}})$ with $X_1, f_1 \leq X_2, f_2$ iff $X_1 \subseteq X_2$ and the function $f_2$ extends the function $f_1$. This poset is not complete but it is such that any directed subset has a least upper bound. It follows that any monotone operator on this poset has a least fixpoint. We define $\mathcal{S}, \phi$ as the least fixpoint of the operator $\Phi(X, f) = Y, g$ where $Y$ and $g$ are defined by the clauses:

- if $A$ is neutral then $A \in Y$ and $g(A) = \underline{\mathcal{B}}$;
- if $A$ is $\Pi x : B.C$ and $B \in X$ and $C(u) \in X$ whenever $u \in f(C)$ then $A \in Y$ and $g(A)$ is the set of all terms $t$ such that $t\ u \in f(C(u))$ whenever $u \in f(C)$.

*Realizability and Impredicativity.* As emphasized earlier, predicativity is crucial to our proof. Indeed, if we try to analyze the present argument with $* : *$, we see there is a problem to define $t \Vdash *$: intuitively, one tries to use $\phi_*$ in the definition of $\phi_*$. In the words of [91], the interpretation of the type $*$ "would so to say have to have been there already before we introduced it". This circularity is broken by using a stratification in two steps: first we proceed with the definition of small types, and then turn to the definition of types. Now if we switch to an impredicative calculus such as the Calculus of Constructions, the circularity reappears since we need the interpretation of a type, namely $*$, for defining the interpretation of a small type, namely $\Pi x : *.x$.

# 4 Beyond Pure Type Systems

Pure Type Systems are minimal languages and lack type-theoretical constructs to carry out practical programming. In this section, we introduce two extensions of PTSs. The first one deals with the representation and manipulation of structures; the second one deals with inductive definitions.

## 4.1 Structures

Introducing structures allows to program in a modular way, to formalize algebraic structures and to represent the notion of subset in type theory. Below we review two standard approaches to introducing structures in dependent type theory. First, we present the traditional approach based on $\Sigma$-types, a straightforward generalization of product types to a dependently typed setting. The second approach we present is based on dependent record types, which provide a more palatable representation of structures.

**$\Sigma$-Types.** In simply typed $\lambda$-calculus, $A \times B$ is the type of pairs whose first and second components respectively inhabit $A$ and $B$. In PTSs, types might depend on terms, so the type $B$ might contain a free variable $x$ of type $A$. The strong sum $\Sigma x\colon A.\, B$ is the type of pairs $\langle M,\ N\rangle_{\Sigma x A.\ B}$ such that $M$ inhabits $A$ and $N$ inhabits $B(M)$. Note that pairs are labeled with their types, so as to ensure uniqueness of types and decidability of type checking.

**Definition 18.**

1. *The set of expressions is extended as follows*

$$\mathcal{T} = \ \ldots \ \mid \Sigma V{:}T.\,T \mid \langle \mathcal{T},\ \mathcal{T}\rangle_{\mathcal{T}} \mid \mathsf{fst}\ \mathcal{T} \mid \mathsf{snd}\ \mathcal{T}$$

2. *$\pi$-reduction is defined by the contraction rules*

$$\begin{array}{c}\mathsf{fst}\ \langle M,\ N\rangle_{\Sigma x:A.\ B} \to_\pi M \\ \mathsf{snd}\ \langle M,\ N\rangle_{\Sigma x:A.\ B} \to_\pi N\end{array}$$

3. *The notion of specification is extended with a set $\mathcal{U} \subseteq \mathcal{S} \times \mathcal{S} \times \mathcal{S}$ of rules for $\Sigma$-types. As usual, we use $(s_1, s_2)$ as an abbreviation for $(s_1, s_2, s_2)$.*
4. *The typing system is extended with the rules of Figure 6. Moreover, the conversion rule is modified so as to include $\pi$-conversion.*

As an example, let us consider an extension of the Calculus of Constructions with strong sums. We start with the rule $(*, *)$, which serves two purposes:

– first, the rule allows to form subsets of small types such as the type of prime numbers $\mathbb{N} : *, \textsc{prime} : \mathbb{N} \to * \ \vdash \ \Sigma n : \mathbb{N}.\ \textsc{prime}\ n : *$. Such a representation of subset types is said to be strong in the sense that one can deduce $\mathsf{prime}\ (\mathsf{fst}\ M)$ from $M : (\Sigma n : \mathbb{N}.\ \mathsf{prime}\ n)$. Alternative formalisms for supporting subsets are discussed e.g. in [129, 136];

$$\frac{\Gamma \vdash A : s_1 \quad \Gamma, x : A \vdash B : s_2}{\Gamma \vdash \Sigma x : A.\ B : s_3} \quad (s_1, s_2, s_3) \in \mathcal{U}$$

$$\frac{\Gamma \vdash M : A \quad \Gamma \vdash N : B\{x := M\} \quad \Gamma \vdash \Sigma x : A.\ B : s}{\Gamma \vdash \langle M,\ N\rangle_{\Sigma x:A.\ B} : \Sigma x : A.\ B}$$

$$\frac{\Gamma \vdash M : \Sigma x : A.\ B}{\Gamma \vdash \mathsf{fst}\ M : A}$$

$$\frac{\Gamma \vdash M : \Sigma x : A.\ B}{\Gamma \vdash \mathsf{snd}\ M : B(\mathsf{fst}\ M)}$$

**Fig. 6.** Typing rules for $\Sigma$-types

– second, the rule captures a strong form of existential quantification that enforces the axiom of choice. In particular, we can extract from a proof $p$ of $\Sigma n : \mathbb{N}.\ \mathsf{prime}\ n$, read as "there exists a prime number $n$", both a witness $\mathsf{fst}\ p$ of type $\mathbb{N}$ and a proof $\mathsf{snd}\ p$ that $\mathsf{fst}\ p$ is prime.

Likewise, the rule $(\Box, *, \Box)$ allows to form "subsets" of kinds. Combined with the rule $(\Box, \Box)$ this rule allows to introduce types of algebraic structures, e.g. the type MONOID of monoids

$$\Sigma \mathsf{el} : *.\ \Sigma \mathsf{o} : \mathsf{el} \to \mathsf{el} \to \mathsf{el}.\ \Sigma \mathsf{e} : \mathsf{el}.\ \text{MLAWS}\ \mathsf{el}\ \mathsf{o}\ \mathsf{e}$$

where MLAWS $\mathsf{el}\ \mathsf{o}\ \mathsf{e}$ state that $\mathsf{o}$ is associative and $\mathsf{e}$ is a neutral element for $\mathsf{o}$. Note that the definition of MLAWS involves conjunction, universal quantification and equality. These are defined in Figure 7.

One may wish to consider further rules but some of them lead to an inconsistency. For example, the rule $(\Box, *)$ allows to form a type $U : *$ isomorphic to $*$; this is known to cause an inconsistency, see Exercise 9.

We conclude this paragraph by sketching an extension of our previous realizability argument to $\Sigma$-types. In fact, it is enough to add the following clauses to the definitions of the interpretations:

– if $A$ is $\Sigma x : B.C$ and $B$ is a small type and $C(u)$ is a small type whenever $u \in \phi_C$ then $A$ is a small type; furthermore, in this case, $\phi_A$ is the set of all terms $t$ such that $\mathsf{fst}\ t \in \phi_B$ and $\mathsf{snd}\ t \in \phi_{C(\mathsf{fst}\ t)}$;
– if $A$ is $\Sigma x : B.C$ and $B$ is a type and $C(u)$ is a type whenever $u \in \psi_C$ then $A$ is a type; furthermore, in this case, $\psi_A$ is the set of all terms $t$ such that $\mathsf{fst}\ t \in \psi_B$ and $\mathsf{snd}\ t \in \psi_{C(\mathsf{fst}\ t)}$.

Under these interpretations, the results of Subsection 3.4 including soundness scale up to $\Sigma$-types.

**Records and Modules.** Dependent record types [12, 27, 28, 47, 124] provide another framework in which to represent structures. In contrast to $\Sigma$-types, records feature labels that can be used to extract every piece of a structure via the dot notation. For example, the type MONOID of monoids of the previous subsection is cast in terms of records as

$$\mathbf{sig}\{\mathsf{el} : *,\ \mathsf{o} : \mathsf{el} \to \mathsf{el} \to \mathsf{el},\ \mathsf{e} : \mathsf{el},\ \mathsf{p} : \text{MLAWS } \mathsf{el}\ \mathsf{o}\ \mathsf{e}\}$$

(in order to enforce decidable type checking, we would need to tag records with their types as for $\Sigma$-types). Using record selection rules, we can extract from any $M$ : MONOID its unit $M.\mathsf{e}$ of type $M.\mathsf{el}$; compare with $\Sigma$-types where the unit of the monoid is $\mathsf{fst}\ (\mathsf{snd}\ (\mathsf{snd}\ M))$.

Dependent records come in different flavors. For example, dependent records can be defined as labeled pairs. In the latter case, dependent record types are of the form $\mathbf{sig}\{L,\ \mathsf{r} : A\}$ and dependent records are of the form $\mathbf{struct}\{l, \mathsf{r} = a\}$. Furthermore, as emphasized in [124], records can be either:

- left-associating, in which case they pass any label that is not theirs to their first component. Left-associating records are extensible in the sense that allow to add a new field to the structure without destroying left-associativity;
- right-associating, in which case they pass any label that is not theirs to their second component; right-associating records show directly how the rest of a package depends on a given field and hence provide support for the specialization of structures. E.g. it is easy to define a type of monoids whose underlying type is $\mathbb{N}$ from a right-associating representation of monoids.

Some formalisms [12, 47] define records as labeled tuples of arbitrary length. For example, the language Cayenne introduces a notion of *record* and *signature* (i.e. record type) so that we can write for instance

$$\mathbf{struct}\{x = a, y = b, z = c\} : \mathbf{sig}\{x : A, y : B(x), z : C(x,y)\}$$

if $a : A$, $b : B(a)$ and $c : C(a,b)$. Furthermore record selection rules can be used to infer from $m : \mathbf{sig}\{x : A, y : B(x), z : C(x,y)\}$ that

$$m.x : A \qquad m.y : B(m.x) \qquad m.z : C(m.x, m.y)$$

Through such a formalism, Cayenne provides a simple module system: a module is essentially simply a record with dependent types. Furthermore, this module system can be used to represent elegantly the notion of class used in Haskell [138]. For instance one can express the class of reflexive relations over a type $A$ as

$$\mathbf{sig}\{\mathsf{r} : A \to A \to *, \mathsf{p} : \Pi x{:}A.\ \mathsf{r}\ x\ x\}$$

There are some further choices in the design of a system with dependently typed records. For example, some type systems [27] include record subtyping as a primitive, whereas other type systems use coercive subtyping [86] to capture record subtyping. Furthermore, some formalisms [12, 47, 48, 124] provide support for *manifest fields* as in

$$\mathbf{sig}\{x : \mathbb{N}, y = 0, z : \mathbb{N}\}$$

If $m$ is an object of this type, then we should have not only $m.x : \mathbb{N}$, $m.z : \mathbb{N}$ but also $m.y = 0$, even if $m$ is a variable. Thus, for this extension, the *evaluation* of a term may depend on the *type* of this term. As typing depends on evaluation through the conversion rule, the theory of such an extension is rather intricate. For example, it is not possible any more to use the convertibility algorithm of Subsection 3.3 nor the realizability interpretation of Subsection 3.4. One possible strategy for factoring out the complexity of type systems with record types and manifest fields is to cast the latter in terms of singleton types which allow to form for every $a : A$ a new type $\{a\}$ whose sole element is $a$. The theory of singleton types is studied e.g. in [10, 50, 135] but many issues remain open.

**Further Reading.** The reader may consult [48, 70, 83, 87, 128] for further information on modules in functional programming languages and dependent type theory.

### 4.2 Inductive Definitions

Inductive definitions provide a mechanism to introduce inductive types, define recursive functions over these types, and in the case of dependent type theory, to prove properties about elements of such inductive types using induction principles. It is therefore not surprising that such definitions are ubiquitous in typed functional programming languages and proof assistants. However the two families of languages do not support the same class of inductive definitions. For example:

- proof assistants allow users to introduce complex inductive definitions such as inductive families. Typical examples of such families are of the form $I \to *$ or $I \to J \to *$, where $I, J$ are inductive types such as the type of natural numbers or the type of expressions of an object language upon which we want to program or reason. Inductive families have been used extensively to give relational specifications of e.g. programming language semantics and cryptographic protocols [31, 115]. In contrast, standard functional programming languages do not support inductive families;
- functional programming languages allow for non-positive type definitions and for non-terminating recursive definitions whereas proof-assistants do not, as the combination of non-termination with dependent types leads to undecidable type checking. To enforce decidable type checking, proof-assistants either require recursive functions to be encoded in terms of recursors or use pattern-matching and check that recursive calls are guarded, as explained below.

In this subsection, we give some examples of inductive definitions in type theory, and briefly discuss the influence of these definitions on termination and decidable type checking.

**Examples.** Basic examples of inductive types include booleans, natural numbers and lists. We also present streams, which form a prime example of coinductive type.

*Booleans.* The small type $\mathbb{B} : *$ of booleans has two constructors $\mathsf{tt} : \mathbb{B}$ and $\mathsf{ff} : \mathbb{B}$. Furthermore, the type $\mathbb{B}$ comes equipped with a recursor $R_{\mathbb{B}}$ that can be used to define functions and prove properties on booleans. The typing rule for $R_{\mathbb{B}}$ is

$$\frac{\Gamma \vdash a : T(\mathsf{tt}) \quad \Gamma \vdash a' : T(\mathsf{ff}) \quad \Gamma \vdash b : \mathbb{B}}{\Gamma \vdash R_{\mathbb{B}}(b, a, a') : T(b)}$$

and its reduction rules are

$$R_{\mathbb{B}}(\mathsf{tt}, a, a') \to a \qquad R_{\mathbb{B}}(\mathsf{ff}, a, a') \to a'$$

We can extend the realizability model of Subsection 3.4 to booleans by casting $\mathbb{B}$ as a small type and defining $t \Vdash \mathbb{B}$ as meaning that $t$ is a neutral term or $\mathsf{tt}$ or $\mathsf{ff}$.

*Natural Numbers.* The small type $\mathbb{N} : *$ of natural numbers has two constructors $0 : \mathbb{N}$ and $\mathsf{s} : \mathbb{N} \to \mathbb{N}$. Furthermore, the type $\mathbb{N}$ comes equipped with a recursor $R_{\mathbb{N}}$ that can be used to define functions and prove properties on natural numbers. The typing rule for $R_{\mathbb{N}}$ is

$$\frac{\Gamma \vdash a : T(0) \quad \Gamma \vdash a' : \Pi x{:}\mathbb{N}.\, T(x) \to T(\mathsf{s}\ x) \quad \Gamma \vdash n : \mathbb{N}}{\Gamma \vdash R_{\mathbb{N}}(n, a, a') : T(n)}$$

and its reduction rules are

$$R_{\mathbb{N}}(0, a, a') \to a \qquad R_{\mathbb{N}}(\mathsf{s}\ n, a, a') \to a'\ n\ R_{\mathbb{N}}(n, a, a')$$

Observe that the usual rule for recursion can be recovered by setting $T$ to be non-dependent: in this case, we get that $R_{\mathbb{N}}(n, a, a') : T$ provided $n : \mathbb{N}$, $a : T$ and $a' : \mathbb{N} \to T \to T$. Also note that adding natural numbers is a strict extension to the language, even if we restrict recursion to the non-dependent case: indeed, the impredicative encoding of natural numbers does not allow to type $R_{\mathbb{N}}$, see e.g. [65].

We can extend the realizability model of Subsection 3.4 to natural numbers by casting $\mathbb{N}$ as a small type and defining $\Vdash \mathbb{N}$ as the smallest set of terms containing neutral terms, 0 and such that, if $t \Vdash \mathbb{N}$ then $\mathsf{s}\ t \Vdash \mathbb{N}$. Notice that this definition is inductive.

*Streams.* The small type $\mathbb{S} : *$ of *streams of booleans* has two destructors $\mathsf{hd} : \mathbb{S} \to \mathbb{B}$ and $\mathsf{tl} : \mathbb{S} \to \mathbb{S}$. Furthermore, the type $\mathbb{S}$ comes equipped with a corecursor $R_{\mathbb{S}}$ that can be used to define constructions on streams. The typing rule for $R_{\mathbb{S}}$ is

$$\frac{\Gamma \vdash a : X \to \mathbb{B} \quad \Gamma \vdash a' : X \to X \quad \Gamma \vdash x : X}{\Gamma \vdash R_{\mathbb{S}}(a, a', x) : \mathbb{S}}$$

and its reduction rules are

$$\mathsf{hd}\ (R_{\mathbb{S}}(x, a, a')) \to a\ x \qquad \mathsf{tl}\ (R_{\mathbb{S}}(x, a, a')) \to R_{\mathbb{S}}(a'\ x, a, a')$$

This definition of streams is closely related to the encoding of abstract datatypes with existential types of J. Mitchell and G. Plotkin [103].

We can extend the realizability model of Subsection 3.4 to streams of booleans by casting $\mathbb{S}$ as a small type and defining $\Vdash \mathbb{S}$ as the greatest set of terms such that if $t \Vdash \mathbb{S}$ then $\mathsf{hd}\ t \Vdash \mathbb{B}$ and $\mathsf{tl}\ t \Vdash \mathbb{S}$ (one can check that if $t$ is neutral then $t \Vdash \mathbb{S}$). Notice that this definition is coinductive.

**Intuitionistic Theory of Inductive Definitions.** The rules for natural numbers given in the previous paragraph were suggested by Martin-Löf, who also gave the rules for ordinals. The small type $\mathbb{O} : *$ of ordinals has three constructors $0 : \mathbb{O}$, $\mathsf{s} : \mathbb{O} \to \mathbb{O}$ and $\mathsf{l} : (\mathbb{N} \to \mathbb{O}) \to \mathbb{O}$. Furthermore, the type $\mathbb{O}$ comes equipped with a recursor $R_{\mathbb{O}}$ that can be used to define functions and prove properties on ordinals. The typing rule for $R_{\mathbb{O}}$ is

$$\frac{\Gamma \vdash a : T(0) \quad \Gamma \vdash a' : \Pi x{:}\mathbb{O}.\, T(x) \to T(\mathsf{s}\ x) \qquad \Gamma \vdash a'' : \Pi u{:}\mathbb{N} \to \mathbb{O}.\, (\Pi x{:}\mathbb{N}.\, T(u\ x)) \to T(\mathsf{l}\ u) \quad \Gamma \vdash o : \mathbb{O}}{\Gamma \vdash R_{\mathbb{O}}(o, a, a', a''') : T(o)}$$

and its reduction rules are

$$\begin{aligned} R_{\mathbb{O}}(0, a, a', a'') &\to a \\ R_{\mathbb{O}}(\mathsf{s}\ o, a, a', a'') &\to a'\ o\ R_{\mathbb{O}}(o, a, a', a'') \\ R_{\mathbb{O}}(\mathsf{l}\ o, a, a', a'') &\to a''\ o\ \lambda n{:}\mathbb{N}.\, R_{\mathbb{O}}(o\ n, a, a', a'') \end{aligned}$$

This is an example of an *iterated* inductive definition, since the definition of $\mathbb{O}$ refers to the previous definition of $\mathbb{N}$. Iterated inductive definitions are very useful in programming, but they also have strong roots in proof theory, see for example [33]. The connections with Type Theory originate from D. Scott's work on constructive validity [130]. Scott's work was itself inspired from [137], where W. Tait studies possible reductions of comprehension principles to the intuitionistic theory of inductive definitions. Such a possibility had been suggested by Gödel, and Tait's work shows that such a reduction is possible for $\Pi^1_1$-comprehension.

The $W$-type schema, introduced by P. Martin-Löf in [93], gives an elegant representation of the inductive definitions introduced by Tait. This schema was further generalized by K. Petersson and D. Synek [109], who give the most general form of Post systems in type theory. Such a formulation may be used to represent interactive systems, as suggested by P. Hancock and A. Setzer [68], but also to encode set theory in type theory, as suggested by P. Aczel [4, 6] and further analyzed by B. Werner [140], see Exercise 17.

Although Martin-Löf's treatment of inductive definitions did not include a general schema for inductive definitions, see however [89], it is natural to want such a schema. Indeed, there have been a number of proposals for such schemata, see e.g. [46, 52, 53, 55, 85, 112, 113, 121].

**Datatypes in Programming Languages.** It is folklore that datatypes can be defined by recursive equations and that recursive functions can be defined using case-expressions and fixpoints. For example, the datatype $\mathbb{N}$ can be defined by the recursive equation $\mathbb{N} = \mathbb{U} + \mathbb{N}$ (where $\mathbb{U}$ denotes the unit type) if we do not use labeled sums and by the recursive equation $\mathbb{N} = 0 + \mathsf{s}\ \mathbb{N}$ if we do; note that constructors are not named in the first case, and named in the second. Furthermore if we use labeled sums to define $\mathbb{N}$, as in [108], then the typing rules for case-expressions and fixpoints are

$$\frac{\Gamma \vdash a : T(0) \quad \Gamma \vdash a' : \Pi x{:}\mathbb{N}.\, T(\mathsf{s}\ x) \quad \Gamma \vdash n : \mathbb{N}}{\Gamma \vdash \mathsf{case}(n, a, a') : T(n)}$$

$$\frac{\Gamma, f : A \to B \vdash e : A \to B}{\Gamma \vdash \mathsf{fix}\ f.\ e : A \to B}$$

and the reduction rules are:

$$\begin{aligned} \mathsf{case}(0, a, a') &\to a \\ \mathsf{case}(\mathsf{s}\ n, a, a') &\to a'\ n \\ \mathsf{fix}\ f.\ e &\to e\{f := \mathsf{fix}\ f.\ e\} \end{aligned}$$

(Such rules raise the question of termination of recursive functions; this question is discussed below.)

Based on these observations, [41] suggests to transfer to type theory the pattern-matching and case notations used in functional programming languages. In this vision, the analogy between proofs and programs can be pushed even further:

- constructors correspond to introduction rules;
- case expressions correspond to deduction by cases;
- recursively defined functions correspond to arguments by structural induction.

*Decidability of Type Checking and Type Inference.* The introduction of datatypes in the language yields new difficulties for type inference and type checking. Two problems arise: the first problem, which arises in a non-dependent setting, is that one needs to define a decidable equality between datatypes. The second problem, which occurs in a dependent setting only, is that checking convertibility between types may require computing with recursive functions. We briefly expose both problems and their possible solutions.

Let us start with defining equality between datatypes. If we view them as solutions to recursive equations, datatypes are infinite objects since

$$\mathbb{N} = 0 + \mathsf{s}\ \mathbb{N} = 0 + \mathsf{s}\ (0 + \mathsf{s}\ \mathbb{N}) = \ldots$$

If we take this view, then it is not immediate to define a decidable notion of equality between datatypes. Two such definitions appear in the literature, depending on the form of recursive equations used to define datatypes:

- if datatypes are defined without using labeled sums, then it is natural that datatypes are compared by structures. This approach has been suggested by L. Cardelli [36] and further analyzed in a non-dependent setting by a number of authors, including R. Amadio and L. Cardelli [9], D. Kozen and J. Palsberg and M. Schwartzback [80], M. Brandt and F. Henglein [32], S. Jha and J. Palsberg and T. Zhao [77, 110];
- if datatypes are defined with labeled sums, then it is natural that constructor names are compared when defining equality, so that the datatype $\mathbb{C} = \mathsf{black}+\mathsf{white}$ is not equal to the datatype $\mathbb{B} = \mathsf{tt} + \mathsf{ff}$.

Let us now turn to checking equality between types in dependent type theory. As emphasized in the introduction, checking equality between types may require checking equality between expressions, which itself may require unfolding recursively defined functions. Hence these functions must be terminating if one is to achieve decidable type checking. Termination of recursively defined functions can be enforced in several ways.

- *Syntactic checks for termination.* [41] introduces a simple guard predicate to ensure termination of fixpoint expressions: in a nutshell, the criterion requires that the definition of $f(e)$ only makes recursive calls of the form $f(e')$ where $e'$ is structurally smaller than $e$. This definition of the guard predicate has been refined e.g. by E. Giménez [62], by A. Abel and T. Altenkirch [1, 3], and by F. Blanqui, J.-P. Jouannaud and M. Okada [30, 79], leading to increasingly complex conditions that allow more expressions to be typed. This line of research bears some similarities with other works on the termination of functional programs, see e.g. [61, 82];
- *Type-based termination.* P.N. Mendler [96, 97] propose systems where the termination of recursive definitions is enforced by the type system. Later, E. Giménez and other authors [2, 8, 62, 63, 22] have pursued a type-based approach to the termination of recursive definitions. In a nutshell, the notion of type is extended to record the size of an element of an inductive type, and the termination of recursive functions is ensured by requiring that, if $e$ is of size $n+1$, then the definition of $f(e)$ only makes recursive calls of the form $f(e')$ where $e'$ is of size smaller or equal to $n$. If we specialize such an approach to natural numbers, one gets the following rules (where contexts are omitted for readability):

$$\frac{}{\vdash 0 : \mathbb{N}^{\hat{\iota}}} \qquad \frac{\vdash n : \mathbb{N}^{\iota}}{\vdash \mathsf{s}\ n : \mathbb{N}^{\hat{\iota}}}$$

$$\frac{\vdash n : \mathbb{N}^{\hat{\iota}} \qquad \vdash f_0 : A \qquad \vdash f_s : \mathbb{N}^{\iota} \to A}{\vdash \mathsf{case}\ n\ \mathsf{of}\{0 \Rightarrow f_0 | \mathsf{s} \Rightarrow f_s\} : A}$$

$$\frac{f : \mathbb{N}^{\iota} \to A \vdash e : \mathbb{N}^{\hat{\iota}} \to A}{\vdash \mathsf{fix}\ f.\ e : \mathbb{N}^{\infty} \to A}$$

where $\iota$ ranges over arbitrary sizes, $\hat{\iota}$ denotes the successor of $\iota$, $\mathbb{N}^{\iota}$ denotes the naturals of length smaller or equal to $\iota$ and $\mathbb{N}^{\infty}$ denotes the naturals of arbitrary length. Again, this approach has some similarities with other work on functional programming [74, 111]. While type-based termination criteria overcome some defects of syntactic criteria, their theory remains to be investigated, especially in the context of dependent types.

**Modularity.** Several functions are "generic" in the data type upon which they operate: for example one can produce generic size and equality functions for each first-order data type. Generic programming [14, 72, 76] is an attempt to provide programmers with facilities to program such functions once and for all. T. Altenkirch and C. McBride [7] have recently shown how generic programming concepts can be programmed in dependent type theory, see also [117, 118].

**Further Reading.** The reader may consult [43, 54, 55, 62, 94, 113] for further information on inductive definitions in dependent type theory.

## 5 Dependent Types in Programming

### 5.1 Cayenne

Cayenne is an Haskell-like language with dependent types developed by L. Augustsson [12]. Although Cayenne is very close to the Agda proof assistant [37], there are some key differences:

- the intended use of Cayenne is the same as a functional language in that one actually wants to run programs using a compiler that produces efficient code (and not only prove theorems). In Cayenne this is achieved by a stripping function that removes all typing information from programs;
- Cayenne allows for arbitrary datatypes and recursive definitions, given that for a programming language there is no formal or moral reason to avoid non-wellfounded datatypes and unrestricted general recursion.

Hence convertibility and type checking are undecidable in Cayenne, i.e. there is no algorithm to decide whether a given program is correct w.r.t. the typing rules of Cayenne. In practice this problem is solved by setting a bound on the number of unfoldings of recursive definitions that are performed during convertibility checking.

Cayenne also features some important differences with functional programming languages. In particular, Cayenne does not have a primitive notion of class or module. As stated in Subsection 4.1, modules are represented in Cayenne using dependent record types with manifest fields. One interesting aspect of this representation is to show that dependent types may be of great help in designing simple module systems.

Cayenne is strictly more expressive than Haskell, in that it types more programs, for example the function `printf`, the SASL tautology function, and interpreters for typed languages, see [12, 13] and Exercise 1.

### 5.2 DML

DML is a dependently typed extension of ML developed by H. Xi and F. Pfenning [141, 145]. The original motivation behind DML is to use dependent types to carry useful information for optimizing legal ML programs [144, 142]. This design choice leads DML to be a conservative extension of ML in the sense that the erasure function $||.||$ that removes type dependencies maps legal DML judgments to legal ML judgments. Further, a legal DML expression $e$ evaluates to a DML value $v$ iff $||e||$ evaluates to a ML value $v'$, in which case $||v|| = v'$.

The key feature of DML is to combine full recursion and dependent types while still enjoying decidability of type checking and a phase distinction [35]. This is achieved by a careful design of the syntax. In a nutshell, DML adopts a layered syntax that distinguishes between types and programs, and singles out a set of pure programs, called indices, that are the only programs allowed to occur in types. Formally, indices are taken to be expressions over a constraint domain $X$ that comes as a parameter of DML and the convertibility relation is defined from the equality relation induced by $X$. It is interesting to note that this notion of convertibility is sometimes more intuitive and powerful than the usual notion of convertibility in dependent type theory. For example, if we take $X$ to be the constraint domain of natural numbers and let $\mathbb{L}\ n\ A$ be the type of $A$-lists of length $n$, then types such as $\mathbb{L}\ (n+m)\ A$ and $\mathbb{L}\ (m+n)\ A$ are convertible because commutativity of addition holds in the underlying constraint domain; see Exercise 15.

In order to provide the type system with sufficient flexibility, DML features restricted subset types, singleton types and existential types that are used to enforce the connection between run-time values and indices, and to interface dependently typed programs with standard programs, such as the ones found in libraries, that are not dependently typed.

Finally, DML shares two important properties of ML that were stated in the definition: first, well-typed DML cannot go wrong. Second, type equality and type inference for DML programs are decidable, provided that the underlying constraint domain is decidable and that the programs are explicitly typed.

### 5.3 Further Reading

[13, 34, 51, 66, 67, 94, 104, 105, 132, 139, 141, 143] address a number of issues related with dependent types in programming.

## Exercises

Throughout the exercises, we let $\lambda x, y, z : A.\ M$ denote $\lambda x : A.\ \lambda y : A.\ \lambda z : A.\ M$.

1. *SASL tautology function.* Define boolean conjunction $\wedge : \mathbb{B} \to \mathbb{B} \to \mathbb{B}$. Next define a function $F : \mathbb{N} \to *$ such that $F\ 0 = \mathbb{B}$ and $F\ (\mathsf{s}\ n) = \mathbb{B} \to F\ n$. Finally define $\tau_{\mathsf{sasl}} : \Pi n : \mathbb{N}.\ F\ n \to \mathbb{B}$ such that $\tau_{\mathsf{sasl}}\ 0\ f = f$ and $\tau_{\mathsf{sasl}}\ (\mathsf{s}\ n)\ f = \wedge\ (\tau_{\mathsf{sasl}}\ n\ (f\ \mathsf{tt}))\ (\tau_{\mathsf{sasl}}\ n\ (f\ \mathsf{ff}))$. Using the realizability model of Section 3.4, prove directly that $\Pi n : \mathbb{N}.\ F\ n \to \mathbb{B}$ is a small type and that $\tau_{\mathsf{sasl}} \Vdash \Pi n : \mathbb{N}.\ F\ n \to \mathbb{B}$.

2. *Set-theoretical models of* $\lambda 2_{\mathrm{x}}$. Recall that one can build a set-theoretical model of simply typed $\lambda$-calculus as follows: starting from sets $A_1 \ldots A_n$, define $[\![st]\!]$ to be the smallest set such that $A_1 \ldots A_n \in [\![*]\!]$ and $X \to Y \in [\![*]\!]$ for every $X, Y \in [\![*]\!]$. The idea is to interpret every type variable as an element of $[\![*]\!]$ and to extend the interpretation to an arbitrary type by setting $[\![A \to B]\!] = [\![A]\!] \to [\![B]\!]$. Extend the interpretation to terms by defining $[\![t]\!]_\rho$ for every valuation $\rho : V \to \bigcup_{A \in [\![*]\!]} A$ and show that the interpretation is sound in the sense that $\Gamma \vdash M : A$ implies $[\![t]\!]_\rho \in [\![A]\!]$ where $\rho$ is a valuation satisfying $\Gamma$. Then extend this model to $\lambda 2_{\mathrm{x}}$.
3. *Encoding arithmetic in* $\lambda P$. The context for arithmetic introduces two base types $\iota$ and $o$, which respectively correspond to individuals, here expressions that denote numbers, and formulae. In addition, there are the usual operations on natural numbers and the usual logical connectives and quantifiers.

$$
\begin{array}{lll}
\iota : *, & o : *, & \wedge : o \to o \to o, \\
0 : \iota, & = : \iota \to \iota \to o, & \vee : o \to o \to o, \\
s : \iota \to \iota, & < : \iota \to \iota \to o, & \supset : o \to o \to o, \\
+ : \iota \to \iota \to \iota, & \forall : (\iota \to o) \to o, & \neg : o \to o \\
\times : \iota \to \iota \to \iota, & \exists : (\iota \to o) \to o, &
\end{array}
$$

The context provides enough structure for terms and formulae of first-order arithmetic to be encoded into the system. To build/manipulate proofs, we encode the basic judgment form '$\phi$ is a logical truth' by adding a declaration

$$\mathsf{true} : o \to *$$

Following [69, Section 4.1], one can then introduce relevant assumptions to encode proofs, see Exercise 4. Prove that the encoding is adequate in the sense of [69, 120].
4. *Impredicative encoding of logic in* $\lambda C$. Define $\lambda$-terms that correspond to the standard natural deduction rules for the connectives and quantifiers of Figure 7. Also, try to define a first and second projection for existential quantification. [Hint: the second projection is not definable.]
5. *Pure Type Systems for Higher-Order Logic.* $\lambda HOL$ is an extension of $\lambda\omega$ that allows variables of type $\Box$ to be introduced in the context of judgments. Formally $\lambda HOL$ is obtained by setting

$$
\begin{aligned}
\mathcal{S} &= \{*, \Box, \triangle\} \\
\mathcal{A} &= \{(*, \Box), (\Box, \triangle)\} \\
\mathcal{R} &= \{(*, *), (\Box, *), (\Box, \Box)\}
\end{aligned}
$$

Show that $\lambda HOL$ captures exactly Church's higher-order logic in the PTS-framework, see e.g. [56].

| Operator | Definition |
|---|---|
| $\forall : \Pi T{:}*. (T \to *) \to *$ | $\equiv \lambda T{:}*. \lambda P{:}T \to *. (\Pi x : T.P x)$ |
| $\exists : \Pi T{:}*. (T \to *) \to *$ | $\equiv \lambda T{:}*. \lambda P{:}T \to *. (\Pi p : *.\Pi x : T.((P\ x) \to p) \to p)$ |
| $\top : *$ | $\equiv \Pi x : *.x \to x$ |
| $\bot : *$ | $\equiv \Pi x : *.x$ |
| $\wedge : * \to * \to *$ | $\equiv \lambda A, B : *{:}(\Pi x : *.A \to B \to x).$ |
| $\vee : * \to * \to *$ | $\equiv \lambda A, B{:}*. (\Pi x : *.(A \to x) \to (B \to x) \to x)$ |
| $\neg : * \to *$ | $\equiv \lambda A{:}*. (A \to \bot)$ |
| $\leftrightarrow : * \to * \to *$ | $\equiv \lambda A, B : *{:}\wedge\ (A \to B)\ (B \to A).$ |
| $\doteq : \Pi T{:}*. T \to T \to *$ | $\equiv \lambda T{:}*\lambda x, y{:}*. \Pi P : T \to *. (Px) \to (Py).$ |

**Fig. 7.** Second-order encoding of logic

6. *The Berardi-Paulin embedding.* The following function $[.]_.$ can be used as a foundation for extracting programs from proofs:

$$[x]_\Gamma = x \qquad x \in V \cup \{*, \Box\}$$

$$[\Pi x{:}\,A.\ B]_\Gamma = \begin{cases} [B]_\Gamma & \text{if } \Gamma \vdash A : * \text{ and } \Gamma \vdash B : \Box \\ \Pi x{:}\,[A]_\Gamma.\ [B]_{\Gamma, x:A} & \text{otherwise} \end{cases}$$

$$[\lambda x{:}A.\ M]_\Gamma = \begin{cases} [M]_{\Gamma, x:A} & \text{if } \Gamma \vdash A : * \text{ and } \Gamma \vdash M : B : \Box \\ \lambda x{:}[A]_\Gamma.\ [M]_\Gamma & \text{otherwise} \end{cases}$$

$$[M\ N]_\Gamma = \begin{cases} [M]_\Gamma & \text{if } \Gamma \vdash M : A : \Box \text{ and } \Gamma \vdash N : B : * \\ [M]_\Gamma\ [N]_\Gamma & \text{otherwise} \end{cases}$$

$$[\langle\rangle] = \langle\rangle$$

$$[\Gamma, x : A] = [\Gamma], x : [A]_\Gamma$$

Show that if $\Gamma \vdash M : A$ is derivable in $\lambda C$ then $[\Gamma] \vdash [M]_\Gamma : [A]_\Gamma$ is derivable in $\lambda\omega$. Conclude that $\lambda C$ is conservative over $\lambda\omega$ in the following sense:

$$\left.\begin{array}{l} \Gamma \vdash A : s \text{ derivable in } \lambda\omega \\ \Gamma \vdash M : A \text{ derivable in } \lambda C \end{array}\right\} \Rightarrow \exists M' \in \mathcal{T}.\, \Gamma \vdash M' : A \text{ derivable in } \lambda C$$

7. *The principle of proof-irrelevance.* The principle, due to N. G. de Bruijn, states that all proofs of a proposition $A$ are equal. There are several possible ways to implement the principle in a type theory. The simplest one is to add $\mathsf{pi} : \Pi A{:}\,*.\ \Pi x, y{:}\,A.\ x \doteq y$ in the context. Using the Berardi-Paulin embedding, show that proof-irrelevance is consistent in the Calculus of Constructions. Then show that the principle is not derivable in the Calculus of Constructions. [Hint: show that there is no pseudo-term $M$ in normal form such that $\vdash M : \Pi A{:}*.\ \Pi x, y{:}\,A.\ x \doteq y$].

8. *Consistency of the axiom of infinity.* The axiom, see e.g. [39], is given by the context $\Gamma_\infty$

$$A : *,\ f : A \to A, a : A,\ R : A \to A \to *,\ h_1 : \Pi x : A.R\ x\ x \to \bot,$$
$$h_2 : \Pi x, y, z : A.R\ x\ y \to R\ y\ z \to R\ x\ z,\ h_3 : \Pi x : A.R\ x\ (f\ x)$$

Intuitively, the context asserts the existence of a small type $A$ with infinitely many elements. Using the consistency of proof-irrelevance, show that the context is not instantiable in $\lambda C$. Then prove that the context is consistent by showing that there is no $M$ in normal form such that $\Gamma_\infty \vdash M : \bot$. [Hint: show first by induction on normal forms, that if we have a term in normal form of type $A$ in this context $\Gamma_\infty$ then this term has the form $f^n\ a$ and if a term in normal form is of type $R\ u\ v$ then we have $u = f^p\ a,\ v = f^q\ a$ with $p < q$.]
9. *Inconsistency of some $\Sigma$-types.* The context $\Gamma_{pip}$ below is inconsistent in $\lambda C$ because it allows for a direct interpretation of $\lambda U$, see [39]:

$$\Gamma_{pip} = B : *,\ E : B \to *,\ \epsilon : * \to B,\ H : \Pi A{:}*.\ A \leftrightarrow (E\ (\epsilon\ A))$$

Conclude that the rule $(\Box, *)$ for $\Sigma$-types is inconsistent. In fact it is possible to provide a direct encoding of $\lambda*$ in $\lambda C$ extended with the rule $(\Box, *)$ for $\Sigma$-types, see [71, 73].
10. *Induction principles for booleans.* The following context $\Gamma_{\mathbb{B}}$, which introduces a type of booleans with its associated induction principle, is not instantiable in $\lambda P2$ and $\lambda C$, see [57]:

$$\Gamma_{\mathbb{B}} = B : *,\ 0, 1 : B,\ h : \Pi C : B \to *.C\ 0 \to C\ 1 \to \Pi x : B.C\ x$$

This is surprising since the Berardi-Paulin embedding $[\Gamma_{\mathbb{B}}]$ of $\Gamma_{\mathbb{B}}$ is instantiable in $\lambda 2$ and hence in $\lambda\omega$ by taking:

$$\begin{aligned} B &= \Pi X : *.\ X \to X \to X \\ 0 &= \lambda X : *.\ \lambda x, y : X.\ x \\ 1 &= \lambda X : *.\ \lambda x, y : X.\ y \\ h &= \lambda C : *.\ \lambda x, y : C.\ \lambda b : B.\ b\ C\ x\ y \end{aligned}$$

The argument is proved via a model construction that has already been used to provide models of $\lambda C$ where the axiom of choice holds [134]. This model is described intuitively as follows. Let us write $A, B, C, \ldots$ terms of type $*$ and $K, L, M, \ldots$ terms of type $\Box$. Let $\Lambda$ be the set of pure (open) $\lambda$-terms. The sort $*$ is interpreted by $\{\emptyset, \Lambda\}$, so that $[\![A]\!]$ is $\emptyset$ or $\Lambda$. The terms $t : A$ are interpreted by stripping away all types/kind information; for instance $\lambda A : *.\lambda x : A.x$ becomes $\lambda x.x \in \Lambda$. More generally, we define:
   - $[\![\lambda x : A.t]\!] = \lambda x.[\![t]\!]$;
   - $[\![\lambda X : K.t]\!] = [\![t]\!]$;
   - $[\![\Pi x : A.B]\!]$ to be the set of all terms $t$ such that if $u \in [\![A]\!]$ then $t\ u \in [\![B]\!]_{x:=u}$;

- $[\![\Pi X : K.B]\!]$ to be the set of all terms $t$ such that if $\alpha \in [\![K]\!]$ then $t \in [\![B]\!]_{X:=\alpha}$;
- $[\![\Pi x : A.L]\!]$ to be the set of all functions $\alpha$ such that if $t \in [\![A]\!]$ then $\alpha(t) \in [\![L]\!]_{x:=t}$;
- application is defined in the obvious way.

Observe that the definition of dependent function space agrees with the interpretation of $*$ because the interpretations of $[\![\Pi x : A.B]\!]$ and $[\![\Pi X : K.B]\!]$ are either $\emptyset$ or $\Lambda$.

Now we reason by contradiction to prove that $\Gamma_{\mathbb{B}}$ is not instantiable by closed expressions $B, 0, 1, h$. If it were, we would have $[\![B]\!] = \Lambda$ because $[\![B]\!]$ is inhabited. Now define $\alpha : \Lambda \to *$ by the clause:

$$\alpha(v) = \{u \in \Lambda \mid v = [\![0]\!] \vee v = [\![1]\!]\}$$

For every $v \in \Lambda$, we have $\alpha(v) \in [\![*]\!]$ since $\alpha(v) = \emptyset$ or $\alpha(v) = \Lambda$. Furthermore $\alpha([\![0]\!]) = \alpha([\![1]\!]) = \Lambda$. Now by definition of the model, we should have, for all $t, u, v \in \Lambda$

$$[\![h]\!]\ t\ u\ v \in \alpha(v)$$

but $\alpha(v)$ may be empty, a contradiction. Hence the context $\Gamma_{\mathbb{B}}$ is not instantiable in $\lambda P2$. Make the argument precise by showing that the construction does provide a model of $\lambda P2$.

11. *Fixpoints in inconsistent Pure Type Systems.* In [75], T. Hurkens provides a strikingly short paradox $Y_H$ for $\lambda U^-$. Check that $Y_H$ is a looping combinator in the sense of [44], and that its domain-free counterpart $Y$ is a fixpoint combinator in the sense that it verifies

$$\vdash Y : \Pi A{:}*. (A \to A) \to A$$

and

$$Y\ A\ f =_{\underline{\beta}} f\ (Y\ A\ f)$$

see [21].

12. *Paradoxical Universes in Pure Type Systems.* The construction of $Y_H$ relies on the existence of a paradoxical universe, that is of a type $\mathcal{U} : \Box$ and two functions $\tau : (\mathcal{U} \to *) \to \mathcal{U}$ and $\sigma : \mathcal{U} \to \mathcal{U} \to *$ such that

$$(\sigma(\tau\ X))\ y \Leftrightarrow \exists x : \mathcal{U}.\ X(x) \wedge y = \tau(\sigma x)$$

Call such a paradoxical universe strong if furthermore $\tau(\sigma x) \twoheadrightarrow_\beta x$. Strong paradoxical universes are of interest because they yield fixpoint combinators. However, show that there is no strong paradoxical universe in a PTS with the axiom $* : \Box$ and rule $(\Box, \Box)$ and for which $M$ is $\beta$-strongly normalizing whenever $\Gamma \vdash M : A$ and $\Gamma \vdash A : \Box$. [Hint: strong paradoxical universes allow to formalize Russell's paradox which yields a non-normalizing expression.]

13. *Pure Type Systems with Fixpoint Combinators.* Consider an extension of PTSs with a fixpoint construct $\mu x : A.\ M$, as given by the typing rule

$$\frac{\Gamma, x : A \vdash M : A \quad \Gamma \vdash A : s}{\Gamma \vdash \mu x : A.\ M : A}$$

and the reduction relation $\to_Y$ given by the contraction rule

$$\mu x : A.\ M \qquad \to_Y \qquad M\{x := \mu x : A.\ M\}$$

Similar extensions are considered e.g. in [11] for the Calculus of Constructions and in [59] for PTSs. Show that type checking is undecidable for the extension of the Calculus of Constructions with a fixpoint construct. One can use a similar argument to conclude that Cayenne has undecidable type checking. [Hint: recall that $N = \Pi X{:}*.\ X \to (X \to X) \to X$ is the second-order encoding of natural numbers. Show that every partial recursive function $f$ is representable by a closed term $F$ s.t. $\vdash F : N \to N$, i.e. for every $n : \mathbb{N}$,

$$f n = m \quad \Leftrightarrow \quad F\ \lceil n \rceil \twoheadrightarrow_{\beta Y} \lceil m \rceil$$

Deduce that convertibility is undecidable. See [125] for a detailed argument.]

14. *Type Checking Domain-Free Pure Type Systems.* Type checking for Domain-Free Pure Type Systems is undecidable in general, even for the Domain-Free variant of $\lambda 2$, but becomes decidable if one restricts oneself to judgments in normal form [23]. Define a type checking algorithm for such judgments.
15. *Leibniz equality vs. convertibility.* In dependent type theory, one can define concatenation APP and inversion REV with the types

$$\begin{array}{l} \text{APP} : \Pi m, n : \mathbb{N}.\ \Pi A : *.\ (\mathbb{L}\ m\ A) \to (\mathbb{L}\ n\ A) \to (\mathbb{L}\ (m+n)\ A) \\ \text{REV} : \Pi m : \mathbb{N}.\ \Pi A : *.\ (\mathbb{L}\ m\ A) \to (\mathbb{L}\ m\ A) \end{array}$$

Now consider the context

$$m : \mathbb{N},\ l : \mathbb{L}\ m\ A,\ n : \mathbb{N},\ l' : \mathbb{L}\ n\ A$$

and introduce the abbreviations

$$\begin{array}{l} l_1 = \text{REV}\ (m+n)\ A\ (\text{APP}\ m\ n\ A\ l\ l') \\ l_2 = \text{APP}\ n\ m\ A\ (\text{REV}\ n\ A\ l')\ (\text{REV}\ m\ A\ l) \end{array}$$

What are the types of $l_1$ and $l_2$? Can we prove $l_1 \doteq l_2$ where $\doteq$ denotes Leibniz equality? Why? [Hint: check whether $m+n$ and $n+m$ are convertible for open expressions $m$ and $n$.]

16. *John Major's equality.* John Major's equality $\simeq$ [94], which is useful for defining functions by pattern-matching in dependent type theory, is given by the typing rules

$$\frac{\Gamma \vdash a : A \quad \Gamma \vdash b : B \quad \Gamma \vdash A, B : s}{\Gamma \vdash a \simeq b : *}$$

$$\frac{\Gamma \vdash a : A \quad \Gamma \vdash A : s}{\Gamma \vdash \mathsf{refl}_{\simeq}\ a : a \simeq a}$$

$$\frac{\begin{array}{cc} \Gamma \vdash a, a' : A & \Gamma \vdash \Phi : \Pi b{:}A.\ (a \simeq b) \to s \\ \Gamma \vdash \phi : \Phi\ a\ (\mathsf{refl}_{\simeq}\ a) & \Gamma \vdash \psi : a \simeq a' \end{array}}{\Gamma \vdash \mathsf{eqelim}\ A\ a\ \Phi\ \phi\ a'\ \psi : \Phi\ a'\ \psi}$$

and by the rewrite rule

$$\mathsf{eqelim}\ A\ a\ \Phi\ \phi\ a\ (\mathsf{refl}_{\simeq}\ a) \to \phi$$

Can we prove $l_1 \simeq l_2$ where $l_1$ and $l_2$ are defined as in the previous exercise? [Note that John Major's equality is not derivable in $\lambda C$.]

17. *W-types.* Given a type $B$ that depends upon $x : A$, one can define the type $Wx : A.\ B$ whose canonical elements have the form *sup* $a\ f$ with $a : A$ and $f : B(a) \to Wx : A.\ B$ (note that this is an inductive definition). Intuitively, elements of $Wx : A.\ B$ are well-founded trees whose possible branchings are indexed by the type $A$. For instance, consider the types $N_0$ with zero element, $N_1$ with one element, and $N_2$ with two elements 0 and 1; further consider the type family $T(x)$ such that $T(0) = N_0$ and $T(1) = N_1$. Then a canonical inhabitant of $Wx : N_2.\ T(x)$ is either a tree with one node, or a tree with one unique subtree in $Wx : N_2.\ T(x)$, hence one can think of $Wx : N_2.\ T(x)$ as a type "isomorphic" to the type of natural numbers.
Show by induction $Wx : A.\ B \to \neg\ \Pi x : A.\ B$, which says intuitively that if $Wx : A.\ B$ is inhabited then it cannot be the case that all $B(x)$ are inhabited. (Classically at least one $B(x)$ is empty.)
Furthermore show by induction that the relation $\sim$ on $Wx : A.\ B$ is an equivalence relation:

$$\begin{array}{rcl} sup\ a_1\ f_1 \sim sup\ a_2\ f_2 & = & \wedge\ (\Pi x_1 : B(a_1).\ \Sigma x_2 : B(a_2).\ \ f_1\ x_1 \sim f_2\ x_2) \\ & & \phantom{\wedge\ }(\Pi x_2 : B(a_2).\ \Sigma x_1 : B(a_1).\ \ f_1\ x_1 \sim f_2\ x_2) \end{array}$$

This inductive definition of equality is due to P. Aczel, who uses it to define $t \in u$ meaning that $t$ is an immediate subtree of $u$ by

$$t \in sup\ a\ f \ = \ \Sigma x : B(a).\ \ t \sim f\ x.$$

These definitions can be used to build a model of constructive set theory [4].

## References


1. A. Abel. On relating type theories and set theories. In T. Coquand, P. Dybjer, B. Nordström, and J. Smith, editors, *Proceedings of TYPES'99*, volume 1956 of *Lecture Notes in Computer Science*, pages 1–20. Springer-Verlag, 2000.
2. A. Abel. Termination checking with types. Technical Report 0201, Institut fur Informatik, Ludwig-Maximilians-Universität München, 2002.
3. A. Abel and T. Altenkirch. A predicative analysis of structural recursion. *Journal of Functional Programming*, 12(1):1–41, January 2002.
4. P. Aczel. The Type Theoretic Interpretation of Constructive Set Theory. In A. MacIntyre, A. Pacholski, and J. Paris, editors, *Proceedings of Logic Colloqium 77*, Studies in Logic and the Foundations of Mathematics, pages 55–66. North-Holland, 1978.
5. P. Aczel. Frege structures and the notions of proposition, truth and set. In J. Barwise, H. J. Keisler, and K. Kunen, editors, *Proceedings of the Kleene Symposium*, volume 101 of *Studies in Logic and the Foundations of Mathematics*, pages 31–59. North-Holland, Amsterdam, 1980.

6. P. Aczel. On Relating Type Theories and Set Theories. In T. Altenkirch, W. Naraschewski, and B. Reus, editors, *Proceedings of TYPES'98*, volume 1657 of *Lecture Notes in Computer Science*, pages 1–18. Springer-Verlag, 1999.
7. T. Altenkirch and C. McBride. Generic programming within dependently typed programming. In J. Gibbons and J. Jeuring, editors, *Proceedings of WCGP'02*. Kluwer Academic Publishers, 2002.
8. R. Amadio and S. Coupet-Grimal. Analysis of a guard condition in type theory. In M. Nivat, editor, *Proceedings of FOSSACS'98*, volume 1378 of *Lecture Notes in Computer Science*, pages 48–62. Springer-Verlag, 1998.
9. R. M. Amadio and L. Cardelli. Subtyping recursive types. *ACM Transactions on Programming Languages and Systems*, 15(4):575–631, September 1993.
10. D. Aspinall. Subtyping with singleton types. In L. Pacholski and J. Tiuryn, editors, *Proceedings of CSL'94*, volume 933 of *Lecture Notes in Computer Science*, pages 1–15. Springer-Verlag, 1994.
11. P. Audebaud. Partial Objects in the Calculus of Constructions. In *Proceedings of LICS'91*, pages 86–95. IEEE Computer Society Press, 1991.
12. L. Augustsson. Cayenne: A language with dependent types. In *Proceedings of ICFP'98*, pages 239–250. ACM Press, 1998.
13. L. Augustsson and M. Carlsson. An exercise in dependent types: A well-typed interpreter. In *Informal Proceedings of DTP'99*, 1999.
14. R. Backhouse, P. Jansson, J. Jeuring, and L. Meertens. Generic programming—an introduction. In S. D. Swierstra, P. R. Henriques, and J. N. Oliveira, editors, *Proceedings of AFP'98*, volume 1608 of *Lecture Notes in Computer Science*, pages 28–115. Springer-Verlag, 1999.
15. S. van Bakel, L. Liquori, S. Ronchi della Rocca, and P. Urzyczyn. Comparing cubes of typed and type assignment systems. *Annals of Pure and Applied Logic*, 86(3):267–303, July 1997.
16. H. Barendregt. Introduction to Generalised Type Systems. *Journal of Functional Programming*, 1(2):125–154, April 1991.
17. H. Barendregt. Lambda calculi with types. In S. Abramsky, D. Gabbay, and T. Maibaum, editors, *Handbook of Logic in Computer Science*, pages 117–309. Oxford Science Publications, 1992. Volume 2.
18. H. Barendregt and H. Geuvers. Proof assistants using dependent type systems. In A. Robinson and A. Voronkov, editors, *Handbook of Automated Reasoning*, volume II, chapter 18, pages 1149–1238. Elsevier Publishing, 2001.
19. G. Barthe. The semi-full closure of Pure Type Systems. In L. Brim, J. Gruska, and J. Zlatuska, editors, *Proceedings of MFCS'98*, volume 1450 of *Lecture Notes in Computer Science*, pages 316–325. Springer-Verlag, 1998.
20. G. Barthe. Type-Checking Injective Pure Type Systems. *Journal of Functional Programming*, 9(6):675–698, 1999.
21. G. Barthe and T. Coquand. On the equational theory of non-normalizing pure type systems. *Journal of Functional Programming*, 200x. To appear.
22. G. Barthe, M. J. Frade, E. Giménez, L. Pinto, and T. Uustalu. Type-based termination of recursive definitions. *Mathematical Structures in Computer Science*, 2002. To appear.
23. G. Barthe and M.H. Sørensen. Domain-free pure type systems. *Journal of Functional Programming*, 10(5):417–452, September 2000.
24. D. Basin and S. Matthews. Logical Frameworks. In D. Gabbay and F. Guenthner, editors, *Handbook of Philosophical Logic*, volume 9. Kluwer Academic Publishers, 2002.

25. L.S. van Benthem Jutting. Typing in pure type systems. *Information and Computation*, 105(1):30–41, July 1993.
26. L.S. van Benthem Jutting, J. McKinna, and R. Pollack. Checking algorithms for pure type systems. In H. Barendregt and T. Nipkow, editors, *Proceedings of TYPES'93*, volume 806 of *Lecture Notes in Computer Science*, pages 19–61. Springer-Verlag, 1994.
27. G. Betarte. *Dependent Record Types and Algebraic Structures in Type Theory.* PhD thesis, Department of Computer Science, Chalmers Tekniska Högskola, 1998.
28. G. Betarte and A. Tasistro. Extension of Martin-Löf's type theory with record types and subtyping. In G. Sambin and J. Smith, editors, *Twenty-five Years of Constructive Type Theory.* Oxford University Press, 1998.
29. R. Bird. *Introduction to Functional Programming using Haskell.* Prenctice Hall, 2 edition, 1998.
30. F. Blanqui, J.-P. Jouannaud, and M. Okada. Inductive Data Type Systems. *Theoretical Computer Science*, 272(1/2):41–68, February 2002.
31. D. Bolignano. Towards a mechanization of cryptographic protocol verification. In O. Grumberg, editor, *Proceedings of CAV'97*, volume 1254 of *Lecture Notes in Computer Science*, pages 131–142. Springer-Verlag, 1997.
32. M. Brandt and F. Henglein. Coinductive axiomatization of recursive type equality and subtyping. *Fundamenta Informaticae*, 33(4):309–338, April 1998.
33. W. Buchholz, S. Feferman, W. Pohlers, and W. Sieg. *Iterated Inductive Definitions and Subsystems of Analysis: Recent Proof-Theoretical Results*, volume 897 of *Lectures Notes in Mathematics.* Springer-Verlag, 1981.
34. L. Cardelli. A polymorphic lambda-calculus with Type:Type. Technical Report 10, SRC, May 1986.
35. L. Cardelli. Phase distinctions in type theory. Unpublished Mansucript, January 1988.
36. L. Cardelli. Structural subtyping and the notion of power type. In *Proceedings of POPL'88*, pages 70–79. ACM Press, 1988.
37. C. Coquand. Agda. See `http://www.cs.chalmers.se/~catarina/agda`.
38. C. Coquand. *Computation in Type Theory.* PhD thesis, Department of Computing Science, Chalmers University of Technology, 1996.
39. T. Coquand. Metamathematical Investigations of a Calculus of Constructions. In P. Odifreddi, editor, *Logic and Computer Science*, pages 91–122. Academic Press, 1990.
40. T. Coquand. An algorithm for testing conversion in type theory. In G. Huet and G. Plotkin, editors, *Logical Frameworks*, pages 255–279. Cambridge University Press, 1991.
41. T. Coquand. Pattern matching with dependent types. In B. Nordström, editor, *Informal proceedings of Logical Frameworks'92*, pages 66–79, 1992.
42. T. Coquand. An algorithm for type-checking dependent types. *Science of Computer Programming*, 26(1–3):167–177, May 1996.
43. T. Coquand and P. Dybjer. Inductive definitions and type theory: an introduction (preliminary version). In P.S. Thiagarajan, editor, *Proceedings of FSTTCS'94*, volume 880 of *Lecture Notes in Computer Science*, pages 60–76. Springer-Verlag, 1994.
44. T. Coquand and H. Herbelin. A-translation and looping combinators in pure type systems. *Journal of Functional Programming*, 4(1):77–88, January 1994.
45. T. Coquand and G. Huet. The Calculus of Constructions. *Information and Computation*, 76(2/3):95–120, February/March 1988.

46. T. Coquand and C. Paulin. Inductively defined types. In P. Martin-Löf and G. Mints, editors, *Proceedings of COLOG'88*, volume 417 of *Lecture Notes in Computer Science*, pages 50–66. Springer-Verlag, 1988.
47. T. Coquand, R. Pollack, and M. Takeyama. Modules as Dependently Typed Records. Manuscript, 2002.
48. J. Courant. *Un calcul de modules pour les systèmes de types purs.* PhD thesis, Ecole Normale Supérieure de Lyon, 1998.
49. G. Cousineau and M. Mauny. *The functional approach to programming.* Cambridge University Press, 1998.
50. K. Crary. Sound and complete elimination of singleton kinds. In R. Harper, editor, *Proceedings of TIC'00*, volume 2071 of *Lecture Notes in Computer Science*, pages 1–26. Springer-Verlag, 2001.
51. K. Crary and S. Weirich. Resource bound certification. In *Proceedings of POPL'00*, pages 184–198. ACM Press, 2000.
52. P. Dybjer. Inductive sets and families in Martin-Löf's type theory and their set-theoretic semantics. In G. Huet and G. Plotkin, editors, *Logical Frameworks*, pages 280–306. Cambridge University Press, 1991.
53. P. Dybjer. Inductive families. *Formal Aspects of Computing*, 6:440–465, 1994.
54. P. Dybjer. Representing inductively defined sets by well-orderings in Martin-Löf's type theory. *Theoretical Computer Science*, 176(1–2):329–335, April 1997.
55. P. Dybjer. A general formulation of simultaneous inductive-recursive definitions in type theory. *Journal of Symbolic Logic*, 65(2):525–549, June 2000.
56. H. Geuvers. *Logics and type systems.* PhD thesis, University of Nijmegen, 1993.
57. H. Geuvers. Induction is not derivable in second order dependent type theory. In S. Abramsky, editor, *Proceedings of TLCA'01*, Lecture Notes in Computer Science, pages 166–181. Springer-Verlag, 2001.
58. H. Geuvers and M.J. Nederhof. A modular proof of strong normalisation for the Calculus of Constructions. *Journal of Functional Programming*, 1(2):155–189, April 1991.
59. H. Geuvers, E. Poll, and J. Zwanenburg. Safe proof checking in type theory with Y. In J. Flum and M. Rodríguez-Artalejo, editors, *Proceedings of CSL'99*, volume 1683 of *Lecture Notes in Computer Science*, pages 439–452. Springer-Verlag, 1999.
60. H. Geuvers and B. Werner. On the Church-Rosser property for expressive type systems and its consequence for their metatheoretic study. In *Proceedings of LICS'94*, pages 320–329. IEEE Computer Society Press, 1994.
61. J. Giesl, C. Walther, and J. Brauburger. Termination analysis for functional programs. In W. Bibel and P. Schmitt, editors, *Automated Deduction - A Basis for Applications*, volume 3 of *Applied Logic Series*, pages 135–164. Kluwer Academic Publishers, 1998.
62. E. Giménez. *Un calcul de constructions infinies et son application à la vérification de systèmes communicants.* PhD thesis, Ecole Normale Superieure de Lyon, 1996.
63. E. Giménez. Structural recursive definitions in Type Theory. In K.G. Larsen, S. Skyum, and G. Winskel, editors, *Proceedings of ICALP'98*, volume 1443 of *Lecture Notes in Computer Science*, pages 397–408. Springer-Verlag, 1998.
64. J-Y. Girard. *Interprétation fonctionnelle et élimination des coupures dans l'arithmétique d'ordre supérieur.* Thèse d'Etat, Université Paris 7, 1972.
65. J.-Y. Girard, Y. Lafont, and P. Taylor. *Proofs and Types.* Number 7 in Tracts in Theoretical Computer Science. Cambridge University Press, 1989.
66. B. Grégoire and X. Leroy. A compiled implementation of strong reduction. In *Proceedings of ICFP'02.* ACM Press, 2002.

67. B. Grobauer. Cost recurrences for DML programs. In *Proceedings of ICFP'01*, pages 253–264. ACM Press, September 2001.
68. P. Hancock and A. Setzer. Interactive programs in dependent type theory. In P. Clote and H. Schwichtenberg, editors, *Proceedings of CSL'00*, volume 1862 of *Lecture Notes in Computer Science*, pages 317–331. Springer-Verlag, 2000.
69. R. Harper, F. Honsell, and G. Plotkin. A framework for defining logics. *Journal of the ACM*, 40(1):143–184, January 1993.
70. R. Harper, J. C. Mitchell, and E. Moggi. Higher-order modules and the phase distinction. In *Proceedings of POPL'90*, pages 341–354. ACM Press, 1990.
71. R. Harper and J.C. Mitchell. On the type structure of Standard ML. *ACM Transactions on Programming Languages and Systems*, 15(2):211–252, April 1993.
72. R. Hinze. A new approach to generic functional programming. In *Proceedings of POPL'00*, pages 119–132. ACM Press, 2000.
73. J. G. Hook and D. J. Howe. Impredicative strong existential equivalent to type:type. Technical Report TR86-760, Cornell University, Computer Science Department, June 1986.
74. J. Hughes, L. Pareto, and A. Sabry. Proving the correctness of reactive systems using sized types. In *Proceedings of POPL'96*, pages 410–423. ACM Press, 1996.
75. A. Hurkens. A Simplification of Girard's Paradox. In M. Dezani-Ciancaglini and G. Plotkin, editors, *Proceedings of TLCA'95*, volume 902 of *Lecture Notes in Computer Science*, pages 266–278. Springer-Verlag, 1995.
76. P. Jansson and J. Jeuring. PolyP—a polytypic programming language extension. In *Proceedings of POPL'97*, pages 470–482. ACM Press, 1997.
77. S. Jha, J. Palsberg, and T. Zhao. Efficient type matching. In M. Nielsen and U. Engberg, editors, *Proceedings of FOSSACS 2002*, volume 2303 of *Lecture Notes in Computer Science*, pages 187–204. Springer-Verlag, 2002.
78. M. P. Jones. Type classes with functional dependencies. In G. Smolka, editor, *Proceedings of ESOP'00*, volume 1782 of *Lecture Notes in Computer Science*, pages 230–244, 2000.
79. J.-P. Jouannaud and M. Okada. Abstract data type systems. *Theoretical Computer Science*, 173(2):349–391, February 1997.
80. D. Kozen, J. Palsberg, and M. Schwartzback. Efficient recursive subtyping. *Mathematical Structures in Computer Science*, 5(1):113–125, March 1995.
81. B. Lampson and R. Burstall. Pebble, a kernel language for modules and abstract data types. *Information and Computation*, 76(2/3):278–346, February/March 1988.
82. C.-S. Lee, N. D. Jones, and A. M. Ben-Amram. The size-change principle for program termination. In *Proceedings of POPL'01*, pages 81–92. ACM Press, 2001.
83. X. Leroy. A modular module system. *Journal of Functional Programming*, 10(3):269–303, May 2000.
84. G. Longo and E. Moggi. Constructive natural deduction and its '$\omega$-set' interpretation. *Mathematical Structures in Computer Science*, 1(2):215–254, July 1991.
85. Z. Luo. *Computation and Reasoning: A Type Theory for Computer Science*. Number 11 in International Series of Monographs on Computer Science. Oxford University Press, 1994.
86. Z. Luo. Coercive subtyping. *Journal of Logic and Computation*, 9(1):105–130, February 1999.
87. D. MacQueen. Using dependent types to express modular structure. In *Proceedings of POPL'86*, pages 277–286. ACM Press, 1986.

88. L. Magnusson. *The implementation of ALF: a proof editor based on Martin-Löf's monomorphic type theory with explicit substitution.* PhD thesis, Department of Computer Science, Chalmers University, 1994.
89. P. Martin-Löf. Hauptsatz for the intuitionistic theory of iterated inductive definitions. In J. E. Fenstad, editor, *Proceedings 2nd Scandinavian Logic Symposium*, volume 63 of *Studies in Logic and the Foundations of Mathematics*, pages 179–216. North-Holland, Amsterdam, 1971.
90. P. Martin-Löf. A theory of types. Technical Report, Stockholm University, February 1971.
91. P. Martin-Löf. An intuitionistic theory of types. Unpublished Manuscript, 1972.
92. P. Martin-Löf. *Intuitionistic Type Theory*, volume 1 of *Studies in Proof Theory.* Bibliopolis, Naples, 1984.
93. P. Martin-Löf. Constructive mathematics and computer programming. In C. A. R. Hoare and J. C. Shepherdson, editors, *Mathematical Logic and Programming Languages*, pages 167–184. Prentice-Hall, 1985.
94. C. McBride. *Dependently typed functional programs and their proofs.* PhD thesis, University of Edinburgh, 2000.
95. C. McBride. Faking It (Simulating Dependent Types in Haskell). *Journal of Functional Programming*, 2002. To appear.
96. N. P. Mendler. Inductive types and type constraints in second-order lambda calculus. In *Proceedings of LICS'87*, pages 30–36. IEEE Computer Society Press, 1987.
97. N. P. Mendler. Inductive types and type constraints in the second-order lambda calculus. *Annals of Pure and Applied Logic*, 51(1-2):159–172, March 1991.
98. R. Milner. A theory of type polymorphism in programming. *Journal of Computer and System Sciences*, 17:348–375, 1978.
99. R. Milner, M. Tofte, and R. Harper. *The Definition of Standard ML.* The MIT Press, 1991.
100. R. Milner, M. Tofte, R. Harper, and D. MacQueen. *The Definition of Standard ML (Revised).* The MIT Press, 1997.
101. A. Miquel. The implicit calculus of constructions. In S. Abramsky, editor, *Proceedings of TLCA'01*, volume 2044 of *Lecture Notes in Computer Science*, pages 344–359. Springer-Verlag, 2001.
102. A. Miquel. *Le Calcul des Constructions implicite: syntaxe et sémantique.* PhD thesis, Université Paris 11, 2001.
103. J. C. Mitchell and G. D. Plotkin. Abstract types have existential type. *ACM Transactions on Programming Languages and Systems*, 10(3):470–502, July 1988.
104. G. C. Necula. Proof-carrying code. In *Proceedings of POPL'97*, pages 106–119. ACM Press, 1997.
105. G. C. Necula and P. Lee. Efficient representation and validation of logical proofs. In *Proceedings of LICS'98*, pages 93–104, 1998.
106. R. Nederpelt, H. Geuvers, and R. de Vrijer, editors. *Selected Papers on Automath*, volume 133 of *Studies in Logic and the Foundations of Mathematics.* North-Holland, 1994.
107. M. Neubauer, P. Thiemann, M. Gasbichler, and M. Sperber. Functional logic overloading. In *Proceedings of POPL'02*, pages 233–244. ACM Press, 2002.
108. B. Nordström. Terminating general recursion. *BIT*, 28(3):605–619, 1988.
109. B. Nordström, K. Petersson, and J. Smith. *Programming in Martin-Löf's Type Theory. An Introduction.* Number 7 in International Series of Monographs on Computer Science. Oxford University Press, 1990.

110. J. Palsberg and T. Zhao. Efficient and flexible matching of recursive types. *Information and Computation*, 171:364–387, November 2001.
111. L. Pareto. *Types for crash prevention.* PhD thesis, Department of Computing, Chalmers Tekniska Högskola, 2000.
112. C. Paulin-Mohring. Inductive definitions in the system Coq. Rules and properties. In M. Bezem and J.F. Groote, editors, *Proceedings of TLCA'93*, volume 664 of *Lecture Notes in Computer Science*, pages 328–345. Springer-Verlag, 1993.
113. C. Paulin-Mohring. *Définitions Inductives en Theorie des Types d'Ordre Superieur.* Habilitation à diriger les recherches, Université Claude Bernard Lyon I, 1996.
114. L. C. Paulson. *ML for the Working Programmer.* Cambridge University Press, 1996.
115. L.C. Paulson. The inductive approach to verifying cryptographic protocols. *Journal of Computer Security*, 6(1/2):85–128, 1998.
116. S. Peyton Jones and E. Meijer. Henk: a typed intermediate language. Appeared as Technical Report BCCS-97-03, Computer Science Department, Boston College, 1997.
117. H. Pfeifer and H. Rueß. Polytypic abstraction in type theory. In R. Backhouse and T. Sheard, editors, *Informal Proceedings of WGP'98.* Department of Computing Science, Chalmers University, June 1998.
118. H. Pfeifer and H. Rueß. Polytypic proof construction. In Y. Bertot, G. Dowek, H. Hirshowitz, C. Paulin, and L. Théry, editors, *Proceedings of TPHOLs'99*, volume 1690 of *Lecture Notes in Computer Science*, pages 55–72. Springer-Verlag, 1999.
119. F. Pfenning. Elf: a meta-language for deductive systems. In A. Bundy, editor, *Proceedings of CADE-12*, volume 814 of *Lecture Notes in Artificial Intelligence*, pages 811–815. Springer-Verlag, 1994.
120. F. Pfenning. Logical Frameworks. In A. Robinson and A. Voronkov, editors, *Handbook of Automated Reasoning*, volume II, chapter 17, pages 1063–1147. Elsevier Publishing, 2001.
121. F. Pfenning and C. Paulin. Inductively Defined Types in the Calculus of Constructions. In M. Main, A. Melton, M. Mislove, and D. Schmidt, editors, *Proceedings of MFPS'89*, volume 442 of *Lecture Notes in Computer Science*, pages 209–228. Springer-Verlag, 1989.
122. R. Pollack. Typechecking in pure type systems. In B. Nordström, editor, *Informal proceedings of Logical Frameworks'92*, pages 271–288, 1992.
123. R. Pollack. *The Theory of LEGO: A Proof Checker for the Extended Calculus of Constructions.* PhD thesis, University of Edinburgh, 1994.
124. R. Pollack. Dependently typed records for representing mathematical structures. In M. Aagard and J. Harrison, editors, *Proceedings of TPHOLs'00*, volume 1869 of *Lecture Notes in Computer Science*, pages 462–479. Springer-Verlag, 2000.
125. M. B. Reinhold. Typechecking is undecidable 'TYPE' is a type. Technical Report MIT/LCS/TR-458, Massachusetts Institute of Technology, December 1989.
126. D. Rémy. Using, Understanding, and Unraveling the OCaml Language—From Practice to Theory and vice versa. This volume.
127. J. W. Roorda. Pure Type Systems for Functional Programming. Master's thesis, Department of Computer Science, University of Utrecht, 2000.
128. C. Russo. *Types For Modules.* PhD thesis, University of Edinburgh, 1998.
129. A. Salvesen and J. Smith. The Strength of the Subset Type in Martin-Löf's Type Theory. In *Proceedings of LICS'88*, pages 384–391. IEEE Computer Society Press, 1988.

130. D. Scott. Constructive validity. In M. Laudet, D. Lacombe, L. Nolin, and M. Schützenberger, editors, *Proceedings of Symposium on Automatic Demonstration*, volume 125 of *Lecture Notes in Mathematics*, pages 237–275. Springer-Verlag, 1970.
131. P. Severi. Type Inference for Pure Type Systems. *Information and Computation*, 143(1):1–23, May 1998.
132. Z. Shao, B. Saha, V. Trifonov, and N. Papaspyrou. A type system for certified binaries. In *Proceedings of POPL'02*, pages 217–232. ACM Press, 2002.
133. M. H. Sørensen and P. Urzyczyn. Lectures on the Curry-Howard Isomorphism. Available as DIKU Rapport 98/14, 1998.
134. M. Stefanova and H. Geuvers. A simple set-theoretic semantics for the Calculus of Constructions. In S. Berardi and M. Coppo, editors, *Proceedings of TYPES'95*, volume 1158 of *Lecture Notes in Computer Science*, pages 249–264. Springer-Verlag, 1996.
135. C. A. Stone and R. Harper. Deciding Type Equivalence with Singleton Kinds. In *Proceedings of POPL'00*, pages 214–227. ACM Press, 2000.
136. M. D. G. Swaen. *Weak and strong sum elimination in intuitionistic type theory.* PhD thesis, Faculty of Mathematics and Computer Science, University of Amsterdam, 1989.
137. W. W. Tait. Constructive reasoning. In *Proceedings of the Third International Congress in Logic, Methodology and Philosophy of Science*, pages 185–199. North-Holland Publishing, 1968.
138. S. Thompson. *Haskell. The Craft of Functional Programming.* Addison-Wesley, 1996.
139. D. Walker. A Type System for Expressive Security Policies. In *Proceedings of POPL'00*, pages 254–267. ACM Press, 2000.
140. B. Werner. Sets in Types, Types in Sets. In M. Abadi and T. Ito, editors, *Proceedings of TACS'97*, volume 1281 of *Lecture Notes in Computer Science*, pages 530–546. Springer-Verlag, 1997.
141. H. Xi. *Dependent types in practical programming.* PhD thesis, Department of Computer Science, Carnegie-Mellon University, 1998.
142. H. Xi. Dead Code Elimination through Dependent Types. In G. Gupta, editor, *Proceedings of PADL'99*, volume 1551, pages 228–242. Springer-Verlag, 1999.
143. H. Xi and R. Harper. A Dependently Typed Assembly Language. In *Proceedings of ICFP'01*, pages 169–180. ACM Press, 2001.
144. H. Xi and F. Pfenning. Eliminating array bound checking through dependent types. In *Proceedings of PLDI'98*, pages 249–257. ACM Press, 1998.
145. H. Xi and F. Pfenning. Dependent types in practical programming. In *Proceedings of POPL'99*, pages 214–227. ACM Press, 1999.

# Monads and Effects

Nick Benton[1], John Hughes[2], and Eugenio Moggi[3,*]

[1] Microsoft Research
[2] Chalmers Univ.
[3] DISI, Univ. di Genova, Genova, Italy
moggi@disi.unige.it

**Abstract.** A tension in language design has been between simple semantics on the one hand, and rich possibilities for side-effects, exception handling and so on on the other. The introduction of monads has made a large step towards reconciling these alternatives. First proposed by Moggi as a way of structuring semantic descriptions, they were adopted by Wadler to structure Haskell programs. Monads have been used to solve long-standing problems such as adding pointers and assignment, inter-language working, and exception handling to Haskell, without compromising its purely functional semantics. The course introduces monads, effects, and exemplifies their applications in programming (Haskell) and in compilation (MLj). The course presents typed metalanguages for monads and related categorical notions, and then describes how they can be further refined by introducing effects.

## Table of Contents



* Research partially supported by MURST and ESPRIT WG APPSEM.

G. Barthe et al. (Eds.): Applied Semantics, LNCS 2395, pp. 42–122, 2002.

# 1 Monads and Computational Types

Monads, sometimes called triples, have been considered in Category Theory (CT) only in the late fifties (see the historical notes in [BW85]). Monads and comonads (the dual of monads) are closely related to adjunctions, probably the most pervasive notion in CT. The connection between monads and adjunctions was established independently by Kleisli and Eilenberg-Moore in the sixties. Monads, like adjunctions, arise in many contexts (e.g. in algebraic theories). There are several CT books covering monads, for instance [Man76,BW85,Bor94]. It is not surprising that monads arise also in applications of CT to Computer Science (CS). We intend to use monads for giving denotational semantics to programming languages, and more specifically as a way of modeling *computational types* [Mog91]:

> ...to interpret a programming language in a category $\mathcal{C}$, we distinguish the object $A$ of values (of type $A$) from the object $TA$ of computations (of type $A$), and take as denotations of programs (of type $A$) the *elements* of $TA$. In particular, we identify the type $A$ with the object of values (of type $A$) and obtain the object of computations (of type $A$) by applying an unary type-constructor $T$ to $A$. We call $T$ a *notion of computation*, since it abstracts away from the type of values computations may produce.

*Example 1.* We give few notions of computation in the category of sets.

- **partiality** $TA = A_\bot$, i.e. $A + \{\bot\}$, where $\bot$ is the *diverging computation*
- **nondeterminism** $TA = \mathcal{P}_{fin}(A)$, i.e. the set of finite subsets of $A$
- **side-effects** $TA = (A \times S)^S$, where $S$ is a set of states, e.g. a set $U^L$ of stores or a set of input/output sequences $U^*$

- **exceptions** $TA = A + E$, where $E$ is the set of exceptions
- **continuations** $TA = R^{(R^A)}$, where $R$ is the set of results
- **interactive input** $TA = (\mu X.A + X^U)$, where $U$ is the set of characters. More explicitly $TA$ is the set of $U$-branching trees with only finite paths and $A$-labelled leaves
- **interactive output** $TA = (\mu X.A + (U \times X))$, i.e. $U^* \times A$ up to iso.

Further examples (in the category of cpos) could be given based on the denotational semantics for various programming languages

*Remark 2.* Many of the examples above are instances of the following one: given a single sorted algebraic theory $Th = (\Sigma, Ax)$, $TA$ is the carrier of the free $Th$-algebra over $A$, i.e. the set $T_\Sigma(A)$ of $\Sigma$-terms over $A$ modulo the equivalence induced by the equational axioms $Ax$. For instance, for nondeterminism $Th$ is the theory of commutative and idempotent monoids, and for exceptions is the theory with one constant for each exception $e \in E$ and no axioms.

More complex examples can be obtained by *combination* of those above, e.g.

- $TA = ((A+E) \times S)^S$ and $TA = ((A \times S) + E)^S$ capture imperative programs with exceptions
- $TA = \mu X.\mathcal{P}_{fin}(A + (Act \times X))$ captures parallel programs interacting via a set *Act* of actions (in fact $TA$ is the set of finite synchronization trees up to strong bisimulation)
- $TA = \mu X.\mathcal{P}_{fin}((A + X) \times S)^S$ captures parallel imperative programs with shared memory.

Wadler [Wad92a] advocates a similar idea to mimic impure programs in a pure functional language. Indeed the Haskell community has gone a long way in exploiting this approach to reconcile the advantages of pure functional programming with the flexibility of imperative (or other styles of) programming. The analogies of computational types with *effect systems* [GL86] have been observed by [Wad92a], but formal relations between the two have been established only recently (e.g. see [Wad98]).

In the denotational semantics of programming languages there are other informal notions modeled using monads, for instance *collection types* in database languages [BNTW95] or *collection classes* in object-oriented languages [Man98]. It is important to distinguish the mathematical notion of monad (or its refinements) from informal notions, such as computational and collection types, which are *defined* by examples. In fact, these informal notions can be modeled with a better degree of approximation by considering monads with additional properties or additional structures. When considering these refinements, it is often the case that what seems a natural requirement for modeling computational types is not appropriate for modeling collection types, for instance:

- most programming languages can express divergent computations and support recursive definitions of programs; hence computational types should have a constant $\bot : TA$ for the divergent computation and a (least) fixpoint combinator $Y : (TA \to TA) \to TA$;

- in database query languages the result of a query is a finite collection of elements; hence it is natural to have an empty collection $\emptyset : TA$ and a way of merging the result of two queries, using a binary operation $+ : TA \to TA \to TA$.

Therefore, programming languages suggest one refinement (of monads), while query languages suggest a different and *incompatible* refinement.

There are at least three equivalent definitions of monad/triple called (see [Man76]): in monoid form (the one usually adopted in CT books), in extension form (the most intuitive one), and in clone form (which takes composition in the Kleisli category as basic). Of these we consider only triples in monoid and extension form.

**Notation 1** *We assume knowledge of basic notions from category theory, such as category, functor and natural transformation. In some cases familiarity with universal constructions (products, sums, exponentials) and adjunction is assumed. We use the following notation:*

- *given a category $\mathcal{C}$ we write:*
  *$|\mathcal{C}|$ for the set/class of its objects,*
  *$\mathcal{C}(A,B)$ for the hom-set of morphisms from $A$ to $B$,*
  *$g \circ f$ and $f;g$ for the composition $A \xrightarrow{f} B \xrightarrow{g} C$,*
  *$\mathrm{id}_A$ for the identity on $A$*
- *$F : \mathcal{C} \to \mathcal{D}$ means that $F$ is a functor from $\mathcal{C}$ to $\mathcal{D}$, and*
  *$\sigma : F \dot{\to} G$ means that $\sigma$ is a natural transformation from $F$ to $G$*
- *$\mathcal{C} \underset{F}{\overset{G}{\underset{\longrightarrow}{\overset{\longleftarrow}{\top}}}} \mathcal{D}$ means that $G$ is right adjoint to $F$ ($F$ is left adjoint to $G$).*

**Definition 3 (Kleisli triple/triple in extension form).** *A* **Kleisli triple** *over a category $\mathcal{C}$ is a triple $(T, \eta, \_^*)$, where $T : |\mathcal{C}| \to |\mathcal{C}|$, $\eta_A : A \to TA$ for $A \in |\mathcal{C}|$, $f^* : TA \to TB$ for $f : A \to TB$ and the following equations hold:*

- $\eta_A^* = \mathrm{id}_{TA}$
- $\eta_A; f^* = f$ *for* $f : A \to TB$
- $f^*; g^* = (f; g^*)^*$ *for* $f : A \to TB$ *and* $g : B \to TC$.

Kleisli triples have an intuitive justification in terms of computational types

- $\eta_A$ is the *inclusion* of values into computations

$$a : A \overset{\eta_A}{\longmapsto} [a] : TA$$

- $f^*$ is the *extension* of a function $f$ from values to computations to a function from computations to computations. The function $f^*$ applied to a computation $c$ returns the computation $\mathrm{let}\, a {\Leftarrow} c \,\mathrm{in}\, f(a)$, which first evaluates $c$ and then applies $f$ to the resulting value $a$

$$\frac{a : A \overset{f}{\longmapsto} f(a) : TB}{c : TA \overset{f^*}{\longmapsto} \mathrm{let}\, a {\Leftarrow} c \,\mathrm{in}\, f(a) : TB}$$

In order to justify the axioms for a Kleisli triple we have first to introduce a category $\mathcal{C}_T$ whose morphisms correspond to programs. We proceed by analogy with the categorical semantics for terms, where types are interpreted by objects and terms of type $B$ with a parameter (free variable) of type $A$ are interpreted by morphisms from $A$ to $B$. Since the denotation of programs of type $B$ are supposed to be elements of $TB$, programs of type $B$ with a parameter of type $A$ ought to be interpreted by morphisms with codomain $TB$, but for their domain there are two alternatives, either $A$ or $TA$, depending on whether parameters of type $A$ are identified with values or computations of type $A$. We choose the first alternative, because it entails the second. Indeed computations of type $A$ are the same as values of type $TA$. So we take $\mathcal{C}_T(A,B)$ to be $\mathcal{C}(A,TB)$. It remains to define composition and identities in $\mathcal{C}_T$ (and show that they satisfy the unit and associativity axioms for categories).

**Definition 4 (Kleisli category).** *Given a Kleisli triple $(T,\eta,\_^*)$ over $\mathcal{C}$, the* **Kleisli category** $\mathcal{C}_T$ *is defined as follows:*

- *the objects of $\mathcal{C}_T$ are those of $\mathcal{C}$*
- *the set $\mathcal{C}_T(A,B)$ of morphisms from $A$ to $B$ in $\mathcal{C}_T$ is $\mathcal{C}(A,TB)$*
- *the identity on $A$ in $\mathcal{C}_T$ is $\eta_A : A \to TA$*
- *$f \in \mathcal{C}_T(A,B)$ followed by $g \in \mathcal{C}_T(B,C)$ in $\mathcal{C}_T$ is $f;g^* : A \to TC$.*

It is natural to take $\eta_A$ as the identity on $A$ in the category $\mathcal{C}_T$, since it maps a parameter $x$ to $[x]$, i.e. to $x$ viewed as a computation. Similarly composition in $\mathcal{C}_T$ has a simple explanation in terms of the intuitive meaning of $f^*$, in fact

$$\frac{x : A \overset{f}{\longmapsto} f\ x : TB \quad y : B \overset{g}{\longmapsto} g\ y : TC}{x : A \overset{f;g^*}{\longmapsto} \mathrm{let}\ y \Leftarrow f(x)\ \mathrm{in}\ g(y) : TC}$$

i.e. $f$ followed by $g$ in $\mathcal{C}_T$ with parameter $x$ is the program which first evaluates the program $f\ x$ and then feed the resulting value as parameter to $g$. At this point we can give also a simple justification for the three axioms of Kleisli triples, namely they are equivalent to the following unit and associativity axioms, which say that $\mathcal{C}_T$ is a category:

- $f;\eta_B^* = f$ for $f : A \to TB$
- $\eta_A; f^* = f$ for $f : A \to TB$
- $(f;g^*);h^* = f;(g;h^*)^*$ for $f : A \to TB$, $g : B \to TC$ and $h : C \to TD$.

*Example 5.* We go through the examples of computational types given in Example 1 and show that they are indeed part of suitable Kleisli triples.

- **partiality** $TA = A_\bot (= A + \{\bot\})$
  $\eta_A$ is the inclusion of $A$ into $A_\bot$
  if $f : A \to TB$, then $f^*\ \bot = \bot$ and $f^*\ a = f\ a$ (when $a \in A$)
- **nondeterminism** $TA = \mathcal{P}_{fin}(A)$
  $\eta_A$ is the singleton map $a \mapsto \{a\}$
  if $f : A \to TB$ and $c \in TA$, then $f^*\ c = \cup\{f\ x | x \in c\}$

- **side-effects** $TA = (A\times S)^S$
  $\eta_A$ is the map $a \mapsto \lambda s : S.(a, s)$
  if $f : A \to TB$ and $c \in TA$, then $f^*\ c = \lambda s : S.\mathrm{let}\,(a, s') = c\ s\,\mathrm{in}\,f\ a\ s'$
- **exceptions** $TA = A + E$
  $\eta_A$ is the injection map $a \mapsto \mathrm{inl}\ a$
  if $f : A \to TB$, then $f^*(\mathrm{inr}\ e) = \mathrm{inr}\ e$ (where $e \in E$) and $f^*(\mathrm{inl}\ a) = f\ a$ (where $a \in A$)
- **continuations** $TA = R^{(R^A)}$
  $\eta_A$ is the map $a \mapsto (\lambda k : R^A.k\ a)$
  if $f : A \to TB$ and $c \in TA$, then $f^*\ c = (\lambda k : R^B.c(\lambda a : A.f\ a\ k))$
- **interactive input** $TA = (\mu X.A + X^U)$
  $\eta_A$ maps $a$ to the tree consisting only of one leaf labelled with $a$
  if $f : A \to TB$ and $c \in TA$, then $f^*\ c$ is the tree obtained by replacing leaves of $c$ labelled by $a$ with the tree $f\ a$
- **interactive output** $TA = (\mu X.A + (U\times X))$
  $\eta_A$ is the map $a \mapsto (\epsilon, a)$
  if $f : A \to TB$, then $f^*\ (s, a) = (s * s', b)$, where $f\ a = (s', b)$ and $s * s'$ is the concatenation of $s$ followed by $s'$.

*Exercise 6.* Define Kleisli triples in the category of cpos similar to those given in Example 5, but ensure that each computational type $TA$ has a least element $\bot$. DIFFICULT: in cpos there are three Kleisli triple for nondeterminism, one for each powerdomain construction.

*Exercise 7.* When modeling a programming language the first choice to make is which category to use. For instance, it is impossible to find a monad over the category of sets which supports recursive definitions of programs, the category of cpos (or similar categories) should be used instead. Moreover, there are other aspects of programming languages that are orthogonal to computational types, e.g. recursive and polymorphic types, that cannot be modeled in the category of sets (but could be modeled in the category of cpos or in *realizability models*). In this exercise we consider modeling a two-level language, where there is a notion of static and dynamic, then the following categories are particularly appropriate

- the category $s(\mathcal{C})$, where $\mathcal{C}$ is a CCC, is defined as follows
  an object is a pair $(A_s, A_d)$ with $A_s, A_d \in |\mathcal{C}|$, $A_s$ is the static and $A_d$ is the dynamic part;
  a morphism in $s(\mathcal{C})((A_s, A_d), (B_s, B_d))$ is a pair $(f_s, f_d)$ with $f_s \in \mathcal{C}(A_s, B_s)$ and $f_d \in \mathcal{C}(A_s\times A_d, B_d)$, thus the static part of the result depends only on the static part of the input.
- the category $Fam(\mathcal{C})$, where $\mathcal{C}$ is a CCC with small limits, is defined as follows
  an object is a family $(A_i|i \in I)$ with $I$ a set and $A_i \in |\mathcal{C}|$ for every $i \in I$;
  a morphism in $Fam(\mathcal{C})((A_i|i \in I), (B_j|j \in J))$ is a pair $(f, g)$ with $f : I \to J$ and $g$ is an $I$-index family of morphisms s.t. $g_i \in \mathcal{C}(A_i, B_{fi})$ for every $i \in I$.

Define Kleisli triples in the categories $s(\mathcal{C})$ and $Fam(\mathcal{C})$ similar to those given in Example 5 (assume that $\mathcal{C}$ is the category of sets). Notice that in a two-level language static and dynamic computations don't have to be the same.

## 1.1 Monads and Related Notions

This section recalls some categorical notions, namely $T$-algebras and monad morphisms, and facts that are not essential to the subsequent developments. First we establish the equivalence of Kleisli triples and monads.

**Definition 8 (Monad/triple in monoid form).** *A* **monad** *over* $\mathcal{C}$ *is a triple* $(T, \eta, \mu)$, *where* $T : \mathcal{C} \to \mathcal{C}$ *is a functor,* $\eta : \mathrm{id}_{\mathcal{C}} \dot{\to} T$ *and* $\mu : T^2 \dot{\to} T$ *are natural transformations and the following diagrams commute:*

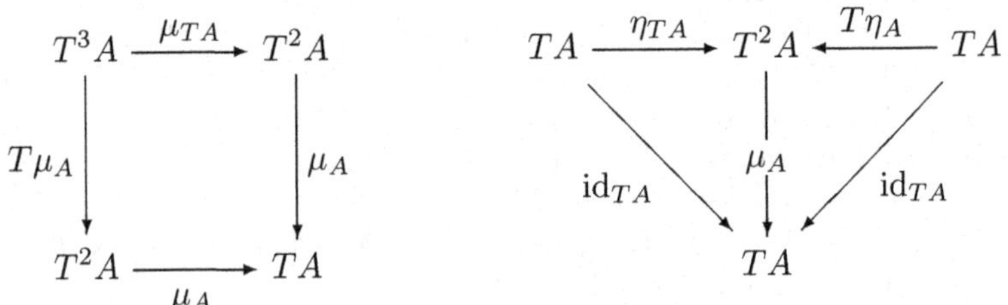


**Proposition 9.** *There is a bijection between Kleisli triples and monads.*

*Proof.* Given a Kleisli triple $(T, \eta, \_^*)$, the corresponding monad is $(T, \eta, \mu)$, where $T$ is the extension of the function $T$ to an endofunctor by taking $T\ f = (f; \eta_B)^*$ for $f : A \to B$ and $\mu_A = \mathrm{id}^*_{TA}$. Conversely, given a monad $(T, \eta, \mu)$, the corresponding Kleisli triple is $(T, \eta, \_^*)$, where $T$ is the restriction of the functor $T$ to objects and $f^* = (T\ f); \mu_B$ for $f : A \to TB$.

Monads are closely related to algebraic theories. In particular, $T$-algebras correspond to models of an algebraic theory.

**Definition 10 (Eilenberg-Moore category).** *Given a monad* $(T, \eta, \mu)$ *over* $\mathcal{C}$, *the* **Eilenberg-Moore category** $\mathcal{C}^T$ *is defined as follows:*

– *the objects of* $\mathcal{C}^T$ *are* $T$-**algebras**, *i.e. morphisms* $\alpha : TA \to A$ *in* $\mathcal{C}$ *s.t.*

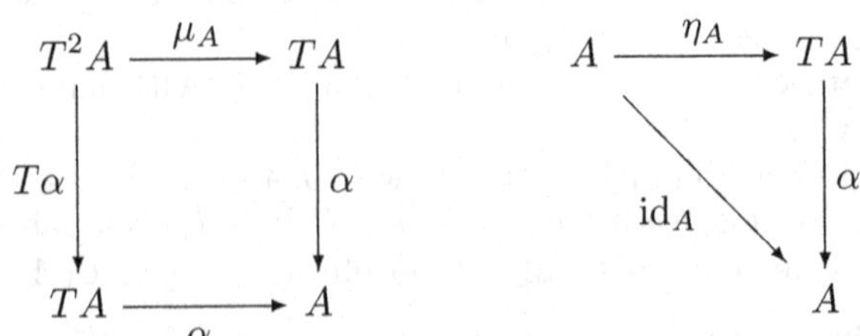


*A is called the* **carrier** *of the* $T$*-algebra* $\alpha$

– *a morphism $f \in \mathcal{C}^T(\alpha, \beta)$ from $\alpha : TA \to A$ to $\beta : TB \to B$ is a morphism $f : A \to B$ in $\mathcal{C}$ s.t.*

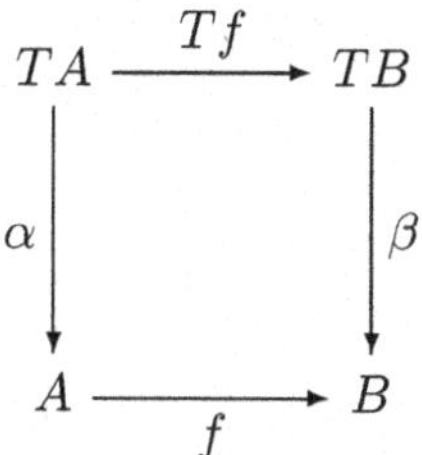


*identity and composition in $\mathcal{C}^T$ are like in $\mathcal{C}$.*

Any adjunction $\mathcal{C} \underset{F}{\overset{G}{\underset{\longrightarrow}{\overset{\longleftarrow}{\top}}}} \mathcal{D}$ induces a monad over $\mathcal{C}$ with $T = F; G$. The Kleisli and Eilenberg-Moore categories can be used to prove the converse, i.e. that any monad over $\mathcal{C}$ is induced by an adjunction. Moreover, the Kleisli category $\mathcal{C}_T$ can be identified with the full sub-category of $\mathcal{C}^T$ of the *free $T$-algebras.*

**Proposition 11.** *Given a monad $(T, \eta, \mu)$ over $\mathcal{C}$ there are two adjunctions*

$$\mathcal{C} \underset{F}{\overset{U}{\underset{\longrightarrow}{\overset{\longleftarrow}{\top}}}} \mathcal{C}^T \qquad\qquad \mathcal{C} \underset{F'}{\overset{U'}{\underset{\longrightarrow}{\overset{\longleftarrow}{\top}}}} \mathcal{C}_T$$

*which induce $T$. Moreover, there is a full and faithful functor $\Phi : \mathcal{C}_T \to \mathcal{C}^T$ s.t.*

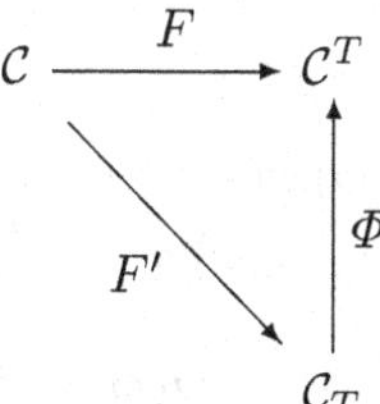


*Proof.* The action of functors on objects is as follows: $U(\alpha : TA \to A) \stackrel{\Delta}{=} A$, $FA \stackrel{\Delta}{=} \mu_A : T^2A \to TA$, $U'A \stackrel{\Delta}{=} TA$, $F'A \stackrel{\Delta}{=} A$, and $\Phi A \stackrel{\Delta}{=} \mu_A : T^2A \to TA$.

**Definition 12 (Monad morphism).** *Given $(T, \eta, \mu)$ and $(T', \eta', \mu')$ monads over $\mathcal{C}$, a* **monad-morphism** *from the first to the second is a natural transformation $\sigma : T \dot{\to} T'$ s.t.*

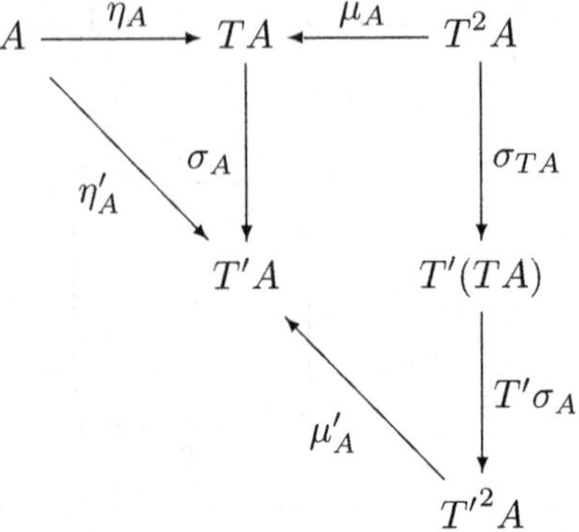


*(note that the morphism $\sigma_{TA}; T'\sigma_A$ is equal to $T\sigma_A; \sigma_{T'A}$, since $\sigma$ is natural). An equivalent definition of monad morphism (in terms of Kleisli triples) is a family of morphisms $\sigma_A : TA \to T'A$ for $A \in |\mathcal{C}|$ s.t.*

- $\eta_A; \sigma_A = \eta'_A$
- $f^*; \sigma_B = \sigma_A; (f; \sigma_B)^{*'}$ *for* $f : A \to TB$

*We write $Mon(\mathcal{C})$ for the* **category of monads over** *$\mathcal{C}$ and monad morphisms.*

There is also a more general notion of monad morphism, which does not require that the monads are over the same category.

Monad morphisms allow to view $T'$-algebras as $T$-algebras with the same underlying *carrier*, more precisely

**Proposition 13.** *There is a bijective correspondence between monad morphisms*

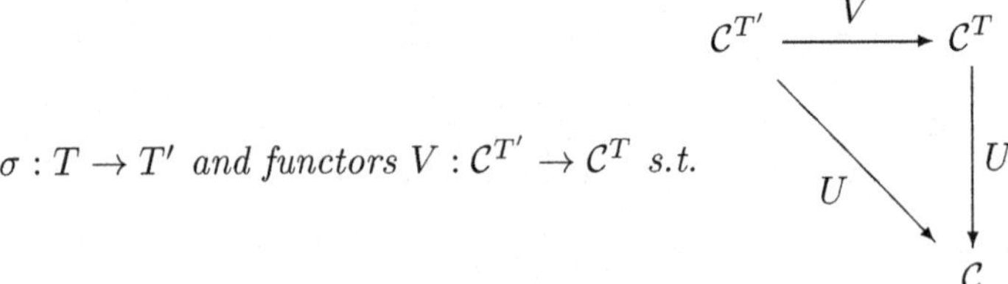


*Proof.* The action of $V$ on objects is $V(\alpha' : T'A \to A) \triangleq \sigma_A; \alpha' : TA \to A$, and $\sigma_A$ is defined in terms of $V$ as $\sigma_A \triangleq TA \xrightarrow{T\eta'_A} T(T'A) \xrightarrow{V\,\mu'_A} T'A$.

*Remark 14.* Filinski [Fil99] uses a *layering* $\zeta_A : T(T'A) \to T'A$ of $T'$ over $T$ in place of a monad morphism $\sigma_A : TA \to T'A$. The two notions are equivalent, in particular $\zeta_A$ is given by $V\,\mu'_A$, i.e. $\sigma_{T'A}; \mu'_A$.

## 2 Metalanguages with Computational Types

It is quite inconvenient to work directly in a specific category or with a specific monad. Mathematical logic provides a simple solution to abstract away from specific models: fix a language, define what is an interpretation of the language in a model, and find a formal system (on the language) that capture the desired properties of models. When the formal system is sound, one can forget about the models and use the formal system instead. Moreover, if the formal system is also complete, then nothing is lost (as far as one is concerned with properties expressible in the language, and valid in all models). Several formal systems have been proved sound and complete w.r.t. certain class of categories:

- many sorted equational logic corresponds to categories with finite products;
- simply typed $\lambda$-calculus corresponds to cartesian closed categories (CCC);
- intuitionistic higher-order logic corresponds to elementary toposes.

*Remark 15.* To ensure soundness w.r.t. the given classes of models, the formal system should cope with the possibility of empty carriers. In contrast, in mathematical logic it is often assumed that all carriers are inhabited. Categorical Logic is the branch of CT devoted mainly at establishing links between formal systems and classes of categorical structures.

Rather than giving a complete formal system, we say how to add computational types to your favorite formal system (for instance higher-order $\lambda$-calculus, or a $\lambda$-calculus with dependent types like a logical framework). The only assumption we make is that the formal system includes many sorted equational logic (this rules out systems like the *linear $\lambda$-calculus*). More specifically we assume that the formal system has the following judgments

| | |
|---|---|
| $\Gamma \vdash$ | $\Gamma$ is a well-formed context |
| $\Gamma \vdash \tau\ type$ | $\tau$ is a well-formed type in context $\Gamma$ |
| $\Gamma \vdash e : \tau$ | $e$ is a well-formed term of type $\tau$ in context $\Gamma$ |
| $\Gamma \vdash \phi\ prop$ | $\phi$ is a well-formed proposition in context $\Gamma$ |
| $\Gamma \vdash \phi$ | the well-formed proposition $\phi$ in context $\Gamma$ is true |

and that the following rules are derivable

- $\dfrac{}{\emptyset \vdash}$ $\quad \dfrac{\Gamma \vdash \tau\ type}{\Gamma, x : \tau \vdash}\ x \text{ fresh in } \Gamma$ $\quad \dfrac{\Gamma \vdash}{\Gamma \vdash x : \tau}\ \tau = \Gamma(x)$
- $\dfrac{\Gamma \vdash e_1 : \tau \quad \Gamma \vdash e_2 : \tau}{\Gamma \vdash (e_1 = e_2 : \tau)\ prop}$ this says when an equation is well-formed
- weak $\dfrac{\Gamma \vdash \tau \quad \Gamma \vdash \phi}{\Gamma, x : \tau \vdash \phi}\ x \text{ fresh in } \Gamma$ $\quad$ sub $\dfrac{\Gamma \vdash e : \tau \quad \Gamma, x : \tau \vdash \phi}{\Gamma \vdash \phi[x := e]}$
- $\dfrac{\Gamma \vdash e : \tau}{\Gamma \vdash e = e : \tau}$ $\quad \dfrac{\Gamma \vdash e_1 = e_2 : \tau}{\Gamma \vdash e_2 = e_1 : \tau}$ $\quad \dfrac{\Gamma \vdash e_1 = e_2 : \tau \quad \Gamma \vdash e_2 = e_3 : \tau}{\Gamma \vdash e_1 = e_3 : \tau}$

  cong $\dfrac{\Gamma, x : \tau \vdash \phi\ prop \quad \Gamma \vdash e_1 = e_2 : \tau \quad \Gamma \vdash \phi[x := e_1]}{\Gamma \vdash \phi[x := e_2]}$

*Remark 16.* More complex formal systems may require other forms of judgment, e.g. equality of types (and contexts), or other *sorts* besides *type* (along the line of Pure Type Systems). The categorical interpretation of typed calculi, including those with dependent types, is described in [Pit00b,Jac99].

The rules for adding computational types are

– $T \dfrac{\Gamma \vdash \tau\ type}{\Gamma \vdash T\tau\ type}$ lift $\dfrac{\Gamma \vdash e : \tau}{\Gamma \vdash [e]_T : T\tau}$

let $\dfrac{\Gamma \vdash e_1 : T\tau_1 \quad \Gamma, x : \tau_1 \vdash e_2 : T\tau_2}{\Gamma \vdash \mathrm{let}_T\, x \Leftarrow e_1\, \mathrm{in}\, e_2 : T\tau_2}\ x \notin \mathrm{FV}(\tau_2)$

$[e]_T$ is the program/computation that simply returns the value $e$, while $\mathrm{let}_T\, x \Leftarrow e_1\, \mathrm{in}\, e_2$ is the computation which first evaluates $e_1$ and binds the result to $x$, then evaluates $e_2$.

– let.$\xi$ $\dfrac{\Gamma \vdash e : T\tau_1 \quad \Gamma, x : \tau_1 \vdash e_1 = e_2 : T\tau_2}{\Gamma \vdash \mathrm{let}_T\, x \Leftarrow e\, \mathrm{in}\, e_1 = \mathrm{let}_T\, x \Leftarrow e\, \mathrm{in}\, e_2 : T\tau_2}\ x \notin \mathrm{FV}(\tau_2)$

this rule expresses congruence for the let-binder.

– assoc $\dfrac{\begin{array}{l}\Gamma \vdash e_1 : T\tau_1 \\ \Gamma, x_1 : \tau_1 \vdash e_2 : T\tau_2 \quad \Gamma, x_2 : \tau_2 \vdash e_3 : T\tau_3\end{array}}{\begin{array}{l}\Gamma \vdash \mathrm{let}_T\, x_2 \Leftarrow (\mathrm{let}_T\, x_1 \Leftarrow e_1\, \mathrm{in}\, e_2)\, \mathrm{in}\, e_3 = \\ \qquad \mathrm{let}_T\, x_1 \Leftarrow e_1\, \mathrm{in}\, (\mathrm{let}_T\, x_2 \Leftarrow e_2\, \mathrm{in}\, e_3) : T\tau_3\end{array}}\ \begin{array}{l}x_1 \notin \mathrm{FV}(\tau_2) \\ \wedge\, x_2 \notin \mathrm{FV}(\tau_3)\end{array}$

this rule says that only the order of evaluation matters (not the parentheses).

– T.$\beta$ $\dfrac{\Gamma \vdash e_1 : \tau_1 \quad \Gamma, x : \tau_1 \vdash e_2 : T\tau_2}{\Gamma \vdash \mathrm{let}_T\, x \Leftarrow [e_1]_T\, \mathrm{in}\, e_2 = e_2[x := e_1] : T\tau_2}\ x \notin \mathrm{FV}(\tau_2)$

T.$\eta$ $\dfrac{\Gamma \vdash e : T\tau}{\Gamma \vdash \mathrm{let}_T\, x \Leftarrow e\, \mathrm{in}\, [x]_T = e : T\tau}$

these rules say how to eliminate trivial computations (i.e. of the form $[e]_T$).

In calculi without dependent types side-conditions like $x \notin \mathrm{FV}(\tau_2)$ are always true, hence they can be ignored.

*Remark 17.* Moggi [Mog91] describes the interpretation of computational types in a simply typed calculus, and establishes soundness and completeness results. In [Mog95] Moggi extends such results to logical systems including the *evaluation modalities* proposed by Pitts.

For interpreting computational types monads are not enough, *parameterized* monads are needed instead. The parameterization is directly related to the form of type-dependency allowed by the typed calculus under consideration. The need to consider parametrized forms of categorical notions is by now a well-understood fact in categorical logic (it is not a peculiarity of computational types).

We sketch the categorical interpretation in a category $\mathcal{C}$ with finite products of a simply typed metalanguage with computational types (see [Mog91] for more details). The general pattern for interpreting a simply typed calculus according to Lawvere's functorial semantics goes as follows

– a context $\Gamma \vdash$ and a type $\vdash \tau$ *type* are interpreted by objects of $\mathcal{C}$, by abuse of notation we indicate these objects with $\Gamma$ and $\tau$ respectively;
– a term $\Gamma \vdash e : \tau$ is interpreted by a morphism $f : \Gamma \to \tau$ in $\mathcal{C}$;

| RULE | SYNTAX | SEMANTICS |
|---|---|---|
| $T$ | | |
| | $\vdash \tau\ type$ | $= \tau$ |
| | $\vdash T\tau\ type$ | $= T\tau$ |
| lift | | |
| | $\Gamma \vdash e : \tau$ | $= f : \Gamma \to \tau$ |
| | $\Gamma \vdash [e]_T : T\tau$ | $= f; \eta_\tau : \Gamma \to T\tau$ |
| let | | |
| | $\Gamma \vdash e_1 : T\tau_1$ | $= f_1 : \Gamma \to T\tau_1$ |
| | $\Gamma, x : \tau_1 \vdash e_2 : T\tau_2$ | $= f_2 : \Gamma \times \tau_1 \to T\tau_2$ |
| | $\Gamma \vdash \mathrm{let}_T\, x \Leftarrow e_1\, \mathrm{in}\, e_2 : T\tau_2$ | $= (\mathrm{id}_\Gamma, f_1); f_2^* : \Gamma \to T\tau_2$ |

**Fig. 1.** Simple interpretation of computational types

– a (well formed) equational $\Gamma \vdash e_1 = e_2 : \tau$ is true iff $f_1 = f_2 : \Gamma \to \tau$ as morphisms in $\mathcal{C}$.

Figure 1 gives the relevant clauses of the interpretation. Notice that the interpretation of let needs a parameterized extension operation $\_^*$, which maps $f : C \times A \to TB$ to $f^* : C \times TA \to TB$.

### 2.1 Syntactic Sugar and Alternative Presentations

It is convenient to introduce some derived notation, for instance:

– an iterated-let ($\mathrm{let}_T\, \overline{x} \Leftarrow \overline{e}\, \mathrm{in}\, e$), which is defined by induction on $|\overline{e}| = |\overline{x}|$

$$\mathrm{let}_T\, \emptyset \Leftarrow \emptyset\, \mathrm{in}\, e \stackrel{\Delta}{\equiv} e \qquad \mathrm{let}_T\, x_0, \overline{x} \Leftarrow e_0, \overline{e}\, \mathrm{in}\, e \stackrel{\Delta}{\equiv} \mathrm{let}_T\, x_0 \Leftarrow e_0\, \mathrm{in}\, (\mathrm{let}_T\, \overline{x} \Leftarrow \overline{e}\, \mathrm{in}\, e)$$

Haskell's do-notation, inspired by monad comprehension (see [Wad92a]), extends the iterated-let by allowing pattern matching and local definitions

In higher-order $\lambda$-calculus, the type- and term-constructors can be replaced by constants:

– $T$ becomes a constant of kind $\bullet \to \bullet$, where $\bullet$ is the kind of all types;
– $[e]_T$ and $\mathrm{let}_T\, x \Leftarrow e_1\, \mathrm{in}\, e_2$ are replaced by polymorphic constants

$$unit_T : \forall X : \bullet . X \to TX \qquad let_T : \forall X, Y : \bullet . (X \to TY) \to TX \to TY$$

where $unit_T \stackrel{\Delta}{=} \Lambda X : \bullet . \lambda x : X . [x]_T$ and $let_T \stackrel{\Delta}{=} \Lambda X, Y : \bullet . \lambda f : X \to TY . \lambda c : TX . \mathrm{let}_T\, x \Leftarrow c\, \mathrm{in}\, f\ x$.

In this way the rule (let.$\xi$) follows from the $\xi$-rule for $\lambda$-abstraction, and the other three equational rules can be replaced with three equational axioms without premises, e.g. $T.\beta$ can be replaced by

$$X, Y : \bullet, x : X, f : X \to TY \vdash \mathrm{let}_T\, x \Leftarrow [x]_T\, \mathrm{in}\, f\ x = f\ x : TY$$

The polymorphic constant $unit_T$ corresponds to the natural transformation $\eta$. In higher-order $\lambda$-calculus it is possible to define also polymorphic constants

$$map_T : \forall X, Y : \bullet.(X \to Y) \to TX \to TY \qquad flat_T : \forall X : \bullet.T^2X \to TX$$

corresponding to the action of the functor $T$ on morphisms and to the natural transformation $\mu$

- $map_T \stackrel{\Delta}{=} \Lambda X, Y : \bullet.\lambda f : X \to Y.\lambda c : TX.\mathrm{let}_T\, x \Leftarrow c\, \mathrm{in}\, [f\ x]_T$
- $flat_T \stackrel{\Delta}{=} \Lambda X : \bullet.\lambda c : T^2X.\mathrm{let}_T\, x \Leftarrow c\, \mathrm{in}\, x$

The axiomatization taking as primitive the polymorphic constants $unit_T$ and $let_T$ amounts to the definition of triple in extension form. There is an alternative axiomatization, corresponding to the definition of triple in monoid form, which takes as primitive the polymorphic constants $map_T$, $unit_T$ and $flat_T$ (see [Wad92a]).

## 2.2 Categorical Definitions in the Metalanguage

The main point for introducing a metalanguage is to provide an alternative to working directly with models/categories. In fact, several categorical notions related to monads, such as algebra and monad morphisms, can be reformulated axiomatically in a metalanguage with computational types.

**Definition 18 (Eilenberg-Moore algebras).** *$\alpha : TA \to A$ is a $T$-algebra iff*

- $x : A \vdash \alpha\ [x]_T = x : A$
- $c : T^2A \vdash \alpha(\mathrm{let}_T\, x \Leftarrow c\, \mathrm{in}\, x) = \alpha(\mathrm{let}_T\, x \Leftarrow c\, \mathrm{in}\, [\alpha\ x]_T) : A$

*$f : A \to B$ is a $T$-algebra morphism from $\alpha : TA \to A$ to $\beta : TB \to B$ iff*

- $c : TA \vdash f(\alpha\ c) = \beta(\mathrm{let}_T\, x \Leftarrow c\, \mathrm{in}\, [fx]_T) : B$

We can consider metalanguages with many computational types, corresponding to different monads on the same category. In particular, to define monad morphisms we use a metalanguage with two computational types $T$ and $T'$.

**Definition 19 (Monad morphism).** *A constant $\sigma : \forall X : \bullet.TX \to T'X$ is a monad morphism from $T$ to $T'$ iff*

- $X : \bullet, x : X \vdash \sigma\ X\ [x]_T = [x]_{T'} : T'X$
- $X, Y : \bullet, c : TX, f : X \to TY \vdash \sigma\ Y\ (\mathrm{let}_T\, x \Leftarrow c\, \mathrm{in}\, f\ x) =$
  $\mathrm{let}_{T'}\, x \Leftarrow \sigma\ X\ c\, \mathrm{in}\, \sigma\ Y\ (f\ x) : T'Y$

## 3 Metalanguages for Denotational Semantics

Translation of a language into another provides a simple and general way to give semantics to the first language in terms of a semantics for the second. In denotational semantics it is quite common to define the semantics of a programming language $PL$ by translating it into a typed metalanguage $ML$. The idea is as old as denotational semantics (see [Sco93]), so the main issue is whether it can be made into a viable technique capable of dealing with complex programming languages. Before being more specific about what metalanguages to use, let us discuss the main advantages of semantics via translation:

- to reuse the same $ML$ for translating several programming languages.

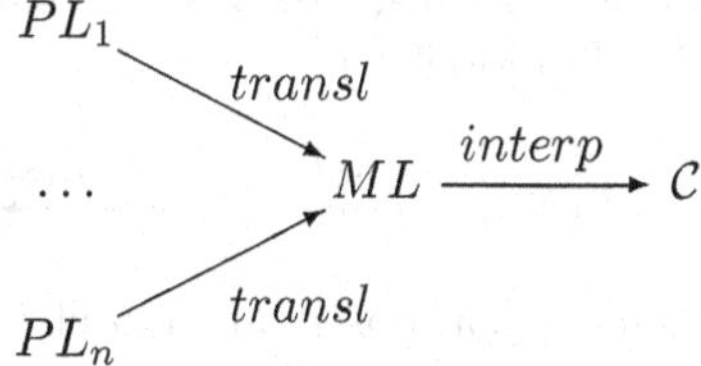


  Here we are assuming that defining a translation from $PL$ to $ML$ is often simpler than directly defining an interpretation of $PL$ in $\mathcal{C}$. In this case it is worth putting some effort in the study of $ML$. In fact, once certain properties of $ML$ have been established (e.g. reasoning principles or computational adequacy), it is usually easy to transfer them to $PL$ via the translation.
- to choose $ML$ according to certain criteria, usually not met by programming languages, e.g.
  - a metalanguage built around few orthogonal concepts is simpler to study, while programming languages often bundle orthogonal concepts in one construct for the benefit of programmers;
  - $ML$ may be equipped with a logic so that it can be used for formalizing reasoning principles or for translating specification languages;
  - $ML$ may be chosen as the *internal language* for a class of categories (e.g. CCC) or for a specific semantic category (e.g. that of sets or cpos).
- to use $ML$ for hiding details of semantic categories (see [Gor79]). For instance, if $ML$ is the internal language for a class of categories, it has one intended interpretation in each of them. A translation into $ML$ will induce a variety of interpretations

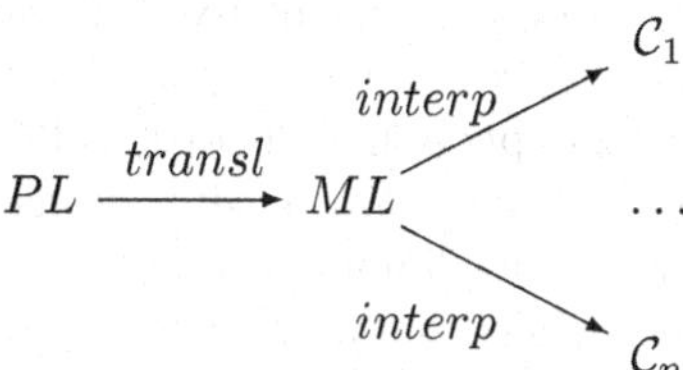


  Even if $ML$ has only one intended interpretation, it may be difficult to work with the semantic category directly. For instance, if the semantic category is a functor category, like those proposed for modeling local variables or dynamic generation of new names (see [Sta96]).

A standard typed λ-calculus is a good starting point for a metalanguage. However, it is more controversial whether the metalanguage should be equipped with some logic (ranging from equational logic to higher-order predicate logic) or have an operational semantics.

After describing the advantages of giving semantics to a programming language $PL$ via translation into a metalanguage $ML$, we explain how metalanguages with computational types can help in structuring the translation from $PL$ to $ML$ by the introduction of **auxiliary notation** (see [Mos92,Mog91])

$$PL \xrightarrow{transl} ML(\Sigma) \xrightarrow{transl} ML$$

and by **incrementally defining auxiliary notation** (as advocated in [Fil99], [LHJ95,LH96] and [CM93,Mog97])

$$PL \xrightarrow{transl} ML(\Sigma_n) \xrightarrow{transl} \ldots \xrightarrow{transl} ML(\Sigma_0) \xrightarrow{transl} ML$$

*Remark 20.* The solutions proposed are closely related to general techniques in *algebraic specifications*, such as abstract datatype, stepwise refinement and hierarchical specifications.

### 3.1 Computational Types and Structuring

Language extension is a typical problem of denotational and operational semantics. For instance, consider extending a pure functional language with side-effects or exceptions, we have to redefine the whole operational/denotational semantics every time we consider a new extension. The problem remains even when the semantics is given via translation in a typed lambda-calculus: one would keep redefining the translation. Mosses [Mos90] identifies this problem very clearly, and he stresses how the use of **auxiliary notation** may help in making semantic definitions more reusable. An approach, that does not make use of monads, has been proposed by Cartwright and Felleisen [CF94].

Moggi [Mog91] identifies monads as an important structuring device for denotational semantics (but not for operational semantics!). The basic idea is that there is a unary type constructor $T$, called a **notion of computation**, and terms of type $T\tau$, should be thought of as programs which compute values of type $\tau$. The interpretation of $T$ is not fixed, it varies according to the *computational features* of the programming language under consideration. Nevertheless, there are operations (for specifying the order of evaluation) and basic properties of them, which should be common to all notions of computation. This suggests to translate a programming language $PL$ into a metalanguage $ML_T(\Sigma)$ with computational types, where the signature $\Sigma$ gives additional operations (and their properties). Hence, the **monadic approach** to define the denotational semantics of a programming language $PL$ consists of three steps:

- identify a suitable metalanguage $ML_T(\Sigma)$, this hides the interpretation of $T$ and $\Sigma$ like an interface hides the implementation of an abstract datatype,

– define a translation of $PL$ into $ML_T(\Sigma)$,
– construct a model of $ML_T(\Sigma)$, e.g. via translation into a metalanguage $ML$ without computational types.

A suitable choice of $\Sigma$ can yield a simple translation from $PL$ to $ML_T(\Sigma)$, which does not have to be redefined when $PL$ is extended, and at the same time keep the translation of $ML_T(\Sigma)$ into $ML$ fairly manageable.

### 3.2 Examples of Translations

To exemplify the use of computational types, we consider several programming languages (viewed as $\lambda$-calculi with constants), and for each of them we define translations into a metalanguage $ML_T(\Sigma)$ with computational types, for a suitable choice of $\Sigma$, and indicate a possible interpretation for computational types and $\Sigma$.

**CBN Translation: Haskell.** We consider a simple explicitly typed fragment of Haskell corresponding to the following typed $\lambda$-calculus:

| | |
|---|---|
| $\tau \in Type_{Haskell} ::= \mathsf{Int}$ | type of integers |
| $\mid \tau_1 \to \tau_2$ | functional type |
| $\mid \tau_1 \times \tau_2$ | product type |
| $e \in Exp_{Haskell} ::= x$ | variable |
| $\mid \mathsf{n} \mid e_0 + e_1$ | numerals and integer addition |
| $\mid \mathsf{if0}\ e_0\ \mathsf{then}\ e_1\ \mathsf{else}\ e_2$ | conditional |
| $\mid \mathrm{let}\, x : \tau = e_1 \,\mathrm{in}\, e_2$ | local definition |
| $\mid \mu x : \tau.e$ | recursive definition |
| $\mid \lambda x : \tau.e$ | abstraction |
| $\mid e_1\ e_2$ | application |
| $\mid (e_1, e_2)$ | pairing |
| $\mid \pi_i\ e$ | projection |

The type system for Haskell derives judgments of the form $\Gamma \vdash e : \tau$ saying that a term $e$ has type $\tau$ in the typing context $\Gamma$. Usually, in denotational semantics only well-formed terms need to be interpreted (since programs rejected by a type-checker are not allowed to run), thus we want to define a translation mapping well-formed terms $\Gamma \vdash_{PL} e : \tau$ of the programming language into well-formed terms $\Gamma \vdash_{ML} e : \tau$ of the metalanguage (with computational types). More precisely, we define a translation $\_^n$ by induction on types $\tau$ and raw terms $e$, called the **CBN translation** (see Figure 2). The signature $\Sigma_n$ for defining the CBN translation of Haskell consists of

– $Y : \forall X : \bullet.(TX \to TX) \to TX$, a (least) fix-point combinator
– a signature for the datatype of integers.

**Lemma 21 (Typing).** *If $\{x_i : \tau_i | i \in m\} \vdash_{PL} e : \tau$ is a well-formed term of Haskell, then $\{x_i : T\tau_i^n | i \in m\} \vdash_{ML} e^n : T\tau^n$ is a well-formed term of the metalanguage with computational types.*

| $\tau \in Type_{Haskell}$ | $\tau^n \in Type(ML_T(\Sigma_n))$ |
|---|---|
| Int | Int |
| $\tau_1 \to \tau_2$ | $T\tau_1^n \to T\tau_2^n$ |
| $\tau_1 \times \tau_2$ | $T\tau_1^n \times T\tau_2^n$ |

| $e \in Exp_{Haskell}$ | $e^n \in Exp(ML_T(\Sigma_n))$ |
|---|---|
| $x$ | $x$ |
| n | $[\mathsf{n}]_T$ |
| $e_0 + e_1$ | $\mathrm{let}_T\, x_0, x_1 \Leftarrow e_0^n, e_1^n \,\mathrm{in}\, [x_0 + x_1]_T$ |
| ifO $e_0$ then $e_1$ else $e_2$ | $\mathrm{let}_T\, x \Leftarrow e_0^n \,\mathrm{in\ if}\ x = 0 \ \mathrm{then}\ e_1^n \ \mathrm{else}\ e_2^n$ |
| $\mathrm{let}\, x : \tau = e_1 \,\mathrm{in}\, e_2$ | $(\lambda x : T\tau^n.e_2^n)\ e_1^n$ |
| $\mu x : \tau.e$ | $Y\ \tau^n\ (\lambda x : T\tau^n.e^n)$ |
| $\lambda x : \tau.e$ | $[\lambda x : T\tau^n.e^n]_T$ |
| $e_1\ e_2$ | $\mathrm{let}_T\, f \Leftarrow e_1^n \,\mathrm{in}\, f\ e_2^n$ |
| $(e_1, e_2)$ | $[(e_1^n, e_2^n)]_T$ |
| $\pi_i\ e$ | $\mathrm{let}_T\, x \Leftarrow e^n \,\mathrm{in}\, \pi_i\ x$ |

$$(\{x_i : \tau_i | i \in m\} \vdash_{PL} e : \tau)^n \stackrel{\Delta}{\equiv} \{x_i : T\tau_i^n | i \in m\} \vdash_{ML} e^n : T\tau^n$$

**Fig. 2.** CBN translation of Haskell

*Remark 22.* The key feature of the CBN translation is that variables in the programming languages are translated into variables ranging over computational types. Another important feature is the translation of types, which basically guides (in combination with operational considerations) the translation of terms.

*Exercise 23.* Extend Haskell with polymorphism, as in 2nd-order $\lambda$-calculus, i.e.

$$\tau \in Type_{Haskell} ::= X \mid \ldots \mid \forall X : \bullet.\tau \qquad e \in Exp_{Haskell} ::= \ldots \mid \Lambda X : \bullet.e \mid e\ \tau$$

where $X$ ranges over type variables. There is a choice in extending the CBN translation to polymorphic types. Either type abstraction delays evaluation, and then $(\forall X : \bullet.\tau)^n$ should be $\forall X : \bullet.T\tau^n$, or it does not, and then $(\forall X : \bullet.\tau)^n$ should be $\forall X : \bullet.\tau^n$. In the latter case there is a problem to extend the CBN translation on terms. A way to overcome the problem is to assume that computational types commute with polymorphic types, i.e. the following map is an iso

$$c\ :\ T(\forall X : \bullet.\tau) \longmapsto \Lambda X : \bullet.\mathrm{let}_T\, x \Leftarrow c \,\mathrm{in}\, [x\ X]_T\ :\ \forall X : \bullet.T\tau$$

In realizability models several monads (e.g. lifting) satisfy this property, indeed the isomorphism is often an identity. In these models, a simpler related property is commutativity of computational types with intersection types.

**Algol Translation.** Some CBN languages (including Algol and PCF) allow computational effects only at base types. Computational types play a limited role in structuring the denotational semantics of these languages. Nevertheless it is worth to compare the translation of such languages with that of Haskell.

| $\tau \in Type_{Algol}$ | $\tau^a \in Type(ML_T(\Sigma_a))$ |
|---|---|
| Loc | $T$Loc |
| Int | $T$Int |
| Cmd | $T1$ |
| $\tau_1 \to \tau_2$ | $\tau_1^a \to \tau_2^a$ |
| $\tau_1 \times \tau_2$ | $\tau_1^a \times \tau_2^a$ |

| $e \in Exp_{Algol}$ | $e^a \in Exp(ML_T(\Sigma_a))$ |
|---|---|
| $x$ | $x$ |
| n | $[\mathsf{n}]_T$ |
| $e_0 + e_1$ | $\mathrm{let}_T\, x_0, x_1 \Leftarrow e_0^a, e_1^a \,\mathrm{in}\, [x_0 + x_1]_T$ |
| ifO $e_0$ then $e_1$ else $e_2$ | $*\mathrm{let}_T\, x \Leftarrow e_0^a \,\mathrm{in\, if}\, x = 0 \,\mathrm{then}\, e_1^a \,\mathrm{else}\, e_2^a$ |
| $\mathrm{let}\, x : \tau = e_1 \,\mathrm{in}\, e_2$ | $(\lambda x : \tau^a . e_2^a)\ e_1^a$ |
| $\mu x : \tau . e$ | $*Y\ \tau^a\ (\lambda x : \tau^a . e^a)$ |
| $\lambda x : \tau . e$ | $\lambda x : \tau^a . e^a$ |
| $e_1\ e_2$ | $e_1^a\ e_2^a$ |
| $(e_1, e_2)$ | $(e_1^a, e_2^a)$ |
| $\pi_i\ e$ | $\pi_i\ e^a$ |
| l | $[\mathsf{l}]_T$ |
| !$e$ | $\mathrm{let}_T\, l \Leftarrow e^a \,\mathrm{in}\, get\ l$ |
| skip | $[()]_T$ |
| $e_0 := e_1$ | $\mathrm{let}_T\, l, n \Leftarrow e_0^a, e_1^a \,\mathrm{in}\, set\ l\ n$ |
| $e_0; e_1$ | $\mathrm{let}_T\, \_ \Leftarrow e_0^a \,\mathrm{in}\, e_1^a$ |

for the definition of $*$let and $*Y$ see Remark 26

$$(\{x_i : \tau_i | i \in m\} \vdash_{PL} e : \tau)^a \stackrel{\Delta}{\equiv} \{x_i : \tau_i^a | i \in m\} \vdash_{ML} e^a : \tau^a$$

**Fig. 3.** Algol translation

We consider an idealized-Algol with a fixed set of locations. Syntactically it is an extension of (simple) Haskell with three base types: Loc for integer locations, Int for integer expressions, and Cmd for commands.

$\tau \in Type_{Algol}$ ::= Loc | Int | Cmd | $\tau_1 \to \tau_2$ | $\tau_1 \times \tau_2$
$e \in Exp_{Algol}$ ::= $x$ | l  location
 | n | $e_0 + e_1$ | !$e$  contents of a location
 | ifO $e_0$ then $e_1$ else $e_2$
 | skip | $e_0 := e_1$  null and assignment commands
 | $e_0; e_1$  sequential composition of commands
 | $\mathrm{let}\, x : \tau = e_1 \,\mathrm{in}\, e_2$ | $\mu x : \tau . e$ | $\lambda x : \tau . e$ | $e_1\ e_2$ | $(e_1, e_2)$ | $\pi_i\ e$

The **Algol translation** $\_^a$ is defined by induction on types $\tau$ and raw terms $e$ (see Figure 3). The signature $\Sigma_a$ for defining the Algol translation consists of

- $Y : \forall X : \bullet.(TX \to TX) \to TX$, like for the Haskell translation
- a signature for the datatype of integers, like for the Haskell translation
- a type Loc of locations, with a fixed set of constants l : Loc, and operations $get$ : Loc $\to T$Int and $set$ : Loc $\to$ Int $\to T1$ to get/store an integer from/into a location.

*Remark 24.* In Algol expressions and commands have different computational effects, namely: expressions can only read the state, while commands can also modify the state. Hence, a precise model would have to consider two monads, $T_{sr}A = A_\bot^S$ for state reading computations and $T_{se}A = (A \times S)_\bot^S$ for computations with side-effects, and a monad morphism from $T_{sr}$ to $T_{se}$.

**Lemma 25 (Typing).** *If* $\{x_i : \tau_i | i \in m\} \vdash_{PL} e : \tau$ *is a well-formed term of Algol, then* $\{x_i : \tau_i^a | i \in m\} \vdash_{ML} e^a : \tau^a$ *is a well-formed term of the metalanguage with computational types.*

*Remark 26.* The Algol translation seems to violate a key principle, namely that the translation of a program should have computational type. But a valid Algol program is a term of base type, and the Algol translation indeed maps base types to computational types. More generally, the Algol translation maps Algol types in (carriers of) $T$-algebras. Indeed $T$-algebras for a (strong) monad are closed under (arbitrary) products and exponentials, more precisely: $A_1 \times A_2$ is the carrier of a $T$-algebra whenever $A_1$ and $A_2$ are, and $B^A$ is the carrier of a $T$-algebra whenever $B$ is [EXERCISE: prove these facts in the metalanguage]. The $T$-algebra structure $\alpha_\tau : T\tau \to \tau$ on the translation $\tau$ of a type in $Type_{Algol}$ is used for defining the translation of terms, namely to extend the let and fix-point combinator from computational types to $T$-algebras:

– *let $$\frac{\Gamma \vdash e_1 : T\tau_1 \quad \Gamma, x : \tau_1 \vdash e_2 : \tau_2}{\Gamma \vdash *\mathrm{let}_T\, x \Leftarrow e_1 \,\mathrm{in}\, e_2 \stackrel{\Delta}{=} \alpha_{\tau_2}(\mathrm{let}_T\, x \Leftarrow e_1 \,\mathrm{in}\, [e_2]_T) : \tau_2}$$

– *Y $$\frac{\Gamma, x : \tau \vdash e : \tau}{\Gamma \vdash *Y\ \tau\ (\lambda x : \tau.e) \stackrel{\Delta}{=} \alpha_\tau(Y\ \tau\ (\lambda c : T\tau.[e[x := \alpha_\tau c]]_T) : \tau}$$

Intuitively, applying $\alpha_\tau$ to a computation pushes its effects *inside* an element of type $\tau$. For instance, if $\tau$ is of the form $\tau_1 \to T\tau_2$, then $\alpha_\tau$ maps a computation $c : T\tau$ of a function to the function $\lambda x : \tau_1.\mathrm{let}_T\, f \Leftarrow c \,\mathrm{in}\, f(x)$.

The Algol translation suggests to put more emphasis on $T$-algebras. Indeed, [Lev99] has proposed a metalanguage with two kinds of types: value types interpreted by objects in $\mathcal{C}$, and computation types interpreted by objects in $\mathcal{C}^T$.

**CBV Translation: SML.** We consider a simple fragment of SML with integer locations. Syntactically the language is a minor variation of idealized Algol. It replaces Cmd by Unit and skip by (), sequential composition of commands has been removed because definable $e_1; e_2$ is definable by $(\lambda\_ : \mathsf{Unit}.e_2)e_1$, recursive definitions are restricted to functional types.

$$\tau \in Type_{SML} ::= \mathsf{Loc} \mid \mathsf{Int} \mid \mathsf{Unit} \mid \tau_1 \to \tau_2 \mid \tau_1 \times \tau_2$$

$$\begin{array}{lll} e \in Exp_{SML} ::= & x \mid \mathsf{l} \mid \mathsf{n} \mid e_0 + e_1 \mid !e \mid \mathsf{if0}\ e_0\ \mathsf{then}\ e_1\ \mathsf{else}\ e_2 \mid () \mid e_0 := e_1 \\ \mid & \mathrm{let}\, x : \tau = e_1 \,\mathrm{in}\, e_2 \mid \mu f : \tau_1 \to \tau_2.\lambda x : \tau_1.e \\ \mid & \lambda x : \tau.e \mid e_1\ e_2 \mid (e_1, e_2) \mid \pi_i\ e \end{array}$$

The **CBV translation** $\_^v$ (see Figure 4) is defined by induction on types $\tau$ and raw terms $e$. When $\{x_i : \tau_i | i \in m\} \vdash_{PL} e : \tau$ is a well-formed term of

| $\tau \in Type_{SML}$ | $\tau^v \in Type(ML_T(\Sigma_v))$ |
|---|---|
| Loc | Loc |
| Int | Int |
| Unit | 1 |
| $\tau_1 \to \tau_2$ | $\tau_1^v \to T\tau_2^v$ |
| $\tau_1 \times \tau_2$ | $\tau_1^v \times \tau_2^v$ |

| $e \in Exp_{SML}$ | $e^v \in Exp(ML_T(\Sigma_v))$ |
|---|---|
| $x$ | $[x]_T$ |
| $\mathsf{n}$ | $[\mathsf{n}]_T$ |
| $e_0 + e_1$ | $\text{let}_T\, x_0, x_1 \Leftarrow e_0^v, e_1^v \text{ in } [x_0 + x_1]_T$ |
| $\mathsf{if0}\ e_0\ \mathsf{then}\ e_1\ \mathsf{else}\ e_2$ | $\text{let}_T\, x \Leftarrow e_0^v \text{ in if } x = 0 \text{ then } e_1^v \text{ else } e_2^v$ |
| $\text{let } x : \tau = e_1 \text{ in } e_2$ | $\text{let}_T\, x \Leftarrow e_1^v \text{ in } e_1^v$ |
| $\mu f : \tau_1 \to \tau_2.\lambda x : \tau_1.e$ | $*Y\ (\tau_1 \to \tau_2)^v\ (\lambda f : (\tau_1 \to \tau_2)^v.\lambda x : \tau_1^v.e^v)$ |
| $\lambda x : \tau.e$ | $[\lambda x : \tau^v.e^v]_T$ |
| $e_1\ e_2$ | $\text{let}_T\, f, x \Leftarrow e_1^v, e_2^v \text{ in } f\ x$ |
| $(e_1, e_2)$ | $\text{let}_T\, x_1, x_2 \Leftarrow e_1^v, e_2^v \text{ in } [(x_1, x_2)]_T$ |
| $\pi_i\ e$ | $\text{let}_T\, x \Leftarrow e^v \text{ in } [\pi_i\ x]_T$ |
| $\mathsf{l}$ | $[\mathsf{l}]_T$ |
| $!e$ | $\text{let}_T\, l \Leftarrow e^v \text{ in } get\ l$ |
| $()$ | $[()]_T$ |
| $e_0 := e_1$ | $\text{let}_T\, l, n \Leftarrow e_0^v, e_1^v \text{ in } set\ l\ n$ |

$$(\{x_i : \tau_i | i \in m\} \vdash_{PL} e : \tau)^v \stackrel{\Delta}{\equiv} \{x_i : \tau_i^v | i \in m\} \vdash_{ML} e^v : T\tau^v$$

**Fig. 4.** CBV translation of SML

SML, one can show that $\{x_i : \tau_i^v | i \in m\} \vdash_{ML} e^v : T\tau^v$ is a well-formed term of the metalanguage with computational types. The signature $\Sigma_v$ for defining the CBV translation is $\Sigma_a$, i.e. that for defining the Algol translation.

*Exercise 27.* So far we have not said how to interpret the metalanguages used as target for the various translations. Propose interpretations of the metalanguages in the category of cpos: first choose a monad for interpreting computational types, then explain how the other symbols in the signature $\Sigma$ should be interpreted.

*Exercise 28.* The translations considered so far allow to validate equational laws for the programming languages, by deriving the translation of the equational laws in the metalanguage. Determine whether $\beta$ and $\eta$ for functional types, i.e. $(\lambda x : \tau_1.e_2)\ e_1 = e_2[x := e_1] : \tau_2$ and $(\lambda x : \tau_1.e\ x) = e : \tau_1 \to \tau_2$ with $x \notin \text{FV}(e)$, are valid in Haskell, Algol or SML. If they are not valid suggest weaker equational laws that can be validated. This exercise indicates that some care is needed in transferring reasoning principles for the $\lambda$-calculus to functional languages.

*Exercise 29.* Consider Haskell with integer locations, and extend the CBN translation accordingly. Which signature $\Sigma$ should be used?

*Exercise 30.* SML has a construct, ref $e$, to create new locations. Consider this extension of SML, and extend the CBV translation accordingly. Which signature $\Sigma$ and monad $T$ in the category of cpos should be used?

*Exercise 31.* Consider SML with locations of any type, and extend the CBV translation accordingly. Which signature $\Sigma$ should be used (you may find convenient to assume that the metalanguage includes higher-order $\lambda$-calculus)? It is very difficult to find monads able to interpret such a metalanguage.

### 3.3 Incremental Approach and Monad Transformers

The monadic approach to denotational semantics has a caveat. If the programming language $PL$ is complex, the signature $\Sigma$ identified by the monadic approach can get fairly large, and the translation of $ML_T(\Sigma)$ into $ML$ may become quite complicated. An **incremental approach** can alleviate the problem of in defining the translation of $ML_T(\Sigma)$ into $ML$. The basic idea is to adapt to this setting the techniques and modularization facilities advocated for formal software development, in particular the desired translation of $ML_T(\Sigma)$ into $ML$ corresponds to the implementation of an abstract datatype (in some given language). In an incremental approach, the desired implementation is obtained by a sequence of steps, where each step constructs an implementation for a more complex datatype from an implementation for a simpler datatype.

> Haskell constructor classes (and to a less extend SML modules) provide a very convenient setting for the incremental approach (see [LHJ95]): the type inference mechanism allows concise and readable definitions, while type-checking detects most errors. What is missing is only the ability to express and validate (equational) properties, which would require extra features typical of Logical Frameworks (see [Mog97]).

This approach requires a collection of *modules* with the following features:

- they should be parametric in $\Sigma$, i.e. for any signature $\Sigma$ (or at least for a wide range of signatures) the module should take an implementation of $\Sigma$ and construct an implementation of $\Sigma + \Sigma_{new}$, where $\Sigma_{new}$ is fixed
- the construction of the signature $\Sigma_{new}$ may depend on some additional parameters of a fixed signature $\Sigma_{par}$.

The first requirement can be easily satisfied, when one can implement $\Sigma_{new}$ without changing the implementation of $\Sigma$ (this is often the case in software development). However, the constructions we are interested in are not *persistent*, since they involve a re-implementation of computational types, and consequently of $\Sigma$. The translations we need to consider are of the form

$$I : ML_T(\Sigma_{par} + \Sigma + \Sigma_{new}) \to ML_T(\Sigma_{par} + \Sigma)$$

where $\Sigma_{new}$ are the new symbols defined by $I$, $\Sigma$ the old symbols *redefined* by $I$, and $\Sigma_{par}$ some fixed parameters of the construction (which are unaffected by $I$). In general $I$ can be decomposed in

- a translation $I_{new} : ML_T(\Sigma_{par} + \Sigma_{new}) \to ML_T(\Sigma_{par})$ defining the new symbols (in $\Sigma_{new}$) and redefining computational types,
- translations $I_{op} : ML_T(\Sigma_{op}) \to ML_T(\Sigma_{par} + \Sigma_{op})$ redefining an old symbol *op* in *isolation* (consistently with the redefinition of computational types), for each possible type of symbol one may have in $\Sigma$.

Filinski [Fil99] has proposed a more flexible approach, which uses metalanguages with several monads $T_i$ (rather than only one), and at each step it introduces a new monad $T'$ and new operations (defined in term of the pre-existing ones), without changing the meaning of the old symbols. Therefore, one is considering *definitional extensions*, i.e. translations of the form

$$I : ML_{T',T_{i\in n}}(\Sigma_{old} + \Sigma'_{new}) \to ML_{T_{i\in n}}(\Sigma_{old})$$

which are the identity on $ML_{T_{i\in n}}(\Sigma_{old})$. In Filinski's approach one can use the translations $I_{new}$ and $I_{op}$, whenever possible, and more ad hoc definitions otherwise. In fact, when Filinski introduces a new monad $T'$, he introduces also two operations called monadic reflection and reification

$$\mathsf{reflect} : \forall X : \bullet.\tau \to T'X \qquad \mathsf{reify} : \forall X : \bullet.T'X \to \tau$$

that establish a bijection between $T'X$ and its implementation $\tau$ (i.e. a type in the pre-existing language). Therefore, we can define operations related to $T'$ by moving back and forth between $T'$ and its implementation (as done in the case of operations defined on an abstract datatype).

Semantically a **monad transformer** is a function $F : |Mon(\mathcal{C})| \to |Mon(\mathcal{C})|$ mapping monads (over a category $\mathcal{C}$) to monads. We are interested in monad transformers for *adding computational effects*, therefore we require that for any monad $T$ there should be a monad morphism $in_T : T \to FT$. It is often the case that $F$ is a functor on $Mon(\mathcal{C})$, and $in$ becomes a natural transformation from $\mathrm{id}_{Mon(\mathcal{C})}$ to $F$. Syntactically a monad transformer is a translation

$$I_F : ML_{T',T}(\Sigma_{par}) \to ML_T(\Sigma_{par})$$

which is the identity on $ML_T(\Sigma_{par})$. In other words we express the new monad $T'$ in terms of the old monad $T$ (and the parameters specified in $\Sigma_{par}$).

### 3.4 Examples of Monad Transformers

In the sequel we describe (in a higher-order $\lambda$-calculus) several monad transformers corresponding to the addition of a new computational effect, more precisely we define

- the new monad $T'$, and the monad morphism $in : T \to T'$
- operations on $T'$-computations associated to the new computational effect
- an operation $op' : \forall X : \bullet.A \to (B \to T'X) \to T'X$ *extending* to $T'$-computations a pre-existing operation $op : \forall X : \bullet.A \to (B \to TX) \to TX$ on $T$-computations.

Intuitively $op\ X : A \to (B \to TX) \to TX$ amounts to having an $A$-indexed family of algebraic operations of arity $B$ on $TX$.

## Monad Transformer $I_{se}$ for Adding Side-Effects

- signature $\Sigma_{par}$ for parameters
  states $S : \bullet$
- signature $\Sigma_{new}$ for new operations
  lookup $lkp' : T'S$
  update $upd' : S \to T'1$
- definition of new monad $T'$ and monad morphism $in : T \to T'$

$$\begin{aligned} T'X &\triangleq S \to T(X \times S) \\ [x]_{T'} &\triangleq \lambda s : S.[(x,s)]_T \\ \mathrm{let}_{T'}\, x{\Leftarrow}c \,\mathrm{in}\, f\ x &\triangleq \lambda s : S.\mathrm{let}_T\,(x,s'){\Leftarrow}c\ s \,\mathrm{in}\, f\ x\ s' \\ in\ X\ c &\triangleq \lambda s : S.\mathrm{let}_T\, x{\Leftarrow}c \,\mathrm{in}\, [(x,s)]_T \end{aligned}$$

  definition of new operations

$$\begin{aligned} lkp' &\triangleq \lambda s : S.[(s,s)]_T \\ upd'\ s &\triangleq \lambda s' : S.[(*,s)]_T \end{aligned}$$

  extension of old operation

$$op'\ X\ a\ f \triangleq \lambda s : S.op\ (X \times S)\ a\ (\lambda b : B.f\ b\ s)$$

*Remark 32.* The operations $lkp'$ and $upd'$ do not fit the format for $op$. However, any $*op : A \to TB$ induces an $op : \forall X : \bullet.A \to (B \to TX) \to TX$ in the right format, namely $op\ X\ a\ f \triangleq \mathrm{let}_T\, b{\Leftarrow} *op\ a \,\mathrm{in}\, f\ b$.

## Monad Transformer $I_{ex}$ for Adding Exceptions

- signature $\Sigma_{par}$ for parameters
  exceptions $E : \bullet$
- signature $\Sigma_{new}$ for new operations
  raise $raise' : \forall X : \bullet.E \to T'X$
  handle $handle' : \forall X : \bullet.(E \to T'X) \to T'X \to T'X$
- definition of new monad $T'$ and monad morphism $in : T \to T'$

$$\begin{aligned} T'X &\triangleq T(X + E) \\ [x]_{T'} &\triangleq [\mathrm{inl}\ x]_T \\ \mathrm{let}_{T'}\, x{\Leftarrow}c \,\mathrm{in}\, f\ x &\triangleq \mathrm{let}_T\, u{\Leftarrow}c \,\mathrm{in}\, (\mathrm{case}\, u \,\mathrm{of}\, x \Rightarrow f\ x \mid n \Rightarrow [\mathrm{inr}\ n]_T) \\ in\ X\ c &\triangleq \mathrm{let}_T\, x{\Leftarrow}c \,\mathrm{in}\, [\mathrm{inl}\ x]_T \end{aligned}$$

  definition of new operations

$$\begin{aligned} raise'\ X\ n &\triangleq [\mathrm{inr}\ n]_T \\ handle'\ X\ f\ c &\triangleq \mathrm{let}_T\, u{\Leftarrow}c \,\mathrm{in}\, (\mathrm{case}\, u \,\mathrm{of}\, x \Rightarrow [\mathrm{inl}\ x]_T \mid n \Rightarrow f\ n) \end{aligned}$$

  extension of old operation

$$op'\ X\ a\ f \triangleq op\ (X + E)\ a\ f$$

*Remark 33.* In this case the definition of $op'$ is particularly simple. In fact, the same definition works for extending any operation of type $\forall X : \bullet.\tau[Y := TX]$, where $\tau$ is a type whose only free type variable is $Y$. The case of an $A$-indexed family of algebraic operations of arity $B$ corresponds to $\tau \equiv A \to (B \to Y) \to Y$.

### Monad Transformer $I_{co}$ for Adding Complexity

- signature $\Sigma_{par}$ for parameters
  monoid $M : \bullet$
  $1 : M$
  $* : M \to M \to M$ (we use infix notation for $*$)
  to prove that $T'$ is a monad, we should add axioms saying that $(M, 1, *)$ is a monoid
- signature $\Sigma_{new}$ for new operations
  cost $tick' : M \to T'1$
- definition of new monad $T'$ and monad morphism $in : T \to T'$

$$T'X \triangleq T(X \times M)$$
$$[x]_{T'} \triangleq [(x, 1)]_T$$
$$\mathrm{let}_{T'}\, x \Leftarrow c \,\mathrm{in}\, f\ x \triangleq \mathrm{let}_T\, (x, m) \Leftarrow c \,\mathrm{in}\, (\mathrm{let}_T\, (y, n) \Leftarrow f\ x \,\mathrm{in}\, [(y, m * n)]_T)$$
$$in\ X\ c \triangleq \mathrm{let}_T\, x \Leftarrow c \,\mathrm{in}\, [(x, 1)]_T$$

  definition of new operations

$$tick'\ m \triangleq [(*, m)]_T$$

  extension of old operation

$$op'\ X\ a\ f \triangleq op\ (X \times M)\ a\ f$$

### Monad Transformer $I_{con}$ for Adding Continuations

- signature $\Sigma_{par}$ for parameters
  results $R : \bullet$
- signature $\Sigma_{new}$ for new operations
  abort $abort' : \forall X : \bullet . R \to T'X$
  call-cc $callcc' : \forall X, Y : \bullet . ((X \to T'Y) \to T'X) \to T'X$
- definition of new monad $T'$ and monad morphism $in : T \to T'$

$$T'X \triangleq (X \to TR) \to TR$$
$$[x]_{T'} \triangleq \lambda k : X \to TR. k\ x$$
$$\mathrm{let}_{T'}\, x \Leftarrow c \,\mathrm{in}\, f\ x \triangleq \lambda k : Y \to TR. c\ (\lambda x. f\ x\ k)$$
$$in\ X\ c \triangleq \lambda k : X \to TR. \mathrm{let}_T\, x \Leftarrow c \,\mathrm{in}\, k\ x$$

  definition of new operations

$$abort'\ X\ r \triangleq \lambda k : X \to TR. [r]_T$$
$$callcc'\ X\ Y\ f \triangleq \lambda k : X \to TR. f\ (\lambda x. \lambda k' : Y \to TR. [k\ x]_T)\ k$$

  extension of old operation

$$op'\ X\ a\ f \triangleq \lambda k : X \to TR. op\ R\ a\ (\lambda b : B. f\ b\ k)$$

*Remark 34.* The operation $callcc'$ and other control operators do not fit the algebraic format, and there is no way to massage them into such format. Unlike the others monad transformers, $I_{con}$ does not extend to a functor on $Mon(\mathcal{C})$.

*Exercise 35.* For each of the monad transformer, prove that $T'$ is a monad. Assume that $T$ is a monad, and use the equational axioms for higher-order $\lambda$-calculus with sums and products, including $\eta$-axioms.

*Exercise 36.* For each of the monad transformer, define a fix-point combinator for the new computational types $Y' : \forall X : \bullet.(T'X \to T'X) \to T'X$ given a fix-point combinator for the old computational types $Y : \forall X : \bullet.(TX \to TX) \to TX$. In some cases one needs the derived fix-point combinator $*Y$ for carriers of $T$-algebras (see Remark 26).

*Exercise 37.* Define a monad transformer $I_{sr}$ for state-readers, i.e. $T'X \triangleq S \to TX$. What could be $\Sigma_{new}$? Define a monad morphism from $T_{sr}$ to $T_{se}$.

*Exercise 38.* Check which monad transformers commute (up to isomorphism). For instance, $I_{se}$ and $I_{ex}$ do not commute, more precisely one gets

- $T_{se+ex}X = S \to T((X+E)\times S)$ when adding first side-effects and then exceptions
- $T_{ex+se}X = S \to T((X\times S)+E)$ when adding first exceptions and then side-effects

*Exercise 39.* For each of the monad transformers, identify equational laws for the new operations specified in $\Sigma_{new}$, and show that such laws are validated by the translation. For instance, $I_{se}$ validates the following equations:

$$\begin{array}{l}
s : S \vdash \mathrm{let}_{T'}\ * \Leftarrow \mathit{upd}'\ s\,\mathrm{in}\,\mathit{lkp}' = \mathrm{let}_{T'}\ * \Leftarrow \mathit{upd}'\ s\,\mathrm{in}\,[s]_{T'} : T'S \\
s, s' : S \vdash \mathrm{let}_{T'}\ * \Leftarrow \mathit{upd}'\ s\,\mathrm{in}\,\mathit{upd}'\ s' = \mathit{upd}'\ s' : T'1 \\
s : S \vdash \mathrm{let}_{T'}\ s \Leftarrow \mathit{lkp}'\,\mathrm{in}\,\mathit{upd}'\ s = [*]_{T'} : T'1 \\
X : \bullet, c : T'X \vdash \mathrm{let}_{T'}\ s \Leftarrow \mathit{lkp}'\,\mathrm{in}\,c = c : T'X
\end{array}$$

*Exercise 40 (Semantics of Effects).* Given a monad $T$ over the category of sets:

- Define predicates for $c \in T'X \triangleq S \to T(X\times S)$ corresponding to the properties "$c$ does not read from $S$" and "$c$ does not write in $S$".
  Such predicates are *extensional*, therefore a computation that reads the state and then rewrites it unchanged, is equivalent to a computation that ignores the state.
- Define a predicate for $c \in T'X \triangleq T(X+E)$ corresponding to the property "$c$ does not raise exceptions in $E$".

## 4 Monads in Haskell

So far we have focussed on applications of monads in denotational semantics, but since Wadler's influential papers in the early 90s [Wad92a,Wad92b,Wad95] they have also become part of the toolkit that Haskell programmers use on a day to day basis. Indeed, monads have proven to be so useful in practice that the language now includes extensions specifically to make programming with them easy. In the next few sections we will see how monads are represented in Haskell, look at some of their applications, and try to explain why they have had such an impact.

## 4.1 Implementing Monads in Haskell

The representation of monads in Haskell is based on the *Kleisli triple* formulation: recall Definition 1.4:

> A **Kleisli triple** over a category $\mathcal{C}$ is a triple $(T, \eta, \_^*)$, where $T : |\mathcal{C}| \to |\mathcal{C}|$, $\eta_A : A \to TA$ for $A \in |\mathcal{C}|$, $f^* : TA \to TB$ for $f : A \to TB$ and the following equations hold: ...

In Haskell, $\mathcal{C}$ is the category with Haskell types as objects and Haskell functions as arrows, $T$ corresponds to a parameterised type, $\eta$ is called `return`, and $\_^*$ is called `>>=`. This would suggest the following types:

```
return :: a -> T a
(>>=) :: (a -> T b) -> (T a -> T b)
```

where `a` and `b` are Haskell type variables, so that these types are polymorphic. But notice that we can consider `>>=` to be a curried function of *two* arguments, with types `(a -> T b)` and `T a`. In practice it is convenient to reverse these arguments, and instead give `>>=` the type

```
(>>=) :: T a -> (a -> T b) -> T b
```

Now the metalanguage notation let $x \Leftarrow e_1$ in $e_2$ can be conveniently expressed as

```
e1 >>= \x -> e2
```

(where `\x -> e` is Haskell's notation for $\lambda x.e$). Intuitively this binds `x` to the result of `e1` in `e2`; with this in mind we usually pronounce "`>>=`" as "bind".

*Example 41.* The monad of **partiality** can be represented using the built-in Haskell type

```
data Maybe a = Just a | Nothing
```

This defines a parameterised type `Maybe`, whose elements are `Just x` for any element `x` of type `a` (representing a successful computation), or `Nothing` (representing failure).

The monad operators can be implemented as

```
return a = Just a

m >>= f = case m of
            Just a -> f a
            Nothing -> Nothing
```

and failure can be represented by

```
failure = Nothing
```

As an example of an application, a division function which operates on possibly failing integers can now be defined as

```
divide :: Maybe Int -> Maybe Int -> Maybe Int
divide a b = a >>= \m ->
             b >>= \n ->
             if n==0 then failure
                     else return (a `div` b)
```

Try unfolding the calls of `>>=` in this definition to understand the gain in clarity that using monadic operators brings.

*Example 42.* As a second example, we show how to implement the monad of **side-effects** in Haskell. This time we will need to define a new type, `State s a`, to represent computations producing an `a`, with a side-effect on a state of type `s`. Haskell provides three ways to define types:

```
type State s a = s -> (s,a)
newtype State s a = State (s -> (s,a))
data State s a = State (s -> (s,a))
```

The first alternative declares a *type synonym*: `State s a` would be in every respect equivalent to the type `s -> (s,a)`. This would cause problems later: since many monads are represented by functions, it would be difficult to tell *just from the type* which monad we were talking about.

The second alternative declares `State s a` to be a new type, different from all others, but isomorphic to `s -> (s,a)`. The elements of the new type are written `State f` to distinguish them from functions. (There is no need for the tag used on elements to have the same name as the type, but it is often convenient to use the same name for both).

The third alternative also declares `State s a` to be a new type, with elements of the form `State f`, but in contrast to `newtype` the `State` constructor is lazy: that is, `State` $\perp$ and $\perp$ are different values. This is because `data` declarations create lifted sum-of-product types, and even when the sum is trivial it is still lifted. Thus `State s a` is *not* isomorphic to `s -> (s,a)` — it has an extra element — and values of this type are more costly to manipulate as a result.

We therefore choose the second alternative. The monad operations are now easy to define:

```
return a = State (\s -> (s,a))

State m >>= f = State (\s -> let (s',a) = m s
                                 State m' = f a
                             in m' s')
```

The state can be manipulated using

```
readState :: State s s
readState = State (\s -> (s,s))

writeState :: s -> State s ()
writeState s = State (\_ -> (s,()))
```

For example, a function to increment the state could be expressed using these functions as

```
increment :: State Int ()
increment = readState >>= \s ->
            writeState (s+1)
```

## 4.2 The Monad Class: Overloading Return and Bind

Haskell programmers make use of many different monads; it would be awkward if `return` and `>>=` had to be given different names for each one. To avoid this, we use *overloading* so that the same names can be used for every monad.

Overloading in Haskell is supported via the *class system*: overloaded names are introduced by defining a *class* containing them. A class is essentially a signature, with a different implementation for each type. The monad operations are a part of a class `Monad`, whose definition is found in Haskell's standard prelude:

```
class Monad m where
  return :: a -> m a
  (>>=) :: m a -> (a -> m b) -> m b
```

Here the class parameter `m` ranges over *parameterised* types; read the declaration as "A parameterised type `m` is a `Monad` if it supports implementations of `return` and `>>=` with the given types".

Implementations of these operations are provided by making a corresponding *instance* declaration, for example:

```
instance Monad Maybe where
  return a = Just a
  m >>= f = case m of
              Just a -> f a
              Nothing -> Nothing
```

which corresponds to the definition of the `Maybe` monad given earlier. For the monad of side-effects, we write

```
instance Monad (State s) where
  return a = State (\s -> (s,a))
  State m >>= f = State (\s -> let (s',a) = m s
                                   State m' = f a
                               in m' s')
```

Notice that although we defined the type `State` with two parameters, and the `Monad` class requires a type with one parameter, Haskell allows us to create the type we need by *partially applying* the `State` type to one parameter: types with many parameters are 'curried'. Indeed, we chose the order of the parameters in the definition of `State` with this in mind.

Now when the monadic operators are applied, the type at which they are used determines which implementation is invoked. This is why we were careful to make `State` a *new* type above.

A great advantage of overloading the monad operators is that it enables us to write code which works with *any* monad. For example, we could define a function which combines two monadic computations producing integers into a computation of their sum:

```
addM a b = a >>= \m ->
           b >>= \n ->
           return (m+n)
```

Since nothing in this definition is specific to a particular monad, we can use this function with any: `addM (Just 2) (Just 3)` is `Just 5`, but we could also use `addM` with the `State` monad. The type assigned to `addM` reflects this, it is[1]

```
addM :: (Monad m) => m Int -> m Int -> m Int
```

The "`(Monad m) =>`" is called a *context*, and restricts the types which may be substituted for `m` to instances of the class `Monad`.

Although `addM` is perhaps too specialised to be really useful, we can derive a very useful higher-order function by generalising over `+`. Indeed, Haskell's standard `Monad` library provides a number of such functions, such as

```
liftM :: Monad m => (a -> b) -> m a -> m b
liftM2 :: Monad m => (a -> b -> c) -> m a -> m b -> m c
sequence :: Monad m => [m a] -> m [a]
```

With these definitions,

```
addM = liftM2 (+)
```

Programming with monads is greatly eased by such a library.

*Exercise 43.* Give a definition of `sequence`. The intention is that each computation in the list is executed in turn, and a list made of the results.

Finally, Haskell provides syntactic sugar for `>>=` to make monadic programs more readable: the do-notation. For example, the definition of `addM` above could equivalently be written as

```
addM a b = do m <- a
              n <- b
              return (m+n)
```

The do-notation is defined by

```
do e          = e

do x <- e     = e >>= (\x -> do c)
   c

do e          = e >>= (\_ -> do c)
   c
```

[1] Actually type inference produces an even more general type, since the arithmetic is also overloaded, but we will gloss over this.

Applying these rules to the definition of addM above rewrites it into the form first presented. The do-notation is simply a shorthand for bind, but does make programs more recognisable, especially for beginners.

*Example 44.* As an example of monadic programming, consider the problem of decorating the leaves of a tree with unique numbers. We shall use a parameterised tree type

```
data Tree a = Leaf a | Bin (Tree a) (Tree a)
```

and define a function

```
unique :: Tree a -> Tree (a,Int)
```

which numbers the leaves from 1 upwards in left-to-right order. For example,

```
unique (Bin (Bin (Leaf 'a') (Leaf 'b')) (Leaf 'c'))
 = Bin (Bin (Leaf ('a',1)) (Leaf ('b',2))) (Leaf ('c',3))
```

Intuitively we think of an integer state which is incremented every time a leaf is encountered: we shall therefore make use of the State monad to define a function

```
unique' :: Tree a -> State Int (Tree (a,Int))
```

First we define a function to increment the state,

```
tick :: State Int Int
tick = do n <- readState
          writeState (n+1)
          return n
```

and then the definition of unique' is straightforward:

```
unique' (Leaf a) = do n <- tick
                      return (Leaf (a,n))
unique' (Bin t1 t2) = liftM2 Bin (unique' t1) (unique' t2)
```

Notice that we use liftM2 to apply the two-argument function Bin to the results of labelling the two subtrees; as a result the notational overhead of using a monad is very small.

Finally we define unique to invoke the monadic function and supply an initial state:

```
unique t = runState 1 (unique' t)

runState s (State f) = snd (f s)
```

It is instructive to rewrite the unique function directly, without using a monad — explicit state passing in the recursive definition clutters it significantly, and creates opportunities for errors that the monadic code completely avoids.

## 5 Applying Monads

So far we have shown how monads are represented in Haskell, and how the language supports their use. But what are monads used *for*? Why have they become so prevalent in Haskell programs? In this section we try to answer these questions.

### 5.1 Input/Output: The Killer Application

Historically, input/output has been awkward to handle in *purely* functional languages. The same applies to foreign function calls: there is no way to *guarantee* that a function written in C, for example, does not have side effects, so calling it directly from a Haskell program would risk compromising Haskell's purely functional semantics.

Yet it is clear enough that input/output can be *modelled* in a purely functional way: we must just consider a program to be a function from the state of the universe before it is run, to the state of the universe afterwards. One possibility is to write the program in this way: every function depending on the external state would take the universe as a parameter, and every function modifying it would return a new universe as a part of its result. For example a program to copy one file to another might be written as

```
copy :: String -> String -> Universe -> Universe
copy from to universe =
  let contents = readFile from universe
      universe' = writeFile to contents universe
  in universe'
```

Such a program has a purely functional semantics, but is not easy to implement. Of course, we cannot really maintain several copies of the universe at the same time, and so 'functions' such as `writeFile` must be implemented by actually writing the new contents to the filestore. If the programmer then accidentally or deliberately returns `universe` instead of `universe'` as the final result of his program, then the purely functional semantics is not correctly implemented. This approach has been followed in Clean though, using a linear type system to guarantee that the programmer manipulates universes correctly [BS96].

However, having seen monads we would probably wish to simplify the program above by using a `State` monad to manage the universe. By defining

```
type IO a = State Universe a
```

and altering the types of the primitives slightly to

```
readFile :: String -> IO String
writeFile :: String -> String -> IO ()
```

then we can rewrite the file copying program as

```
copy :: String -> String -> IO ()
copy from to = do contents <- readFile from
                  writeFile to contents
```

which looks almost like an imperative program for the same task[2].

This program is both purely functional and efficiently implementable: it is quite safe to write the output file destructively. However, there is still a risk that the programmer will define inappropriate operations on the IO type, such as

```
snapshot :: IO Universe
snapshot = State (\univ -> (univ, univ))
```

The solution is just to *make the* IO *type abstract* [JW93]! This does not change the semantics of programs, which remains purely functional, but it *does* guarantee that as long as all the primitive operations on the IO type treat the universe in a proper single-threaded way (which all operations implemented in imperative languages do), then so does any Haskell program which uses them.

Since the IO monad was introduced into Haskell, it has been possible to write Haskell programs which do input/output, call foreign functions directly, and yet still have a purely functional semantics. Moreover, these programs look very like ordinary programs in any imperative language. The contortions previously needed to achieve similar effects are not worthy of description here.

The reader may be wondering what all the excitement is about here: after all, it has been possible to write ordinary imperative programs in other languages for a very long time, including functional languages such as ML or Scheme; what is so special about writing them in Haskell? Two things:

- Input/output can be combined cleanly with the other features of Haskell, in particular higher-order functions, polymorphism, and lazy evaluation. Although ML, for example, combines input/output with the first two, the ability to mix lazy evaluation cleanly with I/O is unique to Haskell with monads — and as the copy example shows, can lead to simpler programs than would otherwise be possible.
- Input/output is combined with a purely functional semantics. In ML, for example, *any* expression may potentially have side-effects, and transformations which re-order computations are invalid without an effect analysis to establish that the computations are side-effect free. In Haskell, no expression has side-effects, but some denote commands with effects; moreover, the potential to cause side-effects is evident in an expression's type. Evaluation order can be changed freely, but monadic computations cannot be reordered because the monad laws do not permit it.

[2] The main difference is that we read and write the entire contents of a file in one operation, rather than byte-by-byte as an imperative program probably would. This may seem wasteful of space, but thanks to lazy evaluation the characters of the input file are only actually read into memory when they are needed for writing to the output. That is, the space requirements are small and constant, just as for a byte-by-byte imperative program.

Peyton-Jones' excellent tutorial [Pey01] covers this kind of monadic programming in much more detail, and also discusses a useful refinement to the semantics presented here.

### 5.2 Imperative Algorithms

Many algorithms can be expressed in a purely functional style with the same complexity as their imperative forms. But some efficient algorithms depend critically on destructive updates. Examples include the UNION-FIND algorithm, many graph algorithms, and the implementation of arrays with constant time access and modification. Without monads, Haskell cannot express these algorithms with the same complexity as an imperative language.

With monads, however, it is easy to do so. Just as the *abstract* `IO` monad enables us to write programs with a purely functional semantics, and give them an imperative implementation, so an abstract *state transformer* monad `ST` allows us to write purely functional programs which update the state destructively [LJ94][3]. Semantically the type `ST a` is isomorphic to `State -> (State,a)`, where `State` is a function from typed references (locations) to their contents. In the implementation, only one `State` ever exists, which is updated destructively in place.

Operations are provided to create, read, and write typed references:

```
newSTRef :: a -> ST (STRef a)
readSTRef :: STRef a -> ST a
writeSTRef :: STRef a -> a -> ST ()
```

Here `STRef a` is the type of a reference containing a value of type `a`. Other operations are provided to create and manipulate arrays.

The reason for introducing a *different* monad `ST`, rather than just providing these operations over the `IO` monad, is that destructive updates to variables in a program are not *externally visible* side-effects. We can therefore encapsulate these imperative effects using a new primitive

```
runST :: ST a -> a
```

which semantically creates a new `State`, runs its argument in it, and discards the final `State` before returning an `a` as its result. (A corresponding function `runIO` would not be implementable, because we have no way to 'discard the final `Universe`'). In the implementation of `runST`, `State`s are represented just by a collection of references stored on the heap; there is no cost involved in creating a 'new' one therefore. Using `runST` we can write pure (non-monadic) functions whose implementation uses imperative features internally.

*Example 45.* The depth-first search algorithm for graphs uses destructively updated marks to identify previously visited nodes and avoid traversing them again.

[3] While the IO monad is a part of Haskell 98, the current standard [JHe+99], the ST monad is not. However, every implementation provides it in some form; the description here is based on the Hugs modules ST and LazyST [JRtYHG+99].

For simplicity, let us represent graph nodes by integers, and graphs using the type

```
type Graph = Array Int [Int]
```

A graph is an array indexed by integers (nodes), whose elements are the list of successors of the corresponding node. We can record which nodes have been visited using an updateable array of boolean marks, and program the depth-first search algorithm as follows:

```
dfs g ns = runST (do marks <- newSTArray (bounds g) False
                     dfs' g ns marks)

dfs' g [] marks = return []
dfs' g (n:ns) marks =
  do visited <- readSTArray marks n
     if visited then dfs' g ns marks
       else do writeSTArray marks n True
               ns' <- dfs' g ((g!n)++ns) marks
               return (n:ns')
```

The function `dfs` returns a list of all nodes reachable from the given list of roots in depth-first order, for example:

```
dfs (array (1,4) [(1,[2,3]), (2,[4]), (3,[4]), (4,[1])]) =
  [1,2,4,3]
```

The *type* of the depth-first search function is

```
dfs :: Graph -> [Int] -> [Int]
```

It is a pure, non-monadic function which can be freely mixed with other non-monadic code.

Imperative features combine interestingly with lazy evaluation. In this example, the output list is produced lazily: the traversal runs only far enough to produce the elements which are demanded. This is possible because, in the code above, `return (n:ns')` can produce a result *before* `ns'` is known. The recursive call of `dfs'` need not be performed until the value of `ns'` is actually needed[4]. Thus we can efficiently use `dfs` even for incomplete traversals: to search for the first node satisfying `p`, for example, we can use

```
head (filter p (dfs g roots))
```

safe in the knowledge that the traversal will stop when the first node is found.

King and Launchbury have shown how the lazy depth-first search function can be used to express a wide variety of graph algorithms both elegantly and efficiently [KL95].

---

[4] Hugs actually provides two variations on the ST monad, with and without lazy behaviour. The programmer chooses between them by importing either ST or LazyST.

The `ST` monad raises some interesting typing issues. Note first of all that its operations cannot be implemented in Haskell with the types given, even inefficiently! The problem is that we cannot represent an indexed collection of values with arbitrary types — if we tried to represent `States` as functions from references to contents, for example, then all the contents would have to have the same type. A purely functional implementation would need at least *dependent types*, to allow the type of a reference's contents to depend on the reference itself — although even given dependent types, it is far from clear how to construct a well-typed implementation.

Secondly, we must somehow prevent references created in one `State` being used in another — it would be hard to assign a sensible meaning to the result. This is done by giving the `ST` type an additional parameter, which we may think of as a 'state identifier', or a *region* [TT97] within which the computation operates: `ST s a` is the type of computations *on state* `s` producing an `a`. Reference types are also parameterised on the state identifier, so the types of the operations on them become:

```
newSTRef :: a -> ST s (STRef s a)
readSTRef :: STRef s a -> ST s a
writeSTRef :: STRef s a -> a -> ST s ()
```

These types guarantee that `ST` computations only manipulate references lying in 'their' `State`.

But what should the type of `runST` be? It is supposed to create a *new* `State` to run its argument in, but if we give it the type

```
runST :: ST s a -> a
```

then it will be applicable to *any* `ST` computation, including those which manipulate references in other `States`. To prevent this, `runST` is given a *rank-2 polymorphic* type:

```
runST :: (forall s. ST s a) -> a
```

("Rank-2 polymorphic" refers to the fact that `forall` appears to the left of a function arrow in this type, so `runST` *requires* a polymorphic argument. Rank-2 polymorphism was added to both Hugs and GHC, just to make this application possible [Jon].) This type ensures that the argument of `runST` can safely be run in *any* `State`, in particular the new one which `runST` creates.

*Example 46.* The expression

```
runST (newSTRef 0)
```

is not well-typed. Since `newSTRef 0` has the type `ST s (STRef s Int)`, then `runST` would have to produce a result of type `STRef s Int` — but the scope of `s` does not extend over the type of the result.

*Example 47.* The expression

```
runST (do r<-newSTRef 0
          return (runST (readSTRef r)))
```

is not well-typed either, because the argument of the inner `runST` is not polymorphic — it depends on the state identifier of the outer one.

The inclusion of the `ST` monad and assignments in Haskell raises an interesting question: just what is a *purely* functional language? Perhaps the answer is: one in which assignment has a funny type!

### 5.3 Domain Specific Embedded Languages

Since the early days of functional programming, *combinator libraries* have been used to define succinct notations for programs in particular domains [Bur75]. There are combinator libraries for many different applications, but in this section we shall focus on one very well-studied area: parsing. A library for writing parsers typically defines a type `Parser a`, of parsers for values of type `a`, and combinators for constructing and invoking parsers. These might include

```
satisfy :: (Char -> Bool) -> Parser Char
```

to construct a parser which accepts a single character satisfying the given predicate,

```
(|||) :: Parser a -> Parser a -> Parser a
```

to construct a parser which accepts an input if *either* of its operands can parse it, and

```
runParser :: Parser a -> String -> a
```

to invoke a parser on a given input.

A parsing library must also include combinators to run parsers in sequence, and to build parsers which invoke functions to compute their results. Wadler realised that these could be provided by declaring the `Parser` type to be a monad [Wad92a]. Further combinators can then be defined in terms of these basic ones, such as a combinator accepting a particular character,

```
literal :: Char -> Parser Char
literal c = satisfy (==c)
```

and a combinator for repetition,

```
many :: Parser a -> Parser [a]
many p = liftM2 (:) p (many p) ||| return []
```

which parses a list of any number of `p`s.

Given such a library, parsing programs can be written very succinctly. As an example, we present a function to evaluate arithmetic expressions involving addition and multiplication:

```
eval :: String -> Int
eval = runParser expr

expr = do t <- term
          literal '+'
          e <- expr
          return (t+e)
   ||| term

term = do c <- closed
          literal '*'
          t <- term
          return (c*t)
   ||| closed

closed = do literal '('
            e <- expr
            literal ')'
            return e
     ||| numeral

numeral = do ds <- many (satisfy isDigit)
             return (read ds)
```

With a good choice of combinators, the code of a parser closely resembles the grammar it parses[5,6]!

In recent years, a different view of such combinator libraries has become popular: we think of them as defining a *domain specific language* (DSL), whose constructions are the combinators of the library [Hud98]. With this view, this little parsing library defines a programming language with special constructions to accept a symbol and to express alternatives.

Every time a functional programmer designs a combinator library, then, we might as well say that he or she designs a domain specific programming language, integrated with Haskell. This is a useful perspective, since it encourages programmers to produce a modular design, with a clean separation between the semantics of the DSL and the program that uses it, rather than mixing combinators and 'raw' semantics willy-nilly. And since monads appear so often in programming language semantics, it is hardly surprising that they appear often in combinator libraries also!

---

[5] In practice the resemblance would be a little less close: real parsers for arithmetic expressions are left-recursive, use a lexical analyser, and are written to avoid expensive backtracking. On the other hand, real parsing libraries provide more combinators to handle these features and make parsers even more succinct! See Hutton's article [HM98] for a good description.

[6] Notice how important Haskell's lazy evaluation is here: without it, these recursive definitions would not make sense!

We will return to the implementation of the parsing library in the next section, after a discussion of monad transformers.

## 6 Monad Transformers in Haskell

The Haskell programmer who makes heavy use of combinators will need to implement a large number of monads. Although it is perfectly possible to define a new type for each one, and implement `return` and `>>=` from scratch, it saves labour to construct monads systematically where possible. The *monad transformers* of section 3.2 offer an attractive way of doing so, as Liang, Hudak and Jones point out [LHJ95].

Recall the definition:

> A **monad transformer** is a function $F : |Mon(\mathcal{C})| \to |Mon(\mathcal{C})|$, i.e. a function mapping monads (over a category $\mathcal{C}$) to monads. We are interested in monad transformers for *adding computational effects*, therefore we require that for any monad $T$ there should be a monad morphism $in_T : T \to FT$.

We represent monad transformers in Haskell by types parameterised on a monad (itself a parameterised type), and the result type — that is, types of kind `(* -> *) -> * -> *`. For example, the partiality monad transformer is represented by the type

```
newtype MaybeT m a = MaybeT (m (Maybe a))
```

According to the definition, `MaybeT m` should be a monad whenever `m` is, which we can demonstrate by implementing `return` and `>>=`:

```
instance Monad m => Monad (MaybeT m) where
  return x = MaybeT (return (Just x))
  MaybeT m >>= f =
    MaybeT (do x <- m
               case x of
                 Nothing -> return Nothing
                 Just a -> let MaybeT m' = f a in m')
```

Moreover, according to the definition of a monad transformer above, there should also be a monad morphism from `m` to `MaybeT m` — that is, it should be possible to transform computations of one type into the other. Since we need to define monad morphisms for many different monad transformers, we use Haskell's overloading again and introduce a *class of monad transformers*

```
class (Monad m, Monad (t m)) => MonadTransformer t m where
  lift :: m a -> t m a
```

Here `t` is the monad transformer, `m` is the monad it is applied to, and `lift` is the monad morphism[7]. Now we can make `MaybeT` into an instance of this class:

```
instance Monad m => MonadTransformer MaybeT m where
  lift m = MaybeT (do x <- m
                      return (Just x))
```

The purpose of the `MaybeT` transformer is to enable computations to fail: we shall introduce operations to cause and handle failures. One might expect their types to be

```
failure :: MaybeT m a
handle :: MaybeT m a -> MaybeT m a -> MaybeT m a
```

However, this is not good enough: since we expect to combine `MaybeT` with other monad transformers, the monad we actually want to apply these operations at may well be of some other form — but as long as it involves the `MaybeT` transformer somewhere, we ought to be able to do so.

We will therefore overload these operations also, and define a class of '`Maybe`-like' monads[8]:

```
class Monad m => MaybeMonad m where
  failure :: m a
  handle :: m a -> m a -> m a
```

Of course, monads of the form `MaybeT m` will be instances of this class, but later we will also see others. In this case, the instance declaration is

```
instance Monad m => MaybeMonad (MaybeT m) where
  failure = MaybeT (return Nothing)
  MaybeT m `handle` MaybeT m' =
    MaybeT (do x <- m
               case x of
                 Nothing -> m'
                 Just a -> return (Just a))
```

Finally, we need a way to 'run' elements of this type. We define

```
runMaybe :: Monad m => MaybeT m a -> m a
runMaybe (MaybeT m) = do x <- m
                         case x of
                           Just a -> return a
```

[7] Here we step outside Haskell 98 by using a *multiple parameter class* – an extension which is, however, supported by Hugs and many other implementations. We make m a parameter of the class to permit the definition of monad transformers which place additional requirements on their argument monad.

[8] Usually the standard Haskell class MonadPlus with operations mzero and mplus is used in this case, but in the present context the names MaybeMonad, failure and handle are more natural.

for this purpose. (We leave undefined how we 'run' an erroneous computation, thus converting an explicitly represented error into a real Haskell one).

We have now seen all the elements of a monad transformer in Haskell. To summarise:

- We define a type to represent the transformer, say `TransT`, with two parameters, the first of which should be a monad.
- We declare `TransT m` to be a `Monad`, under the assumption that `m` already is.
- We declare `TransT` to be an instance of class `MonadTransformer`, thus defining how computations are lifted from `m` to `TransT m`.
- We define a class `TransMonad` of '`Trans`-like monads', containing the operations that `TransT` provides.
- We declare `TransT m` to be an instance of `TransMonad`, thus implementing these operations..
- We define a function to 'run' `(TransT m)`-computations, which produces `m`-computations as a result. In general `runTrans` may need additional parameters — for example, for a state transformer we probably want to supply an initial state.

We can carry out this program to define monad transformers for, among others,

- **state transformers**, represented by

  ```
  newtype StateT s m a = StateT (s -> m (s, a))
  ```

  supporting operations in the class[9]

  ```
  class Monad m => StateMonad s m | m -> s where
    readState :: m s
    writeState :: s -> m ()
  ```

- **environment readers**, represented by

  ```
  newtype EnvT s m a = EnvT (s -> m a)
  ```

  supporting operations in the class

  ```
  class Monad m => EnvMonad env m | m -> env where
    inEnv :: env -> m a -> m a
    rdEnv :: m env
  ```

  where `rdEnv` reads the current value of the environment, and `inEnv` runs its argument in the given environment.

[9] This class declaration uses Mark Jones' *functional dependencies*, supported by Hugs, to declare that the type of the monad's state is determined by the type of the monad itself. In other words, the same monad cannot have two different states of different types. While not strictly necessary, making the dependency explicit enables the type-checker to infer the type of the state much more often, and helps to avoid hard-to-understand error messages about ambiguous typings.

– **continuations**, represented by

```
newtype ContT ans m a = ContT ((a -> m ans) -> m ans)
```

supporting operations in the class

```
class Monad m => ContMonad m where
  callcc :: ((a -> m b) -> m a) -> m a
```

where `callcc f` calls `f`, passing it a function `k`, which if it is ever called terminates the call of `callcc` immediately, with its argument as the final result.

Two steps remain before we can use monad transformers in practice. Firstly, since monad transformers only transform one monad into another, we must define a monad to start with. Although one could start with any monad, it is natural to use a 'vanilla' monad with no computational features – the *identity* monad

```
newtype Id a = Id a
```

The implementations of `return` and `>>=` on this monad just add and remove the `Id` tag.

Secondly, so far the *only* instances in class `MaybeMonad` are of the form `MaybeT m`, the only instances in class `StateMonad` of the form `StateT s m`, and so on. Yet when we combine two or more monads, of course we expect to use the features of *both* in the resulting monad. For example, if we construct the monad `StateT s (MaybeT Id)`, then we expect to be able to use `failure` and `handle` at this type, as well as `readState` and `writeState`.

The only way to do so is to give further instance declarations, which define how to 'lift' the operations of one monad over another. For example, we can lift failure handling to state monads as follows:

```
instance MaybeMonad m => MaybeMonad (StateT s m) where
  failure = lift failure
  StateT m `handle` StateT m' = StateT (\s -> m s `handle` m' s)
```

Certainly this requires $O(n^2)$ instance declarations, one for each pair of monad transformers, but there is unfortunately no other solution.

The payoff for all this work is that, when we need to define a monad, we can often construct it quickly by composing monad transformers, and automatically inherit a collection of useful operations.

*Example 48.* We can implement the parsing library from section 5.3 by combining state transformation with failure. We shall let a parser's state be the input to be parsed; running a parser will consume a part of it, so running two parsers in sequence will parse successive parts of the input. Attempting to run a parser may succeed or fail, and we will often wish to handle failures by trying a different parser instead. We can therefore define a suitable monad by

```
type Parser a = StateT String (MaybeT Id) a
```

whose computations we can run using

```
runParser p s = runId (runMaybe (runState s p))
```

It turns out that the operator we called `|||` earlier is just `handle`, and `satisfy` is simply defined by

```
satisfy :: (s -> Bool) -> Parser s s
satisfy p = do s<-readState
               case s of
                 [] -> failure
                 x:xs -> if p x then do writeState xs
                                        return x
                                else failure
```

There is no more to do.

## 7 Monads and DSLs: A Discussion

It is clear why monads have been so successful for programming I/O and imperative algorithms in Haskell — they offer the only really satisfactory solution. But they have also been widely adopted by the designers of combinator libraries. Why? We have made the analogy between a combinator library and a domain specific language, and since monads can be used to structure denotational semantics, it is not so surprising that they can also be used in combinator libraries. But that something *can* be used, does not mean that it *will* be used. The designer of a combinator library has a choice: he need not slavishly follow the One Monadic Path — why, then, have so many chosen to do so? What are the overwhelming practical benefits that flow from using monads in combinator library design in particular?

Monads offer significant advantages in three key areas. Firstly, they offer a *design principle* to follow. A designer who wants to capture a particular functionality in a library, but is unsure exactly what interface to provide to it, can be reasonably confident that a monadic interface will be a good choice. The monad interface has been tried and tested: we know it allows the library user great flexibility. In contrast, early parsing libraries, for example, used non-monadic interfaces which made some parsers awkward to write.

Secondly, monads can *guide the implementation* of a library. A library designer must choose an appropriate type for his combinators to work over, and his task is eased if the type is a monad. Many monad types can be constructed systematically, as we have seen in the previous section, and so can some parts of the library which operate on them. Given a collection of monad transformers, substantial parts of the library come 'for free', just as when we found there was little left to implement after composing the representation of `Parsers` from two monad transformers.

Thirdly, there are benefits when many libraries *share a part of their interfaces.* Users can learn to use each new library more quickly, because the monadic part of its interface is already familiar. Because of the common interface, it is reasonable to define generic monadic functions, such as `liftM2`, which work with any monadic library. This both helps users, who need only learn to use `liftM2` once, and greatly eases the task of implementors, who find much of the functionality they want to provide comes for free. And of course, it is thanks to the widespread use of monads that Haskell has been extended with syntactic sugar to support them — if each library had its own completely separate interface, then it would be impractical to support them all with special syntax.

Taken together, these are compelling reasons for a library designer to choose monads whenever possible.

## 8 Exercises on Monads

This section contains practical exercises, intended to be solved using Hugs on a computer. Since some readers will already be familiar with Haskell and will have used monads already, while others will be seeing them for the first time, the exercises are divided into different levels of difficulty. Choose those which are right for you.

The Hugs interpreter is started with the command

```
hugs -98
```

The flag informs `hugs` that extensions to Haskell 98 should be allowed — and they are needed for some of these exercises. When Hugs is started it prompts for a command or an expression to evaluate; the command ":?" lists the commands available. Hugs is used by placing definitions in a file, loading the file into the interpreter (with the ":l" or ":r" command), and typing expressions to evaluate. You can obtain information on any defined name with the command ":i", and discover which names are in scope using ":n" followed by a regular expression matching the names you are interested in. Do not try to type definitions in response to the interpreter's prompt: they will not be understood.

### 8.1 Easy Exercises

Choose these exercises if you were previously unfamiliar with monads or Haskell.

*Exercise 49.* Write a function

```
dir :: IO [String]
```

which returns a list of the file names in the current directory. You can obtain them by running `ls` and placing the output in a file, which you then read. You will need to import module `System`, which defines a function `system` to execute shell commands — place "`import System`" on the first line of your file. A string can be split into its constituent words using the standard function `words`, and you can print values (for testing) using the standard function `print`.

*Exercise 50.* Write a function

```
nodups :: [String] -> [String]
```

which removes duplicate elements from a list of strings — the intention is to return a list of strings in the argument, in order of first occurrence. It is easy to write an inefficient version of nodups, which keeps a list of the strings seen so far, but you should use a hash table internally so that each string in the input is compared against only a few others. (The choice of hash function is not particularly important for this exercise, though). Moreover, you should produce the result list *lazily*. Test this by running

```
interact (unlines . nodups . lines)
```

which should echo each line you then type on its first occurrence.

You will need to use Haskell lists, which are written by enclosing their elements in square brackets separated by commas, and the cons operator, which is ":". Import module `LazyST`, and use `newSTArray` to create your hash table, `readSTArray` to read it, and `writeSTArray` to write it. Beware of Haskell's layout rule, which insists that every expression in a `do` begin in the same column — and interprets everything appearing in that column as the start of a new expression.

*Exercise 51.* The implementation of the `MaybeT` transformer is given above, but the implementations of the `StateT`, `EnvT` and `ContT` transformers were only sketched. Complete them. (`ContT` is quite difficult, and you might want to leave it for later).

*Exercise 52.* We define the `MaybeT` type by

```
newtype MaybeT m a = MaybeT (m (Maybe a))
```

What if we had defined it by

```
newtype MaybeT m a = MaybeT (Maybe (m a))
```

instead? Could we still have defined a monad transformer based on it?

*Exercise 53.* We defined the type of `Parsers` above by

```
type Parser a = StateT String (MaybeT Id) a
```

What if we had combined state transformation and failure the other way round?

```
type Parser a = MaybeT (StateT String Id) a
```

Define an instance of `StateMonad` for `MaybeT`, and investigate the behaviour of several examples combining failure handling and side-effects using each of these two monads. Is there a difference in their behaviour?

### 8.2 Moderate Exercises

Choose these exercises if you are comfortable with Haskell, and have seen monads before.

*Exercise 54.* Implement a monad `MaybeST` based on the built-in `ST` monad, which provides updateable typed references, but also supports failure and failure handling. If `m` fails in ``m `handle` h``, then all references should contain the *same* values on entering the handler `h` that they had when `m` was entered.

Can you add an operator

```
commit :: MaybeST ()
```

with the property that updates before a `commit` survive a subsequent failure?

*Exercise 55.* A different way to handle failures is using the type

```
newtype CPSMaybe ans a =
  CPSMaybe ((a -> ans -> ans) -> ans -> ans)
```

This is similar to the monad of continuations, but both computations and continuations take an extra argument — the value to return in case of failure. When a failure occurs, this argument is returned directly and the normal continuation is not invoked.

Make `CPSMaybe` an instance of class `Monad` and `MaybeMonad`, and define `runCPSMaybe`.

Failure handling programs often use a great deal of space, because failure handlers retain data that is no longer needed in the successful execution. Yet once one branch has progressed sufficiently far, we often know that its failure handler is no longer relevant. For example, in parsers we usually combine parsers for quite different constructions, and if the first parser succeeds in parsing more than a few tokens, then we know that the second cannot possibly succeed. Can you define an operator

```
cut :: CPSMaybe ans ()
```

which discards the failure handler, so that the memory it occupies can be reclaimed? How would you use `cut` in a parsing library?

### 8.3 Difficult Exercises

These should give you something to get your teeth into!

*Exercise 56.* Implement a domain specific language for concurrent programming, using a monad `Process s a` and typed channels `Chan s a`, with the operations

```
chan :: Process s (Chan s a)
send :: Chan s a -> a -> Process s ()
recv :: Chan s a -> Process s a
```

to create channels and send and receive messages (synchronously),

```
fork :: Process s a -> Process s ()
```

to start a new concurrent task, and

```
runProcess :: (forall s. Process s a) -> a
```

to run a process. By analogy with the `ST` monad, `s` is a state-thread identifier which is used to guarantee that channels are not created in one call of `runProcess` and used in another. You will need to write the type of `runProcess` *explicitly* — Hugs cannot infer rank 2 types.

*Exercise 57.* Prolog provides so-called *logical variables*, whose values can be referred to before they are set. Define a type `LVar` and a monad `Logic` in terms of `ST`, supporting operations

```
newLVar :: Logic s (LVar s a)
readLVar :: LVar s a -> a
writeLVar :: LVar s a -> a -> Logic s ()
```

where `s` is again a state-thread identifier. The intention is that an `LVar` should be written exactly once, but its value may be read *beforehand*, between its creation and the write — lazy evaluation is at work here. Note that `readLVar` does *not* have a monadic type, and so can be used anywhere. Of course, this can only work if the value written to the `LVar` does not depend on itself. *Hint:* You will need to use

```
fixST :: (a -> ST s a) -> ST s a
```

to solve this exercise — `fixST (\x -> m)` binds `x` to the result produced by `m` during its own computation.

*Exercise 58.* In some applications it is useful to dump the state of a program to a file, or send it over a network, so that the program can be restarted in the same state later or on another machine. Define a monad `Interruptable`, with an operation

```
dump :: Interruptable ()
```

which stops execution and converts a representation of the state of the program to a form that can be saved in a file. The result of running an `Interruptable` computation should indicate whether or not dumping occurred, and if so, provide the dumped state. If `s` is a state dumped by a computation `m`, then `resume m s` should restart `m` in the state that `s` represents. Note that `m` might dump several times during its execution, and you should be able restart it at each point.

You will need to choose a representation for states that can include every type of value used in a computation. To avoid typing problems, convert values to strings for storage using `show`.

You will not be able to make `Interruptable` an instance of class `Monad`, because your implementations of `return` and `>>=` will not be sufficiently polymorphic — they will only work over values that can be converted to strings. This is unfortunate, but you can just choose other names for the purposes of this exercise. One solution to the problem is described by Hughes [Hug99].

## 9 Intermediate Languages for Compilation

We have seen how monads may be used to structure the denotational semantics of languages with computational effects and how they may be used to express effectful computation in languages like Haskell. We now turn to the use of monads in the practical compilation of languages with implicit side effects. Much of this material refers to the MLj compiler for Standard ML [BKR98], and its intermediate language MIL (Monadic Intermediate Language) [BK99].

### 9.1 Compilation by Transformation

It should not be a surprise that ideas which are useful in structuring semantics also turn out to be useful in structuring the internals of compilers since there is a sense in which compilers actually *do* semantics. Compilers for functional languages typically translate source programs into an intermediate form and then perform a sequence of rewrites on that intermediate representation before translating that into lower-level code in the backend. These rewrites should be observational equivalences, since they are intended to preserve the observable behaviour of the user's program whilst improving its efficiency according to some metric. If the transformations are applied locally (i.e. to subterms of the whole program) then they should be instances of an observational *congruence* relation. Of course, deciding whether applying a particular semantic equation is likely to be part of a sequence which eventually yields an improvement is still a very difficult problem. There has been some work on identifying transformations which *never* lead to (asymptotically) worse behaviour, such as the work of Gustavsson and Sands on space usage of lazy programs [GS99], but most compilers simply implement a collection of rewrites which seem to be "usually" worthwhile.

### 9.2 Intermediate Languages

The reasons for having an intermediate language at all, rather than just doing rewriting on the abstract syntax tree of the source program, include:

1. Complexity. Source languages tend to have many syntactic forms (e.g. nested patterns or list comprehensions) which are convenient for the programmer but which can be translated into a simpler core language, leaving fewer cases for the optimizer and code generator to deal with.
2. Level. Many optimizing transformations involve choices which cannot be expressed in the source language because they are at a lower level of abstraction. In other words, they involve distinctions between implementation details which the source language cannot make. For example
   - All functions in ML take a single argument – if you want to pass more than one then you package them up as a single tuple. This is simple and elegant for the programmer, but we don't want the compiled code to pass a pointer to a fresh heap-allocated tuple if it could just pass a couple of arguments on the stack or in registers. Hence MIL (like other intermediate languages for ML) includes both tuples and multiple arguments and transforms some instances of the former into the latter.

  - MIL also includes datastructures with 'holes' (i.e. uninitialized values). These are used to express a transformation which turns some non-tail calls into tail calls and have linear typing rules which prevent holes being dereferenced or filled more than once [Min98].

  There are often many levels of abstraction between the source and target languages, so it is common for compilers to use different intermediate languages in different phases or to have one all-encompassing intermediate datatype, but then to ensure that the input and output of each phase satisfy particular additional constraints.
3. Equational theory. Many important transformations do not involve concepts which are essentially at a lower-level level of abstraction than the source language, but can nevertheless be anywhere between bothersome and impossible to express or implement directly on the source language syntax.

This last point is perhaps slightly subtle: the equational theory of even a simplified core of the source language may be messy and ill-suited to optimization by rewriting. Rather than have a complex rewriting system with conditional rewrites depending on various kinds of contextual information, one can often achieve the same end result by translating into an intermediate language with a better-behaved equational theory. It is typically the case that a 'cleaner' intermediate language makes explicit some aspects of behaviour which are implicit in the source language. For example:

- Some intermediate languages introduce explicit names for every intermediate value. Not only are the names useful in building various auxiliary datastructures, but they make it easy to, for example, share subexpressions. A very trivial case would be

  ```
  let val x = ((3,4),5)
  in (#1 x, #1 x)
  end
  ```

  which we *don't* want to simplify to the equivalent

  ```
  ((3,4),(3,4))
  ```

  because that allocates two identical pairs. One particularly straighforward way to get a better result is to only allow introductions and eliminations to be applied to variables or atomic constants, so the translation of the original program into the intermediate form is

  ```
  let val y = (3,4)
  in let val x = (y,5)
     in (#1 x, #1 x)
     end
  end
  ```

  which rewrites to

```
let val y = (3,4)
in let val x = (y,5)
   in (y, y)
   end
end
```

and then to

```
let val y = (3,4)
in (y, y)
end
```

which is probably what we wanted.

- MIL contains an unusual exception-handling construct because SML's `handle` construct is unable to express some commuting conversion-style rewrites which we wished to perform [BK01].
- Some compilers for higher-order languages use a continuation passing style (CPS) lambda-calculus as their intermediate language (see, for example, [App92,KKR⁺86]). There are translations of call by value (CBV) and call by name (CBN) source languages into CPS. Once a program is in CPS, it is sound to apply the full unrestricted $\beta, \eta$ rules, rather than, say, the more restricted $\beta_v, \eta_v$ rules which are valid for $\lambda_v$ (the CBV lambda calculus). Moreover, Plotkin has shown [Plo75] that $\beta$ and $\eta$ on CPS terms prove strictly more equivalences between translated terms than do $\beta_v$ and $\eta_v$ on the corresponding $\lambda_v$ terms. Hence, a compiler for a CBV language which translates into CPS and uses $\beta\eta$ can perform more transformations than one which just uses $\beta_v$ and $\eta_v$ on the source syntax.
  CPS transformed terms make evaluation order explict (which makes them easier to compile to low-level imperative code in the backend), allow tail-call elimination be be expressed naturally, and are particularly natural if the language contains `call/cc` or other control operators.
  However, Flanagan et al. [FSDF93] argue that compiling CBV lambda-calculus via CPS is an unnecessarily complicated and indirect technique. The translation introduces many new $\lambda$-abstractions and, if performed naively, new and essentially trivial 'administrative redexes' (though there are optimized translations which avoid creating these redexes [DF92,SF93]). To generate good code, and to identify administrative redexes, real CPS compilers treat abstractions introduced by the translation process differently from those originating in the original program and effectively undo the CPS translation in the backend, after having performed transformations. Flanagan et al. show that the same effect can be obtained by using a $\lambda$-calculus with `let` and peforming *A-reductions* to reach an *A-normal form.* A-reductions were introduced in [SF93] and are defined in terms of *evaluation contexts.* Amongst other things, A-normal forms name all intermediate values and only apply eliminations to variables or values. An example of an A-reduction is the following:

$$\mathcal{E}[\text{if } V \text{ then } N_1 \text{ else } N_2] \longrightarrow \text{if } V \text{ then } \mathcal{E}[N_1] \text{ else } \mathcal{E}[N_2]$$

where $\mathcal{E}[\cdot]$ is an evaluation context. Flanagan et al. observe that most non-CPS ('direct style') compilers perform some A-reductions in a more-or-less ad hoc manner, and suggest that doing all of them, and so working with A-normal forms, is both more uniform and leads to faster code.

**Typed Intermediate Languages.** One big decision when designing an intermediate language is whether or not it should be typed. Even when the source language has strong static types, many compilers discard all types after they have been checked, and work with an untyped intermediate language. More recently, typed intermediate languages have become much more popular in compilers and in areas such as mobile code security. Examples of typed compiler intermediate languages include FLINT [Sha97], the GHC intermediate language [Pey96] and MIL [BKR98,BK99]. The advantages of keeping type information around in an intermediate language include:

- Types are increasingly the basis for static analyses, optimizing transformations and representation choices. Type-based optimization can range from the use of sophisticated type systems for static analyses to exploitation of the fact that static types in the source language provide valuable information which it would be foolish to ignore or recompute. For example, the fact that in many languages pointers to objects of different types can never alias can be used to allow more transformations. The MLj compiler uses simple type information to share representations, using a single Java class to implement several different ML closures.
- Type information can be used in generating backend code, for example in interfacing to a garbage collector or allocating registers.
- Type-checking the intermediate representation can help catch many compiler bugs.
- It is particularly natural if the language allows types to be reflected as values.
- It is clearly the right thing to do if the target language is itself typed. This is the case for MLj (since Java bytecode is typed) and for compilers targetting typed assembly language [MWCG99].

But there are disadvantages too:

- Keeping type information around and maintaining it during transformations can be very expensive in both space and time.
- Unless the type system is complex and/or rather non-standard, restricting the compiler to work with typable terms can prohibit transformations. Even something like closure-conversion (packaging functions with the values of their free variables) is not trivial from the point of view of typing [MMH96].

**$\lambda$ML$_T$ as a Compiler Intermediate Language.** Several researchers have suggested that Moggi's computational metalanguage $\lambda\mathrm{ML}_T$ [Mog89,Mog91] might be useful as the basis of a typed intermediate language. $\lambda\mathrm{ML}_T$ certainly has two of properties we have said are desirable in an intermediate language: a good equational theory and explicitness, both at the term level (making order of evaluation explicit) and at the type level (distinguishing between computations and values).

One example of situation in which the computational metalanguage seems applicable is in expressing and reasoning about the optimizations which may be performed as a result of strictness analysis in compilers for CBN languages such as Haskell. Some early work on expressing the use of strictness analysis used a somewhat informal notion of changes in 'evaluation strategy' for fixed syntax. It is much more elegant to reason about changes in *translation* of the source language into some other language which itself has a fixed operational semantics. In the case of a pure CBN source language (such as PCF [Plo77]), however, one cannot (directly) use a source-to-source translation to express strictness-based transformations. Adding a strict `let` construct with typing rule

$$\frac{\Gamma \vdash M : A \qquad \Gamma, x : A \vdash N : B}{\Gamma \vdash \text{let } x = M \text{ in } N : B}$$

where let $x = M$ in $N$ first evaluates $M$ to Weak Head Normal Form (WHNF) before substituting for $x$ in $N$, allows one to express basic strictness optimizations, such as replacing the application $M\ N$ with let $x = N$ in $(M\ x)$ when $M$ is known to be strict. But this is only half the story – we would also like to be able to perform optimizations based on the fact that certain expressions (such as $x$ in our example) are known to be bound to values in WHNF and so need not be represented by thunks or re-evaluated. To capture this kind of information, Benton [Ben92] proposed a variant of the computational metalanguage in which an expression of a *value* type $A$ is always in WHNF and the *computation* type $TA$ is used for potentially unevaluated expressions which, if they terminate, will yield values of type $A$. The default translation of a call-by-name expression of type $A \to B$ is then to an intermediate language expression of type of type $T((A \to B)^n) = T(TA^n \to TB^n)$, i.e. a computation producing a function from computations to computations. An expression denoting a strict function which is only called in strict contexts, by contrast, can be translated into an intermediate language term of type $T(A^n \to TB^n)$ : a computation producing a function from *values* to computations.

The problem of expressing strictness-based transformations has also been addressed by defining translations from strictness-annotated source terms into continuation passing style. This approach has been taken by Burn and Le Métayer [BM92] and by Danvy and Hatcliff [DH93]. Danvy and Hatcliff, for example, derive such a translation by simplifying the result of symbolically composing two translations: first a translation of strictness-annotated CBN terms into a CBV language with explicit suspension operations, and secondly a modified variant of the CBV translation into continuation passing style.

We have already mentioned the work of Flanagan et al. [FSDF93] relating CPS translations with A-normal forms. The reader may now suspect that the computational metalanguage is also closely related, and indeed it is. The connections were expained by Hatcliff and Danvy [HD94], who showed how various CPS transforms could be factored through translations into the computational metalanguage and how the administrative reductions of CPS, and Flanagan et al.'s A-reductions, corresponded to applying the $\beta$-reduction and *commuting conversions* (see Section 12) associated with the computation type constructor in the computational metalanguage. Hatcliff and Danvy also suggested that the computational metalanguage could make an attractive compiler intermediate language. The links between A-normal forms, CPS transforms and Moggi's computational lambda calculus have been investigated further by Sabry and Wadler [SW97].

Another promising application for intermediate languages based on $\lambda\mathrm{ML}_T$ is in common infrastructure for compiling multiple source languages, and perhaps even supporting their interoperability. Peyton Jones et al. [PLST98a] proposed the use of an intermediate language based on the computational metalanguage as a common framework for compiling both call-by-value and call-by-name languages[10].

Barthe et al. [BHT98] add computational types to the pure type systems (PTS) to obtain monadic versions of a whole family of higher-order typed lambda calculi (such as $F_\omega$ and the Calculus of Constructions) and advocate the use of such calculi as compiler intermediate languages for languages which combine polymorphic type and/or module systems with side-effects.

*Exercise 59.* The 'standard' denotational semantics of PCF is in the CCC of pointed $\omega$-cpos and continuous maps, with $[\![\texttt{int}]\!] = \mathbb{Z}_\perp$ and function space interpreted by $[\![A \to B]\!] = [\![B]\!]^{[\![A]\!]}$. This semantics is adequate for a CBN operational semantics in which the notion of observation is termination of closed terms of ground type. It seems natural that one could give a semantics to PCF with a strict let construct just by defining

$$[\![\text{let } x = M \text{ in } N]\!]\rho = \begin{cases} \perp & \text{if } [\![M]\!]\rho = \perp \\ [\![N]\!]\rho[x \mapsto [\![M]\!]\rho] & \text{otherwise} \end{cases}$$

but in fact, the semantics is then no longer adequate. Why? How might one modify the semantics to fix the problem? How good is the modified semantics as a semantics of the original language (i.e. without `let`)?

# 10 Type and Effect Systems

## 10.1 Introduction

The work referred to in the previous section concerns using a well-behaved intermediate language (A-normal forms, CPS or $\lambda\mathrm{ML}_T$) to perform sound rewriting on a programs written in languages with 'impure' features. All those intermediate languages make some kind of separation (in the type system and/or the language syntax) between 'pure' values and 'impure' (potentially side-effecting) computations. The separation is, however, fairly crude and there are often good

[10] The published version of the paper contains an error. A corrigendum can, at the time of writing, be found on the web [PLST98b].

reasons for wanting to infer at compile-time a safe approximation to just *which* side-effects may happen as a result of evaluating a particular expression. This kind of *effect analysis* is really only applicable to CBV languages, since CBN languages do not usually allow any side-effects other than non-termination.

Historically, the first effect analyses for higher order languages were developed to avoid a type soundness problem which occurs when polymorphism is combined naively with updateable references. To see the problem, consider the following (illegal) SML program:

```
let val r = ref (fn x=> x)
in (r := (fn n=>n+1);
    !r true
   )
end
```

Using the 'obvious' extension of the Hindley-Milner type inference rules to cover reference creation, dereferencing and assignment, the program above would type-check:

1. `(fn x=>x)` has type $\alpha \to \alpha$, so
2. `ref (fn x=>x)` has type $(\alpha \to \alpha)$`ref`
3. generalization then gives `r` the type scheme $\forall\alpha.(\alpha \to \alpha)$`ref`
4. so by specialization `r` has type (`int` $\to$ `int`)`ref`, meaning the assignment typechecks
5. and by another specialization, `r` has type (`bool` $\to$ `bool`)`ref`, so
6. `!r` has type `bool` $\to$ `bool`, so the application type checks.

However, it is clear that the program really has a type error, as it will try to increment a boolean.

To avoid this problem, Gifford, Lucassen, Jouvelot, Talpin and others [GL86], [GJLS87], [TJ94] developed *type and effect systems*. The idea is to have a refined type system which infers both the type *and* the possible effects which an expression may have, and to restrict polymorphic generalization to type variables which do not appear in side-effecting expressions. In the example above, one would then infer that the expression `ref (fn x=>x)` creates a new reference cell of type $\alpha \to \alpha$. This prevents the type of `r` being generalized in the `let` rule, so the assignment causes $\alpha$ to be unified with `int` and the application of `!r` to `true` then fails to typecheck.

It should be noted in passing that there are a number of different ways of avoiding the type loophole. For example, Tofte's imperative type discipline [Tof87] using 'imperative type variables' was used in the old (1990) version of the Standard ML Definition, whilst Leroy and Weis proposed a different scheme for tracking 'dangerous' type variables (those appearing free in the types of expressions stored in references) [LW91]. A key motivation for most of that work was to allow as much polymorphic generalization as possible to happen in the `let` rule, whilst still keeping the type system sound. However, expensive and unpredictable inference systems which have a direct impact on which user programs actually typecheck are rarely a good idea. In 1995, Wright published a study [Wri95] indicating that nearly all existing SML code would still typecheck and run identically (sometimes modulo a little $\eta$-expansion) if polymorphic generalization were simply restricted to source expressions which were syntactic values (and thus trivially side-effect free). This simple restriction was adopted in the revised (1997) SML Definition and research into fancy type systems for polymorphism in impure languages seems to have now essentially ceased.

However, there are still very good reasons for wanting to do automatic effect inference. The most obvious is that more detailed effect information allows compilers to perform more aggressive optimizations. Other applications include various kinds of verification tool, either to assist the programmer or to check security policies, for example. In SML, even a seemingly trivial rewrite, such as the dead-code elimination

$$\texttt{let val x = } M_1 \texttt{ in } M_2 \texttt{ end} \quad \longrightarrow \quad M_2 \qquad (\texttt{x} \notin FV(M_2))$$

is generally only valid if the evaluation of $M_1$ doesn't diverge, perform I/O, update the state or throw an exception (though it is still valid if $M_1$ reads from reference cells or allocates new ones). Code like this is frequently created by other rewrites and it is important to be able to clean it up.

## 10.2 The Basic Idea

There are now many different type and effect systems in the literature, but they all share a common core. (The book [NNH99] contains, amongst other things, a fair amount on effect systems and many more references than these notes.) A traditional type system infers judgements of the form

$$x_1 : A_1, \ldots, x_n : A_n \vdash M : B$$

where the $A_i$ and $B$ are types. A type and effect system infers judgements of the form

$$x_1 : A_1, \ldots, x_n : A_n \vdash M : B, \varepsilon$$

which says that in the given typing context, the expression $M$ has type $B$ and effect $\varepsilon$. The effect $\varepsilon$ is drawn from some set $\mathcal{E}$ whose elements denote *sets* of actual effects which may occur at runtime (in other words, they are *abstractions* of runtime effects, just as types are abstractions of runtime values). Exactly what is in $\mathcal{E}$ depends not only on what runtime effects are possible in the language, but also on how precise one wishes to make the analysis. The simplest non-trivial effect system would simply take $\mathcal{E}$ to have two elements, one (usually written $\emptyset$) denoting no effect at all ('pure'), and the other just meaning 'possibly has some effect'. Most effect systems are, as we shall see, a little more refined than this.

The first thing to remark about the form of a type and effect judgement is that an effect appears on the right of the turnstile, but not on the left. This is because we are only considering CBV languages, and that means that at runtime free variables will always be bound to *values*, which have no effect. An effect system for an impure CBN language, were there any such thing, would have pairs of types and effects in the context too[11]. Because variables are always bound to values, the associated type and effect rule will be:

$$\frac{}{\Gamma, x : A \vdash x : A, \emptyset}$$

The second point is that $\mathcal{E}$ actually needs to be an algebra, rather than just a set; i.e. it has some operations for combining effects defined on it. Consider the effectful version of the rule for a simple (strict, non-polymorphic, non-computational) `let` expression:

$$\frac{\Gamma \vdash M : A, \varepsilon_1 \qquad \Gamma, x : A \vdash N : B, \varepsilon_2}{\Gamma \vdash \text{let } x = M \text{ in } N : B, ?}$$

What should the effect of the compound expression be? Dynamically, $M$ will be evaluated, possibly performing some side-effect from the set denoted by $\varepsilon_1$ and, assuming the evaluation of $M$ terminated with a value $V$, then $N[V/x]$ will be evaluated and possibly perform some side-effect from the set denoted by $\varepsilon_2$. How we combine $\varepsilon_1$ and $\varepsilon_2$ depends on how much accuracy we are willing to pay for in our static analysis. If we care about the relative ordering of side-effects then we might take elements of $\mathcal{E}$ to denote sets of *sequences* (e.g. regular languages) over some basic set of effects and then use language concatenation $\varepsilon_1 \cdot \varepsilon_2$ to combine the effects in the `let` rule (see the Nielsons work on analysing concurrent processes [NN94,NNA97], for example). Commonly, however, we abstract away from the relative sequencing and multiplicity of effects and just consider *sets* of basic effects. In this case the natural combining operation for the `let` rule is some abstract union operation[12].

For the conditional expression, the following is a natural rule:

$$\frac{\Gamma \vdash M : \text{bool}, \varepsilon' \qquad \Gamma \vdash N_1 : A, \varepsilon_1 \qquad \Gamma \vdash N_2 : A, \varepsilon_2}{\Gamma \vdash (\text{if } M \text{ then } N_1 \text{ else } N_2) : A, \varepsilon' \cdot (\varepsilon_1 \cup \varepsilon_2)}$$

If we were not tracking sequencing or multiplicity, then the effect in the conclusion of the `if` rule would just be $\varepsilon' \cup \varepsilon_1 \cup \varepsilon_2$, of course.

The other main interesting feature of almost all type and effect systems is the form of the rules for abstraction and application, which make types dependent on effects, in that the function space constructor is now annotated with a 'latent effect' $A \xrightarrow{\varepsilon} B$. The rule for abstraction looks like:

$$\frac{\Gamma, x : A \vdash M : B, \varepsilon}{\Gamma \vdash (\lambda x : A.\, M) : A \xrightarrow{\varepsilon} B, \emptyset}$$

[11] Although the mixture of call by need and side-effects is an unpredictable one, Haskell does actually allow it, via the 'experts-only' `unsafePerformIO` operation. But I'm still not aware of any type and effect system for a lazy language.

[12] Effect systems in the literature often include a binary $\cup$ operation in the formal syntax of effect annotations, which are then considered modulo unit, associativity, commutativity and idempotence. For very simple effect systems, this is unnecessarily syntactic, but it is not so easy to avoid when one also has effect variables and substitution.

because the $\lambda$-abstraction itself is a value, and so has no immediate effect ($\emptyset$) but will have effect $\varepsilon$ when it is applied, as can be seen in the rule for application:

$$\frac{\Gamma \vdash M : A \overset{\varepsilon_1}{\rightarrow} B, \varepsilon_2 \qquad \Gamma \vdash N : A, \varepsilon_3}{\Gamma \vdash M\,N : B, \varepsilon_2 \cdot \varepsilon_3 \cdot \varepsilon_1}$$

The overall effect of evaluating the application is made up of three separate effects – that which occurs when the function is evaluated, that which occurs when the argument is evaluated and finally that which occurs when the body of the function is evaluated. (Again, most effect systems work with sets rather than sequences, so the combining operation in the conclusion of the application rule is just $\cup$.)

The final thing we need to add to our minimal skeleton effect system is some way to weaken effects. The collection $\mathcal{E}$ of effects for a given analysis always has a natural partial order relation $\subseteq$ defined on it such that $\varepsilon \subseteq \varepsilon'$ means $\varepsilon'$ denotes a larger set of possible runtime side-effects than $\varepsilon$. Typically $\subseteq$ is just the subset relation on sets of primitive effects. The simplest rule we can add to make a usable system is the *subeffecting* rule:

$$\frac{\Gamma \vdash M : A, \varepsilon \qquad \varepsilon \subseteq \varepsilon'}{\Gamma \vdash M : A, \varepsilon'}$$

*Exercise 60.* Define a toy simply-typed CBV functional language (integers, booleans, pairs, functions, recursion) with a *fixed* collection of global, mutable integer variables. Give it an operational and/or denotational semantics. Give a type and effect system (with subeffecting) for your language which tracks which global variables may be read and written during the evaluation of each expression (so an effect will be a pair of sets of global variable names). Formulate and prove a soundness result for your analysis. Are there any closed terms in your language which require the use of the subeffect rule to be typable at all?

## 10.3 More Precise Effect Systems

There are a number of natural and popular ways to improve the precision of the hopelessly weak 'simple-types' approach to effect analysis sketched in the previous section.

**Subtyping.** The bidirectional flow of information in type systems or analyses which simply constrain types to be equal frequently leads to an undesirable loss of precision. For example, consider an effect analysis of the following very silly ML program (and forget polymorphism for the moment):

```
let fun f x = ()
    fun pure () = ()
    fun impure () = print "I'm a side-effect"
    val m = (f pure, f impure)
in pure
end
```

If they were typed in isolation, the best type for `pure` would be $\texttt{unit} \xrightarrow{\emptyset} \texttt{unit}$ and `impure` would get $\texttt{unit} \xrightarrow{\{\text{print}\}} \texttt{unit}$ (assuming that the constant `print` has type $\texttt{string} \xrightarrow{\{\text{print}\}} \texttt{unit}$). However, the fact that both of them get passed to the function `f` means that we end up having to make their types, including the latent effects, identical. This we can do by applying the subeffecting rule to the body of `pure` and hence deriving the same type $\texttt{unit} \xrightarrow{\{\text{print}\}} \texttt{unit}$ for both `pure` and `impure`. But then that ends up being the type inferred for the whole expression, when it is clear that we should have been able to deduce the more accurate type $\texttt{unit} \xrightarrow{\emptyset} \texttt{unit}$.

The problem is that both `pure` and `impure` flow to `x`, which therefore has to be given an effectful type. This then propagates back from the use to the *definition* of `pure`. Peyton Jones has given this phenomenon the rather apt name of the *poisoning problem.* One solution is to extend the notion of subeffecting to allow more general *subtyping.* We replace the subeffecting rule with

$$\frac{\Gamma \vdash M : A, \varepsilon \qquad \varepsilon \subseteq \varepsilon' \qquad A \leq A'}{\Gamma \vdash M : A', \varepsilon'}$$

where $\leq$ is a partial order on types defined by rules like

$$\frac{A' \leq A \qquad B \leq B' \qquad \varepsilon \subseteq \varepsilon'}{A \xrightarrow{\varepsilon} B \;\leq\; A' \xrightarrow{\varepsilon'} B'} \quad \text{and} \quad \frac{A \leq A' \qquad B \leq B'}{A \times B \;\leq\; A' \times B'}$$

Note the *contravariance* of the function space constructor in the argument type.

Using the subtyping rule we can now get the type and effect we wouldd expect for our silly example. The definitions of `pure` and `impure` are given different types, but we can apply the subtyping rule (writing 1 for `unit`)

$$\frac{\Gamma, \text{pure} : (1 \xrightarrow{\emptyset} 1) \vdash \text{pure} : (1 \xrightarrow{\emptyset} 1), \emptyset \qquad \dfrac{1 \leq 1 \quad 1 \leq 1 \quad \emptyset \subseteq \{\text{print}\}}{(1 \xrightarrow{\emptyset} 1) \leq (1 \xrightarrow{\{\text{print}\}} 1)} \qquad \emptyset \subseteq \emptyset}{\Gamma, \text{pure} : (1 \xrightarrow{\emptyset} 1) \vdash \text{pure} : (1 \xrightarrow{\{\text{print}\}} 1), \emptyset}$$

to coerce the *use* of `pure` when it is passed to `f` to match the required argument type whilst still using the more accurate type inferred at the point of definition as the type of the whole expression.

**Effect Polymorphism.** Another approach to the poisoning problem is to introduce ML-style polymorphism at the level of effects (this is largely orthogonal to whether we also have polymorphism at the level of types). We allow effects to contain effect variables and then allow the context to bind identifiers to type schemes, which quantify over effect variables.

Consider the following program

```
let fun run f = f ()
    fun pure () = ()
    fun impure () =  print "Poison"
    fun h () = run impure
in run pure
end
```

In this case, even with subtyping, we end up deriving a type and effect of $\texttt{unit}, \{\text{print}\}$ for the whole program, though it actually has no side effect. With effect polymorphism, we can express the fact that there is a dependency between the effect of a particular call to `run` and the latent effect of the function which is passed at that point. The definition of `run` gets the type scheme

$$\forall a.(\texttt{unit} \xrightarrow{a} \texttt{unit}) \xrightarrow{a} \texttt{unit}$$

which is instantiated with $a = \emptyset$ in the application to `pure` and $a = \{\text{print}\}$ in the application to `impure` (which is actually never executed). That lets us deduce a type and effect of $\texttt{unit}, \emptyset$ for the whole program.

**Regions.** One of the most influential ideas to have come out of work on type and effect systems is that of *regions*: static abstractions for sets of dynamically allocated run-time locations. If (as in the earlier exercise) one is designing an effect system to track the use of mutable storage in a language with a *fixed* set of global locations, there are two obvious choices for how precisely one tracks the effects – either one records simply whether or not an expression might read or write some unspecified locations, or one records a set of just *which* locations might be read or written. Clearly the second is more precise and can be used to enable more transformations. For example, the evaluation of an expression whose only effect is to read some locations might be moved from after to before the evaluation of an expression whose effect is to write some locations *if* the set of locations possibly read is disjoint from the set of locations possibly written.

But no real programming language (with the possible exception of ones designed to be compiled to silicon) allows only a statically fixed set of mutable locations. When an unbounded number of new references may be allocated dynamically at runtime, a static effect system clearly cannot name them all in advance. The simple approach of just having one big abstraction for all locations ('the store') and tracking only whether some reading or some writing takes place is still sound, but we would like to be more precise.

In many languages, the existing type system gives a natural way to partition the runtime set of mutable locations into disjoint sets. In an ML-like language, an `int ref` and a `bool ref` are never aliased, so one may obtain a useful increase in precision by indexing read, write and allocation effects by types. Ignoring polymorphism again, we might take

$$\mathcal{E} = \mathbb{P}\{\text{rd}(A), \text{wr}(A), \text{al}(A) \mid A \text{ a type}\}$$

(Note that types and effects are now mutually recursive.)

But we can do even better. Imagine that our language had two quite distinct types of references, say red ones and blue ones, and one always had to say which sort one was creating or accessing. Then clearly a red reference and a blue reference can never alias, we could refine our effect types system to track the colours of references involved in store effects, and we could perform some more transformations (for example commuting an expression which can only write blue integer references with one which only reads red integer references).

In its simplest form, the idea of region inference is to take a typing derivation for a monochrome program and to find a way of colouring each reference type appearing in the derivation subject to preserving the validity of the derivation (so, for example, a function expecting a red reference as an argument can never be applied to a blue one). It should be clear that the aim is to use as many different colours as possible. The colours are conventionally called *regions*, because one can imagine that dynamically all the locations of a given colour are allocated in a particular region of the heap[13].

So now we have three static concepts: type, effect and region. Each of these can be treated monomorphically, with a subwidget relation or polymorphically. The type and effect discipline described by Talpin and Jouvelot in [TJ94] is polymorphic in all three components and indexes reference effects by both regions and types.

Perhaps the most interesting thing about regions is that we can use them to extend our inference system with a rule in which the effect of the conclusion is *smaller* than the effect of the assumption. Consider the following example

```
fun f x = let val r = ref (x+1)
          in !r
          end
```

A simple effect system would assign `f` a type and effect like $\mathtt{int} \stackrel{\{al,rd\}}{\to} \mathtt{int}, \emptyset$, which seems reasonable, since it is indeed a functional value which takes integers to integers with a latent effect of allocating and reading. But the fact that `f` has this latent effect is actually completely unobservable, since the only uses of storage it makes are completely private. In this case it is easy to see that `f` is observationally equivalent to the completely pure successor function

```
fun f' x = x+1
```

which means that, provided the use to which we are going to make of effect information respects observational equivalence[14] we could soundly just forget all

[13] Alternatively, one might think that any runtime location will have a unique allocation site in the code and all locations with the same allocation site will share a colour, so one could think of a region as a set of static program points. But this is a less satisfactory view, since more sophisticated systems allow references allocated at the same program point to be in different regions, depending on more dynamic contextual information, such as which functions appear in the call chain.

[14] This should be the case for justifying optimising transformations or inferring more generous polymorphic types, but might not be in the case of a static analysis tool which helps the programmer reason about, say, memory usage.

about the latent effect of f and infer the type $\mathtt{int} \xrightarrow{\emptyset} \mathtt{int}$ for it instead. How do regions help? A simple type, region and effect derivation looks like this

$$\dfrac{\dfrac{\dfrac{\vdots}{\Gamma, \mathtt{x}\mathtt{:int} \vdash \mathtt{x+1}\mathtt{:int}, \emptyset}}{\Gamma, \mathtt{x}\mathtt{:int} \vdash \mathtt{(ref\ x+1)}\mathtt{:int\ ref}_\rho, \{\mathrm{al}_\rho\}} \qquad \dfrac{\vdots}{\Gamma, \mathtt{x}\mathtt{:int}, \mathtt{r}\mathtt{:int\ ref}_\rho \vdash \mathtt{(!r)}\mathtt{:int}, \{\mathrm{rd}_\rho\}}}{\dfrac{\Gamma, \mathtt{x}\mathtt{:int} \vdash \mathtt{(let\ r=ref\ x+1\ in\ !r)}\mathtt{:int}, \{\mathrm{al}_\rho, \mathrm{rd}_\rho\}}{\Gamma \vdash \mathtt{(fn\ x=>let\ r=ref\ x+1\ in\ !r)} : \mathtt{int} \xrightarrow{\{\mathrm{al}_\rho, \mathrm{rd}_\rho\}} \mathtt{int}, \emptyset}}$$

where $\rho$ is a region. Now this is a valid derivation for *any* choice of $\rho$; in particular, we can pick $\rho$ to be distinct from any region appearing in $\Gamma$. That means that the body of the function does not have any effect involving references imported from its surrounding context. Furthermore, the type of the function body is simply int, so whatever the rest of the program does with the result of a call to the function, it cannot have any dependency on the references used to produce it. Such considerations motivate the *effect masking* rule

$$\frac{\Gamma \vdash M : A, \varepsilon}{\Gamma \vdash M : A, \varepsilon \setminus \{\mathrm{rd}_\rho, \mathrm{al}_\rho, \mathrm{wr}_\rho \mid \rho \notin \Gamma \wedge \rho \notin A\}}$$

Using this rule before just before typing the abstraction in the derivation above does indeed allow us to type f as having no observable latent effect.

One of the most remarkable uses of region analysis is Tofte and Talpin's work on static memory management [TT97]: they assign region-annotated types to every value (rather than just mutable references) in an intermediate language where new lexically-scoped regions are introduced explicitly by a letregion $\rho$ in ...end construct. For a well-typed and annotated program in this language, no value allocated in region $\rho$ will be referenced again after the end of the letregion block introducing $\rho$. Hence that region of the heap may be safely reclaimed on exiting the block. This technique has been successfully applied in a version of the ML Kit compiler in which there is no runtime garbage collector at all. For some programs, this scheme leads to dramatic reductions in runtime space usage compared with traditional garbage collection, whereas for others the results are much worse. Combining the two techniques is possible, but requires some care, since the region-based memory management reclaims memory which will not be referenced again, but to which there may still be pointers accessible from the GC root. The GC therefore needs to avoid following these 'dangling pointers'.

The soundness of effect masking in the presence of higher-type references and of region-based memory management is not at all trivial to prove. Both [TJ94] and [TT97] formulate correctness in terms of a coinductively defined consistency relation between stores and typing judgements. A number of researchers have recently published more elementary proofs of the correctness of region calculi, either by translation into other systems [BHR99,dZG00] or by more direct methods [CHT0x].

# 11 Monads and Effect Systems

## 11.1 Introduction

This section describes how type and effect analyses can be presented in terms of monads and the computational metalanguage. Although this is actually rather obvious, it was only recently that anybody got around to writing anything serious about it. In ICFP 1998, Wadler published a paper [Wad98] (later extended and corrected as [WT99]) showing the equivalence of a mild variant of the effect system of Talpin and Jouvelot [TJ94] and a version of the computational metalanguage in which the computation type constructor is indexed by effects. In the same conference, Benton, Kennedy and Russell described the MLj compiler [BKR98] and its intermediate language MIL, which is a similar effect-refined version of the computational metalanguage. Also in 1998, Tolmach proposed an intermediate representation with a hierarchy of monadic types for use in compiling ML by transformation [Tol98].

The basic observation is that the places where the computation type constructor appears in the call-by-value translation of the lambda calculus into $\lambda ML_T$ correspond precisely to the places where effect annotations appear in type and effect systems. Effect systems put an $\varepsilon$ over each function arrow and on the right-hand side of turnstiles, whilst the CBV translation adds a $T$ to the *end* of each function arrow and on the right hand side of turnstiles. Wadler started with a CBV lambda calculus with a polymorphic types and monomorphic regions and effects, tracking store effects (without masking). He then showed that Moggi's CBV translation of this language into a version of the metalanguage in which the computation type constructor is annotated with a set of effects (and the monadic `let` rule unions these sets) preserves typing, in that

$$\Gamma \vdash_{\mathit{eff}} M : A, \varepsilon \Rightarrow \Gamma^v \vdash_{\mathit{mon}} M^v : T_\varepsilon(A^v)$$

where

$$\begin{aligned} \mathtt{int}^v &= \mathtt{int} \\ (A \xrightarrow{\varepsilon} B)^v &= A^v \to T_\varepsilon(B^v) \end{aligned}$$

Wadler also defined an instrumented operational semantics for each of the two languages and used these to prove subject reduction type soundness results in the style of Wright and Felleisen [WF94]. The instrumented operational semantics records not only the evaluation of an expression and a state to a value and a new state, but also a *trace* of the side effects which occur during the evaluation; part of the definition of type soundness is then that when an expression has a static effect $\varepsilon$, any effect occuring in the dynamic trace of its evaluation must be contained in $\varepsilon$.

Where Wadler's system uses implicit subeffecting, Tolmach's intermediate language has four distinct monads in a linear order and uses explicit monad morphisms used to coerce computations from one monad type to a larger one. The monads are:

1. The identity monad, used for pure, terminating computations;
2. The lifting monad, used to model computations which may fail to terminate but are otherwise pure;
3. The monad of exceptions and non-termination;
4. The ST monad, which combines lifting, exceptions and the possibility of performing output.

Tolmach gives a denotational semantics for his intermediate language (using cpos) and presents a number of useful transformation laws which can be validated using this semantics.

## 11.2 MIL-Lite: Monads in MLj

MIL-lite is a simplified fragment of MIL, the intermediate language used in the MLj compiler. It was introduced by Benton and Kennedy [BK99] as a basis for proving the soundness of some of the effect-based optimizing transformations performed by MLj. Compared with many effect systems in the literature, MIL only performs a fairly crude effect analysis – it doesn't have regions, effect polymorphism or masking. MIL-lite further simplifies the full language by omitting type polymorphism, higher-type references and recursive types as well as various lower level features. Nevertheless, MIL-lite is far from trivial, combining higher-order functions, recursion, exceptions and dynamically allocated state with effect-indexed computation types and subtyping.

**Types and Terms.** MIL-lite is a compiler intermediate language for which we first give an operational semantics and then *derive* an equational theory, so there are a couple of design differences between it and Moggi's equational metalanguage. The first is that types are *stratified* into value types (ranged over by $\tau$) and computation types (ranged over by $\gamma$); computations of computations do not arise. The second difference is that the distinction between computations and values is alarmingly syntactic: the only expressions of value types are normal forms. It is perhaps more elegant to assign value types to a wider collection of pure expressions than just those in normal form. That is the way Wadler's effect-annotated monadic language is presented, and it leads naturally to a stratified operational semantics in which there is one relation defining the pure reduction of expressions of value type to normal form and another defining the possibly side-effecting evaluation of computations. However, the presentation given here more closely matches the language used in the real compiler.

Given a countable set $\mathbb{E}$ of exception names, MIL-lite types are defined by

$$\begin{array}{ll} \tau ::= \mathrm{unit} \mid \mathrm{int} \mid \mathrm{intref} \mid \tau \times \tau \mid \tau + \tau \mid \tau \to \gamma & \\ \gamma ::= \mathbf{T}_{\varepsilon}(\tau) & \varepsilon \subseteq \mathcal{E} = \{\bot, r, w, a\} \uplus \mathbb{E} \end{array}$$

We write bool for unit + unit. Function types are restricted to be from values to computations as this is all we shall need to interpret a CBV source language. The effects which we detect are possible failure to terminate ($\bot$), reading from

$$\frac{}{\Gamma, x:\tau \vdash x:\tau} \quad \frac{}{\Gamma \vdash \underline{n} : \mathrm{int}} \quad \frac{}{\Gamma \vdash () : \mathrm{unit}} \quad \frac{}{\Gamma \vdash \underline{\ell} : \mathrm{intref}}\ \ell \in \mathbb{L}$$

$$\frac{\Gamma \vdash V : \tau_i}{\Gamma \vdash \mathrm{in}_i V : \tau_1 + \tau_2}\ i = 1,2 \qquad \frac{\Gamma \vdash V_1 : \tau_1 \quad \Gamma \vdash V_2 : \tau_2}{\Gamma \vdash (V_1, V_2) : \tau_1 \times \tau_2}$$

$$\frac{\Gamma, x:\tau, f:\tau \to \mathbf{T}_{\varepsilon \cup \{\bot\}}(\tau') \vdash M : \mathbf{T}_\varepsilon(\tau')}{\Gamma \vdash (\mathrm{rec}\ f\ x = M) : \tau \to \mathbf{T}_\varepsilon(\tau')} \qquad \frac{\Gamma \vdash V : \tau_1}{\Gamma \vdash V : \tau_2}\ \tau_1 \leqslant \tau_2$$

$$\frac{\Gamma \vdash V_1 : \tau \to \gamma \quad \Gamma \vdash V_2 : \tau}{\Gamma \vdash V_1\, V_2 : \gamma} \qquad \frac{\Gamma \vdash V : \tau}{\Gamma \vdash \mathrm{val}\ V : \mathbf{T}_\emptyset(\tau)}$$

$$\frac{\Gamma \vdash M : \mathbf{T}_\varepsilon(\tau) \quad \Gamma \vdash H : \mathbf{T}_{\varepsilon'}(\tau') \quad \Gamma, x:\tau \vdash N : \mathbf{T}_{\varepsilon'}(\tau')}{\Gamma \vdash \mathrm{try}\ x \Leftarrow M\ \mathrm{catch}\ H\ \mathrm{in}\ N : \mathbf{T}_{\varepsilon \setminus \mathrm{dom}(H) \cup \varepsilon'}(\tau')} \qquad \frac{}{\Gamma \vdash \mathrm{raise}\ E : \mathbf{T}_{\{E\}}(\tau)}$$

$$\frac{\Gamma \vdash V : \tau_1 \times \tau_2}{\Gamma \vdash \pi_i V : \mathbf{T}_\emptyset(\tau_i)}\ i = 1,2 \qquad \frac{\Gamma \vdash V : \tau_1 + \tau_2 \quad \{\Gamma, x_i : \tau_i \vdash M_i : \gamma\}_{i=1,2}}{\Gamma \vdash (\mathrm{case}\ V\ \mathrm{of}\ \mathrm{in}_1 x_1.M_1\ ;\ \mathrm{in}_2 x_2.M_2) : \gamma}$$

$$\frac{\Gamma \vdash V : \mathrm{int}}{\Gamma \vdash \mathrm{ref}\ V : \mathbf{T}_{\{a\}}(\mathrm{intref})} \qquad \frac{\Gamma \vdash V : \mathrm{intref}}{\Gamma \vdash !V : \mathbf{T}_{\{r\}}(\mathrm{int})} \qquad \frac{\Gamma \vdash V_1 : \mathrm{intref} \quad \Gamma \vdash V_2 : \mathrm{int}}{\Gamma \vdash V_1 := V_2 : \mathbf{T}_{\{w\}}(\mathrm{unit})}$$

$$\frac{\Gamma \vdash V_1 : \mathrm{int} \quad \Gamma \vdash V_2 : \mathrm{int}}{\Gamma \vdash V_1 + V_2 : \mathbf{T}_\emptyset(\mathrm{int})} \qquad \frac{\Gamma \vdash V_1 : \mathrm{int} \quad \Gamma \vdash V_2 : \mathrm{int}}{\Gamma \vdash V_1 = V_2 : \mathbf{T}_\emptyset(\mathrm{bool})} \qquad \frac{\Gamma \vdash M : \gamma_1}{\Gamma \vdash M : \gamma_2}\ \gamma_1 \leqslant \gamma_2$$

**Fig. 5.** Typing rules for MIL-lite

a reference, <u>w</u>riting to a reference, <u>a</u>llocating a new reference cell and raising a particular exception $E \in \mathbb{E}$. Inclusion on sets of effects induces a subtyping relation:

$$\frac{}{\tau \leqslant \tau}\ \tau \in \{\mathrm{unit}, \mathrm{int}, \mathrm{intref}\} \qquad \frac{\varepsilon \subseteq \varepsilon' \qquad \tau \leqslant \tau'}{\mathbf{T}_\varepsilon(\tau) \leqslant \mathbf{T}_{\varepsilon'}(\tau')}$$

$$\frac{\tau_1 \leqslant \tau_1' \qquad \tau_2 \leqslant \tau_2'}{\tau_1 \times \tau_2 \leqslant \tau_1' \times \tau_2'} \qquad \frac{\tau_1 \leqslant \tau_1' \qquad \tau_2 \leqslant \tau_2'}{\tau_1 + \tau_2 \leqslant \tau_1' + \tau_2'} \qquad \frac{\tau' \leqslant \tau \qquad \gamma \leqslant \gamma'}{\tau \to \gamma \leqslant \tau' \to \gamma'}$$

Reflexivity and transitivity are consequences of these rules.

There are two forms of typing judgment: $\Gamma \vdash V : \tau$ for values and $\Gamma \vdash M : \gamma$ for computations, where in both cases $\Gamma$ is a finite map from term variables to *value* types (because the source language is CBV). We assume a countable set $\mathbb{L}$ of locations. The typing rules are shown in Figure 5 and satisfy the usual weakening, strengthening and substitution lemmas. We will sometimes use $G$ to range over both value and computation terms and $\sigma$ to range over both value

$$
\begin{array}{ll}
\lambda x.\, M & \stackrel{\text{def}}{=} \text{rec}\, f\, x = M \quad (f \notin FV(M)) \\
\Omega & \stackrel{\text{def}}{=} (\text{rec}\, f\, x = f\, x)\, () \\
\text{false} & \stackrel{\text{def}}{=} \text{in}_1() \\
\text{true} & \stackrel{\text{def}}{=} \text{in}_2() \\
\text{if}\, V\, \text{then}\, M_2\, \text{else}\, M_1 & \stackrel{\text{def}}{=} \text{case}\, V\, \text{of}\, \text{in}_1 x_1.M_1; \text{in}_2 x_2.M_2 \quad (x_i \notin FV(M_i)) \\
\text{let}\, x \Leftarrow M\, \text{in}\, N & \stackrel{\text{def}}{=} \text{try}\, x \Leftarrow M\, \text{catch}\, \{\}\, \text{in}\, N \\
\text{let}\, x_1 \Leftarrow M_1; x_2 \Leftarrow M_2\, \text{in}\, N & \stackrel{\text{def}}{=} \text{let}\, x_1 \Leftarrow M_1\, \text{in}\, \text{let}\, x_2 \Leftarrow M_2\, \text{in}\, N \\
M; N & \stackrel{\text{def}}{=} \text{let}\, x \Leftarrow M\, \text{in}\, N \quad (x \notin FV(N)) \\
M\, \text{handle}\, H & \stackrel{\text{def}}{=} \text{try}\, x \Leftarrow M\, \text{catch}\, H\, \text{in}\, \text{val}\, x \\
\text{set}\, \{\ell_1 \mapsto n_1, \ldots, \ell_k \mapsto n_k\} & \stackrel{\text{def}}{=} \underline{\ell_1} := \underline{n_1}\, ;\, \ldots\, ;\, \underline{\ell_k} := \underline{n_k}\, ;\, \text{val}\, () \\
\text{assert}\, (\ell, n) & \stackrel{\text{def}}{=} \text{let}\, v \Leftarrow !\underline{\ell}; b \Leftarrow (v = \underline{n})\, \text{in}\, \text{if}\, b\, \text{then}\, \text{val}\, ()\, \text{else}\, \Omega \\
\text{assert}\, \{\ell_1 \mapsto n_1, \ldots, \ell_k \mapsto n_k\} & \stackrel{\text{def}}{=} \text{assert}\, (\ell_1, n_1)\, ;\, \ldots\, ;\, \text{assert}\, (\ell_k, n_k)\, ;\, \text{val}\, ()
\end{array}
$$

**Fig. 6.** Syntactic sugar

and computation types. Most of the terms are unsurprising, but we do use a novel construct

$$\text{try}\, x \Leftarrow M\, \text{catch}\, \{E_1.M_1, \ldots, E_n.M_n\}\, \text{in}\, N$$

which should be read "Evaluate the expression $M$. If successful, bind the result to $x$ and evaluate $N$. Otherwise, if exception $E_i$ is raised, evaluate the exception handler $M_i$ instead, or if no handler is applicable, pass the exception on." A full discussion of the reasons for adopting the try-handle construct may be found in [BK01], but for now observe that it nicely generalises both handle and Moggi's monadic let, as illustrated by some of the syntactic sugar defined in Figure 6.

For ease of presentation the handlers are treated as a set in which no exception $E$ appears more than once. We let $H$ range over such sets, and write $H \setminus E$ to denote $H$ with the handler for $E$ removed (if it exists). We sometimes use map-like notation, for example writing $H(E)$ for the term $M$ in a handler $E.M \in H$, and writing $\text{dom}(H)$ for $\{E \mid E.M \in H\}$. We write $\Gamma \vdash H : \gamma$ to mean that for all $E.M \in H$, $\Gamma \vdash M : \gamma$.

**The Analysis.** The way in which the MIL-lite typing rules express a simple effects analysis should be fairly clear, though some features may deserve further comment. The $\to$ introduction rule incorporates an extremely feeble, but nonetheless very useful, termination test: the more obvious rule would insist that $\bot \in \varepsilon$, but that would prevent $\lambda x.M$ from getting the natural derived typing rule and would cause undesirable non-termination effects to appear in, particularly, curried recursive functions.

Just as with traditional effect systems, the use of subtyping increases the accuracy of the analysis compared with one which just uses simple types or subeffecting.

There are many possible variants of the rules. For example, there is a stronger (try) rule in which the effects of the handlers are not all required to be the same, and only the effects of handlers corresponding to exceptions occurrring in $\varepsilon$ are unioned into the effect of the whole expression.

*Exercise 61.* Give examples which validate the claim that the $\rightarrow$ introduction rule gives better results than the obvious version with $\bot \in \varepsilon$.

MIL-lite does not include recursive types or higher-type references, because they would make proving correctness significantly more difficult. But can you devise candidate rules for an extended language which does include these features? They're not entirely obvious (especially if one tries to make the rules reasonably precise too). It may help to consider

```
datatype U = L of U->U
```

and

```
let val r = ref (fn () => ())
    val _ = r := (fn () => !r ())
in !r
end
```

**Operational Semantics.** We present the operational semantics of MIL-lite using a big-step evaluation relation $\Sigma, M \Downarrow \Sigma', R$ where $R$ ranges over value terms and exception identifiers and $\Sigma \in \text{States} \stackrel{\text{def}}{=} \mathbb{L} \rightharpoonup_{\text{fin}} \mathbb{Z}$.

Write $\Sigma, M \Downarrow$ if $\Sigma, M \Downarrow \Sigma', R$ for some $\Sigma', R$ and $\lfloor G \rfloor$ for the set of location names occuring in $G$. If $\Sigma, \Delta \in \text{States}$ then $(\Sigma \triangleleft \Delta) \in \text{States}$ is defined by $(\Sigma \triangleleft \Delta)(\ell) = \Delta(\ell)$ if that's defined and $\Sigma(\ell)$ otherwise.

In [BK99], we next prove a number of technical results about the operational semantics, using essentially the techniques described by Pitts in his lectures [Pit00a]. Since most of that material is not directly related to monads or effects, we will omit it from this account, but the important points are the following:

- We are interested in reasoning about *contextual equivalence*, which is a *type-indexed* relation between terms *in context*:

$$\Gamma \vdash G =_{\text{ctx}} G' : \sigma$$

- Rather than work with contextual equivalence directly, we show that contextual equivalence coincides with *ciu equivalence* [MT91], which shows that only certain special contexts need be considered to establish equivalence. For MIL-lite, ciu equivalence is the extension to open terms of the relation defined by the following clauses:
  - If $M_1 : \mathbf{T}_\varepsilon(\tau)$ and $M_2 : \mathbf{T}_\varepsilon(\tau)$ we write $M_1 \approx M_2 : \mathbf{T}_\varepsilon(\tau)$ and say $M_1$ *is ciu equivalent to* $M_2$ *at type* $\mathbf{T}_\varepsilon(\tau)$ when $\forall N, H$ such that $x : \tau \vdash N : \gamma$ and $\vdash H : \gamma$, and $\forall \Sigma \in \text{States}$ such that $\text{dom}\, \Sigma \supseteq \lfloor M_1, M_2, H, N \rfloor$ we have
  $$\Sigma, \text{try}\, x \Leftarrow M_1 \,\text{catch}\, H \,\text{in}\, N \Downarrow \quad \Leftrightarrow \quad \Sigma, \text{try}\, x \Leftarrow M_2 \,\text{catch}\, H \,\text{in}\, N \Downarrow$$
  - If $V_1 : \tau$ and $V_2 : \tau$ then we write $V_1 \approx V_2 : \tau$ for $\text{val}\, V_1 \approx \text{val}\, V_2 : \mathbf{T}_\emptyset(\tau)$.

$$\Sigma, \mathrm{val}\, V \Downarrow \Sigma, V \qquad \Sigma, \mathrm{raise}\, E \Downarrow \Sigma, E \qquad \Sigma, \pi_i(V_1, V_2) \Downarrow \Sigma, V_i$$

$$\Sigma, \underline{n} + \underline{m} \Downarrow \Sigma, \underline{n+m} \qquad \Sigma, \underline{n} = \underline{n} \Downarrow \Sigma, \mathrm{true} \qquad \Sigma, \underline{n} = \underline{m} \Downarrow \Sigma, \mathrm{false}\ (n \neq m)$$

$$\Sigma, !\underline{\ell} \Downarrow \Sigma, \underline{\Sigma(\ell)} \qquad \Sigma, \underline{\ell} := \underline{n} \Downarrow \Sigma[\ell \mapsto n], () \qquad \Sigma, \mathrm{ref}\, \underline{n} \Downarrow \Sigma \uplus [\ell \mapsto n], \underline{\ell}$$

$$\frac{\Sigma, M_i[V/x_i] \Downarrow \Sigma', R}{\Sigma, \mathrm{case\ in}_i V \ \mathrm{of\ in}_1 x_1.M_1\ ;\ \mathrm{in}_2 x_2.M_2 \Downarrow \Sigma', R}\ i = 1, 2$$

$$\frac{\Sigma, M[V/x, (\mathrm{rec}\, f\, x = M)/f] \Downarrow \Sigma', R}{\Sigma, (\mathrm{rec}\, f\, x = M)\ V \Downarrow \Sigma', R} \qquad \frac{\Sigma, M \Downarrow \Sigma', V \quad \Sigma', N[V/x] \Downarrow \Sigma'', R}{\Sigma, \mathrm{try}\ x \Leftarrow M\ \mathrm{catch}\ H\ \mathrm{in}\ N \Downarrow \Sigma'', R}$$

$$\frac{\Sigma, M \Downarrow \Sigma', E \quad \Sigma', M' \Downarrow \Sigma'', R}{\Sigma, \mathrm{try}\ x \Leftarrow M\ \mathrm{catch}\ H\ \mathrm{in}\ N \Downarrow \Sigma'', R}\ H(E) = M'$$

$$\frac{\Sigma, M \Downarrow \Sigma', E}{\Sigma, \mathrm{try}\ x \Leftarrow M\ \mathrm{catch}\ H\ \mathrm{in}\ N \Downarrow \Sigma', E}\ E \notin \mathrm{dom}(H)$$

**Fig. 7.** Evaluation relation for MIL-lite

Showing that ciu equivalence conincides with contextual equivalence is non-trivial but uses standard techniques [How96].

### 11.3 Transforming MIL-Lite

**Semantics of Effects.** We want to use the effect information expressed in MIL-lite types to justify some optimizing transformations. Our initial inclination was to prove the correctness of these transformations by using a denotational semantics. However, giving a good denotational semantics of MIL-lite is surprisingly tricky, not really because of the multiple computational types, but because of the presence of dynamically allocated references. Stark's thesis [Sta94] examines equivalence in a very minimal language with dynamically generated names in considerable detail and does give a functor category semantics for a language with higher order functions and integer references. But MIL-lite is rather more complex than Stark's language, requiring a functor category into cpos (rather than sets) and then indexed monads over that. Worst of all, the resulting semantics turns out to be very far from fully abstract – it actually fails to validate some of the most elementary transformations which we wished to perform. So we decided to prove correctness of our transformations using operational techniques instead.

Most work on using operational semantics to prove soundness of effect analyses involves instrumenting the semantics to trace computational effects in some way and then proving that 'well-typed programs don't go wrong' in this modified semantics. This approach is perfectly correct, but the notion of correctness and the meaning of effect annotations is quite intensional and closely tied to the formal system used to infer them. Since we wanted to prove the soundness of using the analysis to justify observational equivalences in an uninstrumented semantics, we instead tried to characterise the meaning of effect-annotated types as properties of terms which are closed under observational equivalence in the uninstrumented semantics. To give a simple example of the difference between the two approaches, a weak effect system (such as that in MIL-lite) will only assign a term an effect which does not contain $w$ if the evaluation of that term really does never perform a write operation. A region-based analysis may infer such an effect if it can detect that the term only writes to private locations. But the property we *really* want to use to justify equations is much more extensional: it's that after evaluating the term, the contents of all the locations which were allocated before the evaluation are indistinguishable from what they were to start with.

The decision not to use an instrumented semantics is largely one of taste, but there is another (post hoc) justification. There are a few places in the MLj libraries where we manually annotate bindings with smaller effect types than could be inferred by our analysis, typically so that the rewrites can dead-code them if they are not used (for example, the initialisation of lookup tables used in the floating point libraries). Since those bindings *do* have the extensional properties associated with the type we force them to have, the correctness result for our optimizations extends easily to these manually annotated expressions.

We capture the intended meaning $[\![\sigma]\!]$ of each type $\sigma$ in MIL-lite as the set of closed terms of that type which pass all of a collection of cotermination tests $\text{Tests}_\sigma \subseteq \text{States} \times \text{Ctxt}_\sigma \times \text{Ctxt}_\sigma$ where $\text{Ctxt}_\sigma$ is the set of closed contexts with a finite number of holes of type $\sigma$. Formally:

$$[\![\sigma]\!] \stackrel{\text{def}}{=} \{\, G : \sigma \mid \forall (\Sigma, M[\cdot], M'[\cdot]) \in \text{Tests}_\sigma . \qquad \lfloor M[G], M'[G] \rfloor \subseteq \text{dom}\,\Sigma \Rightarrow (\Sigma, M[G] \Downarrow \leftrightarrow \Sigma, M'[G] \Downarrow) \,\}$$

We define $\text{Tests}_\sigma$ inductively as shown in Figure 8.

Although these definitions appear rather complex, at value types they actually amount to a familiar-looking logical predicate:

**Lemma 111**

- $[\![\mathit{int}]\!] = \{\underline{n} \mid n \in \mathbb{Z}\}$, $[\![\mathit{intref}]\!] = \{\underline{\ell} \mid \ell \in \mathbb{L}\}$ *and* $[\![\mathit{unit}]\!] = \{()\}$.
- $[\![\tau_1 \times \tau_2]\!] = \{(V_1, V_2) \mid V_1 \in [\![\tau_1]\!], V_2 \in [\![\tau_2]\!]\}$
- $[\![\tau \to \gamma]\!] = \{F : \tau \to \gamma \mid \forall V \in [\![\tau]\!].(F\, V) \in [\![\gamma]\!]\}$
- $[\![\tau_1 + \tau_2]\!] = \bigcup_{i=1,2}\{in_i V \mid V \in [\![\tau_i]\!]\}$ □

**Lemma 112** *If* $\sigma \leqslant \sigma'$ *then* $[\![\sigma]\!] \subseteq [\![\sigma']\!]$. □

We also have to prove an operational version of admissibility for the predicate associated with each type. This follows from a standard 'compactness of evaluation' or 'unwinding' result which is proved using termination induction, but we

$$\text{Tests}_{\text{int}} \stackrel{\text{def}}{=} \{\} \qquad \text{Tests}_{\text{intref}} \stackrel{\text{def}}{=} \{\} \qquad \text{Tests}_{\text{unit}} \stackrel{\text{def}}{=} \{\}$$

$$\text{Tests}_{\tau_1 \times \tau_2} \stackrel{\text{def}}{=} \bigcup_{i=1,2}\{(\Sigma, M[\pi_i[\cdot]], M'[\pi_i[\cdot]]) \mid (\Sigma, M[\cdot], M'[\cdot]) \in \text{Tests}_{\tau_i}\}$$

$$\begin{aligned}\text{Tests}_{\tau_1 + \tau_2} \stackrel{\text{def}}{=} \bigcup_{i=1,2}\{(\Sigma, &\text{case } [\cdot] \text{ of in}_i x.M[x] \;;\; \text{in}_{3-i} y.\Omega, \\ &\text{case } [\cdot] \text{ of in}_i x.M'[x] \;;\; \text{in}_{3-i} y.\Omega) \mid (\Sigma, M[\cdot], M'[\cdot]) \in \text{Tests}_{\tau_i}\}\end{aligned}$$

$$\text{Tests}_{\tau \to \gamma} \stackrel{\text{def}}{=} \{(\Sigma, M[[\cdot]\ V], M'[[\cdot]\ V]) \mid V \in [\![\tau]\!],\ (\Sigma, M[\cdot], M'[\cdot]) \in \text{Tests}_\gamma\}$$

$$\begin{aligned}\text{Tests}_{\mathbf{T}_\varepsilon \tau} \stackrel{\text{def}}{=} \{&(\Sigma, \text{let } x \Leftarrow [\cdot] \text{ in set } \Sigma'; M[x], \text{let } x \Leftarrow [\cdot] \text{ in set } \Sigma'; M'[x]) \\ &\mid (\Sigma', M[\cdot], M'[\cdot]) \in \text{Tests}_\tau,\ \Sigma \in \text{States}\} \cup \textstyle\bigcup_{e \notin \varepsilon} \text{Tests}_{\overline{e},\tau}\end{aligned}$$

where

$$\text{Tests}_{\overline{\bot},\tau} \stackrel{\text{def}}{=} \{(\Sigma, [\cdot], \text{val}\ ()) \mid \Sigma \in \text{States}\}$$

$$\begin{aligned}\text{Tests}_{\overline{w},\tau} \stackrel{\text{def}}{=} \{&(\Sigma, \\ &\text{let } y \Leftarrow !\underline{\ell} \text{ in try } x \Leftarrow [\cdot] \text{ catch } E.M \text{ in } N, \\ &\text{try } x \Leftarrow [\cdot] \text{ catch } E.\text{let } y \Leftarrow !\underline{\ell} \text{ in } M \text{ in let } y \Leftarrow !\underline{\ell} \text{ in } N) \\ &\mid y : \text{int}, x : \tau \vdash N : \gamma, y : \text{int} \vdash M : \gamma, \Sigma \in \text{States}, \ell \in \text{dom}\,\Sigma, E \in \mathbb{E}\}\end{aligned}$$

$$\begin{aligned}\text{Tests}_{\overline{r},\tau} \stackrel{\text{def}}{=} \{&(\Sigma, \\ &\text{d}(\Sigma, \Delta, E); \text{try } x \Leftarrow [\cdot] \text{ catch } E.\text{assert } \Sigma \lhd \Delta; \text{raise } E \text{ in } N, \\ &\text{d}(\Sigma, \Delta, E); \underline{\ell} := \underline{n}; \text{try } x \Leftarrow [\cdot] \text{ catch } E.\text{assert } \Sigma[\ell \mapsto n] \lhd \Delta; \text{raise } E \\ &\text{in assert } (\ell, (\Sigma[\ell \mapsto n] \lhd \Delta)(\ell)); \underline{\ell} := \underline{(\Sigma \lhd \Delta)(\ell)}; N) \\ &\mid E \in \mathbb{E}, \Sigma, \Delta \in \text{States}, \text{dom}\,\Delta \subseteq \text{dom}\,\Sigma \ni \ell, n \in \mathbb{Z}, x : \tau \vdash N : \gamma\} \\ \cup\{&(\Sigma, [\cdot] \text{ handle } E.\Omega, \text{set } \Sigma'; [\cdot] \text{ handle } E.\Omega) \mid \Sigma, \Sigma' \in \text{States}, E \in \mathbb{E}\}\end{aligned}$$

$$\text{Tests}_{\overline{E},\tau} \stackrel{\text{def}}{=} \{(\Sigma, [\cdot], [\cdot] \text{ handle } E.N) \mid \Sigma \in \text{States}, \vdash N : \gamma\}$$

$$\begin{aligned}\text{Tests}_{\overline{a},\tau} \stackrel{\text{def}}{=} \{&(\Sigma, \text{let } x \Leftarrow [\cdot]; y \Leftarrow (\text{set } \Sigma; [\cdot]) \text{ in } N, \text{let } x \Leftarrow [\cdot]; y \Leftarrow \text{val } x \text{ in } N) \\ &\mid \Sigma \in \text{States}, x : \tau, y : \tau \vdash N : \gamma\}\end{aligned}$$

and

$$\text{K}_\Sigma n \stackrel{\text{def}}{=} \{\ell \mapsto n \mid \ell \in \text{dom}(\Sigma)\}$$

$$\begin{aligned}\text{d}(\Sigma, \Delta, E) \stackrel{\text{def}}{=} &\text{set K}_\Sigma 0; (([\cdot]; \text{val}\ ()) \text{ handle } E.\text{val}\ ()); \text{assert K}_\Sigma 0 \lhd \Delta; \\ &\text{set K}_\Sigma 1; (([\cdot]; \text{val}\ ()) \text{ handle } E.\text{val}\ ()); \text{assert K}_\Sigma 1 \lhd \Delta; \text{set } \Sigma\end{aligned}$$

**Fig. 8.** Definition of $\text{Tests}_\sigma$

omit the details. Finally, we can prove the 'Fundamental Theorem' for our logical predicate, which says that the analysis is correct in the sense that whenever a term is given a particular type it actually satisfies the property associated with that type:

**Theorem 62.** *If $\boldsymbol{x_i} : \boldsymbol{\tau_i} \vdash G : \sigma$ and $\boldsymbol{V_i} \in [\![\boldsymbol{\tau_i}]\!]$ then $G[\boldsymbol{V_i}/\boldsymbol{x_i}] \in [\![\sigma]\!]$.* □

The intention is that the extent of $\text{Tests}_{\overline{e},\tau}$ is the set of computations of type $\mathbf{T}_\mathcal{E}(\tau)$ which definitely do *not* have effect $e$. So, passing all the tests in $\text{Tests}_{\overline{\bot},\tau}$

is easily seen to be equivalent to not diverging in any state and passing all the tests in $\text{Tests}_{\overline{E},\tau}$ means not throwing exception $E$ in any state.

The tests concerning store effects are a little more subtle. It is not too hard to see that $\text{Tests}_{\overline{w},\tau}$ expresses not *observably* writing the store. Similarly, $\text{Tests}_{\overline{r},\tau}$ tests (contortedly!) for not observably reading the store, by running the computation in different initial states and seeing if the results can be distinguished by a subsequent continuation.

The most surprising definition is probably that of $\text{Tests}_{\overline{a},\tau}$, the extent of which is intended to be those computations which do not observably allocate any new storage locations. This should include, for example, a computation which allocates a reference and then returns a function which uses that reference to keep count of how many times it has been called, but which never reveals the counter, nor returns different results according to its value. However, the definition of $\text{Tests}_{\overline{a},\tau}$ does not seem to say anything about store extension; what it actually captures is those computations for which two evaluations in equivalent initial states yield indistinguishable results. Our choice of this as the meaning of 'doesn't allocate' was guided by the optimising transformations which we wished to perform rather than a deep understanding of exactly what it means to not allocate observably, but in retrospect it seems quite reasonable.

**Effect-Independent Equivalences.** Figure 9 presents some typed observational congruences that correspond to identities from the equational theory of the computational metalanguage, and Figure 10 presents equivalences that involve local side-effecting behaviour[15]. Directed variants of many of these are useful transformations that are in fact performed by MLj (although the duplication of terms in $cc_2$ is avoided by introducing a special kind of abstraction). These equations can be derived without recourse to our logical predicate, by making use of a rather strong notion of equivalence called *Kleene equivalence* that can easily be shown to be contained in ciu equivalence. Two terms are Kleene equivalent if they coterminate in any initial state with syntactically identical results and the same values in all accessible locations of the store (Mason and Talcott call this 'strong isomorphism' [MT91]).

The beta-equivalences and commuting conversions of Figure 9 together with the equivalences of Figure 10 are derived directly as Kleene equivalences. Derivation of the eta-equivalences involves first deriving a number of extensionality properties using ciu equivalence; similar techniques are used by Pitts [Pit97].

**Effect-Dependent Equivalences.** We now come to a set of equivalences that are dependent on effect information, which are shown in Figure 11. Notice how the first three of these equations respectively subsume the first three local equivalences of Figure 10. Each of these equivalences is proved by considering evaluation of each side in an arbitrary ciu-context and then using the logical predicate

[15] Some side conditions on variables are implicit in our use of contexts. For example, the first equation in Figure 10 has the side condition that $x \notin fv(M)$.

$$\beta\text{-}\times\,\frac{\Gamma\vdash V_1:\tau_1\qquad \Gamma\vdash V_2:\tau_2}{\Gamma\vdash \pi_i(V_1,V_2)\cong \mathrm{val}\ V_i:\mathbf{T}_\emptyset(\tau_i)}\qquad \beta\text{-}\mathbf{T}\,\frac{\Gamma\vdash V:\tau\qquad \Gamma,x:\tau\vdash M:\gamma}{\Gamma\vdash \mathrm{let}\ x\Leftarrow \mathrm{val}\ V\ \mathrm{in}\ M\cong M[V/x]:\gamma}$$

$$\beta\text{-}\rightarrow\,\frac{\Gamma,x:\tau,f:\tau\rightarrow\mathbf{T}_{\varepsilon\cup\{\bot\}}(\tau')\vdash M:\mathbf{T}_\varepsilon(\tau')\qquad \Gamma\vdash V:\tau}{\Gamma\vdash(\mathrm{rec}\ f\ x=M)\ V\cong M[V/x,\mathrm{rec}\ f\ x=M/f]:\mathbf{T}_\varepsilon(\tau')}$$

$$\beta\text{-}+\,\frac{\Gamma\vdash V:\tau_i\qquad \Gamma,x_1:\tau_1\vdash M_1:\gamma\qquad \Gamma,x_2:\tau_2\vdash M_2:\gamma}{\Gamma\vdash \mathrm{case}\ \mathrm{in}_i V\ \mathrm{of}\ \mathrm{in}_1x_1.M_1;\mathrm{in}_2x_2.M_2\cong M_i[V/x_i]:\gamma}$$

$$\eta\text{-}\times\,\frac{\Gamma\vdash V:\tau_1\times\tau_2}{\Gamma\vdash \mathrm{let}\ x_1\Leftarrow\pi_1V;x_2\Leftarrow\pi_2V\ \mathrm{in}\ \mathrm{val}\ (x_1,x_2)\cong \mathrm{val}\ V:\mathbf{T}_\emptyset(\tau_1\times\tau_2)}$$

$$\eta\text{-}+\,\frac{\Gamma\vdash V:\tau_1+\tau_2}{\Gamma\vdash \mathrm{case}\ V\ \mathrm{of}\ \mathrm{in}_1x_1.\mathrm{val}\ (\mathrm{in}_1x_1);\mathrm{in}_2x_2.\mathrm{val}\ (\mathrm{in}_2x_2)\cong \mathrm{val}\ V:\mathbf{T}_\emptyset(\tau_1+\tau_2)}$$

$$\eta\text{-}\rightarrow\,\frac{\Gamma\vdash V:\tau\rightarrow\gamma}{\Gamma\vdash \mathrm{rec}\ f\ x=V\ x\cong V:\tau\rightarrow\gamma}\qquad \eta\text{-}\mathbf{T}\,\frac{\Gamma\vdash M:\gamma}{\Gamma\vdash \mathrm{let}\ x\Leftarrow M\ \mathrm{in}\ \mathrm{val}\ x\cong M:\gamma}$$

$$cc_1\,\frac{\Gamma\vdash M_1:\mathbf{T}_{\varepsilon_1}(\tau_1)\qquad \Gamma,y:\tau_1\vdash M_2:\mathbf{T}_{\varepsilon_2}(\tau_2)\qquad \Gamma,y:\tau_1,x:\tau_2\vdash M_3:\mathbf{T}_{\varepsilon_3}(\tau_3)}{\Gamma\vdash \mathrm{let}\ x\Leftarrow(\mathrm{let}\ y\Leftarrow M_1\ \mathrm{in}\ M_2)\ \mathrm{in}\ M_3\cong \mathrm{let}\ y\Leftarrow M_1;x\Leftarrow M_2\ \mathrm{in}\ M_3:\mathbf{T}_{\varepsilon_1\cup\varepsilon_2\cup\varepsilon_3}(\tau_3)}$$

$$cc_2\,\frac{\Gamma\vdash V:\tau_1+\tau_2\quad \{\Gamma,x_i:\tau_i\vdash M_i:\mathbf{T}_\varepsilon(\tau)\}\quad \Gamma,x:\tau\vdash N:\mathbf{T}_{\varepsilon'}(\tau')}{\Gamma\vdash \mathrm{let}\ x\Leftarrow\mathrm{case}\ V\ \mathrm{of}\ \{\mathrm{in}_ix_i.M_i\}\ \mathrm{in}\ N\cong \mathrm{case}\ V\ \mathrm{of}\ \{\mathrm{in}_ix_i.\mathrm{let}\ x\Leftarrow M_i\ \mathrm{in}\ N\}:\mathbf{T}_{\varepsilon\cup\varepsilon'}(\tau')}$$

$$\beta\text{-}E\,\frac{\Gamma\vdash M:\gamma\qquad \Gamma\vdash H:\gamma\qquad \Gamma,x:\tau\vdash N:\gamma}{\Gamma\vdash \mathrm{try}\ x\Leftarrow\mathrm{raise}\ E\ \mathrm{catch}\ (E.M);H\ \mathrm{in}\ N\cong M:\gamma}$$

$$\eta\text{-}E\,\frac{\Gamma\vdash M:\mathbf{T}_\varepsilon(\tau)\qquad \Gamma\vdash H:\mathbf{T}_{\varepsilon'}(\tau')\qquad \Gamma,x:\tau\vdash N:\mathbf{T}_{\varepsilon'}(\tau')}{\Gamma\vdash \mathrm{try}\ x\Leftarrow M\ \mathrm{catch}\ (E.\mathrm{raise}\ E);H\ \mathrm{in}\ N\cong \mathrm{try}\ x\Leftarrow M\ \mathrm{catch}\ H\ \mathrm{in}\ N:\mathbf{T}_{\varepsilon\cup\varepsilon'}(\tau')}$$

**Fig. 9.** Effect-independent equivalences (1)

to show that if the evaluation terminates then so does the evaluation of the other side in the same context.

### 11.4 Effect-Dependent Rewriting in MLj

In practice, much of the benefit MLj gets from effect-based rewriting is simply from dead-code elimination (*discard* and *dead-try*). A lot of dead code (particularly straight after linking) is just unused top-level function bindings, and these could clearly be removed by a simple syntactic check instead of a type-based effect analysis. Nevertheless, both unused non-values which detectably at most read or allocate and unreachable exception handlers do occur fairly often too, and it is convenient to be able to use a single framework to eliminate them all. Here is an example (from [BK01]) of how tracking exception effects works together with MIL's unusual handler construct to improve an ML program for summing the elements of an array:

$$\textit{deadref}\ \frac{\Gamma \vdash V : \mathrm{int} \qquad \Gamma \vdash M : \mathbf{T}_{\varepsilon}(\tau)}{\Gamma \vdash \mathrm{let}\ x \Leftarrow \mathrm{ref}\ V\ \mathrm{in}\ M \cong M : \mathbf{T}_{\varepsilon \cup \{a\}}(\tau)}$$

$$\textit{deref}\ \frac{\Gamma \vdash V : \mathrm{intref} \qquad \Gamma, x : \mathrm{int}, y : \mathrm{int} \vdash M : \mathbf{T}_{\varepsilon}(\tau)}{\Gamma \vdash \mathrm{let}\ x \Leftarrow !V; y \Leftarrow !V\ \mathrm{in}\ M \cong \mathrm{let}\ x \Leftarrow !V; y \Leftarrow \mathrm{val}\ x\ \mathrm{in}\ M : \mathbf{T}_{\varepsilon \cup \{r\}}(\tau)}$$

$$\frac{[\textit{swapref}]\quad \Gamma \vdash V_1 : \mathrm{int} \qquad \Gamma \vdash V_2 : \mathrm{int} \qquad \Gamma, x_1 : \mathrm{intref}, x_2 : \mathrm{intref} \vdash M : \mathbf{T}_{\varepsilon}(\tau)}{\Gamma \vdash \mathrm{let}\ x_1 \Leftarrow \mathrm{ref}\ V_1; x_2 \Leftarrow \mathrm{ref}\ V_2\ \mathrm{in}\ M \cong \mathrm{let}\ x_2 \Leftarrow \mathrm{ref}\ V_2; x_1 \Leftarrow \mathrm{ref}\ V_1\ \mathrm{in}\ M : \mathbf{T}_{\varepsilon \cup \{a\}}(\tau)}$$

$$\textit{assign}\ \frac{\Gamma \vdash V_1 : \mathrm{intref} \qquad \Gamma \vdash V_2 : \mathrm{int} \qquad \Gamma, x : \mathrm{int} \vdash M : \mathbf{T}_{\varepsilon}(\tau)}{\Gamma \vdash V_1 := V_2; \mathrm{let}\ x \Leftarrow !V_1\ \mathrm{in}\ M \cong V_1 := V_2; M[V_2/x] : \mathbf{T}_{\varepsilon \cup \{r,w\}}(\tau)}$$

**Fig. 10.** Effect-independent equivalences (2)

$$\textit{discard}\ \frac{\Gamma \vdash M : \mathbf{T}_{\varepsilon_1}(\tau_1) \qquad \Gamma \vdash N : \mathbf{T}_{\varepsilon_2}(\tau_2)}{\Gamma \vdash \mathrm{let}\ x \Leftarrow M\ \mathrm{in}\ N \cong N : \mathbf{T}_{\varepsilon_1 \cup \varepsilon_2} \tau_2}$$
$$\text{where } \varepsilon_1 \subseteq \{r, a\}$$

$$\textit{copy}\ \frac{\Gamma \vdash M : \mathbf{T}_{\varepsilon}(\tau) \qquad \Gamma, x : \tau, y : \tau \vdash N : \mathbf{T}_{\varepsilon'}(\tau')}{\Gamma \vdash \mathrm{let}\ x \Leftarrow M; y \Leftarrow M\ \mathrm{in}\ N \cong \mathrm{let}\ x \Leftarrow M; y \Leftarrow \mathrm{val}\ x\ \mathrm{in}\ N : \mathbf{T}_{\varepsilon \cup \varepsilon'}(\tau')}$$
$$\text{where } \{r, a\} \cap \varepsilon = \emptyset \text{ or } \{w, a\} \cap \varepsilon = \emptyset$$

$$\textit{swap}\ \frac{\Gamma \vdash M_1 : \mathbf{T}_{\varepsilon_1}(\tau_1) \qquad \Gamma \vdash M_2 : \mathbf{T}_{\varepsilon_2}(\tau_2) \qquad \Gamma, x_1 : \tau_1, x_2 : \tau_2 \vdash N : \mathbf{T}_{\varepsilon_3}(\tau_3)}{\Gamma \vdash \mathrm{let}\ x_1 \Leftarrow M_1; x_2 \Leftarrow M_2\ \mathrm{in}\ N \cong \mathrm{let}\ x_2 \Leftarrow M_2; x_1 \Leftarrow M_1\ \mathrm{in}\ N : \mathbf{T}_{\varepsilon_1 \cup \varepsilon_2 \cup \varepsilon_3}(\tau_3)}$$
$$\text{where } \varepsilon_1, \varepsilon_2 \subseteq \{r, a, \bot\} \text{ or } \varepsilon_1 \subseteq \{a, \bot\}, \varepsilon_2 \subseteq \{r, w, a, \bot\}$$

$$\textit{dead-try}\ \frac{\Gamma \vdash M : \mathbf{T}_{\varepsilon}(\tau) \qquad \Gamma \vdash H : \mathbf{T}_{\varepsilon'}(\tau') \qquad \Gamma, x : \tau \vdash N : \mathbf{T}_{\varepsilon'}(\tau')}{\Gamma \vdash \mathrm{try}\ x \Leftarrow M\ \mathrm{catch}\ H\ \mathrm{in}\ N \cong \mathrm{try}\ x \Leftarrow M\ \mathrm{catch}\ H \setminus E\ \mathrm{in}\ N : \mathbf{T}_{\varepsilon \cup \varepsilon'}(\tau')}$$
$$\text{where } E \notin \varepsilon$$

**Fig. 11.** Effect-dependent equivalences

```
fun sumarray a =
  let fun s(n,sofar) = let val v = Array.sub(a,n)
                       in s(n+1, sofar+v)
                       end handle Subscript => sofar
  in s(0,0)
  end
```

Because the SML source language doesn't have *try*, the programmer has made the handler cover both the array access and the recursive call to the inner function s. But this would prevent a naïve compiler from recognising that call as tail-recursive. In MLj, the intermediate code for s looks like (in MLish, rather than MIL, syntax):

```
fun s(n,sofar) =
      try val x = try val v = Array.sub(a,n)
                  catch {}
                  in s(n+1, sofar+v)
                  end
      catch Subscript => sofar
      in x
      end
```

A commuting conversion turns this into

```
fun s(n,sofar) = try val v = Array.sub(a,n)
                 catch Subscript => sofar
                 in try val x = s(n+1, sofar+v)
                    catch Subscript => sofar
                    in x
                    end
                 end
```

The effect analysis detects that the recursive call to s cannot, in fact, ever throw the Subscript exception, so the function is rewritten again to

```
fun s(n,sofar) = try val v = Array.sub(a,n)
                 catch Subscript => sofar
                 in s(n+1, sofar+v)
                 end
```

which *is* tail recursive, and so gets compiled as a loop in the final code for sumarray.

Making practical use of the *swap* and *copy* equations is more difficult – although it is easy to come up with real programs which could be usefully improved by sequences of rewrites including those equations, it is hard for the compiler to spot when commuting two computations makes useful progress towards a more significant rewrite. The most significant effect-based code motion transformation which we do perform is pulling constant, pure computations out of functions (in particular, loops), a special case of which is

$$\frac{\Gamma \vdash M : \mathbf{T}_{\emptyset}(\tau_3) \qquad \Gamma, f : \tau_1 \to \mathbf{T}_{\varepsilon\cup\bot}(\tau_2), x : \tau_1, y : \tau_3 \vdash N : \mathbf{T}_{\varepsilon}(\tau_2)}{\Gamma \vdash \mathrm{val}\,(\mathrm{rec}\ f\ x = \mathrm{let}\ y \Leftarrow M\ \mathrm{in}\ N) \cong \mathrm{let}\ y \Leftarrow M\ \mathrm{in}\ \mathrm{val}\,(\mathrm{rec}\ f\ x = N) : \mathbf{T}_{\emptyset}(\tau_1 \to \mathbf{T}_{\varepsilon}(\tau_2))}$$

where there's an implied side condition that neither $f$ nor $x$ is free in $M$. This is not always an improvement (if the function is never applied), but in the absence of more information it's worth doing anyway. Slightly embarassingly, this is not an equivalence which we have proved correct using the techniques described here, however.

One other place where information about which expressions commute could usefully be applied is in a compiler backend, for example in register allocation. We haven't tried this in MLj since a JIT compiler will do its *own* job of allocating real machine registers and scheduling real machine instructions later, which makes doing a very 'good' job of compiling virtual machine code unlikely to produce great improvements in the performance of the final machine code.

An early version of the compiler also implemented a type-directed uncurrying transformation, exploiting the isomorphism

$$\tau_1 \to \mathbf{T}_{\emptyset}(\tau_2 \to \mathbf{T}_{\varepsilon}(\tau_3)) \;\cong\; \tau_1 \times \tau_2 \to \mathbf{T}_{\varepsilon}(\tau_3)$$

but this can lead to extra work being done if the function is actually partially applied, so this transformation also seems to call for auxiliary information to be gathered.

## 11.5 Effect Masking and Monadic Encapsulation

We have seen that it is not too hard to recast simple effect systems in a monadic framework. But what is the monadic equivalent of effect masking? The answer is something like the encapsulation of side-effects provided by `runST` in Haskell, but the full connection has not yet been established.

Haskell allows monadic computations which make purely local use of state to be encapsulated as values with 'pure' types by making use of a cunning trick with type variables which is very similar to the use of regions in effect systems. Briefly (see Section 5 for more information), the state monad is parameterized not only by the type of the state $s$, but also by another 'dummy' type variable $r$[16].

The idea is that the $r$ parameters of types inferred for computations whose states might interfere will be unified, so if a computation can be assigned a type which is parametrically polymorphic in $r$, then its use of state can be encapsulated. This is expressed using the `runST` combinator which is given the rank-2 polymorphic type

$$\texttt{runST} : \forall s, a.(\forall r.(r, s, a)\mathrm{ST}) \to a$$

Just as the soundness of effect masking and of the region calculus is hard to establish, proving the correctness of monadic encapsulation is difficult. Early attempts to prove soundness of encapsulation for lazy languages via subject reduction [LS97] are now known to be incorrect.

Semmelroth and Sabry have defined a CBV language with monadic encapsulation, relating this to a language with effect masking and proving type soundness [SS99]. Moggi and Palumbo have also addressed this problem [MP99], by defining a slightly different form of monadic encapsulation (explicitly parameterizing over the monad and its operations) and proving a type soundness result for a

[16] Actually, Haskell's built-in state monad is not parameterized on the type of the state itself.

language in which the stateful operations are strict. More recently, a type soundness result for a language with lazy state operations has been proved by Moggi and Sabry [MS01].

## 12 Curry-Howard Correspondence and Monads

This section provides a little optional background on a logical reading of the computational metalanguage and explains the term 'commuting conversion'.

Most readers will have some familiarity with the so-called Curry-Howard Correspondence (or Isomorphism, aka the Propositions-as-Types Analogy). This relates types in certain typed lambda calculi to propositions in intuitionistic logics, typed terms in context to (natural deduction) proofs of propositions from assumptions, and reduction to proof normalization. The basic example of the correspondence relates the simply typed lambda calculus with function, pair and disjoint union types to intuitionisitic propositional logic with implication, conjunction and disjunction [GLT89].

It turns out that logic and proof theory can provide helpful insights into the design of programming languages and intermediate languages. Partly this seems to be because proof theorists have developed a number of taxonomies and criteria for 'well-behavedness' of proof rules which turn out to be transferable to the design of 'good' language syntax.

The computational metalanguage provides a nice example of the applicability of proof theoretic ideas [BBdP98,PD01]. If one reads the type rules for the introduction and elimination of the computation type constructor logically, then one ends up with an intuitionistic *modal* logic (which we dubbed 'CL-logic') with a slightly unusual kind of possibility modality, $\diamond$. In sequent-style natural deduction form:

$$\frac{\Gamma \vdash A}{\Gamma \vdash \diamond A}(\diamond_{\mathcal{I}}) \qquad \frac{\Gamma \vdash \diamond A \qquad \Gamma, A \vdash \diamond B}{\Gamma \vdash \diamond B}(\diamond_{\mathcal{E}})$$

Interestingly, not only was (the Hilbert-style presentation of) this logic discovered by Fairtlough and Mendler (who call it 'lax logic') in the context of hardware verification [FM95], but it had even been considered by Curry in 1957 [Cur57]! Moreover, from a logical perspective, the three basic equations of the computational metalanguage arise as inevitable consequences of the form of the introduction and elimination rules, rather than being imposed separately.

The way in which the $\beta$-rule for the computation type constructor arises from the natural deduction presentation of the logic is fairly straightforward – the basic step in normalization is the removal of 'detours' caused by the introduction and immediate elimination of a logical connective:

$$\frac{\dfrac{\begin{array}{c}\vdots\\ A\end{array}}{\diamond A}(\diamond_{\mathcal{I}}) \qquad \begin{array}{c}[A]\cdots[A]\\ \vdots\\ \diamond B\end{array}}{\diamond B}(\diamond_{\mathcal{E}}) \qquad \longrightarrow \qquad \begin{array}{c}\begin{array}{ccc}\vdots & & \vdots\\ {[A]} & \cdots & {[A]}\end{array}\\ \vdots\\ \diamond B\end{array}$$

$$\dfrac{\dfrac{\Gamma \vdash M : A}{\Gamma \vdash \mathrm{val}\, M : TA} \qquad \Gamma, x : A \vdash N : TB}{\Gamma \vdash \mathrm{let}\ x \Leftarrow \mathrm{val}\, M \ \mathrm{in}\ N : TB} \quad \longrightarrow \quad \Gamma \vdash N[M/x] : TB$$

Natural deduction systems can also give rise to a secondary form of normalisation step which are necessary to ensure that normal deductions satisfy the subformula property, for example. These occur when the system contains elimination rules which have a minor premiss – the minor premiss of $(\diamond_{\mathcal{E}})$ is $\diamond B$, for example. (Girard calls this a 'parasitic formula' and refers to the necessity for the extra reductions as 'the shame of natural deduction' [GLT89].) In general, when we have such a rule, we want to be able to commute the last rule in the derivation of the minor premiss down past the rule, or to move the application of a rule to the conclusion of the elimination up past the elimination rule into to the derivation of the minor premiss. The only important cases are moving eliminations up or introductions down. Such transformations are called *commuting conversions.* The elimination rule for disjunction (coproducts) in intuitionisitic logic gives rise to commuting conversions and so does the elimination for the $\diamond$ modality of CL-logic. The restriction on the form of the conclusion of our $(\diamond_{\mathcal{E}})$ rule (it must be modal) means that the rule gives rise to only one commuting conversion:

– A deduction of the form

$$\dfrac{\dfrac{\begin{array}{c}\vdots\\ \diamond A\end{array} \qquad \begin{array}{c}[A]\\ \vdots\\ \diamond B\end{array}}{\diamond B}(\diamond_{\mathcal{E}}) \qquad \begin{array}{c}[B]\\ \vdots\\ \diamond C\end{array}}{\diamond C}(\diamond_{\mathcal{E}})$$

commutes to

$$\dfrac{\begin{array}{c}\vdots\\ \diamond A\end{array} \qquad \dfrac{\begin{array}{c}[A]\\ \vdots\\ \diamond B\end{array} \qquad \begin{array}{c}[B]\\ \vdots\\ \diamond C\end{array}}{\diamond C}(\diamond_{\mathcal{E}})}{\diamond C}(\diamond_{\mathcal{E}})$$

On terms of the computational metalanguage, this commuting conversion induces the 'let of a let' associativity rule (with the free variable condition implicit in the use of $\Gamma$):

$$\dfrac{\dfrac{\Gamma \vdash M : TA \qquad \Gamma, y : A \vdash P : TB}{\Gamma \vdash \mathrm{let}\ y \Leftarrow M \ \mathrm{in}\ P : TB} \qquad \Gamma, x : B \vdash N : TC}{\Gamma \vdash \mathrm{let}\ x \Leftarrow (\mathrm{let}\ y \Leftarrow M \ \mathrm{in}\ P)\ \mathrm{in}\ N : TC} \quad \longrightarrow$$

$$\dfrac{\Gamma \vdash M : TA \qquad \dfrac{\Gamma, y : A \vdash P : TB \qquad \Gamma, y : A, x : B \vdash N : TC}{\Gamma, y : A \vdash \mathrm{let}\ x \Leftarrow P \ \mathrm{in}\ N : TC}}{\Gamma \vdash \mathrm{let}\ y \Leftarrow M \ \mathrm{in}\ (\mathrm{let}\ x \Leftarrow P \ \mathrm{in}\ N) : TC}$$

Commuting conversions are not generally optimizing tranformations in their own right, but they reorganise code so as to expose more computationally significant $\beta$ reductions. They are therefore important in compilation, and most compilers for functional languages perform at least some of them. MLj is somewhat dogmatic in performing *all* of them, to reach what we call *cc-normal form*, from which it also turns out to be particularly straighforward to generate code. As Danvy and Hatcliff observe [HD94], this is closely related to working with A-normal forms, though the logical/proof theoretic notion is an older and more precisely defined pattern.

## Acknowledgements

We are grateful to the anonymous referees for their detailed comments.

## References

[App92] A. W. Appel. *Compiling with Continuations.* Cambridge University Press, 1992.

[BBdP98] P. N. Benton, G. M. Bierman, and V. C. V. de Paiva. Computational types from a logical perspective. *Journal of Functional Programming,* 8(2):177–193, March 1998. Preliminary version appeared as Technical Report 365, University of Cambridge Computer Laboratory, May 1995.

[Ben92] P. N. Benton. *Strictness Analysis of Lazy Functional Programs.* PhD thesis, Computer Laboratory, University of Cambridge, December 1992.

[BHR99] A. Banerjee, N. Heintze, and J. G. Reicke. Region analysis and the polymorphic lambda calculus. In *Fourteenth IEEE Symposium on Logic and Computer Science*, 1999.

[BHT98] G. Barthe, J. Hatcliff, and P. Thiemann. Monadic type systems: Pure type systems for impure settings. In *Proceedings of the Second HOOTS Workshop, Stanford University, Palo Alto, CA. December, 1997*, Electronic Notes in Theoretical Computer Science. Elsevier, February 1998.

[BK99] N. Benton and A. Kennedy. Monads, effects and transformations. In *Third International Workshop on Higher Order Operational Techniques in Semantics (HOOTS), Paris*, volume 26 of *Electronic Notes in Theoretical Computer Science.* Elsevier, September 1999.

[BK01] N. Benton and A. Kennedy. Exceptional syntax. *Journal of Functional Programming*, 11(4):395–410, July 2001.

[BKR98] N. Benton, A. Kennedy, and G. Russell. Compiling Standard ML to Java bytecodes. In *3rd ACM SIGPLAN Conference on Functional Programming*, September 1998.

[BM92] G. L. Burn and D. Le Metayer. Proving the correctness of compiler optimisations based on a global program analysis. Technical Report Doc 92/20, Department of Computing, Imperial College, London, 1992.

[BNTW95] P. Buneman, S. Naqvi, V. Tannen, and L. Wong. Principles of programming with complex objects and collection types. *Theoretical Computer Science*, 149(1), 1995.

[Bor94] F. Borceux. *Handbook of Categorial Algebra.* Cambridge University Press, 1994.

[BS96] Erik Barendsen and Sjaak Smetsers. Uniqueness typing for functional languages with graph rewriting semantics. *Mathematical Structures in Computer Science*, pages 579–612, 1996.

[Bur75] W. Burge. *Recursive Programming Techniques.* Addison-Wesley Publishing Company, Reading, Mass., 1975.

[BW85] M. Barr and C. Wells. *Toposes, Triples and Theories.* Springer, 1985.

[CF94] R. Cartwright and M. Felleisen. Extensible denotational language specifications. In *Theoretical Aspects of Computer Software*, volume 789 of *LNCS*. Springer, 1994.

[CHT0x] C. Calcagno, S. Helsen, and P. Thiemann. Syntactic type soundness results for the region calculus. *Information and Computation*, to appear 200x.

[CM93] P. Cenciarelli and E. Moggi. A syntactic approach to modularity in denotational semantics. In *CTCS 1993*, 1993. CWI Tech. Report.

[Cur57] H. B. Curry. The elimination theorem when modality is present. *Journal of Symbolic Logic*, 17(4):249–265, January 1957.

[DF92] O. Danvy and A. Filinski. Representing control: A study of the CPS transformation. *Mathematical Structures in Computer Science*, 2, 1992.

[DH93] O. Danvy and J. Hatcliff. CPS transformation after strictness analysis. *ACM Letters on Programming Languages and Systems*, 1(3), 1993.

[dZG00] S. dal Zilio and A. Gordon. Region analysis and a $\pi$-calculus with groups. In *25th International Symposium on Mathematical Foundations of Computer Science*, August 2000.

[Fil99] A. Filinski. Representing layered monads. In *POPL'99.* ACM Press, 1999.

[FM95] M. Fairtlough and M. Mendler. An intuitionistic modal logic with applications to the formal verification of hardware. In *Proceedings of Computer Science Logic 1994*, volume 933 of *Lecture Notes in Computer Science.* Springer-Verlag, 1995.

[FSDF93] C. Flanagan, A. Sabry, B. F. Duba, and M. Felleisen. The essence of compiling with continuations. In *Proceedings of the 1993 Conference on Programming Language Design and Implementation.* ACM, 1993.

[GJLS87] D. K. Gifford, P. Jouvelot, J. M. Lucassen, and M. A. Sheldon. FX-87 reference manual. Technical Report MIT/LCS/TR-407, MIT Laboratory for Computer Science, 1987.

[GL86] D.K. Gifford and J.M. Lucassen. Integrating functional and imperative programming. In *ACM Conference on Lisp and Functional Programming.* ACM Press, 1986.

[GLT89] J.-Y. Girard, Y. Lafont, and P. Taylor. *Proofs and Types.* Number 7 in Cambridge Tracts in Theoretical Computer Science. Cambridge University Press, 1989.

[Gor79] M.J.C. Gordon. *Denotational Description of Programming Languages.* Springer, 1979.

[GS99] J. Gustavsson and D. Sands. A foundation for space-safe transformations of call-by-need programs. In A. D. Gordon and A. M.Pitts, editors, *The Third International Workshop on Higher Order Operational Techniques in Semantics*, volume 26 of *Electronic Notes in Theoretical Computer Science.* Elsevier, 1999.

[HD94] J. Hatcliff and O. Danvy. A generic account of continuation-passing styles. In *Proceedings of the 21st Annual Symposium on Principles of Programming Languages.* ACM, January 1994.

[HM98] Graham Hutton and Erik Meijer. Monadic parsing in Haskell. *Journal of Functional Programming*, 8(4):437–444, July 1998.

[How96] D. J. Howe. Proving congruence of bisimulation in functional programming languages. *Information and Computation*, 124(2):103–112, February 1996.

[Hud98] P. Hudak. Modular domain specific languages and tools. In *Fifth International Conference on Software Reuse*, pages 134–142, Victoria, Canada, June 1998.

[Hug99] John Hughes. Restricted Datatypes in Haskell. In *Third Haskell Workshop*. Utrecht University technical report, 1999.

[Jac99] Bart Jacobs. *Categorical Logic and Type Theory.* Number 141 in Studies in Logic and the Foundations of Mathematics. North Holland, 1999.

[JHe+99] Simon Peyton Jones, John Hughes, (editors), Lennart Augustsson, Dave Barton, Brian Boutel, Warren Burton, Joseph Fasel, Kevin Hammond, Ralf Hinze, Paul Hudak, Thomas Johnsson, Mark Jones, John Launchbury, Erik Meijer, John Peterson, Alastair Reid, Colin Runciman, and Philip Wadler. Report on the Programming Language Haskell 98, a Non-strict, Purely Functional Language. Available from `http://haskell.org`, February 1999.

[Jon] Simon Peyton Jones. Explicit quantification in Haskell. http://research.microsoft.com/users/simonpj/Haskell/quantification.html.

[JRtYHG+99] Mark P Jones, Alastair Reid, the Yale Haskell Group, the Oregon Graduate Institute of Science, and Technology. The Hugs 98 user manual. Available from `http://haskell.org/hugs`, 1994-1999.

[JW93] Simon Peyton Jones and Philip Wadler. Imperative functional programming. In *20'th Symposium on Principles of Programming Languages*, Charlotte, North Carolina, January 1993. ACM Press.

[KKR+86] D. Kranz, R. Kelsey, J. Rees, P. Hudak, J. Philbin, and N. Adams. Orbit: An optimizing compiler for Scheme. In *Proceedings of the ACM SIGPLAN Symposium on Compiler Construction*, SIGPLAN Notices, pages 219–233, 1986.

[KL95] D. King and J. Launchbury. Structuring depth-first search algorithms in Haskell. In *Conf. Record 22nd Symp. on Principles of Programming Languages*, pages 344–354, San Francisco, California, 1995. ACM.

[Lev99] P.B. Levy. Call-by-push-value: a subsuming paradigm (extended abstract). In *Typed Lambda-Calculi and Applications*, volume 1581 of *LNCS*. Springer, 1999.

[LH96] S. Liang and P. Hudak. Modular denotational semantics for compiler construction. In *ESOP'96*, volume 1058 of *LNCS*. Springer, 1996.

[LHJ95] S. Liang, P. Hudak, and M. Jones. Monad transformers and modular interpreters. In *POPL'95*. ACM Press, 1995.

[LJ94] J. Launchbury and S. Peyton Jones. Lazy functional state threads. In *Proceedings of the 1994 SIGPLAN Conference on Programming Language Design and Implementation (PLDI)*, June 1994.

[LS97] J. Launchbury and A. Sabry. Monadic state: Axiomatisation and type safety. In *Proceedings of the International Conference on Functional Programming*. ACM, 1997.

[LW91] X. Leroy and P. Weis. Polymorphic type inference and assignment. In *Proceedings of the 1991 ACM Conference on Principles of Programming Languages*. ACM, 1991.

[Man76] E. Manes. *Algebraic Theories.* Graduate Texts in Mathematics. Springer, 1976.

[Man98] E Manes. Implementing collection classes with monads. *Mathematical Structures in Computer Science*, 8(3), 1998.

[Min98] Y. Minamide. A functional represention of data structures with a hole. In *Proceedings of the 25rd Symposium on Principles of Programming Languages*, 1998.

[MMH96] Y. Minamide, G. Morrisett, and R. Harper. Typed closure conversion. In *Conference Record of the 23rd Annual ACM SIGPLAN-SIGACT Symposium on Principles of Programming Languages, St. Petersburg, Florida.* ACM, January 1996.

[Mog89] E. Moggi. Computational lambda-calculus and monads. In *Proceedings of the 4th Annual Symposium on Logic in Computer Science, Asiloomar, CA*, pages 14–23, 1989.

[Mog91] E. Moggi. Notions of computation and monads. *Information and Computation*, 93(1), 1991.

[Mog95] E. Moggi. A semantics for evaluation logic. *Fundamenta Informaticae*, 22(1/2), 1995.

[Mog97] E. Moggi. Metalanguages and applications. In *Semantics and Logics of Computation*, volume 14 of *Publications of the Newton Institute.* Cambridge University Press, 1997.

[Mos90] P. Mosses. Denotational semantics. In J. van Leeuwen, editor, *Handbook of Theoretical Computer Science*, chapter 11. MIT press, 1990.

[Mos92] P. Mosses. *Action Semantics.* Number 26 in Cambridge Tracts in Theoretical Computer Science. Cambridge University Press, 1992.

[MP99] E. Moggi and F. Palumbo. Monadic encapsulation of effects: A revised approach. In *Proceedings of the Third International Workshop on Higher-Order Operational Techniques in Semantics*, Electronic Notes in Theoretical Computer Science. Elsevier, September 1999.

[MS01] E. Moggi and A. Sabry. Monadic encapsulation of effects: A revised approach (extended version). *Journal of Functional Programming*, 11(6), November 2001.

[MT91] I. Mason and C. Talcott. Equivalences in functional languages with effects. *Journal of Functional Programming*, 1:287–327, 1991.

[MWCG99] G. Morrisett, D. Walker, K. Crary, and N. Glew. From System F to typed assembly language. *ACM Transactions on Programming Languages and Systems*, 21(3):528–569, May 1999.

[NN94] F. Nielson and H. R. Nielson. Higher-order concurrent programs with finite communication topology. In *Proceedings of the 21st Annual ACM SIGPLAN-SIGACT Symposium on Principles of Programming Languages*, 1994.

[NNA97] H. R. Nielson, F. Nielson, and T. Amtoft. Polymorphic subtyping for effect analysis: The static semantics. In Mads Dam, editor, *Proceedings of the Fifth LOMAPS Workshop*, number 1192 in Lecture Notes in Computer Science. Springer-Verlag, 1997.

[NNH99] F. Nielson, H. R. Nielson, and C. Hankin. *Principles of Program Analysis.* Springer-Verlag, 1999.

[PD01] F. Pfenning and R. Davies. A judgemental reconstruction of modal logic. *Mathematical Structures in Computer Science*, 11(4), August 2001.

[Pey96] S. L. Peyton Jones. Compiling Haskell by program transformation: A report from the trenches. In *Proceedings of the European Symposium on Programming, Linköping, Sweden*, number 1058 in Lecture Notes in Computer Science. Springer-Verlag, January 1996.

[Pey01] Simon Peyton Jones. Tackling the awkward squad: monadic input/output, concurrency, exceptions, and foreign-language calls in Haskell. In R Steinbrueggen, editor, *Engineering theories of software construction, Marktoberdorf Summer School 2000*, NATO ASI Series. IOS Press, 2001.

[Pit97] A. M. Pitts. Operationally-based theories of program equivalence. In P. Dybjer and A. M. Pitts, editors, *Semantics and Logics of Computation*, Publications of the Newton Institute, pages 241–298. Cambridge University Press, 1997.

[Pit00a] A. M. Pitts. Operational semantics and program equivalence. revised version of lectures at the international summer school on applied semantics. This volume, September 2000.

[Pit00b] A.M. Pitts. Categorical logic. In S. Abramsky, D.M. Gabbay, and T.S.E. Maibaum, editors, *Handbook of Logic in Computer Science*, volume 5. Oxford University Press, 2000.

[Plo75] G. D. Plotkin. Call-by-name, call-by-value and the lambda calculus. *Theoretical Computer Science*, pages 125–159, 1975.

[Plo77] G. D. Plotkin. LCF considered as a programming language. *Theoretical Computer Science*, 5:223–255, 1977.

[PLST98a] S. L. Peyton Jones, J. Launchbury, M. B. Shields, and A. P. Tolmach. Bridging the gulf: A common intermediate language for ML and Haskell. In *Proceedings of POPL'98*. ACM, 1998.

[PLST98b] S. L. Peyton Jones, J. Launchbury, M. B. Shields, and A. P. Tolmach. Corrigendum to bridging the gulf: A common intermediate language for ML and Haskell. Available from http://www.cse.ogi.edu/ mbs/pub, 1998.

[Sco93] D.S. Scott. A type-theoretic alternative to CUCH, ISWIM, OWHY. *Theoretical Computer Science*, 121, 1993.

[SF93] A. Sabry and M. Felleisen. Reasoning about programs in continuation-passing style. *Lisp and Symbolic Computation*, 6(3/4):289–360, 1993.

[Sha97] Z. Shao. An overview of the FLINT/ML compiler. In *Proceedings of the 1997 ACM Workshop on Types in Compilation, Amsterdam*. ACM, June 1997.

[SS99] M. Semmelroth and A. Sabry. Monadic encapsulation in ML. In *Proceedings of the International Conference on Functional Programming*. ACM, 1999.

[Sta94] I. D. B. Stark. *Names and Higher Order Functions*. PhD thesis, Computer Laboratory, University of Cambridge, 1994.

[Sta96] I. Stark. Categorical models for local names. *Lisp and Symbolic Computation*, 9(1), February 1996.

[SW97] Amr Sabry and Philip Wadler. A reflection on call-by-value. *ACM Transactions on Programming Languages and Systems*, 19(6):916–941, November 1997.

[TJ94] J.-P. Talpin and P. Jouvelot. The type and effect discipline. *Information and Computation*, 111(2), June 1994. Revised from LICS 1992.

[Tof87] M. Tofte. *Operational Semantics and Polymorphic Type Inference*. PhD thesis, Department of Computer Science, University of Edinburgh, 1987.

[Tol98] A. Tolmach. Optimizing ML using a hierarchy of monadic types. In *Proceedings of the Workshop on Types in Compilation, Kyoto*, March 1998.

[TT97] M. Tofte and J.-P. Talpin. Region-based memory management. *Information and Computation*, 132(2), February 1997.

[Wad92a] P. Wadler. Comprehending monads. *Mathematical Structures in Computer Science*, 2, 1992.

[Wad92b] P. Wadler. The essence of functional programming. In *Proceedings 1992 Symposium on Principles of Programming Languages*, pages 1–14, Albuquerque, New Mexico, 1992.

[Wad95] P. Wadler. Monads for functional programming. In J. Jeuring and E. Meijer, editors, *Advanced Functional Programming*, number 925 in LNCS, pages 24–52. Springer Verlag, May 1995.

[Wad98] P. Wadler. The marriage of effects and monads. In *International Conference on Functional Programming.* ACM Press, 1998.

[WF94] A. K. Wright and M. Felleisen. A syntactic approach to type soundness. *Information and Computation*, 115(1):38–94, 15 November 1994.

[Wri95] A. Wright. Simple imperative polymorphism. *LISP and Symbolic Computation*, 8:343–355, 1995.

[WT99] P. Wadler and P. Thiemann. The marriage of effects and monads. To appear in ACM Transactions on Computational Logic, 1999.

# Abstract Machines, Control, and Sequents

Pierre-Louis Curien

CNRS – Université Paris VII, France

**Abstract.** We describe simple call-by-value and call-by-name abstract machines, expressed with the help of Felleisen's evaluation contexts, for a toy functional language. Then we add a simple control operator and extend the abstract machines accordingly. We give some examples of their use. Then, restricting our attention to the sole core (typed) $\lambda$-calculus fragment augmented with the control operator, we give a logical status to the machinery. Evaluation contexts are typed "on the left", as they are directed towards their hole, or their input, in contrast to terms, whose type is that of their output. A machine state consists of a term and a context, and corresponds logically to a cut between a formula on the left (context) and a formula on the right (term). Evaluation, viewed logically, is cut-elimination: this is the essence of the so-called Curry-Howard isomorphism. Control operators correspond to classical reasoning principles, as was first observed by Griffin.

## Table of Contents



## 1 A Simple Call-by-Value Evaluator

Consider the following simple functional programming language, whose data types are (nonnegative) integers and lists.

$$\begin{array}{l} M ::= x \mid n \mid \mathtt{T} \mid \mathtt{F} \mid nil \mid ?l \mid \mathtt{h}(l) \mid \mathtt{t}(l) \mid M \; op \; M \\ \qquad\; M \mapsto [M\,,\, M] \mid MM \mid \lambda x.M \mid Yf.M\,. \end{array}$$

Here $op$ denotes collectively operations such as addition, multiplication, consing (notation $a{\cdot}l$), or equality test of two integers (notation $(m = n)$); $nil$ is the empty list, $?l$ tests whether $l$ is empty (i.e., $?nil$ evaluates to $\mathtt{T}$ and $?(a \cdot l)$ evaluates to $\mathtt{F}$), $\mathtt{h}(l)$ and $\mathtt{t}(l)$ allow us to retrieve the first element of a list and the rest of the list, respectively; $M \mapsto [N\,,\, P]$ passes control to $N$ ($P$) if $M$ evaluates to $\mathtt{T}$ ($\mathtt{F}$); $MN$ is function application; $\lambda x.M$ is function abstraction; finally, $Yf.M$ denotes a recursive function definition. The more familiar construct (`let rec` $fx =$ `in rec` $N$) is defined from it as $(\lambda f.N)(Yf.(\lambda x.M))$.

G. Barthe et al. (Eds.): Applied Semantics, LNCS 2395, pp. 123–136, 2002.

Next, we specify an interpreter for the mini-language. The interpreter progressively transforms the whole program to be evaluated, and at each step maintains a pointer to a subprogram, in which the current work is done. Felleisen and Friedman [4] have formalized this using evaluation contexts, which are programs with a (single) hole that in our case are built recursively as follows:

$$\begin{array}{l} E ::= [\,] \mid E[[\,]M] \mid E[M[\,]] \\ \quad \mid E[[\,]\, op\, M] \mid E[M\, op\, [\,]] \mid E[\mathtt{h}([\,])] \mid E[\mathtt{t}([\,])] \mid E[?[\,]] \mid E[[\,] \mapsto [M\,,\, M]] \end{array}$$

The notation should be read as follows: $E$ is a term with a hole, and $E[[\,]M]$ is the context whose single occurrence of $[\,]$ has been replaced by $[\,]M$: thus, in $E[[\,]M]$, the external square brackets refer to the hole of $E$, while the internal ones refer to the hole of $E[[\,]M]$. For example, $[\,][[\,]M] = [\,]M$, and if this context is called $E$, then $E[[\,]N] = ([\,]N)M$. (The above syntax is in fact too liberal, see exercise 2

The abstract machine rewrites expressions $E[N]$, that we write $\langle\, N \mid E \,\rangle$ to stress the interaction (and the symmetry) of terms and contexts. We call such pairs $\langle\, N \mid E \,\rangle$ *states*, or *commands*. The initial command is of the form $\langle\, M \mid [\,] \,\rangle$. The rules (in call-by-value) are as follows:

$$\begin{array}{lll}
\langle\, MN \mid E \,\rangle & \to \langle\, M \mid E[[\,]N] \,\rangle & \\
\langle\, \lambda x.P \mid E[[\,]N] \,\rangle & \to \langle\, N \mid E[(\lambda x.P)[\,]] \,\rangle & \\
\langle\, V \mid E[(\lambda x.P)[\,]] \,\rangle & \to \langle\, P[x \leftarrow V] \mid E \,\rangle & \\
 & & \\
\langle\, Yf.M \mid E \,\rangle & \to \langle\, M[f \leftarrow Yf.M] \mid E \,\rangle & \\
 & & \\
\langle\, M\, op\, N \mid E \,\rangle & \to \langle\, M \mid E[[\,]\, op\, N] \,\rangle & \\
\langle\, m \mid E[[\,]\, op\, N] \,\rangle & \to \langle\, N \mid E[m\, op\, [\,]] \,\rangle & \\
\langle\, n \mid E[m\, op\, [\,]] \,\rangle & \to \langle\, m\, op\, n \mid E \,\rangle & \text{(operation performed)} \\
 & & \\
\langle\, \star(M) \mid E \,\rangle & \to \langle\, M \mid E[\star([\,])] \,\rangle & (\star = ?, \mathtt{h}, \mathtt{t}) \\
\langle\, nil \mid E[?([\,])] \,\rangle & \to \langle\, \mathtt{T} \mid E \,\rangle & \\
\langle\, a \cdot l \mid E[?([\,])] \,\rangle & \to \langle\, \mathtt{F} \mid E \,\rangle & \\
\langle\, a \cdot l \mid E[\mathtt{h}([\,])] \,\rangle & \to \langle\, a \mid E \,\rangle & \\
\langle\, a \cdot l \mid E[\mathtt{t}([\,])] \,\rangle & \to \langle\, l \mid E \,\rangle & \\
\langle\, M \mapsto [N\,,\, P] \mid E \,\rangle & \to \langle\, M \mid E[[\,] \mapsto [N\,,\, P]] \,\rangle & \\
\langle\, \mathtt{T} \mid E[[\,] \mapsto [N\,,\, P]] \,\rangle & \to \langle\, N \mid E \,\rangle & \\
\langle\, \mathtt{F} \mid E[[\,] \mapsto [N\,,\, P]] \,\rangle & \to \langle\, P \mid E \,\rangle &
\end{array}$$

The first rule amounts to moving the pointer to the left son: thus the evaluator is also left-to-right. The second rule expresses call-by-value: the argument $N$ of the function $\lambda x.P$ must be evaluated before being passed to $\lambda x.P$. In the third rule, $V$ denotes a value – that is, a function $\lambda x.P$, an integer $n$, or a list $l$ which is either $nil$ or $a \cdot l'$ where $a$ is a value and $l'$ is a value (later, we shall add more values) –, that can be passed, i.e., that can be substituted for the formal parameter $x$. The fourth rule allows us to unfold the definition of a recursive function. The last rules specify the (left-to-right) evaluation of the binary operations, and the precise meaning of the unary operations $?, \mathtt{h}$ and $\mathtt{t}$, as well as of $M \mapsto [N\,,\, P]$.

Notice that the above system of rules is deterministic, as at each step at most one rule may apply.

*Exercise 1.* Characterize the final states, i.e. the states which cannot be rewritten.

*Exercise 2.* Design a more restricted syntax for call-by-value evalaution contexts (hint: replace $E[M[\,]]$ by $E[V[\,]]$, etc...).

*Remark 1.* The call-by-name abstract machine is slightly simpler. The context formation rule $E[M[\,]]$ disappears, as well as the third rule above. The only rule which changes is the rule for $\lambda x.P$, which is now

$$\langle\, \lambda x.P \mid E[[\,]N]\,\rangle \;\rightarrow\; \langle\, P[x \leftarrow N] \mid E\,\rangle$$

i.e., $N$ is passed unevaluated to the function $\lambda x.P$. All the other rules stay the same.

*Remark 2.* In call-by-name, the left-to-right order of evaluation given by the rule $\langle\, MN \mid E\,\rangle \rightarrow \langle\, M \mid E[[\,]N]\,\rangle$ is forced upon us: we should not attempt to evaluate $N$ first. But in call-by-value, both $M$ and $N$ have to be evaluated, and the right-to-left order of evaluation becomes an equally valid strategy. In this variant, the first three rules are modified as follows:

$$\begin{array}{ll}\langle\, MN \mid E\,\rangle & \rightarrow \langle\, N \mid E[M[\,]]\,\rangle \\ \langle\, V \mid E[M[\,]]\,\rangle & \rightarrow \langle\, M \mid E[[\,]V]\,\rangle \\ \langle\, \lambda x.P \mid E[[\,]V]\,\rangle & \rightarrow \langle\, P[x \leftarrow V] \mid E\,\rangle \end{array}$$

Below, we give a few examples of execution. We first consider a program that takes a natural number $x$ as input and returns the product of all prime numbers not greater than $x$. One supposes given an operation $\pi?$ that tests its argument for primality, i.e., $\pi?(n)$ evaluates to $\mathtt{T}$ if $n$ is prime, and to $\mathtt{F}$ if $n$ is not prime. The program is a mere transcription of the specification of the problem:

$$\pi_\times \;=\; Yf.\lambda n.\,(n=1) \mapsto [\,1\,,\,(\pi?(n) \mapsto [\,n \times f(n-1)\,,\,f(n-1)\,])\,]$$

Here is the execution of this program with input 4:

$$\begin{array}{rl}\langle\, \pi_\times(4) \mid [\,]\,\rangle \rightarrow & \langle\, (4=1) \mapsto [\,1\,,\,(\pi?(4) \mapsto [\,4 \times \pi_\times(4-1)\,,\,\pi_\times(4-1)\,])\,] \mid [\,]\,\rangle \\ \rightarrow & \langle\, \pi?(4) \mapsto [\,4 \times \pi_\times(4-1)\,,\,\pi_\times(4-1)\,] \mid [\,]\,\rangle \\ \rightarrow & \langle\, \pi_\times(4-1) \mid [\,]\,\rangle \\ \rightarrow^\star & \langle\, \pi_\times(3) \mid [\,]\,\rangle \\ \rightarrow^\star & \langle\, 3 \times \pi_\times(3-1) \mid [\,]\,\rangle \\ \rightarrow^\star & \langle\, \pi_\times(2) \mid 3 \times [\,]\,\rangle \\ \rightarrow^\star & \langle\, \pi_\times(1) \mid 3 \times (2 \times [\,])\,\rangle \\ \rightarrow^\star & \langle\, 1 \mid 3 \times (2 \times [\,])\,\rangle \\ \rightarrow & \langle\, 2 \mid 3 \times [\,]\,\rangle \\ \rightarrow & \langle\, 6 \mid [\,]\,\rangle \end{array}$$

Our next example is the function that takes an integer $n$ and a list $l$ as arguments and returns $l$ if $n$ does not occur in $l$, or else the list of the elements of $l$ found after the last occurrence of $n$ in $l$. For example, when applied to 3 and $1 \cdot (3 \cdot (2 \cdot (3 \cdot (4 \cdot nil))))$, the function returns the list $4 \cdot nil$. The following program for this function makes use of an auxiliary list, that can be called an accumulator:

$$F \;=\; \lambda n.\lambda l.(Y f.\lambda l_1.\lambda l_2.\, ?l_1 \mapsto [\, l_2 \,,\, \mathtt{h}(l_1) = n \mapsto [\, f\, \mathtt{t}(l_1)\, \mathtt{t}(l_1) \,,\, f\, \mathtt{t}(l_1)\, l_2 \,]\,])\, l\, l$$

We present the execution of $F$ with inputs 3 and $1 \cdot (3 \cdot (2 \cdot (3 \cdot (4 \cdot nil))))$. We set:

$$\epsilon = Y f.\lambda l_1.\lambda l_2.?l_1 \mapsto [\, l_2 \,,\, \mathtt{h}(l_1) = 3 \mapsto [\, f\, \mathtt{t}(l_1)\, \mathtt{t}(l_1) \,,\, f\, \mathtt{t}(l_1)\, l_2 \,]\,]$$

We have:

$$\begin{array}{l}
\langle\, (F\, 3)\, (1 \cdot (3 \cdot (2 \cdot (3 \cdot (4 \cdot nil))))) \mid [\,]\,\rangle \\
\quad \to^\star \langle\, \epsilon\, (1 \cdot (3 \cdot (2 \cdot (3 \cdot (4 \cdot nil)))))\, (1 \cdot (3 \cdot (2 \cdot (3 \cdot (4 \cdot nil))))) \mid [\,]\,\rangle \\
\quad \to^\star \langle\, \epsilon\, (3 \cdot (2 \cdot (3 \cdot (4 \cdot nil))))\, (1 \cdot (3 \cdot (2 \cdot (3 \cdot (4 \cdot nil))))) \mid [\,]\,\rangle \\
\quad \to^\star \langle\, \epsilon\, (2 \cdot (3 \cdot (4 \cdot nil)))\, (2 \cdot (3 \cdot (4 \cdot nil))) \mid [\,]\,\rangle \\
\quad \to^\star \langle\, \epsilon\, (3 \cdot (4 \cdot nil))\, (2 \cdot (3 \cdot (4 \cdot nil))) \mid [\,]\,\rangle \\
\quad \to^\star \langle\, \epsilon\, (4 \cdot nil)\, (4 \cdot nil) \mid [\,]\,\rangle \\
\quad \to^\star \langle\, \epsilon\, nil\, (4 \cdot nil) \mid [\,]\,\rangle \\
\quad \to^\star \langle\, 4 \cdot nil \mid [\,]\,\rangle
\end{array}$$

Note that the execution is tail-recursive: the evaluation context remains empty. This is good for efficiency, but, conceptually, handling the auxiliary list is somewhat "low level".

*Remark 3.* Similarly, our first example can be programmed in a tail recursive way, as

$$Y f.\lambda(n, c).\, n = 1 \mapsto [\, c(1) \,,\, f\, (n - 1, \pi?(n) \mapsto [\, \lambda p.c(n \times p) \,,\, c\,])\,]$$

Here, $c$ is an additional parameter, called the *continuation*, which is a function from natural numbers to natural numbers. This is the *continuation passing style* (CPS). We encourage the reader to run this new program on input $(4, \lambda x.x)$, and to check that the execution is indeed tail-recursive.

## 2 Control Operators

We now add two primitive operations, in addition to those of the previous section:

$$M ::= \cdots \mid \kappa k.M \mid \star_E$$

The second construction allows us to consider, or *reflect* evaluation contexts as values (in addition to those considered above). It is then possible to bind a variable $k$ to a (reflected) context, and thus to memorize and reuse contexts. This is what the first construction $\kappa k.M$ does. It exists in programming languages like SCHEME, where it is written as (`call/cc` (`lambda` ($k$) $M$))). We add two rules to the abstract machine:

$$\begin{array}{ll} \langle\, \kappa k.M \mid E \,\rangle & \rightarrow \langle\, M[k \leftarrow \star_E] \mid E \,\rangle \\ \langle\, \star_{E_1} \mid E_2[[\,]N] \,\rangle & \rightarrow \langle\, N \mid E_1 \,\rangle \end{array}$$

The second rule throws away the current evaluation context $E_2$ and replaces it with a context $E_1$ captured earlier using the first rule. Note that $N$ is unevaluated (compare with the rule for $\lambda$ which swaps function and argument).

We illustrate the new primitives through some examples. First, consider the function that takes as input a list of integers and returns the product of the elements of the list. A naïve program for this function is:

$$\Pi_1 \;=\; Yf.\lambda l.\, ?l \mapsto [\,1\,,\, \mathtt{h}(l) \times f(\mathtt{t}(l))\,]$$

The execution of this program applied to the list [2,4,3,0,7,8,1,13] involves the full multiplication $2\times(4\times(3\times(0\times(7\times(8\times(1\times 13))))))$, which is not particularly perspicuous, given that 0 is absorbing for $\times$. A better try is:

$$\Pi_2 \;=\; Yf.\lambda l.\, ?l \mapsto [\,1\,,\, (\mathtt{h}(l)=0) \mapsto [\,0\,,\, \mathtt{h}(l) \times f(\mathtt{t}(l))\,]\,]$$

Here, the final multiplications by 7, 8, 1, and 13 have been avoided. But the execution still involves the successive multiplications of 0 by 3, 4, and 2. The following program, which makes use of the control operator $\kappa$, takes care of this:

$$\Pi_3 \;=\; Yf.\lambda l.\kappa k.\, ?l \mapsto [\,1\,,\, (\mathtt{h}(l)=0) \mapsto [\,k\,0\,,\, \mathtt{h}(l) \times f(\mathtt{t}(l))\,]\,]$$

It is easily checked that the execution on the same input [2,4,3,0,7,8,1,13] now returns 0 without performing any multiplication.

*Remark 4.* We can reach the same goal (of avoiding any multiplication by 0) using CPS (cf. Remark 3). The CPS tail-recursive version of $\Pi_2$ is:

$$\Pi_4 \;=\; Yf.\lambda l\lambda k''.\, ?l \mapsto [\,k''\,1\,,\, (\mathtt{h}(l)=0) \mapsto [\,k''\,0\,,\, f(\mathtt{t}(l))(\lambda x.k''(\mathtt{h}(l) \times x))\,]\,]$$

It should be clear how tail-recursiveness is achieved: the additional parameter $k''$ is an abstraction of the stack/context. If $k''$ currently stands for $E$, then $\lambda x.k''(\mathtt{h}(l)\times x)$ stands for $E[\mathtt{h}(l)\times[]]$. The program $\Pi_4$ does no better than $\Pi_2$, as it does not avoid to multiply by zero back along the recursive calls. But the following program $\Pi_5$ avoids this:

$$\Pi_5 \;=\; Yf.\lambda l\lambda k'.\, ?l \mapsto [\,k'\,1\,,\, (\mathtt{h}(l)=0) \mapsto [\,0\,,\, f(\mathtt{t}(l))(\lambda x.k'(\mathtt{h}(l) \times x))\,]\,]$$

We owe to Olivier Danvy the following rationale for a smooth transformation from $\Pi_4$ to $\Pi_5$. The program $\Pi_4$ takes a list and a function from `nat` (the type of natural numbers) to `nat` as arguments and returns a natural number. Now, natural numbers split into 0 and (strictly) positive numbers, let us write this as

$\mathtt{nat} = 0 + \mathtt{nat}^\star$. There is a well-known isomorphism between $(A+B) \to C$ and $(A \to C) \times (B \to C)$. By all this, we can rewrite $\Pi_4$ as

$$\Pi_5' \;=\; Yf.\lambda l \lambda k \lambda k'.\, ?l \mapsto [\, k'\,1\,,\, (\mathtt{h}(l) = 0) \mapsto [\, k\,0\,,\, f(\mathtt{t}(l))(\lambda x. k'(\mathtt{h}(l) \times x))\,]\,]$$

(with $k : 0 \to \mathtt{nat}$ and $k' : \mathtt{nat}^\star \to \mathtt{nat}$, where $(k, k')$ represents $k'' : \mathtt{nat} \to \mathtt{nat}$). We then remark that $k$ is not modified along the recursive calls, hence there is no need to carry it around. Assuming that $k$ was initially mapping 0 to 0, we obtain $\Pi_5$. So, the CPS program $\Pi_5$ gets rid of $k$ and retains only $k'$. Quite dually, we could say that the program $\Pi_3$ gets rid of $k'$ (which has the normal control behaviour) and retains only $k$ (whose exceptional control behaviour is handled via the $\kappa$ abstraction).

A similar use of $\kappa$ abstraction leads to a more "natural" way of programming the function underlying program $F$ of section 1:

$$\begin{aligned} F' = \lambda n.\lambda l.\kappa k.(Yf.\lambda l_1.\, ?l_1 \mapsto [\, \mathit{nil}\,,\, (\mathtt{h}(l_1) = n) \\ \mapsto [\, k(f(\mathtt{t}(l_1)))\,,\, \mathtt{h}(l_1) \cdot f(\mathtt{t}(l_1))\,]\,])\, l \end{aligned}$$

We set $\epsilon' \;=\; Yf.\lambda l_1.?l_1 \mapsto [\, \mathit{nil}\,,\, (\mathtt{h}(l_1) = 3) \mapsto [\, \star_{[]}(f(\mathtt{t}(l_1)))\,,\, \mathtt{h}(l_1) \cdot f(\mathtt{t}(l_1))\,]\,])\, l$, and we abbreviate $4 \cdot \mathit{nil}$ as 4. Here is the execution of $F'$ on the same input as above:

$$\begin{aligned} \langle\, F'(3)(1 \cdot (3 \cdot (2 \cdot (3 \cdot 4)))) \mid [\,]\,\rangle &\to^\star \langle\, \epsilon'\,(1 \cdot (3 \cdot (2 \cdot (3 \cdot 4)))) \mid [\,]\,\rangle \\ &\to^\star \langle\, \epsilon'\,(3 \cdot (2 \cdot (3 \cdot 4))) \mid 1 \cdot [\,]\,\rangle \\ &\to^\star \langle\, \star_{[]}(\epsilon'(2 \cdot (3 \cdot 4))) \mid 1 \cdot [\,]\,\rangle \\ &\to^\star \langle\, \epsilon'(2 \cdot (3 \cdot 4)) \mid [\,]\,\rangle \\ &\to^\star \langle\, 4 \mid [\,]\,\rangle \end{aligned}$$

*Exercise 3.* [6] Consider a slight variation of the toy language, in which lists are replaced by binary trees whose leaves are labeled by integers. This is achieved by reusing the operations $\cdot$, $\mathtt{h}$, $\mathtt{t}$, ?, and by removing *nil*: a tree $t$ is either a number or is of the form $t_1 \cdot t_2$; the meaning of $\mathtt{h}$ and $\mathtt{t}$ are "left immediate subtree" and "right immediate subtree", respectively; $?t$ is now a function from trees to a sum type whose values are $\mathtt{F}$ or integers, it returns $\mathtt{F}$ if $t = t_1 \cdot t_2$ and $n$ if $t = n$. The weight of a tree is computed as follows: $w(n) = n$, and $w(t_1 \cdot t_2) = w(t_1) + w(t_2) + 1$. A tree is called well-balanced if $t = n$, or if $t = t_1 \cdot t_2$ and $w(t_1) = w(t_2)$ and $t_1, t_2$ are well-balanced. Write three programs for testing if a tree is well-balanced. All programs should traverse the input tree only once. The second program should save on weight computations, the third one should also save on successive returns of the negative information that the tree is not well-balanced. (Hint: for the first two programs, make use of the above sum type.)

So far, we have only demonstrated how the $\kappa$ construct allows us to escape from an evaluation context. The following exercises propose examples where continuations are passed around in more sophisticated ways. Exercises 5 and 6 are variations on the theme of *coroutines.* Coroutines are two programs that are designed to be executed in an interleaving mode, each with its own stack of execution. Each program works in turn for a while until it calls the other. Call them $P$ and $Q$, respectively. When $P$ calls $Q$, the execution of $P$ is suspended until $P$ is called back by $Q$, and then $P$ resumes its execution in the context it had reached at the time of its last suspension.

*Exercise 4.* [11, 12] The following programs illustrate the reuse of evaluation contexts or continuations. What do they compute?

$$(\kappa k.\lambda x.k(\lambda y.x+y))\,6$$
$$\kappa l.(\lambda(a,h).h(a+7))(\tau(3,l))\;(\tau=\lambda(n,p).\kappa k.(\lambda m.k(m,p))(\kappa q.k(n,q)))$$

*Exercise 5.* [12] Consider the following programs:

$$\pi=\lambda a.\phi(\lambda x.\,write\,a;x)\quad\text{and}\quad\phi=\lambda f.\lambda h.\kappa k.h(fk)$$

where the new command *write* applies to a character string, say, *'toto*, and is executed as follows:

$$\langle\,write\,'toto;M\mid E\,\rangle\to\langle\,M\mid E\,\rangle\,!toto$$

by which we mean that the execution prints or displays *toto* and then proceeds. Describe the execution of $((\pi\,'ping)(\pi\,'pong))((\pi\,'ping)(\pi\,'pong))$. Does it terminate? Which successive strings are printed? (Hint: setting $P=(\pi\,'ping)(\pi\,'pong)$, $V_a=\lambda h.\kappa k.h((\lambda x..\,write\,a;x)k)$ , and $E=[\,]P$, here are some intermediate commands: $\langle\,PP\mid[\,]\,\rangle\to^{\star}\langle\,V_{'pong}\mid E[V_{'ping}[\,]]\,\rangle\to^{\star}\langle\,\star_E\mid$ $\mid E[[]((\lambda x..\,write\,'pong;x)\star_E)]\,\rangle\to\langle\,(\lambda x..\,write\,'pong;x)\star_E\mid E\,\rangle$.)

*Exercise 6.* [8] The toy language is extended with references and commands:

$$M:=\cdots\mid\texttt{let}\;x\;=\;\texttt{ref}\;V\;\texttt{in}\;M\mid\,!x\mid x:=V\mid M;M$$

(a variable defined wih the `ref` construct is called a reference). The machine states have now a store component (a list $S$ of term/reference associations), notation $\langle\,M\mid E\,\rangle_S$. The evaluation rules are as follows:

$$\begin{array}{l}
\langle\,M\mid E\,\rangle_S\to\langle\,M'\mid E'\,\rangle_S\qquad\text{(for all the above rules }\langle\,M\mid E\,\rangle\to\langle\,M'\mid E'\,\rangle\text{)}\\
\langle\,\texttt{let}\;x\;=\;\texttt{ref}\;V\;\texttt{in}\;N\mid E\,\rangle_S\to\langle\,N\mid E\,\rangle_{S[x\leftarrow V]}\qquad(x\text{ not defined in }S)\\
\langle\,!x\mid E\,\rangle_S\to\langle\,S(x)\mid E\,\rangle_S\\
\langle\,x:=V\mid E\,\rangle_S\to\langle\,\mid E\,\rangle_{S[x\leftarrow V]}\\
\langle\,M;N\mid E\,\rangle_S\to\langle\,M\mid E[[];N]\,\rangle_S\\
\langle\,\mid E[[];N]\,\rangle_S\to\langle\,N\mid E[]\,\rangle_S
\end{array}$$

Write two programs `get_first` and `get_next` that work on a binary tree (cf. exercise 2) and whose effects are the following: (`get_first` $t$) returns the value of the first leave (in left-to-right traversal) of $t$, and then evaluations of `get_next` return the values of the leaves of $t$ in turn, suspending the traversal between two `get_next` calls. (Hints: define two references and two auxiliary functions `start` and `suspend` that use $\kappa$ abstraction to store the stack in the respective references: `start` is invoked by `get_first` and `get_next` at the beginning (storing the context of the caller who communicates with the tree via these `get` functions), while `suspend` is invoked when the value of a leaf is returned (storing the context that will guide the search for the next leave).)

## 3 Curry-Howard

In this section, we assign typing judgements to terms $M$, contexts $E$, and commands $c = \langle M \mid E \rangle$. We restrict our attention to $\lambda$-calculus, extended with the above control operations. We also switch to call-by-name, for simplicity (cf. remark 1). In this section, we adopt the alternative notation $M \cdot E$ for $E[[\,]M]$ ("push $M$ on top of $E$ considered as a stack"). The resulting syntax is as follows:

$$\begin{array}{l} M ::= x \mid MN \mid \lambda x.M \mid \kappa k.M \mid \star_E \\ E ::= [\,] \mid M \cdot E \end{array}$$

The abstract machine for this restricted language, called $\lambda\kappa$-calculus [2], boils down to the following four rules:

$$\begin{array}{rcl} \langle MN \mid E \rangle & \to & \langle M \mid N \cdot E \rangle \\ \langle \lambda x.M \mid N \cdot E \rangle & \to & \langle M[x \leftarrow N] \mid E \rangle \\ \langle \kappa k.M \mid E \rangle & \to & \langle M[k \leftarrow \star_E] \mid E \rangle \\ \langle \star_{E_1} \mid M \cdot E_2 \rangle & \to & \langle M \mid E_1 \rangle \end{array}$$

Note that the first rule suggests that the application and the push operation are redundant. As a matter of fact, we shall remove the application from the syntax in a short while.

As is well-known, terms are usually typed through judgements $\Gamma \vdash M : A$, where $\Gamma$ is a sequence $x_1 : A_1, \ldots, x_n : A_n$ of variable declarations, and where $M$ can also be interpreted as a notation for a proof tree of the sequent $A_1, \ldots, A_n \vdash A$. Let us recall the notion of sequent, due do the logician Gentzen (for an introduction to sequent calculus, we refer to, say, [5]). A sequent is given by two lists of formulas, separated by the sign $\vdash$ (which one reads as "proves"):

$$A_1, \ldots, A_m \vdash B_1, \ldots, B_n$$

The intended meaning is: "if $A_1$ and ... and $A_m$, then $B_1$ or ... or $B_n$". The $A_i$'s are the assumptions, and the $B_i$'s are the conclusions. Notice that there may be several formulas on the right of $\vdash$. In sequent calculus, limiting the right hand side list to consist of exactly one formula corresponds to intuitionistic logic. As a hint as to why multiple conclusions have to do with classical reasoning, let us examine how we can derive the excluded middle $\neg A \vee A$ (the typical non-constructive tautology of classical logic) from the very innocuous axiom $A \vdash A$. First, we denote false as $\perp$, and we encode $\neg A$ as $A \to \perp$ (a simple truth-table check will convince the reader that the encoding is sensible). Then, we use the multi-conclusion facility to do a right *weakening*. Weakening means adding more assumptions, or more conclusions (or both), its validity corresponds to something like "one who can do the most can do less". And finally, one gets the excluded middle by right implication introduction (see below):

$$\dfrac{\dfrac{A \vdash A}{A \vdash \bot, A}}{\vdash \neg A, A}$$

As we shall see, control operators lead us outside of intuitionistic logic, so we shall adopt unconstrained sequents rightaway.

Sequents may be combined to form proofs, through a few deduction rules. Here are two of them:

$$\dfrac{\Gamma \,|\, A \vdash \Delta \quad \Gamma \vdash A \,|\, \Delta}{\Gamma \vdash \Delta} \qquad \dfrac{\Gamma, A \vdash B \,|\, \Delta}{\Gamma \vdash A \to B \,|\, \Delta}$$

The first rule is the cut rule, that can be interpreted backwards as "proving a theorem with the help of a lemma": in order to prove $\Delta$ from assumptions $\Gamma$, we first prove an auxiliary property $A$, and then prove $\Delta$, taking the auxiliary property as an additional assumption. The second rule is the one corresponding to $\lambda$-abstraction. Read $A \to B$ as a function type. Then a program of type $B$ depending on a parameter $x$ of type $A$ can be viewed as a function of type $A \to B$. (The role of the vertical bars in the sequents is explained in the next paragraph.)

More generally, the Curry-Howard isomorphism says that there is a one-to-one correspondence between proofs and programs. We shall extend here the correspondence to let also contexts and commands fit into it. We shall consider three sorts of sequents, corresponding to terms, contexts, and commands, respectively. They are given in the following table:

$$\left.\begin{array}{r} \ldots, A_i, \ldots \vdash B \,|\, \ldots, B_j, \ldots \\ \ldots, A_i, \ldots \,|\, A \vdash \ldots, B_j, \ldots \\ \ldots, A_i, \ldots \vdash \ldots, B_j, \ldots \end{array}\right\} \longleftrightarrow \left\{\begin{array}{l} \ldots, x_i : A_i, \ldots \vdash M : B \,|\, \ldots, \alpha_j : B_j, \ldots \\ \ldots, x_i : A_i, \ldots \,|\, E : A \vdash \ldots, \alpha_j : B_j, \ldots \\ c : (\ldots, x_i : A_i, \ldots \vdash \ldots, \alpha_j : B_j, \ldots) \end{array}\right.$$

In the sequents corresponding to terms, one conclusion is singled out as the current one, and is placed between the $\vdash$ and the vertical bar. Symmetrically, in the sequents corresponding to contexts, one assumption is singled out as the current one, and is placed between the vertical bar and the $\vdash$. Note that a context is typed *on the left*: what we type is the hole of the context, that standds for the input it is wainting for. A command is obtained by cutting a conclusion that is singled out against an assumption that is singled out, and the resulting sequent has no conclusion nor assumption singled out.

We now turn to the typing rules. But we first note that the evaluation rule for $\kappa$ is rather complicated: it involves copying the context, and transforming one of the copies into a term. It turns out that both $\kappa k.M$ and $\star_E$ can be encoded simply using a more primitive operation: Parigot's $\mu$-abstraction [9], which has the following behaviour:

$$\langle\, \mu\alpha.c \,|\, E \,\rangle \;\rightarrow\; c[\alpha \leftarrow E]$$

Moreover, the application can also be encoded with the help of the $\mu$ abstraction. The encodings are as follows (cf. also [3]):

$$\begin{array}{ll} \star_E = \lambda x.\mu\alpha.\langle\, x \,|\, E \,\rangle & (\alpha \text{ not free in } E) \\ \kappa k.M = \mu\beta.\langle\, \lambda k.M \,|\, \star_\beta \cdot \beta \,\rangle & (\beta \text{ not free in } M) \\ MN = \mu\alpha.\langle\, M \,|\, N \cdot \alpha \,\rangle & (\alpha \text{ not free in } M, N) \end{array}$$

*Exercise 7.* Check that the encodings simulate the evaluation rules for $\star_E$, $\kappa k.M$, and $MN$.

*Exercise 8.* Prove the following equality:

$$(\kappa k.M)N = \kappa k'.M[k \leftarrow \lambda m.k'(mN)]N\,.$$

More precisely, prove that the encodings of the two sides of this equality have a common reduct.

Note that the $\mu$ operation involves an explicit continuation variable (that may be bound to a context), while $\kappa$ does not (it involves an ordinary variable that may be bound to a term representing a context). We shall give typing rules for the following more primitive syntax, called $\overline{\lambda}\mu$-calculus [1]:

$$\begin{array}{l} M ::= x \mid \lambda x.M \mid \mu\alpha.c \\ E ::= \alpha \mid M \cdot E \\ c ::= \langle\, M \,|\, E \,\rangle \end{array}$$

with the following reduction rules:

$$\begin{array}{l} \langle\, \lambda x.M \,|\, N \cdot E \,\rangle \;\rightarrow\; \langle\, M[x \leftarrow N] \,|\, E \,\rangle \\ \langle\, \mu\alpha.c \,|\, E \,\rangle \;\rightarrow\; c[\alpha \leftarrow E] \end{array}$$

Note that in addition to the ordinary variables $(x, y, k, k', \ldots)$, there are now first-class continuation variables $\alpha$, in place of the (constant) empty context (the top-level continuation). We can now revisit the three sorts of typing judgements. All judgements allow us to type an expression containing free ordinary variables $\ldots, x_i : A_i, \ldots$ and continuation variables $\ldots, \alpha_j : B_j, \ldots$. The judgements $\ldots, x_i : A_i, \ldots \vdash M : B \,|\, \ldots, \alpha_j : B_j, \ldots$, $\ldots, x_i : A_i, \ldots \,|\, E : A \vdash \ldots, \alpha_j : B_j, \ldots$, and $c : (\ldots, x_i : A_i, \ldots \vdash \ldots, \alpha_j : B_j, \ldots)$ say that $M$ delivers a value of type $B$, that $E$ accepts a term of type $A$, and that $c$ is a well-formed command, respectively. The typing rules are as follows:

$$\frac{}{\Gamma \,|\, \alpha : A \vdash \alpha : A, \Delta} \qquad \frac{}{\Gamma, x : A \vdash x : A \,|\, \Delta}$$

$$\frac{\Gamma \vdash M : A \,|\, \Delta \qquad \Gamma \,|\, E : B \vdash \Delta}{\Gamma \,|\, (M \cdot E) : A \to B \vdash \Delta} \qquad \frac{\Gamma, x : A \vdash M : B \,|\, \Delta}{\Gamma \vdash \lambda x.M : A \to B \,|\, \Delta}$$

$$\frac{c : (\Gamma \vdash \beta : B\,,\ \Delta)}{\Gamma \vdash \mu\beta.c : B \,|\, \Delta} \qquad \frac{\Gamma \vdash M : A \,|\, \Delta \qquad \Gamma \,|\, E : A \vdash \Delta}{\langle\, M \mid E \,\rangle : (\Gamma \vdash \Delta)}$$

Let us read the rules logically. The first two rules are variations of the axiom: a sequent holds if one formula $A$ is both among the assumptions and the conclusions. The following two rules correspond to the introduction of the implication on the right and on the left: this is typical of sequent calculus style. Let us spell out the left introduction rule, returning to the old notation $E[[\,]M]$. This expression has two bracketings $[\;]$: call them the inner hole and the outer hole. If $M$ has type $A$, then the inner hole (which is the hole of $E[[\,]M]$) must have a type $A \to B$, hence $[\,]M$ has type $B$, and the outer hole (which is the hole of $E$) must have type $B$. Thus, sequent calculus' left introduction is interpreted as "push $M$ on stacke $E$". The rule for $\mu$ can be viewed as a sort of coercion: the sequent to be proved does not vary, but the status of the sequent changes from having no assumption or conclusion singled out to having one conclusion singled out, which is a key step in writing a cut. The final rule is the cut rule: $\langle\, M \mid E \,\rangle$ is well-formed when $M$ has the type that $E$ expects.

*Remark 5 (for the logically oriented reader).* In this typing system, we have left contraction (e.g., from $\Gamma, A, A \vdash \Delta$ deduce $\Gamma, A \vdash \Delta$) and weakening implicit: weakening is built-in in the two axioms for variables and continuation variables (when $\Gamma$ or $\Delta$ or both are non-empty), and contraction is implicit in the "push" rule $(M \cdot E)$ and in the cut rule $(\langle\, M \mid E \,\rangle)$.

Beyond the particularity of having a conclusion or an assumption singled out, the above rules are nothing but the rules of sequent calculus, and the above encoding of application is the essence of the translation from natural deduction style to sequent calculus style [5].

*Exercise 9.* Give a technical contents to the second part of remark 5, by defining a translation from $\lambda$-calculus to $\overline{\lambda}\mu$-calculus that preserves reductions. (Note that in the $\overline{\lambda}\mu$-calculus, the evaluation rules are not deterministic anymore: since commands are recursively part of the syntax, it makes sense to reduce not only at the root.)

Now we can derive the typing rules for $\kappa k.M$ and $\star_E$:

$$\dfrac{\dfrac{\dfrac{\Gamma, x : A \vdash x : A \mid \Delta \qquad \Gamma \mid E : A \vdash \Delta}{\langle x \mid E \rangle : (\Gamma, x : A \vdash \Delta)}}{\Gamma, x : A \vdash \mu\alpha.\langle x \mid E \rangle : R \mid \Delta}}{\Gamma \vdash \star_E : A \to R \mid \Delta}$$

Here, $R$ is an arbitrary (fixed) formula/type of *results*. Note that we have slightly departed from the typing rules as written above, in order to make the essential use of weakening explicit: $\alpha : R$ is a fresh variable.

$$\dfrac{\dfrac{\dfrac{\dfrac{\Gamma \mid \beta : A \vdash \Delta, \beta : A}{\Gamma \vdash \star_\beta : A \to R \mid \Delta, \beta : A} \quad \Gamma \mid \beta : A \vdash \Delta, \beta : A}{\Gamma \mid \star_\beta \cdot \beta : (A \to R) \to A \vdash \Delta, \beta : A} \qquad \dfrac{\Gamma, k : \boldsymbol{A \to R} \vdash M : \boldsymbol{A} \mid \Delta}{\Gamma \vdash \lambda k.M : (A \to R) \to A \mid \Delta}}{\langle \lambda k.M \mid \star_\beta \cdot \beta \rangle : (\Gamma \vdash \Delta, \beta : A)}}{\Gamma \vdash \kappa k.M : \boldsymbol{A} \mid \Delta}$$

The last derivation reveals one of these unexpected mysteries that makes research so fascinating. The control feature encoded by $\kappa$ abstraction corresponds under the Curry-Howard correspondence to reasoning by contradiction, as first discovered in [7]. Indeed, think of $R$ as $\bot$. Then $A \to R$ is $\neg A$, and

$$\dfrac{\Gamma, k : \boldsymbol{A \to R} \vdash M : \boldsymbol{A} \mid \Delta}{\Gamma \vdash \kappa k.M : \boldsymbol{A} \mid \Delta}$$

reads as: "if we can prove $A$ assuming $\neg A$, then we reach a contradiction, and hence $A$ is proved". The implication $((A \to R) \to A) \to A$ is known as Peirce's law. The reader will find related classical reasoning principles in the following exercise.

*Exercise 10.* We call the sequents $\neg\neg A \vdash A$ and $\bot \vdash A$ double negation elimination and $\bot$ elimination, respectively.

(1) Show that Peirce's law plus $\bot$ elimination imply double negation elimination (hint: apply the contravariance of implication, i.e., if $A'$ implies $A$, then $A \to B$ implies $A' \to B$).

(2) Show that double negation elimination implies $\bot$ elimination (hint: prove that $\bot$ implies $\neg\neg B$).

(3) Show that double negation elimination implies Peirce's law (hint: use (2)).

*Remark 6.* Double negation elimination (cf. exercise 10) corresponds to another control operator, Felleisen's $\mathcal{C}$, whose behaviour is the following:

$$\langle \mathcal{C}(M) \mid E \rangle \to \langle M \mid \star_E \cdot [\,] \rangle$$

Thus, $\mathcal{C}(\lambda k.M)$ is quite similar to $\kappa k.M$, except that the stack is not copied, but only captured. The $\lambda\mu$ counterpart of $\mathcal{C}(M)$ is given by $\mu\beta.\langle M \,\|\, \star_\beta \cdot \alpha \rangle$ where the variables $\beta$ and $\alpha$ are not free in $M$; $\alpha$ can be understood as a name for the toplevel continuation. The typing, as literally induced by the encoding, is as follows

$$\frac{\Gamma \vdash M : (A \to R) \to R \,|\, \Delta}{\Gamma \vdash \mathcal{C}(M) : A \,|\, \alpha : R, \Delta}$$

It looks a little odd, because $\alpha$ is a variable not mentioned in the $\mathcal{C}$ construction. One way out is to assimilate $R$ with $\bot$, which amounts to viewing $R$ as the (unique) type of *final* results. Then we can remove altogether $\alpha : \bot$ from the judgement (as "$\Delta$ or $\bot$" is the same as $\Delta$), and obtain:

$$\frac{\Gamma \vdash M : (A \to \bot) \to \bot \,|\, \Delta}{\Gamma \vdash \mathcal{C}(M) : A \,|\, \Delta}$$

i.e., "$\mathcal{C}$ is double negation elimination" [7].

## 4 Conclusion

We have shown some basic relations between continuations and control operators, abstract machines, and sequent caclulus. The connection with logic is lost when we admit recursion into the language (section 2). But the detour through logic is extremely useful, as it brings to light a deep symmetry between terms and contexts.

The $\overline{\lambda}\mu$ calculus can be extracted from the logical considerations and can then be considered as an untyped calculus *per se*. An extension of the $\overline{\lambda}\mu$-calculus that allows for a completely symmetric account of call-by-name and call-by-value is presented in [1].

## References


1. Curien, P.-L., and Herbelin, H., The duality of computation, Proc. International Conference on Functional Programming 2000, IEEE (2000).
2. Danos, V., and Krivine, J.-L., Disjunctive tautologies and synchronisation schemes, Proc. Computer Science Logic 2000.
3. de Groote, Ph., On the relation between the $\lambda\mu$-calculus and the syntactic theory of sequential control, in Proc. Logic Programming and Automated Reasoning '94, Lecture Notes in Computer Science 822, Springer (1994).
4. Felleisen, M., and Friedman, D., Control operators, the SECD machine, and the $\lambda$-calculus, in Formal Description of Programming Concepts III, 193-217, North Holland (1986).
5. Girard, J.-Y., Lafont, Y., and Taylor, P., Proofs and Types, Cambridge University Press (1989).
6. Greussay, P., Contribution à la définition interprétative et à l'implémentation des lambda-langages, Thèse d'Etat, Université Paris VII (1977).

7. Griffin, T., A formula-as-types notion of control, in Proc. Principles of Programming Languages 1990, IEEE (1990).
8. Gunter, C., Rémy, D., and Riecke, J., A generalization of exceptions and control in ML-like languages, in Proc. Functional Programming and Computer Architecture '95, ACM Press (1995).
9. Parigot, M. $\lambda\mu$-calculus: An algorithmic interpretation of classical natural deduction, Proc. of the International Conference on Logic Programming and Automated Reasoning, St. Petersburg, Lecture Notes in Computer Science 624 (1992).
10. Prawitz, D., Natural deduction, a proof-theoretical study, Almqvist & Wiskell (1965).
11. Reynolds, J., Theories of programming languages, Cambridge University Press (1998).
12. Thielecke, H., Categorical structure of continuation passing style, PhD Thesis, Univ. of Edinburgh (1997).

# Normalization and Partial Evaluation

Peter Dybjer[1] and Andrzej Filinski[2,*]

[1] Department of Computing Science
Chalmers University of Technology, Göteborg, Sweden
peterd@cs.chalmers.se
[2] Department of Computer Science
University of Copenhagen, Denmark
andrzej@diku.dk

**Abstract.** We give an introduction to normalization by evaluation and type-directed partial evaluation. We first present normalization by evaluation for a combinatory version of Gödel System T. Then we show normalization by evaluation for typed lambda calculus with $\beta$ and $\eta$ conversion. Finally, we introduce the notion of binding time, and explain the method of type-directed partial evaluation for a small PCF-style functional programming language. We give algorithms for both call-by-name and call-by-value versions of this language.

## Table of Contents



* Part of this work was carried out at BRICS (Basic Research in Computer Science, www.brics.dk), funded by the Danish National Research Foundation.

G. Barthe et al. (Eds.): Applied Semantics, LNCS 2395, pp. 137–192, 2002.

## 1 Introduction

*Normalization.* By "normalization" we mean the process known from proof theory and lambda calculus of simplifying proofs or terms in logical systems. Normalization is typically specified as a stepwise simplification process. Formally, one introduces a relation $\texttt{red}_1$ of step-wise reduction: $E \ \texttt{red}_1 \ E'$ means that $E$ reduces to $E'$ in one step, where $E$ and $E'$ are terms or proof trees.

A "normalization proof" is a proof that a term $E$ can be step-wise reduced to a normal form $E'$ where no further reductions are possible. One distinguishes between "weak" normalization, where one only requires that there exists a reduction to normal form, and "strong" normalization where all reduction sequences must terminate with a normal form.

*Partial Evaluation.* By "partial evaluation" we refer to the process known from computer science of simplifying a program where some of the inputs are known (or "static"). The simplified (or "residual") program is typically obtained by executing operations which only depend on known inputs. More precisely, given a program $\vdash P : \tau_s \times \tau_d \to \tau_r$ of two arguments, and a fixed static argument $s : \tau_s$, we wish to produce a *specialized* program $\vdash P_s : \tau_d \to \tau_r$ such that for all remaining "dynamic" arguments $d : \tau_d$, $\mathrm{eval}\big(P_s\, d\big) = \mathrm{eval}\big(P\,(s, d)\big)$. Hence, running the specialized program $P_s$ on an arbitrary dynamic argument is equivalent to running the original program on both the static and the dynamic ones. In general we may have several static and several dynamic arguments. Writing a partial evaluator is therefore like proving an $\mathrm{S}^m_n$-theorem for the programming language: given a program with $m + n$ inputs, $m$ of which are static (given in advance) and $n$ are dynamic, the partial evaluator constructs another program with $n$ inputs which computes the same function of these dynamic inputs as the original one does (with the static inputs fixed). Of course, the goal is not to construct *any* such program but an efficient one!

In a functional language, it is easy to come up with a specialized program $P_s$: just take $P_s = \lambda d.\, P\,(s, d)$. That is, we simply invoke the original program with a constant first argument. But this $P_s$ is likely to be suboptimal: the knowledge of $s$ may already allow us to perform some simplifications that are independent of $d$. For example, consider the power function:

$$\mathit{power}\,(n, x) \stackrel{\text{rec}}{=} \textbf{if } n = 0 \textbf{ then } 1 \textbf{ else } x \times \mathit{power}(n-1, x)$$

Suppose we want to compute the third power of several numbers. We can achieve this by using the trivially specialized program:

$$\mathsf{power}_3 = \lambda x.\,\mathsf{power}(3, x)$$

But using a few simple rules derived from the semantics of the language, we can safely transform $\mathsf{power}_3$ to the much more efficient

$$\mathsf{power}'_3 = \lambda x.x \times (x \times (x \times 1))$$

Using further arithmetic identities, we can easily eliminate the multiplication by 1. On the other hand, if only the argument $x$ were known, we could not simplify much: the specialized program would in general still need to contain a recursive definition and a conditional test in addition to the multiplication. (Note that, even when $x$ is 0 or 1, the function should diverge for negative values of $n$.)

*Partial Evaluation as Normalization.* Clearly partial evaluation and normalization are related processes. In partial evaluation, one tries to simplify the original program by executing those operations that only depend on the static inputs. Such a simplification is similar to what happens in normalization. In a functional language, in particular, we can view specialization as a general-purpose simplification of the trivially specialized program $\lambda d.\,P(s, d)$: contracting $\beta$-redexes and eliminating static operations as their inputs become known. For example, $\mathsf{power}_3$ is transformed into $\mathsf{power}'_3$ by normalizing $\mathsf{power}_3$ according to the reduction rules mentioned above.

In these lecture notes, we address the question of whether one can apply methods developed for theoretical purposes in proof theory and lambda calculus to achieve partial evaluation of programs. Specifically, we show how the relatively recent idea of *normalization by evaluation*, originally developed by proof-theorists, provides a new approach to the partial evaluation of functional programs, yielding *type-directed partial evaluation*.

*Evaluation.* By "evaluation" we mean the process of computing the output of a program when given all its inputs. In lambda calculus "evaluation" means normalization of a closed term, usually of base type.

It is important here to contrast (a) *normalization* and *partial evaluation* and (b) the *evaluation* of a complete program. In (a) there are still unknown (dynamic) inputs, whereas in (b) all the inputs are known.

*Normalization by Evaluation (NBE).* Normalization by evaluation is based on the idea that one can obtain a normal form by first interpreting the term in a suitable model, possibly a non-standard one, and then write a function "reify" which maps an object in this model to a normal form representing it. The normalization function is obtained by composing reify with the non-standard interpretation function $[\![-]\!]$:

$$\text{norm } E = \text{reify } [\![E]\!]$$

We want a term to be convertible (provably equal, in some formal system) to its normal form

$$\vdash E = \text{norm}\ E$$

and therefore we require that reify is a left inverse of $[\![-]\!]$. The other key property is that the interpretation function should map convertible terms to equal objects in the model

$$\text{if}\ \vdash E = E'\ \text{then}\ [\![E]\!] = [\![E']\!]$$

because then the normalization function maps convertible terms to syntactically equal terms

$$\text{if}\ \vdash E = E'\ \text{then norm}\ E = \text{norm}\ E'$$

It follows that the normalization function picks a representative from each equivalence class of convertible terms

$$\vdash E = E'\ \text{iff norm}\ E = \text{norm}\ E'$$

If the norm-function is computable, we can thus decide whether two terms are convertible by computing their normal forms and comparing them.

This approach bypasses the traditional notion of reduction formalized as a binary relation, and is therefore sometimes referred to as “reduction-free normalization”.

Normalization by evaluation was invented by Martin-Löf [ML75b]. In the original presentation it just appears as a special way of presenting an ordinary normalization proof. Instead of proving that every term has a normal form, one writes a function which returns the normal form, together with a proof that it actually is a normal form. This way of writing a normalization proof is particularly natural from a constructive point of view: to prove that there *exists* a normal form of an arbitrary term, means to actually be able to compute this normal form from the term.

Martin-Löf viewed this kind of normalization proof as a kind of normalization by intuitionistic model construction: he pointed out that equality (convertibility) in the object-language is modelled by “definitional equality” in the meta-language [ML75a]. Thus the method of normalization works because the simplification according to this definitional equality is carried out by the evaluator of the intuitionistic (!) meta-language: hence “normalization by evaluation”. If instead we work in a classical meta-language, then some extra work would be needed to implement the meta-language function in a programming language.

Martin-Löf's early work on NBE dealt with normalization for intuitionistic type theory [ML75b]. This version of type theory had a weak notion of reduction, where no reduction under the λ-sign was allowed. This kind of reduction is closely related to reduction of terms in combinatory logic, and we shall present this case in Section 2.

Normalization by evaluation for typed lambda calculus with $\beta$ and $\eta$ conversion was invented by Berger and Schwichtenberg [BS91]. Initially, they needed a normalization algorithm for their proof system MINLOG, and normalization by evaluation provided a simple solution. Berger then noticed that the NBE program could be extracted from a normalization proof using Tait's method [Ber93]. The method has been refined using categorical methods [AHS95,ČDS98], and also extended to System F [AHS96] and to include strong sums [ADHS01].

*Type-Directed Partial Evaluation (TDPE).* Type-directed partial evaluation stems from the study of "two-level $\eta$-expansions", a technique for making programs specialize better [DMP95]. This technique had already been put to use to write a "one-pass" CPS transformation [DF90] and it turned out to be one of the paths leading to the discovery of NBE [DD98].

Because of its utilization of a standard evaluator for a functional language to achieve normalization, TDPE at first also appeared as a radical departure from traditional, "syntax-directed" partial-evaluation techniques. It only gradually became apparent that the core of TDPE could in fact be seen as a generalization of earlier work on $\lambda$-MIX [Gom91], a prototypical partial evaluator for lambda-terms. In particular, the semantic justifications for the two algorithms are structurally very similar. In these notes we present such a semantic reconstruction of the TDPE algorithm as an instance of NBE, based on work by Filinski [Fil99b,Fil01].

*Meta-Languages for Normalization by Evaluation and Type-Directed Partial Evaluation.* NBE is based on the idea that normalization is achieved by interpreting an object-language term as a meta language term and then evaluating the latter. For this purpose one can use different meta languages, and we make use of several such in these notes.

In Section 2 we follow Martin-Löf [ML75b] and Coquand and Dybjer [CD93b] who used an intuitionistic meta-language, which is both a mathematical language and a programming language. Martin-Löf worked in an informal intuitionistic meta-language, where one uses that a function is a function in the intuitionistic sense, that is, an algorithm. Coquand and Dybjer [CD93b] implemented a formal construction similar to Martin-Löf's in the meta-language of Martin-Löf's intuitionistic type theory using the proof assistant ALF [MN93]. This NBE-algorithm makes essential use of the dependent type structure of that language. It is important to point out that the development in Section 2 can be directly understood as a mathematical description of a normalization function also from a classical, set-theoretic point of view. The reason is that Martin-Löf type theory has a direct set-theoretic semantics, where a function space is interpreted classically as the set of all functions in the set-theoretic sense. However, if read with classical eyes, nothing guarantees a priori that the constructed normalization function is computable, so some further reasoning to prove this property would be needed.

We also show how to program NBE-algorithms using a more standard functional language such as Standard ML. Without dependent types we collect all object-language terms into one type and all semantic objects needed for the interpretation into another. With dependent types we can index both the syntactic sets of terms $\mathrm{T}(\tau)$ and the semantic sets $[\![\tau]\!]$ by object-language types $\tau$.

Another possibility, not pursued here, is to use an untyped functional language as a meta-language. For example, Berger and Schwichtenberg's first implementation of NBE in the MINLOG system was written in Scheme.

In type-directed partial evaluation one wishes to write NBE-functions which do not necessarily terminate. Therefore one cannot use Martin-Löf type theory, since it only permits terminating functions. Nevertheless, the dependent type structure would be useful here too, and one might want to use a version of dependent type theory, such as the programming language Cayenne [Aug98], which allows non-terminating functions. We do not pursue this idea further here either.

*Notation.* NBE-algorithms use the interpretation of an object language in a meta-language. Since our object- and meta-languages are similar (combinatory and lambda calculi), we choose notations which clearly distinguish object- and meta-level but at the same time enhance their correspondence. To this end we use the following conventions.

- Alphabetic object-language constants are written in sans serif and meta-language constants in roman. For example, SUCC denotes the syntactic successor combinator in the language of Section 2 and succ denotes the semantic successor function in the meta-language.
- For symbolic constants, we put a dot above a meta-language symbol to get the corresponding object-language symbol. For example, $\dot{\rightarrow}$ is object-language function space whereas $\rightarrow$ is meta-language function space; $\dot{\lambda}$ is lambda abstraction in the object-language whereas $\lambda$ is lambda abstraction in the meta-language.
- We also use some special notations. For example, syntactic application is denoted by a dot $(F \cdot E)$ whereas semantic application is denoted by juxtaposition $(f\ e)$ as usual. Syntactic pairing uses round brackets $(E, E')$ whereas semantic pairing uses angular ones $\langle e, e' \rangle$.

*Plan.* The remainder of the chapter is organized as follows.

In Section 2 we introduce a combinatory version of Gödel System T, that is, typed combinatory logic with natural numbers and primitive recursive functionals. We show how to write an NBE-algorithm for this language by interpreting it in a non-standard "glueing" model. The algorithm is written in the dependently typed functional language of Martin-Löf type theory, and a correctness proof is given directly inside this language. Furthermore, we show how to modify the proof of the correctness of the NBE-algorithm to a proof of weak normalization and Church-Rosser for the usual notion of reduction for typed combinatory logic. Finally, we show how to implement this NBE-algorithm in Standard ML.

We begin Section 3 by discussing the suitability of the combinatory NBE-algorithm for the purpose of partial evaluation. We identify some of its shortcomings, such as the need for extensionality. Then we present the pure NBE algorithm for the typed lambda calculus with $\beta$ and $\eta$ conversion. This algorithm employs a non-standard interpretation of base types as term families.

In Section 4 we turn to type-directed partial evaluation, by which we mean the application of NBE to partial evaluation in more realistic programming languages. To this end we extend the pure typed lambda calculus with constants for arithmetic operations, conditionals, and fixed point computations yielding a version of the functional language PCF. In order to perform partial evaluation for this language we need to combine the pure NBE algorithm with the idea of off-line partial evaluation. We therefore introduce a notion of binding times, that allows us to separate occurrences of constant symbols in source programs into "static" and "dynamic" ones: the former are eliminated by the partial-evaluation process, while the latter remain in the residual code.

Finally, in Section 5, we show how the normalization technique is adapted from a semantic notion of equivalence based on $\beta\eta$-equality to one based on equality in the computational $\lambda$-calculus, which is the appropriate setting for call-by-value languages with computational effects.

*Background Reading.* The reader of these notes is assumed to have some prior knowledge about lambda calculus and combinators, partial evaluation, functional programming, and semantics of programming languages, and we therefore list some links and reference works which are suitable for background reading.

For sections 2 and 3 we assume a reader familiar with combinatory logic and lambda calculus, including their relationship, type systems, models, and the notions of reduction and conversion. We recommend the following reference books as background reading. Note of course, that only a few of the basic concepts described in these books will be needed.

- Lecture notes on functional programming by Paulson [Pau00].
- Several reference articles by Barendregt on lambda calculi and functional programming [Bar77,Bar90,Bar92].

We use both dependent type theory and Standard ML (SML) as implementation languages, and assume that the reader is familiar with these languages. Knowledge of other typed functional languages such as OCAML or Haskell is of course also useful.

- Tutorials on Standard ML can be found at `http://cm.bell-labs.com/cm/cs/what/smlnj/doc/literature.html#tutorials`.
- For background reading about OCAML, see the chapter on *Objective CAML* by Didier Remy in this volume.
- For background reading about Haskell, see references in the chapter on *Monads and Effects* by Nick Benton, John Hughes, and Eugenio Moggi in this volume.
- For background reading about dependent types, see the chapter on *Dependent Types in Programming* by Gilles Barthe and Thierry Coquand in this volume.

For Sections 4 and 5, we also assume some knowledge of domains and continuous functions, monads, and continuations.

- A good introduction to domains and their use in denotational semantics is Winskel's textbook [Win93].
- For background reading about monads, see the chapter on *Monads and Effects* by Nick Benton, John Hughes, and Eugenio Moggi in this volume.
- Three classic articles on continuations are by Reynolds [Rey72], Strachey and Wadsworth [SW74], and Plotkin [Plo75], although we will not make use of any specific results presented in those references.

Previous knowledge of some of the basic ideas from partial evaluation, including the notion of binding time is also useful. Some references:

- The standard textbook by Jones, Gomard, and Sestoft [JGS93].
- Tutorial notes on partial evaluation by Consel and Danvy [CD93a].
- Lecture notes on type-directed partial evaluation by Danvy [Dan98].

*Acknowledgments.* We gratefully acknowledge the contributions of our APPSEM 2000 co-lecturer Olivier Danvy to these notes, as well as the feedback and suggestions from the other lecturers and students at the meeting.

## 2 Normalization by Evaluation for Combinators

### 2.1 Combinatory System T

In this section we use a combinatory version of Gödel System T of primitive recursive functionals. In addition to the combinators K and S, this language has combinators ZERO for the number 0, SUCC for the successor function, and REC for primitive recursion.

The set of types is defined by

$$\vdash \mathsf{nat}\ \mathit{type} \qquad \frac{\vdash \tau_1\ \mathit{type} \quad \vdash \tau_2\ \mathit{type}}{\vdash \tau_1 \dashrightarrow \tau_2\ \mathit{type}}$$

The typing rules for terms are

$$\frac{\vdash_{\mathrm{CL}} E : \tau_1 \dashrightarrow \tau_2 \qquad \vdash_{\mathrm{CL}} E' : \tau_1}{\vdash_{\mathrm{CL}} E \cdot E' : \tau_2}$$

$$\begin{aligned}
\vdash_{\mathrm{CL}} \mathsf{K}_{\tau_1\tau_2} &: \tau_1 \dashrightarrow \tau_2 \dashrightarrow \tau_1 \\
\vdash_{\mathrm{CL}} \mathsf{S}_{\tau_1\tau_2\tau_3} &: (\tau_1 \dashrightarrow \tau_2 \dashrightarrow \tau_3) \dashrightarrow (\tau_1 \dashrightarrow \tau_2) \dashrightarrow \tau_1 \dashrightarrow \tau_3 \\
\vdash_{\mathrm{CL}} \mathsf{ZERO} &: \mathsf{nat} \\
\vdash_{\mathrm{CL}} \mathsf{SUCC} &: \mathsf{nat} \dashrightarrow \mathsf{nat} \\
\vdash_{\mathrm{CL}} \mathsf{REC}_\tau &: \tau \dashrightarrow (\mathsf{nat} \dashrightarrow \tau \dashrightarrow \tau) \dashrightarrow \mathsf{nat} \dashrightarrow \tau
\end{aligned}$$

We will often drop the subscripts of $\mathsf{K}, \mathsf{S}$, and $\mathsf{REC}$, when they are clear from the context. Furthermore, we let $\mathrm{T}(\tau) = \{E \mid \vdash_{\mathrm{CL}} E : \tau\}$.

We now introduce the relation conv of convertibility of combinatory terms. We usually write $\vdash_{\mathrm{CL}} E = E'$ for $E \,\mathtt{conv}\, E'$. It is the least equivalence relation closed under the following rules

$$\frac{\vdash_{\mathrm{CL}} F = F' \qquad \vdash_{\mathrm{CL}} E = E'}{\vdash_{\mathrm{CL}} F{\cdot}E = F'{\cdot}E'}$$

$$\vdash_{\mathrm{CL}} \mathsf{K}_{\tau_1\tau_2}{\cdot}E{\cdot}E' = E$$

$$\vdash_{\mathrm{CL}} \mathsf{S}_{\tau_1\tau_2\tau_3}{\cdot}G{\cdot}F{\cdot}E = G{\cdot}E{\cdot}(F{\cdot}E)$$

$$\vdash_{\mathrm{CL}} \mathsf{REC}_\tau{\cdot}E{\cdot}F{\cdot}\mathsf{ZERO} = E$$

$$\vdash_{\mathrm{CL}} \mathsf{REC}_\tau{\cdot}E{\cdot}F{\cdot}(\mathsf{SUCC}{\cdot}N) = F{\cdot}N{\cdot}(\mathsf{REC}_\tau{\cdot}E{\cdot}F{\cdot}N)$$

## 2.2 Standard Semantics

In the standard semantics we interpret a type $\tau$ as a set $[\![\tau]\!]$:

$$\begin{aligned} [\![\tau_1 \dashrightarrow \tau_2]\!] &= [\![\tau_1]\!] \to [\![\tau_2]\!] \\ [\![\mathsf{nat}]\!] &= \mathbb{N} \end{aligned}$$

where $\mathbb{N}$ is the set of natural numbers in the meta-language.

The interpretation $[\![E]\!] \in [\![\tau]\!]$ of an object $E \in \mathrm{T}(\tau)$ is defined by induction on $E$:

$$\begin{aligned} [\![\mathsf{K}_{\tau_1\tau_2}]\!] &= \lambda x^{[\![\tau_1]\!]}.\, \lambda y^{[\![\tau_2]\!]}.\, x \\ [\![\mathsf{S}_{\tau_1\tau_2\tau_3}]\!] &= \lambda g^{[\![\tau_1]\!]}.\, \lambda f^{[\![\tau_2]\!]}.\, \lambda x^{[\![\tau_3]\!]}.\, g\ x\ (f\ x) \\ [\![F{\cdot}E]\!] &= [\![F]\!]\ [\![E]\!] \\ [\![\mathsf{ZERO}]\!] &= 0 \\ [\![\mathsf{SUCC}]\!] &= \mathrm{succ} \\ [\![\mathsf{REC}_\tau]\!] &= \mathrm{rec}_{[\![\tau]\!]} \end{aligned}$$

where $\mathrm{succ} \in \mathbb{N} \to \mathbb{N}$ is the meta-language successor function

$$\mathrm{succ}\ n = n + 1$$

and $\mathrm{rec}_C \in C \to (\mathbb{N} \to C \to C) \to \mathbb{N} \to C$ is the meta-language primitive recursion operator defined by

$$\begin{aligned} \mathrm{rec}_C\ e\ f\ 0 &= e \\ \mathrm{rec}_C\ e\ f\ (\mathrm{succ}\ n) &= f\ n\ (\mathrm{rec}_C\ e\ f\ n) \end{aligned}$$

**Theorem 1.** *If* $\vdash_{\mathrm{CL}} E = E'$ *then* $[\![E]\!] = [\![E']\!]$.

**Proof.** By induction on the proof that $\vdash_{\mathrm{CL}} E = E'$.

### 2.3 Normalization Algorithm

The interpretation function into the standard model is not injective and hence cannot be inverted. For example, both $\mathsf{S}\cdot\mathsf{K}\cdot\mathsf{K}$ and $\mathsf{S}\cdot\mathsf{K}\cdot(\mathsf{S}\cdot\mathsf{K}\cdot\mathsf{K})$ denote identity functions. They are however not convertible, since they are distinct normal forms. (This follows from the normalization theorem below.)

We can construct a non-standard interpretation where the functions are interpreted as pairs of syntactic and semantic functions:

$$\begin{aligned} [\![\mathsf{nat}]\!]^{\mathrm{Gl}} &= \mathbb{N} \\ [\![\tau_1 \dashrightarrow \tau_2]\!]^{\mathrm{Gl}} &= \mathrm{T}(\tau_1 \dashrightarrow \tau_2) \times ([\![\tau_1]\!]^{\mathrm{Gl}} \to [\![\tau_2]\!]^{\mathrm{Gl}}) \end{aligned}$$

We say that the model is constructed by "glueing" a syntactic and a semantic component, hence the notation $[\![-]\!]^{\mathrm{Gl}}$. (The glueing technique is also used in some approaches to partial evaluation [Asa02,Ruf93,SK01].)

Now we can write a function $\mathrm{reify}_\tau \in [\![\tau]\!]^{\mathrm{Gl}} \to \mathrm{T}(\tau)$ defined by

$$\begin{aligned} \mathrm{reify}_{\mathsf{nat}}\ 0 &= \mathsf{ZERO} \\ \mathrm{reify}_{\mathsf{nat}}\ (\mathrm{succ}\ n) &= \mathsf{SUCC}\cdot(\mathrm{reify}_{\mathsf{nat}}\ n) \\ \mathrm{reify}_{\tau_1 \dashrightarrow \tau_2}\ \langle F, f\rangle &= F \end{aligned}$$

and which inverts the interpretation function $[\![-]\!]^{\mathrm{Gl}}_\tau \in \mathrm{T}(\tau) \to [\![\tau]\!]^{\mathrm{Gl}}$:

$$\begin{aligned} [\![\mathsf{K}]\!]^{\mathrm{Gl}} &= \langle \mathsf{K}, \lambda p.\, \langle \mathsf{K}\cdot(\mathrm{reify}\ p), \lambda q.\, p\rangle\rangle \\ [\![\mathsf{S}]\!]^{\mathrm{Gl}} &= \langle \mathsf{S}, \lambda p.\, \langle \mathsf{S}\cdot(\mathrm{reify}\ p), \lambda q.\, \langle \mathsf{S}\cdot(\mathrm{reify}\ p)\cdot(\mathrm{reify}\ q), \\ &\qquad\qquad \lambda r.\, \mathrm{appsem}\ (\mathrm{appsem}\ p\ r)(\mathrm{appsem}\ q\ r)\rangle\rangle\rangle \\ [\![F\cdot E]\!]^{\mathrm{Gl}} &= \mathrm{appsem}\ [\![F]\!]^{\mathrm{Gl}}\ [\![E]\!]^{\mathrm{Gl}} \\ [\![\mathsf{ZERO}]\!]^{\mathrm{Gl}} &= 0 \\ [\![\mathsf{SUCC}]\!]^{\mathrm{Gl}} &= \langle \mathsf{SUCC}, \mathrm{succ}\rangle \\ [\![\mathsf{REC}]\!]^{\mathrm{Gl}} &= \langle \mathsf{REC}, \lambda p.\, \langle \mathsf{REC}\cdot(\mathrm{reify}\ p), \lambda q.\, \langle \mathsf{REC}\cdot(\mathrm{reify}\ p)\cdot(\mathrm{reify}\ q), \\ &\qquad\qquad \mathrm{rec}\ p\ (\lambda n r.\, \mathrm{appsem}\ (\mathrm{appsem}\ q\ n)\ r)\rangle\rangle\rangle \end{aligned}$$

We have here omitted type labels in lambda abstractions, and used the following application operator in the model:

$$\mathrm{appsem}\ \langle F, f\rangle\ q = f\ q$$

It follows that the conversion rules are satisfied in this model, for example

$$[\![\mathsf{K}\cdot E\cdot E']\!]^{\mathrm{Gl}} = [\![E]\!]^{\mathrm{Gl}}$$

**Theorem 2.** *If* $\vdash_{\mathrm{CL}} E = E'$ *then* $[\![E]\!]^{\mathrm{Gl}} = [\![E']\!]^{\mathrm{Gl}}$.

The normal form function can now be defined by

$$\mathrm{norm}\ E = \mathrm{reify}\ [\![E]\!]^{\mathrm{Gl}}$$

**Corollary 1.** *If* $\vdash_{\mathrm{CL}} E = E'$ *then* norm $E$ = norm $E'$.

**Theorem 3.** $\vdash_{\mathrm{CL}} E = \text{norm } E$, *that is,* reify *is a left inverse of* $[\![-]\!]^{\mathrm{Gl}}$.

**Proof.** We use *initial algebra semantics* to structure our proof. A model of Gödel System T is a typed combinatory algebra extended with operations for interpreting ZERO, SUCC, and REC, such that the two equations for primitive recursion are satisfied. The syntactic algebra $\mathrm{T}(\tau)/\mathtt{conv}$ of terms under convertibility is an initial model. The glueing model here is another model. The interpretation function $[\![-]\!]^{\mathrm{Gl}}_{\tau} \in \mathrm{T}(\tau)/\mathtt{conv} \to [\![\tau]\!]^{\mathrm{Gl}}$ is the unique homomorphism from the initial model: if we could prove that $\text{reify}_{\tau} \in [\![\tau]\!]^{\mathrm{Gl}} \to \mathrm{T}(\tau)/\mathtt{conv}$ also is a homomorphism, then it would follow that $\text{norm}_{\tau} \in \mathrm{T}(\tau)/\mathtt{conv} \to \mathrm{T}(\tau)/\mathtt{conv}$, the composition of $[\![\ ]\!]^{\mathrm{Gl}}_{\tau}$ and $\text{reify}_{\tau}$, is also a homomorphism. Hence it must be equal to the identity homomorphism, and hence $\vdash_{\mathrm{CL}} E = \text{norm } E$.

But reify does not preserve application. However, we can construct a submodel of the non-standard model, such that the restriction of $\text{reify}_{\tau}$ to this submodel is a homomorphism. We call this the *glued* submodel; this construction is closely related to the glueing construction in category theory, see Lafont [Laf88, Appendix A].

In the submodel we require that a value $p \in [\![\tau]\!]^{\mathrm{Gl}}$ satisfies the property $\mathrm{Gl}_{\tau}\ p$ defined by induction on the type $\tau$:

- $\mathrm{Gl}_{\mathsf{nat}}\ n$ holds for all $n \in \mathbb{N}$.
- $\mathrm{Gl}_{\tau_1 \to \tau_2}\ q$ holds *iff* for all $p \in [\![\tau_1]\!]^{\mathrm{Gl}}$ if $\mathrm{Gl}_{\tau_1}\ p$ then $\mathrm{Gl}_{\tau_2}(\text{appsem } q\ p)$ and $\vdash_{\mathrm{CL}} (\text{reify } q) \cdot (\text{reify } p) = \text{reify } (\text{appsem } q\ p)$

Notice that this construction can be made from any model, and not only the term model. In this way we can define the normalization function abstractly over any initial algebra for our combinatory system T.

**Lemma 1.** *The glued values* $\{p \in [\![\tau_1]\!]^{\mathrm{Gl}} \mid \mathrm{Gl}_{\tau_1} p\}$ *form a model of Gödel System T.*

**Proof.** We show the case of K, and leave the other cases to the reader.

*Case* K. We wish to prove

$$\mathrm{Gl}_{\tau_1 \to \tau_2 \to \tau_1}\ \langle \mathsf{K}, \lambda p.\ \langle \mathsf{K} \cdot (\text{reify } p), \lambda q.\ p \rangle \rangle$$

But this property follows immediately by unfolding the definition of $\mathrm{Gl}_{\tau_1 \to \tau_2 \to \tau_1}$ and using

$$\vdash_{\mathrm{CL}} \mathsf{K} \cdot (\text{reify } p) \cdot (\text{reify } q) = \text{reify } p$$

**Lemma 2.** reify *is a homomorphism from the algebra of glued values to the term algebra.*

The definition of glued value is such that reify commutes with syntactic application. The other cases are immediate from the definition.

It now follows that norm is an identity homomorphism as explained above.

**Corollary 2.** $\vdash_{\mathrm{CL}} E = E'$ *iff* norm $E =$ norm $E'$.

**Proof.** If norm $E =$ norm $E'$ then $\vdash_{\mathrm{CL}} E = E'$, by theorem 4. The reverse implication is theorem 3.

## 2.4 Weak Normalization and Church-Rosser

We end this section by relating the "reduction-free" approach and the standard, reduction-based approach to normalization. We thus need to introduce the binary relation `red` of reduction (in zero or more steps) for our combinatory version of Gödel System T. This relation is inductively generated by exactly the same rules as convertibility, except that the rule of symmetry is omitted.

We now prove *weak* normalization by modifying the glueing model and replacing $\vdash_{\mathrm{CL}} - = -$ in the definition of Gl by `red`:

- $\mathrm{Gl}_{\mathsf{nat}}\ n$ holds for all $n \in \mathbb{N}$.
- $\mathrm{Gl}_{\tau_1 \dashrightarrow \tau_2}\ q$ holds *iff* for all $p \in [\![\tau_1]\!]^{\mathrm{Gl}}$ if $\mathrm{Gl}_{\tau_1}\ p$ then $\mathrm{Gl}_{\tau_2}(\mathrm{appsem}\ q\ p)$ and $(\mathrm{reify}\ q)\cdot(\mathrm{reify}\ p)$ `red` $(\mathrm{reify}\ (\mathrm{appsem}\ q\ p))$

**Theorem 4.** *Weak normalization:* $E$ `red` norm $E$ *and* norm $E$ *is irreducible.*

**Proof.** The proof of $\vdash_{\mathrm{CL}} E =$ norm $E$ is easily modified to a proof that $E$ `red` norm $E$.

It remains to prove that norm $E$ is a normal form (an irreducible term). A normal natural number is built up by SUCC and ZERO. Normal function terms are combinators standing alone or applied to insufficiently many normal arguments. If we let $\vdash^{\mathrm{nf}}_{\mathrm{CL}} E : \tau$ mean that $E$ is a normal form of type $\tau$ we can inductively define it by the following rules:

$$\vdash^{\mathrm{nf}}_{\mathrm{CL}} \mathsf{ZERO} : \mathsf{nat}$$

$$\vdash^{\mathrm{nf}}_{\mathrm{CL}} \mathsf{SUCC} : \mathsf{nat} \dashrightarrow \mathsf{nat} \qquad \frac{\vdash^{\mathrm{nf}}_{\mathrm{CL}} E : \mathsf{nat}}{\vdash^{\mathrm{nf}}_{\mathrm{CL}} \mathsf{SUCC}\cdot E : \mathsf{nat}}$$

$$\vdash^{\mathrm{nf}}_{\mathrm{CL}} \mathsf{K} : \tau_1 \dashrightarrow \tau_2 \dashrightarrow \tau_1 \qquad \frac{\vdash^{\mathrm{nf}}_{\mathrm{CL}} E : \tau_1}{\vdash^{\mathrm{nf}}_{\mathrm{CL}} \mathsf{K}\cdot E : \tau_2 \dashrightarrow \tau_1}$$

$$\vdash^{\mathrm{nf}}_{\mathrm{CL}} \mathsf{S} : (\tau_1 \dashrightarrow \tau_2 \dashrightarrow \tau_3) \dashrightarrow (\tau_1 \dashrightarrow \tau_2) \dashrightarrow \tau_1 \dashrightarrow \tau_3$$

$$\frac{\vdash^{\mathrm{nf}}_{\mathrm{CL}} G : \tau_1 \dashrightarrow \tau_2 \dashrightarrow \tau_3}{\vdash^{\mathrm{nf}}_{\mathrm{CL}} \mathsf{S}\cdot G : (\tau_1 \dashrightarrow \tau_2) \dashrightarrow \tau_1 \dashrightarrow \tau_3}$$

$$\frac{\vdash^{\mathrm{nf}}_{\mathrm{CL}} G : \tau_1 \dashrightarrow \tau_2 \dashrightarrow \tau_3 \qquad \vdash^{\mathrm{nf}}_{\mathrm{CL}} F : \tau_1 \dashrightarrow \tau_2}{\vdash^{\mathrm{nf}}_{\mathrm{CL}} \mathsf{S}\cdot G\cdot F : \tau_1 \dashrightarrow \tau_3}$$

$$\vdash^{\mathrm{nf}}_{\mathrm{CL}} \mathsf{REC} : \tau \dashrightarrow (\mathsf{nat} \dashrightarrow \tau \dashrightarrow \tau) \dashrightarrow \mathsf{nat} \dashrightarrow \tau$$

$$\frac{\vdash^{\mathrm{nf}}_{\mathrm{CL}} E : \tau}{\vdash^{\mathrm{nf}}_{\mathrm{CL}} \mathsf{REC}\cdot E : (\mathsf{nat} \dashrightarrow \tau \dashrightarrow \tau) \dashrightarrow \mathsf{nat} \dashrightarrow \tau}$$

$$\frac{\vdash^{\mathrm{nf}}_{\mathrm{CL}} E : \tau \qquad \vdash^{\mathrm{nf}}_{\mathrm{CL}} F : \mathsf{nat} \dot{\to} \tau \dot{\to} \tau}{\vdash^{\mathrm{nf}}_{\mathrm{CL}} \mathsf{REC}{\cdot}E{\cdot}F : \mathsf{nat} \dot{\to} \tau}$$

Let $\mathrm{T}^{\mathrm{nf}}(\tau) = \{E \mid \vdash^{\mathrm{nf}}_{\mathrm{CL}} E : \tau\}$ be the set of normal forms of type $\tau$. If we redefine

$$[\![\tau_1 \dot{\to} \tau_2]\!]^{\mathrm{Gl}} \;=\; \mathrm{T}^{\mathrm{nf}}(\tau_1 \dot{\to} \tau_2) \times ([\![\tau_1]\!]^{\mathrm{Gl}} \to [\![\tau_2]\!]^{\mathrm{Gl}})$$

then we can verify that reify and norm have the following types

$$\begin{aligned} \mathrm{reify}_\tau &\in [\![\tau]\!]^{\mathrm{Gl}} \to \mathrm{T}^{\mathrm{nf}}(\tau) \\ \mathrm{norm}_\tau &\in \mathrm{T}(\tau) \to \mathrm{T}^{\mathrm{nf}}(\tau) \end{aligned}$$

and hence $\mathrm{norm}_\tau E \in \mathrm{T}^{\mathrm{nf}}(\tau)$ for $E \in \mathrm{T}(\tau)$.

**Corollary 3.** *Church-Rosser: if $E$ `red` $E'$ and $E$ `red` $E''$ then there exists an $E'''$ such that $E'$ `red` $E'''$ and $E''$ `red` $E'''$.*

**Proof.** It follows that $\vdash_{\mathrm{CL}} E' = E''$ and hence by theorem 3 that norm $E' =$ norm $E''$. Let $E''' =$ norm $E' =$ norm $E''$ and hence $E'$ `red` $E'''$ and $E''$ `red` $E'''$.

### 2.5 The Normalization Algorithm in Standard ML

We now show a sample implementation of the above algorithm in a conventional functional language[1]. We begin by defining the datatype `syn` of untyped terms:

```
datatype syn = S
             | K
             | APP of syn * syn
             | ZERO
             | SUCC
             | REC
```

We don't have dependent types in Standard ML so we have to collect all terms into this one type `syn`.

We implement the semantic natural numbers using SML's built-in type `int` of integers. The primitive recursion combinator can thus be defined as follows:

```
(* primrec : 'a * (int -> 'a -> 'a) -> int -> 'a *)

fun primrec (z, s)
    = let fun walk 0
              = z
            | walk n
              = let val p = n-1
                in s p (walk p)
                end
      in walk
      end
```

[1] All the code in these notes is available electronically at `http://www.diku.dk/~andrzej/papers/NaPE-code.tar.gz`

In order to build the non-standard interpretation needed for the normalization function, we introduce the following reflexive datatype sem of semantic values:

```
datatype sem = FUN of syn * (sem -> sem)
             | NAT of int
```

The function reify is implemented by

```
(* reify : sem -> syn *)

fun reify (FUN (syn, _))
    = syn
  | reify (NAT n)
    = let fun reify_nat 0
                = ZERO
            | reify_nat n
                = APP (SUCC, reify_nat (n-1))
      in reify_nat n
      end
```

Before writing the non-standard interpretation function we need some auxiliary semantic functions:

```
(* appsem : sem * sem -> sem
   succsem : sem -> sem
   recsem : 'a * (int -> 'a -> 'a) -> sem -> 'a *)

exception NOT_A_FUN

fun appsem (FUN (_, f), arg)
    = f arg
  | appsem (NAT _, arg)
    = raise NOT_A_FUN

exception NOT_A_NAT

fun succsem (FUN _)
    = raise NOT_A_NAT
  | succsem (NAT n)
    = NAT (n+1)

fun recsem (z, s) (FUN _)
    = raise NOT_A_NAT
  | recsem (z, s) (NAT n)
    = primrec (z, s) n
```

And thus we can write the non-standard interpretation function:

```
(* eval : syn -> sem *)

fun eval S
    = FUN (S,
           fn f => let val Sf = APP (S, reify f)
                   in FUN (Sf,
```

```
                              fn g => let val Sfg = APP (Sf, reify g)
                                      in FUN (Sfg,
                                              fn x
                                              => appsem (appsem (f, x),
                                                         appsem (g, x)))
                                      end)
                  end)
  | eval K
    = FUN (K,
           fn x => let val Kx = APP (K, reify x)
                   in FUN (Kx,
                           fn _ => x)
                   end)
  | eval (APP (e0, e1))
    = appsem (eval e0, eval e1)
  | eval ZERO
    = NAT 0
  | eval SUCC
    = FUN (SUCC,
           succsem)
  | eval REC
    = FUN (REC,
           fn z
           => let val RECz = APP (REC, reify z)
              in FUN (RECz,
                      fn s
                      => let val RECzs = APP (RECz, reify s)
                         in FUN (RECzs,
                                 recsem (z,
                                         fn n
                                         => fn c
                                            => appsem (appsem (s,
                                                               NAT n),
                                                       c)))
                         end)
              end)
```

Finally, the normalization function is

```
(* norm : syn -> syn *)

fun norm e
    = reify (eval e)
```

How do we know that the SML program is a correct implementation of the dependently typed (or "mathematical") normalization function? This is a non-trivial problem, since we are working in a language where we can write non-terminating well-typed programs. So, unlike before we cannot use the direct mathematical normalization proof, but have to resort to the operational or denotational semantics of SML. Note in particular the potential semantic complications of using the reflexive type `sem`.

Nevertheless, we claim that for any two terms `E, E' : syn` which represent elements of $\mathrm{T}(\tau)$, `norm E` and `norm E'` both terminate with identical values of `syn` iff `E` and `E'` represent convertible terms.

### 2.6 Exercises

*Exercise 1.* Extend NBE and its implementation to some or all of the following combinators:

```
    I x = x                C f x y = f y x
B f g x = f (g x)            W f x = f x x
```

*Exercise 2.* Extend the datatype `sem` to have a double (that is, syntactic and semantic) representation of natural numbers, and modify NBE to cater for this double representation. Is either the simple representation or the double representation more efficient, and why?

*Exercise 3.* Because ML follows call by value, a syntactic witness is constructed for each intermediate value, even though only the witness of the final result is needed. How would you remedy that?

*Exercise 4.* Where else does ML's call by value penalize the implementation of NBE? How would you remedy that?

*Exercise 5.* Program a rewriting-based lambda calculus reducer and compare it to NBE in efficiency.

*Exercise 6.* Implement NBE in a language with dependent types such as Cayenne.

## 3 Normalization by Evaluation for the $\lambda_{\beta\eta}$-Calculus

In the next section, we shall see how normalization by evaluation can be exploited for the practical task of type-directed partial evaluation (TDPE) [Dan98]. TDPE is not based on the NBE-algorithm for combinators given in the previous section, but on the NBE-algorithm returning long $\beta\eta$-normal forms first presented by Berger and Schwichtenberg [BS91]. There are several reasons for this change:

*Syntax.* Most obviously, SK-combinators are far from a practical programming language. Although the algorithm extends directly to a more comprehensive set (e.g., SKBCI-combinators), we still want to express source programs in a more conventional lambda-syntax with variables. To use any combinator-based normalization algorithm, we would thus need to convert original programs to combinator form using bracket abstraction, and then either somehow evaluate combinator code directly, or convert it back to lambda-syntax (without undoing normality in the process – simply replacing the combinators with their definitions would not work!).

Thus, we prefer an algorithm that works on lambda-terms directly. As a consequence, however, we need to keep track of bound-variable names, and in particular avoid inadvertent clashes. While this is simple enough to do informally, we must be careful to express the process precisely enough to be analyzed, while keeping the implementation efficient.

*Extensionality.* As shown by Martin-Löf [ML75b] and by Coquand and Dybjer [CD93b], the glueing technique from the previous section can also be used for normalizing terms in a version of lambda-syntax. A problem with both variants, however, is the lack of extensionality. As we already mentioned, $\mathsf{S}{\cdot}\mathsf{K}{\cdot}\mathsf{K}$ and $\mathsf{S}{\cdot}\mathsf{K}{\cdot}(\mathsf{S}{\cdot}\mathsf{K}{\cdot}\mathsf{K})$ are both normal forms representing the identity function, which is somewhat unsatisfactory.

Even more problematically, these algorithms only compute *weak* normal forms. That is, the notion of conversion does not include (the combinatory analog of) the $\xi$-rule, which allows normalization under lambdas. Being able to reduce terms with free variables is a key requirement for partial evaluation. Consider, for example, the addition function in pseudo-lambda-syntax (with $\lambda^*$ denoting bracket abstraction),

$$\begin{aligned} \mathit{add} &= \lambda^* m.\,\lambda^* n.\,\mathsf{REC}{\cdot}m{\cdot}(\lambda^* a.\,\lambda^* x.\,\mathsf{SUCC}{\cdot}x){\cdot}n \\ &= \lambda^* m.\,\mathsf{REC}{\cdot}m{\cdot}(\mathsf{K}{\cdot}\mathsf{SUCC}) \\ &= \mathsf{S}{\cdot}\mathsf{REC}{\cdot}(\mathsf{K}{\cdot}(\mathsf{K}{\cdot}\mathsf{SUCC})) \end{aligned}$$

$\mathit{add}{\cdot}m{\cdot}n$ applies the successor function $n$ times to $m$. Given the reduction equations $\mathsf{REC}{\cdot}b{\cdot}f{\cdot}\mathsf{ZERO} = b$ and $\mathsf{REC}{\cdot}b{\cdot}f{\cdot}(\mathsf{SUCC}{\cdot}n) = f{\cdot}n{\cdot}(\mathsf{REC}{\cdot}b{\cdot}f{\cdot}n)$, we would hope that a partially applied function such as

$$\lambda^* m.\,\mathit{add}{\cdot}m{\cdot}(\mathsf{SUCC}{\cdot}(\mathsf{SUCC}{\cdot}\mathsf{ZERO})) = \mathsf{S}{\cdot}\mathit{add}{\cdot}(\mathsf{K}{\cdot}(\mathsf{SUCC}{\cdot}(\mathsf{SUCC}{\cdot}\mathsf{ZERO})))$$

could be normalized into $\lambda^* m.\,\mathsf{SUCC}{\cdot}(\mathsf{SUCC}{\cdot}m)$, i.e., eliminating the primitive recursion. But unfortunately, the combinatory term above is already in normal form with respect to the rewriting rules for $\mathsf{S}$, $\mathsf{K}$ and $\mathsf{REC}$, because all the combinators are unsaturated (i.e., applied to fewer arguments than their rewrite rules expect). Thus, we cannot unfold computations based on statically known data when the computation is also parameterized over unknown data.

It is fairly simple to extend the glueing-based normalization algorithms with top-level free variables; effectively, we just treat unknown inputs as additional, uninterpreted constants. With this extension the addition example goes through. However, the problem is not completely solved since we still do not simplify under *internal* lambdas in the program. For example, with

$$\mathit{mul} = \lambda^* m.\,\lambda^* n.\,\mathsf{REC}{\cdot}\mathsf{ZERO}{\cdot}(\lambda^* a.\,\lambda^* x.\,\mathit{add}{\cdot}x{\cdot}n){\cdot}m\,,$$

we would want the open term $\mathit{mul}{\cdot}m{\cdot}(\mathsf{SUCC}{\cdot}(\mathsf{SUCC}{\cdot}\mathsf{ZERO}))$ to normalize to something like

$$\mathsf{REC}{\cdot}\mathsf{ZERO}{\cdot}(\lambda^* a.\,\lambda^* x.\,\mathsf{SUCC}{\cdot}(\mathsf{SUCC}{\cdot}x)){\cdot}m\,,$$

i.e., to eliminate at least the primitive recursion inside *add*; but again the necessary reductions will be blocked.

*Native implementation.* A final problem with the glueing-based algorithm is that the non-standard interpretation of terms differs significantly from the standard one for function spaces. This means that we have to construct a special-purpose evaluator; even if we already had an efficient standard evaluator for combinatory System T, we would not be able to use it directly for the task of normalization. The same problem appears for lambda-terms: we do have very efficient standard evaluators for functional programs, but we may not be able to use them if the interpretation of lambda-abstraction and application is seriously non-standard.

In this section, we present a variant of the Berger and Schwichtenberg NBE algorithm. (The main difference to the original is that we use a somewhat simpler scheme for avoiding variable clashes.) Again, we stress that the dimensions of syntax and convertibility are largely independent: one can also devise NBE-like algorithms for lambda-syntax terms based on $\beta$-conversion only [Mog92]. Likewise, it is also perfectly possible to consider $\beta\eta$-convertibility in a combinatory setting, especially for a different basis, such as categorical combinators [AHS95]. The following (obviously incomplete) table summarizes the situation:

| | notion of conversion | | |
|---|---|---|---|
| syntax | weak $\beta$ | strong $\beta$ | $\beta\eta$ |
| combinators | [CD97] | | [AHS95] |
| lambda-terms | [ML75b,CD93b] | [Mog92] | [BS91] |

We should also mention that a main advantage with the glueing technique is that it extends smoothly to datatypes. We showed only how to treat natural numbers in the previous section, but the approach extends smoothly to arbitrary strictly positive datatypes such as the datatype of Brouwer ordinals [CD97]. For TDPE it is of course essential to deal with functions on datatypes, and in Section 4 we show how to deal with this problem by combining the idea of binding-time separation with normalization by evaluation.

### 3.1 The Setting: Simply Typed Lambda Calculus

For the purpose of presenting the algorithm, let us ignore for the moment constant symbols and concentrate on pure lambda-terms only. Accordingly, consider a fixed collection of base types $b$; the *simple types* $\tau$ are then generated from those by the rules

$$\frac{}{\vdash b\ \mathit{type}} \qquad \frac{\vdash \tau_1\ \mathit{type} \quad \vdash \tau_2\ \mathit{type}}{\vdash \tau_1 \dashrightarrow \tau_2\ \mathit{type}}$$

For a typing context $\Delta$, assigning simple types to variables, the well-typed lambda-terms over $\Delta$, $\Delta \vdash E : \tau$, are inductively generated by the usual rules:

$$\frac{\Delta(x) = \tau}{\Delta \vdash x : \tau} \qquad \frac{\Delta, x\colon \tau_1 \vdash E : \tau_2}{\Delta \vdash \underline{\lambda} x^{\tau_1}.E : \tau_1 \dashrightarrow \tau_2} \qquad \frac{\Delta \vdash E_1 : \tau_1 \dashrightarrow \tau_2 \qquad \Delta \vdash E_2 : \tau_1}{\Delta \vdash E_1 \cdot E_2 : \tau_2}$$

We write $E =_\alpha E'$ if $E'$ can be obtained from $E$ by a consistent, capture-avoiding renaming of bound variables. We introduce the notion of $\beta\eta$-convertibility as a judgment $\vdash E =_{\beta\eta} E'$, generated by the following rules, together with reflexivity, transitivity, symmetry, and $\alpha$-conversion:

$$\frac{\vdash E_1 =_{\beta\eta} E_1' \qquad \vdash E_2 =_{\beta\eta} E_2'}{\vdash E_1 \cdot E_2 =_{\beta\eta} E_1' \cdot E_2'} \qquad \frac{\vdash E =_{\beta\eta} E'}{\vdash \underline{\lambda} x.\, E =_{\beta\eta} \underline{\lambda} x.\, E'}$$

$$\frac{}{\vdash (\underline{\lambda} x.\, E_1) \cdot E_2 =_{\beta\eta} E_1[E_2/x]} \qquad \frac{}{\vdash \underline{\lambda} x.\, E \cdot x =_{\beta\eta} E}\;(x \notin FV(E))$$

Here $E_1[E_2/x]$ denotes the capture-avoiding substitution of $E_2$ for free occurrences of $x$ in $E_1$ (which in general may require an initial $\alpha$-conversion of $E_1$; the details are standard).

Let us also recall the usual notion of $\beta\eta$-long normal form for lambda-terms. In the typed setting, it is usually expressed using two mutually recursive judgments enumerating terms in *normal* and *atomic* (also known as *neutral*) forms:

$$\frac{\Delta \vdash^{\mathrm{at}} E : b}{\Delta \vdash^{\mathrm{nf}} E : b} \qquad \frac{\Delta, x\!: \tau_1 \vdash^{\mathrm{nf}} E : \tau_2}{\Delta \vdash^{\mathrm{nf}} \underline{\lambda} x^{\tau_1}.\, E : \tau_1 \underline{\to} \tau_2}$$

$$\frac{\Delta(x) = \tau}{\Delta \vdash^{\mathrm{at}} x : \tau} \qquad \frac{\Delta \vdash^{\mathrm{at}} E_1 : \tau_1 \underline{\to} \tau_2 \qquad \Delta \vdash^{\mathrm{nf}} E_2 : \tau_1}{\Delta \vdash^{\mathrm{at}} E_1 \cdot E_2 : \tau_2}$$

One can show that any well-typed lambda-term $\Delta \vdash E : \tau$ is $\beta\eta$-convertible to exactly one (up to $\alpha$-conversion) term $\tilde{E}$ such that $\Delta \vdash^{\mathrm{nf}} \tilde{E} : \tau$.

### 3.2 An Informal Normalization Function

The usual way of computing long $\beta\eta$-normal forms is to repeatedly perform $\beta$-reduction steps until no $\beta$-redexes remain, and then $\eta$-expand the result until all variables are applied to as many arguments as their type suggests. We now present an alternative way of computing such normal forms.

Let $\mathbf{V}$ be a set of variable names and $\mathbf{E}$ be some set of elements suitable for representing lambda-terms. More precisely, we assume that there exist injective functions with disjoint ranges,

$$\mathrm{VAR} \in \mathbf{V} \to \mathbf{E} \qquad \mathrm{LAM} \in \mathbf{V} \times \mathbf{E} \to \mathbf{E} \qquad \mathrm{APP} \in \mathbf{E} \times \mathbf{E} \to \mathbf{E}$$

Perhaps the simplest choice is to take $\mathbf{E}$ as the set of (open, untyped) syntactic lambda-terms. But we could also take $\mathbf{V} = \mathbf{E} = \mathbb{N}$ with some form of Gödel-coding. More practically, we could take $\mathbf{V} = \mathbf{E}$ as the set of ASCII strings or the set of Lisp/Scheme S-expressions. In particular, we do not require that $\mathbf{E}$ does not contain elements other than the representation of lambda-terms.

*Remark 1.* It would be possible to let $\mathbf{E}$ be an object-type-indexed set family, as in the previous section, rather than a single set. We will not pursue such an approach for two reasons, though. First, for practical applications, it is important that correctness of the algorithm can be established in a straightforward way even when it is expressed in a non-dependently typed functional language.

And second, there are additional complications in expressing the normalization algorithm for the call-by-value setting in the next section in a dependent-typed setting. The problems have to do with the interaction between computational effects such as continuations with a dependent type structure; at the time of writing, we do not have a viable dependently-typed algorithm for that case.

In any case, we can define a representation function $\ulcorner - \urcorner$ from well-formed lambda-terms with variables from $\mathbf{V}$ to elements of $\mathbf{E}$ by

$$\ulcorner x \urcorner = \mathrm{VAR}\, x \qquad \ulcorner \lambda x^\tau . E \urcorner = \mathrm{LAM}\,\langle x, \ulcorner E \urcorner \rangle \qquad \ulcorner E_1 \cdot E_2 \urcorner = \mathrm{APP}\,\langle \ulcorner E_1 \urcorner, \ulcorner E_2 \urcorner \rangle$$

(Note that we do not include the type tags for variables in representations of lambda-abstraction; the extension to do this is completely straightforward. See Exercise 7.) Because of the injectivity and disjointness requirements, for any $e \in \mathbf{E}$, there is then at most one $E$ such that $\ulcorner E \urcorner = e$.

We now want to construct a *residualizing* interpretation, such that from the residualizing meaning of a term, we can extract its normal form, like before. Moreover, we want to interpret function types as ordinary function spaces. A natural first try at such an interpretation would thus be to assign to every type $\tau$ a set $[\![\tau]\!]^{\mathrm{r}}$ as follows:

$$\begin{aligned} [\![b]\!]^{\mathrm{r}} &= \mathbf{E} \\ [\![\tau_1 \dashrightarrow \tau_2]\!]^{\mathrm{r}} &= [\![\tau_1]\!]^{\mathrm{r}} \to [\![\tau_2]\!]^{\mathrm{r}} \end{aligned}$$

The interpretation of terms is then completely standard: let $\rho$ be a $\Delta$-environment, that is, a function assigning an element of $[\![\tau]\!]^{\mathrm{r}}$ to every $x$ with $\Delta(x) = \tau$. Then we define the residualizing meaning of a well-typed term $\Delta \vdash E : \tau$ as an element $[\![E]\!]^{\mathrm{r}}_\rho \in [\![\tau]\!]^{\mathrm{r}}$ by structural induction:

$$\begin{aligned} [\![x]\!]^{\mathrm{r}}_\rho &= \rho\,(x) \\ [\![\lambda x^\tau . E]\!]^{\mathrm{r}}_\rho &= \lambda a^{[\![\tau]\!]^{\mathrm{r}}} . [\![E]\!]^{\mathrm{r}}_{\rho[x \mapsto a]} \\ [\![E_1 \cdot E_2]\!]^{\mathrm{r}}_\rho &= [\![E_1]\!]^{\mathrm{r}}_\rho\, [\![E_2]\!]^{\mathrm{r}}_\rho \end{aligned}$$

This turns out to be a good attempt: for any type $\tau$, it allows us to construct the following pair of functions, conventionally called *reification* and *reflection*:

$$\begin{aligned} \downarrow_\tau &\in [\![\tau]\!]^{\mathrm{r}} \to \mathbf{E} \\ \downarrow_b &= \lambda t^{\mathbf{E}} . t \\ \downarrow_{\tau_1 \dashrightarrow \tau_2} &= \lambda f^{[\![\tau_1]\!]^{\mathrm{r}} \to [\![\tau_2]\!]^{\mathrm{r}}} . \mathrm{LAM}\,\langle v, \downarrow_{\tau_2} (f\,(\uparrow_{\tau_1} (\mathrm{VAR}\, v)))\rangle \qquad (v \in \mathbf{V}, \text{“fresh”}) \end{aligned}$$

$$\begin{aligned} \uparrow_\tau &\in \mathbf{E} \to [\![\tau]\!]^{\mathrm{r}} \\ \uparrow_b &= \lambda e^{\mathbf{E}} . e \\ \uparrow_{\tau_1 \dashrightarrow \tau_2} &= \lambda e^{\mathbf{E}} . \lambda a^{[\![\tau_1]\!]^{\mathrm{r}}} . \uparrow_{\tau_2} (\mathrm{APP}\,\langle e, \downarrow_{\tau_1} a\rangle) \end{aligned}$$

Reification extracts a syntactic representation of a term from its residualizing semantics (as in the combinatory logic algorithm). Conversely, reflection wraps up a piece of syntax to make it act as an element of the corresponding type interpretation.

Together, these functions allow us to extract syntactic representations of closed lambda-terms from their denotations in the residualizing interpretation. For example,

$$\begin{aligned}
&\downarrow_{(b\to b)\to b\to b} [\![\underline{\lambda} s.\, \underline{\lambda} z.\, s \cdot (s \cdot z)]\!]^{\mathrm{r}}_{\emptyset} = \downarrow_{(b\to b)\to b\to b} (\lambda\phi.\, \lambda a.\, \phi\,(\phi\, a)) \\
&\quad = \mathrm{LAM}\,\langle x_1, \downarrow_{b\to b} ((\lambda\phi.\, \lambda a.\, \phi\,(\phi\, a))\,(\uparrow_{b\to b} (\mathrm{VAR}\, x_1)))\rangle \\
&\quad = \mathrm{LAM}\,\langle x_1, \downarrow_{b\to b} ((\lambda\phi.\, \lambda a.\, \phi\,(\phi\, a))\,(\lambda a.\, \mathrm{APP}\,\langle \mathrm{VAR}\, x_1, a\rangle))\rangle \\
&\quad = \mathrm{LAM}\,\langle x_1, \downarrow_{b\to b} (\lambda a.\, \mathrm{APP}\,\langle \mathrm{VAR}\, x_1, \mathrm{APP}\,\langle \mathrm{VAR}\, x_1, a\rangle\rangle)\rangle \\
&\quad = \mathrm{LAM}\,\langle x_1, \mathrm{LAM}\,\langle x_2, (\lambda a.\, \mathrm{APP}\,\langle \mathrm{VAR}\, x_1, \mathrm{APP}\,\langle \mathrm{VAR}\, x_1, a\rangle\rangle)\,(\mathrm{VAR}\, x_2)\rangle\rangle \\
&\quad = \mathrm{LAM}\,\langle x_1, \mathrm{LAM}\,\langle x_2, \mathrm{APP}\,\langle \mathrm{VAR}\, x_1, \mathrm{APP}\,\langle \mathrm{VAR}\, x_1, \mathrm{VAR}\, x_2\rangle\rangle\rangle\rangle
\end{aligned}$$

where we have arbitrarily chosen the fresh variable names $x_1, x_2 \in \mathbf{V}$ in the definition of reification at function types. Note that all the equalities in this derivation express definitional properties of functional abstraction and application in our set-theoretic metalanguage, as distinct from formal convertibility in the object language.

Given this extraction property for normal forms, it is now easy to see that $\downarrow_\tau [\![-]\!]^{\mathrm{r}}$ must be a normalization function, because $\beta\eta$-convertible terms have the same semantic denotation. Thus, for example, we would have obtained the same syntactic result if we had started instead with $\downarrow [\![\underline{\lambda} s.\, (\underline{\lambda} r.\, \underline{\lambda} z.\, r \cdot (s \cdot z)) \cdot (\underline{\lambda} x.\, s \cdot x)]\!]^{\mathrm{r}}_{\emptyset}$.

### 3.3 Formalizing Unique Name Generation

On closer inspection, our definition of reification above is mathematically unsatisfactory. The problem is the "$v$ fresh" condition: what exactly does it mean? Unlike such conditions as "$x$ does not occur free in $E$", it is not even locally checkable whether a variable is fresh; freshness is a global property, defined with respect to a term that may not even be fully constructed yet.

Needless to say, having such a vague notion at the core of an algorithm is a serious impediment to any formal analysis; we need a more precise way of talking about freshness. The concept can in fact be characterized rigorously in a framework such as Fraenkel-Mostowski sets, and even made accessible to the programmer as a language construct [GP99]. However, such an approach removes us a level from a direct implementation in a traditional, widely available functional language.

Instead, we explicitly generate non-clashing variable names. It turns out that we can do so fairly simply, if instead of working with individual term representations, we work with families of $\alpha$-equivalent representations. The families will have the property that it is easy to control which variable names may occur bound in any particular member of the family. (This numbering scheme was also used by Berger [Ber93] and is significantly simpler than that in the original presentation of the algorithm [BS91].)

**Definition 1.** *Let* $\{g_0, g_1, g_2, \dots\} \subseteq \mathbf{V}$ *be a countably infinite set of variable names. We then define the set of* term families,

$$\hat{\mathbf{E}} = \mathbb{N} \to \mathbf{E}$$

*together with the* wrapper functions

$$\begin{aligned}
\widehat{\mathrm{VAR}} \in \mathbf{V} \to \hat{\mathbf{E}} &= \lambda v.\, \lambda i.\, \mathrm{VAR}\, v \\
\widehat{\mathrm{LAM}} \in (\mathbf{V} \to \hat{\mathbf{E}}) \to \hat{\mathbf{E}} &= \lambda f.\, \lambda i.\, \mathrm{LAM}\, \langle g_i, f\, g_i\, (i+1)\rangle \\
\widehat{\mathrm{APP}} \in \hat{\mathbf{E}} \times \hat{\mathbf{E}} \to \hat{\mathbf{E}} &= \lambda \langle e_1, e_2\rangle.\, \lambda i.\, \mathrm{APP}\, \langle e_1\, i, e_2\, i\rangle
\end{aligned}$$

We can construct term families using only these wrappers, then apply the result to a starting index $i_0$ and obtain a concrete representative not using any $g_i$'s with $i < i_0$ as bound variables. For example,

$$\begin{aligned}
&(\widehat{\mathrm{LAM}}\, (\lambda v_1.\, \widehat{\mathrm{LAM}}\, (\lambda v_2.\, \widehat{\mathrm{APP}}\, (\widehat{\mathrm{VAR}} v_2, \widehat{\mathrm{APP}}\, (\widehat{\mathrm{VAR}} v_2, \widehat{\mathrm{VAR}}\, v_1)))))\, 7 = \cdots \\
&\quad = \mathrm{LAM}\, \langle g_7, \mathrm{LAM}\, \langle g_8, \mathrm{APP}\, \langle \mathrm{VAR}\, g_7, \mathrm{APP}\, \langle \mathrm{VAR}\, g_7, \mathrm{VAR}\, g_8\rangle\rangle\rangle\rangle
\end{aligned}$$

In general, each bound variable will be named $g_i$ where $i$ is the sum of the starting index and the number of lambdas enclosing the binding location. (This naming scheme is sometimes known as *de Bruijn levels* – not to be confused with *de Bruijn indices*, which assign numbers to individual uses of variables, not to their introductions.)

We now take for the residualizing interpretation,

$$\begin{aligned}
[\![b]\!]^{\mathrm{r}} &= \hat{\mathbf{E}} \\
[\![\tau_1 \dashrightarrow \tau_2]\!]^{\mathrm{r}} &= [\![\tau_1]\!]^{\mathrm{r}} \to [\![\tau_2]\!]^{\mathrm{r}}
\end{aligned}$$

and define corresponding reification and reflection functions:

$$\begin{aligned}
\downarrow_\tau &\in [\![\tau]\!]^{\mathrm{r}} \to \hat{\mathbf{E}} \\
\downarrow_b &= \lambda t^{\hat{\mathbf{E}}}.\, t \\
\downarrow_{\tau_1 \dashrightarrow \tau_2} &= \lambda f^{[\![\tau_1]\!]^{\mathrm{r}} \to [\![\tau_2]\!]^{\mathrm{r}}}.\, \widehat{\mathrm{LAM}}\, (\lambda v^{\mathbf{V}}.\, \downarrow_{\tau_2} (f\, (\uparrow_{\tau_1} (\widehat{\mathrm{VAR}}\, v)))) \\
\uparrow_\tau &\in \hat{\mathbf{E}} \to [\![\tau]\!]^{\mathrm{r}} \\
\uparrow_b &= \lambda e^{\hat{\mathbf{E}}}.\, e \\
\uparrow_{\tau_1 \dashrightarrow \tau_2} &= \lambda e^{\hat{\mathbf{E}}}.\, \lambda a^{[\![\tau_1]\!]^{\mathrm{r}}}.\, \uparrow_{\tau_2} (\widehat{\mathrm{APP}}\, \langle e, \downarrow_{\tau_1} a\rangle)
\end{aligned}$$

Finally we can state,

**Definition 2.** *We define the normalization function* norm *as follows: For any well-typed closed term* $\vdash E : \tau$, norm $E$ *is the unique* $\tilde{E}$ *(if it exists) such that* $\ulcorner \tilde{E} \urcorner = \downarrow_\tau [\![E]\!]^{\mathrm{r}}_{\emptyset}\, 0$.

**Theorem 5 (Correctness).** *We formulate correctness of* norm *as three criteria:*

1. norm *is total and type preserving: for any* $\vdash E : \tau$, norm $E$ *denotes a well-defined* $\tilde{E}$, *and* $\vdash \tilde{E} : \tau$. *Moreover,* $\tilde{E}$ *is in normal form,* $\vdash^{\mathrm{nf}} \tilde{E} : \tau$.
2. $\vdash \mathrm{norm}\, E =_{\beta\eta} E$.
3. *If* $\vdash E =_{\beta\eta} E'$ *then* $\mathrm{norm}\, E = \mathrm{norm}\, E'$.

Several approaches are possible for the proof. Perhaps the simplest proceeds as follows: If $\tilde{E}$ is already in normal form, then it is fairly simple to show that $\mathrm{norm}\, \tilde{E} =_\alpha \tilde{E}$. (This follows by structural induction on the syntax of normal forms; the only complication is keeping track of variable renamings.) Moreover, as we observed in the informal example with "magic" fresh variables, if $E =_{\beta\eta} \tilde{E}$ then $[\![E]\!]^{\mathrm{r}}_\emptyset = [\![\tilde{E}]\!]^{\mathrm{r}}_\emptyset$, and hence $\mathrm{norm}\, E = \mathrm{norm}\, \tilde{E} =_\alpha \tilde{E}$ directly by the definition of norm. All the claims of the theorem then follow easily from the (non-trivial) fact that every term is $\beta\eta$-equivalent to one in normal form.

### 3.4 Implementation

An SML implementation of the $\lambda_{\beta\eta}$-normalizer is shown in Figure 1. Note that, unlike in the combinatory case, the central function `eval` is essentially the same as in a standard interpreter for a simple functional language. In the next section, we will see how we can take advantage of this similarity, by replacing the custom-coded interpretation function with the native evaluator of a functional language.

## 4 Type-Directed Partial Evaluation for Call-by-Name

In this section, we will see how the general idea of normalization by evaluation can be exploited for the practical task of type-directed partial evaluation (TDPE) of functional programs [Dan98]. The main issues addressed here are:

*Interpreted constants.* A problem with the NBE algorithm for the pure $\lambda_{\beta\eta}$-calculus given in the previous section is that it is not clear how to extend it to, for example, System T, where we need to deal with primitive constants such as primitive recursion. Clearly, we cannot expect to interpret nat standardly, as we did for the combinatory version of System T: we cannot expect that all extensionally indistinguishable functions from natural numbers to natural numbers have the same normal form.

To recover a simple notion of equivalence, we need to introduce an explicit notion of *binding times* in the programs. That is, we must distinguish clearly between the *static* subcomputations, which should be carried out during normalization, and the *dynamic* ones, that will only happen when the normalized program itself is executed.

An *offline binding-time annotation* allows us to determine which parts of the program are static, even without knowing the actual static values. We can then distinguish between static and dynamic *occurrences* of operators, with their associated different conversion rules. This distinction will allow us to re-introduce interpreted constants, including recursion.

```
datatype term =
  VAR of string | LAM of string * term | APP of term * term

type termh = int -> term

fun VARh v = fn i => VAR v
fun LAMh f =
      fn i => let val v = "x" ^ Int.toString i in LAM (v, f v (i+1)) end
fun APPh (e1, e2) = fn i => APP (e1 i, e2 i)

datatype sem =
  TM of termh | FUN of sem -> sem

fun eval (VAR x) r = r x
  | eval (LAM (x, t)) r =
      FUN (fn a => eval t (fn x' => if x' = x then a else r x'))
  | eval (APP (e1, e2)) r =
      let val FUN f = eval e1 r in f (eval e2 r) end

datatype tp =
  BASE of string | ARROW of tp * tp

fun reify (BASE _) (TM e) = e
  | reify (ARROW (t1, t2)) (FUN f) =
      LAMh (fn v => reify t2 (f (reflect t1 (VARh v))))
and reflect (BASE _) e = TM e
  | reflect (ARROW (t1, t2)) e =
      FUN (fn a => reflect t2 (APPh (e, reify t1 a)))

fun norm t e =
      reify t (eval e (fn x => raise Fail ("Unbound: " ^ x))) 0

val test =
    norm (ARROW (ARROW (BASE "a", BASE "b"), ARROW (BASE "a", BASE "b")))
         (LAM ("f", LAM ("x", APP (LAM ("y", APP (VAR "f", VAR "y")),
                                   APP (VAR "f", VAR "x")))));
(* val test =
   LAM ("x0",LAM ("x1",APP (VAR "x0",APP (VAR "x0",VAR "x1")))) : term *)
```

**Fig. 1.** An implementation of the $\lambda_{\beta\eta}$-normalizer in SML

*Recursion.* When we want to use NBE for conventional functional programs, we get an additional complication in the form of unrestricted recursion. While many uses of general recursion can be replaced with suitable notions of primitive recursion, this is unfortunately not the case for one of the primary applications of partial evaluation, namely programming-language interpreters: since the interpreted program may diverge, the interpreter cannot itself be a total function either.

In fact, normalization of programs with interpreted constants is often expressed more naturally with respect to a *semantic* notion of equivalence, rather than syntactic $\beta\eta$-convertibility with additional rules. And in particular, to properly account for general recursion, it becomes natural to consider domain-theoretic models for both the standard and the non-standard interpretations, rather than purely set-theoretic ones.

## 4.1 The Setting: A Domain-Theoretic Semantics of PCF

Our prototypical functional language has the following set of well-formed types, $\vdash_\Sigma \sigma\ \mathit{type}$:

$$\frac{b \in \Sigma}{\vdash_\Sigma b\ \mathit{type}} \qquad \frac{\vdash_\Sigma \sigma_1\ \mathit{type} \quad \vdash_\Sigma \sigma_2\ \mathit{type}}{\vdash_\Sigma \sigma_1 \dashrightarrow \sigma_2\ \mathit{type}}$$

where the signature $\Sigma$ contains a collection of base types $b$. (Note that the change from $\tau$ to $\sigma$ as a metavariable for object types, and $\Delta$ to $\Gamma$ for typing contexts below, is deliberate, in preparation for the next section.) Although we are limiting ourselves to base and function types for conciseness, adding finite-product types would be straightforward.

Each base type $b$ is equipped with a countable collection of *literals* (numerals, truth values, etc.) $\Xi(b)$. These represent the observable results of program execution.

A typing context $\Gamma$ is a finite mapping of variable names to well-formed types over $\Sigma$. Then the well-typed $\Sigma$-terms over $\Gamma$, $\Gamma \vdash_\Sigma E : \sigma$, are much as before:

$$\frac{l \in \Xi(b)}{\Gamma \vdash_\Sigma l : b} \qquad \frac{\Sigma(c_{\sigma_1,\ldots,\sigma_n}) = \sigma}{\Gamma \vdash_\Sigma c_{\sigma_1,\ldots,\sigma_n} : \sigma} \qquad \frac{\Gamma(x) = \sigma}{\Gamma \vdash_\Sigma x : \sigma}$$

$$\frac{\Gamma, x{:}\, \sigma_1 \vdash_\Sigma E : \sigma_2}{\Gamma \vdash_\Sigma \lambda x^{\sigma_1}.E : \sigma_1 \dashrightarrow \sigma_2} \qquad \frac{\Gamma \vdash_\Sigma E_1 : \sigma_1 \dashrightarrow \sigma_2 \qquad \Gamma \vdash_\Sigma E_2 : \sigma_1}{\Gamma \vdash_\Sigma E_1 \cdot E_2 : \sigma_2}$$

Here $x$ ranges over a countable set of variables, and $c$ over a set of function constants in $\Sigma$. Note that some constants, such as conditionals, are actually polymorphic families of constants. We must explicitly pick out the relevant instance using type subscripts. We say that a well-typed term is a *complete program* if it is closed and of base type.

Since we want to model general recursion, we use a domain-theoretic model instead of a simpler set-theoretic one. (However, it is possible to understand most of the following constructions by ignoring the order structure and continuity, and simply thinking of domains as sets; only the formal treatment of fixpoints suffers from such a simplification.)

Accordingly, we say that an *interpretation* of a signature $\Sigma$ is a triple $\mathcal{I} = (\mathcal{B}, \mathcal{L}, \mathcal{C})$. $\mathcal{B}$ maps every base type $b$ in $\Sigma$ to a predomain, that is, a possibly bottomless cpo, usually discretely ordered. Then we can interpret every type phrase $\sigma$ over $\Sigma$ as a domain (pointed cpo):

$$\begin{aligned} [\![b]\!]^{\mathcal{I}} &= \mathcal{B}(b)_\bot \\ [\![\sigma_1 \dashrightarrow \sigma_2]\!]^{\mathcal{I}} &= [\![\sigma_1]\!]^{\mathcal{I}} \to_c [\![\sigma_2]\!]^{\mathcal{I}} \end{aligned}$$

(For any cpo $A$, we write $A_\bot = A \cup \{\bot\}$ for its lifting, where the additional element $\bot$ signifies divergence. The interpretation of function types is the usual continuous-function space. Since we only deal with continuous functions in the semantics, we generally omit the subscript $c$ from now on.)

Then, for any base type $b$ and literal $l \in \Xi(b)$, the interpretation must specify an element $\mathcal{L}_b(l) \in \mathcal{B}(b)$; and for every type instance of a polymorphic constant, an element $\mathcal{C}(c_{\sigma_1,\ldots,\sigma_n}) \in [\![\Sigma(c_{\sigma_1,\ldots,\sigma_n})]\!]^{\mathcal{I}}$. For simplicity, we assume that $\mathcal{L}_b$ is surjective, that is, that every element of $\mathcal{B}(b)$ is denoted by a literal.

We interpret a typing assignment $\Gamma$ as a labelled product:

$$[\![\Gamma]\!]^{\mathcal{I}} = \prod_{x \in \mathrm{dom}\,\Gamma} [\![\Gamma(x)]\!]^{\mathcal{I}}$$

(Note that this is now a finite product of domains, ordered pointwise, i.e., $\rho \sqsubseteq \rho'$ iff $\forall x \in \mathrm{dom}\,\Gamma.\, \rho\,x \sqsubseteq_{\Gamma(x)} \rho'\,x$.)

To make a smooth transition to the later parts, let us express the semantics of terms with explicit reference to the *lifting monad* $(-_\bot, \eta^\bot, \star^\bot)$, where $\eta^\bot\, a$ is the *inclusion* of $a \in A$ into $A_\bot$, and $t \star^\bot f$ is the *strict extension* of $f \in A \to B_\bot$ applied to $t \in A_\bot$, given by $\bot_A \star^\bot f = \bot_B$ and $(\eta^\bot\, a) \star^\bot f = f\,a$. We then give the semantics of a term $\Gamma \vdash E : \tau$ as a (total) continuous function $[\![E]\!]^{\mathcal{I}} \in [\![\Gamma]\!]^{\mathcal{I}} \to [\![\tau]\!]^{\mathcal{I}}$:

$$\begin{aligned}
[\![l]\!]^{\mathcal{I}}\rho &= \eta^\bot(\mathcal{L}_b(l)) \\
[\![c_{\sigma_1,\ldots,\sigma_n}]\!]^{\mathcal{I}}\rho &= \mathcal{C}(c_{\sigma_1,\ldots,\sigma_n}) \\
[\![x]\!]^{\mathcal{I}}\rho &= \rho\,x \\
[\![\lambda x^\sigma.\,E]\!]^{\mathcal{I}}\rho &= \lambda a^{[\![\sigma]\!]^{\mathcal{I}}}.\,[\![E]\!]^{\mathcal{I}}(\rho[x \mapsto a]) \\
[\![E_1 \cdot E_2]\!]^{\mathcal{I}}\rho &= [\![E_1]\!]^{\mathcal{I}}\rho([\![E_2]\!]^{\mathcal{I}}\rho)
\end{aligned}$$

Finally, given an interpretation $\mathcal{I}$ of $\Sigma$ we define the partial function returning the observable result of evaluating a complete program:

$$\mathrm{eval}^{\mathcal{I}} \in \{E \mid \vdash_\Sigma E : b\} \rightharpoonup \Xi(b)$$

by

$$\mathrm{eval}^{\mathcal{I}}\,E = \begin{cases} l & \text{if } [\![E]\!]^{\mathcal{I}}\emptyset = \eta^\bot(\mathcal{L}_b(l)) \\ \text{undefined} & \text{if } [\![E]\!]^{\mathcal{I}}\emptyset = \bot \end{cases}$$

where $\emptyset$ is the empty environment.

**Definition 3 (standard static language).** *We define a simple functional language (essentially PCF [Plo77]) by taking the signature $\Sigma_{\mathrm{s}}$ as follows. The base types are* int *and* bool*; the literals,* $\Xi(\mathsf{int}) = \{\ldots, \text{-}1, 0, 1, 2, \ldots\}$ *and* $\Xi(\mathsf{bool}) = \{\mathsf{true}, \mathsf{false}\}$*; and the constants,*

$$\begin{aligned}
+, -, \times &: \mathsf{int} \dashrightarrow \mathsf{int} \dashrightarrow \mathsf{int} & \qquad \mathsf{if}_\sigma &: \mathsf{bool} \dashrightarrow \sigma \dashrightarrow \sigma \dashrightarrow \sigma \\
=, < &: \mathsf{int} \dashrightarrow \mathsf{int} \dashrightarrow \mathsf{bool} & \mathsf{fix}_\sigma &: (\sigma \dashrightarrow \sigma) \dashrightarrow \sigma
\end{aligned}$$

*(We use infix notation for applications of binary operations, for example, $x + y$ instead of $+ \cdot x \cdot y$.)*

*Similarly, the standard interpretation of this signature is also as expected:*

$$
\begin{aligned}
\mathcal{B}_s(\mathsf{bool}) &= \mathbb{B} = \{\text{true}, \text{false}\} \\
\mathcal{B}_s(\mathsf{int}) &= \mathbb{Z} = \{\ldots, -1, 0, 1, 2, \ldots\} \\
\mathcal{C}_s(\diamond) &= \lambda x^{\mathbb{Z}_\perp}.\lambda y^{\mathbb{Z}_\perp}.x \star^\perp \lambda n.y \star^\perp \lambda m.\eta^\perp(m \diamond n) \quad {\scriptstyle \diamond \in \{+,-,\times,=,<\}} \\
\mathcal{C}_s(\mathsf{if}_\sigma) &= \lambda x^{\mathbb{B}_\perp}.\lambda a_1^{[\![\sigma]\!]}.\lambda a_2^{[\![\sigma]\!]}.x \star^\perp \lambda b.\,\text{if } b \text{ then } a_1 \text{ else } a_2 \\
\mathcal{C}_s(\mathsf{fix}_\sigma) &= \lambda f^{[\![\sigma]\!]\to[\![\sigma]\!]}.\bigsqcup_{i\in\omega} f^i \perp_{[\![\sigma]\!]}
\end{aligned}
$$

*(where the conditional* if $b$ then $x$ else $y$ *chooses between* $x$ *and* $y$ *based on the truth value* $b$*.)*

It is well known (computational adequacy of the denotational semantics for call-by-name evaluation [Plo77]) that with this interpretation, $\text{eval}^{\mathcal{I}_s}$ is computable.

*Remark 2.* This PCF semantics differs from the standard semantics of Haskell in that there is no extra lifting of function types; Haskell would have $[\![\tau_1 \dot{\to} \tau_2]\!] = ([\![\tau_1]\!] \to [\![\tau_2]\!])_\perp$. One can show that this makes no difference, as long as we cannot observe termination at higher types. That is, with the typing restriction on complete programs, our denotational semantics is actually computationally adequate whether we evaluate programs in PCF or in Haskell.

Note that being able to observe termination at higher types breaks the validity of $\eta$-conversion as a semantic equivalence ($\dot{\lambda} x.f \cdot x$ and $f$ become operationally distinguishable when $f$ can be replaced with a non-terminating term), for no clear gain in convenience or expressive power.

### 4.2 Binding-Time Separation and Static Normal Forms

For partial evaluation, we distinguish between operations that can be performed knowing only the static input, and those that also require dynamic data. A particularly useful way of making this distinction is through an *off-line binding-time annotation (BTA)*, where knowledge about which arguments to a program's top-level function will be static, and which will be dynamic, is propagated throughout the program in a separate phase. Note that this can be done without knowing the actual *values* of the static arguments.

The annotation can either be performed by a program (so called binding-time analysis), or explicitly by the programmer as the program is written. The latter is quite practical when the usage pattern is fixed – for example, an interpreter may be specialized with respect to a program, but practically never with respect to the program's input data.

Traditional binding-time annotations for typed languages are often expressed in terms of two-level types [NN88], where types and type constructors (such as function spaces and products) are annotated as static or dynamic. Type-directed partial evaluation is unusual in that the binding-time annotations are expressed in an essentially standard type system, which allows the annotations to be verified by an ML type checker. It also means that the annotated programs remain directly executable.

Specifically, BTA in TDPE is performed by expressing the program as a term over a *binding-time separated signature*, where the declarations of base types and constants are divided into a static and a dynamic part. That is, $\Sigma = \Sigma_\mathrm{s} \cup \Sigma_\mathrm{d}$ where each of $\Sigma_\mathrm{s}$ and $\Sigma_\mathrm{d}$ is itself a signature. Following the tradition, we will write type and term constants from the static part overlined, and the dynamic ones underlined.

For simplicity, we require that the dynamic base types do not come with any new literals, that is, $\Xi(\underline{b}) = \emptyset$. (If needed, they can be added as dynamic constants.) However, some base types will be *persistent*, that is, have both static and dynamic versions with the same intended meaning. In that case, we also include *lifting functions*

$$\$_b : \overline{b} \mathrel{\dot{\to}} \underline{b}$$

in the dynamic signature.

We say that a type $\tau$ is *fully dynamic* if it is constructed from dynamic base types only:

$$\frac{\underline{b} \in \Sigma_\mathrm{d}}{\underline{b}\ dtype} \qquad \frac{\tau_1\ dtype \quad \tau_2\ dtype}{\tau_1 \mathrel{\dot{\to}} \tau_2\ dtype}$$

We also reserve $\Delta$ for typing assumptions assigning fully dynamic types to all variables. All term constants in $\Sigma_\mathrm{d}$ must have fully dynamic types, and in particular, polymorphic dynamic constants must only be instantiated by dynamic types, ensuring that the type of every instance is fully dynamic, for example, $\Sigma_\mathrm{d}(\underline{\mathsf{if}}_\tau) = \underline{\mathsf{bool}} \mathrel{\dot{\to}} \tau \mathrel{\dot{\to}} \tau \mathrel{\dot{\to}} \tau$. On the other hand, constants from $\Sigma_\mathrm{s}$ can be instantiated at both static and dynamic types.

We will always take the language from Definition 3 with the standard semantics $\mathcal{I}_\mathrm{s} = (\mathcal{B}_\mathrm{s}, \mathcal{L}, \mathcal{C}_\mathrm{s})$ as the static part. The dynamic signature typically also has some intended *evaluating interpretation* $\mathcal{I}_\mathrm{d}^\mathrm{e}$; in particular, when $\Sigma_\mathrm{d}$ is merely a copy of $\Sigma_\mathrm{s}$, we can use $\mathcal{I}_\mathrm{s}$ directly for $\mathcal{I}_\mathrm{d}^\mathrm{e}$ (interpreting all lifting functions as identities). Later, however, we will also introduce a "code-generating", residualizing interpretation of the dynamic signature.

*Example 1.* Given the functional term

$$\mathsf{power} : \iota \mathrel{\dot{\to}} \iota \mathrel{\dot{\to}} \iota \equiv \dot{\lambda} x^{\iota}.\, \mathsf{fix}_{\iota \dot{\to} \iota} \cdot (\dot{\lambda} p^{\iota \dot{\to} \iota}.\, \dot{\lambda} n^{\iota}.\, \mathsf{if}_{\iota} \cdot (n = 0) \cdot 1 \cdot (x \times p \cdot (n - 1)))$$

(abbreviating $\mathsf{int}$ as $\iota$), we can binding-time annotate it in four different ways, depending on which arguments will be statically known:

$$\begin{aligned}
\mathsf{power}_{ss} : \overline{\iota} \mathrel{\dot{\to}} \overline{\iota} \mathrel{\dot{\to}} \overline{\iota} &\equiv \dot{\lambda} x^{\overline{\iota}}.\, \overline{\mathsf{fix}}_{\overline{\iota} \dot{\to} \overline{\iota}} \cdot (\dot{\lambda} p^{\overline{\iota} \dot{\to} \overline{\iota}}.\, \dot{\lambda} n^{\overline{\iota}}.\, \overline{\mathsf{if}}_{\overline{\iota}} \cdot (n \mathrel{\overline{=}} 0) \cdot 1 \cdot (x \mathbin{\overline{\times}} p \cdot (n \mathbin{\overline{-}} 1))) \\
\mathsf{power}_{sd} : \overline{\iota} \mathrel{\dot{\to}} \underline{\iota} \mathrel{\dot{\to}} \underline{\iota} &\equiv \dot{\lambda} x^{\overline{\iota}}.\, \underline{\mathsf{fix}}_{\underline{\iota} \dot{\to} \underline{\iota}} \cdot (\dot{\lambda} p^{\underline{\iota} \dot{\to} \underline{\iota}}.\, \dot{\lambda} n^{\underline{\iota}}.\, \underline{\mathsf{if}}_{\underline{\iota}} \cdot (n \mathrel{\underline{=}} \$ \cdot 0) \cdot (\$ \cdot 1) \cdot (\$ \cdot x \mathbin{\underline{\times}} p \cdot (n \mathbin{\underline{-}} \$ \cdot 1))) \\
\mathsf{power}_{ds} : \underline{\iota} \mathrel{\dot{\to}} \overline{\iota} \mathrel{\dot{\to}} \underline{\iota} &\equiv \dot{\lambda} x^{\underline{\iota}}.\, \overline{\mathsf{fix}}_{\overline{\iota} \dot{\to} \underline{\iota}} \cdot (\dot{\lambda} p^{\overline{\iota} \dot{\to} \underline{\iota}}.\, \dot{\lambda} n^{\overline{\iota}}.\, \overline{\mathsf{if}}_{\underline{\iota}} \cdot (n \mathrel{\overline{=}} 0) \cdot (\$ \cdot 1) \cdot (x \mathbin{\underline{\times}} p \cdot (n \mathbin{\overline{-}} 1))) \\
\mathsf{power}_{dd} : \underline{\iota} \mathrel{\dot{\to}} \underline{\iota} \mathrel{\dot{\to}} \underline{\iota} &\equiv \lambda x^{\underline{\iota}}.\, \underline{\mathsf{fix}}_{\underline{\iota} \dot{\to} \underline{\iota}} \cdot (\dot{\lambda} p^{\underline{\iota} \dot{\to} \underline{\iota}}.\, \dot{\lambda} n^{\underline{\iota}}.\, \underline{\mathsf{if}}_{\underline{\iota}} \cdot (n \mathrel{\underline{=}} \$ \cdot 0) \cdot (\$ \cdot 1)(x \mathbin{\underline{\times}} p \cdot (n \mathbin{\underline{-}} \$ \cdot 1)))
\end{aligned}$$

Note how the fixed-point and conditional operators are classified as static or dynamic, depending on the binding time of the second argument.

Some of the usual concerns of binding-time annotation arise for TDPE as well: for example, an unannotated term such as $(d+3)+s$, where $d$ is a dynamic variable and $s$ a static one, must be annotated as $(x \underline{+} \$\cdot 3) \underline{+} \$\cdot s$. That is, neither of the additions can be performed even with knowledge of $s$'s value. Had we instead written the term as $d + (3 + s)$, we could annotate it as $d \underline{+} \$\cdot(3 \overline{+} s)$, allowing the second addition to be eliminated at specialization time. Such rewritings are called *binding-time improvements.*

In keeping with the idea that computations involving dynamic constants should be left in the normalized program, we introduce a new notion of program equivalence, compatible with any future interpretation of the dynamic operators:

**Definition 4 (Static Equivalence).** *We say that $E$ and $E'$ are statically equivalent (wrt. a given static interpretation $\mathcal{I}_s$ of $\Sigma_s$), written $\mathcal{I}_s \models E = E'$, if for every interpretation $\mathcal{I}_d$ of $\Sigma_d$, $[\![E]\!]^{\mathcal{I}_s \cup \mathcal{I}_d} = [\![E']\!]^{\mathcal{I}_s \cup \mathcal{I}_d}$.*

(More generally, one can imagine an intermediate between static and dynamic constants: we may consider equivalence in all interpretations of $\Sigma_d$ satisfying some additional constraints [Fil01].)

Note that static equivalence includes not only full $\beta\eta$-convertibility, but also equalities involving static constants, such as $\mathcal{I}_s \models \overline{\mathsf{fix}}\cdot f = f\cdot(\overline{\mathsf{fix}}\cdot f)$. However, in the particular case where the static signature contains no term constants, one can show that static equivalence coincides with $\beta\eta$-convertibility. (This is known as Friedman's completeness theorem for the full continuous type frame [Mit96, Theorem 8.4.6].)

### 4.3 A Residualizing Interpretation

To normalize a term with respect to static equivalence, we first adjust our syntactic characterization of normal forms: we allow constants from the dynamic signature only, and all literals must appear as arguments to \$. That is, we add the following two rules for atomic forms:

$$\frac{\Sigma_d(c_{\tau_1,\ldots,\tau_n}) = \tau}{\Delta \vdash^{\mathrm{at}} c_{\tau_1,\ldots,\tau_n} : \tau} \qquad \frac{l \in \Xi(\overline{b})}{\Delta \vdash^{\mathrm{at}} \$_b\cdot l : \underline{b}}$$

Also, corresponding to our extension of the language, we assume that in addition to VAR, LAM, and APP, we have two further syntax-constructor functions (again with ranges disjoint from those of the others),

$$\mathrm{CST} \in \mathbf{V} \to \mathbf{E} \qquad \mathrm{LIT}_b \in \mathcal{B}_s(b) \to \mathbf{E} \text{ (for each } b \text{ in } \Sigma_d)$$

As we only need to represent programs in normal form, we extend the representation equations as follows:

$$\ulcorner c_{\tau_1,\ldots,\tau_n} \urcorner = \mathrm{CST}\, c \qquad \ulcorner \$_b\cdot l \urcorner = \mathrm{LIT}_b\,(\mathcal{L}_b(l))$$

(For simplicity, we assume that elements of $\mathbf{V}$ can also be used to represent constant names. Also, we omit type tags in the generated representation of constants; like for lambda-abstraction, adding them is straightforward.)

Moreover, since we are working with domains, we need to take into account the possibility of nontermination at normalization time; that is, the reification function may need to return a $\bot$-result. Thus we take

$$\hat{\mathbf{E}} = \mathbb{Z}_\bot \to \mathbf{E}_\bot$$

where $\mathbf{E}$ is our set of term representations viewed as a discrete cpo. Elements of $\hat{\mathbf{E}}$ are ordered pointwise, that is $e \sqsubseteq e'$ iff for all $i \in \mathbb{Z}_\bot$, $e\,i = \bot$ or $e\,i = e'\,i$. For the purpose of the semantic presentation, we could have used $\mathbb{N}$ instead of $\mathbb{Z}_\bot$ ($\hat{\mathbf{E}}$ would still be a pointed cpo with that choice), but we will make use of the revised definition in Section 4.4: unlike $\mathbb{N} \to \mathbf{E}_\bot$, $\mathbb{Z}_\bot \to \mathbf{E}_\bot$ is actually the denotation of a type in our standard static signature.

Correspondingly, we define our new wrapper functions taking lifting into account:

$$\begin{aligned}
\widehat{\mathrm{LIT}}_b \in \mathcal{B}_{\mathrm{s}}(b)_\bot \to \hat{\mathbf{E}} &= \lambda d.\,\lambda i.\,d \star^\bot \lambda n.\,\eta^\bot\,(\mathrm{LIT}_b\,n)\\
\widehat{\mathrm{CST}} \in \mathbf{V}_\bot \to \hat{\mathbf{E}} &= \lambda d.\,\lambda i.\,d \star^\bot \lambda v.\,\eta^\bot\,(\mathrm{CST}\,v)\\
\widehat{\mathrm{VAR}} \in \mathbf{V}_\bot \to \hat{\mathbf{E}} &= \lambda d.\,\lambda i.\,d \star^\bot \lambda v.\,\eta^\bot\,(\mathrm{VAR}\,v)\\
\widehat{\mathrm{LAM}} \in (\mathbf{V}_\bot \to \hat{\mathbf{E}}) \to \hat{\mathbf{E}} &= \\
&\lambda f.\,\lambda i.\,i \star^\bot \lambda j.\,f\,(\eta^\bot\,g_j)\,(\eta^\bot\,(j+1)) \star^\bot \lambda l.\,\eta^\bot\,(\mathrm{LAM}\,\langle g_j, l\rangle)\\
\widehat{\mathrm{APP}} \in \hat{\mathbf{E}} \times \hat{\mathbf{E}} \to \hat{\mathbf{E}} &= \lambda\langle e_1, e_2\rangle.\,\lambda i.\,e_1\,i \star^\bot \lambda l_1.\,e_2\,i \star^\bot \lambda l_2.\,\eta^\bot\,(\mathrm{APP}\,\langle l_1, l_2\rangle)
\end{aligned}$$

For the residualizing interpretation on types, we now specify

$$\mathcal{B}^{\mathrm{r}}_{\mathrm{d}}(\underline{b}) = \hat{\mathbf{E}}$$

Together with the standard interpretation of the static base types, this determines the semantics of any type $\sigma$ over $\Sigma_{\mathrm{s}} \cup \Sigma_{\mathrm{d}}$.

The reification functions can be written exactly as before: for any dynamic type $\tau$, we define a pair of continuous functions by induction on the structure of $\tau$:

$$\begin{aligned}
\downarrow_\tau &\in [\![\tau]\!]^{\mathcal{I}_{\mathrm{s}} \cup \mathcal{I}^{\mathrm{r}}_{\mathrm{d}}} \to \hat{\mathbf{E}}\\
\downarrow_{\underline{b}} &= \lambda t.\,t\\
\downarrow_{\tau_1 \to \tau_2} &= \lambda f.\,\widehat{\mathrm{LAM}}\,(\lambda v.\downarrow_{\tau_2}(f\,(\uparrow_{\tau_1}(\widehat{\mathrm{VAR}}\,v))))\\
\uparrow_\tau &\in \hat{\mathbf{E}} \to [\![\tau]\!]^{\mathcal{I}_{\mathrm{s}} \cup \mathcal{I}^{\mathrm{r}}_{\mathrm{d}}}\\
\uparrow_{\underline{b}} &= \lambda e.\,e\\
\uparrow_{\tau_1 \to \tau_2} &= \lambda e.\,\lambda a.\uparrow_{\tau_2}(\widehat{\mathrm{APP}}\,(e, \downarrow_{\tau_1} a))
\end{aligned}$$

Finally, we can construct the residualizing interpretation of terms. Again, we give only the interpretation of $\Sigma_{\mathrm{d}}$'s term constants; the semantics of lambda-abstraction and application are fixed by the semantic framework. We take:

$$\mathcal{C}^{\mathrm{r}}_{\mathrm{d}}(\underline{c}_{\tau_1,\ldots,\tau_n}) = \uparrow_{\Sigma_{\mathrm{d}}(\underline{c}_{\tau_1,\ldots,\tau_n})} (\widehat{\mathrm{CST}}\, c) \qquad \mathcal{C}^{\mathrm{r}}_{\mathrm{d}}(\$_b) = \widehat{\mathrm{LIT}}_b$$

That is, a general dynamic constant is simply interpreted as the reflection of its name, while a lifting function forces evaluation of its argument and constructs a representation of the literal result. (It is this forcing of static subcomputations that may cause the whole specialization process to diverge.)

Finally, we are again ready to define the normalization function:

**Definition 5.** *For any dynamic type $\tau$, define the auxiliary function*

$$\mathrm{reify}_\tau \in [\![\tau]\!]^{\mathcal{I}_{\mathrm{s}} \cup \mathcal{I}^{\mathrm{r}}_{\mathrm{d}}} \to \mathbf{E}_\perp, \qquad \mathrm{reify}_\tau = \lambda a. \downarrow_\tau a\, (\eta^\perp 0)$$

*Then for any closed term $\vdash E : \tau$, define the partial function,*

$$\mathrm{norm}^{\mathcal{I}_{\mathrm{s}}}\, E = \begin{cases} \tilde{E} & \text{if } \mathrm{reify}_\tau\, ([\![E]\!]^{\mathcal{I}_{\mathrm{s}} \cup \mathcal{I}^{\mathrm{r}}_{\mathrm{d}}}\, \emptyset) = \eta^\perp \ulcorner \tilde{E} \urcorner \\ \text{undefined} & \text{otherwise} \end{cases}$$

And again, we can state three properties of the normalization function:

**Theorem 6 (Partial Correctness).** *Let $\vdash_{\Sigma_{\mathrm{s}} \cup \Sigma_{\mathrm{d}}} E : \tau$ be a closed term of fully dynamic type. Then*

1. $\mathrm{norm}^{\mathcal{I}_{\mathrm{s}}}$ *is type-preserving (but not necessarily total): if* $\mathrm{norm}^{\mathcal{I}_{\mathrm{s}}}\, E = \tilde{E}$ *for some* $\tilde{E}$ *then* $\vdash_{\Sigma_{\mathrm{d}}} \tilde{E} : \tau$ *and* $\vdash^{\mathrm{nf}} \tilde{E} : \tau$.
2. *If* $\mathrm{norm}^{\mathcal{I}_{\mathrm{s}}}\, E = \tilde{E}$ *for some* $\tilde{E}$ *then* $\mathcal{I}_{\mathrm{s}} \models \tilde{E} = E$.
3. *If* $\mathcal{I}_{\mathrm{s}} \models E = E'$ *then* $\mathrm{norm}^{\mathcal{I}_{\mathrm{s}}}\, E$ *and* $\mathrm{norm}^{\mathcal{I}_{\mathrm{s}}}\, E'$ *are either both undefined or both defined and equal.*

The proof is somewhat more involved than in the pure lambda calculus case, since we can no longer exploit that any term over the full signature is statically equivalent to one in normal form (terms involving static fixed points may have no normal forms). We can, however, adapt an explicit normalization proof based on Kripke logical relations to the domain-theoretic case without too much additional trouble. The details can be found in [Fil99b], which also sketches how the normalization result relates to the correctness proof of the Lambda-mix partial evaluator [JGS93, Section 8.8].

Without strong normalization, another notion from rewriting enters: in general it may be that one series of reductions brings a term to normal form, while another gives rise to an infinite reduction sequence. We usually say that a reduction strategy is *complete* if it terminates with a normal form whenever the term can be reduced to normal form at all. For the pure, untyped lambda calculus, for example, one can show that always contracting the leftmost-outermost redex is a complete strategy for $\beta$-normalization. A similar property holds for our normalizer:

**Theorem 7 (Completeness).** *If for a term $E$, there exists an $\tilde{E}$ satisfying the conclusions of parts (1) and (2) of Theorem 6, then* $\mathrm{norm}^{\mathcal{I}_s} E$ *is in fact defined.*

The proof proceeds by showing (through another simple logical-relations argument) that for any $\vdash_{\Sigma_d} \tilde{E} : \tau$, $\mathrm{norm}^{\mathcal{I}_s} \tilde{E}$ is defined. Thus, if $\mathcal{I}_s \models E = \tilde{E}$, then, by Property (3) of Theorem 6, $\mathrm{norm}^{\mathcal{I}_s} E = \mathrm{norm}^{\mathcal{I}_s} \tilde{E}$ and thus $\mathrm{norm}^{\mathcal{I}_s} E$ must be defined. Again, the details can be found in [Fil99b].

### 4.4 A Normalization Algorithm

Note that, so far, we have only been considering a mathematical normalization function: from the denotation of a term in a particular domain-theoretic model, we can extract a syntactic representation of the normal form of the term, if it exists. We will now consider how to exploit this result to actually compute that normal form using a functional program.

The benefit of limiting the variation of interpretation to just base types and constants should now be apparent: instead of constructing an implementation of a non-standard denotational semantics, we can construct it in terms of an existing implementation of a standard semantics. We only need to construct a syntactic counterpart to the notion of a residualizing interpretation. This can be formalized as follows:

**Definition 6.** *A* realization $\Phi$ *of a signature* $\Sigma$ *over a signature* $\Sigma'$ *is a type-preserving substitution that assigns to every type constant of* $\Sigma$ *a type phrase (not necessarily atomic) over* $\Sigma'$*, and to every term constant of* $\Sigma$ *a term over* $\Sigma'$*. Applying such a substitution to a* $\Sigma$*-phrase (type or term)* $\theta$*, we obtain a* $\Sigma'$*-phrase* $\theta\{\Phi\}$*.*

We assume now that we have a PCF-like programming language with signature $\Sigma_{\mathrm{pl}} \supseteq \Sigma_{\mathrm{s}}$ and interpretation $\mathcal{I}_{\mathrm{pl}}$ agreeing with $\mathcal{I}_{\mathrm{s}}$ on $\Sigma_{\mathrm{s}}$, as well as an executable implementation of the corresponding evaluation function $\mathrm{eval}^{\mathcal{I}_{\mathrm{pl}}}$. For notational simplicity, we will also require that the programming language includes binary product types. (This is not essential, as we could have made all functions curried.)

Assume further that our programming language includes base types $\mathsf{var}$ and $\mathsf{exp}$, with $\mathcal{B}_{\mathrm{pl}}(\mathsf{var}) = \mathbf{V}$ and $\mathcal{B}_{\mathrm{pl}}(\mathsf{exp}) = \mathbf{E}$. Moreover, let $\Sigma_{\mathrm{pl}}$ contain constructor constants corresponding to the semantic constructor functions, for example,

$$\Sigma_{\mathrm{pl}}(\mathsf{VAR}) = \mathsf{var} \rightharpoonup \mathsf{exp} \qquad \mathcal{C}_{\mathrm{pl}}(\mathsf{VAR}) = \lambda d^{\mathbf{V}_\perp}. d \star^{\perp} \lambda v. \eta^{\perp} (\mathrm{VAR}\, v)$$

(Note that we extend the semantic constructor function from sets to flat domains to fit into the interpretation of types.) Finally, we assume a function constant $\mathsf{mkvar} : \mathsf{int} \rightharpoonup \mathsf{var}$ such that for all $i \in \mathbb{N}$, $\mathcal{C}_{\mathrm{pl}}(\mathsf{mkvar})\,(\eta^{\perp}\, i) = \eta^{\perp}\, g_i$.

For the type part of the residualizing interpretation, we first define the abbreviation

$$\mathit{expf} \equiv \mathsf{int} \rightharpoonup \mathsf{exp}$$

and then take, for all dynamic base types $\underline{b}$,

$$\Phi^{\mathrm{r}}(\underline{b}) = \mathit{expf}$$

This gives us exactly $[\![\underline{b}\{\Phi^{\mathrm{r}}\}]\!]^{\mathcal{I}_{\mathrm{pl}}} = \hat{\mathbf{E}} = [\![\underline{b}]\!]^{\mathcal{I}_{\mathrm{s}} \cup \mathcal{I}_{\mathrm{d}}^{\mathrm{r}}}$, and thus $[\![\tau\{\Phi^{\mathrm{r}}\}]\!]^{\mathcal{I}_{\mathrm{pl}}} = [\![\tau]\!]^{\mathcal{I}_{\mathrm{s}} \cup \mathcal{I}_{\mathrm{d}}^{\mathrm{r}}}$ for all $\tau$.

The wrapper functions are likewise denotable by $\Sigma_{\mathrm{pl}}$-terms, for example,

$$\mathit{LAMF} : (\mathsf{var} \dashrightarrow \mathit{expf}) \dashrightarrow \mathit{expf}, \qquad \mathit{LAMF} \equiv \lambda f.\, \lambda i.\, \mathsf{LAM}\cdot(\mathsf{mkvar}\cdot i, f\cdot(i+1))$$

with $[\![\mathit{LAMF}]\!]^{\mathcal{I}_{\mathrm{pl}}} = \widehat{\mathrm{LAM}}$, and analogously for the other wrappers. Note that the explicit forcing in the semantic terms comes for free from the strict behavior of the term-constructor and arithmetic constants. We can then express the realizations of reflection and reification analogously to their semantic definitions:

$$\begin{aligned}
\mathit{reifyf}_{\tau} &: \tau\{\Phi^{\mathrm{r}}\} \dashrightarrow \mathit{expf} \\
\mathit{reifyf}_{\underline{b}} &\equiv \lambda e.\, e \\
\mathit{reifyf}_{\tau_1 \dashrightarrow \tau_2} &\equiv \lambda f.\, \mathit{LAMF}\cdot(\lambda v.\, \mathit{reifyf}_{\tau_2}\cdot(f\cdot(\mathit{reflectf}_{\tau_1}\cdot(\mathit{VARF}\cdot v)))) \\
\mathit{reflectf}_{\tau} &: \mathit{expf} \dashrightarrow \tau\{\Phi^{\mathrm{r}}\} \\
\mathit{reflectf}_{\underline{b}} &\equiv \lambda e.\, e \\
\mathit{reflectf}_{\tau_1 \dashrightarrow \tau_2} &\equiv \lambda e.\, \lambda a.\, \mathit{reflectf}_{\tau_2}\cdot(\mathit{APPF}\cdot(e, \mathit{reifyf}_{\tau_1}\cdot a))
\end{aligned}$$

with $[\![\mathit{reifyf}_{\tau}]\!]^{\mathcal{I}_{\mathrm{pl}}}\,\emptyset = \downarrow_{\tau}$ and $[\![\mathit{reflectf}_{\tau}]\!]^{\mathcal{I}_{\mathrm{pl}}}\,\emptyset = \uparrow_{\tau}$. And as the residualizing realization of the term constants in $\Sigma_{\mathrm{d}}$, we finally take,

$$\begin{aligned}
\Phi^{\mathrm{r}}(\underline{c}_{\tau_1,\ldots,\tau_n}) &= \mathit{reflectf}_{\Sigma_{\mathrm{d}}(\underline{c}_{\tau_1,\ldots,\tau_n})}\cdot(\mathit{CSTF}\cdot c) \\
\Phi^{\mathrm{r}}(\$_{b}) &= \mathit{LITF}_{b}
\end{aligned}$$

It is now straightforward to show:

**Theorem 8 (Implementing the CBN normalizer).** *For any dynamic type $\tau$, we define the term*

$$\mathit{reify}_{\tau} : \tau\{\Phi^{\mathrm{r}}\} \dashrightarrow \mathsf{exp}, \qquad \mathit{reify}_{\tau} \equiv \lambda a.\, \mathit{reifyf}_{\tau}\cdot a\cdot 0$$

*Then the static normal form function of any closed term $\vdash_{\Sigma_{\mathrm{s}} \cup \Sigma_{\mathrm{d}}} E : \tau$ can be computed as:*

$$\mathrm{norm}^{\mathcal{I}_{\mathrm{s}}}\, E = \tilde{E} \;\; \mathit{iff} \;\; \mathrm{eval}^{\mathcal{I}_{\mathrm{pl}}}(\mathit{reify}_{\tau}\cdot E\{\Phi^{\mathrm{r}}\}) = \ulcorner \tilde{E} \urcorner$$

In particular, for partial evaluation, if we have a function of two arguments, where the second argument and the result type are classified as dynamic, that is,

$$\vdash_{\Sigma_{\mathrm{s}} \cup \Sigma_{\mathrm{d}}} F : \sigma \dashrightarrow \tau \dashrightarrow \tau'$$

then for any static value $\vdash_{\Sigma_{\mathrm{s}} \cup \Sigma_{\mathrm{d}}} s : \sigma$, we can compute $\mathrm{norm}^{\mathcal{I}_{\mathrm{s}}}(F\cdot s)$ to obtain the specialized program $\vdash_{\Sigma_{\mathrm{d}}} \widetilde{F_s} : \tau \dashrightarrow \tau'$.

*Remark 3.* The semantics of the type exp is actually a bit subtle. Note that our analysis assumes that $\mathcal{B}_{\rm pl}(\mathsf{exp})$ is a flat domain, with strict constructor functions. This is trivially satisfied if we take exp as, for example, the type of strings. However, if we simply use a Haskell-style datatype to define exp, it will also include many "partially defined" values because of the extra liftings of sum types. Worse, the constructor functions will not be strict, and the reification function may in fact produce partially defined results when static subcomputations diverge. Only when the normalized term has been completely printed can we be sure that the normalization function was in fact defined.

*Remark 4.* When there are no dynamic constants in the signature, the substitution $\Phi^{\rm r}$ simply replaces all occurrences of $\underline{b}$ in type tags with exp. In a polymorphic language such as Haskell or ML, this allows a shortcut: one can simply leave all dynamic types in $E$ as uninstantiated polymorphic type variables; the application of *reify* will instantiate them to exp. Moreover, any (monomorphic) dynamic constants can also be handled using explicit lambda-abstractions. This approach was used in early presentations of TDPE [Dan96], but gets awkward for larger examples. The functor-based approach described below scales up more gracefully.

*Example 2.* Returning to the possible annotations of the power function from Example 1, we get

$$
\begin{aligned}
\mathrm{norm}\,(\$\cdot(\mathit{power}_{ss}\cdot 3\cdot 4)) &= \$\cdot 81 \\
\mathrm{norm}\,(\lambda\!\!\!{}^{-} x^{\underline{\mathsf{int}}}.\,\mathit{power}_{ds}\cdot x\cdot 3) &= \underline{\lambda} g_0^{\mathsf{int}}.\,g_0 \mathbin{\underline{\times}} (g_0 \mathbin{\underline{\times}} (g_0 \mathbin{\underline{\times}} \$\cdot 1)) \\
\mathrm{norm}\,(\lambda\!\!\!{}^{-} x^{\underline{\mathsf{int}}}.\,\mathit{power}_{ds}\cdot x\cdot\text{-}2) & \quad \text{undefined}
\end{aligned}
$$

Note first that ordinary evaluation is just a special case of static normalization. The second example shows how static normalization achieves the partial-evaluation goal of the introduction. Finally, some terms have no static normal form at all; in that case, the normalization function must diverge.

As a further refinement, the signatures and realizations can be very conveniently expressed in terms of parameterized modules in a Standard ML-style module system. The program to be specialized is simply written as the body of a functor parameterized by the signature of dynamic operations. The functor can then be applied to either an evaluating ($\Phi^{\rm e}$) or a residualizing ($\Phi^{\rm r}$) structure. That is, applying the relevant substitutions does not even require an explicit syntactic traversal of the program, making it possible to enrich the static fragment of the language (for example, with pattern matching) without any modification to the partial evaluator itself.

It is also worth noting that the $\tau$-indexed families above can be concisely defined even in ML's type system: consider the type abbreviation

$$\mathit{rr}(\alpha) \equiv (\alpha \dashrightarrow \mathit{expf}) \times (\mathit{expf} \dashrightarrow \alpha)\,.$$

Then for any dynamic type $\tau$, we can construct a term of type $\mathit{rr}(\tau\{\Phi^{\mathrm{r}}\})$ whose value is the pair $(\mathit{reifyf}_\tau, \mathit{reflectf}_\tau)$. We do this by defining once and for all two ML-typable terms

$$\mathit{base} : \mathit{rr}(\mathit{expf}) \qquad \mathit{arrow} : \forall\alpha,\beta.\, \mathit{rr}(\alpha) \,\underline{\times}\, \mathit{rr}(\beta) \,\underline{\to}\, \mathit{rr}(\alpha \,\underline{\to}\, \beta)\,,$$

with which we can then systematically construct the required value. The technique is explained in more detail elsewhere [Yan98].

Finally, the dynamic polymorphic constants (for example, $\underline{\mathrm{fix}}$) now take explicit representations of the types at which they are being instantiated as extra arguments. In the evaluating realization, these extra arguments are ignored, since the standard interpretations of dynamic constants are parametrically polymorphic; but the residualizing realization uses the type representations to construct the reify-reflect pair for $\Sigma(\underline{c}_{\tau_1,\ldots,\tau_n})$ given corresponding pairs for $\tau_1, \ldots, \tau_n$.

We do not show actual runnable code here, since there is no widely adopted CBN language with SML-style functors, allowing multiple implementations of a given signature to coexist in the same program. On the other hand, while the terms above can certainly be coded in ML, their behavior would be suspect for anything involving recursion. We refer the reader to Section 5.5 for actual SML code implementing normalization in a call-by-value language; the corresponding code for CBN is virtually identical, except for the actual definitions of the reification and reflection functions.

# 5 TDPE for Call-by-Value and Computational Effects

To complete the transition to practical programming, we need to account for the fact that execution of functional programs may involve general computational effects, both "internal" (such as catching and throwing exceptions) and "external" (such as performing I/O operations). It is well known that reasoning about such programs requires a more refined notion of equivalence than full $\beta\eta$-conversion.

We will look at computational effects in an ML-like call-by-value setting, where it will turn out that both the semantic and syntactic characterizations of normal forms differ significantly from the purely functional ones. We expect, however, that the results in this section can be adapted to programs in purely functional languages, written in "monadic style": we would then effectively be normalizing with respect to an equational theory including not only $\beta\eta$-conversion, but also the three monad laws.

The effectful setting is where the semantic notion of convertibility really shines: being able to reason about interpreted constants in terms of their denotations, rather than their operational behavior, proves to be a substantial help when proving the correctness of the final normalization-by-evaluation algorithm, since that algorithm itself is implemented in terms of computational effects.

### 5.1 A Call-by-Value Language Framework

As before, a program is a term over a signature of type and term constants. This time, however, the basic language is a bit richer. We add three new components:

- A let-expression for explicitly expressing sequencing.
- Binary products. (This is mainly for cosmetic reasons, as curried arithmetic primitives get somewhat ugly in CBV.)
- A primitive type of booleans and an if-expression. We could easily generalize to general disjoint-union types (see Exercise 8), but simple booleans illustrate the basic principles.

The set of types over $\Sigma$ is therefore now:

$$\frac{b \in \Sigma}{\vdash_\Sigma b\ \mathit{type}} \qquad \frac{\vdash_\Sigma \sigma_1\ \mathit{type} \quad \vdash_\Sigma \sigma_2\ \mathit{type}}{\vdash_\Sigma \sigma_1 \rightharpoonup \sigma_2\ \mathit{type}}$$

$$\frac{\vdash_\Sigma \sigma_1\ \mathit{type} \quad \vdash_\Sigma \sigma_2\ \mathit{type}}{\vdash_\Sigma \sigma_1 \times \sigma_2\ \mathit{type}} \qquad \frac{}{\vdash_\Sigma \mathbf{bool}\ \mathit{type}}$$

The terms are much as before, with the straightforward addition of the following constructors:

$$\frac{\Gamma \vdash_\Sigma E_1 : \sigma_1 \quad \Gamma, x{:}\, \sigma_1 \vdash_\Sigma E_2 : \sigma_2}{\Gamma \vdash_\Sigma \mathbf{let}\ x = E_1\ \mathbf{in}\ E_2 : \sigma_2} \qquad \frac{\Gamma \vdash_\Sigma E_1 : \sigma_1 \quad \Gamma \vdash_\Sigma E_2 : \sigma_2}{\Gamma \vdash_\Sigma (E_1, E_2) : \sigma_1 \times \sigma_2}$$

$$\frac{\Gamma \vdash_\Sigma E : \sigma_1 \times \sigma_2 \quad \Gamma, x_1{:}\, \sigma_1, x_2{:}\, \sigma_2 \vdash_\Sigma E' : \sigma}{\Gamma \vdash_\Sigma \mathbf{match}\ (x_1, x_2) = E\ \mathbf{in}\ E' : \sigma}$$

$$\frac{}{\Gamma \vdash_\Sigma \mathbf{true} : \mathbf{bool}} \qquad \frac{}{\Gamma \vdash_\Sigma \mathbf{false} : \mathbf{bool}}$$

$$\frac{\Gamma \vdash_\Sigma E_1 : \mathbf{bool} \quad \Gamma \vdash_\Sigma E_2 : \sigma \quad \Gamma \vdash_\Sigma E_3 : \sigma}{\Gamma \vdash_\Sigma \mathbf{if}\ E_1\ \mathbf{then}\ E_2\ \mathbf{else}\ E_3 : \sigma}$$

(We use a pattern-matching construct instead of explicit projections, which could be defined like $\mathbf{fst}\, E \equiv \mathbf{match}\ (x, y) = E\ \mathbf{in}\ x$. This gives a more uniform treatment of normal forms, but is not essential. In practice, one would typically extend the language to allow general pattern matching in lambda- and let-bindings. See Exercise 9.)

Again, we say that a complete program is a closed term of base type.

For the semantics, we get a new component: an interpretation is now a quadruple $\mathcal{I} = (\mathcal{B}, \mathcal{L}, \mathcal{C}, \mathcal{T})$, where $\mathcal{T} = (T, \eta, \star)$ is a *monad* modeling the spectrum of effects in the language. To model recursion we require that $\mathcal{T}$ admits a monad morphism from the lifting monad, ensuring that any $A_\perp$-computation can be meaningfully seen as a $TA$-computation. Technically, the condition amounts to requiring that the cpo $TA$ is pointed for any $A$, and that the function $\lambda t.\, t \star f \in TA \to TB$ is strict for any $f \in A \to TB$, that is, that $\perp_{TA} \star f = \perp_{TB}$.

(Of course, one can take the monad $\mathcal{T}$ to be simply lifting, but we will see in a moment why baking this choice into the semantic framework will prevent us from using NBE.)

We can then define the CBV semantics of types:

$$\begin{aligned}
[\![b]\!]^{\mathcal{I}}_{\mathrm{v}} &= \mathcal{B}(b) \\
[\![\mathbf{bool}]\!]^{\mathcal{I}}_{\mathrm{v}} &= \mathbb{B} \\
[\![\sigma_1 \times \sigma_2]\!]^{\mathcal{I}}_{\mathrm{v}} &= [\![\sigma_1]\!]^{\mathcal{I}}_{\mathrm{v}} \times [\![\sigma_2]\!]^{\mathcal{I}}_{\mathrm{v}} \\
[\![\sigma_1 \dashrightarrow \sigma_2]\!]^{\mathcal{I}}_{\mathrm{v}} &= [\![\sigma_1]\!]^{\mathcal{I}}_{\mathrm{v}} \to \mathcal{T}[\![\sigma_2]\!]^{\mathcal{I}}_{\mathrm{v}}
\end{aligned}$$

Note that the meaning of a type is now a cpo that is not necessarily pointed. The meaning of a type assignment is still a product cpo,

$$[\![\Gamma]\!]^{\mathcal{I}}_{\mathrm{v}} = \prod_{x \in \mathrm{dom}\,\Gamma} [\![\Gamma(x)]\!]^{\mathcal{I}}_{\mathrm{v}}$$

but it will not in general be pointed, either.

The meaning of a term $\Gamma \vdash_{\Sigma} E : \sigma$ is now a continuous function $[\![E]\!]^{\mathcal{I}}_{\mathrm{v}} \in [\![\Gamma]\!]^{\mathcal{I}}_{\mathrm{v}} \to \mathcal{T}[\![\sigma]\!]^{\mathcal{I}}_{\mathrm{v}}$,

$$\begin{aligned}
[\![l]\!]^{\mathcal{I}}_{\mathrm{v}}\,\rho &= \eta\,(\mathcal{L}_b(l)) \\
[\![c_{\sigma_1,\ldots,\sigma_n}]\!]^{\mathcal{I}}_{\mathrm{v}}\,\rho &= \eta\,(\mathcal{C}(c_{\sigma_1,\ldots,\sigma_n})) \\
[\![\mathbf{true}]\!]^{\mathcal{I}}_{\mathrm{v}}\,\rho &= \eta\,\mathrm{true} \\
[\![\mathbf{false}]\!]^{\mathcal{I}}_{\mathrm{v}}\,\rho &= \eta\,\mathrm{false} \\
[\![x]\!]^{\mathcal{I}}_{\mathrm{v}}\,\rho &= \eta\,(\rho x) \\
[\![(E_1, E_2)]\!]^{\mathcal{I}}_{\mathrm{v}}\,\rho &= [\![E_1]\!]^{\mathcal{I}}_{\mathrm{v}}\,\rho \star \lambda a_1.\,[\![E_2]\!]^{\mathcal{I}}_{\mathrm{v}}\,\rho \star \lambda a_2.\,\eta\,\langle a_1, a_2\rangle \\
[\![\mathbf{match}\,(x_1, x_2) = E\ \mathbf{in}\ E']\!]^{\mathcal{I}}_{\mathrm{v}}\,\rho &= [\![E]\!]^{\mathcal{I}}_{\mathrm{v}}\,\rho \star \lambda\langle a_1, a_2\rangle.\,[\![E']\!]^{\mathcal{I}}_{\mathrm{v}}\,(\rho[x_1 \mapsto a_1, x_2 \mapsto a_2]) \\
[\![\lambda x^{\sigma}.\,E]\!]^{\mathcal{I}}_{\mathrm{v}}\,\rho &= \eta\,(\lambda a^{[\![\sigma]\!]^{\mathcal{I}}_{\mathrm{v}}}.\,[\![E]\!]^{\mathcal{I}}_{\mathrm{v}}\,(\rho[x \mapsto a])) \\
[\![E_1 \cdot E_2]\!]^{\mathcal{I}}_{\mathrm{v}}\,\rho &= [\![E_1]\!]^{\mathcal{I}}_{\mathrm{v}}\,\rho \star \lambda f.\,[\![E_2]\!]^{\mathcal{I}}_{\mathrm{v}}\,\rho \star \lambda a.\,f\,a \\
[\![\mathbf{if}\ E_1\ \mathbf{then}\ E_2\ \mathbf{else}\ E_3]\!]^{\mathcal{I}}_{\mathrm{v}}\,\rho &= [\![E_1]\!]^{\mathcal{I}}_{\mathrm{v}}\,\rho \star \lambda b.\,\mathrm{if}\ b\ \mathrm{then}\ [\![E_2]\!]^{\mathcal{I}}_{\mathrm{v}}\,\rho\ \mathrm{else}\ [\![E_3]\!]^{\mathcal{I}}_{\mathrm{v}}\,\rho \\
[\![\mathbf{let}\ x = E_1\ \mathbf{in}\ E_2]\!]^{\mathcal{I}}_{\mathrm{v}}\,\rho &= [\![E_1]\!]^{\mathcal{I}}_{\mathrm{v}}\,\rho \star \lambda a.\,[\![E_2]\!]^{\mathcal{I}}_{\mathrm{v}}\,(\rho[x \mapsto a])
\end{aligned}$$

(Note that the let-construct appears redundant, because we have

$$[\![\mathbf{let}\ x = E_1\ \mathbf{in}\ E_2]\!]^{\mathcal{I}}_{\mathrm{v}} = [\![(\lambda x.\,E_2)\,E_1]\!]^{\mathcal{I}}_{\mathrm{v}}\,,$$

but it turns out that including it gives a nicer syntactic characterization of normal forms.)

The standard static signature is similar to that of Definition 3, except that we no longer include the type constant $\mathsf{bool}$, the associated literals $\mathsf{true}$ and $\mathsf{false}$, or the constant $\mathsf{if}$ in $\Sigma_{\mathrm{s}}$: those are now part of the fixed language core. Also, since it only makes sense to define recursive values of functional type, the fixed-point constants are now parameterized by two types,

$$\mathsf{fix}_{\sigma_1,\sigma_2} : ((\sigma_1 \dashrightarrow \sigma_2) \dashrightarrow \sigma_1 \dashrightarrow \sigma_2) \dashrightarrow \sigma_1 \dashrightarrow \sigma_2$$

Finally, we make the arithmetic and comparison operators uncurried, so that the infix operation $x + y$ now stands for $+\cdot(x, y)$, etc.

The standard interpretation of the constants is also what could be expected:

$$\begin{aligned}
\mathcal{B}_{\mathsf{s}}(\mathsf{int}) &= \mathbb{Z} \\
\mathcal{C}_{\mathsf{s}}(\diamond) &= \lambda(x,y)^{\mathbb{Z}\times\mathbb{Z}}.\eta\,(x \diamond y) \quad {\scriptstyle \diamond\in\{+,-,\times,=,<\}} \\
\mathcal{C}_{\mathsf{s}}(\mathsf{fix}_{\sigma_1,\sigma_2}) &= \lambda f^{([\![\sigma_1]\!]\to T[\![\sigma_2]\!])\to T([\![\sigma_1]\!]\to T[\![\sigma_2]\!])}. \\
&\qquad \eta\,(\textstyle\bigsqcup_{i\in\omega}(\lambda g^{[\![\sigma_1]\!]\to T[\![\sigma_2]\!]}.\,\lambda a^{[\![\sigma_1]\!]}.\,f\,g \star \lambda g'.\,g'\,a)^i\,(\lambda a^{[\![\sigma_1]\!]}.\,\bot_{T[\![\sigma_2]\!]}))
\end{aligned}$$

Note how we make crucial use of the requirement that $T[\![\sigma_2]\!]$ must have a least element, for the interpretation of fix.

### 5.2 Binding Times and Static Normalization

As before, we consider a binding-time annotated program to be expressed over a signature which has been explicitly partitioned into a static and a dynamic part. We still say that a general type is fully dynamic if it is constructed using base types from only the dynamic part of the signature.

For the interpretation of a partitioned signature, we require that all static constants have meanings *parametric* in the choice of monad, being able to rely only on $TA$ being pointed, but not on any other structure of $\mathcal{T}$; this still allows us to include operations such as the fixed-point operator above, and possibly additional primitive partial functions. On the other hand, the meanings of the dynamic constants may be expressed with respect to a *specific* monad. Thus, in a combined interpretation $\mathcal{I}_{\mathsf{s}} \cup \mathcal{I}_{\mathsf{d}}$, all the constants can still be given a consistent interpretation based on the monad of $\mathcal{I}_{\mathsf{d}}$. As before, we can then define a notion of static equivalence: $\mathcal{I}_{\mathsf{s}} \models_{\mathsf{v}} E = E'$ iff for all $\mathcal{I}_{\mathsf{d}}$ interpreting the dynamic types, constants, and monad, $[\![E]\!]_{\mathsf{v}}^{\mathcal{I}_{\mathsf{s}}\cup\mathcal{I}_{\mathsf{d}}} = [\![E']\!]_{\mathsf{v}}^{\mathcal{I}_{\mathsf{s}}\cup\mathcal{I}_{\mathsf{d}}}$.

This notion of static equivalence captures transformations that are safe for any CBV language with monadic effects. For example, when $x$ does not occur free in $E_3$, we always have

$$\mathcal{I}_{\mathsf{s}} \models_{\mathsf{v}} (\textbf{let } y = (\textbf{let } x = E_1 \textbf{ in } E_2) \textbf{ in } E_3) = (\textbf{let } x = E_1 \textbf{ in let } y = E_2 \textbf{ in } E_3)$$

*Remark 5.* Another interesting static equivalence is the following:

$$\mathcal{I}_{\mathsf{s}} \models_{\mathsf{v}} f\cdot(\textbf{if } E_1 \textbf{ then } E_2 \textbf{ else } E_3) = \textbf{if } E_1 \textbf{ then } f\cdot E_2 \textbf{ else } f\cdot E_3$$

This static equivalence is particularly remarkable since it does *not* hold in the CBN semantics, unless $f$ is known to denote a strict function, or $E_1$ is guaranteed to converge. This equation, sometimes known as a commuting conversion, allows us to eliminate all **bool**-typed variables as soon as they are introduced (by a lambda-, match- or let-binding), which enables a simple CBV NBE result for booleans and sums. An NBE result for sum types in a CBN-like setting was obtained very recently [ADHS01], but the details are considerably more involved than for the CBV case treated below.

It is easy to show that the computational lambda calculus [Mog89] is sound with respect to static equivalence. (Under certain circumstances, one can also show that it is complete, much like $\beta\eta$-conversion was complete with respect to CBN static equivalence.)

For a syntactic characterization of normal forms, somewhat analogous to the CBN case, we now have notions of *normal values* and *normal computations*:

$$\frac{\Delta(x) = \underline{b}}{\Delta \vdash^{\mathrm{nv}} x : \underline{b}} \qquad \frac{l \in \Xi(b)}{\Delta \vdash^{\mathrm{nv}} \$\cdot l : \underline{b}} \qquad \frac{\Delta \vdash^{\mathrm{nv}} E_1 : \tau_1 \qquad \Delta \vdash^{\mathrm{nv}} E_2 : \tau_2}{\Delta \vdash^{\mathrm{nv}} (E_1, E_2) : \tau_1 \times \tau_2}$$

$$\frac{}{\Delta \vdash^{\mathrm{nv}} \mathbf{true} : \mathbf{bool}} \qquad \frac{}{\Delta \vdash^{\mathrm{nv}} \mathbf{false} : \mathbf{bool}} \qquad \frac{\Delta, x\colon \tau_1 \vdash^{\mathrm{nc}} E : \tau_2}{\Delta \vdash^{\mathrm{nv}} \lambda x^{\tau_1}. E : \tau_1 \rightarrow \tau_2}$$

$$\frac{\Delta \vdash^{\mathrm{nv}} E : \tau}{\Delta \vdash^{\mathrm{nc}} E : \tau} \qquad \frac{\Delta(x) = \mathbf{bool} \qquad \Delta \vdash^{\mathrm{nc}} E_1 : \tau \qquad \Delta \vdash^{\mathrm{nc}} E_2 : \tau}{\Delta \vdash^{\mathrm{nc}} \mathbf{if}\ x\ \mathbf{then}\ E_1\ \mathbf{else}\ E_2 : \tau}$$

$$\frac{\Delta(x) = \tau_1 \times \tau_2 \qquad \Delta, x_1\colon \tau_1, x_2\colon \tau_2 \vdash^{\mathrm{nc}} E : \tau}{\Delta \vdash^{\mathrm{nc}} \mathbf{match}\ (x_1, x_2) = x\ \mathbf{in}\ E : \tau}$$

$$\frac{\Delta(x_2) = \tau_1 \rightarrow \tau_2 \qquad \Delta \vdash^{\mathrm{nv}} E_1 : \tau_1 \qquad \Delta, x_1\colon \tau_2 \vdash^{\mathrm{nc}} E_2 : \tau}{\Delta \vdash^{\mathrm{nc}} \mathbf{let}\ x_1 = x_2 \cdot E_1\ \mathbf{in}\ E_2 : \tau}$$

$$\frac{\Sigma(c) = \tau_1 \rightarrow \tau_2 \qquad \Delta \vdash^{\mathrm{nv}} E_1 : \tau_1 \qquad \Delta, x\colon \tau_2 \vdash^{\mathrm{nc}} E_2 : \tau}{\Delta \vdash^{\mathrm{nc}} \mathbf{let}\ x = c \cdot E_1\ \mathbf{in}\ E_2 : \tau}$$

In particular, for terms not involving boolean or product types, a normal value is either a base-typed constant or variable, or of the form

$$\lambda x.\, \mathbf{let}\ x_1 = f_1 \cdot V_1\ \mathbf{in}\ \cdots\ \mathbf{let}\ x_n = f_n \cdot V_n\ \mathbf{in}\ V_{n+1} \quad (n \geq 0)\ ,$$

where all the $V_i$ are normal values, and each $f_i$ is a function-typed constant or variable.

(These rules are actually a bit too permissive, in that they admit both variants of statically equivalent terms, such as

$$\lambda x^{\mathbf{bool}}.\, \mathbf{if}\ x\ \mathbf{then}\ 3\ \mathbf{else}\ 4 \quad \text{and} \quad \lambda x^{\mathbf{bool}}.\, \mathbf{if}\ x\ \mathbf{then}\ 3\ \mathbf{else}\ \mathbf{if}\ x\ \mathbf{then}\ 5\ \mathbf{else}\ 4$$

Of course, a proper normalization function can only return one of those. To get a more precise syntactic characterization of normal forms, one needs to further restrict the occurrences of sum- and product-typed variables, and to pick a canonical order for their elimination. This can be done fairly straightforwardly using a split typing context [Fil01]; we omit the details here.)

*Remark 6.* The observant reader may note that the rules for normal forms essentially correspond (modulo implicit uses of contraction and weakening) to the left- and right-introduction rules for a Gentzen-style intuitionistic sequent calculus. (The general form of the if-rule as a case expression introduces bound variables corresponding to the disjuncts.) Moreover, the typing of the general let corresponds to a cut. In other words, reducing CBV terms to normal form is closely related to cut-elimination. On the other hand, for the CBN normalizer, the rules correspond to the usual introduction and elimination rules in a natural-deduction calculus. It would be interesting to further investigate these connections to standard proof-normalization theory. Some results in this direction have already been obtained by Ohori [Oho99]; see [Fil01] for a more detailed discussion of this issue.

### 5.3 A Residualizing Interpretation for CBV

We now aim to find an NBE result for the CBV setting. Note that for the residualizing interpretation, we need a more "powerful" effect than simple partiality (as embodied by the lifting monad), because we need to distinguish between terms such as

$$E_1 \equiv \dot{\lambda} f.\,\dot{\lambda} x.\,(\dot{\lambda} y.\,x)\cdot(f\cdot x) \quad \text{and} \quad E_2 \equiv \dot{\lambda} f.\,\dot{\lambda} x.\,x$$

which have observably different behavior (even when the effect is only partiality), and therefore should have different normal forms. But taking partiality as the residualizing effect will not allow us to extract enough information from the residualizing interpretations of those two terms to reconstruct them accurately: for any $\mathcal{I}$ whose $\mathcal{T}$ is the lifting monad, we have $[\![E_1]\!]^{\mathcal{I}}_{\mathrm{v}}\,\rho \sqsubseteq [\![E_2]\!]^{\mathcal{I}}_{\mathrm{v}}\,\rho$ (with the strictness of the inequality demonstrated by application of both sides to $\lambda a.\,\bot$). But $\ulcorner E_1 \urcorner \not\sqsubseteq \ulcorner E_2 \urcorner$, so there can be no *monotone* (let alone continuous) function $\mathrm{reify} \in [\![(b \dot{\rightarrow} b) \dot{\rightarrow} b \dot{\rightarrow} b]\!]^{\mathcal{I}}_{\mathrm{v}} \rightarrow \mathbf{E}_\bot$ such that $\mathrm{reify}([\![E_1]\!]^{\mathcal{I}}_{\mathrm{v}}\,\emptyset) = \eta^\bot \ulcorner E_1 \urcorner$ and $\mathrm{reify}([\![E_2]\!]^{\mathcal{I}}_{\mathrm{v}}\,\emptyset) = \eta^\bot \ulcorner E_2 \urcorner$.

Instead, we pick for the residualizing interpretation a "universal" effect, which will ensure that we can probe the residualizing semantic interpretations closely enough to make all the required distinctions.

Incidentally, such a choice also allows the task of fresh-name generation to be folded into the residualization monad, instead of requiring us to work with term families such as $\hat{\mathbf{E}}$. We can now use an effect-based notion of freshness, generating "globally unique" variable names; with a suitable effect structure, we can actually make this concept precise.

We first define the name-generation monad. This is just a state-passing monad on top of partiality; the state is the "next free index":

$$\begin{aligned} T^{\mathrm{g}} A &= \mathbb{Z} \rightarrow (A \times \mathbb{Z})_\bot \\ \eta^{\mathrm{g}}\, a &= \lambda i.\,\eta^\bot \langle a, i \rangle \\ t \star^{\mathrm{g}} f &= \lambda i.\,t\,i \star^\bot \lambda \langle a, i' \rangle.\,f\,a\,i' \end{aligned}$$

(As in CBN, we use integers rather than natural numbers for the index, in anticipation of embedding the construction into an existing programming language.)

Using $T^{\mathrm{g}}$ we can define an effectful computation that generates a fresh name, and one that initializes the counter for a delimited subcomputation:

$$\begin{array}{rcl} \mathrm{new} & \in & T^{\mathrm{g}}\mathbf{V} \\ \mathrm{new} & = & \lambda i.\,\eta^{\perp}\,\langle g_i, i+1\rangle \end{array} \qquad \begin{array}{rcl} \mathrm{withct}_A & \in & T^{\mathrm{g}}A \to T^{\mathrm{g}}A \\ \mathrm{withct}_A & = & \lambda t.\,\lambda i.\,t\,0 \star^{\perp} \lambda\langle a, i'\rangle.\,\eta^{\perp}\,\langle a, i\rangle \end{array}$$

Further, we define $T^{\mathrm{c}}$ to be the continuation monad with answer domain chosen as $T^{\mathrm{g}}\mathbf{E}$:

$$\begin{array}{rcl} T^{\mathrm{c}}A & = & (A \to T^{\mathrm{g}}\mathbf{E}) \to T^{\mathrm{g}}\mathbf{E} \\ \eta^{\mathrm{c}}\,a & = & \lambda\kappa.\,\kappa\,a \\ t \star^{\mathrm{c}} f & = & \lambda\kappa.\,t\,(\lambda a.\,f\,a\,\kappa) \end{array}$$

Every $T^{\mathrm{g}}$-computation can be seen as a $T^{\mathrm{c}}$-computation without control effects, through the monad morphism $\gamma_A^{\mathrm{g,c}} \in T^{\mathrm{g}}A \to T^{\mathrm{c}}A$ given by

$$\gamma_A^{\mathrm{g,c}}\,t = \lambda\kappa^{A \to T^{\mathrm{g}}\mathbf{E}}.\,t \star^{\mathrm{g}} \kappa.$$

In particular, we can "lift" the name-generation functions to $T^{\mathrm{c}}$-computations as

$$\begin{array}{rcl} \mathrm{cnew} & \in & T^{\mathrm{c}}\mathbf{V} \\ \mathrm{cnew} & = & \lambda\kappa.\,\lambda i.\,\kappa\,g_i\,(i+1) \end{array} \qquad \begin{array}{rcl} \mathrm{cwithct}_A & \in & T^{\mathrm{c}}A \to T^{\mathrm{c}}A \\ \mathrm{cwithct}_A\,t & = & \lambda\kappa.\,\lambda i.\,t\,(\lambda a.\,\lambda i'.\,\kappa\,a\,i)\,0 \end{array}$$

These satisfy the natural equations $\mathrm{cnew} = \gamma^{\mathrm{g,c}}\,\mathrm{new}$ and $\mathrm{cwithct}\,(\gamma^{\mathrm{g,c}}\,t) = \gamma^{\mathrm{g,c}}\,(\mathrm{withct}\,t)$.

In any continuation monad, we can define operators for capturing complete continuations (such as Scheme's `call/cc`). However, for our particular choice of answer domain, we can also define operations for working with *delimited* or *composable* continuations [DF90]:

$$\begin{array}{rcl} \mathrm{reset} & \in & T^{\mathrm{c}}\mathbf{E} \to T^{\mathrm{c}}\mathbf{E} \\ \mathrm{reset}\,t & = & \gamma_{\mathbf{E}}^{\mathrm{g,c}}\,(t\,\eta^{\mathrm{g}}) = \lambda\kappa.\,t\,\eta^{\mathrm{g}} \star^{\mathrm{g}} \kappa \\ \mathrm{shift}_A & \in & ((A \to T^{\mathrm{c}}\mathbf{E}) \to T^{\mathrm{c}}\mathbf{E}) \to T^{\mathrm{c}}A \\ \mathrm{shift}_A\,h & = & \lambda\kappa.\,h\,(\lambda a.\,\gamma_{\mathbf{E}}^{\mathrm{g,c}}\,(\kappa\,a))\,\eta^{\mathrm{g}} = \lambda\kappa.\,h\,(\lambda a.\,\lambda\kappa'.\,\kappa\,a \star^{\mathrm{g}} \kappa')\,\eta^{\mathrm{g}} \end{array}$$

Here, $\mathrm{reset}\,t$ evaluates $t$ with an empty continuation, thus encapsulating any control effects $t$ might have. $\mathrm{shift}\,h$ captures and removes the current continuation (up to the nearest enclosing reset), and passes it to $h$ as a control-effect-free function.

These definitions are somewhat awkward to work with directly. However, we can easily check that they validate the following equational reasoning principles:

$$\begin{array}{rcl} \mathrm{reset}\,(\eta^{\mathrm{c}}\,a) & = & \eta^{\mathrm{c}}\,a \\ \mathrm{reset}\,(\mathrm{shift}\,h \star^{\mathrm{c}} f) & = & \mathrm{reset}\,(h\,(\lambda a.\,\mathrm{reset}\,(f\,a))) \\ \mathrm{reset}\,(\gamma^{\mathrm{g,c}}t \star^{\mathrm{c}} f) & = & \gamma^{\mathrm{g,c}}t \star^{\mathrm{c}} \lambda a.\,\mathrm{reset}\,(f\,a) \end{array}$$

The first of these says that a reset does not affect effect-free computations. The second specifies the behavior of a delimited shift-operation. (Remember that $\mathrm{shift}\, h = \mathrm{shift}\, h \star^{\mathrm{c}} \eta^{\mathrm{c}}$, and $(\mathrm{shift}\, h \star^{\mathrm{c}} f) \star^{\mathrm{c}} g = \mathrm{shift}\, h \star^{\mathrm{c}} (\lambda a.\, f\, a \star^{\mathrm{c}} g)$ by the usual monad laws, so the equation is widely applicable.) The third allows computations such as cnew (without control effects, but not necessarily completely effect-free) to be moved outside a reset. For example, we can derive

$$\begin{aligned}
&\mathrm{reset}\,\big(\mathrm{shift}\,(\lambda k.\, k\, 3 \star^{\mathrm{c}} \lambda x.\, \eta^{\mathrm{c}}\,(x+1)) \star^{\mathrm{c}} \lambda r.\, \eta^{\mathrm{c}}\,(2 \times r)\big) \star^{\mathrm{c}} \lambda a.\, \eta^{\mathrm{c}}\,(-a)\\
&\quad = \mathrm{reset}\,\big((\lambda k.\, k\, 3 \star^{\mathrm{c}} \lambda x.\, \eta^{\mathrm{c}}\,(x+1))\,(\lambda a.\, \mathrm{reset}\,(\eta^{\mathrm{c}}\,(2 \times a)))\big) \star^{\mathrm{c}} \lambda a.\, \eta^{\mathrm{c}}\,(-a)\\
&\quad = \mathrm{reset}\,\big(\mathrm{reset}\,(\eta^{\mathrm{c}}\, 6) \star^{\mathrm{c}} \lambda x.\, \eta^{\mathrm{c}}\,(x+1)\big) \star^{\mathrm{c}} \lambda a.\, \eta^{\mathrm{c}}\,(-a)\\
&\quad = \mathrm{reset}\,\big(\eta^{\mathrm{c}}\, 6 \star^{\mathrm{c}} \lambda x.\, \eta^{\mathrm{c}}\,(x+1)\big) \star^{\mathrm{c}} \lambda a.\, \eta^{\mathrm{c}}\,(-a)\\
&\quad = \mathrm{reset}\,(\eta^{\mathrm{c}}\, 7) \star^{\mathrm{c}} \lambda a.\, \eta^{\mathrm{c}}\,(-a) = \eta^{\mathrm{c}}\,(-7)
\end{aligned}$$

Note how the doubling operation (which uses the result of shift directly) gets captured as part of $k$, while the outer negation (which is protected by a reset) is not. It is this ability of shift to reschedule "future" computations that will allow us to properly arrange the residual code as it is being incrementally generated.

We can now take as the non-standard interpretation of dynamic base types and effects,

$$\mathcal{B}^{\mathrm{r}}_{\mathrm{d}}(\underline{b}) = \mathbf{E} \qquad \text{and} \qquad \mathcal{T}^{\mathrm{r}} = \mathcal{T}^{\mathrm{c}}$$

which again allows us to define reification and reflection functions:

$$\begin{aligned}
\downarrow^{\mathrm{v}}_{\tau} &\in [\![\tau]\!]^{\mathcal{I}_{\mathrm{s}} \cup \mathcal{I}^{\mathrm{r}}_{\mathrm{d}}}_{\mathrm{v}} \to T^{\mathrm{r}}\mathbf{E}\\
\downarrow^{\mathrm{v}}_{\underline{b}} &= \lambda e.\, \eta^{\mathrm{r}}\, e\\
\downarrow^{\mathrm{v}}_{\mathbf{bool}} &= \lambda b.\, \mathrm{if}\ b\ \mathrm{then}\ \eta^{\mathrm{r}}\, \mathrm{TRUE}\ \mathrm{else}\ \eta^{\mathrm{r}}\, \mathrm{FALSE}\\
\downarrow^{\mathrm{v}}_{\tau_1 \underline{\times} \tau_2} &= \lambda\langle a_1, a_2\rangle.\, \downarrow^{\mathrm{v}}_{\tau_1} a_1 \star^{\mathrm{r}} \lambda e_1.\, \downarrow^{\mathrm{v}}_{\tau_2} a_2 \star^{\mathrm{r}} \lambda e_2.\, \eta^{\mathrm{r}}\,(\mathrm{PAIR}\,\langle e_1, e_2\rangle)\\
\downarrow^{\mathrm{v}}_{\tau_1 \underline{\to} \tau_2} &=\\
&\lambda f.\, \mathrm{cnew} \star^{\mathrm{r}} \lambda v.\, \mathrm{reset}\,\big(\uparrow^{\mathrm{v}}_{\tau_1}(\mathrm{VAR}\, v) \star^{\mathrm{r}} \lambda a.\, f\, a \star^{\mathrm{r}} \lambda b.\, \downarrow^{\mathrm{v}}_{\tau_2} b\big) \star^{\mathrm{r}} \lambda e.\, \eta^{\mathrm{r}}\,(\mathrm{LAM}\,\langle v, e\rangle)
\end{aligned}$$

$$\begin{aligned}
\uparrow^{\mathrm{v}}_{\tau} &\in \mathbf{E} \to T^{\mathrm{r}}[\![\tau]\!]^{\mathcal{I}_{\mathrm{s}} \cup \mathcal{I}^{\mathrm{r}}_{\mathrm{d}}}_{\mathrm{v}}\\
\uparrow^{\mathrm{v}}_{\underline{b}} &= \lambda e.\, \eta^{\mathrm{r}}\, e\\
\uparrow^{\mathrm{v}}_{\mathbf{bool}} &= \lambda e.\, \mathrm{shift}\,(\lambda k.\, k\, \mathrm{true} \star^{\mathrm{r}} \lambda e_1.\, k\, \mathrm{false} \star^{\mathrm{r}} \lambda e_2.\, \eta^{\mathrm{r}}\,(\mathrm{IF}\,\langle e, e_1, e_2\rangle))\\
\uparrow^{\mathrm{v}}_{\tau_1 \underline{\times} \tau_2} &=\\
&\lambda e.\, \mathrm{shift}\,(\lambda k.\, \mathrm{cnew} \star^{\mathrm{r}} \lambda v_1.\, \mathrm{cnew} \star^{\mathrm{r}} \lambda v_2.\\
&\qquad\qquad \mathrm{reset}\,\big(\uparrow^{\mathrm{v}}_{\tau_1}(\mathrm{VAR}\, v_1) \star^{\mathrm{r}} \lambda a_1.\, \uparrow^{\mathrm{v}}_{\tau_2}(\mathrm{VAR}\, v_2) \star^{\mathrm{r}} \lambda a_2.\, k\,\langle a_1, a_2\rangle\big) \star^{\mathrm{r}} \lambda e'.\\
&\qquad\qquad\quad \eta^{\mathrm{r}}\,(\mathrm{MATCH}\,\langle\langle v_1, v_2\rangle, e, e'\rangle))\\
\uparrow^{\mathrm{v}}_{\tau_1 \underline{\to} \tau_2} &= \lambda e.\, \eta^{\mathrm{r}}(\lambda a.\, \mathrm{cnew} \star^{\mathrm{r}} \lambda v.\\
&\qquad\qquad \mathrm{shift}\,(\lambda k.\, \downarrow^{\mathrm{v}}_{\tau_1} a \star^{\mathrm{r}} \lambda e'.\, \mathrm{reset}\,(\uparrow^{\mathrm{v}}_{\tau_2}(\mathrm{VAR}\, v) \star^{\mathrm{r}} k) \star^{\mathrm{r}} \lambda e''.\\
&\qquad\qquad\quad \eta^{\mathrm{r}}\,(\mathrm{LET}\,\langle v, \mathrm{APP}\,\langle e, e'\rangle, e''\rangle)))
\end{aligned}$$

Observe how the non-trivial reflection functions use shift to wrap a syntactic binding or a test around their invocation points, which are expecting semantic results. Note also how reflection of a boolean expression sequentially traces through both possibilities for the boolean value returned, by passing both true and false to the continuation $k$.

*Remark 7.* It is evident that a new variable is generated every time the pseudo-semantic function returned by $\uparrow_{\tau_1 \to \tau_2} e$ is applied. Had we instead, incorrectly, written $\uparrow_{\tau_1 \to \tau_2}$ as $\lambda e.\,\mathrm{cnew} \star^{\mathrm{r}} \lambda v.\,\eta^{\mathrm{r}}\,(\lambda a.\,\mathrm{shift}\,\cdots)$, all such applications would share the same let-variable name, causing clashes. This illustrates how monads allow us to be precise about "freshness" in a way that informal annotations of definitions do not readily support.

The residualizing interpretation of dynamic constants and lifting is now:

$$\begin{aligned} \mathcal{C}^{\mathrm{r}}_{\mathrm{d}}(\underline{c}_{\tau_1,\ldots,\tau_n}) &= \uparrow^{\mathrm{v}}_{\Sigma(c_{\tau_1,\ldots,\tau_n})} (\mathrm{CST}\, c) \\ \mathcal{C}^{\mathrm{r}}_{\mathrm{d}}(\$_b) &= \lambda n^{\mathcal{B}_{\mathrm{s}}(b)}.\,\eta^{\mathrm{r}}\,(\mathrm{LIT}_b\, n) \end{aligned}$$

Finally, we can again define a static-normalization function. For CBN, we could restrict ourselves to normalizing closed terms, because free variables could be lambda-abstracted without changing the result. For CBV, we make the additional restriction that the term to be normalized must be a formal value (constant, variable, lifted literal, or lambda-abstraction); we can always wrap a non-value term $E$ in a dummy lambda-abstraction $\underline{\lambda} d.\, E$. We thus take:

**Definition 7.** *For any dynamic type $\tau$, define the auxiliary function*

$$\mathrm{reify}^{\mathrm{v}}_{\tau} \in [\![\tau]\!]^{\mathcal{I}_{\mathrm{s}} \cup \mathcal{I}^{\mathrm{r}}_{\mathrm{d}}}_{\mathrm{v}} \to T^{\mathrm{r}}\mathbf{E}, \qquad \mathrm{reify}^{\mathrm{v}}_{\tau} = \lambda a.\,\mathrm{cwithct}_{\mathbf{E}}\,(\downarrow^{\mathrm{v}}_{\tau} a)$$

*(Note how initialization of the counter now happens using computational effects.) Then, for any closed value $\vdash_{\Sigma_{\mathrm{s}} \cup \Sigma_{\mathrm{d}}} E : \tau$, we define the normalization function*

$$\mathrm{norm}^{\mathcal{I}_{\mathrm{s}}}_{\mathrm{v}}\, E = \begin{cases} \tilde{E} & \textit{if } \mathrm{reify}^{\mathrm{v}}_{\tau}\,([\![E]\!]^{\mathcal{I}_{\mathrm{s}} \cup \mathcal{I}^{\mathrm{r}}_{\mathrm{d}}}_{\mathrm{v}}\, \emptyset) = \eta^{\mathrm{r}} \ulcorner \tilde{E} \urcorner \\ \textit{undefined} & \textit{otherwise} \end{cases}$$

Again, we can summarize the result:

**Theorem 9 (Correctness of CBV normalizer).** *Partial correctness:*

1. *For any closed value $\vdash_{\Sigma_{\mathrm{s}} \cup \Sigma_{\mathrm{d}}} E : \tau$, if $\mathrm{norm}^{\mathcal{I}_{\mathrm{s}}}_{\mathrm{v}}\, E = \tilde{E}$ for some $\tilde{E}$ then $\vdash^{\mathrm{nv}}_{\Sigma_{\mathrm{d}}} \tilde{E} : \tau$.*
2. *If $\mathrm{norm}^{\mathcal{I}_{\mathrm{s}}}_{\mathrm{v}}\, E = \tilde{E}$ then $\mathcal{I}_{\mathrm{s}} \models_{\mathrm{v}} E = \tilde{E}$.*
3. *if $\mathcal{I}_{\mathrm{s}} \models_{\mathrm{v}} E = E'$ then $\mathrm{norm}^{\mathcal{I}_{\mathrm{s}}}_{\mathrm{v}}\, E = \mathrm{norm}^{\mathcal{I}_{\mathrm{s}}}_{\mathrm{v}}\, E'$ (both defined and equal, or both undefined).*

*Completeness: If $E$ is statically equivalent to some term in normal form, $\mathrm{norm}^{\mathcal{I}_{\mathrm{s}}}_{\mathrm{v}}\, E$ is defined.*

The proofs for both halves are similar to the CBN case, but somewhat more elaborate, due to the extra parameterization on a dynamic monad, and the more complicated reification and reflection functions.

*Remark 8.* It is possible to define a CBV normalization function using only a suitable state monad in the residualizing interpretation, rather than continuations [SK01, Section 4]. This approach, however, does not allow the normalizer to handle booleans and sum types as part of the semantic framework.

### 5.4 A CBV Normalization Algorithm

Again, we can formulate the semantic normalization results in terms of a syntactic realization of the components. As before, we assume that our programming language has types var, exp, and constants corresponding to the constructor functions, for example,

$$\Sigma_{\text{pl}}(\mathsf{APP}) = \mathsf{exp} \times \mathsf{exp} \rightharpoonup \mathsf{exp} \qquad \mathcal{C}_{\text{pl}}(\mathsf{APP}) = \lambda\langle e_1, e_2\rangle.\, \eta^{\text{r}}\,(\text{APP}\,\langle e_1, e_2\rangle)$$

(Note that, unlike for the CBN case, the arguments of the constructor functions are values, not computations)

We also assume that $\mathcal{T}_{\text{pl}} = \mathcal{T}^{\text{r}}$, and that we have constants whose interpretations correspond to the semantic functions for name generation and control primitives:

$$\begin{aligned} \Sigma_{\text{pl}}(\mathsf{gensym}) &= 1 \to \mathsf{var} & \mathcal{C}_{\text{pl}}(\mathsf{gensym}) &= \lambda\langle\rangle.\,\text{cnew} \\ \Sigma_{\text{pl}}(\mathsf{withct}_\sigma) &= (1 \to \sigma) \to \sigma & \mathcal{C}_{\text{pl}}(\mathsf{withct}_\sigma) &= \lambda t.\,\text{cwithct}\,(t\,\langle\rangle) \\ \Sigma_{\text{pl}}(\mathsf{reset}) &= (1 \to \mathsf{exp}) \to \mathsf{exp} & \mathcal{C}_{\text{pl}}(\mathsf{reset}) &= \lambda t.\,\text{reset}\,(t\,\langle\rangle) \\ \Sigma_{\text{pl}}(\mathsf{shift}_\sigma) &= ((\sigma \to \mathsf{exp}) \to \mathsf{exp}) \to \sigma & \mathcal{C}_{\text{pl}}(\mathsf{shift}_\sigma) &= \text{shift}_{[\![\sigma]\!]} \end{aligned}$$

Like in the CBN case, a practical programming language usually has many further types and constants, beyond what we need to construct the residualizing interpretation of the dynamic signature. Additionally, a CBV language typically has a wider spectrum of effects than captured by the residualizing monad $T^{\text{r}}$. (For example, it may allow functions to have side effects or to perform I/O operations.) And it is not obvious that this additional generality of the programming language will not get in the way of our result.

What we require is that we can *simulate* the behavior of a $T^{\text{r}}$-computation using whatever more general monad the programming language provides. In fact, we only need to consider evaluation of programs without top-level residualization-specific effects. In other words, we only require that the evaluation partial function for complete programs (closed terms of base type) satisfies:

$$\text{eval}_{\text{v}}^{\mathcal{I}_{\text{pl}}}\, E = \begin{cases} l & \text{if } [\![E]\!]_{\text{v}}^{\mathcal{I}_{\text{pl}}}\,\emptyset = \eta^{\text{pl}}\,(\mathcal{L}_b\,(l)) \\ \text{undefined} & \text{if } [\![E]\!]_{\text{v}}^{\mathcal{I}_{\text{pl}}}\,\emptyset = \bot \end{cases}$$

Note that, unlike the case for CBN, these two possibilities are not exhaustive: the result of $\text{eval}_{\text{v}}^{\mathcal{I}_{\text{pl}}}$ is unspecified for programs with top-level effects other than divergence, for example, those that try to capture the top-level continuation, or rely on the initial value of the gensym counter. Evaluation of such programs may abort, diverge, or even return unpredictable results. Of course, the program $E$ that we evaluate to execute the normalization algorithm will not have such effects.

One can show that an $\mathrm{eval}_{\mathrm{v}}^{\mathcal{I}_{\mathrm{pl}}}$ with the above properties can be implemented through a further realization of $\Sigma_{\mathrm{pl}}$ in any general-purpose functional language that supports first-class continuations and references [Fil99a]. (In fact, we can implement a whole hierarchy of monads by such an embedding, and thus avoid the need to explicitly lift many monad operations, such as withct to cwithct.) The details are beyond the scope of these notes, but we do show the actual construction in Section 5.5.

We can now simply take the residualizing realizations of all dynamic base types as the type of term representations,

$$\Phi_{\mathrm{v}}^{\mathrm{r}}(\underline{b}) = \mathsf{exp}$$

and express the CBV reification and reflection functions as $\Sigma_{\mathrm{pl}}$-terms with effects:

$$\begin{aligned}
\mathit{reifyve}_{\tau} &: \tau\{\Phi_{\mathrm{v}}^{\mathrm{r}}\} \dot{\rightarrow} \mathsf{exp} \\
\mathit{reifyve}_{\underline{b}} &\equiv \dot{\lambda} e.\, e \\
\mathit{reifyve}_{\mathbf{bool}} &\equiv \dot{\lambda} b.\, \mathbf{if}\ b\ \mathbf{then}\ \mathsf{TRUE}\ \mathbf{else}\ \mathsf{FALSE} \\
\mathit{reifyve}_{\tau_1 \dot{\times} \tau_2} &\equiv \dot{\lambda} p.\, \mathbf{match}\ (x_1, x_2) = p\ \mathbf{in}\ \mathsf{PAIR}\cdot(\mathit{reifyve}_{\tau_1}\cdot a_1, \mathit{reifyve}_{\tau_2}\cdot a_2) \\
\mathit{reifyve}_{\tau_1 \dot{\rightarrow} \tau_2} &\equiv \dot{\lambda} f.\, \mathbf{let}\ v = \mathsf{gensym}\cdot() \\
&\qquad \mathbf{in}\ \mathsf{LAM}\cdot(v, \mathsf{reset}\cdot(\dot{\lambda}().\, \mathit{reifyve}_{\tau_2}\cdot(f\cdot(\mathit{reflectve}_{\tau_1}\cdot(\mathsf{VAR}\cdot v)))))
\end{aligned}$$

$$\begin{aligned}
\mathit{reflectve}_{\tau} &: \mathsf{exp} \dot{\rightarrow} \tau\{\Phi_{\mathrm{v}}^{\mathrm{r}}\} \\
\mathit{reflectve}_{\underline{b}} &\equiv \dot{\lambda} e.\, e \\
\mathit{reflectve}_{\mathbf{bool}} &\equiv \dot{\lambda} e.\, \mathsf{shift}\cdot(\dot{\lambda} k.\, \mathsf{IF}\cdot(e, k\cdot\mathbf{true}, k\cdot\mathbf{false})) \\
\mathit{reflectve}_{\tau_1 \dot{\times} \tau_2} &\equiv \\
&\dot{\lambda} e.\, \mathbf{let}\ v_1 = \mathsf{gensym}\cdot() \\
&\quad \mathbf{in}\ \mathbf{let}\ v_2 = \mathsf{gensym}\cdot() \\
&\qquad \mathbf{in}\ \mathsf{shift}\cdot(\dot{\lambda} k.\, \mathsf{MATCH}\cdot((v_1, v_2), e, \\
&\qquad\qquad \mathsf{reset}\cdot(\dot{\lambda}().\, k\cdot(\mathit{reflectve}_{\tau_1}\cdot(\mathsf{VAR}\cdot v_1), \mathit{reflectve}_{\tau_2}\cdot(\mathsf{VAR}\cdot v_2))))) \\
\mathit{reflectve}_{\tau_1 \dot{\rightarrow} \tau_2} &\equiv \dot{\lambda} e.\, \dot{\lambda} a.\, \mathbf{let}\ v = \mathsf{gensym}\cdot() \\
&\qquad \mathbf{in}\ \mathsf{shift}(\lambda k.\, \mathsf{LET}\cdot(v, \mathsf{APP}\cdot(e, \mathit{reifyve}_{\tau_1}\cdot a), \\
&\qquad\qquad \mathsf{reset}\cdot(\dot{\lambda}().\, k\cdot(\mathit{reflectve}_{\tau_2}\cdot(\mathsf{VAR}\cdot v)))))
\end{aligned}$$

Note that, although these terms are significantly more complicated than their CBN counterparts, they still share some basic structure. For reification at functional type, we still reflect a new VAR, apply the function, reify the result, and generate a LAM. Similarly, for reflection, we reify the function argument, generate an APP, and reflect the result (bound to an intermediate variable this time.) The main conceptual change is in the added shift and reset operations to suitably rearrange the generated code.

We complete the residualizing realization of the dynamic signature by taking

$$\Phi^{\mathrm{r}}_{\mathrm{v}}(\underline{c}_{\tau_1,\ldots,\tau_n}) = \mathit{reflectve}_{\Sigma(\underline{c}_{\tau_1,\ldots,\tau_n})}\cdot(\mathsf{CST}\cdot c)$$
$$\Phi^{\mathrm{r}}_{\mathrm{v}}(\$_b) = \lambda n.\,\mathsf{LIT}_b\cdot n$$

Finally, we can state again a procedure for computing CBV normal forms:

**Theorem 10 (Implementing the CBV normalizer).** *We define the auxiliary term*

$$\mathit{reifyv}_\tau : \tau\{\Phi^{\mathrm{r}}_{\mathrm{v}}\} \rightarrow \mathsf{exp}, \qquad \mathit{reifyv}_\tau \equiv \lambda a.\,\mathsf{withct}_{\mathsf{exp}}\cdot(\lambda().\,\mathit{reifyve}_\tau\cdot a)$$

*Then for any closed value* $\vdash_{\Sigma_s \cup \Sigma_d} E : \tau$, *its CBV static normal form can be computed as*

$$\mathrm{norm}^{\mathcal{I}_s}_{\mathrm{v}}\, E = \tilde{E} \;\; \mathit{iff} \;\; \mathrm{eval}^{\mathcal{I}_{\mathrm{pl}}}_{\mathrm{v}}(\mathit{reifyv}_\tau\cdot E\{\Phi^{\mathrm{r}}_{\mathrm{v}}\}) = \ulcorner\tilde{E}\urcorner$$

For partial evaluation, we again take the $E$ to be normalized as the partial application of the binding-time separated original program to the static argument:

*Example 3.* Let us revisit the power function from Example 1 in a CBV setting. With conditionals now being part of the framework, here are the two interesting annotations of power:

$$\mathit{power}_{ds} : \underline{\iota} \rightarrow \overline{\iota} \rightarrow \underline{\iota} = \lambda x.\,\overline{\mathsf{fix}}_{\overline{\iota},\underline{\iota}}\cdot(\lambda p.\,\lambda n.\,\mathbf{if}\ n \,\overline{=}\, 0\ \mathbf{then}\ \$\cdot 1\ \mathbf{else}\ x \,\underline{\times}\, p\cdot(n \,\overline{-}\, 1))$$
$$\mathit{power}_{sd} : \overline{\iota} \rightarrow \underline{\iota} \rightarrow \underline{\iota} =$$
$$\lambda x.\,\underline{\mathsf{fix}}_{\underline{\iota},\underline{\iota}}\cdot(\lambda p.\,\lambda n.\,\mathbf{if}\ n \,\underline{=}\, \$\cdot 0\ \mathbf{then}\ \$\cdot 1\ \mathbf{else}\ \$\cdot x \,\underline{\times}\, p\cdot(n \,\underline{-}\, \$\cdot 1))$$

(Note that, unlike for the CBN variant, the "ifs" are not binding-time annotated.) Computing the normal form of $\lambda x.\,\mathit{power}_{ds}\cdot x\cdot 3$, we get

$$\lambda g_0.\,\mathbf{let}\ g_1 = g_0 \,\underline{\times}\, \$\cdot 1\ \mathbf{in}\ \mathbf{let}\ g_2 = g_0 \,\underline{\times}\, g_1\ \mathbf{in}\ \mathbf{let}\ g_3 = g_0 \,\underline{\times}\, g_2\ \mathbf{in}\ g_3$$

Conversely, if we specialize with respect to the base, by computing the normal form of $\lambda n.\,\mathit{power}_{sd}\cdot 5\cdot n$, we obtain essentially just the let-normal form of the original program, with the literal argument 5 inlined:

$$\begin{array}{l}\lambda g_0.\,\mathbf{let}\ g_1 = \underline{\mathsf{fix}}_{\underline{\iota},\underline{\iota}}\cdot(\lambda g_2.\,\lambda g_3.\,\mathbf{let}\ g_4 = (g_3 \,\underline{=}\, \$\cdot 0)\\ \qquad\qquad\qquad\qquad\qquad\quad \mathbf{in}\ \mathbf{if}\ x_4\ \mathbf{then}\ \$\cdot 1\\ \qquad\qquad\qquad\qquad\qquad\qquad \mathbf{else}\ \mathbf{let}\ g_5 = g_3 \,\underline{-}\, \$\cdot 1\\ \qquad\qquad\qquad\qquad\qquad\qquad\qquad \mathbf{in}\ \mathbf{let}\ g_6 = g_2\cdot g_5\\ \qquad\qquad\qquad\qquad\qquad\qquad\qquad\quad \mathbf{in}\ \mathbf{let}\ g_7 = \$\cdot 5 \,\underline{\times}\, g_6\ \mathbf{in}\ g_7)\\ \quad \mathbf{in}\ \mathbf{let}\ g_8 = g_1\cdot g_0\ \mathbf{in}\ g_8\end{array}$$

*Remark 9.* Note that the normalized forms contain what seems to be excessive let-sequentialization of trivial arithmetic functions. This is because the residualizing interpretation specifically does not know anything about the intended evaluating interpretation of those constants, and in particular whether they might have computational effects that must not be reordered, discarded, or duplicated.

While the explicit naming of all intermediate results may be useful if the specialized programs are to be further machine-processed, it makes them hard to read for humans. Of course, one could unfold the "trivial" lets in a separate post-processing phase, but doing so loses some of the appeal of generating code directly from the semantics.

However, it is actually possible to annotate the types of "pure" arithmetic primitives to make them let-unfoldable at generation time, much as for CBN functions [Dan96]. Formally, such an annotation corresponds to imposing constraints on possible behaviors of the dynamic interpretations of $\times$, $=$, etc., so that these constants may only be interpreted as semantic functions that factor through the $\eta$ of the dynamic monad.

### 5.5 Complete Code for CBV Normalization

For completeness, we include below the full code for the implementation of the CBV normalizer. The implementation of shift/reset in Figure 2 is equivalent to the one from [Fil99a], but streamlined a bit for SML/NJ's notion of first-class continuation. Figure 3 shows the implementation of type-indexed function families and presents the dynamic signature. Figure 4 shows the evaluating and residualizing interpretations of the dynamic signature, as well as an example of a binding-time separated term parameterized over the dynamic signature. (The function `power_ds` uses the evaluating interpretation explicitly, to highlight the parallels with `power_sd`. In practice, the static operations in `power_ds` would usually be expressed directly in terms of the corresponding native ML constructs.) Finally, Figure 5 shows a few concrete execution examples of evaluating and residualizing the power function.

### 5.6 Exercises

*Exercise 7.* Make the ML implementation of TDPE generate residual terms with explicit type tags for lambda-abstractions and polymorphic constants.

*Exercise 8.* Extend the ML implementation of TDPE with disjoint unions (sums).

*Exercise 9.* Extend TDPE to generate pattern-matching bindings for let and lambda instead of using an explicit match construct.

*Exercise 10.* The first Futamura projection is defined as the specialization of an interpreter with respect to a program [Fut71,Fut99]; it is a standard exercise in partial evaluation. In this open exercise, you are asked to write an interpreter for a simple imperative language, and to specialize it with respect to a program of your choice.

Specifically, you should write a core interpreter, in denotational style, as the body of a functor; this functor should be parameterized with the generic interpretation of each elementary operation that has to be happen at runtime (such

```
functor Control (type ans) :
sig
   val reset : (unit -> ans) -> ans
   val shift : (('a -> ans) -> ans) -> 'a
end =
struct
   open SMLofNJ.Cont
   exception MissingReset
   val mk : ans cont option ref = ref NONE
   fun abort x =
      case !mk of SOME k => throw k x | NONE => raise MissingReset

   type ans = ans
   fun reset t =
      let val m = !mk
          val r = callcc (fn k => (mk := SOME k; abort (t ())))
      in mk := m; r end
   fun shift h =
      callcc (fn k => abort (h (fn v => reset (fn () => throw k v))))
end;

type var = string
datatype exp =
   VAR of var
 | CST of var
 | LIT_int of int
 | PAIR of exp * exp
 | TRUE
 | FALSE
 | LAM of var * exp
 | APP of exp * exp
 | LET of var * exp * exp
 | MATCH of (string * string) * exp * exp
 | IF of exp * exp * exp;

structure Aux :
sig
   val gensym : unit -> var
   val withct : (unit -> 'a) -> 'a
   val reset : (unit -> exp) -> exp
   val shift : (('a -> exp) -> exp) -> 'a
end =
struct
   val n = ref 0
   fun gensym () =
      let val x = "x" ^ (Int.toString (!n)) in n := (!n+1); x end
   fun withct t = let val on = !n
                  in n := 0; let val r = t () in n := on; r end end

   structure C = Control (type ans = exp)
   val reset = C.reset
   val shift = C.shift
end;
```

**Fig. 2.** Auxiliary definitions

```
structure Norm =
struct
   open Aux
   datatype 'a rr = RR of ('a -> exp) * (exp -> 'a)

   val dint = RR (fn e => e, fn e => e)
   val bool = RR (fn b => if b then TRUE else FALSE,
                  fn e => shift (fn k => IF (e, k true, k false)))
   fun prod (RR (rya, rta), RR (ryb, rtb)) =
        RR (fn p => PAIR (rya (#1 p), ryb (#2 p)),
            fn e => let val v1 = gensym ()
                        val v2 = gensym ()
                    in shift (fn k =>
                         MATCH ((v1,v2), e,
                                reset (fn () => k (rta (VAR v1),
                                                   rtb (VAR v2)))))
                    end)
   fun arrow (RR (rya, rta), RR (ryb, rtb)) =
        RR (fn f => let val v = gensym ()
                    in LAM (v, reset (fn () => ryb (f (rta (VAR v)))))
                    end,
            fn e => fn a => let val v = gensym ()
                            in shift (fn k =>
                                 LET (v, APP (e, rya a),
                                      reset (fn () => k (rtb (VAR v)))))
                            end)

   fun reify (RR (ry, rt)) a = withct (fn () => ry a)
   fun reflect (RR (ry, rt)) = rt
end;

signature DYN =
sig
   type dint
   type 'a rep

   val dint : dint rep
   val bool : bool rep
   val prod : 'a rep * 'b rep -> ('a * 'b) rep
   val arrow : 'a rep * 'b rep -> ('a -> 'b) rep

   val lift_int : int -> dint

   val plus : dint * dint -> dint
   val minus : dint * dint -> dint
   val times : dint * dint -> dint
   val equal : dint * dint -> bool
   val less : dint * dint -> bool

   val fix : ('a rep * 'b rep) -> (('a -> 'b) -> 'a -> 'b) -> 'a -> 'b
end;
```

**Fig. 3.** Normalization algorithm and dynamic signature

```
structure EvalD : DYN =
struct
   type dint = int
   type 'a rep = unit

   val dint = ()
   val bool = ()
   fun prod ((),()) = ()
   fun arrow ((),()) = ()

   fun lift_int n = n
   val plus = op +       val minus = op -       val times = op *
   val equal = op =      val less = op <

   fun fix ((),()) f = fn x => f (fix ((),()) f) x
end;

structure ResD : DYN =
struct
   open Aux Norm
   type dint = exp
   type 'a rep = 'a rr

   val lift_int = LIT_int
   val plus = reflect (arrow (prod (dint, dint), dint)) (CST "+")
   val minus = reflect (arrow (prod (dint, dint), dint)) (CST "-")
   val times = reflect (arrow (prod (dint, dint), dint)) (CST "*")
   val equal = reflect (arrow (prod (dint, dint), bool)) (CST "=")
   val less = reflect (arrow (prod (dint, dint), bool)) (CST "<")

   fun fix (rra, rrb) =
      reflect (arrow (arrow (arrow (rra, rrb), arrow (rra, rrb)),
                      arrow (rra, rrb)))
              (CST "fix")
end;

functor Power (D : DYN) =
struct
   fun power_ds x =
      EvalD.fix (EvalD.dint, EvalD.dint)
        (fn p => fn n =>
            if EvalD.equal (n, EvalD.lift_int 0)
            then D.lift_int 1
            else D.times (x, p (EvalD.minus(n, EvalD.lift_int 1))))

   fun power_sd x =
      D.fix (D.dint, D.dint)
        (fn p => fn n =>
            if D.equal (n, D.lift_int 0)
            then D.lift_int 1
            else D.times (D.lift_int x, p (D.minus (n, D.lift_int 1))))
end;
```

**Fig. 4.** Evaluating and residualizing realizations

```
structure PE = Power (EvalD);

val n1 = PE.power_ds (EvalD.lift_int 5) 3;
(* val n1 = 125 : EvalD.dint *)

val n2 = PE.power_sd 5 (EvalD.lift_int 3);
(* val n2 = 125 : EvalD.dint *)

structure PR = Power (ResD);

val t1 = Norm.reify (Norm.arrow (Norm.dint, Norm.dint))
                    (fn x => PR.power_ds x 3);
(*
val t1 =
  LAM
    ("x0",
     LET
       ("x1",APP (CST "*",PAIR (VAR "x0",LIT_int 1)),
        LET
          ("x2",APP (CST "*",PAIR (VAR "x0",VAR "x1")),
           LET ("x3",APP (CST "*",PAIR (VAR "x0",VAR "x2")),VAR "x3"))))
  : exp
*)

val t2 = Norm.reify (Norm.arrow (Norm.dint, Norm.dint))
                    (fn n => PR.power_sd 5 n);
(*
val t2 =
  LAM
    ("x0",
     LET
       ("x1",
        APP
          (CST "fix",
           LAM
             ("x2",
              LAM
                ("x3",
                 LET
                   ("x4",APP (CST "=",PAIR (VAR "x3",LIT_int 0)),
                    IF
                      (VAR "x4",LIT_int 1,
                       LET
                         ("x5",APP (CST "-",PAIR (VAR "x3",LIT_int 1)),
                          LET
                            ("x6",APP (VAR "x2",VAR "x5"),
                             LET
                               ("x7",
                                APP (CST "*",PAIR (LIT_int 5,VAR "x6")),
                                VAR "x7")))))))),
        LET ("x8",APP (VAR "x1",VAR "x0"),VAR "x8"))) : exp
*)
```

**Fig. 5.** Examples: evaluating and specializing power

as arithmetic, state lookup and modification, I/O operations, and fixpoints for loops), much as in the power example. You should also write two structures: one for the static interpretations of all elementary constructs, and one for their dynamic interpretations. Again, as in the power example, instantiating the functor with the static structure should yield an interpreter, while instantiating it with the dynamic structure and should yield the core of a compiler.

Some inspiration for solving this exercise can be found in Danvy's lecture notes on type-directed partial evaluation [Dan98], in Grobauer and Yang's treatment of the second Futamura projection [GY01], and in Danvy and Vestergaard's take on semantics-based compiling by type-directed partial evaluation [DV96].

## 6 Summary and Conclusions

We have shown two different versions of NBE in Sections 2 and 3, and in Sections 4 and 5 we showed how to generalize the idea of NBE to TDPE. Some of the key properties of NBE which we have exploited for TDPE are:

– Normal forms are characterized in terms of undirected equivalence, rather than directed reduction.
– The notion of equivalence is sound for equality with respect to a wide variety of interpretations.
– Among those interpretations, we pick a particular, quasi-syntactic one, which allows us to extract syntactic terms from denotations.

On the other hand, we also wish to emphasize some important adaptations and changes:

– TDPE introduces a notion of binding times, in the form of a distinction between interpreted (static) and uninterpreted (dynamic) base types and constants.
– We characterize equivalence in TDPE semantically (equality of interpretations in all models), rather than syntactically (convertibility).
– We consider a language with computational effects – either just potential divergence, or general monadic effects – not only a direct set-theoretic interpretation of functions.

Type-directed partial evaluation can be seen as a prime example of "applied semantics": while the basic TDPE algorithm, even for call-by-value, can be expressed in a few lines, we only get a proper understanding of how and why it works by considering its semantic counterpart.

It is somewhat surprising that the notion of normalization by evaluation is so robust and versatile. It may well be possible to find other instances within computer science – even outside of the field of programming-language theory – where an NBE view allows us to drastically simplify and speed up computations of canonical representatives of an equivalence class.

## References


[ADHS01] Thorsten Altenkirch, Peter Dybjer, Martin Hofmann, and Philip Scott. Normalization by evaluation for typed lambda calculus with coproducts. In *Proceedings of the 16th Annual IEEE Symposium on Logic in Computer Science*, pages 303–310, Boston, Massachusetts, June 2001.

[AHS95] Thorsten Altenkirch, Martin Hofmann, and Thomas Streicher. Categorical reconstruction of a reduction free normalization proof. In D. Pitt, D. E. Rydeheard, and P. Johnstone, editors, *Category Theory and Computer Science, 6th International Conference*, number 953 in Lecture Notes in Computer Science, Cambridge, UK, August 1995.

[AHS96] Thorsten Altenkirch, Martin Hofmann, and Thomas Streicher. Reduction-free normalization for a polymorphic system. In *Proceedings of the 11th Annual IEEE Symposium on Logic in Computer Science*, pages 98–106, New Brunswick, New Jersey, July 1996.

[Asa02] Kenichi Asai. Binding-time analysis for both static and dynamic expressions. *New Generation Computing*, 20(1):27–51, 2002. Preliminary version available in the proceedings of SAS 1999 (LNCS 1694).

[Aug98] Lennart Augustsson. Cayenne – a language with dependent types. In *ACM SIGPLAN International Conference on Functional Programming*, pages 239–250, Baltimore, Maryland, September 1998.

[Bar77] Henk Barendregt. The type free lambda calculus. In *Handbook of Mathematical Logic*, pages 1092–1132. North-Holland, 1977.

[Bar90] Henk Barendregt. Functional programming and lambda calculus. In *Handbook of Theoretical Computer Science*, pages 323–363. Elsevier, 1990.

[Bar92] Henk P. Barendregt. Lambda calculi with types. In *Handbook of Logic in Computer Science*, volume 2, pages 117–309. Oxford University Press, 1992.

[Ber93] Ulrich Berger. Program extraction from normalization proofs. In M. Bezem and J. F. Groote, editors, *Typed Lambda Calculi and Applications*, number 664 in Lecture Notes in Computer Science, pages 91–106, Utrecht, The Netherlands, March 1993.

[BS91] Ulrich Berger and Helmut Schwichtenberg. An inverse of the evaluation functional for typed λ-calculus. In *Proceedings of the Sixth Annual IEEE Symposium on Logic in Computer Science*, pages 203–211, Amsterdam, The Netherlands, July 1991.

[CD93a] Charles Consel and Olivier Danvy. Tutorial notes on partial evaluation. In *Proceedings of the Twentieth Annual ACM Symposium on Principles of Programming Languages*, pages 493–501, 1993.

[CD93b] Thierry Coquand and Peter Dybjer. Intuitionistic model constructions and normalization proofs. In H. Barendregt and T. Nipkow, editors, *Types for Proofs and Programs, International Workshop TYPES'93*, number 806 in Lecture Notes in Computer Science, Nijmegen, The Netherlands, May 1993.

[CD97] Thierry Coquand and Peter Dybjer. Intuitionistic model constructions and normalization proofs. *Mathematical Structures in Computer Science*, 7:75–94, 1997.

[ČDS98] Djordje Čubrić, Peter Dybjer, and Philip Scott. Normalization and the Yoneda embedding. *Mathematical Structures in Computer Science*, 8:153–192, 1998.

[Dan96] Olivier Danvy. Pragmatics of type-directed partial evaluation. In O. Danvy, R. Glück, and P. Thiemann, editors, *Partial Evaluation*, number 1110 in Lecture Notes in Computer Science, pages 73–94, Dagstuhl, Germany, February 1996. Springer-Verlag. Extended version available as the technical report BRICS RS-96-15.

[Dan98] Olivier Danvy. Type-directed partial evaluation. In J. Hatcliff, T. Æ. Mogensen, and P. Thieman, editors, *Partial Evaluation – Practice and Theory; Proceedings of the 1998 DIKU Summer School*, number 1706 in Lecture Notes in Computer Science, pages 367–411. Springer-Verlag, Copenhagen, Denmark, July 1998.

[DD98] Olivier Danvy and Peter Dybjer, editors. *Proceedings of the 1998 APPSEM Workshop on Normalization by Evaluation, NBE '98,* (Gothenburg, Sweden, May 8–9, 1998), number NS-98-8 in Note Series, Department of Computer Science, University of Aarhus, May 1998. BRICS.

[DF90] Olivier Danvy and Andrzej Filinski. Abstracting control. In *Proceedings of the 1990 ACM Conference on Lisp and Functional Programming*, pages 151–160, Nice, France, June 1990.

[DMP95] Olivier Danvy, Karoline Malmkjær, and Jens Palsberg. The essence of eta-expansion in partial evaluation. *Lisp and Symbolic Computation*, 8(3):209–227, 1995.

[DV96] Olivier Danvy and René Vestergaard. Semantics-based compiling: A case study in type-directed partial evaluation. In *Eighth International Symposium on Programming Language Implementation and Logic Programming*, number 1140 in Lecture Notes in Computer Science, pages 182–197, Aachen, Germany, September 1996.

[Fil99a] Andrzej Filinski. Representing layered monads. In *Proceedings of the 26th ACM SIGPLAN-SIGACT Symposium on Principles of Programming Languages*, pages 175–188, San Antonio, Texas, January 1999.

[Fil99b] Andrzej Filinski. A semantic account of type-directed partial evaluation. In G. Nadathur, editor, *International Conference on Principles and Practice of Declarative Programming*, number 1702 in Lecture Notes in Computer Science, pages 378–395, Paris, France, September 1999.

[Fil01] Andrzej Filinski. Normalization by evaluation for the computational lambda-calculus. In S. Abramsky, editor, *Typed Lambda Calculi and Applications*, number 2044 in Lecture Notes in Computer Science, pages 151–165, Krakow, Poland, May 2001.

[Fut71] Yoshihiko Futamura. Partial evaluation of computation process – an approach to a compiler-compiler. *Systems, Computers, Controls*, 2(5):721–728, 1971. Reprinted in *Higher-Order and Symbolic Computation*, 12(4):381–391, 1999.

[Fut99] Yoshihiko Futamura. Partial evaluation of computation process, revisited. *Higher-Order and Symbolic Computation*, 12(4):377–380, 1999.

[Gom91] Carsten K. Gomard. A self-applicable partial evaluator for the lambda calculus: Correctness and pragmatics. *ACM Transactions on Programming Languages and Systems*, 12(4):147–172, April 1991.

[GP99] Murdoch Gabbay and Andrew Pitts. A new approach to abstract syntax involving binders. In *Proceedings of the 14th Annual IEEE Symposium on Logic in Computer Science*, pages 214–224, Trento, Italy, July 1999.

[GY01] Bernd Grobauer and Zhe Yang. The second Futamura projection for type-directed partial evaluation. *Higher-Order and Symbolic Computation*, 14(2/3):173–219, 2001.

[JGS93] Neil D. Jones, Carsten K. Gomard, and Peter Sestoft. *Partial Evaluation and Automatic Program Generation.* Prentice Hall International Series in Computer Science. Prentice-Hall, 1993. Available electronically at `http://www.dina.dk/~sestoft/pebook/`.

[Laf88] Yves Lafont. *Logiques, Catégories et Machines.* PhD thesis, Université de Paris VII, Paris, France, January 1988.

[Mit96] John C. Mitchell. *Foundations for Programming Languages.* The MIT Press, 1996.

[ML75a] Per Martin-Löf. About models for intuitionistic type theories and the notion of definitional equality. In S. Kanger, editor, *Proceedings of the 3rd Scandinavian Logic Symposium*, pages 81–109, 1975.

[ML75b] Per Martin-Löf. An intuitionistic theory of types: Predicative part. In H. E. Rose and J. C. Shepherdson, editors, *Logic Colloquium '73*, pages 73–118. North-Holland, 1975.

[MN93] Lena Magnusson and Bengt Nordström. The ALF proof editor and its proof engine. In H. Barendregt and T. Nipkow, editors, *Types for Proofs and Programs, International Workshop TYPES'93*, number 806 in Lecture Notes in Computer Science, pages 213–237, Nijmegen, The Netherlands, May 1993.

[Mog89] Eugenio Moggi. Computational lambda-calculus and monads. In *Proceedings of the Fourth Annual Symposium on Logic in Computer Science*, pages 14–23, Pacific Grove, California, June 1989. IEEE.

[Mog92] Torben Æ. Mogensen. Efficient self-interpretation in lambda calculus. *Journal of Functional Programming*, 2(3):345–364, July 1992.

[NN88] Flemming Nielson and Hanne Riis Nielson. Two-level semantics and code generation. *Theoretical Computer Science*, 56(1):59–133, January 1988.

[Oho99] Atsushi Ohori. A Curry-Howard isomorphism for compilation and program execution. In J.-Y. Girard, editor, *Typed Lambda Calculi and Applications*, number 1581 in Lecture Notes in Computer Science, pages 280–294, L'Aquila, Italy, April 1999.

[Pau00] Lawrence C. Paulson. Foundations of functional programming. Notes from a course given at the Computer Laboratory of Cambridge University, available from `http://www.cl.cam.ac.uk/users/lcp/papers/#Courses`, 2000.

[Plo75] Gordon D. Plotkin. Call-by-name, call-by-value and the λ-calculus. *Theoretical Computer Science*, 1(2):125–159, December 1975.

[Plo77] Gordon D. Plotkin. LCF considered as a programming language. *Theoretical Computer Science*, 5(3):223–255, December 1977.

[Rey72] John C. Reynolds. Definitional interpreters for higher-order programming languages. In *Proceedings of 25th ACM National Conference*, pages 717–740, Boston, Massachusetts, August 1972. Reprinted in *Higher-Order and Symbolic Computation*, 11(4):363–397, 1998.

[Ruf93] Erik Ruf. *Topics in Online Partial Evaluation.* PhD thesis, Stanford University, Stanford, California, February 1993. Technical report CSL-TR-93-563.

[SK01] Eijiro Sumii and Naoki Kobayashi. A hybrid approach to online and offline partial evaluation. *Higher-Order and Symbolic Computation*, 14(2/3):101–142, 2001.

[SW74] Christopher Strachey and Christopher P. Wadsworth. Continuations: A mathematical semantics for handling full jumps. Technical Monograph PRG-11, Oxford University Computing Laboratory, Programming Research Group, Oxford, England, 1974. Reprinted in *Higher-Order and Symbolic Computation*, 13(1/2):135–152, April 2000.

[Win93] Glynn Winskel. *The Formal Semantics of Programming Languages: An Introduction.* The MIT Press, 1993.

[Yan98] Zhe Yang. Encoding types in ML-like languages. In *ACM SIGPLAN International Conference on Functional Programming*, pages 289–300, Baltimore, Maryland, September 1998. Extended version to appear in TCS.

# Computing with Real Numbers

## I. The LFT Approach to Real Number Computation

## II. A Domain Framework for Computational Geometry

Abbas Edalat[1] and Reinhold Heckmann[2]

[1] Department of Computing, Imperial College
180 Queens Gate, London SW7 2BZ, UK
ae@doc.ic.ac.uk

[2] AbsInt Angewandte Informatik GmbH
Stuhlsatzenhausweg 69, D-66123 Saarbrücken, Germany
heckmann@absint.com

**Abstract.** We introduce, in Part I, a number representation suitable for exact real number computation, consisting of an exponent and a mantissa, which is an infinite stream of signed digits, based on the interval $[-1, 1]$. Numerical operations are implemented in terms of *linear fractional transformations* (LFT's). We derive lower and upper bounds for the number of argument digits that are needed to obtain a desired number of result digits of a computation, which imply that the complexity of LFT application is that of multiplying $n$-bit integers. In Part II, we present an accessible account of a domain-theoretic approach to computational geometry and solid modelling which provides a data-type for designing robust geometric algorithms, illustrated here by the convex hull algorithm.

## Table of Contents



G. Barthe et al. (Eds.): Applied Semantics, LNCS 2395, pp. 193–267, 2002.

# Part I: The LFT Aproach to Real Number Computation

## 1 Introduction

Computing with real numbers is one of the main applications of "computers". Yet real numbers are infinite mathematical objects (digit sequences, Cauchy sequences, nested sequences of intervals, or the like). Within finite time, one may only hope to obtain a finite part of a real number, giving an approximation to some accuracy.

This also means that comparison on real numbers is undecidable. Consider the predicate $x > 0$ applied to the number $x$ represented as the nested sequence of intervals $([-\frac{1}{n}, \frac{1}{n}])_{n \geq 0}$. Within finite time, only a finite number of these intervals can be inspected, which always contain positive as well as negative numbers so that no decision on the sign of $x$ is possible.

The problems mentioned above can be avoided by restricting attention to some subset of real numbers which can be finitely described. An obvious choice are the *rational numbers*, but this means that operations such as square root or tangent are not possible. A larger such set consists of the *algebraic numbers*, i.e., the roots of integer polynomials. With algebraic numbers, square roots and higher roots are possible, but trigonometric functions such as sine, cosine or tangent are still not supported.

Usually, a different approach is chosen. A finite set of machine-representable *floating-point numbers* is singled out, and fast operations are provided which approximate the standard operations and functions: if, say, the square root of a floating-point number is computed, then the resulting floating-point number is usually not the exact mathematical answer, but a number very close to it. The errors introduced by these approximations are known as *round-off errors*, and the easiest approach is to simply ignore them because they are so small. Yet in certain situations, round-off errors may accumulate to yield a big error. An example where this happens is the following number sequence defined by Jean-Michel Muller (found in [40]):

$$a_0 = \frac{11}{2}, \qquad a_1 = \frac{61}{11}, \qquad a_{n+1} = 111 - \frac{1130 - \frac{3000}{a_{n-1}}}{a_n}.$$

With the Unix program bc, one can compute with an arbitrary, but fixed number of decimal places. Let $a_n^{(k)}$ be the sequence element $a_n$ computed with an accuracy of $k$ decimal places. Computing with 5 decimal places yields the following results (rounded to 3 places for presentation):

| | |
|---|---|
| $a_0^{(5)}$ | 5.500 |
| $a_1^{(5)}$ | 5.545 |
| $a_2^{(5)}$ | 5.590 |
| $a_3^{(5)}$ | 5.632 |

| | |
|---|---|
| $a_4^{(5)}$ | 5.648 |
| $a_5^{(5)}$ | 5.242 |
| $a_6^{(5)}$ | −3.241 |
| $a_7^{(5)}$ | 283.1 |

| | |
|---|---|
| $a_8^{(5)}$ | 103.738 |
| $a_9^{(5)}$ | 100.209 |
| $a_{10}^{(5)}$ | 100.012 |
| $a_{11}^{(5)}$ | 100.001 |

From this, one gets the impression that the sequence converges to 100. To confirm this impression, we compute the number $a_{100}$ with an increasing number of decimal places:

| | |
|---|---|
| $a_{100}^{(5)}$ | $100.0^41$ |
| $a_{100}^{(30)}$ | $100.0^{29}1$ |
| $a_{100}^{(60)}$ | $100.0^{57}997$ |
| $a_{100}^{(100)}$ | $100.0^{17}98\ldots$ |

| | |
|---|---|
| $a_{100}^{(110)}$ | $100.0^792\ldots$ |
| $a_{100}^{(120)}$ | $-3.790\ldots$ |
| $a_{100}^{(130)}$ | $5.9^78697\ldots$ |
| $a_{100}^{(140)}$ | $5.9^787925\ldots$ |

Here, the "exponents" indicate the number of repetitions; for instance, $100.0^41$ means 100.00001. As expected, the computations with 5, 30, and 60 decimal places show that $a_{100}$ is close to the presumable limit 100. They are consistent in their result value, and it is tempting to think "I know that round-off errors may lead to wrong results, but if I increase the precision from 30 to 60 and the result obtained with 30 digits is confirmed, then it must be accurate." Yet the computations with 100 and 110 decimal places indicate that $a_{100}$ is less close to 100 than expected, and worse, the computations with 120, 130, and 140 decimal places show that all the decimals obtained from the less precise computations were wrong. Or do the more precise computations yield wrong answers? What is the correct answer after all? Using the approach to exact real arithmetic presented in the sequel, one can verify that the number $a_{100}^{(140)}$ computed with 140 decimal places is an accurate approximation of the real value of $a_{100}$ (and with a bit of mathematical reasoning, one can show that the sequence converges to 6, not to 100). Thus, on the positive side, we see that there is a precision (140) which yields the right answer for $a_{100}$, but in programs such as bc, one has to fix this precision in advance, and without a detailed analysis of the problem, it is unclear which precision will be sufficient (all precisions up to 110 give completely wrong, but consistent answers near 100).

In the approach to Exact Real Arithmetic presented here, one need not specify a fixed precision in advance. Instead, a real number is set up by some operations and functions, and then one may ask the system to evaluate this number up to a certain precision. The result will be an interval which approximates the real number with the required precision, and it is actually *guaranteed* that the number really is contained in this interval: with this arithmetic, it is impossible to get wrong answers (well, sometimes it may take very long to get an answer, but once the answer is there, it is trustworthy).

### 1.1 Overview

In Section 2, we introduce a number representation suitable for our purposes, consisting of an exponent and a mantissa, which is an infinite stream of signed digits. A few simple operations like $-x$ and $|x|$ are implemented directly on this representation. All other operations are implemented in terms of *linear fractional transformations* (LFT's). Individual LFT's act on number representations and digit streams in a uniform way which is fixed once and for all. Thus they provide a high-level framework for implementing functions without the need to think about their action on the low-level digit streams.

LFT's and basic LFT operations are introduced in Section 3. Section 4 studies monotonicity properties of general functions, in particular LFT's. Such properties are useful in the design and analysis of algorithms. In Section 5, we characterize those LFT's which map the *base interval* $[-1, 1]$ into itself (*refining LFT's*). The action of refining LFT's on digit streams is defined in Section 6: the absorption of argument digits into an LFT, and the emission of result digits from an LFT. Absorption and emission are the main ingredients of an algorithm that computes the result of applying an LFT to a real number (Section 6.3). Section 6.5 contains some example runs of this algorithm.

In Section 7, we derive lower and upper bounds for the number of argument digits that are needed to obtain a desired number of result digits of an LFT application. This information is complemented by information about the complexity of individual absorptions and emissions (Section 8). Taken together, these results imply that LFT application is quadratic in the number $n$ of emitted digits—provided that digits are absorbed and emitted one by one. If many digits are absorbed and emitted at once, the complexity can be reduced to that of multiplying $n$-bit integers (Section 9).

All basic arithmetic operations are special instances of LFT application. In Section 10, the results about general LFT application are specialized to addition, multiplication, and reciprocal $1/x$. Transcendental functions can be implemented as infinite LFT expansions. Section 11 defines the semantics of such expansions, and shows how they can be derived from Taylor expansions (Section 11.4) or continued fraction expansions (Section 11.5). In Section 12, this knowledge is used to implement exponential function and natural logarithm; other functions are handled in the exercises.

Sections 13–18 present a domain-theoretic framework for computational geometry. Section 19 contains historical remarks to both parts, and Section 20 contains exercises.

## 2 Digit Streams

In the approach to real number computation presented here, (computable) real numbers are represented as potentially infinite streams of digits. At any time, a finite prefix of this stream has already been evaluated, e.g., $\pi = 3.14159\cdots$, and there is a method to compute larger finite prefixes on demand.

A finite prefix of the digit stream denotes an interval, namely the set of all real numbers whose digit streams start with this prefix. For instance, the prefix 3.14 denotes the interval $[3.14, 3.15]$ since all numbers starting with 3.14 are between $3.14000\cdots$ and $3.14999\cdots = 3.15$. The longer the prefix, the smaller the interval, e.g., 3.141 denotes $[3.141, 3.142]$. In this way, the digit stream denotes by means of its prefixes a nested sequence of intervals whose intersection contains exactly one number, namely the real number given by the digit stream.

The closed intervals of $\mathbb{R}$ form a *domain* when ordered under opposite inclusion. A nested sequence of intervals is an increasing chain in this domain, with its intersection as the least upper bound. The real numbers themselves are in one-to-one correspondence to the maximal elements of this domain, namely the degenerate intervals $[x, x]$. The Scott topology of the interval domain induces the usual topology on $\mathbb{R}$ via this embedding.

## 2.1 The Failure of Standard Number Systems

The examples above are based on the familiar *decimal system*, which is actually unsuitable for exact arithmetic (Brouwer [10]). We shall demonstrate this by means of an example, and note that similar examples exist for bases different from 10, i.e., this is a principal problem affecting all standard positional number systems.

Consider the task of computing the product $y = 3 \cdot x$ where $x$ is given by the decimal representation $\xi = 0.333\cdots$. Mathematically, the result is given by the decimal representation $\eta = 0.999\cdots$, but is it possible to compute this result? Recall that at any time, only a finite prefix of $\xi$ is known, and this finite prefix is the only source of information available to produce a finite prefix of the result $\eta$.

Assume we know the prefix 0.333 of $\xi$. Is this sufficient to determine the first digit of $\eta$? Unfortunately not, because the prefix 0.333 denotes the interval $[0.333, 0.334]$, which gives $[0.999, 1.002]$ when multiplied by 3. So we know that $\eta$ should start with 0. or 1., but we do not yet know which is the right one, since neither the interval $[0, 1]$ denoted by 0. nor the interval $[1, 2]$ denoted by 1. covers the output interval $[0.999, 1.002]$. Worse, it is easy to see that this happens with all prefixes of the form $0.33\cdots3$. Hence if $\xi$ is the stream $0.333\cdots$ with '3' forever, we can never output the first digit of $\eta$ since no finite amount of information from $\xi$ is sufficient to decide whether $\eta$ should start with 0. or 1..

A solution to this problem is to admit negative digits ($-1, \ldots, -9$ in base 10). If we now find that $\xi$ begins with 0.333, we may safely output '1.' (even 1.00) as a prefix of $\eta$ since we can compensate by negative digits if it turns out later that the number represented by $\xi$ is less than $1/3$, and so the result is actually smaller than 1. More formally, the interval denoted by the prefix 0.333 is now $[0.332, 0.334]$, since the smallest possible extension of 0.333 is no longer $0.33300\cdots$, but $0.333(-9)(-9)\cdots$. This interval yields $[0.996, 1.002]$ when multiplied by 3, which is contained in the interval $[0.99, 1.01]$ represented by the prefix 1.00, i.e., we can safely output 1.00 as the beginning of the output stream.

## 2.2 Signed Positional Systems

Signed positional systems are variants of standard positional systems which admit negative as well as positive digits. Like the standard systems, they are characterised by a base $r$, which is an integer $r \geq 2$. Once the base is fixed, the set of possible digits is taken as $D_r = \{d \in \mathbb{Z} \mid |d| < r\}$. For $r = 10$, we obtain $D_{10} = \{-9, -8, \ldots, 0, 1, \ldots, 9\}$ (*signed decimal system*), but the *signed binary system* with $r = 2$ and $D_2 = \{-1, 0, 1\}$ is practically more important. Most of these lecture notes deal with the case of base 2, which will therefore be the default case when the index $r$ is omitted.

To avoid a special notation for the "decimal" (or "binary") point, let's assume it is always at the beginning of the digit stream. Then an (infinite) digit stream $\xi = \langle d_1, d_2, d_3, \cdots \rangle$ with $d_i \in D_r$ represents the real number $[\xi]_r = \sum_{i=1}^{\infty} d_i r^{-i}$ as usual. A finite digit sequence $\delta$ represents the set $[\delta]_r$ of all numbers $[\delta\xi]_r$ which are represented by extensions of $\delta$ to an infinite stream. For $\delta = \langle d_1, d_2, \cdots, d_n \rangle$, this set can be determined as the interval $[\delta]_r = [\sum_{i=1}^{n} d_i r^{-i} - r^{-n}, \sum_{i=1}^{n} d_i r^{-i} + r^{-n}]$ of length $2r^{-n}$. Note that the empty prefix $\langle\rangle$ $(n = 0)$ denotes the interval $[-1, 1]$, which is the set of all real numbers representable by now. For the other ones, see Section 2.3 below.

In the sequel, we shall usually omit the parentheses and commas in digit sequences to obtain a more compact notation. Instead, we shall write concrete examples of digits and digit sequences in a special style, e.g., **4711** for $\langle 4, 7, 1, 1 \rangle$, to distinguish these sequences as syntactic objects from the numbers they denote. For further notational convenience, the minus sign becomes a bar within digit sequences, e.g., we write $\mathbf{1\bar{1}01}$ for the sequence $\langle 1, -1, 0, 1 \rangle$. The digit sequence which results from attaching a single digit $d$ to a sequence $\xi$ will be written as $d : \xi$ (like "cons" in the lazy functional languages Haskell and Miranda). Unlike these languages, we shall abbreviate $d_1 : d_2 : \xi$ by $d_1 d_2 : \xi$.

What is then the proper semantic meaning of this "cons" operation? For infinite streams, we may calculate

$$[d : \xi]_r = d \cdot r^{-1} + \sum_{i=2}^{\infty} \xi_{i-1} r^{-i} = \frac{1}{r}\left(d + \sum_{i=1}^{\infty} \xi_i r^{-i}\right) = \frac{1}{r}(d + [\xi]_r).$$

Hence, we have $[d : \xi]_r = A_d^r([\xi]_r)$ where $A_d^r$ denotes the affine function with $A_d^r(x) = \frac{x+d}{r}$. A similar calculation can be done for finite digit sequences denoting intervals; the result is again $[d : \xi]_r = A_d^r([\xi]_r)$, but this time, both sides are intervals, and for an interval $I$, $A_d^r(I)$ is the image of $I$ under $A_d^r$, which may as well be obtained as $A_d^r([u, v]) = [A_d^r(u), A_d^r(v)]$. For finite digit sequences, these considerations lead to an alternative characterisation of $[d_1 \cdots d_n]_r$ as $A_{d_1}^r(\cdots A_{d_n}^r([-1, 1]) \cdots)$.

In contrast to the "cons" operation, the "tail" operation (omitting the first digit) has no semantic meaning. In base 2, $\mathbf{010}\ldots$ and $\mathbf{1\bar{1}0}\ldots$ both represent the number $\frac{1}{4}$, but their tails $\mathbf{10}\ldots$ and $\mathbf{\bar{1}0}\ldots$ represent two different numbers ($\frac{1}{2}$ and $-\frac{1}{2}$).

Let's now consider the practically important case $r = 2$, $D = \{-1, 0, 1\}$ more closely. Here, we have (suppressing the index 2) $A_{\bar{1}}(x) = \frac{1}{2}(x-1)$, $A_0(x) = \frac{1}{2}x$, and $A_1(x) = \frac{1}{2}(x+1)$. All possible digit sequences up to length 2 and the intervals denoted by them are given by the following table:

$$
\begin{array}{lcccc}
 & & & [\mathbf{11}] & = [\frac{1}{2}, 1] \\
 & [\mathbf{1}] = [0,1] & & [\mathbf{10}] & = [\frac{1}{4}, \frac{3}{4}] \\
 & & [\mathbf{01}] = & [\mathbf{1\bar{1}}] & = [0, \frac{1}{2}] \\
[\,] = [-1,1] & [\mathbf{0}] = [-\frac{1}{2}, \frac{1}{2}] & [\mathbf{00}] & & = [-\frac{1}{4}, \frac{1}{4}] \\
 & & [\mathbf{0\bar{1}}] = & [\mathbf{\bar{1}1}] & = [-\frac{1}{2}, 0] \\
 & [\mathbf{\bar{1}}] = [-1,0] & & [\mathbf{\bar{1}0}] & = [-\frac{3}{4}, -\frac{1}{4}] \\
 & & & [\mathbf{\bar{1}\bar{1}}] & = [-1, -\frac{1}{2}]
\end{array}
$$

We see that the intervals overlap considerably, and some intervals are outright equal, e.g., $[\mathbf{1\bar{1}}]$ and $[\mathbf{01}]$. The latter observation can be strengthened to the fact that for all finite or infinite digit sequences $\delta$, the sequences $\mathbf{1\bar{1}} : \delta$ and $\mathbf{01} : \delta$ are equivalent in the sense that they denote the same interval (finite case) or the same real number (infinite case). The semantic reason for this is $A_1 \circ A_{\bar{1}} = A_0 \circ A_1 = (x \mapsto \frac{1}{4}(x+1))$. Similarly, $\mathbf{\bar{1}1} : \delta$ and $\mathbf{0\bar{1}} : \delta$ are always equivalent.

Therefore, most real numbers have several (often infinitely many) different digit stream representations. This redundancy, or more precisely the overlapping which causes it is important for computability: if an output range crosses the border point 0 of $[\mathbf{\bar{1}}]$ and $[\mathbf{1}]$ and is sufficiently small, then it will be contained in $[\mathbf{0}]$, i.e., the digit $\mathbf{0}$ may be output. This observation may be strengthened as follows:

- If an interval $J \subseteq [-1, 1]$ has length $\ell(J) \leq \frac{1}{2}$, then it is contained in (at least) one of the three digit intervals $[\mathbf{\bar{1}}]$, $[\mathbf{0}]$, $[\mathbf{1}]$.

An interval $J$ with $\frac{1}{2} < \ell(J) \leq 1$ may or may not fit into one of the three digit intervals; consider $[-\epsilon, \frac{1}{2} + \epsilon]$ which does not fit for $\epsilon > 0$, and $[0, l]$ which fits into $[\mathbf{1}] = [0, 1]$ for $l \leq 1$. Finally, an interval $J$ with $\ell(J) > 1$ cannot fit into any of the three digit intervals.

These observations can be generalised to digit sequences of length greater than 1 and arbitrary bases $r$ as follows:

**Proposition 2.1.** *Let $J \subseteq [-1, 1]$ be an interval.*

1. *If $\ell(J) \leq r^{-n}$, then $J \subseteq [\delta]_r$ for some digit sequence $\delta$ of length $n$ in base $r$.*
2. *If $J \subseteq [\delta]_r$ for some digit sequence $\delta$ of length $n$ in base $r$, then $\ell(J) \leq 2r^{-n}$.*

### 2.3 Exponents

We have seen that a signed positional number system as defined above can only represent numbers $x$ with $|x| \leq 1$ by digit streams. To obtain representations for real numbers $x$ of any size, one may write $x$ as $r^e \cdot x'$ where $r^e$ is a power of the base and $x'$ satisfies $|x'| \leq 1$ so that it can be represented by a digit stream. In principle, exponents $e \geq 0$ are sufficient, but allowing arbitrary $e \in \mathbb{Z}$ has its virtues. Thus, we arrive at representations $(e \parallel \xi)$ where $e$ is an integer (called *exponent*) and $\xi$ is a digit stream (called *mantissa*), and $(e \parallel \xi)$ represents $[(e \parallel \xi)]_r = r^e \cdot [\xi]_r$. Semantically, the attachment of the exponent can again be captured by an affine map, namely $[(e \parallel \xi)]_r = E^r_e([\xi]_r)$, where $E^r_e$ is given by $E^r_e(x) = r^e \cdot x$.

The resulting number representation is similar to the familiar exponent-mantissa representation. The differences are that the mantissa is (potentially) infinite and may contain negative digits, and that no leading sign is required to represent negative numbers. (A further syntactic difference is that the exponent comes first; this reflects the fact that all algorithms deal with the exponent first before working with the mantissa.)

Clearly, the exponent in the number representation is not unique. Since $[\mathbf{0} : \xi]_r = \frac{1}{r}[\xi]_r$, a representation $(e \parallel \xi)$ can always be replaced by $(e+1 \parallel \mathbf{0} : \xi)$, or more generally by $(e + k \parallel \mathbf{0}^k : \xi)$, where $\mathbf{0}^k : \xi$ means that $k$ **0**-digits are attached to the beginning of $\xi$. On the other hand, we may remove leading **0**-digits from $\xi$ and reduce (*refine*) the exponent accordingly: $[(e \parallel \mathbf{0} : \xi)]_r = [(e-1 \parallel \xi)]_r$, or more generally $[(e \parallel \mathbf{0}^k : \xi)]_r = [(e - k \parallel \xi)]_r$.

Note that **0**-digits may be squeezed out of a digit stream even if it does not begin with a **0**-digit. For instance, in base $r = 2$, we have seen that $\mathbf{1\bar{1}} : \xi$ and $\mathbf{01} : \xi$ are equivalent, and so are $\mathbf{\bar{1}1} : \xi$ and $\mathbf{0\bar{1}} : \xi$. Thus, we have $[(e \parallel \mathbf{1\bar{1}} : \xi)] = [(e - 1 \parallel \mathbf{1} : \xi)]$ and $[(e \parallel \mathbf{\bar{1}1} : \xi)] = [(e - 1 \parallel \mathbf{\bar{1}} : \xi)]$.

Refinement of the exponent is no longer possible iff the mantissa $\xi$ starts with one of $\mathbf{10}$, $\mathbf{11}$, $\mathbf{\bar{1}0}$, or $\mathbf{\bar{1}\bar{1}}$. We call a representation with this property *normalised*. A normalised mantissa represents a number $x$ with $\frac{1}{4} \leq |x| \leq 1$. All real numbers except 0 have normalised representations, but in contrast to the familiar case of unsigned digits, the exponents of two normalised representations for the same number may still differ by 1, e.g., $\frac{1}{3} = [(-1 \parallel (\mathbf{10})^\omega)] = [(0 \parallel \mathbf{1}(\mathbf{0\bar{1}})^\omega)]$.

The computation of a real number $y$ (more exactly, one of its representations) generally proceeds in the following stages:

1. Obtain an upper bound for the exponent of $y$.
2. Refine the exponent until it is sufficiently small or the representation is normalised.
3. Compute prefixes of the mantissa according to the required precision.

In simple cases, the exponent of the result is immediately known, but sometimes, considerable work is to be done in the first two stages.

### 2.4 Calculations with Digit Streams

Suppose we want to implement a function $f : \mathbb{R} \to \mathbb{R}$ which takes real numbers to real numbers. Then we need to find a corresponding function $\varphi$ on *representations*, i.e., a function $\varphi$ that maps representations $(e \parallel \xi)$ of $x$ into representations $(e' \parallel \eta)$ of $f(x)$. Often, this function will be based on some function $\varphi_0$ that maps digit streams into digit streams. Algorithms for such stream functions can usually be specified recursively in the spirit of a lazy functional programming language such as Haskell or Miranda.

We are now ready to present the implementations of a few simple functions (and constants), always assuming base $r = 2$. We shall usually not distinguish between a stream $\xi$ and its denotation $[\xi]$, nor between a function $f$ and its representation $\varphi$.

*Zero* may be represented by $(0 \parallel \mathbf{0}^\omega)$, and *one* by $(0 \parallel \mathbf{1}^\omega)$ or $(1 \parallel \mathbf{10}^\omega)$.

*Negation* $-x$ can be implemented by leaving the exponent alone, and negating (the number represented by) the mantissa: $-(e \parallel \xi) = (e \parallel -\xi)$.
The latter can be done by flipping all digits around:

$$-(\mathbf{1} : \xi) = \bar{\mathbf{1}} : (-\xi), \qquad -(\mathbf{0} : \xi) = \mathbf{0} : (-\xi), \qquad -(\bar{\mathbf{1}} : \xi) = \mathbf{1} : (-\xi).$$

*Absolute value* $|x|$ can also be realised by acting on the mantissa:
$|(e \parallel \xi)| = (e \parallel |\xi|)$.
As long as the leading digit of $\xi$ is $\mathbf{0}$, we do not know whether $[\xi]$ is positive or negative. But because of $[\mathbf{0} : \xi] = \frac{1}{2}[\xi]$ and $|\frac{1}{2}x| = \frac{1}{2}|x|$ we can safely output a $\mathbf{0}$-digit for every $\mathbf{0}$-digit we meet: $|\mathbf{0} : \xi| = \mathbf{0} : |\xi|$.
Once the first non-zero digit has been found, we know $[\xi] \geq 0$ or $[\xi] \leq 0$, and can switch to the identity stream function or negation:

$$|\mathbf{1} : \xi| = \mathbf{1} : \xi, \qquad |\bar{\mathbf{1}} : \xi| = \mathbf{1} : (-\xi)\,.$$

*Other Operations.* Implementations of the minimum function $\min(x, y)$ and addition $x + y$ in this framework are straightforward (see also Exercise 1). Multiplication is a bit more difficult, but division already requires some ingenuity, and there is no immediate way to obtain functions like square root, exponential, logarithm, etc. Fortunately, *linear fractional transformations* (LFT's) provide a high-level framework that makes the implementation of such real number operations much easier. Individual LFT's act on number representations and digit streams in a uniform way which is fixed once and for all. The desired real number operations may then be implemented in terms of LFT expressions, without the need to think about their action on the low-level digit streams. (Another approach was used by Plume [42] who worked on digit streams using auxiliary representations and an auxiliary limit function. These also provide an abstraction from the underlying digit streams.)

# 3 Linear Fractional Transformations (LFT's)

We have already seen that the semantic meaning of digits and exponents can be captured by certain *affine transformations*: $[d : \xi]_r = A^r_d([\xi]_r)$ with $A^r_d(x) = \frac{x+d}{r}$, and $[(e \parallel \xi)]_r = E^r_e([\xi]_r)$ with $E^r_e(x) = r^e \cdot x$. The general form of these affine transformations is $A(x) = ax + b$ with two fixed parameters $a$ and $b$. Considering affine transformations would already be sufficient to obtain some useful results, but to handle division and certain transcendental functions, one needs the more general linear fractional transformations or LFT's.

## 3.1 One-Dimensional LFT's (1-LFT's) and Matrices

A *one-dimensional linear fractional transformation* (1-LFT), also called *Möbius transformation*, is a function of the form $L(x) = \frac{ax+c}{bx+d}$ with four fixed parameters $a$, $b$, $c$, and $d$. In general, these parameters are arbitrary real (or even complex) numbers, but we shall usually only consider 1-LFT's with integer parameters.

The notion of 1-LFT includes that of affine transformation. A 1-LFT $\frac{ax+c}{bx+d}$ is *affine* if and only if $b = 0$; in this case it becomes $\frac{a}{d}x + \frac{c}{d}$.

For ease of notation, we abbreviate the function $x \mapsto \frac{ax+c}{bx+d}$ by $\left\langle\begin{smallmatrix} a & c \\ b & d \end{smallmatrix}\right\rangle$. The following are some examples of 1-LFT's:

| | | | |
|---|---|---|---|
| $x \mapsto x$ | $\left\langle\begin{smallmatrix} 1 & 0 \\ 0 & 1 \end{smallmatrix}\right\rangle$ | $x \mapsto -x$ | $\left\langle\begin{smallmatrix} -1 & 0 \\ 0 & 1 \end{smallmatrix}\right\rangle$ |
| $x \mapsto x + 1$ | $\left\langle\begin{smallmatrix} 1 & 1 \\ 0 & 1 \end{smallmatrix}\right\rangle$ | $x \mapsto 3x$ | $\left\langle\begin{smallmatrix} 3 & 0 \\ 0 & 1 \end{smallmatrix}\right\rangle$ |
| $x \mapsto \frac{1}{x}$ | $\left\langle\begin{smallmatrix} 0 & 1 \\ 1 & 0 \end{smallmatrix}\right\rangle$ | $x \mapsto \frac{2x+3}{4x+5}$ | $\left\langle\begin{smallmatrix} 2 & 3 \\ 4 & 5 \end{smallmatrix}\right\rangle$ |
| $x \mapsto A^r_d(x) = \frac{x+d}{r}$ | $\left\langle\begin{smallmatrix} 1 & d \\ 0 & r \end{smallmatrix}\right\rangle$ | $x \mapsto E^r_e(x) = r^e \cdot x$ | $\left\langle\begin{smallmatrix} r^e & 0 \\ 0 & 1 \end{smallmatrix}\right\rangle$ |

The notation $\left\langle\begin{smallmatrix} a & c \\ b & d \end{smallmatrix}\right\rangle$ for 1-LFT's looks similar to a 2-2-matrix $M = \left(\begin{smallmatrix} a & c \\ b & d \end{smallmatrix}\right)$. Indeed, any such matrix $M = \left(\begin{smallmatrix} a & c \\ b & d \end{smallmatrix}\right)$ defines a 1-LFT, namely $\langle M \rangle = \left\langle\begin{smallmatrix} a & c \\ b & d \end{smallmatrix}\right\rangle$, with $\langle M \rangle(x) = \frac{ax+c}{bx+d}$. Yet this correspondence is not one-to-one: in a 1-LFT, common factors of the four parameters do not matter; $\left\langle\begin{smallmatrix} a & c \\ b & d \end{smallmatrix}\right\rangle$ and $\left\langle\begin{smallmatrix} ka & kc \\ kb & kd \end{smallmatrix}\right\rangle$ are the same 1-LFT if $k$ is a non-zero number. Thus, we have $\langle M \rangle = \langle kM \rangle$ for $k \neq 0$. In fact, the opposite direction also holds: if $\langle M_1 \rangle = \langle M_2 \rangle$, then $M_1$ and $M_2$ differ only by a non-zero multiplicative factor. In particular, we have $\langle M \rangle = \langle -M \rangle$. As a slight normalisation, we usually present 1-LFT's in a way such that the lower right entry is non-negative ($d \geq 0$).

The matrix-like notation for 1-LFT's carries mathematical meaning because of the following:

**Proposition 3.1.** *The composition of two 1-LFT's $L_1$ and $L_2$ is again a 1-LFT. Composition of 1-LFT's corresponds to matrix multiplication: $\langle M_1 \rangle \circ \langle M_2 \rangle = \langle M_1 \cdot M_2 \rangle$ (Exercise 2).*

Recall from linear algebra how two matrices are multiplied:

$$\begin{pmatrix} a & c \\ b & d \end{pmatrix} \cdot \begin{pmatrix} a' & c' \\ b' & d' \end{pmatrix} = \begin{pmatrix} aa' + cb' & ac' + cd' \\ ba' + db' & bc' + dd' \end{pmatrix} \tag{1}$$

If $b = b' = 0$, then also $ba' + db' = 0$, hence affinity is preserved by multiplication. The neutral element of matrix multiplication is the *identity matrix* $\mathrm{E} = \left(\begin{smallmatrix} 1 & 0 \\ 0 & 1 \end{smallmatrix}\right)$, whose 1-LFT $\left\langle\begin{smallmatrix} 1 & 0 \\ 0 & 1 \end{smallmatrix}\right\rangle$ is the identity function. Recall further the important notion of the *determinant* of a matrix

$$\det \begin{pmatrix} a & c \\ b & d \end{pmatrix} = ad - bc \tag{2}$$

and its basic properties:

$$\det \mathrm{E} = 1 \qquad \det(A \cdot B) = \det A \cdot \det B \qquad \det(kM) = k^2 \cdot \det M \tag{3}$$

Because of the last equation above, the determinant is not a well-defined property of a 1-LFT (remember that $\langle kM \rangle = \langle M \rangle$ for $k \neq 0$). Yet the *sign* of the determinant is a perfect 1-LFT property because for $k \neq 0$, $\det(kM) \gtreqless 0$ iff $\det M \gtreqless 0$.

A matrix $M$ is *non-singular* iff $\det M \neq 0$. The *inverse* of a non-singular matrix $M = \left(\begin{smallmatrix} a & c \\ b & d \end{smallmatrix}\right)$ is given by $\left(\begin{smallmatrix} a & c \\ b & d \end{smallmatrix}\right)^{-1} = \frac{1}{\det M}\left(\begin{smallmatrix} d & -c \\ -b & a \end{smallmatrix}\right)$. For 1-LFT's, the factor $\frac{1}{\det M}$ does not matter, and we may define the *pseudo inverse* $M^*$ instead:

$$\begin{pmatrix} a & c \\ b & d \end{pmatrix}^* = \begin{pmatrix} d & -c \\ -b & a \end{pmatrix} \tag{4}$$

Note that the pseudo inverse of an integer matrix is again an integer matrix, and affinity ($b = 0$) is preserved as well. The following are the main properties of this notion (in the matrix world):

$$\begin{aligned} \mathrm{E}^* &= \mathrm{E} & (M^*)^* &= M \\ (k \cdot M)^* &= k \cdot M^* & (A \cdot B)^* &= B^* \cdot A^* \\ \det M^* &= \det M & M \cdot M^* = M^* \cdot M &= \det M \cdot \mathrm{E} \end{aligned} \tag{5}$$

Since *non-zero* factors do not matter for 1-LFT's, the last property gives the 1-LFT equation $\langle M^* \rangle \circ \langle M \rangle = \langle M \rangle \circ \langle M^* \rangle = \mathrm{id}$ for $\det M \neq 0$, i.e., $\langle M^* \rangle$ is the inverse function of $\langle M \rangle$.

### 3.2 Two-Dimensional LFT's (2-LFT's) and Tensors

The 1-LFT's defined above are functions of one argument, and as such, not suitable to capture the standard binary operations of addition $x+y$, subtraction $x-y$, multiplication $x \cdot y$, and division $x/y$. For this purpose, we introduce LFT's of two arguments (two-dimensional LFT's, shortly 2-LFT's).

A *two-dimensional linear fractional transformation* (2-LFT) is a function of the form $L(x,y) = \frac{axy+cx+ey+g}{bxy+dx+fy+h}$ with eight fixed parameters $a$, $b$, $c$, $d$, $e$, $f$, $g$, and $h$. For ease of notation, we write this function as $\left\langle\begin{smallmatrix} a & c & e & g \\ b & d & f & h\end{smallmatrix}\right\rangle$. The following are some examples of 2-LFT's:

| | | | |
|---|---|---|---|
| $(x,y) \mapsto x+y$ | $\left\langle\begin{smallmatrix} 0 & 1 & 1 & 0 \\ 0 & 0 & 0 & 1\end{smallmatrix}\right\rangle$ | $(x,y) \mapsto x-y$ | $\left\langle\begin{smallmatrix} 0 & 1 & -1 & 0 \\ 0 & 0 & 0 & 1\end{smallmatrix}\right\rangle$ |
| $(x,y) \mapsto x \cdot y$ | $\left\langle\begin{smallmatrix} 1 & 0 & 0 & 0 \\ 0 & 0 & 0 & 1\end{smallmatrix}\right\rangle$ | $(x,y) \mapsto x/y$ | $\left\langle\begin{smallmatrix} 0 & 1 & 0 & 0 \\ 0 & 0 & 1 & 0\end{smallmatrix}\right\rangle$ |
| $(x,y) \mapsto \frac{x+y}{1-xy}$ | $\left\langle\begin{smallmatrix} 0 & 1 & 1 & 0 \\ -1 & 0 & 0 & 1\end{smallmatrix}\right\rangle$ | $(x,y) \mapsto \frac{2x+3}{4y+5}$ | $\left\langle\begin{smallmatrix} 0 & 2 & 0 & 3 \\ 0 & 0 & 4 & 5\end{smallmatrix}\right\rangle$ |

The notation $\left\langle\begin{smallmatrix} a & c & e & g \\ b & d & f & h\end{smallmatrix}\right\rangle$ for 2-LFT's looks similar to a 2-4-matrix $T = \left(\begin{smallmatrix} a & c & e & g \\ b & d & f & h\end{smallmatrix}\right)$, called *tensor*. The relation between tensors and 2-LFT's is similar to the relation between matrices and 1-LFT's. Any tensor $T$ defines a 2-LFT $\langle T\rangle$. Two tensors define the same 2-LFT if and only if their entries differ by a non-zero multiplicative factor. Thus, $\langle T\rangle = \langle kT\rangle$ for $k \neq 0$; in particular $\langle T\rangle = \langle -T\rangle$. We usually present 2-LFT's in a way such that the lower right entry is non-negative ($h \geq 0$).

If the second argument of a 2-LFT $F = \left\langle\begin{smallmatrix} a & c & e & g \\ b & d & f & h\end{smallmatrix}\right\rangle$ is a fixed number $y$, then $F|^y$ is a function in one argument, given by

$$F|^y(x) = F(x,y) = \frac{(ay+c)x+(ey+g)}{(by+d)x+(fy+h)} = \left\langle\begin{matrix} ay+c & ey+g \\ by+d & fy+h\end{matrix}\right\rangle(x)\,.$$

A similar calculation can be done if the first argument is a fixed number $x$, leading to another 1-LFT $F|_x$. Thus, if we define for tensors $T = \left(\begin{smallmatrix} a & c & e & g \\ b & d & f & h\end{smallmatrix}\right)$

$$T|_x = \begin{pmatrix} ax+e & cx+g \\ bx+f & dx+h\end{pmatrix} \quad\text{and}\quad T|^y = \begin{pmatrix} ay+c & ey+g \\ by+d & fy+h\end{pmatrix} \tag{6}$$

then $\langle T|_x\rangle(y) = T(x,y)$ and $\langle T|^y\rangle(x) = T(x,y)$.

While there is no obvious way to compose two 2-LFT's in the framework presented here, there are several ways to compose a 2-LFT and a 1-LFT (or to multiply a tensor and a matrix). Let for the following $M$ be a matrix and $T$ a tensor.

First, the function $F$ defined by $F(x,y) = \langle M\rangle(\langle T\rangle(x,y))$ is again a 2-LFT, namely $F = \langle MT\rangle$, where $MT$ is an instance of ordinary matrix multiplication:

$$\begin{pmatrix} a' & c' \\ b' & d'\end{pmatrix}\begin{pmatrix} a & c & e & g \\ b & d & f & h\end{pmatrix} = \begin{pmatrix} a'a+c'b & a'c+c'd & a'e+c'f & a'g+c'h \\ b'a+d'b & b'c+d'd & b'e+d'f & b'g+d'h\end{pmatrix} \tag{7}$$

Second, the function $G$ defined by $G(x,y) = \langle T\rangle(\langle M\rangle(x),y)$ is again a 2-LFT, namely $G = \langle T \circledL M\rangle$, where $T \circledL M$ is a special purpose operation defined by

$$\begin{pmatrix} a & c & e & g \\ b & d & f & h\end{pmatrix} \circledL \begin{pmatrix} a' & c' \\ b' & d'\end{pmatrix} = \begin{pmatrix} aa'+eb' & ca'+gb' & ac'+ed' & cc'+gd' \\ ba'+fb' & da'+hb' & bc'+fd' & dc'+hd'\end{pmatrix} \tag{8}$$

Third, the function $H$ defined by $H(x,y) = \langle T\rangle(x, \langle M\rangle(y))$ is again a 2-LFT, namely $H = \langle T ® M\rangle$, where $T ® M$ is a special purpose operation defined by

$$\begin{pmatrix} a & c & e & g \\ b & d & f & h \end{pmatrix} ® \begin{pmatrix} a' & c' \\ b' & d' \end{pmatrix} = \begin{pmatrix} aa'+cb' & ac'+cd' & ea'+gb' & ec'+gd' \\ ba'+db' & bc'+dd' & fa'+hb' & fc'+hd' \end{pmatrix} \tag{9}$$

All these operations are connected by various algebraic laws:

$$(M_1 \cdot M_2) \cdot T = M_1 \cdot (M_2 \cdot T) \qquad (T Ⓛ M_1) ® M_2 = (T ® M_2) Ⓛ M_1 \tag{10}$$

$$(M_1 \cdot T) Ⓛ M_2 = M_1 \cdot (T Ⓛ M_2) \qquad (M_1 \cdot T) ® M_2 = M_1 \cdot (T ® M_2) \tag{11}$$

$$(T Ⓛ M_1) Ⓛ M_2 = T Ⓛ (M_1 \cdot M_2) \qquad (T ® M_1) ® M_2 = T ® (M_1 \cdot M_2) \tag{12}$$

### 3.3 Zero-Dimensional LFT's (0-LFT's) and Vectors

In analogy to 1-LFT's which take one argument and 2-LFT's which take two arguments, there are also 0-LFT's $\left\langle \begin{smallmatrix} a \\ b \end{smallmatrix} \right\rangle$ which take no argument at all, but deliver the constant $\frac{a}{b}$.

The notation $\left\langle \begin{smallmatrix} a \\ b \end{smallmatrix} \right\rangle$ for 0-LFT's looks similar to a vector $\left( \begin{smallmatrix} a \\ b \end{smallmatrix} \right)$. Clearly, two vectors correspond to the same 0-LFT if and only if they differ by a non-zero multiplicative factor.

A 1-LFT $\left\langle \begin{smallmatrix} a & c \\ b & d \end{smallmatrix} \right\rangle$ can be applied to a 0-LFT $\left\langle \begin{smallmatrix} u \\ v \end{smallmatrix} \right\rangle$ resulting in a new 0-LFT $\left\langle \begin{smallmatrix} au+cv \\ bu+dv \end{smallmatrix} \right\rangle$. If the first argument of a 2-LFT $F = \left\langle \begin{smallmatrix} a & c & e & g \\ b & d & f & h \end{smallmatrix} \right\rangle$ is a fixed 0-LFT $w = \left\langle \begin{smallmatrix} u \\ v \end{smallmatrix} \right\rangle$, then $F|_w$ is the 1-LFT $\left\langle \begin{smallmatrix} au+ev & cu+gv \\ bu+fv & du+hv \end{smallmatrix} \right\rangle$. Similarly, $F|^w = \left\langle \begin{smallmatrix} au+cv & eu+gv \\ bu+dv & fu+hv \end{smallmatrix} \right\rangle$.

These absorption rules can be used to deal with rational numbers in the real arithmetic. An expression like $\frac{1}{3}\pi$ can be set up as $\left\langle \begin{smallmatrix} 1 & 0 & 0 & 0 \\ 0 & 0 & 0 & 1 \end{smallmatrix} \right\rangle (\left\langle \begin{smallmatrix} 1 \\ 3 \end{smallmatrix} \right\rangle, \pi)$ using the tensor for multiplication, and then simplified to $\left\langle \begin{smallmatrix} 1 & 0 \\ 0 & 3 \end{smallmatrix} \right\rangle (\pi)$. If only rational operations on rational numbers are performed, this is equivalent to a rational arithmetic, with the disadvantage that in general, denominators double in their bit size in every addition and multiplication. Alternatively, a rational number can be treated like any real number and transformed into a digit stream.

## 4 Monotonicity

By interval, we always mean a closed interval $[u, v]$ with $u \le v$ in $\mathbb{R}$. If $I$ is an interval and $f : I \to \mathbb{R}$ a continuous function, then its image $f(I)$ is again an interval. To actually determine the end points of $f(I)$, it is useful to know about the monotonicity of $f$.

A function $f : I \to \mathbb{R}$ is

- *increasing* if $x \le y$ in $I$ implies $f(x) \le f(y)$,
- *decreasing* if $x \le y$ in $I$ implies $f(x) \ge f(y)$,
- *strictly increasing* if $x < y$ in $I$ implies $f(x) < f(y)$,

- *strictly decreasing* if $x < y$ in $I$ implies $f(x) > f(y)$,
- *monotonic* if it is increasing (on the whole of $I$) or decreasing (on the whole of $I$).

For monotonic functions, we also speak of their *monotonicity type*, which is $\uparrow$ for increasing functions, and $\downarrow$ for decreasing functions. Clearly, $f([u,v]) = [f(u), f(v)]$ for increasing $f$, and $f([u,v]) = [f(v), f(u)]$ for decreasing $f$. Hence for monotonic $f$, $f([u,v])$ is the interval spanned by the two values $f(u)$ and $f(v)$, extending from their minimum to their maximum. If $J$ is another interval, then $f([u,v]) \subseteq J$ if and only if both $f(u)$ and $f(v)$ are in $J$.

Let $\langle M \rangle$ be a 1-LFT such that the denominator $bx + d$ of $\langle M \rangle(x) = \frac{ax+c}{bx+d}$ is non-zero for all $x$ in an interval $I$. We call such a 1-LFT *bounded* on $I$ since it avoids the value $\infty$ which formally occurs as a fraction with denominator 0. Analogous notions can be introduced for 2-LFT's.

A 1-LFT $f = \langle M \rangle$ which is bounded on $I$ is a continuous function $f : I \to \mathbb{R}$, given by $f(x) = \frac{ax+c}{bx+d}$. Clearly, this function is differentiable with derivative $f'(x) = \frac{ad-bc}{(bx+d)^2}$. In this fraction, the denominator is always greater than 0 (it cannot be 0 since $f$ was supposed to be bounded on $I$), while the numerator is a constant, namely $\det M$. Thus, the monotonicity behaviour of $\langle M \rangle$ depends only on the sign of $\det M$ (which is a meaningful notion for a 1-LFT):

- If $\det M > 0$, then $\langle M \rangle'(x) > 0$ for all $x$ in $I$, hence $\langle M \rangle$ is strictly increasing.
- If $\det M < 0$, then $\langle M \rangle'(x) < 0$ for all $x$ in $I$, hence $\langle M \rangle$ is strictly decreasing.
- If $\det M = 0$, then $\langle M \rangle'(x) = 0$ for all $x$ in $I$, hence $\langle M \rangle$ is constant on $I$.

In any case, $\langle M \rangle$ is monotonic, and therefore, the remarks on monotonic functions given above apply. All this relies on the fact that we let the 1-LFT act on an interval; for instance, $\left\langle \begin{smallmatrix} 0 & 1 \\ 1 & 0 \end{smallmatrix} \right\rangle = (x \mapsto \frac{1}{x})$ with $\det \left( \begin{smallmatrix} 0 & 1 \\ 1 & 0 \end{smallmatrix} \right) = -1$ is decreasing on $[1,2]$ and on $[-2,-1]$, but not on $[-1,1] \setminus \{0\}$.

We now turn to functions of two arguments. Let $I$ and $J$ be two intervals. Geometrically, their product set $I \times J$ is a rectangle. For a function $F : I \times J \to \mathbb{R}$, we define $F|_x : J \to \mathbb{R}$ for fixed $x$ in $I$ by $F|_x(y) = F(x,y)$, and dually $F|^y : I \to \mathbb{R}$ for fixed $y$ in $J$ by $F|^y(x) = F(x,y)$; these functions are the *sections* of $F$.

A function $F : I \times J \to \mathbb{R}$ is *monotonic* if all its sections $F|_x$ for $x \in I$ and $F|^y$ for $y \in J$ are monotonic. Recall that all the sections of a 2-LFT are 1-LFT's, and therefore monotonic by the results above. Hence, every 2-LFT is monotonic on every rectangle where it is bounded (i.e., its denominator avoids 0).

**Proposition 4.1.** *If $F : [u_1, u_2] \times [v_1, v_2] \to \mathbb{R}$ is continuous and monotonic, then its image $F([u_1, u_2] \times [v_1, v_2])$ is the interval spanned by the four corner values $F(u_1, v_1)$, $F(u_1, v_2)$, $F(u_2, v_1)$, and $F(u_2, v_2)$, i.e., it extends from the smallest of these values to the largest.*

**Corollary 4.2.** *If $F : [u_1, u_2] \times [v_1, v_2] \to \mathbb{R}$ is continuous and monotonic, then for all intervals $J$, the inclusion $F([u_1, u_2] \times [v_1, v_2]) \subseteq J$ holds if and only if all the corner values $F(u_1, v_1)$, $F(u_1, v_2)$, $F(u_2, v_1)$, and $F(u_2, v_2)$ are in $J$.*

If $F : I \times J \to \mathbb{R}$ is monotonic, then it may happen that some of the sections $F|^y$ are increasing, while some other sections $F|^y$ are decreasing. We say $F$ is *increasing in the first argument* if all sections $F|^y$ for $y \in J$ are increasing. The properties to be decreasing in the first (or second) argument are defined analogously. We say $F$ *has type* $(\uparrow, \downarrow)$ if $F$ is increasing in the first argument and decreasing in the second. The 3 other types $(\uparrow, \uparrow)$, $(\downarrow, \uparrow)$, and $(\downarrow, \downarrow)$ are defined similarly.

Let's consider some examples. On $I_0 \times I_0 = [-1, 1]^2$, addition $F(x, y) = x + y$ has type $(\uparrow, \uparrow)$, subtraction $F(x, y) = x - y$ has type $(\uparrow, \downarrow)$, while multiplication $F(x, y) = x \cdot y$ is of course monotonic like all other 2-LFT's, but does not have any of the four types. For, $F|^1(x) = x$ is increasing, but $F|^{-1}(x) = -x$ is decreasing.

## 5 Bounded and Refining LFT's

Later, we shall apply LFT's to arguments given by digit streams. Of course, this makes only sense if the LFT is well-defined for arguments from the *"base interval"* $I_0 = [-1, 1]$, i.e., is *bounded* in the sense that its denominator avoids 0 for arguments from $I_0$. If we want the result to be represented by a digit stream as well, then the LFT should moreover be *refining*, i.e., map $I_0$ into itself.

In this section, we shall derive some criteria for LFT's to be bounded and refining, and prove some properties of these notions. These proofs involve some manipulations of absolute values, so that it is worthwhile to establish some properties of absolute values in the beginning. Recall

$$|x| = \max(x, -x) \qquad -|x| = \min(x, -x) \tag{13}$$

for real numbers $x$. The following lemma will be useful in dealing with sums.

**Lemma 5.1.**
$\max(|x + y|, |x - y|) = |x| + |y|$ *and* $|x + y| + |x - y| = 2\max(|x|, |y|)$.

### 5.1 Bounded 1-LFT's

A 1-LFT $\langle \begin{smallmatrix} a & c \\ b & d \end{smallmatrix} \rangle$ is *bounded* iff the denominator $D(x) = bx + d$ is non-zero for all $x \in I_0$. Since $I_0$ is an interval and $D$ is continuous, this means either $D(x) > 0$ for all $x$ in $I_0$, or $D(x) < 0$ for all $x$ in $I_0$. Under the general assumption $d \geq 0$, the second case is ruled out because $D(0) = d$. To check $D(x) > 0$ for all $x \in I_0$, it suffices to consider the minimal value of $D$ on $[-1, 1]$. For $b \geq 0$, this is $D(-1) = d - b$, and for $b \leq 0$, it is $D(1) = d + b$. In any case, the minimum is $d - |b|$. Therefore, we obtain:

**Proposition 5.2.** $\langle \begin{smallmatrix} a & c \\ b & d \end{smallmatrix} \rangle$ *with* $d \geq 0$ *is bounded if and only if* $d > |b|$. *In this case, the denominator* $bx + d$ *is positive for all* $x$ *in* $I_0$.

### 5.2 Bounded 2-LFT's

For a 2-LFT $F = \left\langle\begin{smallmatrix} a & c & e & g \\ b & d & f & h \end{smallmatrix}\right\rangle$, the denominator is $D(x,y) = bxy + dx + fy + h$. We say $F$ is bounded if $D$ avoids 0 for $(x,y)$ in $I_0^2$. Under the general assumption $h = D(0,0) \geq 0$, this is again equivalent to positivity of $D$ on $I_0^2$. Function $D$ is monotonic; this is most easily seen by noting that $D = \left\langle\begin{smallmatrix} b & d & f & h \\ 0 & 0 & 0 & 1 \end{smallmatrix}\right\rangle$ is a 2-LFT. Hence, the range of possible values of $D$ on $I_0^2$ is spanned by the four corner values $D(\pm 1, \pm 1)$. Thus, $F$ is bounded iff the four values $b+d+f+h$, $-b-d+f+h$, $-b+d-f+h$, and $b-d-f+h$ are positive. Equivalently, this means

$$h > \max(b+d-f, b-d+f, -b+d+f, -b-d-f)\,. \tag{14}$$

In case of $b = 0$, the condition can be simplified to $h > |d| + |f|$ with the help of Lemma 5.1.

**Proposition 5.3.** *If* $\left\langle\begin{smallmatrix} a & c & e & g \\ b & d & f & h \end{smallmatrix}\right\rangle$ *with* $h \geq 0$ *is bounded, then* $h > \max(|b|, |d|, |f|)$.

*Proof.* We start with (14). Adding the two relations $h > b+d-f$ and $h > b-d+f$ gives $2h > 2b$, and adding $h > -b+d+f$ and $h > -b-d-f$ yields $2h > -2b$. Together, $h > |b|$ follows. In a similar way, $h > |d|$ and $h > |f|$ can be derived. □

### 5.3 Refining 1-LFT's

A bounded 1-LFT $f = \left\langle\begin{smallmatrix} a & c \\ b & d \end{smallmatrix}\right\rangle$ is *refining* if $f(I_0) \subseteq I_0$. Since $f$ is monotonic, this is equivalent to the two conditions $f(-1) \in I_0$ and $f(1) \in I_0$, or $|f(-1)| \leq 1$ and $|f(1)| \leq 1$. With the assumption $d \geq 0$, the denominator of $f(x) = \frac{ax+c}{bx+d}$ is positive. Hence, the two conditions can be reformulated as $|c-a| \leq d-b$ and $|c+a| \leq d+b$, or $d \geq \max(|c-a|+b, |c+a|-b) = \max(c+a-b, c-a+b, -c+a+b, -c-a-b)$.

Note the similarity of this condition to the condition for a 2-LFT to be bounded (14); the only difference lies in the variable names and the relation symbol. Hence everything what has been said about bounded 2-LFT's holds here as well in an analogous way:

**Proposition 5.4.**
*An affine 1-LFT* $\left\langle\begin{smallmatrix} a & c \\ 0 & d \end{smallmatrix}\right\rangle$ *with* $d > 0$ *is refining if and only if* $d \geq |a| + |c|$.

**Proposition 5.5.** *If* $\left\langle\begin{smallmatrix} a & c \\ b & d \end{smallmatrix}\right\rangle$ *with* $d \geq 0$ *is refining, then* $d \geq \max(|a|, |b|, |c|)$.

### 5.4 Refining 2-LFT's

A bounded 2-LFT $F = \left\langle\begin{smallmatrix} a & c & e & g \\ b & d & f & h \end{smallmatrix}\right\rangle$ is *refining* if $F(I_0^2) \subseteq I_0$. Since $F$ is monotonic, this is equivalent to the condition that all four corner values $F(\pm 1, \pm 1)$

are in $I_0$, or $|F(\pm 1, \pm 1)| \leq 1$. With the assumption $h \geq 0$, all denominators are positive. Hence, the four conditions can be reformulated as

$$\begin{array}{llll} |a+c+e+g| \leq b+d+f+h & |-a-c+e+g| \leq -b-d+f+h \\ |a-c-e+g| \leq b-d-f+h & |-a+c-e+g| \leq -b+d-f+h \end{array} \quad (15)$$

We now show that the lower right entry $h$ of a refining 2-LFT dominates all other ones (under the assumption $h \geq 0$). First, we know from Prop. 5.3 that $h > |b|, |d|, |f|$. Adding the two equations in the first column of (15) gives $\max(|a + g|, |c + e|) \leq h + b$ with the help of Lemma 5.1. Similarly, adding the second column yields $\max(|a - g|, |c - e|) \leq h - b$. Next, adding $|a + g| \leq h + b$ and $|a - g| \leq h - b$ gives $\max(|a|, |g|) \leq h$, and adding the other two relations yields $\max(|c|, |e|) \leq h$.

**Proposition 5.6.** *If* $\left\langle \begin{smallmatrix} a & c & e & g \\ b & d & f & h \end{smallmatrix} \right\rangle$ *with* $h \geq 0$ *is refining, then* $h \geq |a|, |c|, |e|, |g|$ *and* $h > |b|, |d|, |f|$.

## 6 LFT's and Digit Streams

Now we consider the application of (refining) LFT's to arguments from $I_0$. The LFT's will be represented by matrices, and the arguments and results by digit streams (exponents are handled later). We take the freedom to occasionally identify LFT's and their representing matrices, and thus to apply the LFT notions bounded, refining, monotonic etc. to the representing matrices as well.

### 6.1 Absorption of Argument Digits

**Absorption into Matrices.** Let $f = \langle M \rangle$ be a 1-LFT to be applied to a digit stream. Remember that a digit $k$ in base $r$ corresponds to an affine transformation $A_k^r$ with $A_k^r(x) = \frac{x+k}{r}$. This is a special case of a 1-LFT, with matrix $A_k^r = \left( \begin{smallmatrix} 1 & k \\ 0 & r \end{smallmatrix} \right)$. Using this matrix, we may calculate

$$\langle M \rangle([k : \xi]_r) = \langle M \rangle(\langle A_k^r \rangle([\xi]_r)) = \langle M \cdot A_k^r \rangle([\xi]_r).$$

Thus, we may *absorb* the first digit of the argument stream into the matrix $M$ by multiplying $M$ with $A_k^r$ from the right:

– Absorption: $M(k : \xi) = (M \cdot A_k^r)(\xi)$.

An explicit formula for the product $M \cdot A_k^r$ may be obtained by specialising Equation (1):

$$M \cdot A_k^r = \begin{pmatrix} a & c \\ b & d \end{pmatrix} \cdot \begin{pmatrix} 1 & k \\ 0 & r \end{pmatrix} = \begin{pmatrix} a & rc + ka \\ b & rd + kb \end{pmatrix} \quad (16)$$

For the following, let $M = \left( \begin{smallmatrix} a & c \\ b & d \end{smallmatrix} \right)$ and $M' = M \cdot A_k^r = \left( \begin{smallmatrix} a' & c' \\ b' & d' \end{smallmatrix} \right)$, where the actual values of $a'$ etc. are given by (16).

1. If $M$ is bounded with positive denominator, then so is $M'$.
   Proof: Let $D(x) = bx + d$ be the denominator of $M$, and $D'(x) = b'x + d'$ the denominator of $M'$. Both $D$ and $D'$ are 1-LFT's, namely $D = \left(\begin{smallmatrix} b & d \\ 0 & 1 \end{smallmatrix}\right)$ and $D' = \left(\begin{smallmatrix} b & rd+kb \\ 0 & 1 \end{smallmatrix}\right)$. By (16), $D \cdot A_k^r$ is $D'' = \left(\begin{smallmatrix} b & rd+kb \\ 0 & r \end{smallmatrix}\right)$. By hypothesis, $D(x) > 0$ for all $x$ in $I_0$. Hence, $D(x) > 0$ for all $x \in A_k^r(I_0) \subseteq I_0$, and therefore, $D''(x) = D(A_k^r(x)) > 0$ for all $x$ in $I_0$. From this, positivity of $D'(x) = r \cdot D''(x)$ immediately follows.
2. If $M$ is refining, then so is $M'$.
   Proof: If $M(I_0) \subseteq I_0$, then $M'(I_0) = M(A_k^r(I_0)) \subseteq M(I_0) \subseteq I_0$.
3. If $M$ is increasing (decreasing), then so is $M'$.
   Proof: $M'$ is $M$ composed with the increasing function $A_k^r$.

**Absorption into Tensors.** The absorption of a digit into a tensor $T$ rests on a similar semantic foundation. It comes in two versions, depending on whether the digit is taken from the left or the right argument.

- Left absorption: $T\,(k : \xi,\ \eta) = (T \circledL A_k^r)\,(\xi,\ \eta)$.
- Right absorption: $T\,(\xi,\ k : \eta) = (T \circledR A_k^r)\,(\xi,\ \eta)$.

Explicit formulae for the products $T \circledL A_k^r$ and $T \circledR A_k^r$ may be obtained by specialising (8) and (9):

$$T \circledL A_k^r = \begin{pmatrix} a & c & e & g \\ b & d & f & h \end{pmatrix} \circledL \begin{pmatrix} 1 & k \\ 0 & r \end{pmatrix} = \begin{pmatrix} a & c & re+ka & rg+kc \\ b & d & rf+kb & rh+kd \end{pmatrix} \tag{17}$$

$$T \circledR A_k^r = \begin{pmatrix} a & c & e & g \\ b & d & f & h \end{pmatrix} \circledR \begin{pmatrix} 1 & k \\ 0 & r \end{pmatrix} = \begin{pmatrix} a & rc+ka & e & rg+ke \\ b & rd+kb & f & rh+kf \end{pmatrix} \tag{18}$$

For the following, let $T' = T \circledL A_k^r$ or $T' = T \circledR A_k^r$.

1. If $T$ is bounded with positive denominator, then so is $T'$.
2. If $T$ is refining, then so is $T'$.
3. If $T$ has a monotonicity type, e.g., $(\uparrow, \uparrow)$, then $T'$ has the same type.

The proofs of these statements are analogous to the corresponding ones for matrices.

### 6.2 Emission of Result Digits

Of course, absorption is not enough; we also need a method to *emit* digits of the output stream representing the result of a computation.

**Emission from Matrices.** Let $M$ be a matrix and $\xi$ a digit stream. To emit a digit $k$ of $\langle M\rangle([\xi]_r)$, we must transform this value into the form $[k : \eta]_r = \langle A_k^r\rangle([\eta]_r)$. This can be done by writing $M$ as product $A_k^r \cdot M'$ for some matrix $M'$. The equation $M = A_k^r \cdot M'$ yields $M' = A_k^{r*} \cdot M$ using the inverse of $A_k^r$. Thus, emission is performed by $M(\xi) = k : (A_k^{r*} \cdot M)(\xi)$.

An explicit formula for the product $A_k^{r*} \cdot M$ is obtained by specialising (1):

$$A_k^{r*} \cdot M = \begin{pmatrix} r & -k \\ 0 & 1 \end{pmatrix} \cdot \begin{pmatrix} a & c \\ b & d \end{pmatrix} = \begin{pmatrix} ra - kb & rc - kd \\ b & d \end{pmatrix} \tag{19}$$

Of course, we cannot emit an arbitrary digit. If the output stream is to begin with $k$, then the result of the computation should be in the corresponding digit interval $[k]_r$; otherwise the method would be unsound. Thus, we can only emit $k$ from $M(\xi)$ if we know that its value is contained in $[k]_r$. Without looking into $\xi$, we know nothing about it. Thus, the condition $M(\xi) \in [k]_r$ must hold for all digit streams $\xi$, which is equivalent to $M(I_0) \subseteq [k]_r$.

– Emission: $M(\xi) = k : (A_k^{r*} \cdot M)(\xi)$.
  This operation is permitted only if $M(I_0) \subseteq [k]_r$.

For the following invariance properties, let $M' = A_k^{r*} \cdot M$.

1. If $M$ is bounded with positive denominator, then so is $M'$.
   Proof: This is obvious since $M$ and $M'$ have the same denominator.
2. If $M$ is refining and the emission leading to $M'$ was permitted, then $M'$ is refining again. Proof: If $M(I_0) \subseteq [k]_r = A_k^r(I_0)$, then $M'(I_0) = A_k^{r*}(M(I_0)) \subseteq A_k^{r*}(A_k^r(I_0)) = I_0$.
3. If $M$ is increasing (decreasing), then so is $M'$. Proof: $M'$ is $M$ composed with the increasing function $A_k^{r*}$.

**Emission from Tensors.** Emission from a tensor works similar to emission from a matrix:

– Emission: $T(\xi, \eta) = k : (A_k^{r*} \cdot T)(\xi, \eta)$.
  This operation is permitted only if $T(I_0^2) \subseteq [k]_r$.

An explicit formula for the product $A_k^{r*} \cdot T$ is obtained by specialising (7):

$$\begin{pmatrix} r & -k \\ 0 & 1 \end{pmatrix} \cdot \begin{pmatrix} a & c & e & g \\ b & d & f & h \end{pmatrix} = \begin{pmatrix} ra - kb & rc - kd & re - kf & rg - kh \\ b & d & f & h \end{pmatrix} \tag{20}$$

This variant of emission satisfies invariance properties 1–3 analogous to those for matrices.

### 6.3 Sketch of an Algorithm

We are now able to sketch an algorithm for applying a refining 1-LFT given by a matrix $M$ to a digit stream:

**Algorithm 1**
*Let* $M_0 = M$. *Then for every* $n \geq 0$ *do:*
*If there is a digit* $k$ *such that* $M_n(I_0) \subseteq [k]_r$,
*then output digit* $k$ *and let* $M_{n+1} = A_k^{r*} \cdot M_n$,
*else read the next digit* $k$ *from the input stream and let* $M_{n+1} = M_n \cdot A_k^r$.

The matrices $M_0$, $M_1$, etc. represent the internal state of the algorithm. Hence, we refer to them collectively as the *state matrix*. (In an imperative language, they would all occupy the same variable.)

For tensors an additional problem comes up: if no emission is possible, should we absorb a digit from the left argument or from the right? A simple strategy is to alternate between left and right absorption, while a more sophisticated strategy could look into the tensor to see which absorption is more likely to lead to a subsequent emission.

## 6.4 The Emission Conditions

Algorithm 1 was not very specific on how to find a digit $k$ such that the image of the LFT is contained in $[k]_r$, or to find out that such a digit does not exist. These questions will be handled for base $r = 2$ only since this case allows for a simple solution: try the 3 possibilities $k = \mathbf{1}, \mathbf{0}, \bar{\mathbf{1}}$ in turn. (An idea of what to do for a general base can be obtained by looking at Section 9.3 below.)

The actual computation is simplified if we know some properties of the state matrix (or tensor) in question. Remember that some LFT properties are preserved by absorptions and permitted emissions. Thus, if the initial matrix is refining and bounded with positive denominator, then so will be all state matrices encountered in Alg. 1. Moreover, if the initial matrix has some specific monotonicity property, then all state matrices will have this property. Thus, for the following, we always assume a refining bounded matrix with positive denominator, and we shall try to exploit monotonicity as far as possible.

**Base 2: Matrices.** Let $M$ be a refining bounded matrix with positive denominator. First, we consider the case that $M$ is increasing, so that $M(I_0) = [M(-1), M(1)]$. Since $M$ is refining, we know $M(I_0) \subseteq I_0$, or $M(-1) \geq -1$ and $M(1) \leq 1$. Then $M(I_0) \subseteq [\mathbf{1}]_2 = [0, 1]$ iff $M(-1) \geq 0$ and $M(1) \leq 1$, where the second condition is redundant. The first condition reads $\frac{-a+c}{-b+d} \geq 0$. Since the denominator is positive, this is equivalent to $a \leq c$. Similarly, $M(I_0) \subseteq [\bar{\mathbf{1}}]_2 = [-1, 0]$ iff $M(-1) \geq -1$ and $M(1) \leq 0$, where the first condition is redundant. The second condition reads $\frac{a+c}{b+d} \leq 0$. Since the denominator is positive, this is equivalent to $-a \geq c$.

Finally, $M(I_0) \subseteq [\mathbf{0}]_2 = [-\frac{1}{2}, \frac{1}{2}]$ iff $M(-1) \geq -\frac{1}{2}$ and $M(1) \leq \frac{1}{2}$, where no condition is redundant. The first condition reads $\frac{-a+c}{-b+d} \geq -\frac{1}{2}$, or $2(c-a) \geq b-d$. The second condition reads $\frac{a+c}{b+d} \leq \frac{1}{2}$, or $2(c+a) \leq b+d$. Checking these two conditions becomes more efficient if they contain common subexpressions that can be evaluated ahead. Indeed, the first condition can be transformed into $b - 2c \leq d - 2a$, and the second into $2c - b \leq d - 2a$. Hence, the two conditions may be even combined into one, namely $|2c - b| \leq d - 2a$.

If $M$ is decreasing, the roles of $M(1)$ and $M(-1)$ are interchanged. This means that in the emission conditions, $a$ and $b$ have to be replaced by $-a$ and $-b$, respectively, while $c$ and $d$ remain unchanged. Thus, the condition $a \leq c$ for emission of **1** becomes $-a \leq c$, the condition $-a \geq c$ for emission of $\bar{\mathbf{1}}$ becomes $a \geq c$, and finally, the condition $|2c - b| \leq d - 2a$ becomes $|2c + b| \leq d + 2a$. All conditions are summarised in the following table:

| Type | **1** | $\bar{\mathbf{1}}$ | **0** |
|---|---|---|---|
| $\uparrow$ | $a \leq c$ | $-a \geq c$ | $\|2c - b\| \leq d - 2a$ |
| $\downarrow$ | $-a \leq c$ | $a \geq c$ | $\|2c + b\| \leq d + 2a$ |

Since the condition for **0** is more complicated than the other two, we propose to check the conditions in the order **1**, $\bar{\mathbf{1}}$, **0**. This has the additional advantage that there is a situation where some tests can be avoided because they are bound to fail. Suppose the checks of the emission conditions for **1** and $\bar{\mathbf{1}}$ both failed, but the check for **0** succeeded. Then the digit **0** is emitted, and the current matrix $\left(\begin{smallmatrix} a & c \\ b & d \end{smallmatrix}\right)$ is replaced by $\left(\begin{smallmatrix} 2a & 2c \\ b & d \end{smallmatrix}\right)$ according to (19). Yet the relationship between $\pm 2a$ and $2c$ is the same as between $\pm a$ and $c$, which means that the emission conditions for **1** and $\bar{\mathbf{1}}$ will again fail; therefore, only the condition for **0** needs to be checked again.

**Base 2: Tensors.** Now let $T$ be a refining bounded tensor with positive denominator. First, we consider the case that $T$ is of type $(\uparrow, \uparrow)$, so that $T(I_0^2) = [T(-1,-1), T(1,1)]$. Then $T(I_0^2) \subseteq [\mathbf{1}]_2 = [0,1]$ iff $T(-1,-1) \geq 0$; the other condition $T(1,1) \leq 1$ holds anyway since $T$ is refining. The relevant condition reads $\frac{a-c-e+g}{b-d-f+h} \geq 0$. Since the denominator is positive, this is equivalent to $c+e \leq g+a$. Similarly, $T(I_0^2) \subseteq [\bar{\mathbf{1}}]_2 = [-1,0]$ iff $T(1,1) = \frac{a+c+e+g}{b+d+f+h} \leq 0$, which is equivalent to $c + e \leq -(g + a)$.

Finally, $T(I_0^2) \subseteq [\mathbf{0}]_2 = [-\frac{1}{2}, \frac{1}{2}]$ iff $T(-1,-1) \geq -\frac{1}{2}$ and $T(1,1) \leq \frac{1}{2}$. The first condition reads $\frac{a-c-e+g}{b-d-f+h} \geq -\frac{1}{2}$, or $-2(a - c - e + g) \leq b - d - f + h$. The second condition reads $\frac{a+c+e+g}{b+d+f+h} \leq \frac{1}{2}$, or $2(a + c + e + g) \leq b + d + f + h$. The first condition can be transformed into $d + f - 2a - 2g \leq h + b - 2c - 2e$, and the second into $2a + 2g - d - f \leq h + b - 2c - 2e$. Again, these two conditions can be combined into one, namely $|2(g+a) - (d+f)| \leq (h+b) - 2(c+e)$. Note that $g + a$ and $c + e$ also occur in the tests for **1** and $\bar{\mathbf{1}}$; they need only be evaluated once.

If $T$ is of type $(\uparrow, \downarrow)$ instead, then $T(-1,-1)$ must be replaced by $T(-1,1)$, and $T(1,1)$ by $T(1,-1)$. This corresponds to negation of $a$, $b$, $e$, $f$, while the other four parameters are unchanged. The other two monotonicity types can be handled by similar negations. The results are collected in the following table:

| Type | $\mathbf{1}$ | $\bar{\mathbf{1}}$ | $\mathbf{0}$ |
|---|---|---|---|
| $(\uparrow,\uparrow)$ | $c+e \le g+a$ | $c+e \le -(g+a)$ | $\|2(g+a)-(d+f)\| \le (h+b)-2(c+e)$ |
| $(\uparrow,\downarrow)$ | $c-e \le g-a$ | $c-e \le -(g-a)$ | $\|2(g-a)-(d-f)\| \le (h-b)-2(c-e)$ |
| $(\downarrow,\uparrow)$ | $e-c \le g-a$ | $e-c \le -(g-a)$ | $\|2(g-a)-(f-d)\| \le (h-b)-2(e-c)$ |
| $(\downarrow,\downarrow)$ | $-c-e \le g+a$ | $-c-e \le -(g+a)$ | $\|2(g+a)+(d+f)\| \le (h+b)+2(c+e)$ |

If $T$ is of unknown monotonicity type or does not have any type at all, then the conjunction of the four conditions in each column must be considered. The four conditions for $\mathbf{1}$ can be combined into the two conditions $|c+e| \le g+a$ and $|c-e| \le g-a$, and similarly for $\bar{\mathbf{1}}$, while no simplification seems to be possible in case of $\mathbf{0}$.

Again, the conditions for $\mathbf{0}$ are more complicated then the other two. If the order $\mathbf{1}$, $\bar{\mathbf{1}}$, $\mathbf{0}$ is chosen, then as in the matrix case, $\mathbf{1}$ and $\bar{\mathbf{1}}$ need not be checked again after emission of $\mathbf{0}$.

## 6.5 Examples

*Example 6.1.* Let's first consider the matrix $M = \left(\begin{smallmatrix}3 & 0\\ 0 & 4\end{smallmatrix}\right)$ which means multiplication by $\frac{3}{4}$. The $d$-entry 4 is positive, and the determinant 12 is positive as well. The function is bounded ($d = 4 > |b| = 0$), and refining ($[M(-1), M(1)] = [-\frac{3}{4}, \frac{3}{4}] \subseteq I_0$). Therefore, we can use the emission conditions in the $\uparrow$ row of the matrix table. Generally, we check the conditions in the order $\mathbf{1}$, $\bar{\mathbf{1}}$, $\mathbf{0}$, except after emission of $\mathbf{0}$, where the conditions for $\mathbf{1}$ and $\bar{\mathbf{1}}$ are skipped because they are known to fail as pointed out above. We also take any opportunity to cancel common factors of the four parameters of the state matrix. Let's assume the digit sequence denoting the argument starts with $\mathbf{101}$.

**Start:** $M = \left(\begin{smallmatrix}3 & 0\\ 0 & 4\end{smallmatrix}\right)$
$a \le c \Leftrightarrow 3 \le 0$ fails, $-a \ge c \Leftrightarrow -3 \ge 0$ fails, $|2c-b| \le d-2a \Leftrightarrow 0 \le -2$ fails.
**Absorb 1** and set $M$ to $\left(\begin{smallmatrix}3 & 3\\ 0 & 8\end{smallmatrix}\right)$.
$a \le c \Leftrightarrow 3 \le 3$ succeeds.
**Emit 1** and set $M$ to $\begin{pmatrix}6 & -2\\ 0 & 8\end{pmatrix}$. **Cancel** a factor of 2 so that $M = \begin{pmatrix}3 & -1\\ 0 & 4\end{pmatrix}$.
$a \le c \Leftrightarrow 3 \le -1$ fails, $-a \ge c \Leftrightarrow -3 \ge -1$ fails, $|2c-b| \le d-2a \Leftrightarrow 2 \le -2$ fails.
**Absorb 0** and set $M$ to $\begin{pmatrix}3 & -2\\ 0 & 8\end{pmatrix}$.
$a \le c \Leftrightarrow 3 \le -2$ fails, $-a \ge c \Leftrightarrow -3 \ge -2$ fails, $|2c-b| \le d-2a \Leftrightarrow 4 \le 2$ fails.
**Absorb 1** and set $M$ to $\left(\begin{smallmatrix}3 & -1\\ 0 & 16\end{smallmatrix}\right)$.
$a \le c \Leftrightarrow 3 \le -1$ fails, $-a \ge c \Leftrightarrow -3 \ge -1$ fails,
but $|2c-b| \le d-2a \Leftrightarrow 2 \le 10$ succeeds.
**Emit 0** and set $M$ to $\left(\begin{smallmatrix}6 & -2\\ 0 & 16\end{smallmatrix}\right)$. **Cancel** a factor of 2 so that $M = \begin{pmatrix}3 & -1\\ 0 & 8\end{pmatrix}$.
$|2c-b| \le d-2a \Leftrightarrow 2 \le 2$ succeeds.
**Emit 0** and set $M$ to $\begin{pmatrix}6 & -2\\ 0 & 8\end{pmatrix}$. **Cancel** a factor of 2 so that $M = \begin{pmatrix}3 & -1\\ 0 & 4\end{pmatrix}$.
$|2c-b| \le d-2a \Leftrightarrow 2 \le -2$ fails.

Now, we should absorb a new digit, but we only assumed the prefix **101** to be known. Thus, the algorithm transforms the argument prefix **101** into the result prefix **100**. Note that $[\mathbf{101}] = [\frac{1}{2}, \frac{3}{4}]$ and $\mathbf{100} = [\frac{3}{8}, \frac{5}{8}] \supseteq [\frac{3}{8}, \frac{9}{16}] = M([\frac{1}{2}, \frac{3}{4}])$, as it should be. In practice, a demand for more output digits will automatically generate a demand for more input digits, which will be computed by the process computing the argument.

*Example 6.2.* Let's consider another example which involves something more complicated than multiplication by $\frac{3}{4}$, namely computing $\frac{1}{x+2}$. In contrast to $\frac{3}{4}x$, it is not immediate how a digit stream for $\frac{1}{x+2}$ can be computed from a digit stream for $x$. Yet the algorithm developed above provides the answer.

The function $x \mapsto \frac{1}{x+2}$ is a 1-LFT with matrix $\left(\begin{smallmatrix} 0 & 1 \\ 1 & 2 \end{smallmatrix}\right)$. The entry $d = 2$ is positive, but the determinant $-1$ is negative. The function is bounded ($d = 2 > |b| = 1$), and refining ($[M(1), M(-1)] = [\frac{1}{3}, 1] \subseteq I_0$). Thus, the algorithm can be applied—with the emission conditions from the $\downarrow$ row of the table for matrices.

**Start:** $M = \left(\begin{smallmatrix} 0 & 1 \\ 1 & 2 \end{smallmatrix}\right)$
$-a \leq c \Leftrightarrow 0 \leq 1$ succeeds. **Emit 1** and set $M$ to $\left(\begin{smallmatrix} -1 & 0 \\ 1 & 2 \end{smallmatrix}\right)$.
$-a \leq c \Leftrightarrow 1 \leq 0$ fails, $a \geq c \Leftrightarrow -1 \geq 0$ fails, $|2c + b| \leq d + 2a \Leftrightarrow 1 \leq 0$ fails.
**Absorb 1** and set $M$ to $\left(\begin{smallmatrix} -1 & -1 \\ 1 & 5 \end{smallmatrix}\right)$.
$-a \leq c \Leftrightarrow 1 \leq -1$ fails, $a \geq c \Leftrightarrow -1 \geq -1$ succeeds.
**Emit $\bar{\mathbf{1}}$** and set $M$ to $\left(\begin{smallmatrix} -1 & 3 \\ 1 & 5 \end{smallmatrix}\right)$.
$-a \leq c \Leftrightarrow 1 \leq 3$ succeeds. **Emit 1** and set $M$ to $\left(\begin{smallmatrix} -3 & 1 \\ 1 & 5 \end{smallmatrix}\right)$.
$-a \leq c \Leftrightarrow 3 \leq 1$ fails, $a \geq c \Leftrightarrow -3 \geq 1$ fails, $|2c + b| \leq d + 2a \Leftrightarrow 3 \leq -1$ fails.
**Absorb 0** and set $M$ to $\left(\begin{smallmatrix} -3 & 2 \\ 1 & 10 \end{smallmatrix}\right)$.
$-a \leq c \Leftrightarrow 3 \leq 2$ fails, $a \geq c \Leftrightarrow -3 \geq 2$ fails, $|2c + b| \leq d + 2a \Leftrightarrow 5 \leq 4$ fails.
**Absorb 1** and set $M$ to $\left(\begin{smallmatrix} -3 & 1 \\ 1 & 21 \end{smallmatrix}\right)$.
$-a \leq c \Leftrightarrow 3 \leq 1$ fails, $a \geq c \Leftrightarrow -3 \geq 1$ fails, $|2c + b| \leq d + 2a \Leftrightarrow 3 \leq 15$ succeeds.
**Emit 0** and set $M$ to $\left(\begin{smallmatrix} -6 & 2 \\ 1 & 21 \end{smallmatrix}\right)$.
$|2c + b| \leq d + 2a \Leftrightarrow 5 \leq 9$ succeeds. **Emit 0** and set $M$ to $\left(\begin{smallmatrix} -12 & 4 \\ 1 & 21 \end{smallmatrix}\right)$.
$|2c + b| \leq d + 2a \Leftrightarrow 9 \leq -3$ fails.

Thus, the algorithm maps the input prefix **101**, which denotes the interval $[\frac{1}{2}, \frac{3}{4}]$, into the output prefix $\mathbf{1\bar{1}100}$, which denotes the interval $[\frac{11}{32}, \frac{13}{32}]$. This interval really contains $M([\frac{1}{2}, \frac{3}{4}]) = [\frac{4}{11}, \frac{2}{5}]$ as it should be.

Note that in Example 6.1, a common factor of 2 could occasionally be cancelled, while in Example 6.2, no cancellation was possible. We will return to this point in Section 8.1. Note further the way in which absorptions (A) and emissions (E) alternate. In the first example, the sequence is AEAAEE, and in the second, it is EAEEAAEE. In both cases, the next would be an A. There appears to be some randomness in these sequences, but it is not too bad; there seem to be no strings of 3 consecutive A's or E's.

The question how many absorptions are needed to achieve a certain number of emissions is important for the performance of the algorithm. We would not like situations where a large number of absorptions is needed before the next emission is possible. The worst possibility were a situation where the algorithm keeps on absorbing for ever without ever being able to emit something (like in the problem of computing $3 \cdot 0.333\cdots$ in ordinary decimal notation). Fortunately, we can prove that this cannot happen; apart from some finite start-up phase in the beginning, absorptions and emissions will approximately alternate. This will be shown in the next section.

# 7 Contractivity and Expansivity

Our next goal is to derive bounds for the number of absorptions that are required to achieve a certain number of emissions. Such bounds can be obtained from bounds of the derivative(s) of the LFT. In fact, we are able to obtain theoretical bounds for an even larger class of functions.

## 7.1 Functions of One Argument

Let $I$ be an interval (as always closed) and $F : I \to \mathbb{R}$ a $C^1$-function, i.e., a continuous function which is differentiable with continuous derivative $F'$. The *mean value theorem* of analysis states that for all $x$, $y$ in $I$, there is some $z$ between $x$ and $y$ (hence in $I$) such that $F(x) - F(y) = F'(z) \cdot (x - y)$. This property gives bounds for the length of the interval $F(I)$. First, we have for $I = [u, v]$

$$\ell(F(I)) \geq |F(v) - F(u)| \geq \inf_{z \in I} |F'(z)| \cdot (v - u) = \exp^I F \cdot \ell(I) \tag{21}$$

where $\exp^I F = \inf_{z \in I} |F'(z)|$ is the *expansivity* of $F$ on $I$.

Second, we have

$$\ell(F(I)) = \sup_{x,y \in I} |F(x) - F(y)| \leq \sup_{z \in I} |F'(z)| \cdot \sup_{x,y \in I} |x - y| = \operatorname{con}^I F \cdot \ell(I) \tag{22}$$

where $\operatorname{con}^I F = \sup_{z \in I} |F'(z)|$ is the *contractivity* of $F$ on $I$. Since $F' : I \to \mathbb{R}$ is continuous, the contractivity is always finite, and so we have $0 \leq \exp^I F \leq \operatorname{con}^I F < \infty$.

Together with Prop. 2.1, the bounds derived above will provide information about possible emissions. Assume $F$ is a $C^1$-function defined on the base interval $I_0 = [-1, 1]$ with $F(I_0) \subseteq I_0$. We now look for theoretical lower and upper bounds for the number of digits required from a digit stream $\xi$ representing an argument $x$ if we want to compute a certain number $n$ of digits of a stream representing the result $F(x)$. We work with a general base $r \geq 2$.

If a prefix $\delta$ of length $m$ of the argument stream $\xi$ is known, then $x$ is in the interval $I = [\delta]_r$ of length $\ell(I) = 2r^{-m}$. Hence, $F(x)$ is in the interval $F(I)$, whose length $l$ is bounded by $\exp^I F \cdot 2r^{-m} \leq l \leq \operatorname{con}^I F \cdot 2r^{-m}$. The dependence on the actual interval $I$ can be removed by replacing $\exp^I F$ by $\exp^{I_0} F \leq \exp^I F$, and $\operatorname{con}^I F$ by $\operatorname{con}^{I_0} F \geq \operatorname{con}^I F$. Dropping the index $I_0$, we obtain $\exp F \cdot 2r^{-m} \leq l \leq \operatorname{con} F \cdot 2r^{-m}$. (Yet note for later that we may work with $\exp^J F$ and $\operatorname{con}^J F$ instead, if we are interested in arguments taken from a subinterval $J \subseteq I_0$.)

By Prop. 2.1, we know that (at least) $n$ result digits can be emitted if $l \leq r^{-n}$. Hence, $n$ digits can be emitted if $\operatorname{con} F \cdot 2r^{-m} \leq r^{-n}$, or $r^m \geq 2 \operatorname{con} F \cdot r^n$, or $m \geq \log_r(2 \operatorname{con} F) + n$. Thus, to emit $n$ output digits, we need at most $\lceil \log_r(2 \operatorname{con} F) \rceil + n$ input digits. This statement even applies to the case $\operatorname{con} F = 0$, where the logarithm is $-\infty$. For, in this case, $F$ is constant, and any number of output digits can be obtained without looking at the input at all.

By Prop. 2.1, we also know that $l \leq 2r^{-n}$ if (at least) $n$ result digits can be emitted. Thus, $\exp F \cdot 2r^{-m} \leq 2r^{-n}$, or $m \geq \log_r(\exp F) + n$ if $n$ result digits can be emitted. Hence, we need at least $\lceil \log_r(\exp F) \rceil + n$ input digits to obtain $n$ result digits. In case of $\exp F = 0$ where the logarithm is $-\infty$, this statement still holds (trivially), but does not yield any useful information.

**Theorem 7.1.** *Let $F$ be a $\mathrm{C}^1$-function defined on the base interval $I_0$. To obtain $n$ digits of $F(x)$ for $x$ in $I_0$, one needs at least $c^< + n$ and at most $c^> + n$ digits of $x$, where*

$$c^< = \lceil \log_r(\exp F) \rceil \quad \textit{and} \quad c^> = \lceil \log_r(2 \operatorname{con} F) \rceil$$

*where $r$ is the base of the number system, $\exp F = \inf_{x \in I_0} |F'(x)|$ and $\operatorname{con} F = \sup_{x \in I_0} |F'(x)|$.*

For functions with $\operatorname{con} F \geq \exp F > 0$, the theorem implies that asymptotically, the number of absorptions and emissions will be equal, i.e., on the long run and on average, one absorption is required for every emission. Locally, we see that for $n$ emissions, at least $c^< + n$ absorptions are needed, while for $n+1$ emissions, at most $c^> + n + 1$ are required. Hence, after any emission, we need at most $c^> - c^< + 1$ absorptions, before the next emission is permitted. In particular, it can never happen that an infinite amount of absorptions does not lead to any emission.

For affine $F$, i.e., $F(x) = ax + b$, $F'$ is constant and so $\exp F$ and $\operatorname{con} F$ coincide. In this case, the two bounds in Theorem 7.1 are close together: For base 2, they always differ by one, while for large bases, they are even identical in most cases, allowing the exact prediction of the number of required argument digits. For non-affine $F$, $\exp F$ and $\operatorname{con} F$ may differ considerably, leading to less accurate estimations.

Let's now consider the case that $F$ is a 1-LFT which is bounded on $I_0$, given by a matrix $M = \begin{pmatrix} a & c \\ b & d \end{pmatrix}$ with non-negative $d$. Recall from Section 4 that $M$ is $\mathrm{C}^1$ with $M'(x) = \frac{\det M}{(bx+d)^2}$. From Prop. 5.2 and its proof, we know that $bx + d$ is positive for $x \in I_0$, with least value $d - |b|$. It is not hard to see that its largest value is $d + |b|$, and therefore

$$\operatorname{con} M = \frac{|\det M|}{(d-|b|)^2} \quad \text{and} \quad \exp M = \frac{|\det M|}{(d+|b|)^2}. \tag{23}$$

For affine matrices ($b = 0$), both expressions simplify to $\frac{|ad|}{d^2} = \frac{|a|}{d}$.

With these values, Theorem 7.1 not only describes the theoretical complexity of obtaining $M(x)$, but also the actual complexity of Algorithm 1. For, the algorithm detects an opportunity for emission as soon as it arises because its tests are logically equivalent to the emission condition.

In Example 6.1, we have $M = \left(\begin{smallmatrix} 3 & 0 \\ 0 & 4 \end{smallmatrix}\right)$, hence $\exp M = \operatorname{con} M = \frac{3}{4}$, and so $c^< = \lceil \log_2 \frac{3}{4} \rceil = 0$ and $c^> = \lceil \log_2 \frac{3}{2} \rceil = 1$. Hence, between $n$ and $n+1$ absorptions are needed for $n$ emissions, and the maximum number of absorptions between any two emissions is $1 - 0 + 1 = 2$.

In Example 6.2, we have $M = \left(\begin{smallmatrix} 0 & 1 \\ 1 & 2 \end{smallmatrix}\right)$, hence $\exp M = \frac{1}{9}$ and $\operatorname{con} M = 1$, and so $c^< = \lceil \log_2 \frac{1}{9} \rceil = -3$ and $c^> = \lceil \log_2 2 \rceil = 1$. Hence, between $n-3$ and $n+1$ absorptions are needed for $n$ emissions, and the maximum number of absorptions between any two emissions is $1 - (-3) + 1 = 5$.

Note that for 1-LFT's $M$, we have $\exp M = 0$ iff $\operatorname{con} M = 0$ iff $\det M = 0$ iff $M$ is a constant function. Hence, there are only two cases: if $\det M \neq 0$, the number of absorptions and emissions is asymptotically equal, while for $\det M = 0$, any number of digits can be emitted without absorbing anything.

### 7.2 Functions of Two Arguments

Let $I$ and $J$ be two intervals (as always closed) and $F : I \times J \to \mathbb{R}$ a $C^1$-function, i.e., a continuous function which is differentiable in both arguments with continuous derivatives $\frac{\partial F}{\partial x}$ and $\frac{\partial F}{\partial y}$. Thus, for fixed $x$ in $I$, $F|_x : J \to \mathbb{R}$ with $F|_x(y) = F(x, y)$ is a $C^1$-function on $J$, and for fixed $y$ in $J$, $F|^y : I \to \mathbb{R}$ with $F|^y(x) = F(x, y)$ is a $C^1$-function on $I$.

Let's first derive a lower bound for $\ell(F(I, J))$. For every $y$ in $J$, (21) implies

$$\ell(F(I \times J)) \geq \ell(F|^y(I)) \geq \exp^I(F|^y) \cdot \ell(I) \geq {\exp_{\mathrm{L}}}^{I,J} F \cdot \ell(I) \tag{24}$$

where

$${\exp_{\mathrm{L}}}^{I,J} F = \inf_{y \in J} \exp^I(F|^y) = \inf_{x \in I, y \in J} |\tfrac{\partial F}{\partial x}(x, y)| \tag{25}$$

is the left *expansivity* of $F$ on $I \times J$. Dually, we have

$$\ell(F(I \times J)) \geq {\exp_{\mathrm{R}}}^{I,J} F \cdot \ell(J) \quad \text{where} \quad {\exp_{\mathrm{R}}}^{I,J} F = \inf_{x \in I, y \in J} |\tfrac{\partial F}{\partial y}(x, y)| \tag{26}$$

is the right *expansivity* of $F$ on $I \times J$.

For an upper bound, consider $x_1, x_2 \in I$ and $y_1, y_2 \in J$. With (22), we obtain

$$\begin{aligned} |F(x_1, y_1) - F(x_2, y_2)| &\leq |F(x_1, y_1) - F(x_2, y_1)| + |F(x_2, y_1) - F(x_2, y_2)| \\ &\leq \operatorname{con}^I(F|^{y_1}) \cdot \ell(I) + \operatorname{con}^J(F|_{x_2}) \cdot \ell(J) \\ &\leq {\operatorname{con}_{\mathrm{L}}}^{I,J} F \cdot \ell(I) + {\operatorname{con}_{\mathrm{R}}}^{I,J} F \cdot \ell(J) \end{aligned} \tag{27}$$

where $\quad \mathrm{con_L}^{I,J} F = \sup_{y \in J} \mathrm{con}^I(F|^y) = \sup_{x \in I, y \in J} |\frac{\partial F}{\partial x}(x,y)|$

and $\quad \mathrm{con_R}^{I,J} F = \sup_{x \in I} \mathrm{con}^J(F|_x) = \sup_{x \in I, y \in J} |\frac{\partial F}{\partial y}(x,y)|$.

Note that these numbers are finite because the partial derivatives are continuous. Finally, Relation (27) yields $\ell(F(I \times J)) =$

$$\sup_{x_1,x_2 \in I} \sup_{y_1,y_2 \in J} |F(x_1,y_1) - F(x_2,y_2)| \leq \mathrm{con_L}^{I,J} F \cdot \ell(I) + \mathrm{con_R}^{I,J} F \cdot \ell(J) . \quad (28)$$

Assume now $F$ is a $\mathrm{C}^1$-function defined on $I_0^2 = [-1,1] \times [-1,1]$ with $F(I_0^2) \subseteq I_0$. Assume further that $F(x_1,x_2)$ is to be computed where each $x_i$ is given by a digit stream $\xi_i$, and we want to find out how many argument digits are needed to obtain $n$ digits of the result $F(x_1,x_2)$.

If a prefix $\delta_i$ of length $m_i$ of the argument stream $\xi_i$ is known, then $x_i$ is in the interval $I_i = [\delta_i]_r$ of length $\ell(I_i) = 2r^{-m_i}$. Hence, $F(x_1,x_2)$ is in the interval $F(I_1,I_2)$, whose length $l$ is bounded by $l^< \leq l \leq l^>$, where

$$l^< = \max(\mathrm{exp_L}^{I_1,I_2} F \cdot 2r^{-m_1}, \mathrm{exp_R}^{I_1,I_2} F \cdot 2r^{-m_2})$$

$$l^> = \mathrm{con_L}^{I_1,I_2} F \cdot 2r^{-m_1} + \mathrm{con_R}^{I_1,I_2} F \cdot 2r^{-m_2}$$

Again, the dependence on the actual intervals $I_1$ and $I_2$ can be removed by enlarging both of them to $I_0$. We call the resulting bounds $l^{\ll}$ and $l^{\gg}$. For ease of notation, we drop the indices in $\mathrm{exp_L}^{I_0,I_0}$, etc.

By Prop. 2.1, we know that (at least) $n$ result digits can be emitted if $l \leq r^{-n}$, which is the case if $l^{\gg} \leq r^{-n}$. Hence, $n$ digits can be emitted if $\mathrm{con_L}\, F \cdot 2r^{-m_1} \leq \frac{1}{2}r^{-n}$ and $\mathrm{con_R}\, F \cdot 2r^{-m_2} \leq \frac{1}{2}r^{-n}$. The first condition is equivalent to $r^{m_1} \geq 4\,\mathrm{con_L}\, F \cdot r^n$, or $m_1 \geq \log_r(4\,\mathrm{con_L}\, F) + n$. Thus, to emit $n$ output digits, $\lceil \log_r(4\,\mathrm{con_L}\, F)\rceil + n$ digits from the left argument and $\lceil \log_r(4\,\mathrm{con_R}\, F)\rceil + n$ digits from the right argument are sufficient.

By Prop. 2.1, we also know that $l \leq 2r^{-n}$ if (at least) $n$ result digits can be emitted. Thus, if $n$ digits can be emitted, then $l^{\ll} \leq 2r^{-n}$, or $\mathrm{exp_L}\, F \cdot 2r^{-m_1} \leq 2r^{-n}$ and $\mathrm{exp_R}\, F \cdot 2r^{-m_2} \leq 2r^{-n}$, or $m_1 \geq \log_r(\mathrm{exp_L}\, F) + n$ and $m_2 \geq \log_r(\mathrm{exp_R}\, F) + n$. These relations indicate how many digits from the two arguments are at least needed to obtain $n$ result digits.

**Theorem 7.2.** *Let $F$ be a $\mathrm{C}^1$-function with two arguments defined on $I_0^2$. To obtain $n$ digits in base $r$ of $F(x_1,x_2)$ for $x_1$, $x_2$ in $I_0$, one needs at least $c_\mathrm{L}^{\leq} + n$ digits of $x_1$ and $c_\mathrm{R}^{\leq} + n$ digits of $x_2$, where*

$$c_\mathrm{L}^{\leq} = \lceil \log_r(\mathrm{exp_L}\, F)\rceil \quad \textit{and} \quad c_\mathrm{R}^{\leq} = \lceil \log_r(\mathrm{exp_R}\, F)\rceil .$$

*On the other hand, $c_\mathrm{L}^{\geq} + n$ digits of $x_1$ and $c_\mathrm{R}^{\geq} + n$ digits of $x_2$ are sufficient to obtain (at least) $n$ output digits, where*

$$c_\mathrm{L}^{\geq} = \lceil \log_r(4\,\mathrm{con_L}\, F)\rceil \quad \textit{and} \quad c_\mathrm{R}^{\geq} = \lceil \log_r(4\,\mathrm{con_R}\, F)\rceil .$$

For functions with $\exp_L F > 0$ and $\exp_R F > 0$, the theorem implies that on the long run and on average, one absorption from each argument is required for every emission. Analogously to the case of one argument, one can show that it can never happen that an infinite amount of absorptions from both sides does not lead to any emission.

Unlike the case of matrices, there are no simple formulae for the left and right contractivities and expansivities of a general tensor. The reason is that the general forms of the partial derivatives are too complicated. Yet for some special tensors, concrete bounds can be obtained easily.

The tensor for addition is not refining, but $T = \left(\begin{smallmatrix} 0 & 1 & 1 & 0 \\ 0 & 0 & 0 & 2 \end{smallmatrix}\right)$ with $T(x,y) = \frac{1}{2}(x+y)$ is refining. Since $\frac{\partial T}{\partial x}(x,y) = \frac{\partial T}{\partial y}(x,y) = \frac{1}{2}$, we have $\exp_L T = \exp_R T = \operatorname{con}_L T = \operatorname{con}_R T = \frac{1}{2}$. Hence in base 2, at least $n-1$ digits and at most $n+1$ digits must be absorbed from both sides to obtain $n$ output digits. (In practice, $n-1$ digits are not sufficient.)

The tensor $T = \left(\begin{smallmatrix} 1 & 0 & 0 & 0 \\ 0 & 0 & 0 & 1 \end{smallmatrix}\right)$ with $T(x,y) = xy$ is refining. Since $\frac{\partial T}{\partial x}(x,y) = y$ and $\frac{\partial T}{\partial y}(x,y) = x$, we have $\exp_L T = \exp_R T = 0$ and $\operatorname{con}_L T = \operatorname{con}_R T = 1$. Hence in base 2, $n+2$ digits from both sides are sufficient to obtain $n$ output digits, but we do not get useful lower bounds. Indeed, we have $(\mathbf{0} : \xi) \cdot \eta = \mathbf{0} : (\xi \cdot \eta)$, and therefore, an arbitrary number of output digits can be obtained without looking at the second argument if the first argument is $\mathbf{0}^\omega$.

# 8 The Size of the Entries

When a non-singular refining matrix is applied to a digit stream, we know from Theorem 7.1 that between $c^< + 2n$ and $c^> + 2n$ *transactions* (absorptions plus emissions) are needed to obtain $n$ output digits. At first glance, these transactions (and the emission tests) seem to require only constant time (see (16) and (19)), but we need to take into account the size of the four entries of the state matrix. In Example 6.2, the entries seem to grow during the course of the computation, and the time required by the integer operations in the transactions and tests (mainly addition and comparison) is linear in the bit size of the involved numbers. Thus, we should try to obtain bounds for the entries of the state matrix (or tensor) in order to obtain proper complexity results.

## 8.1 Common Factors

Cancellation of common factors of the entries of the state matrix could help to keep the entries small. In Example 6.1, a common factor of 2 could occasionally be cancelled, while there were no common factors at all in Example 6.2.

We first show that the range of possible common factors is quite limited.

**Proposition 8.1.** *Let $M$ be a matrix or tensor in lowest terms (i.e., no non-trivial common factors in the entries), and let $M'$ be the result of performing one transaction in base $r$ (absorption or emission) at $M$. Then any common factor of $M'$ divides $r$.*

*Proof.* Let $M = \left(\begin{smallmatrix} a & c \\ b & d \end{smallmatrix}\right)$ as usual. If $M'$ results from absorbing digit $k$, then $M' = \left(\begin{smallmatrix} a & rc+ka \\ b & rd+kb \end{smallmatrix}\right)$. Any common factor $g$ of $a$, $b$, $rc+ka$, and $rd+kb$ is also a common factor of $ra$, $rb$, $rc$, and $rd$. Since $a$, $b$, $c$, and $d$ are relatively prime by assumption, $g$ must divide $r$. The arguments for emission, where $M' = \left(\begin{smallmatrix} ra-kb & rc-kd \\ b & d \end{smallmatrix}\right)$, and for tensors are similar. □

Even the limited amount of cancellation admitted by Prop. 8.1 does not show up in most cases. Note that without cancellation of common factors, neither absorption nor emission affect the $b$-entry of the state matrix or tensor. If $b$ is odd like in Example 6.2, then it remains odd for ever, and there will never be any common factors in base 2. If $b$ is even and non-zero, then common factors may occur, but only as often as the exponent of the largest power of 2 contained in $b$. After this amount of common factors has been cancelled out, the resulting value of $b$ will be odd, and no further cancellations will be possible. Only if $b = 0$, an unlimited number of cancellations may occur. In the following two subsections, we study the two cases $b = 0$ and $b \neq 0$ for matrices more closely.

## 8.2 Affine Matrices

For an affine matrix ($b = 0$), the transactions simplify a bit:

$$\begin{pmatrix} a & c \\ 0 & d \end{pmatrix} \cdot A_k^r = \begin{pmatrix} a & rc+ka \\ 0 & rd \end{pmatrix} \qquad A_k^{r*} \cdot \begin{pmatrix} a & c \\ 0 & d \end{pmatrix} = \begin{pmatrix} ra & rc-kd \\ 0 & d \end{pmatrix} \tag{29}$$

Hence, the result of first absorbing $k$ and then emitting $l$, or the other way round, is

$$A_l^{r*} \cdot \begin{pmatrix} a & c \\ 0 & d \end{pmatrix} \cdot A_k^r = \begin{pmatrix} ra & r^2c+rka-rld \\ 0 & rd \end{pmatrix} \tag{30}$$

which has a common factor of $r$. After cancelling it, we obtain $\left(\begin{smallmatrix} a & rc+ka-ld \\ 0 & d \end{smallmatrix}\right)$, which is the same as the original matrix, except for the $c$-entry. Similarly, we obtain a common factor $r^k$ after performing $k$ absorptions and $k$ emissions in any order, and cancelling $r^k$ will produce a matrix with the same $a$ and $d$ entries as the original one. The $d$-entry will only increase if there is an excess of absorptions over emissions; this increase consists of a factor of $r$ for every additional absorption.

By Theorem 7.1, we know that at most $c^> + n$ absorptions are needed for $n$ emissions. Thus, immediately before the last of these $n$ emissions, $n-1$ emissions and at most $c^> + n$ absorptions have happened; the maximal possible excess is therefore $c^> + 1$. Recall $c^> = \lceil \log_r(2 \operatorname{con} M) \rceil = \lceil \log_r(2\frac{|a|}{d}) \rceil$. By Prop. 5.4, $|a| \leq d$ holds, whence $c^> \leq 1$. Therefore, the maximal possible excess of absorptions over emissions is 2.

**Theorem 8.2.** *Let* $M_0 = \left(\begin{smallmatrix} a_0 & c_0 \\ 0 & d_0 \end{smallmatrix}\right)$ *be an affine refining matrix with* $d_0 \geq 0$, *and* $(M_n)_{n \geq 0}$ *the sequence of matrices which results from Algorithm 1, with the* *additional provision that after each step, all common factors are cancelled out. Then all entries of $M_n$ are bounded by $r^2 \cdot d_0$.*

This bound is sharp as can be seen from Example 6.1: The starting value is $d_0 = 4$, and so the theoretical upper bound is $2^2 \cdot 4 = 16$, which indeed occurs after four transactions. But Theorem 8.2 ensures that it cannot get worse.

Because of the constant upper bound in Theorem 8.2, the additions and comparisons needed to execute the algorithm take only constant time.

**Corollary 8.3.** *If an affine refining 1-LFT is applied to a digit stream, each transaction (absorption or emission) takes only constant time. Hence, $n$ output digits can be computed in time $O(n)$.*

## 8.3 Non-affine Matrices

Remember that $b$ in $\left(\begin{smallmatrix} a & c \\ b & d \end{smallmatrix}\right)$ is invariant under absorptions and emissions. Hence in case $b \neq 0$, all common factors that may appear during the calculation are factors of $b$, and thus, cancellation of common factors can only lead to a constant size reduction. (In the special case $|b| = 1$, there will be no non-trivial common factors at all.)

Let us consider entry $d$, which is an upper bound for all other entries by Prop. 5.5. Emission does not affect $d$, while absorption of $A_k^r$ transforms $d$ into $d' = rd + kb$. Because of $|k| \leq r - 1$, one obtains $d' \leq rd + (r-1)|b|$ and $d' \geq rd - (r-1)|b|$, which lead to $d' + |b| \leq r(d + |b|)$ and $d' - |b| \geq r(d - |b|)$. These estimations can easily be iterated. Taking into account possible cancellations by common factors in the lower bound, one obtains:

**Theorem 8.4.** *Let $M_0 = \left(\begin{smallmatrix} a & c \\ b & d \end{smallmatrix}\right)$ be a refining matrix with $d \geq 0$ and $b \neq 0$, and let $M_m = \begin{pmatrix} a_m & c_m \\ b_m & d_m \end{pmatrix}$ be a matrix which results from $M_0$ by $m$ absorptions in base $r$, any number of emissions, and cancellation of all common factors. Then $d_m \geq \frac{d-|b|}{|b|} r^m + 1$ and $d_m \leq (d + |b|) r^m - |b|$ holds (where the coefficients of $r^m$ are positive by Prop. 5.2).*

For the matrix $\left(\begin{smallmatrix} 0 & 1 \\ 1 & 2 \end{smallmatrix}\right)$ of Example 6.2, we obtain in base 2 the estimations $2^m + 1 \leq d_m \leq 3 \cdot 2^m - 1$. For $m = 0, \ldots, 3$, the lower bounds are 2, 3, 5, 9, the upper bounds 2, 5, 11, 23, and the observed values of $d_m$ are 2, 5, 10, 21, close to the upper bounds.

On the positive side, Theorem 8.4 ensures that the bit size of the $d$-entry (and with it all other entries by Prop. 5.5) is at most linear in the number of absorptions. On the negative side, it indicates that it really has linear bit size; the increase of the size of the $d$-entry cannot be avoided. The $a$- and $c$-entries may grow as well, but they need not, while $b$ is guaranteed to remain small because it is invariant.

Theorem 8.4 also has a negative effect on efficiency. Remember (Theorem 7.1) that $n$ emissions require $O(n)$ absorptions, and thus lead to a $d$-entry of bit size

$O(n)$. The next execution of the loop in Algorithm 1 will thus need time $O(n)$ because it requires the calculation of either $2c - d$ (emission of $\mathbf{1}$), or $2c + d$ (emission of $\bar{\mathbf{1}}$), or $d - 2a$ (in the test whether $\mathbf{0}$ can be emitted). Therefore we obtain:

**Theorem 8.5.** *The calculation of the first $n$ digits of the result of applying a non-affine refining 1-LFT to a digit stream needs time $O(n^2)$ if Algorithm 1 is used.*

## 8.4 Size Bounds for Tensors

For tensors, similar results hold, but their proofs are much more involved. Here, we present only the main results.

**Proposition 8.6.** *Let $T_0 = \left(\begin{smallmatrix} a & c & e & g \\ b & d & f & h \end{smallmatrix}\right)$ be a refining tensor with $h \geq 0$, and let $T_m$ be a tensor which results from $T_0$ by $m$ absorptions in base $r$, any number of emissions, and cancellation of all common factors. Then all entries of $T_m$ are bounded by $r^m(h + |f| + |d| + |b|)$.*

**Proposition 8.7.** *For every refining tensor $T_0 = \left(\begin{smallmatrix} a & c & e & g \\ b & d & f & h \end{smallmatrix}\right)$ with $h \geq 0$, there is an integer $m_0 \geq 0$ such that after $m \geq m_0$ absorptions, any number of emissions,* but no cancellations, *the lower right entry $h'$ of the resulting tensor satisfies $h' \geq r^{m-m_0}$.*

## 8.5 Cancellation in Tensors

From (17), (18), and (20), it follows that the entry $b$ in $\left(\begin{smallmatrix} a & c & e & g \\ b & d & f & h \end{smallmatrix}\right)$ is invariant under emissions and absorptions. Hence, only a finite amount of cancellation is possible if $b \neq 0$, and so, $h$ will have size $\Theta(r^m)$ after $m$ absorptions. Only in the case $b = 0$, an infinite amount of cancellations is possible. The result of emitting $A_k^r$ from $\left(\begin{smallmatrix} a & c & e & g \\ 0 & d & f & h \end{smallmatrix}\right)$ is

$$\begin{pmatrix} ra & rc-kd & re-kf & rg-kh \\ 0 & d & f & h \end{pmatrix}.$$

The results of left and right absorption of $A_k^r$ into $\left(\begin{smallmatrix} a & c & e & g \\ 0 & d & f & h \end{smallmatrix}\right)$ are the tensors

$$\begin{pmatrix} a & c & re+ka & rg+kc \\ 0 & d & rf & rh+kd \end{pmatrix} \quad \text{and} \quad \begin{pmatrix} a & rc+ka & e & rg+ke \\ 0 & rd & f & rh+kf \end{pmatrix}.$$

These three tensors reveal that the three entries $a$, $d$, and $f$ either remain the same or are multiplied by $r$. Hence—under the condition $b = 0$—the three conditions $a = 0$, $d = 0$, and $f = 0$ are invariant under absorptions and emissions, i.e., zeros at these positions will stay for ever. Yet the three tensors do not exhibit any opportunity for cancellation in themselves.

In the case of matrices, the opportunity for cancelling $r$ appears only if an absorption and an emission are considered together. Analogously, we now consider the combined effect of absorbing $k_1$ from the left and $k_2$ from the right, and emitting $l$ at $\begin{pmatrix} a & c & e & g \\ b & d & f & h \end{pmatrix}$ (a *round*). The result, which does not depend on the temporal order of these three transactions, has a common factor of $r$ in its 8 entries. Cancelling this factor leads to

$$\begin{pmatrix} a & rc + k_2a - ld & re + k_1a - lf & G \\ 0 & d & f & rh + k_1d + k_2f \end{pmatrix} \tag{31}$$

where $G = r^2g + rk_1c + rk_2e + k_1k_2a - rlh - k_1ld - k_2lf$.
Thus, in each round, a factor of $r$ can be cancelled. Yet this is not enough: since a round contains two absorptions, the lower right entry increases by a factor of approximately $r^2$ in each round, i.e., with the cancellation, it still increases by approximately $r$. At least, it will be only half as big (in terms of bit size) as in the case $b \neq 0$. Note also that $a$, $d$, and $f$ attain their original values after a round with cancellation. On the positive side, this means that these three entries are bounded, reducing both space and time complexity of the calculations. On the negative side, it implies that if at least one of these three values is non-zero, then only a finite amount of further cancellations is possible (none at all if at least one of $a$, $d$, $f$ is 1 or $-1$). Thus, we may only hope for a further infinite amount of cancellations if $a = d = f = 0$. Under this assumption, there is indeed another common factor of $r$ in Tensor (31). Its cancellation leads to

$$\begin{pmatrix} 0 & c & e & rg + k_1c + k_2e - lh \\ 0 & 0 & 0 & h \end{pmatrix} \tag{32}$$

Hence, the entries $c$, $e$, and $h$ attain their original values. As $h$ is the dominant entry, one may argue further as in the case of matrices that all entries are bounded during the calculation. Summarising, we have the following three cases for $\begin{pmatrix} a & c & e & g \\ b & d & f & h \end{pmatrix}$ if all possible cancellations are performed:

1. If $b \neq 0$, then there are only finitely many cancellations possible. After $m$ rounds, $h$ has bit size $2m + O(1)$.
2. If $b = 0$, then it stays 0 for ever, and so do each of $a$, $d$, $f$ in this case. If not all of $a$, $d$, $f$ are zero, then a factor of $r$ can be cancelled in each round, but apart from these, there are only finitely many cancellations possible. After $m$ rounds, $h$ has bit size $m + O(1)$.
3. If $b = a = d = f = 0$, then this remains true for ever, and a factor of $r^2$ can be cancelled in each round. All entries of the tensor have size $O(1)$.

Like in the case of matrices, these results imply that a calculation with a tensor $T$ needs quadratic time, unless $b = a = d = f = 0$ or $\exp_L T = 0$ or $\exp_R T = 0$.

# 9 Handling Many Digits at Once

The complexity analysis given above has shown that apart from some exceptional cases, the computation of $n$ output digits from $M(x)$ or $T(x,y)$ needs quadratic time $O(n^2)$—if Algorithm 1 is used which works digit by digit, handling each individual digit by a transaction. In this section, we show that handling many digits at once leads to a reduction in the complexity.

## 9.1 Multi-digits

The key observation is that the product of two (and hence many) digit matrices is again a digit matrix, in a bigger base. The product of two digit matrices

$$\begin{pmatrix} 1 & k_1 \\ 0 & r_1 \end{pmatrix} \cdot \begin{pmatrix} 1 & k_2 \\ 0 & r_2 \end{pmatrix} = \begin{pmatrix} 1 & k_1 r_2 + k_2 \\ 0 & r_1 r_2 \end{pmatrix} \tag{33}$$

looks like a digit matrix again; indeed, the conditions $|k_i| \le r_i - 1$ imply

$$|k_1 r_2 + k_2| \le (r_1 - 1)\, r_2 + (r_2 - 1) = r_1 r_2 - 1$$

so that the result really is a digit matrix in base $r_1 r_2$. Iterating (33) yields

$$A^r_{k_1} \cdot \ldots \cdot A^r_{k_n} = A^R_K \quad \text{where} \quad R = r^n \ \text{ and } \ K = \sum_{i=1}^{n} k_i r^{n-i} . \tag{34}$$

Thus, instead of considering the digit sequence $k_1 \ldots k_n$, one may instead consider the single number $K$ and the length $n$ of the sequence. The number $K$ with $|K| \le r^n - 1$ will be called an *$n$-multi-digit* in base $r$.

If a real number $x \in I_0$ is given, then we may ask for the first $n$ digits of a possible digit stream representation of $x$; this request is written as $n?\,x$. According to the considerations above, we may accept that the answer is not given as a digit stream of length $n$, but as an $n$-multi-digit $K$. The number $K$ with $|K| \le r^n - 1$ is a correct answer to the request $n?\,x$ iff $x$ is in $[\frac{K-1}{r^n}, \frac{K+1}{r^n}]$. We write $K = n?\,x$ if $K$ is a correct answer for $n?\,x$ (but note that there are usually two different correct answers, e.g., $1?\,\frac{1}{3}$ has the correct answers 0 and 1).

## 9.2 Multi-digit Computation

Assume we are given a refining non-singular matrix $M$ and an argument $x$ in $I_0$, and we are asked for $n$ digits of $M(x)$ in base 2. Theorem 7.1 provides two integers $c^<$ and $c^>$ such that at least $c^< + n$ and at most $c^> + n$ digits from $x$ are needed to obtain $n$ digits of $M(x)$. Thus we must ask for some number $m$ of digits of $x$, but we only know $c^< + n \le m \le c^> + n$. There are two strategies that can be used:

1. Ask for $m = c^< + n$ digits from $x$ and let $K = m?\,x$. Absorb $A_K^{2^m}$ into $M$ and check whether $n$ digits can be emitted from the resulting matrix $M'$. If yes, then do the emission, but if not, absorb one more digit from $x$, check again, etc. Alternatively, one may determine the number $c'^<$ belonging to $M'$ and ask for $c'^< - c^<$ more digits from $x$, absorb these new digits into $M'$ and check again whether $n$ digits can be emitted, etc.
2. Ask for $m = c^> + n$ digits from $x$ and let $K = m?\,x$. Absorb $A_K^{2^m}$ into $M$ and emit $n$ digits from the resulting matrix (which is guaranteed to be possible).

Strategy (1) ensures that as few as possible digits are read from $x$, but it is algorithmically more involved than strategy (2) since it involves checking whether the emission is possible, and if this fails, either degenerates to the old digit-by-digit algorithm, or involves finding out how many more argument digits are at least needed. Here, we shall follow strategy (2), which is easier to describe.

Assume $M = \left(\begin{smallmatrix} a & c \\ b & d \end{smallmatrix}\right)$ is given where the four entries are small. We need to determine $c^> = \lceil \log_2(2 \operatorname{con} M) \rceil = \lceil \log_2(\frac{2|\det M|}{(d-|b|)^2}) \rceil$. The rounded logarithm can be obtained by counting how often the denominator $(d - |b|)^2$ must be doubled until it is bigger than the numerator, or the other way round, depending on which is bigger in the beginning. Alternatively, the calculation may be based on bit sizes. Clearly, it is sufficient to compute $c^>$ once for $M$ to serve several requests $n?\,M(x)$ with different $n$ and $x$.

To handle a request $n?\,M(x)$, we compute $m = c^> + n$ and ask for $K = m?\,x$. Then we absorb $A_K^{2^m}$ into $M$:

$$M \cdot A_K^{2^m} = \begin{pmatrix} a & c \\ b & d \end{pmatrix} \cdot \begin{pmatrix} 1 & K \\ 0 & 2^m \end{pmatrix} = \begin{pmatrix} a & 2^m c + Ka \\ b & 2^m d + Kb \end{pmatrix} \tag{35}$$

Since the original entries are assumed to be small and $2^m$ and $K$ have a bit size of $O(m) = O(n)$, the computations in (35) can be done in linear time $O(n)$. Let the result be $M' = \left(\begin{smallmatrix} a & C \\ b & D \end{smallmatrix}\right)$ with small $a$ and $b$, and big $C$ and $D$.

The next step is to find a suitable integer $L$ with $|L| \le 2^n - 1$ such that $A_L^{2^n}$ can be emitted from $M'$, which is possible iff $M'(I_0) \subseteq [\frac{L-1}{2^n}, \frac{L+1}{2^n}]$. If $M$ and hence $M'$ are increasing, then $M'(I_0) = [\frac{C-a}{D-b}, \frac{C+a}{D+b}]$, and if $M$ is decreasing, then $M'(I_0) = [\frac{C+a}{D+b}, \frac{C-a}{D-b}]$. Anyway, we know what $M'(I_0)$ is. In the next subsection, we shall show how to determine a suitable $L$ from this information.

Before we come to this, we consider the case of tensors. Assume we are given a refining tensor $T$ and two arguments $x_1$ and $x_2$ in $I_0$, and we are asked to compute the first $n$ digits of a representation of the result $T(x_1, x_2)$. Although we did not show how to do this, it is in principle possible to compute the two integers $c_{\mathrm{L}}^> = \lceil \log_2(4 \operatorname{con}_{\mathrm{L}} T) \rceil$ and $c_{\mathrm{R}}^> = \lceil \log_2(4 \operatorname{con}_{\mathrm{R}} T) \rceil$ from Theorem 7.2. Then we may request $m_1 = c_{\mathrm{L}}^> + n$ digits from $x_1$ and $m_2 = c_{\mathrm{R}}^> + n$ digits from $x_2$ which will be delivered as multi-digits $K_1 = m_1?\,x_1$ and $K_2 = m_2?\,x_2$.

Absorbing these multi-digits into $T = \begin{pmatrix} a & c & e & g \\ b & d & f & h \end{pmatrix}$ yields

$$T' = \begin{pmatrix} a & C & E & G \\ b & D & F & H \end{pmatrix} = T \circledL A_{K_1}^{2^{m_1}} \circledR A_{K_2}^{2^{m_2}}$$

where $T'$ is given by

$$\begin{pmatrix} a & 2^{m_2}c + K_2 a & 2^{m_1}e + K_1 a & 2^{m_1+m_2}g + 2^{m_1}K_2 e + 2^{m_2}K_1 c + K_1 K_2 a \\ b & 2^{m_2}d + K_2 b & 2^{m_1}f + K_1 b & 2^{m_1+m_2}h + 2^{m_1}K_2 f + 2^{m_2}K_1 d + K_1 K_2 b \end{pmatrix} \tag{36}$$

In contrast to the matrix case, we do not get away with a linear computation. The product $K_1 K_2$ is a product of two $n$-bit integers which needs time $\psi(n) > O(n)$. Currently, the best known algorithms yield $\psi_0(n) = O(n \log n \log\log n)$, but many software packages for big integer arithmetic come up with a multiplication which needs more time than $\psi_0(n)$, but is still more efficient than $O(n^2)$.

Apart from the product $K_1 K_2$, all other operations, including multiplication by the powers of 2, can be performed in linear time $O(n)$. Thus we still have linear time if $a = b = 0$; in this case, some power of 2 may be cancelled.

Again, the next step is to find a suitable $L$ with $|L| \leq r^n - 1$ such that $A_L^{r^n}$ can be emitted from $T'$, which is possible iff $T'(I_0^2) \subseteq [\frac{L-1}{2^n}, \frac{L+1}{2^n}]$. The two end points of $T'(I_0^2)$ are the smallest and the largest of the four corner values $T'(\pm 1, \pm 1)$, respectively. If the monotonicity type of $T$ and hence of $T'$ is known, then it is clear which of the corner values are the smallest and the largest.

## 9.3 Multi-digit Emission

The treatment in the previous section has left us with the following problem: given an integer $n > 0$ and a rational interval $[u, v] \subseteq I_0$, which arose as $M'(I_0)$ or $T'(I_0^2)$, find an integer $L$ such that $|L| \leq 2^n - 1$ and $[u, v] \subseteq [\frac{L-1}{2^n}, \frac{L+1}{2^n}]$. Because we used the upper bounds for absorption, we know that such an $L$ exists, but for the sake of generality, we also derive a condition for the existence of $L$.

The interval inclusion above can be written as $u \geq \frac{L-1}{2^n}$ and $v \leq \frac{L+1}{2^n}$, which is equivalent to $2^n v - 1 \leq L \leq 2^n u + 1$. Since $L$ is required to be an integer, this in turn is equivalent to $v' \leq L \leq u'$, where $v' = \lceil 2^n v - 1 \rceil$ and $u' = \lfloor 2^n u + 1 \rfloor$. Note that $v'$ and $u'$ are integers.

Thus, the following seems to be the appropriate method: Compute the integers $v'$ and $u'$. If $v' > u'$, then the emission of $n$ digits is not possible. Otherwise, any integer $L$ with $v' \leq L \leq u'$ can be emitted, for instance $L = v'$ or $L = u'$.

There is one remaining difficulty though: as an $n$-multi-digit, the chosen integer $L$ should satisfy $|L| \leq 2^n - 1$. Yet if $u = 1$, then $u' = 2^n + 1$, and if $1 - 2^{-n} \leq u < 1$, then $u' = 2^n$; in both cases, the choice $L = u'$ is forbidden. Similarly, $v' = -2^n - 1$ or $v' = -2^n$ may happen if $v \leq -1 + 2^{-n}$, rendering the choice $L = v'$ unsuitable.

These problems may be solved as follows: remember $u \geq -1$, whence $u' \geq -2^n + 1$. Hence, $u'$ is a suitable choice if $u' \leq 2^n - 1$. This condition can be expressed in terms of $u$ as follows:

$$u' = \lfloor 2^n u + 1 \rfloor \leq 2^n - 1 \iff 2^n u + 1 < 2^n \iff u < 1 - 2^{-n}. \tag{37}$$

Since $n > 0$, this is certainly the case if $u \leq 0$. Analogously, one may show that $v'$ is suitable if $v \geq 0$. Since $u \leq v$, one of these two conditions is always satisfied. Actually, the decision which of $u'$ and $v'$ to take can be based on the sign of any element $w \in [u, v]$; for, $w \leq 0$ implies $u \leq 0$, and $w \geq 0$ implies $v \geq 0$.

**Algorithm 2**

***Input:*** *An integer $n > 0$ and a rational interval $[u, v] \subseteq I_0$.*

***Output:*** *An $n$-multi-digit $L$ which can be emitted, or the information that such a digit does not exist.*

***Method:***

$u' = \lfloor 2^n u + 1 \rfloor$; $v' = \lceil 2^n v - 1 \rceil$;
*if* $u' < v'$ *then no such digit exists*
*else if* $w \geq 0$ *then* $L = v'$ *else* $L = u'$
*(where $w$ is any convenient test value from $[u, v]$).*

This algorithm is sufficient to deal with the various cases of LFT's which have been handled in the previous section. Since we followed strategy (2) and absorbed sufficiently many digits to guarantee the emission, the test $u' < v'$ can be omitted.

In the matrix case, we have $[u, v] = M'(I_0)$ where $M' = \begin{pmatrix} a & C \\ b & D \end{pmatrix}$. If $M'$ is increasing, then $u = \frac{C-a}{D-b}$ and $v = \frac{C+a}{D+b}$. A simple test value $w$ in-between is $M'(0) = C/D$. The test $C/D \geq 0$ is equivalent to $C \geq 0$ since $D > 0$ by our general assumption. Hence, we obtain the following algorithm (which also includes the absorption phase):

**Algorithm 3**

***Input:*** *A refining increasing matrix $M = \begin{pmatrix} a & c \\ b & d \end{pmatrix}$ with $c^>$, an argument $x$, and the desired number $n > 0$ of output digits.*

***Output:*** *An $n$-multi-digit $L = n?\,M(x)$.*

***Method:***

$m = c^> + n$;
*if* $m > 0$ *then* $K = m?\,x$; $C = 2^m c + Ka$; $D = 2^m d + Kb$
*else* $C = c$; $D = d$;
*if* $C \geq 0$ *then* $L = \left\lceil \frac{2^n(C+a)}{D+b} \right\rceil - 1$ *else* $L = \left\lfloor \frac{2^n(C-a)}{D-b} \right\rfloor + 1$.

For a decreasing matrix, the algorithm has to be suitably modified.

The two numbers $\left\lfloor \frac{2^n(C-a)}{D-b} \right\rfloor$ and $\left\lceil \frac{2^n(C+a)}{D+b} \right\rceil$ are obtained by integer divisions of the $2n$-bit integers $2^n(C \pm a)$ by the $n$-bit integers $D \pm b$, resulting in $n$-bit integers. The complexity of such a division is the same as the complexity $\psi(n)$ of multiplying two $n$-bit integers. Apart from the two divisions, all other operations, including multiplication by $2^n$, can be performed in linear time $O(n)$. Thus, we have managed to decrease the time needed to obtain $n$ output digits from $O(n^2)$ (for non-affine matrices) to $\psi(n)$.

But what about affine matrices ($b = 0$) where the single digit algorithm already performed in time $O(n)$? Well, if $b = 0$, the fractions $\frac{2^n(C \pm a)}{D \pm b}$ simplify to $\frac{2^n(C \pm a)}{2^m d}$, where a power of 2 can be cancelled before the quotients are computed. After cancellation, these are divisions of an $n$ bit integer by a small integer which can be done in linear time $O(n)$.

For tensors of known monotonicity type, similar variants of the general Algorithm 2 can be developed. For general tensors, the algorithm becomes more complicated.

# 10 Algebraic Operations

These are the basic arithmetic operations like addition and multiplication. For each operation, we shall show how exponents can be handled, and how its action on mantissas can be implemented by LFT's. The general algorithm for multi-digits (Alg. 2) can be specialised to the various cases (here only shown for addition). These specialised multi-digit operations will not depend on LFT's any more. Later, we consider transcendental functions like exponential and logarithm, where LFT's will be indispensable.

## 10.1 Addition $x_1 + x_2$

*Exponents.* If both arguments happen to have the same exponent, it can be taken out since $2^e x_1 + 2^e x_2 = 2^e(x_1 + x_2)$. If the exponents are different, then the smaller one can be increased because of $[\xi]_2 = 2^e[\mathbf{0}^e : \xi]_2$. If the exponents have been successfully handled, we are left with adding the mantissas. Unfortunately, the base interval $[-1, 1]$ is not closed under addition, but writing $x_1 + x_2$ as $2(x_1 \oplus x_2)$ with $x_1 \oplus x_2 = \frac{x_1 + x_2}{2}$ solves the problem. Hence the exponent handling can be done as follows:

$$(e_1 \,\|\, \xi_1) + (e_2 \,\|\, \xi_2) \;=\; (e + 1 \,\|\, (\mathbf{0}^{e-e_1} : \xi_1) \oplus (\mathbf{0}^{e-e_2} : \xi_2)) \quad \text{where } e = \max(e_1, e_2).$$

*Single-digit algorithm.* The operation '$\oplus$' is a refining 2-LFT $T = \left(\begin{smallmatrix} \mathit{0} & 1 & 1 & 0 \\ \mathit{0} & \mathit{0} & \mathit{0} & 2 \end{smallmatrix}\right)$ of type $(\uparrow, \uparrow)$. By the analysis in Section 8.5 we know that the zeros written as $\mathit{0}$ are persistent, and that there are sufficient opportunities for cancellation so that the entries remain bounded. Thus, the single-digit algorithm for addition can be run with tensors of the form $\left(\begin{smallmatrix} \mathit{0} & c & e & g \\ \mathit{0} & \mathit{0} & \mathit{0} & h \end{smallmatrix}\right)$, i.e., four parameters which are small integers. Since the entries are bounded, only finitely many tensors may show up during the single-digit algorithm. Hence, the algorithm can be turned into the action of a finite state transducer operating on digits as pure symbols.

*Multi-digit algorithm.* Algorithm 2 can be adapted to the special case of addition. Because of $\frac{\partial T}{\partial x}(x,y) = \frac{\partial T}{\partial y}(x,y) = \frac{1}{2}$, we know $\text{con}_\text{L}\, T = \text{con}_\text{R}\, T = \frac{1}{2}$, whence $c_\text{L}^> = c_\text{R}^> = 1$. Thus, $n+1$ digits from the two arguments are sufficient to obtain $n$ result digits. With $K_i = (n+1)?\,\xi_i$ for $i = 1,2$, we have $u = \frac{K_1-1}{2^{n+1}} \oplus \frac{K_2-1}{2^{n+1}} = \frac{K_1+K_2-2}{2^{n+2}}$ and $v = \frac{K_1+K_2+2}{2^{n+2}}$. A convenient test value $w$ in-between is $\frac{K_1+K_2}{2^{n+2}}$; the condition $w \geq 0$ is equivalent to $K_1 + K_2 \geq 0$. The two integer candidates are $u' = \lfloor 2^n u + 1 \rfloor = \lfloor (K_1 + K_2 + 2)/4 \rfloor$ and $v' = \lceil (K_1 + K_2 - 2)/4 \rceil$. Thus, the algorithm looks as follows:

For $L = n?\,(\xi_1 \oplus \xi_2)$ do:
$K_1 = (n+1)?\,\xi_1$; $K_2 = (n+1)?\,\xi_2$; $K = K_1 + K_2$;
if $K \geq 0$ then $L = \lceil (K-2)/4 \rceil$ else $L = \lfloor (K+2)/4 \rfloor$.

Subtraction is very similar to addition and not included here.

## 10.2 Multiplication $x_1 * x_2$

*Exponents.* $(e_1 \parallel \xi_1) * (e_2 \parallel \xi_2) = (e_1 + e_2 \parallel \xi_1 * \xi_2)$.

*Zero Digits.* Multiplication '$*$' is a refining 2-LFT $T = \left(\begin{smallmatrix} 1 & 0 & 0 & 0 \\ 0 & 0 & 0 & 1 \end{smallmatrix}\right)$ which has no monotonicity type since $\xi_1 * \xi_2$ is increasing in $\xi_1$ for $\xi_2 \geq 0$, but decreasing for $\xi_2 \leq 0$. If $\xi_2$ starts with $\mathbf{1}$ or $\bar{\mathbf{1}}$, we are in one of these two cases, but $\mathbf{0}$ does not provide the necessary information. Yet we may push out any zero digits without bothering about monotonicity and without changing the state tensor: $(\mathbf{0} : \xi_1) * \xi_2 = \mathbf{0} : (\xi_1 * \xi_2)$, $\quad \xi_1 * (\mathbf{0} : \xi_2) = \mathbf{0} : (\xi_1 * \xi_2)$.
This process requires only linear time in the number of emitted digits. It ends if enough digits have been emitted or both arguments are normalised.

*Single-Digit Algorithm.* If there are no more zero digits to be emitted, then the signs of the arguments can be read off from their first non-zero digits. From these signs, the monotonicity type to be used in the rest of the computation can be determined, e.g., $\xi_1 \geq 0$ and $\xi_2 \leq 0$ implies type $(\downarrow, \uparrow)$. By the analysis in Section 8.5 we know that $\left(\begin{smallmatrix} 1 & 0 & 0 & 0 \\ 0 & 0 & 0 & 1 \end{smallmatrix}\right)$ has three persistent zeros and belongs to the medium class of tensors that permit one cancellation in every round, which does not suffice to obtain bounded entries. The general form of the state tensor will be $\left(\begin{smallmatrix} a & C & E & G \\ 0 & 0 & 0 & H \end{smallmatrix}\right)$ with small $a$ and big $C$, $E$, $G$, and $H$. The algorithm cannot be optimised to a finite state transducer, but some optimisations are possible because of the persistent zero entries. (Konecny [39] characterized the functions that can be computed by finite state transducers. Multiplication is not among these functions.)

## 10.3 Reciprocal $1/x$

This operation presents the difficulty that it is undefined for $x = 0$. To compute $1/x$, we first need to normalise the argument $x$ by squeezing out zeros from the mantissa and reducing the exponent accordingly (see Section 2.3). This process does not terminate for $x = 0$ and may take very long for $x \approx 0$. A possible solution is to provide a lower bound for the exponent and to indicate a "potential division by 0" if this bound is reached.

If normalisation terminates, we know $x \neq 0$ and $\frac{1}{4} \leq |\xi| \leq 1$ for the final mantissa of $x$. Then $1 \leq \frac{1}{|\xi|} \leq 4$, whence $|\frac{1}{4\xi}| \leq 1$. This shows how to proceed after normalisation:

$$1/(e \parallel \xi) \;=\; (-e+2 \parallel R(\xi)) \quad \text{where} \quad R(\xi) = \tfrac{1}{4\xi}$$

Function $R$ is a 1-LFT, $R = \left(\begin{smallmatrix} 0 & 1 \\ 4 & 0 \end{smallmatrix}\right)$. It is decreasing, bounded and refining on the two intervals $[\frac{1}{4}, 1]$ and $[-1, -\frac{1}{4}]$. This is sufficient to use the single-digit algorithm for computing $R(\xi)$. Practically, this can be done by first absorbing the initial two digits of $\xi$, which are **11**, **10**, $\bar{\mathbf{1}}\mathbf{0}$, or $\bar{\mathbf{1}}\bar{\mathbf{1}}$ because of normalisation. Absorption of **11** leads to $\left(\begin{smallmatrix} 0 & 1 \\ 1 & 3 \end{smallmatrix}\right)$ (after cancellation), absorption of **10** leads to $\left(\begin{smallmatrix} 0 & 1 \\ 1 & 2 \end{smallmatrix}\right)$ etc. These matrices are ordinary decreasing refining matrices as required by the single-digit algorithm ($\left(\begin{smallmatrix} 0 & 1 \\ 1 & 2 \end{smallmatrix}\right)$ is exactly the matrix used in Example 6.2).

## 11 Infinite LFT Expressions

### 11.1 Infinite Matrix Products

We shall later see that many familiar constants like $\pi$ or e can be written as (formal) infinite products $\prod_{n=0}^{\infty} M_n$ of matrices with integer entries. This is a generalisation of the infinite sequences (or products) of digit matrices that we have already seen. Moreover, functions like $\mathrm{e}^x$ can be realised as infinite products of matrices whose entries depend on the argument $x$.

Before we continue, we need to clarify what such an infinite product actually means. As finite products of matrices are again matrices, one should expect the same for an infinite product. The standard way to define the infinite product $\prod_{n=0}^{\infty} M_n$ would be that it is the limit of the finite products $\prod_{n=0}^{m} M_n$ as $m$ goes to infinity. Yet such a definition would involve a notion of limit for matrices, or rather 1-LFT's. While it is not impossible to define such a limit notion, it is beyond the scope of these notes. To avoid this problem, we only define the results of applying infinite products to arguments (numbers or intervals); the product itself remains meaningless and is considered mainly as another way to present a sequence of matrices.

Given a real number argument $y_0$, it is straightforward to define $\prod_{n=0}^{\infty} M_n(y_0)$ as the limit of the sequence of real numbers $y_n = M_0 \cdots M_{n-1}(y_0)$, provided all the numbers $y_n$ are well-defined (no division by 0) and the limit exists. Using this new notion, we obtain for instance the real number $y = \sum_{i=1}^{\infty} d_i 2^{-i}$ denoted by the digit stream $d_1 d_2 \cdots$ as $\prod_{n=1}^{\infty} A_{d_n}(0)$, because $A_{d_1} \cdots A_{d_n}(0) = (\sum_{i=1}^{n} d_i 2^{n-i})/2^n$ converges to $y$. Actually, the argument 0 can be replaced by any real number $y_0$ since $A_{d_1} \cdots A_{d_n}(y_0) = (y_0 + \sum_{i=1}^{n} d_i 2^{n-i})/2^n$ also converges to $y$.

Now we replace the argument $y_0$ by an interval $J_0$. In analogy to the number case we consider the intervals

$$J_n \; = \; M_0 \cdots M_{n-1}(J_0). \tag{38}$$

The sequence $(J_n)_{n\geq 0}$ of intervals is *nested* if $J_n \supseteq J_{n+1}$ for all $n \geq 1$ (this does not include the inclusion $J_0 \supseteq J_1$ which is disregarded deliberately). The inclusion $J_n \supseteq J_{n+1}$ means $M_0 \cdots M_{n-1}(J_0) \supseteq M_0 \cdots M_n(J_0)$. If the matrices $M_0, \ldots, M_{n-1}$ are non-singular, this is equivalent to $M_n(J_0) \subseteq J_0$. Therefore in the non-singular case, the sequence of intervals is nested iff all LFT's $M_n$ with $n \geq 1$ are refining w.r.t. the interval $J_0$. Note that $M_0$ need not be refining, but it should be bounded on $J_0$ so that $J_1 = M_0(J_0)$ and all other intervals are well-defined.

Following these considerations, an infinite product $\prod_{n=0}^{\infty} M_n(J_0)$ is called *refining* if $M_0$ is bounded on $J_0$ and all $M_n$ for $n \geq 1$ are refining for $J_0$. This includes the sequences of our signed number representation, where $M_0$ is an exponent matrix, which is bounded on the base interval $I_0$, and the remaining matrices are digit matrices, which are refining for $I_0$.

We say that the refining product $\prod_{n=0}^{\infty} M_n(J_0)$ has as value the real number $y$ if the intersection of the nested sequence of intervals $J_1 \supseteq J_2 \supseteq \cdots$ is the singleton set $\{y\}$. For instance, the product $E_e \prod_{n=1}^{\infty} A_{d_n}(I_0)$ corresponding to the number representation $(e \parallel d_1 d_2 \ldots)$ has as value the real number $2^e \cdot \sum_{i=1}^{\infty} d_i 2^{-i}$ denoted by the representation.

Application of an infinite product to a number and to an interval are clearly related. If $y = \prod_{n=0}^{\infty} M_n(J_0)$, then also $y = \prod_{n=0}^{\infty} M_n(y_0)$ for all $y_0$ in $J_0$. On the other hand, the interval notion is more restricted and hence more powerful than the point notion because it includes the fact that the interval sequence is nested, which provides lower and upper bounds for all sequences $(y_n)_{n\geq 0}$ coming from arguments $y_0 \in J_0$.

## 11.2 Convergence Criteria

A nested sequence of intervals $J_n = [u_n, v_n]$ converges to some single point iff $\ell(J_n) = v_n - u_n \to 0$ as $n \to \infty$. This single point is then the common limit of $(u_n)_{n\geq 1}$ and $(v_n)_{n\geq 1}$. Because of this observation, a convergence criterion may be obtained from the notion of contractivity. Iterating Relation (22) yields

$$\ell(J_n) \; = \; \ell((M_0 \cdots M_{n-1})(J_0)) \; \leq \; \mathrm{con}^{J_0} M_0 \cdot \ldots \cdot \mathrm{con}^{J_0} M_{n-1} \cdot \ell(J_0)\,.$$

Thus, we obtain the following:

**Theorem 11.1.**
*A refining infinite product* $\prod_{n=0}^{\infty} M_n(J_0)$ *converges if* $\prod_{n=0}^{\infty} \mathrm{con}^{J_0} M_n = 0$.

Usually, we shall not directly apply this criterion, but the following corollary:

**Corollary 11.2.** *If* $\prod_{n=0}^{\infty} M_n(J_0)$ *is a refining infinite product with the property* $\lim_{n\to\infty} \mathrm{con}^{J_0} M_n < 1$, *then the product converges to a real number.*

## 11.3 Transformation of Infinite Products

(Formal) infinite products can be transformed by algebraic manipulation with the hope that the result of the transformation has better convergence properties than the original product.

Given $\prod_{n=0}^{\infty} M_n$, select a sequence $(U_n)_{n\geq 1}$ of *non-singular* matrices. Then finite products can be transformed as follows:

$$M_0 \cdots M_{n-1}\, U_n \;=\; M_0\, U_1\, U_1^*\, M_1\, U_2 \cdots U_{n-1}^*\, M_{n-1}\, U_n \;=\; \widetilde{M_0}\, \widetilde{M_1} \cdots \widetilde{M}_{n-1} \tag{39}$$

using the new matrices

$$\widetilde{M_0} \;=\; M_0\, U_1 \qquad \text{and} \qquad \widetilde{M_n} \;=\; U_n^*\, M_n\, U_{n+1} \quad \text{for } n \geq 1. \tag{40}$$

Because any infinite product $\prod_{n=0}^{\infty} M_n$ of non-singular matrices can be transformed into any other product $\prod_{n=0}^{\infty} \widetilde{M_n}$ by choosing $U_1 = M_0^* \widetilde{M_0}$ and $U_{n+1} = M_n^* U_n \widetilde{M_n}$, one needs separate arguments for the convergence of the new product to the same value as the old one.

If the original product is applied to a real number $y_0$, then its value is the limit of the sequence $y_n = M_0 \cdots M_{n-1}(y_0)$. If there is a real number $\widetilde{y}_0$ such that $U_n(\widetilde{y}_0) = y_0$ for all $n \geq 1$, then the number sequence induced by the new matrices at $\widetilde{y}_0$ is the same as the sequence induced by the old matrices at $y_0$ because of $\widetilde{M_0} \cdots \widetilde{M}_{n-1}(\widetilde{y}_0) = M_0 \cdots M_{n-1} U_n(\widetilde{y}_0) = y_n$ using (39). Hence we obtain:

**Proposition 11.3.** *If $\prod_{n=0}^{\infty} \widetilde{M_n}$ results from transforming $\prod_{n=0}^{\infty} M_n$ with $(U_n)_{n\geq 1}$ and $y_0$ and $\widetilde{y}_0$ are two real numbers satisfying $U_n(\widetilde{y}_0) = y_0$ for all $n \geq 1$, then $\prod_{n=0}^{\infty} \widetilde{M_n}(\widetilde{y}_0) = \prod_{n=0}^{\infty} M_n(y_0)$ (this means, the first expression converges if and only if the second converges, and if they converge, they have the same value).*

## 11.4 Infinite Products from Taylor Series

We want to implement transcendental functions by infinite products, and so we need methods to obtain such products from more familiar representations. One such representation is the Taylor power series $f(x) = \sum_{n=0}^{\infty} a_n x^n$, e.g., $e^x = \sum_{n=0}^{\infty} \frac{x^n}{n!}$.

There are several ways to transform Taylor series into infinite products. Among the methods explored so far, the one described in the sequel turned out to be the most useful one for the intended applications [29]. It can be applied whenever $a_n \neq 0$ for $n \geq 1$ and uses the matrices

$$M_0 \;=\; \begin{pmatrix} a_1 x & a_0 + a_1 x \\ 0 & 1 \end{pmatrix} \;\text{ and }\; M_n \;=\; \begin{pmatrix} x & x \\ 0 & q_n \end{pmatrix} \;\text{ for } n \geq 1 \tag{41}$$

where $q_n = \frac{a_n}{a_{n+1}}$. To show that these matrices correspond to the Taylor series, we claim that their finite products have the following form (up to scaling):

$$P_n = M_0 \cdots M_{n-1} = \begin{pmatrix} a_n x^n & \sum_{i=0}^{n} a_i x^i \\ 0 & 1 \end{pmatrix} \tag{42}$$

This claim can be verified by induction. For $n = 1$, we have $P_1 = M_0$, which clearly has the claimed form. For the step from $n$ to $n+1$, we compute $P_{n+1} =$

$$P_n M_n = \begin{pmatrix} a_n x^n & \sum_{i=0}^{n} a_i x^i \\ 0 & 1 \end{pmatrix} \begin{pmatrix} x & x \\ 0 & q_n \end{pmatrix} = \begin{pmatrix} a_n x^{n+1} & a_n x^{n+1} + q_n (\sum_{i=0}^{n} a_i x^i) \\ 0 & q_n \end{pmatrix}$$

Dividing all four entries by $q_n \neq 0$ yields the required form because of $a_n / q_n = a_{n+1}$.

From (42), $P_n(0) = \sum_{i=0}^{n} a_i x^i$ follows. Hence, the product $\prod_{n=0}^{\infty} M_n(0)$ converges if and only if the Taylor series converges, and yields the desired value $\sum_{i=0}^{\infty} a_i x^i$.

Of course, we do not want to apply the product to the real number 0, but to the base interval $I_0 = [-1, 1]$ of our number representation. Clearly, all matrices $M_n$ are bounded (under the assumption $a_n \neq 0$ for $n \geq 1$). The matrices $\left(\begin{smallmatrix} x & x \\ 0 & q_n \end{smallmatrix}\right)$ are refining iff $|x| + |x| \leq |q_n|$ (Prop. 5.4). Hence, $\prod_{n=0}^{\infty} M_n(I_0)$ is refining for $|x| \leq q/2$, where $q = \inf_{n \geq 1} |q_n|$. The contractivity of $M_n$ is $|x|/|q_n| \leq |x|/q$, which is at most $1/2$ for $|x| \leq q/2$. Thus, for $|x| \leq q/2$, $\prod_{n=0}^{\infty} M_n(I_0)$ is a refining convergent product. Since $I_0$ contains 0, its value coincides with $\prod_{n=0}^{\infty} M_n(0) = \sum_{n=0}^{\infty} a_n x^n$ as desired.

## 11.5 Infinite Products from Continued Fractions

Another, less familiar source of infinite products are continued fraction expansions. A continued fraction is an infinite expression

$$a_0 + \cfrac{b_1}{a_1 + \cfrac{b_2}{\cdots}} \tag{43}$$

parameterised by numbers $(a_n)_{n \geq 0}$ and $(b_n)_{n \geq 1}$. It denotes the limit of the sequence of partial continued fractions

$$a_0, \quad a_0 + \frac{b_1}{a_1}, \quad a_0 + \cfrac{b_1}{a_1 + \cfrac{b_2}{a_2}}, \quad \ldots$$

provided that this limit exists. For ease of notation, the infinite expression (43) is written as $\langle a_0; b_1, a_1; b_2, a_2; \ldots \rangle$.

Like for Taylor series, there are several ways to turn a continued fraction into an infinite product. We use the following:

$$M_0 = \begin{pmatrix} 1 & a_0 \\ 0 & 1 \end{pmatrix} \quad \text{and} \quad M_n = \begin{pmatrix} 0 & b_n \\ 1 & a_n \end{pmatrix} \quad \text{for } n \geq 1. \tag{44}$$

Since $M_0(y) = a_0 + y$ and $M_n(y) = \frac{b_n}{a_n+y}$, the partial products $M_0 \cdots M_{n-1}(0)$ are exactly the partial continued fractions so that $\prod_{n=0}^{\infty} M_n(0)$ converges if and only if the continued fraction converges, and yields the same value.

In practical applications, this infinite product must usually be transformed into a more appropriate one before the argument can successfully be extended to the base interval $I_0$. Often, the transformation matrices are chosen as $U_n = \left(\begin{smallmatrix} 1 & 0 \\ 0 & u_n \end{smallmatrix}\right)$. Since 0 is a fixed point of these matrices ($U_n(0) = 0$), the transformed infinite product still has the value of the continued fraction when applied to 0 by Prop. 11.3. For the actual transformation, it is useful to note that

$$\begin{pmatrix} a & c \\ b & d \end{pmatrix} \begin{pmatrix} 1 & 0 \\ 0 & u_{n+1} \end{pmatrix} = \begin{pmatrix} a & c\,u_{n+1} \\ b & d\,u_{n+1} \end{pmatrix} \tag{45}$$

$$\begin{pmatrix} 1 & 0 \\ 0 & u_n \end{pmatrix}^* \begin{pmatrix} a & c \\ b & d \end{pmatrix} \begin{pmatrix} 1 & 0 \\ 0 & u_{n+1} \end{pmatrix} = \begin{pmatrix} u_n\,a & u_n\,c\,u_{n+1} \\ b & d\,u_{n+1} \end{pmatrix} \tag{46}$$

### 11.6 The Evaluation of Infinite Products

Before we come to the implementation of the various transcendental functions by infinite products, we give hints on how to use the products in a practical implementation. For simplicity, we only consider refining products applied to the base interval $[-1, 1]$.

If all the matrices in $\prod_{n=0}^{\infty} M_n(I_0)$ have integer entries, there is a choice of several different evaluation algorithms. We only consider single digit approaches, but corresponding multi-digit realisations do exist. Generally, one has to assume that a matrix $M_n$ can be created from its index $n$. First, the matrices may be put into a list which initially contains only $M_0$. In this list, each matrix absorbs the digits that are emitted from its right neighbour. Whenever the rightmost matrix $M_n$ needs to absorb a digit, the next matrix $M_{n+1}$ is created and appended to the list.

Second, the algorithm may be run with a state matrix which initially is $M_0$. Whenever the state matrix cannot emit a digit, it absorbs the next matrix $M_n$ down the list of matrices which has not been absorbed before. This next matrix is created on the fly from its index $n$. Thus, only one matrix must be stored (and the index of the next one to be absorbed), while in the first method, a whole list of matrices must be maintained. On the other hand, the upper bounds for space and time complexity of the ordinary single-digit algorithm do not hold here, since the matrices that are absorbed are usually much more complicated than the simple digit matrices.

Usually, the matrices in the infinite product depend on an argument $x$, like in the product derived from the Taylor series expansion. If the argument is a given rational, the matrices can be converted into integer matrices by suitable scaling, and we are back to the previous case. In the general case of an arbitrary real argument, this cannot be done; instead, the matrices must be converted into tensors. This is always possible if their four entries depend linearly on $x$, by using (6):

$$\begin{pmatrix} ax+e & cx+g \\ bx+f & dx+h \end{pmatrix} = \begin{pmatrix} a & c & e & g \\ b & d & f & h \end{pmatrix}\Bigg|_x$$

If $T_n$ is the tensor belonging to $M_n$, the product $f(x) = \prod_{n=0}^{\infty} M_n(I_0)$ becomes the infinite tensor expression $f(x) = T_0(x, T_1(x, \ldots))$. Such an expression can only be evaluated by the first method indicated above: a list of tensors must be maintained which initially consists of $T_0$ only. Each tensor absorbs argument digits from the left, and from the right the digits emitted from the next tensor. If the last tensor needs a digit from its right argument, a new tensor is created and added to the list. This algorithm works if the tensors are sufficiently contractive so that (almost) each tensor needs strictly less than $n$ digits from its right argument to emit $n$ digits.

## 12 Transcendental Functions

### 12.1 Exponential Function

*Argument Reduction.* The infinite products derived below will only behave well for $|x| \leq 1$, which is equivalent to the exponent of $x$ being at most 0. Yet an arbitrary real argument can be brought into this region by exploiting the fact $\mathrm{e}^{2x} = (\mathrm{e}^x)^2$. Hence, an exponent $n \geq 0$ may be handled by $\mathrm{e}^{(n\|\xi)} = S^n(\mathrm{e}^{\xi})$ where $S^n$ means $n$ applications of the squaring operation $S$. (Admittedly, this can become quite inefficient for larger exponents.) Negative exponents $n < 0$ can be handled by putting the corresponding number of zero digits in front of the mantissa: $\mathrm{e}^{(n\|\xi)} = \mathrm{e}^{\xi'}$ where $\xi' = \mathbf{0}^{|n|} : \xi$.

*Taylor Series Realisation.* The well-known Taylor series for $\mathrm{e}^x$ is $\sum_{n=0}^{\infty} \frac{x^n}{n!}$. All coefficients $a_n = 1/n!$ are non-zero, so that the method of Section 11.4 can be applied. The quotient $q_n = a_n/a_{n+1}$ is $n+1$, so that $q = \inf_{n\geq 1} |q_n| = 2$. Thus we have

$$\mathrm{e}^x = \begin{pmatrix} x & x+1 \\ 0 & 1 \end{pmatrix} \prod_{n=1}^{\infty} \begin{pmatrix} x & x \\ 0 & n+1 \end{pmatrix} (I_0) \quad \text{for } |x| \leq 1. \tag{47}$$

All $M_n$ with $n \geq 1$ have contractivity $\frac{|x|}{n+1} \leq \frac{1}{n+1}$.

As already mentioned, a representation such as (47) is open to two different interpretations. For rational arguments $x$, it is (equivalent to) an infinite product of integer matrices, e.g., $\mathrm{e} = \left(\begin{smallmatrix} 1 & 2 \\ 0 & 1 \end{smallmatrix}\right) \prod_{n=1}^{\infty} \left(\begin{smallmatrix} 1 & 1 \\ 0 & n+1 \end{smallmatrix}\right) (I_0)$. For general (real) arguments however, representation (47) should be turned into the infinite tensor expression $\mathrm{e}^x = T_0(x, T_1(x, T_2(x, \ldots)))$ with

$$T_0 = \begin{pmatrix} 1 & 1 & 0 & 1 \\ \mathit{0} & \mathit{0} & \mathit{0} & 1 \end{pmatrix} \quad \text{and} \quad T_n = \begin{pmatrix} 1 & 1 & 0 & 0 \\ \mathit{0} & \mathit{0} & \mathit{0} & n+1 \end{pmatrix}$$

where each tensor has 3 persistent zeros, indicated by $\mathit{0}$.

The tensors $T_n$ for $n \geq 0$ realise the functions $T_n(x,y) = x(y+1)/(n+1)$ which are increasing in $x$ because $y+1 \geq 0$ for $y \in I_0$, but are not monotonic in $y$. They can be handled similar to multiplication: leading zero digits of $x$ can be pushed out without changing the tensor, and then the first non-zero digit decides the monotonicity behaviour.

The front tensor $T_0(x,y) = x(y+1)+1$ has the same monotonicity behaviour, but cannot be handled immediately in the same way; notice also that it is bounded, but not refining, so that it must emit an exponent matrix first.

- For $x \in [0,1]$ (leading digit $\mathbf{1}$), $T_0$ has type $(\uparrow,\uparrow)$ and image $[1,3]$, so that the appropriate exponent is 2 (and $\mathbf{10}$ can be emitted after emitting the exponent matrix).
- For $x \in [-1,0]$ (leading digit $\bar{\mathbf{1}}$), $T_0$ has type $(\uparrow,\downarrow)$ and image $[-1,1]$, so that the appropriate exponent is 0.
- For $x \in [-\frac{1}{2},\frac{1}{2}]$ (leading digit $\mathbf{0}$), $T_0$ has image $[0,2]$, so that the appropriate exponent is 1, and $\mathbf{1}$ can be emitted after the exponent matrix. The tensor resulting from these emissions is (up to scaling) $T_0' = \left(\begin{smallmatrix} 1 & 1 & 0 & 0 \\ 0 & 0 & 0 & 1 \end{smallmatrix}\right)$ with $T_0'(x,y) = x(y+1)$. Hence, all leading zeros of $x$ can be pushed out without modifying $T_0'$, and the first non-zero digit decides the monotonicity behaviour.

*Continued Fraction Realisation.* A continued fraction for the exponential function is

$$\mathrm{e}^x = \langle 1;\ x,\ 1-\frac{x}{2};\ \frac{x^2}{16\cdot 1^2-4},\ 1;\ \frac{x^2}{16\cdot 2^2-4},\ 1;\ \ldots\rangle.$$

It corresponds to the product representation

$$\mathrm{e}^x = \begin{pmatrix} 1 & 1 \\ 0 & 1 \end{pmatrix} \begin{pmatrix} 0 & x \\ 1 & 1-x/2 \end{pmatrix} \prod_{n=1}^{\infty} \begin{pmatrix} 0 & x^2/(16n^2-4) \\ 1 & 1 \end{pmatrix} (0).$$

The product of the first two matrices is (up to scaling) $M_0 = \left(\begin{smallmatrix} 2 & 2+x \\ 2 & 2-x \end{smallmatrix}\right)$. The infinite product cannot directly be extended to the base interval $I_0 = [-1,1]$ since the denominators of the matrices $M_n = \left(\begin{smallmatrix} 0 & x^2/(16n^2-4) \\ 1 & 1 \end{smallmatrix}\right)$ become 0 at $-1$. This problem is solved by transforming the product with the matrices $U_n = \left(\begin{smallmatrix} 1 & 0 \\ 0 & 4(2n-1) \end{smallmatrix}\right)$ $(n \geq 1)$, which have the form considered in Section 11.5. By (45), the new front matrix is

$$\widetilde{M_0} = \begin{pmatrix} 2 & 4(2+x) \\ 2 & 4(2-x) \end{pmatrix} \cong \begin{pmatrix} 1 & 4+2x \\ 1 & 4-2x \end{pmatrix}$$

which is bounded on $I_0$ for $|x| \leq 1$. By (46), the other matrices are

$$\widetilde{M_n} = \begin{pmatrix} 0 & x^2\frac{16(2n-1)(2n+1)}{4(2n-1)(2n+1)} \\ 1 & 4(2n+1) \end{pmatrix} = \begin{pmatrix} 0 & 4x^2 \\ 1 & 4(2n+1) \end{pmatrix}$$

These matrices are refining on $I_0$ for $|x| \leq 1$. By (23), the contractivity of $\widetilde{M}_n$ is $\frac{4x^2}{(8n+3)^2} \leq \frac{x^2}{16n^2}$ which is better (i.e., smaller) than the value $\frac{|x|}{n+1} \leq \frac{1}{n+1}$ achieved by the Taylor expansion. Therefore, $\prod_{n=0}^{\infty} \widetilde{M}_n(I_0)$ converges, and since $0 \in I_0$, it converges to $\prod_{n=0}^{\infty} \widetilde{M}_n(0) = \prod_{n=0}^{\infty} M_n(0) = \mathrm{e}^x$.

Like the Taylor product, the continued fraction product consists of integer matrices for rational arguments, e.g., $\mathrm{e} = \begin{pmatrix} 1 & 6 \\ 1 & 2 \end{pmatrix} \prod_{n=1}^{\infty} \begin{pmatrix} 0 & 4 \\ 1 & 8n+4 \end{pmatrix} (I_0)$. In contrast to the Taylor case, these matrices are not affine and hence more difficult to handle, but they have better contractivity.

For general (real) arguments, the representation must be turned into the infinite tensor expression $\mathrm{e}^x = T_0\,(x, T_1\,(x^2, T_2\,(x^2, \ldots)))$ which uses both $x$ and $x^2$. The tensors are

$$T_0 = \begin{pmatrix} \mathit{0} & 2 & 1 & 4 \\ \mathit{0} & -2 & 1 & 4 \end{pmatrix} \quad \text{and} \quad T_n = \begin{pmatrix} \mathit{0} & 4 & 0 & 0 \\ \mathit{0} & \mathit{0} & 1 & 8n+4 \end{pmatrix}$$

where each tensor except $T_0$ has 3 persistent zeros, indicated by $\mathit{0}$. Taking into account that their left argument $x^2$ is $\geq 0$, the tensors $T_n$ for $n \geq 1$ have type $(\uparrow, \downarrow)$. Leading zero digits of $x$ are doubled by squaring and can be pushed out of $T_n$ without modifying it. Moreover, each $T_n$ can emit $\mathbf{1}$ after reading $\mathbf{1}$ from $x^2$. The front tensor $T_0$ is a bit more complicated, but can be handled essentially like the front tensor of the Taylor expansion.

### 12.2 Logarithm

*Definition.* Natural logarithm $\ln x$ is the inverse of the exponential function. Thus it is only defined for arguments $x > 0$. To deal with negative arguments, we propose to actually compute the function $f(x) = \ln|x|$, which is the anti-derivative (indefinite integral) of the reciprocal function $1/x$.

*Argument Normalisation.* Like the reciprocal itself, $f$ is still undefined for 0. The handling of this special case is similar to the handling of $1/0$ in Section 10.3: To compute $f(x)$, we first normalise the argument $x$ by squeezing out zeros from the mantissa and reducing the exponent accordingly (see Section 2.3). If normalisation terminates, we know $x \neq 0$ and $\frac{1}{4} \leq |\xi| \leq 1$ for the final mantissa of $x$. This mantissa will start with the digit $\mathbf{1}$ or $\bar{\mathbf{1}}$. The following description tells what to do in the positive case; the negative case is dual.

*Argument Reduction.* Here, we use the fact that a (positive) normalised mantissa starts with $\mathbf{10}$ or $\mathbf{11}$: $\ln(e \parallel \mathbf{1} : \xi) = \ln(2^e \cdot (\xi+1)/2) = (e-1) \cdot \ln 2 + \ln(1+\xi)$. For the constant $\ln 2$ see below. The first digit of $\xi$ is $\mathbf{0}$ or $\mathbf{1}$; hence $\xi \in [-\frac{1}{2}, 1]$.

*Continued Fraction Expansion.* A continued fraction for the function $\ln(1+x)$ is

$$\langle 0;\ x,\ 1;\ x/2,\ 1;\ v_1,\ 1;\ w_1,\ 1;\ v_2,\ 1;\ w_2,\ 1;\ \ldots \rangle$$

where $v_n = \frac{nx}{4n+2}$ and $w_n = \frac{(n+1)x}{4n+2}$. We now write this continued fraction as an infinite product like in Section 11.5, and immediately transform this product by $U_n = \begin{pmatrix} 1 & 0 \\ 0 & 4 \end{pmatrix}$, using (45) and (46) in the step marked by '$\stackrel{\mathrm{T}}{=}$'. In the last step, the matrices are converted into tensors.

$$\begin{aligned}
\ln(1+x) &= \begin{pmatrix} 1 & 0 \\ 0 & 1 \end{pmatrix} \begin{pmatrix} 0 & x \\ 1 & 1 \end{pmatrix} \begin{pmatrix} 0 & x/2 \\ 1 & 1 \end{pmatrix} \prod_{n=1}^{\infty} \begin{pmatrix} 0 & v_n \\ 1 & 1 \end{pmatrix} \begin{pmatrix} 0 & w_n \\ 1 & 1 \end{pmatrix} (0) \\
&= \begin{pmatrix} x & x \\ 1 & x/2+1 \end{pmatrix} \prod_{n=1}^{\infty} \begin{pmatrix} v_n & v_n \\ 1 & w_n+1 \end{pmatrix} (0) \\
&= \begin{pmatrix} 2x & 2x \\ 2 & x+2 \end{pmatrix} \prod_{n=1}^{\infty} \begin{pmatrix} nx & nx \\ 4n+2 & (n+1)x+4n+2 \end{pmatrix} (0) \\
&\stackrel{\mathrm{T}}{=} \begin{pmatrix} 2x & 2x\cdot 4 \\ 2 & (x+2)\cdot 4 \end{pmatrix} \prod_{n=1}^{\infty} \begin{pmatrix} 4\cdot nx & 4\cdot nx\cdot 4 \\ 4n+2 & ((n+1)x+4n+2)\cdot 4 \end{pmatrix} (0) \\
&= \begin{pmatrix} x & 4x \\ 1 & 2x+4 \end{pmatrix} \prod_{n=1}^{\infty} \begin{pmatrix} 2nx & 8nx \\ 2n+1 & (2n+2)x+8n+4 \end{pmatrix} (0) \\
&= \begin{pmatrix} 1 & 4 & 0 & 0 \\ 0 & 2 & 1 & 4 \end{pmatrix}\Big|_x \prod_{n=1}^{\infty} \begin{pmatrix} 2n & 8n & 0 & 0 \\ 0 & 2n+2 & 2n+1 & 8n+4 \end{pmatrix}\Big|_x (0)
\end{aligned}$$

The tensors in the last line will be called $T_n$ ($n \geq 0$), and the corresponding matrices in the second but last line $M_n$ ($n \geq 0$). All tensors $T_n$ exhibit one persistent zero, in the lower left corner. They are bounded on $I_0^2$ since the right entry in their second line is bigger than the sum of the two middle entries. The determinants of the matrices are $\det M_0 = 2x^2 \geq 0$ and $\det M_n = 4n(n+1)x^2 \geq 0$ for $n \geq 1$. Hence, all tensors are increasing in their second argument, for any $x$. For $y \in I_0$, one may also verify $\det(T_n|^y) \geq 0$, i.e., all the tensors have type $(\uparrow, \uparrow)$ in $I_0^2$. They are *not* refining for $I_0$, but remember that we only consider $x \in [-\frac{1}{2}, 1]$. For such $x$, the matrices $M_n$ with $n \geq 1$ *are* refining. By (23), the contractivity of these matrices is

$$\frac{4n(n+1)x^2}{((2n+2)x+6n+3)^2} \stackrel{n\to\infty}{\longrightarrow} \frac{4x^2}{(2x+6)^2} = \left(\frac{x}{x+3}\right)^2$$

For $x = -\frac{1}{2}, 0, \frac{1}{2}, 1$, this gives $\frac{1}{25}, 0, \frac{1}{49}, \frac{1}{16}$, respectively.

*The Constant* $\ln 2$ can be derived from the general case as

$$\ln(1+1) = \begin{pmatrix} 1 & 4 \\ 1 & 6 \end{pmatrix} \prod_{n=1}^{\infty} \begin{pmatrix} 2n & 8n \\ 2n+1 & 10n+6 \end{pmatrix} (I_0)$$

with contractivity $\frac{1}{16}$ (in the limit). Another possibility is to exploit the fact $\ln 2 = -\ln(\frac{1}{2}) = -\ln(1-\frac{1}{2})$, which leads to a product with contractivity $\frac{1}{25}$ (in the limit):

$$\ln 2 = \begin{pmatrix} 1 & 4 \\ 2 & 6 \end{pmatrix} \prod_{n=1}^{\infty} \begin{pmatrix} -n & -4n \\ 2n+1 & 7n+3 \end{pmatrix} (I_0) \, .$$

# Part II: A Domain Framework for Computational Geometry

## 13 Introduction

In Part I we presented a framework for exact real number computation, where we developed a data type for real numbers and presented algorithms for computing elementary functions. We now turn our attention to computational geometry, where we are interested in computing geometric objects, such as lines, curves, planes, surfaces, convex hulls and Voronoi diagrams. In a broad sense, we can say that this represents an extension of exact arithmetic in that we now need to compute a subset of the Euclidean space rather than just a real number. In fact, the undecidability of comparison of real numbers in exact arithmetic has a close counterpart in computational geometry, namely the undecidability of the membership predicate for proper subsets of the Euclidean space. Thus, in computational geometry one has to deal with somewhat similar problems as in exact arithmetic. However, there are some other fundamental new issues which are not encountered in exact arithmetic, making computational geometry an independent subject of its own.

Computational geometry and solid modelling, as in Computer Aided Design (CAD), are fundamental in the design and manufacturing of all physical objects. However, these disciplines suffer from the lack of a proper and sound data-type. The current frameworks in these subjects are based, on the one hand, on discontinuous predicates and Boolean operations, and, on the other hand, on comparison of real numbers, which is undecidable. These essential foundations of the existing theory and implementations are both unjustified and unrealistic; they give rise to unreliable programs in practice.

Topology and geometry, as mainstream mathematical disciplines, have been developed to study continuous transformations on spaces. It is therefore an irony that the main building blocks in these subjects, namely the membership predicate of a set, the subset inclusion predicate, and the basic operations such as intersection are generally not continuous and therefore non-computable.

For example, in any Euclidean space $\mathbb{R}^n$ the membership predicate $\in_S$ of any subset $S \subseteq \mathbb{R}^n$ defined as

$$\begin{aligned} \in_S \colon \mathbb{R}^n &\to \{\mathsf{tt}, \mathsf{ff}\} \\ x &\mapsto \begin{cases} \mathsf{tt} \text{ if } x \in S \\ \mathsf{ff} \text{ if } x \notin S \end{cases} \end{aligned}$$

with the discrete topology on $\{\mathsf{tt}, \mathsf{ff}\}$ is continuous if and only if $S$ is both open and closed, i.e. if $S$ is either empty or the whole space. In fact, the membership predicate of any proper subset of $\mathbb{R}^n$ is discontinuous at the boundary of the subset.

Similarly, consider the intersection operator as a binary operator on the collection $\mathcal{C}(\mathbb{R}^n)$ of compact subsets of $\mathbb{R}^n$ equipped with the Hausdorff distance $d_H$ defined on closed subsets by

$$d_H(C,D) = \max(\sup_{d\in D} \inf_{c\in C} |c-d|, \sup_{c\in C} \inf_{d\in D} |c-d|),$$

with the convention that $d_H(\emptyset,\emptyset)=0$ and for $C\neq\emptyset$, $d_H(\emptyset,C)=\infty$:

$$\begin{array}{ll} -\cap - : \mathcal{C}(\mathbb{R}^n)\times\mathcal{C}(\mathbb{R}^n) & \to \mathcal{C}(\mathbb{R}^n) \\ \qquad (A,B) & \mapsto A\cap B \end{array}$$

Then, $-\cap-$ is discontinuous whenever $A$ and $B$ just touch each other.

The non-continuity of the basic predicates and operations creates a foundational problem in computation, which has so far been essentially neglected. In fact, in order to construct a sound computational model for solids and geometry, one needs a framework in which these elementary building blocks are continuous and computable.

In practice, correctness of algorithms in computational geometry is usually proved using the Real RAM machine model of computation, in which comparison of real numbers is considered to be decidable. Since this model is not realistic, correct algorithms, when implemented, turn into unreliable programs.

A simple example is provided by computing, in any floating point format, first the intersection point $x$ in the plane of two straight lines $L_1$ and $L_2$ meeting under a small angle, and then computing the minimum distance $d(x,L_1)$ and $d(x,L_2)$ from $x$ to each of the two lines. In general, $d(x,L_1)$ and $d(x,L_2)$ are both positive and distinct.

A more sophisticated example is given by the implementation in floating point of any algorithm to compute the convex hull of a finite number of points in the plane. If there are three nearly collinear points $A,B,C$ as in the picture, then depending upon the floating point format, the program can give, instead of the two edges $AB$ and $BC$, any of the following:

(i) $AB$ only.
(ii) $AC$ only.
(iii) $BC$ only.
(iv) none of them.

In any of the above four cases, we get a logical inconsistency as the edges returned by the program do not give the correct convex hull and in the cases (i), (iii) and (iv) do not give a closed polygon at all.

In CAGD modelling operators, the effect of rounding errors on consistency and robustness of actual implementations is an open question, which is handled in industrial software by various heuristics.

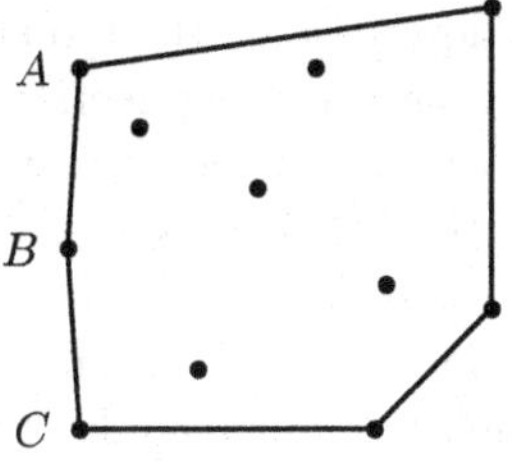


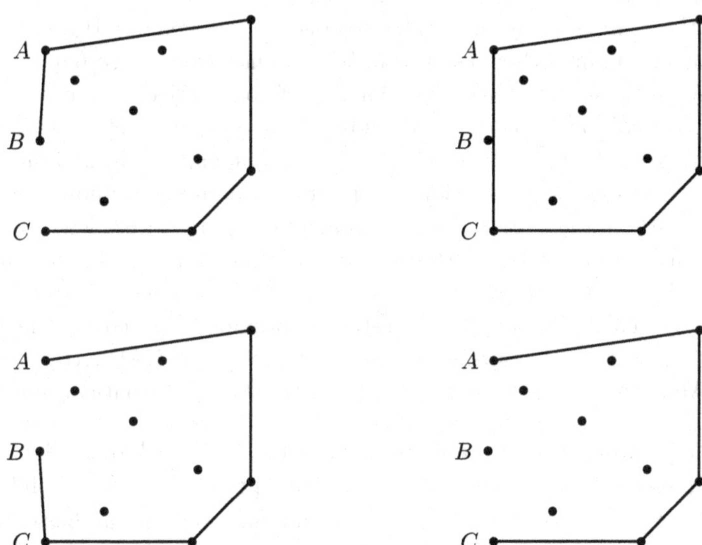


**Fig. 1.** The convex hull of a finite number of points (top picture) and four possible errors arising from floating point implementations.

The solid modelling framework provided by classical analysis, which allows discontinuous behaviour and comparison of exact real numbers, is not realistic as a model of our interaction with the physical world in terms of measurement and manufacturing. Nor is it realistic as a basis for the design of algorithms implemented on realistic machines, which can only deal with finite data. Industrial solid modelling software used for CAGD (Computer Aided Geometric Design), CAM (Computer Aided Manufacturing) or robotics is therefore infected by the disparity between the classical analysis paradigm and feasible computations. This disparity, as well as the representation of uncertainties in the geometry of the solid objects, is handled case by case, by various expensive and unsatisfactory "up to epsilon" ad-hoc heuristics. It is difficult, if at all possible, to improve and generalise these techniques, since their relatively poor success depends on the skill and experience of software engineers rather than on a well formalised methodology. In practice, the maintenance cost of some central geometric operators such as the Boolean operations or some specific variants of the Minkowski sum has always remained critical.

A robust algorithm is one whose correctness is proved with the assumption of a realistic machine model. Recursive analysis defines precisely what it means, in the context of the realistic Turing machine model of computation, to compute objects belonging to non-countable sets such as the set of real numbers.

Here, we use a domain-theoretic approach to recursive analysis to develop the foundation of an effective framework for solid modelling and computational geometry. It is based on the work of the second author with André Lieutier. In fact these notes form an abridged version of two papers [14, 15]; full details of proofs and many other results can be obtained from these papers.

We present the continuous domain of solid objects which gives a concrete model of computation on solids close to the actual practice of CAD engineers. In this model, the basic predicates, such as membership and subset inclusion, and operations, such as union and intersection, are continuous and computable. The set-theoretic aspects of solid modelling are revisited, leading to a theoretically motivated model. Within this model, some unavoidable limitations of solid modelling computations are shown and a sound framework to design specifications for feasible modelling operators is provided. Moreover, the model is able to capture the uncertainties of input data in actual CAD situations.

We need the following requirements for the mathematical model:

1. the notion of computability of solids has to be well defined,
2. the model has to reflect the observable properties of real solids,
3. it has to be closed under the Boolean operations and all basic predicates and operations have to be computable,
4. non-regular sets[1] have to be captured by the model as well as regular solids,
5. the model has to support a design methodology for actual robust algorithms.

A general methodology for the specification of feasible operators and the design of robust algorithms should rely on a sound mathematical model. This is why the domain-theoretic approach is a powerful framework both to model partial or uncertain data and to guide the design of robust software.

## 14 The Solid Domain

In this section, we introduce the solid domain, a mathematical model for representing rigid solids. The reader should refer to the Appendix for a basic introduction to the domain-theoretic notions required in the rest of this article. We focus

[1] An open set is regular if it is the interior of its closure.

here on the set-theoretic aspects of solid modelling. Our model is motivated by requirements 1 to 5 given above.

We first recall some basic notions in topology. For any subset A of a topological space $X$, the closure, $\overline{A}$, of $A$ is the intersection of all closed sets containing $A$, the interior, $A^\circ$, of $A$ is the union of all open sets contained in $A$ and the boundary, $\partial A$, of $A$ is the set of points $x \in X$ such that any neighbourhood of $x$ (i.e. any open set containing $x$) intersects both $A$ and its complement $A^c$. Recall that an open set is *regular* if it is the interior of its closure; dually, a closed set is regular if it is the closure of its interior. The complement of a regular open set then is a regular closed set and vice versa. A subset $C \subseteq X$ is *compact* if for every collection of open subsets $\langle O_i \rangle_{i\in I}$ with $C \subseteq \bigcup_{i\in I} O_i$ there exists a finite set $J \subseteq I$ with $C \subseteq \bigcup_{i\in J} O_i$. A subset of $\mathbb{R}^d$ is compact iff it is bounded and closed.

Given any proper subset $S \subseteq \mathbb{R}^n$, the classical membership predicate $\in_S$: $\mathbb{R}^n \to \{\mathsf{tt}, \mathsf{ff}\}$ is continuous except on $\partial S$. Recall that a predicate is semi-decidable if there is an algorithm to confirm in finite time that it is true whenever the predicate is actually true. For example, membership of a point in an open set in $\mathbb{R}^n$ is semi-decidable, since if the point is given in terms of a shrinking sequence of rational rectangles, then in finite time one such rational rectangle will be completely inside the open set. On the other hand, if $S$ is an open or closed set, then its boundary has empty interior and it is not semi-decidable that a point is on the boundary. For example if $n = 1$ and $S$ is the set of positive numbers, then a real number $x \in \mathbb{R}$ is on the boundary of $S$ iff $x = 0$ which is not decidable in computable analysis. It therefore makes sense from a computational viewpoint to redefine the membership predicate as the continuous function:

$$\begin{aligned} \in'_S \colon \mathbb{R}^n &\to \{\mathsf{tt}, \mathsf{ff}\}_\perp \\ x &\mapsto \begin{cases} \mathsf{tt} & \text{if } x \in S^\circ \\ \mathsf{ff} & \text{if } x \in S^{c\circ} \\ \perp & \text{otherwise.} \end{cases} \end{aligned}$$

Here, $\{\mathsf{tt}, \mathsf{ff}\}_\perp$ is the three element poset with least element $\perp$ and two incomparable elements tt and ff. In the Scott topology $\{\mathsf{tt}\}$ and $\{\mathsf{ff}\}$ are open sets but $\{\perp\}$ is not open. We call this the *continuous membership predicate.* Then, two subsets, or two solid objects, are equivalent if and only if they have the same continuous membership predicate, i.e. if they have the same interior and the same exterior (interior of complement). By analogy with general set theory for which a set is completely defined by its membership predicate, we can define a solid object in $\mathbb{R}^n$ to be any continuous map of type $\mathbb{R}^n \to \{\mathsf{tt}, \mathsf{ff}\}_\perp$. The definition of the solid domain is then consistent with requirement 1 since a computable membership predicate has to be continuous.

Note that a solid object, given by a continuous map $f : \mathbb{R}^n \to \{\mathsf{tt}, \mathsf{ff}\}_\perp$, is determined precisely by two disjoint open sets, namely $f^{-1}(\mathsf{tt})$ and $f^{-1}(\mathsf{ff})$. Moreover, the interior $(f^{-1}(\mathsf{tt}) \cup f^{-1}(\mathsf{ff}))^{c\circ}$ of the complement of the union of these two open sets can be non-empty. If we now consider a second continuous function $g : \mathbb{R}^n \to \{\mathsf{tt}, \mathsf{ff}\}_\perp$ with $f \sqsubseteq g$, then we have $f^{-1}(\mathsf{tt}) \subseteq g^{-1}(\mathsf{tt})$ and $f^{-1}(\mathsf{ff}) \subseteq g^{-1}(\mathsf{ff})$. This means that a more defined solid object has a larger interior and a larger exterior. We can think of the pair $f^{-1}(\mathsf{tt}), f^{-1}(\mathsf{ff})$ as the points of the interior and the exterior of a solid object as determined at some finite stage of computation. At a later stage, we obtain a more refined approximation $g$ which gives more information about the solid object, i.e. more points of its interior and more points of its exterior.

**Definition 14.1.** *The* solid domain $(\mathbf{S}\mathbb{R}^n, \sqsubseteq)$ *of* $\mathbb{R}^n$ *is the set of ordered pairs* $(A, B)$ *of disjoint open subsets of* $\mathbb{R}^n$ *endowed with the information order:* $(A_1, B_1) \sqsubseteq (A_2, B_2) \iff A_1 \subseteq A_2$ *and* $B_1 \subseteq B_2$.

An element $(A, B)$ of $\mathbf{S}\mathbb{R}^n$ is called a *partial solid.* The sets $A$ and $B$ are intended to capture, respectively, the interior and the exterior (interior of the complement) of a solid object, possibly, at some finite stage of computation. Note that $(\mathbf{S}\mathbb{R}^n, \sqsubseteq)$ is a directed complete partial order with $\bigsqcup_{i\in I}(A_i, B_i) = (\bigcup_{i\in I} A_i, \bigcup_{i\in I} B_i)$ and is isomorphic with the function space $\mathbb{R}^n \to \{\mathsf{tt}, \mathsf{ff}\}_\perp$. By duality of open and closed sets, $(\mathbf{S}\mathbb{R}^n, \sqsubseteq)$ is also isomorphic with the collection of ordered pairs $(A, B)$ of closed subsets of $\mathbb{R}^n$ with $A \cup B = \mathbb{R}^n$ with the information ordering: $(A_1, B_1) \sqsubseteq (A_2, B_2) \iff A_2 \subseteq A_1$ and $B_2 \subseteq B_1$.

**Proposition 14.2.** *The partial solid* $(A, B) \in (\mathbf{S}\mathbb{R}^n, \sqsubseteq)$ *is a maximal element iff* $A = B^{c\circ}$ *and* $B = A^{c\circ}$.

*Proof.* Let $(A, B)$ be maximal. Since $A$ and $B$ are disjoint open sets, it follows that $A \subseteq B^{c\circ}$. Hence, $(A, B) \sqsubseteq (B^{c\circ}, B)$ and thus $A = B^{c\circ}$. Similarly, $B = A^{c\circ}$. This proves the "only if" part. For the "if" part, suppose that $A = B^{c\circ}$ and $B = A^{c\circ}$. Then, any proper open superset of $A$ will have non-empty intersection with $B$ and any proper open superset of $B$ will have non-empty intersection with $A$. It follows that $(A, B)$ is maximal. □

**Corollary 14.3.** *If* $(A, B)$ *is a maximal element, then* $A$ *and* $B$ *are regular open sets. Conversely, for any regular open set* $A$*, the partial solid* $(A, A^{c\circ})$ *is maximal.*

*Proof.* For the first part, note that $A$ is the interior of the closed set $B^c$ and is, therefore, regular; similarly $B$ is regular. For the second part, observe that $A^{c\circ c\circ} = (\overline{A})^\circ = A$. □

We define $(A, B) \in \mathbf{S}\mathbb{R}^n$ to be a *classical* solid object if $\overline{A} \cup \overline{B} = \mathbb{R}^n$.

**Proposition 14.4.** *Any maximal element is a classical solid object.*

*Proof.* Suppose $(A, B)$ is maximal. Then $\mathbb{R}^n = A \cup \partial A \cup A^{c\circ} = \overline{A} \cup \overline{B}$, since $\overline{A} = A \cup \partial A$ and $A^{c\circ} \subseteq \overline{A^{c\circ}} = \overline{B}$. □

Classical solid objects form a larger family than the maximal elements, i.e. regular solids. For example, if $A = \{z \in \mathbb{R}^2 \mid |z| \leq 1\} \cup \{(x, 0) \in \mathbb{R}^2 \mid |x| \leq 2\}$, then $A$ is represented in our model by the classical (non-regular) object $(A^\circ, A^c)$.

**Theorem 14.5.** *The solid domain* $(\mathbf{S}\mathbb{R}^n, \sqsubseteq)$ *is a bounded complete* $\omega$*-continuous domain and* $(A_1, B_1) \ll (A_2, B_2)$ *iff* $\overline{A_1}$ *and* $\overline{B_1}$ *are compact subsets of* $A_2$ *and* $B_2$ *respectively.*

*Proof.* To characterise the way-below relation, first assume that $\overline{A_1}$ and $\overline{B_1}$ are compact subsets of $A_2$ and $B_2$ respectively. If $A_2 \subseteq \bigcup_{i \in I} U_i$ and $B_2 \subseteq \bigcup_{i \in I} V_i$, where the unions are assumed to be directed, then we get $\overline{A_1} \subseteq A_2 \subseteq \bigcup_{i \in I} U_i$ and $\overline{B_1} \subseteq B_2 \subseteq \bigcup_{i \in I} V_i$. By compactness of $\overline{A_1}$ and $\overline{B_1}$ it follows that there exists $i \in I$ with $\overline{B_1} \subseteq U_i$ and $\overline{B_2} \subseteq V_i$. Conversely, assume that $(A_1, B_1) \ll (A_2, B_2)$. There exist directed collections of open sets $(U_i)_{i \in I}$ and $(V_i)_{i \in I}$ with union $A_2$ and $B_2$ respectively such that $\overline{U_i}$ and $\overline{V_i}$ are compact subsets of $A_2$ and $B_2$ for each $i \in I$. By the definition of the way-below relation, there exists $i \in I$ with $A_1 \subseteq U_i$ and $B_1 \subseteq V_i$ from which it follows that $\overline{A_1}$ and $\overline{B_1}$ are compact subsets of $A_2$ and $B_2$ respectively. Every open subset of $\mathbb{R}^n$ can be obtained as the union of an increasing sequence of open rational polyhedra (i.e. polyhedra whose vertices have rational coordinates) way-below the open set. The collection of all pairs of disjoint open rational polyhedra thus provides a countable basis for $\mathbf{S}\mathbb{R}^n$. □

In practice, we are often interested in the subdomain $\mathbf{S}_b\mathbb{R}^n$ of *bounded* partial solids which is defined as $\mathbf{S}_b\mathbb{R}^n = \{(A, B) \in \mathbf{S}\mathbb{R}^n \mid B^c \text{ is bounded}\} \cup \{(\emptyset, \emptyset)\}$, ordered by inclusion. It is easy to see that $\mathbf{S}_b\mathbb{R}^n$ is a subdcpo of $\mathbf{S}\mathbb{R}^n$. Moreover, it is left as an exercise to show that:

**Proposition 14.6.** *The dcpo* $\mathbf{S}_b\mathbb{R}^n$ *is* $\omega$*-continuous with the way-below relation given by* $(A_1, B_1) \ll (A_2, B_2)$ *iff* $\overline{A_1} \subseteq A_2$ *and* $B_2^c \subseteq {B_1}^{c\circ}$.

We say $(A, B) \in \mathbf{S}[-a, a]^n$ is a *proper* element if $(A, B) \neq (\emptyset, [-a, a]^n)$ and $(A, B) \neq ([-a, a]^n, \emptyset)$. Consider the collection $\mathcal{R}([-a, a]^n)$ of non-empty regular closed subsets of $[-a, a]^n$ with the metric given by,

$$d(A, B) = \max(d_H(A, B), d_H(\overline{A^c}, \overline{B^c}),$$

where $d_H$ is the Hausdorff metric.

**Theorem 14.7.** *The collection of proper maximal elements of* $\mathbf{S}[-a, a]^n$ *is the continuous image of the space* $(\mathcal{R}([-a, a]^n), d)$ *of the non-empty regular closed subsets of* $[-a, a]^n$.

*Proof.* It is convenient to work with the representation of $\mathbf{S}[-a, a]^n$ by pairs $(A, B)$ of closed subsets of $[-a, a]^n$, with $A \cup B = [-a, a]^n$, ordered by reverse inclusion. Any pair of open sets $(U, V)$ of $[-a, a]^n$ provides a basic Scott open set $O_{(U,V)}$ of $\mathbf{S}[-a, a]^n$ given by $O_{(U,V)} = \{(A, B) \in \mathbf{S}[-a, a]^n \mid A \subset U \,\&\, B \subset V\}$. Now consider the map $\Gamma : \mathcal{R}([-a, a]^n) \to \mathbf{S}[-a, a]^n$ defined by $\Gamma(A) = (A, \overline{A^c})$. Clearly, $\Gamma$ is a function onto the set of proper maximal elements of $\mathbf{S}[-a, a]^n$. To show that it is continuous, suppose $(A, \overline{A^c}) \in O_{(U,V)}$, i.e. $A \subset U$ and $\overline{A^c} \subset V$. Let $k = \min(r(A, U^c), r(\overline{A^c}, V^c))$ where $r(Y, Z)$ is the minimum distance between compact sets $Y$ and $Z$. Then for $D \in \mathcal{R}([-a,a]^n)$ with $d(C,D) < k$, the inequalities $d_H(C,D) < k$ and $d_H(\overline{C^c}, \overline{D^c}) < k$ imply $D \subset U$ and $\overline{D^c} \subset V$. This shows that $\Gamma$ is continuous. □

We can define a metric on the non-empty closed subsets of $\mathbb{R}^n$ by putting: $d'_H(A,B) = \max(d_H(A,B), 1)$. We leave it as an exercise for the reader to show that the collection of proper maximal elements of $\mathbf{S}\mathbb{R}^n$ is the continuous image of the space $(\mathcal{R}(\mathbb{R}^n), d')$ of the non-empty regular closed subsets of $\mathbb{R}^n$ with the metric defined by

$$d'(A,B) = \max(d'_H(A,B), d'_H(\overline{A^c}, \overline{B^c})). \tag{48}$$

## 15 Predicates and Operations on Solids

Our definition is also consistent with requirement 2 in a closely related way. We consider the idealisation of a machine used to measure mechanical parts. Two parts corresponding to equivalent subsets cannot be distinguished by such a machine. Moreover, partial solids, and, more generally, domain-theoretically defined data types allow us to capture partial, or uncertain input data encountered in realistic CAD situations. In order to be able to compute the continuous membership predicate, we extend it to the interval domain $\mathbf{I}\mathbb{R}^n$ and define $- \in - : \mathbf{I}\mathbb{R}^n \times \mathbf{S}\mathbb{R}^n \to \{\mathrm{tt}, \mathrm{ff}\}_\perp$ with:

$$C \in (A,B) = \begin{cases} \mathrm{tt} & \text{if } C \subseteq A \\ \mathrm{ff} & \text{if } C \subseteq B \\ \perp & \text{otherwise} \end{cases}$$

(see Figure 2). Note that we use the infix notation for predicates and Boolean operations.

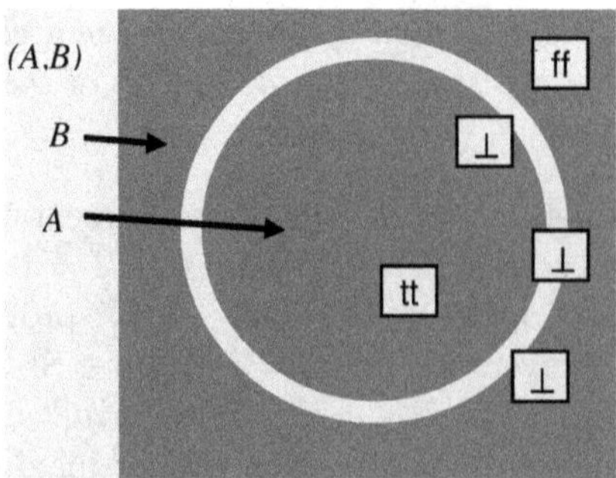


**Fig. 2.** The membership predicate of a partial solid object of the unit square.

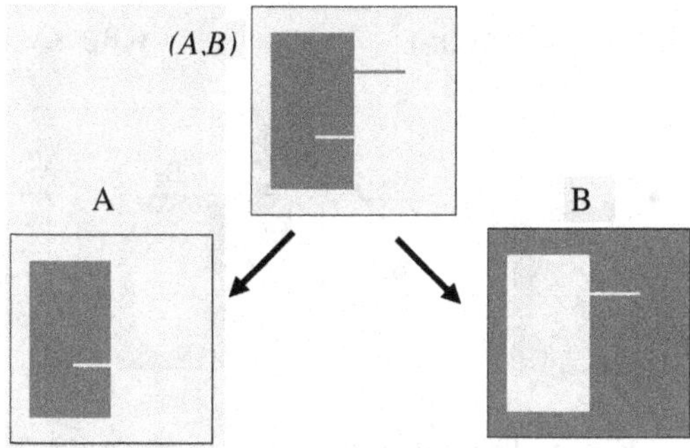


**Fig. 3.** Representation of a non-regular solid.

We define the predicate $- \subseteq - : \mathbf{S}_b\mathbb{R}^n \times \mathbf{S}\mathbb{R}^n \to \{\mathsf{tt}, \mathsf{ff}\}_\perp$, by

$$(A,B) \subseteq (C,D) = \begin{cases} \mathsf{tt} & \text{if } B \cup C = \mathbb{R}^n \\ \mathsf{ff} & \text{if } A \cap D \neq \emptyset \\ \perp & \text{otherwise} \end{cases}$$

The restriction to $\mathbf{S}_b\mathbb{R}^n$ will ensure that $- \subseteq -$ is continuous, as we will see in one of the exercises below. Starting with the continuous membership predicate, the natural definition for the complement would be to swap the values tt and ff. This means that the complement of $(A, B)$ is $(B, A)$, cf. requirement 3.

As for requirement 4, Figure 3 represents a subset $S$ of $[0, 1]^2$ that is not regular. Its regularization removes both the external and internal "dangling edge". Here and in subsequent figures, the two components A and B of the partial solid are, for clarity, depicted separately below each picture.

Bearing in mind that for a partial solid object $(A, B)$, the open sets $A$ and $B$ respectively capture the interior and the exterior of the solid, we can deduce the definition of Boolean operators on partial solids:

$$\begin{aligned}(A_1, B_1) \cup (A_2, B_2) &= (A_1 \cup A_2, B_1 \cap B_2) \\ (A_1, B_1) \cap (A_2, B_2) &= (A_1 \cap A_2, B_1 \cup B_2).\end{aligned}$$

One can likewise define the $m$-ary union and the $m$-ary intersection of partial solids. Note that, given two partial solids representing adjacent boxes, their union would not represent the set-theoretic union of the boxes, as illustrated in Figure 4.

**Theorem 15.1.** *The following maps are continuous:*

*(i) The predicate* $- \in - : \mathbf{I}\mathbb{R}^n \times \mathbf{S}\mathbb{R}^n \to \{\mathsf{tt}, \mathsf{ff}\}_\perp$.
*(ii) The binary union* $- \cup - : \mathbf{S}\mathbb{R}^n \times \mathbf{S}\mathbb{R}^n \to \mathbf{S}\mathbb{R}^n$ *and more generally the* $m$*-ary union* $\bigcup : (\mathbf{S}\mathbb{R}^n)^m \to \mathbf{S}\mathbb{R}^n$.
*(iii) The binary intersection* $- \cap - : \mathbf{S}\mathbb{R}^n \times \mathbf{S}\mathbb{R}^n \to \mathbf{S}\mathbb{R}^n$ *and more generally the* $m$*-ary intersection* $\bigcap : (\mathbf{S}\mathbb{R}^n)^m \to \mathbf{S}\mathbb{R}^n$.

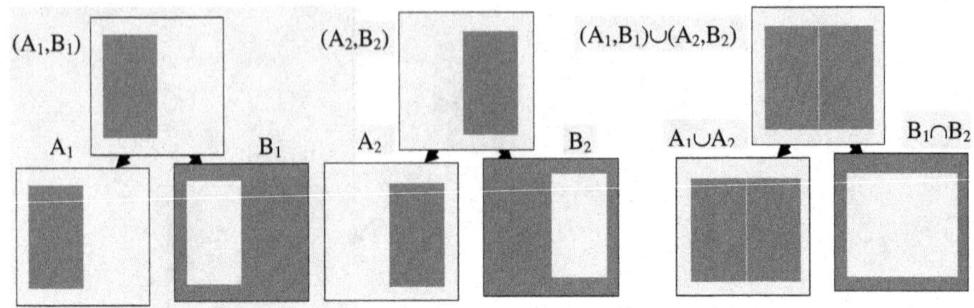


**Fig. 4.** The union operation on the solid domain.

*Proof.* (i) A function of two variables on domains is continuous iff it is continuous in each variable separately when the other variable is fixed. From this, we obtain the required continuity by observing that a non-empty compact set is contained in the union of an increasing sequence of open sets iff it is contained in one such open set.

(ii) This follows from the distributivity of ∪ over ∩.

(iii) Follows from (ii) by duality. □

### 15.1 The Minkowski Operator

We now introduce the Minkowski sum operation for partial solids of $\mathbb{R}^n$. Recall that the Minkowski sum of two subsets $S_1, S_2 \subseteq \mathbb{R}^n$ is defined as

$$S_1 \oplus S_2 = \{x + y \mid x \in S_1, y \in S_2\}$$

where $x + y$ is the vector addition in $\mathbb{R}^n$. For convenience we will use the same notation $\oplus$ for the Minkowski sum on the solid domain, which is defined as a function $- \oplus - : (\mathbf{S}_b\mathbb{R}^n) \times (\mathbf{S}\mathbb{R}^n) \to \mathbf{S}\mathbb{R}^n$ by:

$$(A_1, B_1) \oplus (A_2, B_2) = ((A_1 \oplus A_2), (B_1^c \oplus B_2^c)^c).$$

It can be shown that $- \oplus - : (\mathbf{S}_b\mathbb{R}^d) \times (\mathbf{S}\mathbb{R}^d) \to \mathbf{S}\mathbb{R}^d$ is well-defined and continuous.

## 16 Computability on the Solid Domain

We can provide an effective structure for $\mathbf{S}\mathbb{R}^n$ as follows. Consider the collection of all pairs of disjoint open rational polyhedra of the form $K = (L_1, L_2)$. Take an effective enumeration $(K_i)_{i\in\omega}$ with $K_i = (\pi_1(K_i), \pi_2(K_i))$ of this collection.

We say $(A, B)$ is a *computable* partial solid if there exists a total recursive function $\beta : \mathbb{N} \to \mathbb{N}$ such that $(A, B) = (\bigcup_{n\in\omega} \pi_1(K_{\beta(n)}), \bigcup_{n\in\omega} \pi_2(K_{\beta(n)}))$.

One can similarly define an effective structure on $\mathbf{I}\mathbb{R}^n$, by taking an effective enumeration of rational intervals.

It follows from the general domain-theoretic definition (see the Appendix) that a function $F : (\mathbf{S}\mathbb{R}^n)^2 \to \mathbf{S}\mathbb{R}^n$ is *computable* if the relation $\{(i, j, k) \mid K_k \ll F(K_i, K_j)\}$ is r.e.. The definition extends in the natural way to functions of other types. A sequence $((A_n, B_n))_{n\in\omega}$ of partial solids is *computable* if there exists a total recursive function $\alpha : \mathbb{N} \times \mathbb{N} \to \mathbb{N}$ such that $(A_n, B_n) = \bigsqcup_{i\in\omega} K_{\alpha(n,i)}$, with $(K_{\alpha(n,i)})_{i\in\omega}$ an increasing chain for each $n \in \omega$. For domains in general, it can be shown that a function is computable iff it sends computable sequences to computable sequences.

**Proposition 16.1.** *The following functions are computable with respect to the effective structures on* $\mathbf{I}\mathbb{R}^n$, $\mathbf{S}\mathbb{R}^n$ *and* $\mathbf{S}[-a, a]^n$.

*(i)* $- \in - : \mathbf{I}\mathbb{R}^n \times \mathbf{S}\mathbb{R}^n \to \{\mathrm{tt}, \mathrm{ff}\}_\perp$.
*(ii)* $- \cup - : \mathbf{S}\mathbb{R}^n \times \mathbf{S}\mathbb{R}^n \to \mathbf{S}\mathbb{R}^n$.
*(iii)* $- \cap - : \mathbf{S}\mathbb{R}^n \times \mathbf{S}\mathbb{R}^n \to \mathbf{S}\mathbb{R}^n$.
*(iv)* $- \subseteq - : \mathbf{S}[-a, a]^n \times \mathbf{S}[-a, a]^n \to \{\mathrm{tt}, \mathrm{ff}\}_\perp$.

*Proof.* We show (ii) and leave the rest as exercise. We have to show that the relation $K_k \ll K_i \cup K_j$ is r.e. Writing this relation in detail, it reduces to

$$(\pi_1(K_k), \pi_2(K_k)) \ll (\pi_1(K_i) \cup \pi_1(K_j), \pi_2(K_i) \cap \pi_2(K_j)),$$

i.e. $\overline{\pi_1(K_k)} \subseteq \pi_1(K_i) \cup \pi_1(K_j)$ and $\overline{\pi_2(K_k)} \subseteq \pi_2(K_i) \cap \pi_2(K_j)$, which are both decidable. □

## 17 Lebesgue and Hausdorff Computability

Our domain-theoretic notion of computability so far has the essential weakness of lacking a quantitative measure for the rate of convergence of basis elements to a computable element. This shortcoming can be redressed by enriching the domain-theoretic notion of computability with an additional requirement which allows a quantitative degree of approximation. We will see in this section that this can be done in at least two different ways. The reader should refer to the appendix for various notions of computability in this section.

### 17.1 Lebesgue Computability

The Lebesgue measure $\mu$ in $\mathbb{R}^n$, which measures the volume of subsets of $\mathbb{R}^n$, gives us a notion of approximation which is stable under Boolean operations. For simplicity, we confine ourselves to the solid domain of a large cube in $\mathbb{R}^n$. We say that $(A, B) \in \mathbf{S}[-a, a]^n$ is *Lebesgue computable* if there exists a total recursive function $\beta : \mathbb{N} \to \mathbb{N}$ such that $(A, B) = (\bigcup_{n\in\omega} \pi_1(K_{\beta(n)}), \bigcup_{n\in\omega} \pi_2(K_{\beta(n)}))$ with $\mu(A) - \mu(\pi_1(K_{\beta(n)})) < 2^{-n}$ and $\mu(B) - \mu(\pi_2(K_{\beta(n)})) < 2^{-n}$. The definition extends naturally to computable elements of $(\mathbf{S}X)^m$ for any positive integer $m$.

**Proposition 17.1.** *If $a$ is a computable real number and $(A, B) \in \mathbf{S}[-a, a]^n$ is a computable maximal element with $\mu(\partial A) = 0$, then $(A, B)$ is Lebesgue computable.*

The sequence $((A_n, B_n))_{n\in\omega}$ is said to be Lebesgue computable if it is computable and if $(\mu(A_n))_{n\in\omega}$ and $(\mu(B_n))_{n\in\omega}$ are computable sequences of real numbers. As for computable elements, the definition extends naturally to computable sequences of $(\mathbf{S}X)^m$ for any positive integer $m$.

A computable function $f : (\mathbf{S}X)^m \to \mathbf{S}X$ is said to be *Lebesgue computable* if it takes any Lebesgue computable sequence of $m$-tuples of partial solids to a Lebesgue computable sequence of partial solids. The main result here is the following.

**Theorem 17.2.** *Boolean operations are Lebesgue computable.*

### 17.2 Hausdorff Computability

Another appropriate form for the quantitative degree of approximation of solids is provided by the Hausdorff distance. We say $(A, B) \in \mathbf{S}[-a, a]^n$ is *Hausdorff computable* if there exists a total recursive function $\beta : \mathbb{N} \to \mathbb{N}$ such that $(A, B) = (\bigcup_{n\in\omega} \pi_1(K_{\beta(n)}), \bigcup_{n\in\omega} \pi_2(K_{\beta(n)}))$ with $d_H(\pi_1(K_{\beta(n)}), A) < 2^{-n}$ and $d_H(\pi_2(K_{\beta(n)}), B) < 2^{-n}$.

We can define the notion of a Hausdorff computable map similar to the way we defined a Lebesgue computable map. The Hausdorff distance provides a good way of approximating solids; in fact, objects with small Hausdorff distance with each other are visually close. However, it can be shown by a non-trivial example that the binary Boolean operations do not preserve Hausdorff computability. The main positive result is the following.

**Theorem 17.3.** *A computable maximal element of $\mathbf{S}[-a, a]^n$ is Hausdorff computable.*

## 18 The Convex Hull

We have already seen that points of $\mathbb{R}^n$ can be modelled using the domain $\mathbf{I}\mathbb{R}^n$ of the compact rectangles in $\mathbb{R}^n$ ordered by reverse inclusion. Using the domain-theoretic model, one can construct other basic notions in geometry, such as line segments, lines and hyperplanes. We demonstrate this by describing the simplest non-trivial geometric object, namely a line segment.

We define the *partial line segment map* $f : (\mathbf{I}\mathbb{R}^n)^2 \to \mathbf{S}\mathbb{R}^n$ with $f(x_1, x_2)$, called the *partial line segment* through the partial points $x_1$ and $x_2$, given by $f(x_1, x_2) = (\emptyset, E)$ where the exterior $E$ is the empty set if $x_1 \cap x_2 \neq \emptyset$ and is otherwise the complement of the convex hull of the $2 \times 2^n$ vertices of $x_1$ and $x_2$; see Figure 5. It is easy to check that $f$ is Scott continuous and computable. Likewise, one can define Scott continuous maps for partial lines through two partial points, and other basic geometric objects.

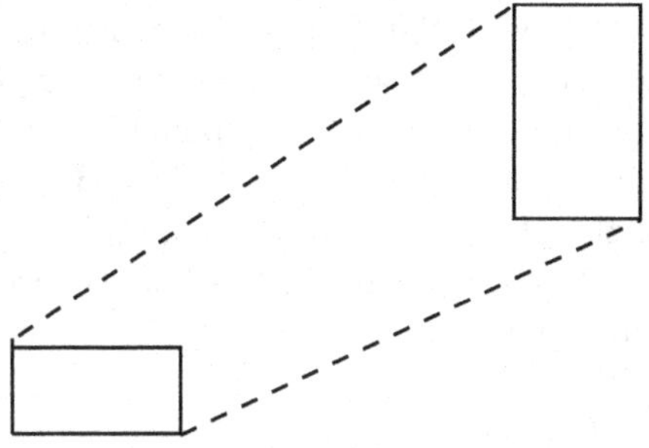

**Fig. 5.** A partial line segment.

We will now describe an algorithm to compute the convex hull of a finite number of points in the plane in the context of the solid domain. Assume we have $m$ points in the plane. Each of these points is approximated by a shrinking nested sequence of rational rectangles; at each finite stage of computation we have approximations to the $m$ points by $m$ rational rectangles, considered as imprecise points, as in Figure 6.

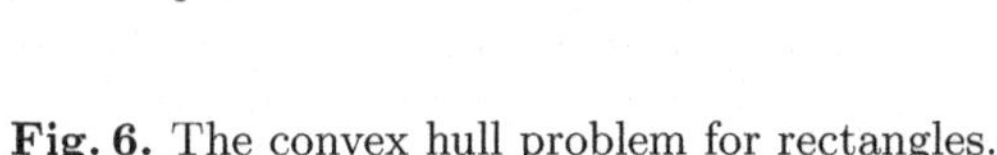

**Fig. 6.** The convex hull problem for rectangles.

For these $m$ rational rectangles we obtain a partial solid object with an interior open rational polygon, which is contained in the interior of the convex hull of the $m$ points, and an exterior open rational polygon, which is contained in the exterior of the convex hull of the $m$ points. The union of the interior (respectively, the exterior) open rational polygons obtained for all finite stages of computation gives the interior (respectively, the exterior) of the convex hull of the $m$ points.

More formally, we define a map $C_m : (\mathbf{I}\mathbb{R}^2)^m \to \mathbf{S}\mathbb{R}^2$, where $\mathbf{I}\mathbb{R}^2$ is the domain of the planar rectangles, the collection of all rectangles of the plane partially ordered by reverse inclusion. Let $\mathcal{C}(\mathbb{R}^2)$ be the collection of non-empty compact subsets of $\mathbb{R}^2$ with the Hausdorff metric and let $H_m : (\mathbb{R}^2)^m \to \mathcal{C}(\mathbb{R}^2)$ be the classical function which sends any $m$-tuple of planar points to its convex hull regarded as a compact subset of the plane.

We first define $C_m$ on the basis $(\mathbf{I}\mathbb{Q}^2)^m$ of $(\mathbf{I}\mathbb{R}^2)^m$ consisting of $m$-tuples of rational rectangles. Let $x = (R_1, R_2, \cdots, R_m) \in (\mathbf{I}\mathbb{Q}^2)^m$ be an $m$-tuple of rational rectangles. Each rectangle $R_i$ has four vertices denoted, anti-clockwise starting with the bottom left corner, by $R_i^1$, $R_i^2$, $R_i^3$ and $R_i^4$. We define $C_m(x) = (I_m(x), E_m(x))$ with

$$E_m(x) = (H_{4m}((R_i^1, R_i^2, R_i^3, R_i^4))_{i=1}^m)^c, \qquad I_m(x) = (\bigcap_{1 \le j \le 4} H_m(R_i^j)_{i=1}^m)^\circ.$$

In words, $E_m(x)$ is the complement of the convex hull of the $4m$ vertices of all rectangles (Figure 7), whereas $I_m(x)$ is the interior of the intersection of the 4 convex hulls of the bottom left, bottom right, top right and top left vertices (Figure 8). Since the intersection of convex sets is convex, $I_m(x)$ as well as $E_m(x)$ are both convex open rational polygons.

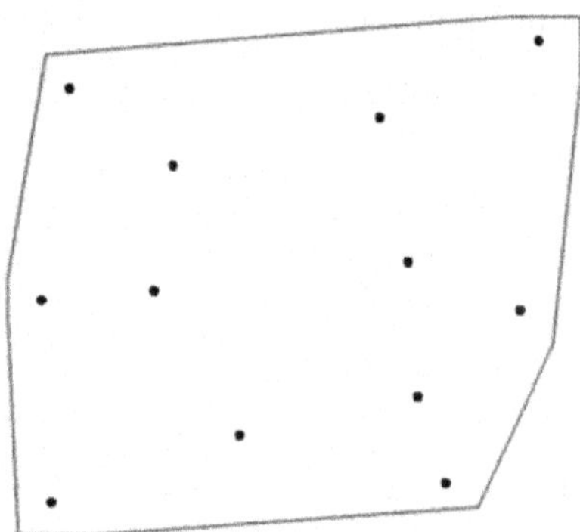

**Fig. 7.** The exterior convex hull of rectangles.

With more accurate input data about the planar points, the boundaries of the inner and outer convex hulls get closer to each other as in Figure 9. In the limit, the inner and outer convex hulls will be simply the interior and the exterior of the convex hull of the planar points (Figure 10).

Since we work completely with rational arithmetic, we will not encounter any round-off errors and, as comparison of rational numbers is decidable, we will not get inconsistencies.

Clearly the complexity of these algorithms to compute $I_m(x)$ and $E_m(x)$ is $O(m \log m)$ each. We have therefore obtained a robust algorithm for the convex hull which has the same complexity as the non-robust classical algorithm. Moreover, the algorithm extends in the obvious way to $\mathbb{R}^d$. In 3d, we still have the complexity $O(m \log m)$; see [15] for the complexity in higher dimension.

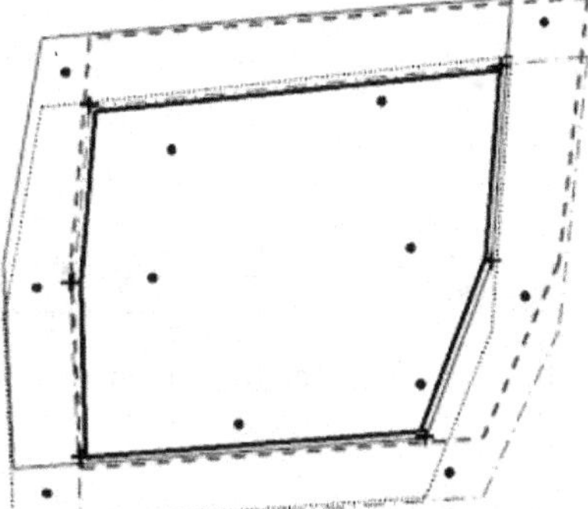


**Fig. 8.** The interior convex hull of rectangles.

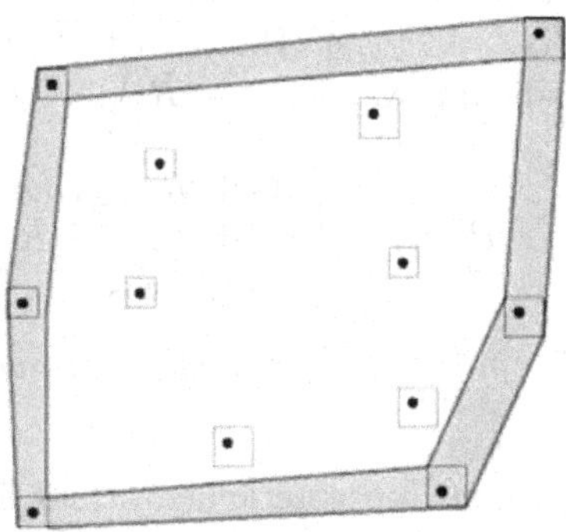

**Fig. 9.** Convergence of the interior and exterior convex hulls.

We now define $\hat{C}_m : (\mathbf{I}\mathbb{R}^2)^m \to \mathbf{S}\mathbb{R}^2$ on tuples of rectangles $y \in (\mathbf{I}\mathbb{R}^2)^m$ by putting $\hat{C}_m(y) = \bigsqcup\{C(x) \mid x \in (\mathbf{I}\mathbb{Q})^m \text{ with } x \ll y\}$. It can be checked that $\hat{C}_m(x) = C_m(x)$ for $x \in (\mathbf{I}\mathbb{Q}^2)^m$, and that, therefore, we can simply write $\hat{C}_m$ as $C_m$ which will be a continuous function between domains.

The map $C_m$ computes the convex hull of $m$ planar points as follows. Note that a maximal element $x = (R_i)_{i=1}^m$ of $(\mathbf{I}\mathbb{R}^2)^m$ consists of an $m$-tuple of degenerate rectangles, i.e., an $m$-tuple of planar points $(r_i)_{i=1}^m$, where $R_i^j = r_i$, for $j = 1, 2, 3, 4$. It can be shown that, for such maximal $x$, we have $C_m(x) = (I_m(x), E_m(x))$ where $I_m(x) = (H_m((r_i)_{i=1}^m))^\circ$ and $E_m(x) = (H_m((r_i)_{i=1}^m))^c$.

**Theorem 18.1.** *The map $C_m$ is Lebesgue computable and Hausdorff computable.*

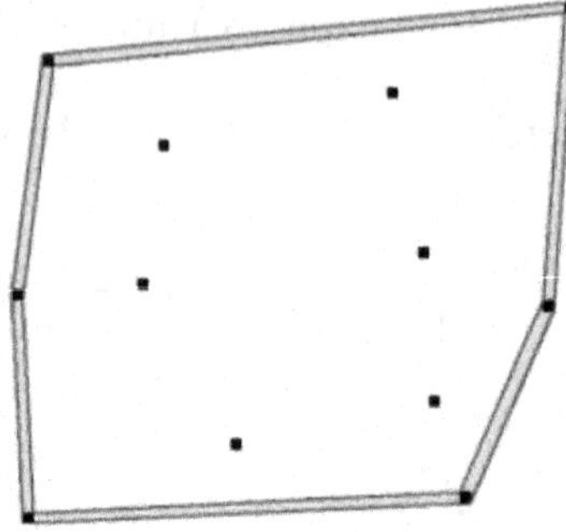

**Fig. 10.** Limit of interior and exterior convex hulls.

We can also study the domain-theoretic version of the following classical question: Given $N$ points $x_1, \ldots, x_N$ in $\mathbb{R}^2$, does $x_k$, for $1 \leq k \leq N$, lie on the boundary of the convex hull of these $N$ points? With imprecise input, i.e. for $N$ input rectangles, the answer is either "surely yes", or "surely not" or "cannot say". More precisely, we define the *boundary rectangle* predicate $P_k : (\mathbf{I}\mathbb{R}^2)^N \to \{\mathsf{tt}, \mathsf{ff}\}_\bot$. For $\overline{R} = (R_1, \ldots, R_N) \in (\mathbf{I}\mathbb{R}^2)^N$, let $\overline{R}(k) \in (\mathbf{I}\mathbb{R}^2)^{N-1}$ be the ordered list of the $N-1$ dyadic interval vertices: $\overline{R}(k) = (R_1, \ldots, R_{k-1}, R_{k+1}, \ldots, R_N)$. We have:

$$P_k(\overline{R}) = \begin{cases} \mathsf{tt} \text{ if } R_k \subseteq E(\overline{R}(k)), \\ \mathsf{ff} \text{ if } R_k \subseteq I(\overline{R}), \\ \bot \text{ otherwise.} \end{cases} \tag{49}$$

**Theorem 18.2.** *The predicate $P_k$ is Scott continuous and computable for each $k = 1, \ldots, N$.*

Finally, we note that domain-theoretic algorithms for Voronoi diagram and Delaunay triangulation have also been developed; see [38].

## 19 Historical Remarks and Pointers to Literature

### 19.1 Real Number Computation

In the late 1980's, two frameworks for exact real number computation were proposed. In the approach of Boehm and Cartwright [5, 6], a computable real number is approximated by rational numbers of the form $K/r^n$ where $r$ is the base and $K$ is a (usually big) integer. This approach was further developed and implemented by Valérie Ménissier-Morain [40]. For any basic function in analysis a feasible algorithm has been presented in order to produce an approximation to the value of the function at a given computable real number up to any threshold of accuracy. However, the computation is not incremental in the sense that to obtain a more accurate approximation one has to compute from scratch. Furthermore, the algorithms are constructed using various ad-hoc techniques and therefore, except for the simplest arithmetic operations, it is rather difficult to verify their correctness. Actually, this method is not so different from the multi-digit approach presented here, except that our transcendental operations are based on LFT's, which provide a general underlying framework that simplifies the finding of the algorithms and makes the proofs of their correctness automatic.

Vuillemin [57] proposed a representation of computable real numbers by continued fractions and presented various incremental algorithms for basic arithmetic operations using the earlier work of Gosper [24], and for some transcendental functions. However, this representation is rather complicated and the resulting algorithms are relatively inefficient.

Plume [42] studied and implemented Exact Real Arithmetic based on the number representation of Section 2 (exponent plus a stream of signed binary digits). His division algorithm employs an auxiliary representation with dyadic rationals as digits. Transcendental functions are based on an auxiliary function computing the real number defined by a (computable) nested sequence of real intervals whose lengths tend to 0.

In the early and mid 90's Di Gianantonio [12,13] and Escardó [20] studied extensions of the theoretical language PCF with a real number data type based on domain theory. At Imperial College, a new approach was then developed which is almost entirely based on LFT's and combines domain theory and the digit approach with continued fraction algorithms [45,16,46,43,44]. Within this approach, Peter Potts derived algorithms for transcendental functions from continued fraction expansions. He also developed the single-digit approach with the absorption and emission of digit matrices, and made first steps towards a multi-digit approach. The approach was implemented in functional languages such as Miranda, Haskell and CAML, and in imperative languages such as C. The LFT framework for real number computation has also been studied in the context of extensions of PCF with a real number data type by Edalat, Escardó, Potts and Sünderhauf [47,17].

In contrast to the notes at hand, Potts and Edalat used the base interval $[0,\infty]$, and accordingly, digit matrices which were different from the ones presented here. This approach includes $\infty$ with the same rights as any finite real number. The number $\infty$ represents both $+\infty$ and $-\infty$. Its presence makes the reciprocal function total by $\frac{1}{0} = \infty$ and $\frac{1}{\infty} = 0$. Yet on the other hand, addition and multiplication, which are total if $\infty$ is excluded, become partial with $\infty$ since $\infty + \infty$ and $0 \cdot \infty$ are not defined.

In this approach, exponent matrices cannot be used. Instead, each number representation begins with a *sign matrix.* There are four sign matrices, for numbers in the intervals $[0,\infty]$, $[-1,1]$, $[\infty,0]$, and $[1,-1] = \{x \mid |x| \geq 1\}$. Edalat and Potts name two advantages of $[0,\infty]$: First, the image $M[0,\infty]$ of $[0,\infty]$ under a non-singular LFT $M = \left(\begin{smallmatrix} a & c \\ b & d \end{smallmatrix}\right)$ can be easily obtained from the entries of $M$: $M[0,\infty] = [\frac{c}{d}, \frac{a}{b}]$ if $\det M > 0$, and $[\frac{a}{b}, \frac{c}{d}]$ if $\det M < 0$. In contrast, the calculation of $M[-1,1]$ requires some additions. Second, a matrix or tensor is refining for $[0,\infty]$ iff all its entries are non-negative and all its column sums are positive (if the matrix or tensor is weakly normalised so that the sum of its entries is non-negative). This condition is much simpler than the conditions we have derived for refinement w.r.t. $[-1, 1]$ in Section 5. The emission conditions for the two base intervals are similar, but the actual emissions and absorptions are simpler in $[-1, 1]$. A huge practical advantage of $[-1, 1]$ are the persistent zeros which can be found in basically all the tensors for the standard operations. With $[0, \infty]$, there are no persistent zeros at all, and no entries which are invariant under absorption and emission.

On the theoretical side as well, the base interval $[-1, 1]$ has clear advantages. It avoids the troublesome value $\infty$ that poses difficulties in algebraic transformations and size estimations. Furthermore, one may work with the standard metric $(\ell([u, v]) = v - u)$ and standard derivatives in $[-1, 1]$, while working with $[0, \infty]$ excludes the standard metric. In fact, [16, 43, 28] use a metric on $[0, \infty]$ that is derived from the standard metric on $[-1, 1]$. Here, working in $[-1, 1]$ directly drastically simplifies the reasoning.

Results on the growth of the entries of matrices and tensors were presented in [26, 27]—for the base interval $[0, \infty]$. With this base interval, matrices $\left(\begin{smallmatrix} a & c \\ b & d \end{smallmatrix}\right)$ cannot be classified according to $b = 0$ and $b \neq 0$ as in Section 8; the crucial value is instead $(c + d) - (a + b)$. Given this, it is not surprising that a complete classification of tensors w.r.t. the opportunities for cancellations was never found under the reign of $[0, \infty]$. The classification presented in Section 8.5 of these notes was recently found by Reinhold Heckmann and never published before.

The contractivity was already studied by Potts, and considered in greater detail by Heckmann in [28] (for $[0, \infty]$). In [30], Heckmann switched over to $[-1, 1]$ and studied contractivity there.

Peter Potts was a master in the derivation of infinite products from continued fractions (for $[0, \infty]$). The few derivations presented here are new because of the new base interval. They start from the same continued fractions, but are generally shorter. The derivation of products from Taylor series is taken from [29].

### 19.2 Computational Geometry

The quest for reliable geometric algorithms in recent years has been a most challenging problem. In the words of C. M. Hoffmann, a leading expert in computational geometry: "Despite the pressing need, devising accurate and robust geometric algorithms has proved elusive for many important science and engineering applications" [31].

In the existing frameworks and implementations of geometric algorithms, great efforts are required to use various, often ad hoc, techniques in order to avoid potential inconsistencies and degeneracies. These methods include: (i) the so-called exact arithmetic approach [41, 37, 51, 23, 52, 3, 61, 9, 8, 22, 11], combined with lazy implementation [4, 53] and symbolic perturbation [19, 51, 60] in which numerical computations are performed to a high degree of accuracy in order to ensure the correct logical and topological decisions; (ii) the logical and topological oriented technique [52, 55, 56], which seeks to place the highest priority on the consistency of the logical and topological properties of geometric algorithms, using numerical results only when they are consistent with these properties; and, (iii) the intermediate methods, such as $\epsilon$-geometry [25], the interval arithmetic technique [49, 32–34] and the tolerance approach [50, 21, 36], which determine an upper bound for the numerical error whenever a computation takes place in order to decide if a computation is reliable or not. While there are pros and cons for each of these methods in any given category of algorithms [54]; no single method gives an overall satisfactory solution for geometric modelling as a whole.

The traditional frameworks for geometric modelling are not founded on computable analysis: there is no reference to a notion of data type or computability in the standard literature of computational geometry or geometric modelling. Indeed, these frameworks are all based on classical topology and geometry in which the basic predicates and Boolean operations are not continuous, and hence not computable, the source of non-robustness of the resulting algorithms.

Brattka and Weihrauch [7] have studied the question of computability of classical subsets of the Euclidean space in the type two theory of computability [59] but it is not at all clear how their framework can be used in any practical geometric computation.

The domain-theoretic framework for solid modelling and computational geometry was first formulated in [14] and algorithms for the convex hull and for Voronoi diagram/Delaunay triangulation in the domain-theoretic setting were presented in [15] and [38] respectively. Continuous geometric operations have also been discussed in [35].

# 20 Exercises

## 20.1 Real Arithmetic

*Exercise 20.1.* Implement addition $x+y$ directly on the number representations by exponents and signed binary digit streams (cf. Section 2.4). Deal first with exponents and use the mean value operation $x \oplus y = \frac{x+y}{2}$ on mantissas.

*Exercise 20.2.* Prove Prop. 3.1 (using Equation (1)).

*Exercise 20.3.* Let $M_0 = \left(\begin{smallmatrix} 0 & 1 \\ 1 & 3 \end{smallmatrix}\right)$.

a) What is the function represented by $M_0$?
b) Compute $\det M_0$ (Equation (2)) and deduce the monotonicity type of $M_0$ (Section 4).
c) Check that $M_0$ is bounded (Prop. 5.2) and refining (Section 5.3) on $I_0$.
d) Assuming that the digit stream $\xi$ starts with **101**, determine the first *four* digits of $M_0(\xi)$ as in Section 6.5.
e) Compute $\exp M_0$ and $\operatorname{con} M_0$ (23) and derive the numbers $c^<$ and $c^>$ of Theorem 7.1.

f) Redo part (d) in the multi-digit approach, i.e., answer the request 4? $M_0(\xi)$. Run Algorithm 3, but consider the monotonicity type of $M_0$. Use the fact that $\xi$ begins with **101** to find the answer of the required request to $\xi$.
g) Compare the results of parts (d) and (f), but remember that there are often two possible answers to a request, differing by 1.

*Exercise 20.4.* Let $T = \left(\begin{smallmatrix} 0 & 1 & 0 & 1 \\ 0 & 0 & 1 & 3 \end{smallmatrix}\right)$.

a) What is the function represented by $T$?
b) Compute $\det(T|_x)$ and $\det(T|^y)$ (Equations (6)) and deduce the monotonicity type of $T$ for arguments $x, y \in I_0$ (Section 4).
c) Check that $T$ is bounded (14) and refining on $I_0$. For the latter, you may use (15) or Cor. 4.2, taking the monotonicity type into account.
d) Determine $\mathrm{con}_\mathrm{L}\, T$ and $\mathrm{con}_\mathrm{R}\, T$ and derive the numbers $c_\mathrm{L}^{>}$ and $c_\mathrm{R}^{>}$ of Theorem 7.2.

*Exercise 20.5.* Let $T = \left(\begin{smallmatrix} 0 & 1 & 1 & 0 \\ 0 & 0 & 1 & 1 \end{smallmatrix}\right)$. Given $x \geq 0$, solve the equation $y = T(x, y)$ for $y \geq 0$. (Thus you see how an important function can be implemented. The equation $y = T(x, y)$ can be considered as an infinite product $y = T(x, T(x, \ldots))$, or more efficiently, as a feed-back loop where everything emitted from $T$ is fed back into $T$ via its right argument.)

*Exercise 20.6.* (Taylor series)
Use the method presented in Section 11.4 to derive an infinite product for the cosine function from the Taylor series $\cos x = \sum_{n=0}^{\infty} \frac{(-1)^n}{(2n)!}(x^2)^n$. (By writing this in terms of $x^2$ instead of $x$, zero coefficients are avoided.) Determine for which $x$ this product is valid, and calculate the contractivities of its matrices.

## 20.2 Computational Geometry and Solid Modelling

*Exercise 20.7.* Show that the map $- \sqsubseteq - : \mathbf{S}_b\mathbb{R}^n \times \mathbf{S}\mathbb{R}^n \to \{\mathrm{tt}, \mathrm{ff}\}_\perp$ is continuous.

*Exercise 20.8.* Prove Proposition 14.6.

*Hint:* Use the following fact for Euclidean spaces. For an open set $O$ and a decreasing sequence of compact subsets $\langle C_i \rangle_{i\omega}$, the relation $\bigcap_{i \in \omega} C_i \subseteq O$ implies the existence of $i \in \omega$ with $C_i \subseteq O$.

*Exercise 20.9.* Show that the collection of proper maximal elements of $\mathbf{S}\mathbb{R}^n$ is the continuous image of the space $(\mathcal{R}(\mathbb{R}^n), d')$ of the non-empty regular closed subsets of $\mathbb{R}^n$ with the metric defined by Equation 48.

*Hint:* Follow the steps of proof in Theorem 14.7 and note that in the representation of $\mathbf{S}\mathbb{R}^n$ by closed sets ordered by reverse inclusion we have: $(A_1, B_1) \ll (A_2, B_2)$ iff $A_2$ and $B_2$ are compact subsets of $A_1^\circ$ and $B_1^\circ$ respectively.

*Exercise 20.10.* Draw the inner and outer convex hulls of the following three rectangles.

$$\begin{aligned}
R_1 &= \{(-2,0),(-1,0),(-1,-1),(-2,-1)\}\\
R_2 &= \{(-1,3),(0,3),(0,2),(-1,2)\}\\
R_3 &= \{(1,1),(2,1),(2,0),(1,0)\}.
\end{aligned}$$

*Exercise 20.11.* In the domain-theoretic convex hull algorithm, compute the boundary rectangle predicate $P_k$ for $1 \le k \le 11$.

$$\begin{aligned}
R_1 &= \{(-7/2,-3),(-7/2,-2),(-5/2,-2),(-5/2,-3)\}\\
R_2 &= \{(-7/2,-1),(-7/2,-1/2),(-3,-1/2),(-3,-1)\}\\
R_3 &= \{(-4,4/3),(-4,5/3),(-3,5/3),(-3,4/3)\}\\
R_4 &= \{(-2,-4),(-2,-7/2),(-3/2,-7/2),(-3/2,-4)\}\\
R_5 &= \{(-2,3),(-2,7/2),(-3/2,7/2),(-3/2,3)\}\\
R_6 &= \{(0,-4),(0,-7/2),(1/2,-7/2),(1/2,-4)\}\\
R_7 &= \{(0,0),(0,1),(1,1),(1,0)\}\\
R_8 &= \{(0,4),(0,5),(1,5),(1,4)\}\\
R_9 &= \{(4,-3),(4,-2),(5,-2),(5,-3)\}\\
R_{10} &= \{(5,-1),(5,-1/2),(27/5,-1/2),(27/5,-1)\}\\
R_{11} &= \{(5,2),(5,3),(6,3),(6,2)\}.
\end{aligned}$$

*Hint:* Note that a rectangle is a boundary rectangle if it lies completely inside the exterior convex hull of the other rectangles.

## Appendix: Basic Domain Theory

We give here the formal definitions of a number of notions in domain theory used in these notes; see [1, 2, 18] for more detail. We think of a partially ordered set (poset) $(P, \sqsubseteq)$ as the set of output of some computation such that the partial order is an order of information: in other words, $a \sqsubseteq b$ indicates that $a$ has less information than $b$. For example, the set $\{0,1\}^\infty$ of all finite and infinite sequences of bits 0 and 1 with $a \sqsubseteq b$ if the sequence $a$ is an initial segment of the sequence $b$ is a poset and $a \sqsubseteq b$ simply means that $b$ has more bits of information than $a$. A non-empty subset $A \subseteq P$ is *directed* if for any pair of elements $a, b \in A$ there exists $c \in A$ such that $a \sqsubseteq c$ and $b \sqsubseteq c$. A directed set is therefore a consistent set of output elements of a computation: for every pair of output $a$ and $b$, there is some output $c$ with more information than $a$ and $b$. A *directed complete partial order (dcpo)* or a *domain* is a partial order in which every directed subset has a least upper bound (lub). We say that a dcpo is *pointed* if it has a least element which is denoted by $\bot$ and is called *bottom*.

For two elements $a$ and $b$ of a dcpo we say $a$ is *way-below* or *approximates* $b$, denoted by $a \ll b$, if for every directed subset $A$ with $b \sqsubseteq \bigsqcup A$ there exists $c \in A$ with $a \sqsubseteq c$. The idea is that $a$ is a finitary approximation to $b$: whenever the lub of a consistent set of output elements has more information than $b$, then already one of the input elements in the consistent set has more information than $a$. In $\{0,1\}^\infty$, we have $a \ll b$ iff $a \sqsubseteq b$ and $a$ is a finite sequence. The closed subsets of the *Scott topology* of a domain are those subsets $C$ which are downward closed (i.e. $x \in C \;\&\; y \sqsubseteq x \;\Rightarrow\; y \in C$) and closed under taking lub's of directed subsets (i.e. for every directed subset $A \subseteq C$ we have $\bigsqcup A \in C$).

A basis of a domain $D$ is a subset $B \subseteq D$ such that for every element $x \in D$ of the domain the set $B_x = \{y \in B \mid y \ll x\}$ of elements in the basis way-below $x$ is directed with $x = \bigsqcup B_x$. An *($\omega$)-continuous* domain is a dcpo with a (countable) basis. In other words, every element of a continuous domain can be expressed as the lub of the directed set of basis elements which approximate it. In a continuous dcpo $D$, subsets of the form $\twoheaduparrow a = \{x \in D \mid a \ll x\}$, for $a \in D$, form a basis for the Scott topology. A domain is *bounded complete* if every bounded subset has a lub; in such a domain every non-empty subset has an infimum or greatest lower bound.

It can be shown that a function $f : D \to E$ between dcpo's is continuous with respect to the Scott topology if and only if it is *monotone* (i.e. $a \sqsubseteq b \Rightarrow f(a) \sqsubseteq f(b)$) and preserves lub's of directed sets i.e. for any directed $A \subseteq D$, we have $f(\bigsqcup_{a\in A} a) = \bigsqcup_{a \in A} f(a)$. Moreover, if $D$ is an $\omega$-continuous dcpo, then $f$ is continuous iff it is monotone and preserves lub's of increasing sequences (i.e. $f(\bigsqcup_{i\in\omega} x_i) = \bigsqcup_{i\in\omega} f(x_i)$, for any increasing $(x_i)_{i\in\omega}$).

The collection, $D \to E$, of continuous functions $f : D \to E$ between dcpo's $D$ and $E$ can be ordered pointwise: $f \sqsubseteq g$ iff $\forall x \in D.\, f(x) \sqsubseteq g(x)$. With this partial order, $D \to E$ becomes a dcpo with $\bigsqcup_{i\in I} f_i$ given by $(\bigsqcup_{i\in I} f_i)(x) = \bigsqcup_{i\in I} f_i(x)$. Moreover, if $D$ and $E$ are bounded complete $\omega$-continuous dcpo's, so is $D \to E$.

The *interval domain* $\mathbf{I}[0,1]^n$ of the unit box $[0,1]^n \subseteq \mathbb{R}^n$ is the set of all non-empty $n$-dimensional sub-rectangles in $[0,1]^n$ ordered by reverse inclusion. A basic Scott open set is given, for every open subset $O$ of $\mathbb{R}^n$, by the collection of all rectangles contained in $O$. The map $x \mapsto \{x\} : [0,1]^n \to \mathbf{I}[0,1]^n$ is an embedding onto the set of maximal elements of $\mathbf{I}[0,1]^n$. Every maximal element $\{x\}$ can be obtained as the least upper bound (lub) of an increasing chain of elements, i.e. a shrinking, nested sequence of sub-rectangles, each containing $\{x\}$ in its interior and thereby giving an approximation to $\{x\}$ or equivalently to $x$. The set of sub-rectangles with rational coordinates provides a countable basis. One can similarly define, for example, the interval domain $\mathbf{I}\mathbb{R}^n$ of $\mathbb{R}^n$.

An important feature of domains, in the context of these notes, is that they can be used to obtain computable approximations to operations which are classically non-computable. For example, comparison of a real number with 0 is not computable. However, the function $N : \mathbf{I}[-1,1] \to \{\mathrm{tt}, \mathrm{ff}\}_\perp$ with

$$N([a,b]) = \begin{cases} \mathsf{tt} & \text{if } b < 0 \\ \mathsf{ff} & \text{if } 0 < a \\ \bot & \text{otherwise} \end{cases}$$

is the computable approximation to the comparison predicate. Here, $\{\mathsf{tt}, \mathsf{ff}\}_\bot$ is the *lift* of $\{\mathsf{tt}, \mathsf{ff}\}$, i.e. the three element pointed domain with two incomparable maximal elements tt and ff.

An $\omega$-continuous domain $D$ with a least element $\bot$ is *effectively given* wrt an effective enumeration $b : \mathbb{N} \to B$ of a countable basis $B$ if the set $\{\langle m, n\rangle \mid b_m \ll b_n\}$ is recursive, where $\langle .,. \rangle : \mathbb{N} \times \mathbb{N} \to \mathbb{N}$ is the standard pairing function i.e. the isomorphism $(x, y) \mapsto \frac{(x+y)(x+y+1)}{2} + x$. This means that for each pair of basis elements $(b_m, b_n)$, it is possible to decide in finite time whether or not $b_m \ll b_n$. We say $x \in D$ is *computable* if the set $\{n | b_n \ll x\}$ is r.e. This is equivalent to say that there is a master program which outputs exactly this set. It is also equivalent to the existence of a recursive function $g$ such that $(b_{g(n)})_{n\in\omega}$ is an increasing chain in $D$ with $x = \bigsqcup_{n\in\omega} b_{g(n)}$. If $D$ is also effectively given wrt to another basis $B' = \{b'_0, b'_1, b'_2, \cdots\}$ such that the sets $\{\langle m, n\rangle \mid b_m \ll b'_n\}$ and $\{\langle m, n\rangle \mid b'_m \ll b_n\}$ are both decidable, then $x$ will be computable wrt $B$ iff it is computable wrt $B'$. We say that $B$ and $B'$ are *recursively equivalent.*

We can define an effective enumeration $\xi$ of the set $D_c$ of all computable elements of $D$. Let $\theta_n$, $n \in \omega$, be the $n$th partial recursive function. It can be shown [18] that there exists a total recursive function $\sigma$ such that $\xi : \mathbb{N} \to D_c$ with $\xi_n := \bigsqcup_{i\in\omega} b_{\theta_{\sigma(n)}(i)}$, with $(b_{\theta_{\sigma(n)}(i)})_{i\in\omega}$ an increasing chain for each $n \in \omega$, is an effective enumeration of $D_c$. A sequence $(x_i)_{i\in\omega}$ is *computable* if there exists a total recursive function $h$ such that $x_i = \xi_{h(i)}$ for all $i \in \omega$.

We say that a continuous map $f : D \to E$ of effectively given $\omega$-continuous domains $D$ (with basis $\{a_0, a_1 \cdots\}$) and $E$ (with basis $\{b_0, b_1 \cdots\}$) is *computable* if the set $\{\langle m, n\rangle \mid b_m \ll f(a_n)\}$ is r.e. This is equivalent to say that $f$ maps computable sequences to computable sequences. Computable functions are stable under change to a recursively equivalent basis. Every computable function can be shown to be a continuous function [58, Theorem 3.6.16]. It can be shown [18] that these notions of computability for the domain $\mathbf{I}\mathbb{R}$ of intervals of $\mathbb{R}$ induce the same class of computable real numbers and computable real functions as in the classical theory [48].

We also need the following classical definitions for sequences of real numbers. A sequence $(r_i)_{i\in\omega}$ of rational numbers is *computable* if there exist three total recursive functions $a$, $b$, and $s$ such that $b(i) \neq 0$ for all $i \in \omega$ and

$$r_i = (-1)^{s(i)} \frac{a(i)}{b(i)}.$$

A computable double sequence of rational numbers is defined in a similar way. A sequence $(x_i)_{i\in\omega}$ of real numbers is *computable* if there exists a computable double sequence $(r_{ij})_{i,j\in\omega}$ of rational numbers such that

$$|r_{ij} - x_i| \leq 2^{-j} \qquad \text{for all } i \text{ and } j$$

A computable double sequence of real numbers is defined analogously. If $(x_{nk})_{n,k\in\omega}$ is a computable double sequence of real numbers which converges to a sequence $(x_n)_{n\in\omega}$ effectively in $k$ and $n$ (i.e. there exists a total recursive function $e : \mathbb{N} \times \mathbb{N} \to \mathbb{N}$ such that $|x_{nk} - x_n| \leq 2^{-N}$ for all $k \geq e(n, N)$), then the sequence $(x_n)_{n\in\omega}$ is computable [48, Page 20].

## References

1. S. Abramsky and A. Jung. Domain theory. In S. Abramsky, D. M. Gabbay, and T. S. E. Maibaum, editors, *Handbook of Logic in Computer Science*, volume 3. Clarendon Press, 1994.
2. R. M. Amadio and P.-L. Curien. *Domains and Lambda-Calculi.* Cambridge Tracts in Theoretical Computer Science, 1998.
3. F. Avnaim, J. D. Boissonnat, O. Devillers, F. Preparata, and M. Yvinec. Evaluation of a new method to compute signs of determinants. In *Proc. Eleventh ACM Symposium on Computational Geometry*, June 1995.
4. M. Benouamer, D. Michelucci, and B. Peroche. Error-free boundary evaluation using lazy rational arithmetic - a detailed implementation. In *Proceeding of the 2nd Symposium on Solid Modeling and Applications*, pages 115–126, 1993.
5. H. J. Boehm and R. Cartwright. Exact real arithmetic: Formulating real numbers as functions. In Turner. D., editor, *Research Topics in Functional Programming*, pages 43–64. Addison-Wesley, 1990.
6. H. J. Boehm, R. Cartwright, M. Riggle, and M. J. O'Donnell. Exact real arithmetic: A case study in higher order programming. In *ACM Symposium on Lisp and Functional Programming*, 1986.
7. V. Brattka and K. Weihrauch. Computability on subsets of Euclidean space I: Closed and compact subsets. *Theoretical Computer Science*, 219:65–93, 1999.
8. H. Brönimann, J. Emiris, V. Pan, and S. Pion. Computing exact geometric predicates using modular arithmetic with single precision. *ACM Conference on Computational Geometry*, 1997.
9. H. Brönnimann and M. Yvinec. Efficient exact evaluation of signs of determinants. In *Proc. Thirteenth ACM Symposium on Computational Geometry*, pages 136–173, June 1997.
10. L. E. J. Brouwer. Besitzt jede reelle zahl eine dezimalbruchentwicklung? *Math Ann*, 83:201–210, 1920.
11. O. Devillers, A. Fronville, B. Mourrain, and M. Teillaud. Algebraic methods and arithmetic filtering for exact predicates on circle arcs. In *Proc. Sixteenth ACM Symposium on Computational Geometry*, pages 139–147, June 2000.
12. P. Di Gianantonio. *A functional approach to real number computation.* PhD thesis, University of Pisa, 1993.
13. P. Di Gianantonio. Real number computability and domain theory. *Information and Computation*, 127(1):11–25, May 1996.
14. A. Edalat and A. Lieutier. Foundation of a computable solid modeling. In *Proceedings of the fifth symposium on Solid modeling and applications*, ACM Symposium on Solid Modeling and Applications, pages 278–284, 1999. Full paper to appear in TCS.
15. A. Edalat, A. Lieutier, and E. Kashefi. The convex hull in a new model of computation. In *Proc. 13th Canad. Conf. Comput. Geom.*, pages 93–96, 2001.

16. A. Edalat and P. J. Potts. A new representation for exact real numbers. In *Proceedings of Mathematical Foundations of Programming Semantics 13*, volume 6 of *Electronic Notes in Theoretical Computer Science*. Elsevier Science B. V., 1997. Available from URL: http://www.elsevier.nl/locate/entcs/volume6.html.
17. A. Edalat, P. J. Potts, and P. Sünderhauf. Lazy computation with exact real numbers. In *Proceedings of the Third ACM SIGPLAN International Confrence on Functional Programming*, pages 185–194. ACM, 1998.
18. A. Edalat and P. Sünderhauf. A domain theoretic approach to computability on the real line. *Theoretical Computer Science*, 210:73–98, 1998.
19. H. Edelsbrunner and E. P. Mucke. Simulation of simplicity - a technique to cope with degenerate cases in geometric algorithms. In *Proceeding of the 4th ACM Annual Symposium on Computational Geometry*, pages 118–133, 1998.
20. M. H. Escardó. PCF extended with real numbers. *Theoretical Computer Science*, 162(1):79–115, August 1996.
21. S. Fang, B. Bruderlin, and X. Zhu. Robustness in solid modeling: a tolerance-based intuitionistic approach. *Computer-Aided Design*, 25(9):567–577, 1993.
22. S. Fortune. Polyhedral modeling with multi-precision integer arithmetic. *Computer-Aided Design*, 29(2):123–133, 1997.
23. S. Fortune and C. von Wyk. Efficient exact arithmetic for computational geometry. In *Proceeding of the 9th ACM Annual Symposium on Computational Geometry*, pages 163–172, 1993.
24. W. Gosper. *Continued Fraction Arithmetic*. HAKMEM Item 101B, MIT Artificial Intelligence Memo 239. MIT, 1972.
25. L. Guibas, D. Salesin, and J. Stolfi. Epsilon geometry - building robust algorithms for imprecise computations. In *Proceeding of the 5th ACM Annual Symposium on Computational Geometry*, pages 208–217, 1989.
26. R. Heckmann. The appearance of big integers in exact real arithmetic based on linear fractional transformations. In *Proc. Foundations of Software Science and Computation Structures (FoSSaCS '98)*, volume 1378 of *LNCS*, pages 172–188. Springer-Verlag, 1998.
27. R. Heckmann. Big integers and complexity issues in exact real arithmetic. In *Third Comprox workshop (Sept. 1997 in Birmingham)*, volume 13 of *Electronic Notes in Theoretical Computer Science*, 1998. URL: `http://www.elsevier.nl/locate/entcs/volume13.html`.
28. R. Heckmann. Contractivity of linear fractional transformations. In J.-M. Chesneaux, F. Jézéquel, J.-L. Lamotte, and J. Vignes, editors, *Third Real Numbers and Computers Conference (RNC3)*, pages 45–59, April 1998. An updated version will appear in TCS.
29. R. Heckmann. Translation of Taylor series into LFT expansions. Submitted to Proceedings of Dagstuhl Seminar "Symbolic Algebraic Methods and Verification Methods", November 1999.
30. R. Heckmann. How many argument digits are needed to produce $n$ result digits? In *RealComp '98 Workshop (June 1998 in Indianapolis)*, volume 24 of *Electronic Notes in Theoretical Computer Science*, 2000. URL: `http://www.elsevier.nl/locate/entcs/volume24.html`.
31. C. M. Hoffmann. The problems of accuracy and robustness in geometric computation. *IEEE Comput.*, 22(3):31–41, 1989.
32. C. Y. Hu, T. Maekawa, E. C. Shebrooke, and N. M. Patrikalakis. Robust interval algorithm for curve intersections. *Computer-Aided Design*, 28(6/7):495–506, 1996.
33. C. Y. Hu, N. M. Patrikalakis, and X. Ye. Robust interval solid modeling, part i: representations. *CAD*, 28:807–818, 1996.

34. C. Y. Hu, N. M. Patrikalakis, and X. Ye. Robust interval solid modeling, part ii: boundary evaluation. *CAD*, 28:819–830, 1996.
35. V. Stoltenberg-Hansen J. Blanck and J. V. Tucker. Domain representations of partial functions, with applications to spatial objects and constructive volume geometry. *Theoretical Computer Science*. To appear.
36. D. Jackson. Boundary representation modeling with local tolerances. In *ACM Symposium on Solid Modeling and Applications*, pages 247–253, 1995.
37. M. Karasick, D. Lieber, and L. R. Nackman. Efficient Delaunay triangulation using rational arithmetic. *ACM Trans. Graphics*, 10:71–91, 1991.
38. A. A. Khanban, A. Edalat, and A. Lieutier. Delaunay triangulation and Voronoi diagram with imprecise input data. Submitted. Available from `http://www.doc.ic.ac.uk/~khanban/`.
39. M. Konecny. *Many-valued Real Functions Computable by Finite Transducers using IFS Representations*. PhD thesis, School of Computer Science, University of Birmingham, 2000. Available via URL `http://www.cs.bham.ac.uk/~axj/former-students.html`.
40. V. Menissier-Morain. Arbitrary precision real arithmetic: design and algorithms. submitted to *J. Symbolic Computation*, 1996.
41. T. Ottmann, G. Thiemt, and C. Ullrich. Numerical stability of geometric algorithms. In *Proceeding of the 3rd ACM Annual Symposium on Computational Geometry*, pages 119–125, 1987.
42. D. Plume. A calculator for exact real number computation. Available from `http://www.dcs.ed.ac.uk/home/mhe/plume/index.html`, 1998.
43. P. J. Potts. Efficient on-line computation of real functions using exact floating point. Available from: `http://www.purplefinder.com/~potts`, 1997.
44. P. J. Potts. *Exact Real Arithmetic Using Mobius Transformations*. PhD thesis, Imperial College, 1998. Available from: `http://www.purplefinder.com/~potts`.
45. P. J. Potts and A. Edalat. Exact Real Arithmetic based on Linear Fractional Transformations, December 1996. Draft, Imperial College, available from `http://www-tfm.doc.ic.ac.uk/~pjp`.
46. P. J. Potts and A. Edalat. Exact Real Computer Arithmetic, March 1997. Department of Computing Technical Report DOC 97/9, Imperial College, available from `http://theory.doc.ic.ac.uk/~ae`.
47. P. J. Potts, A. Edalat, and M. Escardó. Semantics of exact real arithmetic. In *Twelfth Annual IEEE Symposium on Logic in Computer Science*. IEEE, 1997.
48. M. B. Pour-El and J. I. Richards. *Computability in Analysis and Physics*. Springer-Verlag, 1988.
49. T. W. Sederberg and R. T. Farouki. Approximation by interval Bezier curves. *IEEE Comput. Graph. Appl.*, 15(2):87–95, 1992.
50. M. Segal. Using tolerances to guarantee valid polyhedral modeling results. *Computer Graphics*, 24(4):105–114, 1990.
51. K. Sugihara. A simple method for avoiding numerical errors and degeneracy in Voronoi diagram construction. *IEICE Trans. Fundamentals*, 1992.
52. K. Sugihara. A robust and consistent algorithm for intersecting convex polyhedra. In *Computer Graphics Forum, EUROGRAPHICS'94*, pages C–45–C–54, 1994.
53. K. Sugihara. Experimental study on acceleration of an exact-arithmetic geometric algorithm. In *Proceeding of the International Conference on Shape Modeling and Applications*, pages 160–168, 1997.
54. K. Sugihara. How to make geometric algorithms robust. *IEICE Trans. Inf. & Syst.*, E833-D(3):447–454, 2000.

55. K. Sugihara and M. Iri. Construction of the Voronoi diagram for one million generators in single-precision arithmetic. *Proc. IEEE*, 80:1471–1484, 1992.
56. K. Sugihara and M. Iri. A robust topology-oriented incremental algorithm for Voronoi diagrams. *International Journal of Computational Geometry and Applications*, pages 179–228, 1994.
57. J. E. Vuillemin. Exact real computer arithmetic with continued fractions. *IEEE Transactions on Computers*, 39(8):1087–1105, 1990.
58. K. Weihrauch. *Computability*, volume 9 of *EATCS Monographs on Theoretical Computer Science.* Springer-Verlag, 1987.
59. K. Weihrauch. A foundation for computable analysis. In D.S. Bridges, C.S. Calude, J. Gibbons, S. Reeves, and I.H. Witten, editors, *Combinatorics, Complexity, and Logic*, Discrete Mathematics and Theoretical Computer Science, pages 66–89, Singapore, 1997. Springer-Verlag. Proceedings of DMTCS'96.
60. C. Yap. A geometric consistency theorem for a symbolic perturbation theorem. In *Proc. Fourth ACM Symp. on Computer Geometry*, pages 134–142, June 1988.
61. C. K. Yap. The exact computation paradigm. In D. Z. Du and F. Hwang, editors, *Computing in Euclidean Geometry.* World Scientific, 1995.

# The Join Calculus: A Language for Distributed Mobile Programming

Cédric Fournet[1] and Georges Gonthier[2,*]

[1] Microsoft Research
[2] INRIA Rocquencourt

**Abstract.** In these notes, we give an overview of the join calculus, its semantics, and its equational theory. The join calculus is a language that models distributed and mobile programming. It is characterized by an explicit notion of locality, a strict adherence to local synchronization, and a direct embedding of the ML programming language. The join calculus is used as the basis for several distributed languages and implementations, such as JoCaml and functional nets.

Local synchronization means that messages always travel to a set destination, and can interact only after they reach that destination; this is required for an efficient implementation. Specifically, the join calculus uses ML's function bindings and pattern-matching on messages to program these synchronizations in a declarative manner.

Formally, the language owes much to concurrency theory, which provides a strong basis for stating and proving the properties of asynchronous programs. Because of several remarkable identities, the theory of process equivalences admits simplifications when applied to the join calculus. We prove several of these identities, and argue that equivalences for the join calculus can be rationally organized into a five-tiered hierarchy, with some trade-off between expressiveness and proof techniques.

We describe the mobility extensions of the core calculus, which allow the programming of agent creation and migration. We briefly present how the calculus has been extended to model distributed failures on the one hand, and cryptographic protocols on the other.

## Table of Contents



* This work is partly supported by the RNRT project MARVEL 98S0347

G. Barthe et al. (Eds.): Applied Semantics, LNCS 2395, pp. 268–332, 2002.

## Introduction

Wide-area distributed systems have become an important part of modern programming, yet most distributed programs are still written using traditional languages, designed for sequential architectures. Distribution issues are typically relegated to libraries and informal design patterns, with little support in the language for asynchrony and concurrency. Conversely, distributed constructs are influenced by the local programming model, with for instance a natural bias towards RPCs or RMIs rather than asynchronous message passing.

Needless to say, distributed programs are usually hard to write, much harder to understand and to relate to their specifications, and almost impossible to debug. This is due to essential difficulties, such as asynchrony or partial failures. Nonetheless, it should be possible to provide some high-level language support to address these issues.

The join calculus is an attempt to provide language support for asynchronous, distributed, and mobile programming. While it is clearly not the only approach, it has a simple and well-defined model, which has been used as the basis for several language implementations and also as a specification language for studying the properties of such programs. These notes give an overview of the model, with an emphasis on its operational semantics and its equational theory.

JoCaml [30] is the latest implementation of the join calculus; it is a distributed extension of Objective Caml [32], a typed high-level programming language with a mix of functional, object-oriented, and imperative features. OCaml already provides native-code and bytecode compilers, which is convenient for mobile code. The JoCaml language extends OCaml, in the sense that OCaml programs and libraries are just a special kind of JoCaml programs and libraries. JoCaml also implements strong mobility and provides support for distributed execution, including a dynamic linker and a garbage collector. The language documentation includes extensive tutorials; they can be seen as a concrete counterpart for the material presented in these notes (Sect. 1 and 5) with larger programming examples.

In these notes, we present a core calculus, rather than a full-fledged language. This minimalist approach enables us to focus on the essential features of the language, and to develop a simple theory: the calculus provides a precise description of how the distributed implementation should behave and, at the same time, it yields a formal model that is very close to the actual programming language. Thus, one can directly study the correctness of distributed programs, considering them as executable specifications. Ideally, the model should provide strong guiding principles for language design and, conversely, the model should reflect the implementation constraints.

The join calculus started out as an attempt to take the models and methods developed by concurrency theory, and to adapt and apply them to the programming of systems distributed over a wide area network. The plan was to start from Milner's pi calculus [36, 35, 49], extend it with constructs for locality and mobility, and bring to bear the considerable body of work on process calculi and their equivalences on the problem of programming mobile agents. During the course of this work, the implementation constraints of asynchronous systems suggested changing the pi calculus's CCS-based communication model. The idea was that the model had to stick to what all basic protocol suites do, and decouple transmission from synchronization, so that synchronization issues can always be resolved locally.

To us, the natural primitives for doing this in a higher-order setting were message passing, function call, and pattern-matching, and these suggested a strong link with the programming language ML. This connection allowed us to reuse a significant portion of the ML programming technology—notably the ML type system—for the "programming" part of our project. Thus the join calculus was born out of the synergy between asynchronous process calculi and ML.

Many of the ideas that we adapted from either source took new meaning in the location-sensitive, asynchronous framework of the join calculus. The connection with ML illuminates the interaction between functional and imperative features, down to their implications for typing. The highly abstract chemical abstract machine of Berry and Boudol [10] yields a much more operational instance for the join calculus. The intricate lattice of equivalences for synchronous and asynchronous calculi [21] simplifies remarkably in the pure asynchronous setting of the join calculus, to the point that we can reasonably concentrate on a single five-tiered hierarchy of equivalences, where each tier can be clearly argued for. These lecture notes contain a summary of these results, as well as much of the rationale that joins them into a coherent whole.

These notes are organized as follows. In Sect. 1, we gradually introduce the join calculus as a concurrent extension of ML, describe common synchronization patterns, and give its chemical semantics. In Sect. 2, we define and motivate our main notions of observational equivalences, and illustrate the main proof techniques for establishing equivalences between processes. In Sect. 3, we refine our framework for reasoning about processes. We introduce intermediate notions of equivalence that account for fairness and gradual commitment, and organize all our equivalences in a hierarchy, according to their discriminating power. In Sect. 4, we supplement this framework with labeled semantics, and discuss their relation. In Sect. 5, we finally refine the programming model to account for locality information and agent migration.

# 1 The Core Join Calculus

Although the join calculus was designed as a process calculus for distributed and mobile computation, it turned out to be a close match to ML-style (impure) functional programming. In these notes we will use this connection to motivate and explain the computational core of the calculus.

First we will introduce the primitives of the join calculus by showing how they mesh in a typical 'mini-ML' lambda-like calculus. At a more concrete level, there is a similar introduction to the JoCaml language as an extension of the OCaml programming language [30].

We will then show how a variety of synchronization primitives can be easily encoded in the join calculus and argue that the general join calculus itself can be encoded by its "asynchronous" fragment, i.e., that function calls are just a form of message passing. This allows us to limit the formal semantics of the join calculus to its asynchronous core.

We conclude the section by exposing the computational model that underlies the formal semantics of the join calculus. This simple model guarantees that distributed computation can be faithfully represented in the join calculus.

## 1.1 Concurrent Functional Programming

Our starting point is a small ML-like syntax for the call-by-value polyadic lambda calculus:

| | | |
|---|---|---|
| $E, F ::=$ | | expressions |
| | $x, y, f$ | variable |
| $\vert$ | $f(\tilde{E})$ | function call |
| $\vert$ | $\texttt{let}\ x = E\ \texttt{in}\ F$ | local value definition |
| $\vert$ | $\texttt{let}\ f(\tilde{x}) = E\ \texttt{in}\ F$ | local recursive function definition |

The notation $\tilde{x}$ stands for a possibly empty comma-separated tuple $x_1, x_2, \ldots, x_n$ of variables; similarly $\tilde{E}$ is a tuple of expressions. We casually assume that the usual Hindley-Milner type system ensures that functions are always called with the proper number of arguments.

We depart from the lambda calculus by taking the ML-style function definition as primitive, rather than $\lambda$-expressions, which can be trivially recovered as $\lambda x.E \stackrel{\text{def}}{=} \texttt{let}\ f(x) = E\ \texttt{in}\ f$. This choice is consistent with the usual ML programming practice, and will allow us to integrate smoothly primitives with side effects, such as the join calculus primitives, because the `let` provides a syntactic "place" for the state of the function. An immediate benefit, however, is that values in this calculus consist only of *names*: (globally) free variables, or `let`-defined function names. This allows us to omit altogether curried function calls from our syntax, since the function variable in a call can only be replaced by a function name in a call-by-value computation.

We are going to present the join calculus as an extension of this functional calculus with concurrency. The most straightforward way of doing this would be to add a new `run` $E$ primitive that returns immediately after starting a concurrent evaluation of $E$. However, we want to get a model in which we can reason about concurrent behavior, not just a programming language design. In order to develop an operational semantics, we also need a syntax that describes the situation *after* `run` $E$ returns, and the evaluation of $E$ and the evaluation of the expression $F$ that contained the `run` $E$ proceed concurrently. It would be quite awkward to use `run` for this, since it would force us to treat $E$ and $F$ asymmetrically.

It is more natural to denote the concurrent computation of $E$ and $F$ by $E \mid F$, using a symmetric operator '|' for parallel composition. However, $E \mid F$ is not quite an "expression", since an expression denotes a computation that returns a result, and there is no natural way of defining a unique "result" for $E \mid F$. Therefore, we extend our calculus with a second sort for *processes*, i.e., computations that aren't expected to produce a result (and hence, don't terminate). In fact, the operands $E$ and $F$ of $E \mid F$ should also be processes, rather than expressions, since they aren't expected to return a result either. Thus, '|' will simply be an operation on processes.

We will use the letters $P, Q, R$ for processes. We still need the `run` $P$ primitive to launch a process from an expression; conversely, we allow `let` constructs in processes, so that processes can evaluate expressions.

| | | |
|---|---|---|
| $P, Q, R ::=$ | | processes |
| | $\texttt{let}\ x = E\ \texttt{in}\ P$ | compute expression |
| \| | $\texttt{let}\ f(\tilde{x}) = E\ \texttt{in}\ P$ | local recursive function definition |
| \| | $P \mid Q$ | parallel composition |
| \| | $\mathbf{0}$ | inert process |

| | | |
|---|---|---|
| $E, F ::=$ | | expressions |
| | ... | |
| \| | $\texttt{run}\ P$ | spawn process |

In this minimal syntax, invoking an abstraction for a process $P$ is quite awkward, since it involves computing an expression that calls a function whose body will execute `run` $P$. To avoid this, we also add a "process abstraction" construct to mirror the function abstraction construct; besides, we use a different keyword '**def**' and different call brackets '$\langle\ \rangle$' to enforce the separation of expressions and processes:

$$
\begin{array}{lll}
P, Q, R ::= & & \text{processes} \\
& \dots & \\
& \mid\ p\langle\tilde{E}\rangle & \text{execute abstract process} \\
& \mid\ \mathtt{def}\ p\langle\tilde{x}\rangle \triangleright P\ \mathtt{in}\ Q & \text{process abstraction} \\
E, F ::= & & \text{expressions} \\
& \dots & \\
& \mid\ \mathtt{def}\ p\langle\tilde{x}\rangle \triangleright P\ \mathtt{in}\ E & \text{process abstraction}
\end{array}
$$

Operationally, "executing" an abstract process really means computing its parameters and shipping their values to the '**def**', where a new copy of the process body can be started. Hence, we will use the term *channel* for the "abstract process" defined by a `def`, and *message send* for a "process call" $p\langle\tilde{E}\rangle$.

Our calculus allows the body $E$ of a function $f$ to contain a subprocess $P$. From $P$'s point of view, returning the value for $f$'s computation is just sending data away on a special "channel"; we extend our calculus with a `return` primitive to do just that. Since messages carry a tuple of values, the `return` primitive also gives us a notation for returning several values from a function; we just need to extend the `let` so it can bind a tuple of variables to the result of such tuple-valued functions.

$$
\begin{array}{lll}
P, Q, R ::= & & \text{processes} \\
& \dots & \\
& \mid\ \mathtt{return}\ \tilde{E}\ \mathtt{to}\ f & \text{return value(s) to function call} \\
& \mid\ \mathtt{let}\ \tilde{x} = E\ \mathtt{in}\ P & \text{compute expression} \\
E, F ::= & & \text{expressions} \\
& \dots & \\
& \mid\ \mathtt{let}\ \tilde{x} = E\ \mathtt{in}\ F & \text{local definition(s)}
\end{array}
$$

Note that the tuple may be empty, for functions that only perform side effects; we write the matching `let` statement $E; P$ (or $E; F$) rather than `let` $= E$ `in` $P$. Also, we will omit the `to` part for `return`s that return to the closest lexically enclosing function.

With the $E; P$ and `return` statements, it is now more convenient to write function bodies as processes rather than expressions. We therefore extend the `def` construct to allow for the direct definition of functions with processes.

$$
\begin{array}{lll}
P, Q, R ::= & & \text{processes} \\
& \dots & \\
& \mid\ \mathtt{def}\ f(\tilde{x}) \triangleright P\ \mathtt{in}\ Q & \text{recursive function definition} \\
E, F ::= & & \text{expressions} \\
& \dots & \\
& \mid\ \mathtt{def}\ f(\tilde{x}) \triangleright P\ \mathtt{in}\ E & \text{recursive function definition}
\end{array}
$$

Hence **def** $f(\tilde{x}) \triangleright P$ is equivalent to `let` $f(\tilde{x}) =$ `run` $P$. Conversely, `let` $f(\tilde{x}) = E$ is equivalent to `def` $f(\tilde{x}) \triangleright$ `return` $E$, so, in preparation for the next section, we take the `def` form as primitive, and treat the `let` $f(\tilde{x}) = \ldots$ form as an abbreviation for a `def`.

### 1.2 Synchronization by Pattern-Matching

Despite its formal elegance, the formalism we have developed so far has limited expressiveness. While it allows for the generation of concurrent computation, it provides no means for joining together the results of two such computations, or for having any kind of interaction between them, for that matter. Once spawned, a process will be essentially oblivious to its environment.

A whole slew of stateful primitives have been proposed for encapsulating various forms of inter-process interaction: concurrent variables, semaphores, message passing, futures, rendez-vous, monitors, ... just to name a few. The join calculus distinguishes itself by using that basic staple of ML programming, *definition by pattern-matching*, to provide a declarative means for specifying inter-process synchronization, thus leaving state inside processes, where it rightfully belongs.

Concretely, this is done by allowing the joint definition of several functions and/or channels by matching concurrent call and message patterns; in a nutshell, by allowing the '|' operator on the left of the '$\triangleright$' definition symbol. The syntax for doing this is a bit more complex, partly because we also want to allow for multiple patterns, so we create new categories for *definitions* and *join patterns*.

| | | |
|---|---|---|
| $P, Q, R ::=$ | | processes |
| | $\ldots$ | |
| | $\mid$ `def` $D$ `in` $P$ | process/function definition |
| $E, F ::=$ | | expressions |
| | $\ldots$ | |
| | $\mid$ `def` $D$ `in` $E$ | process/function definition |
| $D ::=$ | | definitions |
| | $J \triangleright P$ | execution rule |
| | $\mid D \wedge D'$ | alternative definitions |
| | $\mid \top$ | empty definition |
| $J ::=$ | | join patterns |
| | $x\langle\tilde{y}\rangle$ | message send pattern |
| | $\mid x(\tilde{y})$ | function call pattern |
| | $\mid J \mid J'$ | synchronization |

Definitions whose join pattern consists of a single message pattern (or a single call pattern) correspond to the abstract processes (or functions) presented above. More interestingly, the meaning of a joint definition $p\langle x\rangle \mid q\langle y\rangle \triangleright P$ is that, each time messages are concurrently sent on *both* the $p$ and $q$ channels, the process $P$

is run with the parameters $x$ and $y$ set to the contents of the $p$ and $q$ messages, respectively. For instance, this two-message pattern may be used to join the results of two concurrent computations:

$$\begin{array}{l} \texttt{def}\ \mathit{jointCall}(f_1, f_2, t) \rhd \\ \quad \texttt{def}\ p\langle x\rangle \,|\, q\langle y\rangle \rhd \texttt{return}\ x, y\ \texttt{in} \\ \quad p\langle f_1(t)\rangle \mid q\langle f_2(t)\rangle\ \texttt{in} \\ \texttt{let}\ x, y = \mathit{jointCall}(\cos, \sin, 0.1)\ \texttt{in} \ldots \end{array}$$

In this example, each call to $\mathit{jointCall}(f_1, f_2, t)$ starts two processes $p\langle f_1(t)\rangle$ and $q\langle f_2(t)\rangle$ that compute $f_1(t)$ and $f_2(t)$ in parallel and send their values on the local channels $p$ and $q$, respectively. When both messages have been sent, the inner `def` rule joins the two messages and triggers the `return` process, which returns the pair $f_1(t), f_2(t)$ to the caller of $\mathit{jointCall}(f_1, f_2, t)$.

If there is at least a function call in the pattern $J$ of a rule $J \rhd P$, then the process body $P$ may contain a `return` for that call, as in the functional core. We can thus code a local asynchronous pi calculus "channel" $x$ as follows

$$\begin{array}{l} \texttt{def}\ \overline{x}\langle v\rangle \,|\, x() \rhd \texttt{return}\ v\ \texttt{in} \\ \ldots \overline{x}\langle E\rangle \ldots \mid \texttt{let}\ u = x()\ \texttt{in}\ P \end{array}$$

Since a pi calculus channel $x$ supports two different operations, sending and receiving, we need two join calculus names to implement it: a channel name $\overline{x}$ for sending, and a function name $x$ for receiving a value. The meaning of the joint definition is that a call to $x()$ returns a value $v$ that was sent on an $\overline{x}\langle\rangle$ message. Note that the pi calculus term $\overline{x}\langle v\rangle$, which denotes a primitive "send" operation on a channel $x$, gets encoded as $\overline{x}\langle v\rangle$, which sends a message on the (ordinary) channel name $\overline{x}$ in the join calculus. The primitive pi calculus reception process $x(u).P$, which runs $P\{v/u\}$ after receiving a single $\overline{x}\langle v\rangle$ message, gets encoded as `let` $u = x()$ `in` $P$. Finally, the two names $\overline{x}$ and $x$ are bound by their definition, hence the example above implements a *restricted* pi calculus channel $(\nu x. \ldots)$.

In the example above, $u$ will be thus bound to the value of $E$ for the execution of $P$—if there are no other $x()$ calls or $\overline{x}\langle v\rangle$ messages around. If there are, then the behavior is not deterministic: the join calculus semantics does ensure that each $x()$ call grabs at most one $\overline{x}\langle v\rangle$ message, and that each $\overline{x}\langle v\rangle$ message fulfills at most one $x()$ call (the `def` rule *consumes* its join pattern), but it does not specify how the available $x()$ and $\overline{x}\langle v\rangle$ are paired. Any leftover calls or messages (there cannot be both[1]) simply wait for further messages or calls to complete; however the calculus makes no guarantee as to the order in which they will complete. To summarize, running

$$\overline{x}\langle 1\rangle \mid \overline{x}\langle 2\rangle \mid \overline{x}\langle 3\rangle \mid (\mathit{print}(x()); \mathit{print}(x()); \mathbf{0})$$

can print `1 2` and stop with a leftover $\overline{x}\langle 3\rangle$ message, or print `3 2` and stop with a leftover $\overline{x}\langle 1\rangle$ message, etc. The join calculus semantics allows any of these possibilities. On the other hand,

[1] Under the fairness assumptions usually provided by implementations, and implied by most process equivalences (see Sect. 3.2).

$$\overline{x}\langle 1\rangle \mid \big(print(x()); (\overline{x}\langle 2\rangle \mid print(x()); \mathbf{0})\big)$$

can only print `1 2`, as the $\overline{x}\langle 2\rangle$ message is sent only after the first $x()$ call has completed.

We can use higher-order constructs to encapsulate this encoding in a single *newChannel* function that creates new channels and returns their interface:

$$\begin{array}{l} \texttt{def}\ newChannel() \triangleright \\ \quad \texttt{def}\ send\langle v\rangle \mid receive() \triangleright \texttt{return}\ v\ \texttt{in} \\ \quad \texttt{return}\ send, receive\ \texttt{in} \\ \texttt{let}\ \overline{x}, x = newChannel()\ \texttt{in} \\ \texttt{let}\ \overline{y}, y = newChannel()\ \texttt{in} \ldots \end{array}$$

(Because the join calculus has no data structures, we encode the channel "objects" by the tuple of join calculus names *send*, *receive* that implement their operations. In JoCaml, we would return a record.)

This kind of higher-order abstraction allows us to return only some of the names that define an object's behavior, so that the other names remain *private*. An especially common idiom is to keep the *state* of a concurrent object in a single private message, and to use function names for the *methods*. Since the state remains private, it is trivial to ensure that there is always exactly one state message available. For example, here is the join calculus encoding of a "shared variable" object.

$$\begin{array}{l} \texttt{def}\ newVar(v_0) \triangleright \\ \quad \texttt{def}\ put(w) \mid val\langle v\rangle \triangleright val\langle w\rangle \mid \texttt{return} \\ \quad\ \ \wedge\ get() \mid val\langle v\rangle \triangleright val\langle v\rangle \mid \texttt{return}\ v\ \texttt{in} \\ \quad val\langle v_0\rangle \mid \texttt{return}\ put, get\ \texttt{in} \ldots \end{array}$$

The inner definition has two rules that define three names—two functions *put* and *get*, and a channel *val*. The *val* name remains private and always carries a single state message with the current value; it initially carries the value $v_0$ passed as a parameter when the shared variable is created. Note that since the state must be joined with a call to run a method, it is easy to ensure that at most one method runs at a time, by reissuing the state message only when the method completes. This is the classical *monitor* construct (also known as a *synchronized object*).

It is often natural to use different channel names to denote different synchronization states of an object. Compare, for instance, the encoding for a shared variable above with the encoding for a one-place buffer:

$$\begin{array}{l} \texttt{def}\ newBuf() \triangleright \\ \quad \texttt{def}\ put(v) \mid empty\langle\rangle \triangleright full\langle v\rangle \mid \texttt{return} \\ \quad\ \ \wedge\ get() \mid full\langle v\rangle \triangleright empty\langle\rangle \mid \texttt{return}\ v\ \texttt{in} \\ \quad empty\langle\rangle \mid \texttt{return}\ put, get\ \texttt{in} \ldots \end{array}$$

The join calculus gives us considerably more flexibility for describing the synchronization behavior of the object. For instance, the state may at times be divided among several concurrent asynchronous state messages, and method calls may be joined with several of these messages. In short, we may use a Petri net rather than a finite state machine to describe the synchronization behavior. For example, a concurrent two-place buffer might be coded as

$$\begin{array}{l}\texttt{def}\ \mathit{newBuf2}() \triangleright \\ \quad \texttt{def}\ \mathit{put}(v) \mid \mathit{emptyTail}\langle\rangle \triangleright \mathit{fullTail}\langle v\rangle \mid \texttt{return} \\ \quad\ \ \wedge\ \mathit{emptyHead}\langle\rangle \mid \mathit{fullTail}\langle v\rangle \triangleright \mathit{fullHead}\langle v\rangle \mid \mathit{emptyTail}\langle\rangle \\ \quad\ \ \wedge\ \mathit{get}() \mid \mathit{fullHead}\langle v\rangle \triangleright \mathit{emptyHead}\langle\rangle \mid \texttt{return}\ v\ \texttt{in} \\ \quad \mathit{emptyHead}\langle\rangle \mid \mathit{emptyTail}\langle\rangle \mid \texttt{return}\ \mathit{put}, \mathit{get}\ \texttt{in} \ldots\end{array}$$

Note that these concurrent objects are just a programming idiom; there is nothing specific to them in the join calculus, which can accommodate other programming models equally well. For instance, we get the *actors* model if we make the "methods" asynchronous, and put the methods' code inside the state, i.e., the state contains a function that processes the method message and returns a function for processing the next message:

$$\begin{array}{l}\texttt{def}\ \mathit{newActor}(\mathit{initBehavior}) \triangleright \\ \quad \texttt{def}\ \mathit{request}\langle v\rangle \mid \mathit{state}\langle \mathit{behavior}\rangle \triangleright \mathit{state}\langle \mathit{behavior}(v)\rangle\ \texttt{in} \\ \quad \mathit{state}\langle \mathit{initBehavior}\rangle \mid \texttt{return}\ \mathit{request}\ \texttt{in} \ldots\end{array}$$

We can also synchronize several calls, to model for instance the CCS *synchronous channels.* (In this case, we have to specify to which calls the `return` statements return).

$$\begin{array}{l}\texttt{def}\ \mathit{newCCSchan}() \triangleright \\ \quad \texttt{def}\ \mathit{send}(v) \mid \mathit{receive}() \triangleright \texttt{return to}\ \mathit{send} \mid \texttt{return}\ v\ \texttt{to}\ \mathit{receive}\ \texttt{in} \\ \texttt{return}\ \mathit{send}, \mathit{receive}\ \texttt{in} \\ \ldots\end{array}$$

The Ada *rendez-vous* can be modeled similarly; in this case, the "acceptor" task sends a message-processing function, and the function result is returned to the "caller" task:

$$\begin{array}{l}\texttt{def}\ \mathit{newRendezVous}() \triangleright \\ \quad \texttt{def}\ \mathit{call}(v) \mid \mathit{accept}(f) \triangleright \\ \quad\quad \texttt{let}\ r = f(v)\ \texttt{in}\ (\texttt{return}\ r\ \texttt{to}\ \mathit{call} \mid \texttt{return to}\ \mathit{accept})\ \texttt{in} \\ \quad \texttt{return}\ \mathit{call}, \mathit{accept}\ \texttt{in} \ldots\end{array}$$

The `let` ensures that the acceptor is suspended until the rendez-vous processing has completed, so that the message-processing "function" can freely access the acceptor's imperative variables without race conditions. An `accept` $e(x)$ `do` $E$ `end` Ada statement would thus be modeled as $\mathit{accept}_e(\lambda x.E)$.

In theory, adding any of the above constructs—even the imperative variable—to the concurrent lambda calculus of Sect. 1.1 gives a formalism equivalent to the join calculus in terms of expressiveness. What are, then, the advantages of the join pattern construct? If a specific synchronization device is taken as primitive (say, the one-place buffer), other devices must be coded in terms of that primitive. These encodings are usually abstracted as functions (often the only available form of abstraction). This means that the synchronization behavior of an application that relies mostly on non-primitive devices is mostly hidden in the side effects of functions. On the contrary, the join calculus encodings we have presented above make the synchronization behavior of the encoding devices explicit. The join calculus gives us a general language for writing synchronization devices; devices are just common idioms in that language. This makes it much easier to turn from one type of device to another, to use several kinds of devices, or even to *combine* devices, e.g., provide method rendez-vous for a synchronized object.

Also, the join calculus syntax favors statically binding code to a synchronization event. This increases the "referential transparency"[2] of join calculus programs, because this code is easily found by a lexical lookup of the functions and channels involved in the event. In other words, this code gives a first approximation of what happens when the corresponding functions are called, and the corresponding messages are sent. The longer the code in the definition, the better the approximation. It should be noted that for most of the devices we have presented here this static code is very short. The pi calculus asynchronous channel encoding is probably a worst case. It only says "a value sent on $\overline{x}$ can be returned by an $x()$ call", so that any other properties of the channel have to be inferred from the dynamic configuration of the program.

Finally—and this was actually the main motivation for the join calculus design—the join calculus synchronization can always be performed *locally*. Any contention between messages and/or calls is resolved at the site that holds their joint definition. The transmission of messages, calls, and returns, on the other hand, can never cause contention. As we will see in section 4, this property is required if the calculus is to be used for modeling distributed systems, and *a fortiori* mobility.

This property is the reason for which the CCS (or pi calculus) "external choice" operator is conspicuously absent from our list of encodings : this device can express an atomic choice between communication offers on arbitrary channels, and thus intrinsically creates non-local contention. Its join calculus encoding would necessarily include some rather cumbersome mechanism for resolving this contention (see [41]). We should however point out that global atomic choice is a rarely needed device, and that the join calculus provides versatile local choice in the form of alternative rules.

Even without choice, the pi calculus does not enjoy the locality property (unlike many other models, such as monitors or actors, which do exhibit locality). This is because the contention between senders on one hand, and receivers on the other hand, cannot be both resolved simultaneously and locally at a sender or at a receiver site. Typical implementations of the pi calculus, such as PICT [45], eventually map channels to local data structures, but this mapping is not reflected in the language. Similarly, the join calculus encoding introduces an

[2] A misnomer, of course, since a language with synchronization must have side effects.

explicit "channel definition" for every pi calculus channel, in which the resolution can take place.

## 1.3 The Asynchronous Core

In spite of some simplifications at the end of Sect. 1.1, the syntax of the general join calculus is rather large and complex. It would be preferable to carry out a few other simplifications before trying to formulate a precise operational semantics for the calculus. In particular, the semantics of rendez-vous type definitions, where two calls are synchronized, is going to be painful to describe formally.

A standard trick in operational semantics is to use $Q\{E/f(\tilde{v})\}$ to denote a state where $Q$ is computing an expression $E$ for the function call $f(\tilde{v})$. This neatly averts the need for a new syntax for such states, but clearly does not work if $E$ is run by a rendez-vous between two calls $f(\tilde{v})$ and $g(\tilde{w})$; we would need new syntax for that. For that matter, we would also need new syntax for the case where $E$ has forked off a separate process $P$ that contains some `return` $F$ `to` $f$ primitives. We would also need special rules to allow messages (and possibly definitions) to move in and out of such "inner processes".

Fortunately, we can avoid these complications by *defining* function calls by a message protocol. We will take literally the analogy we used to introduce the `return` primitive, and actually implement the `return` with a message send on a continuation channel. The function call will be implemented by a message carrying both the arguments and the continuation channel. The precise "wiring" of the continuations will specify exactly the evaluation order.

We assume that, for each function name $f$, we have a fresh channel name $\kappa_f$ for the return channel of $f$ (we will reuse the function name $f$ for the call channel). Then the continuation-passing style (CPS) encoding of function calls in the join calculus can be specified by the equations:

$$
\begin{aligned}
f(\tilde{x}) &\stackrel{\text{def}}{=} f\langle\tilde{x}, \kappa_f\rangle \qquad\qquad \text{(in join patterns } J\text{)}\\
\texttt{return}\ \tilde{E}\ \texttt{to}\ f &\stackrel{\text{def}}{=} \kappa_f\langle\tilde{E}\rangle\\
p\langle E_1, \ldots, E_n\rangle &\stackrel{\text{def}}{=} \texttt{let}\ v_1 = E_1\ \texttt{in}\\
&\qquad \vdots\\
&\quad\ \ \texttt{let}\ v_n = E_n\ \texttt{in}\ p\langle v_1, \ldots, v_n\rangle\\
&\quad\ \ \text{(when at least one } E_i \text{ is not a variable)}\\
\texttt{let}\ v = u\ \texttt{in}\ P &\stackrel{\text{def}}{=} P\{u/v\}\\
\texttt{let}\ \tilde{x} = f(\tilde{E})\ \texttt{in}\ P &\stackrel{\text{def}}{=} \texttt{def}\ \kappa\langle\tilde{x}\rangle \triangleright P\ \texttt{in}\ f\langle\tilde{E}, \kappa\rangle\\
\texttt{let}\ \tilde{x} = \texttt{def}\ D\ \texttt{in}\ E\ \texttt{in}\ P &\stackrel{\text{def}}{=} \texttt{def}\ D\ \texttt{in}\ \texttt{let}\ \tilde{x} = E\ \texttt{in}\ P\\
\texttt{let}\ \tilde{x} = \texttt{let}\ \tilde{y} = F\ \texttt{in}\ E\ \texttt{in}\ P &\stackrel{\text{def}}{=} \texttt{let}\ \tilde{y} = F\ \texttt{in}\ \texttt{let}\ \tilde{x} = E\ \texttt{in}\ P\\
\texttt{let}\ \ = \texttt{run}\ P\ \texttt{in}\ Q &\stackrel{\text{def}}{=} P \mid Q
\end{aligned}
$$

The equations above make the general assumption that there are no spurious variable captures : the names $\kappa$ and $v_1, \ldots, v_n$ are fresh, and the names defined by $D$ or bound by $\tilde{y}$ are not free in $P$ in the `let-def` and `let-let` equations. Expanded repeatedly, these definitions translate up to alpha-conversion any full

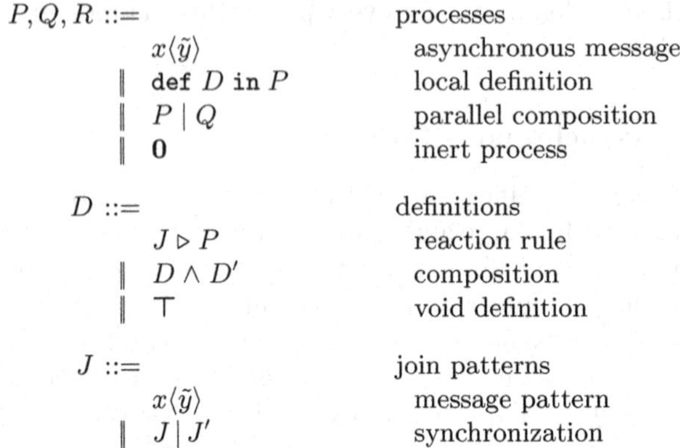

**Fig. 1.** Syntax for the core join calculus

join calculus process into an equivalent asynchronous join calculus process—one that does not involve function calls or `let`, `return`, or `run` primitives.

In addition to choosing an evaluation order, the translation assigns a "continuation capture" semantics to multiple returns: if several `return`s are executed for the same function call, then the calling context will be executed several times with different return values. While this feature may be useful for implementing, e.g., a fail-retry construct, it is not really compatible with the stack implementation of function calls, so JoCaml for instance puts severe syntactic restrictions on the use of `return` statements to rule out multiple returns.

We could apply further internal encodings to remove other "complex" features from the join calculus: alternative definitions, $n$-way join patterns for $n \neq 2$, $n$-ary messages for $n \neq 1$, even $\mathbf{0}$... However, none of these "simplifications" would really simplify the operational semantics, and the behavior of the encoding would be significantly more complex than behavior of the encoded term. This is not the case for the CPS encoding presented above; we are simply providing, within the asynchronous join calculus, the "extra syntax" that was called for at the top of this section.

### 1.4 Operational Semantics

Since in the asynchronous join calculus the only expressions are variables, we can altogether do away with the "expressions" syntactic class. The remaining syntax, summarized in Fig. 1, is quite regular: messages and parallel composition in both processes and patterns, plus definitions in processes.

The precise binding rules for the asynchronous join calculus are those of mutually-recursive functions in ML:

(*i*) A rule $x_1\langle\tilde{y}_1\rangle \mid \cdots \mid x_n\langle\tilde{y}_n\rangle \triangleright P$ binds the formal parameters $\tilde{y}_1, \ldots, \tilde{y}_n$ with scope $P$; the variables in each tuple $\tilde{y}_i$ must be distinct, and the tuples must be pairwise disjoint. Also, the rule *defines* the channel names $x_1, \ldots, x_n$.

(*ii*) A definition **def** $J_1 \triangleright P_1 \wedge \ldots \wedge J_k \triangleright P_k$ **in** $Q$ recursively binds in $Q, P_1, \ldots, P_k$ all the channel names defined in $J_1 \triangleright P_1, \ldots, J_k \triangleright P_k$.

We will denote $\mathrm{rv}(J)$ the set of variables bound by a join-pattern $J$ in (*i*), and $\mathrm{dv}(D)$ the set of channel names defined by a definition $D$ in (*ii*). We will denote $\mathrm{fv}(P)$ the set of free names or variables in a process $P$. Similarly, $\mathrm{fv}(D)$ will denote the set of free variables in a definition $D$; by convention we take $\mathrm{dv}(D) \subseteq \mathrm{fv}(D)$. The inductive definition for $\mathrm{rv}(J)$, $\mathrm{dv}(D)$, $\mathrm{fv}(D)$, and $\mathrm{fv}(P)$ appears in Fig. 5 page 313.

Since we have eliminated all the synchronous primitives by internal translation, our operational semantics only needs to define two operations:

(a) sending a message on a channel name
(b) triggering a definition rule whose join pattern has been fulfilled.

Operation (a) means moving the message from its sending site to its definition site. This operation is not quite as trivial as it might first appear to be, because this move might conflict with the scoping rules of the join calculus: some of the message's arguments might be locally defined channel names, as in

$$\texttt{def}\ p\langle x\rangle \triangleright P\ \texttt{in}\ (\texttt{def}\ q\langle y\rangle \triangleright Q\ \texttt{in}\ p\langle q\rangle)$$

In the lambda calculus, this problem is solved by combining the sending and triggering operations, and directly replacing $p\langle q\rangle$ by $P\{q/x\}$ in the process above. This solution does not work for the join calculus in general, however, since a rule might need several messages from several sites to trigger, as in

$$\texttt{def}\ p\langle x\rangle \mid p'\langle x'\rangle \triangleright P\ \texttt{in}\ (\texttt{def}\ q\langle y\rangle \triangleright Q\ \texttt{in}\ p\langle q\rangle) \mid (\texttt{def}\ q\langle y\rangle \triangleright Q'\ \texttt{in}\ p'\langle q\rangle)$$

The solution, which was first discovered for the pi calculus [37], lies in doing things the other way around: rather than moving the contents of the outer definition inside the inner one, we extend the scope of the argument's definition to include that of the message's channel. This operation is called a *scope extrusion*. This is a fairly complex operation, since it involves doing preliminary alpha-conversion to avoid name captures, and moving a full definition, along with all the messages associated with it.

In contrast, the trigger operation (b) means selecting a particular rule $J \triangleright P$, assembling a group $M$ of messages that match the rule's join pattern $J$, and simply replacing $M$ with an appropriate instance of $P$ (with the arguments of $M$ substituted for the parameters $\mathrm{rv}(J)$ of the rule).

Although it might seem much simpler, only operation (b) has real computational contents in the core join calculus (for the distributed join calculus, moving a message across sites does impact computation in subtle ways—see Sect. 5). Operation (a) only rearranges the order of subterms in a way that preserves all bindings. The selecting and assembling steps of operation (b) can also be viewed as similar rearrangements. Finally, we note that such rearrangements never take place in *guarded* subterms (subterms of a process $P$ that appears on the right hand side of a definition rule $J \triangleright P$).

Thus, if we denote by $P \equiv Q$ the *structural equivalence* relation "$P$ and $Q$ are the same up to alpha-conversion and rearrangement of unguarded subterms that preserve bindings", then the entire operational semantics of the join calculus can be expressed by a single rule:

$$\frac{\begin{array}{c} R \equiv \texttt{def}\ J \triangleright P \wedge D\ \texttt{in}\ J\rho \mid Q \\ R' \equiv \texttt{def}\ J \triangleright P \wedge D\ \texttt{in}\ P\rho \mid Q \\ \rho \text{ maps variables in } \mathrm{rv}(J) \text{ to channel names} \end{array}}{R \longrightarrow R'}$$

where the process $R$ is decomposed as follows: $J \triangleright P$ is the active rule, $J\rho$ are the messages being consumed, and $D$ and $Q$ collect all other rules and processes of $R$. The '$\equiv$' in the second premise could be replaced by '$=$' since it is only necessary to shift messages and definitions around before the trigger step. However, this '$\equiv$' gives us additional flexibility in writing series of reduction steps, since it allows us to keep the syntactic shape of the term by undoing the "rule selection" steps, and moving back the process $P\rho$ to the original place of one of the triggering messages.

The structural equivalence relation $\equiv$ itself is easily (but tediously) axiomatized as the least equivalence relation such that:

$$\begin{array}{rll}
P \equiv P' & & \text{if } P \text{ and } P' \text{ are alpha-equivalent} \\
D \equiv D' & & \text{if } D \text{ and } D' \text{ are alpha-equivalent} \\
P \mid Q \equiv P' \mid Q' & & \text{if } P \equiv P' \text{ and } Q \equiv Q' \\
\texttt{def}\ D\ \texttt{in}\ P \equiv \texttt{def}\ D'\ \texttt{in}\ P' & & \text{if } D \equiv D' \text{ and } P \equiv P' \\
D_1 \wedge D_2 \equiv D_1' \wedge D_2' & & \text{if } D_1 \equiv D_1' \text{ and } D_2 \equiv D_2' \\
P \mid \mathbf{0} \equiv P & & \\
P \mid (Q \mid R) \equiv (Q \mid P) \mid R & & \\
D \wedge \top \equiv D & & \\
D_1 \wedge (D_2 \wedge D_3) \equiv (D_2 \wedge D_1) \wedge D_3 & & \\
\texttt{def}\ \top\ \texttt{in}\ P \equiv P & & \\
(\texttt{def}\ D\ \texttt{in}\ P) \mid Q \equiv \texttt{def}\ D\ \texttt{in}\ (P \mid Q) & & \text{provided } \mathrm{dv}(D) \cap \mathrm{fv}(Q) = \emptyset \\
\texttt{def}\ D_1\ \texttt{in}\ \texttt{def}\ D_2\ \texttt{in}\ P \equiv \texttt{def}\ D_1 \wedge D_2\ \texttt{in}\ P & & \text{provided } \mathrm{dv}(D_2) \cap \mathrm{fv}(D_1) = \emptyset
\end{array}$$

### 1.5 The Reflexive Chemical Abstract Machine

The operational semantics we just described may be technically sound and convenient to manipulate, but it does not quite give an intuitively satisfying account of the execution of processes. The reason is that, in order to simplify the exposition, we have lumped together and hidden in the "trivial rearrangements" equivalence '$\equiv$' a number of operations that must occur in a real implementation:

1. Programmed parallelism (the '$|$' operator) must be turned into runtime parallelism (multiple kernel or virtual machine threads) and, conversely, threads must terminate with either the null process $\mathbf{0}$ or with a message send.
2. The alpha-conversions required for scope extrusion are usually implemented by dynamically allocating a new data structure for the names of each local definition.

3. The selection of the definition containing the next rule to be triggered is done by thread scheduling.
4. The selection of the actual rule within the definition is done by a finite state automaton that tracks the names of messages that have arrived. This automaton also enables the scheduling of the definition in 3.
5. Messages must be routed to their definition, where they are sorted by name and queued.

All this should concern us, because there might be some other implementation issue that is hidden in the use of '$\equiv$' and that could not be resolved like the above. For instance, the asynchronous pi calculus has an equivalence-based semantics that is very similar to that of the join calculus. It has a single reduction rule, up to unguarded contexts and '$\equiv$':

$$\overline{x}\langle\tilde{v}\rangle \mid x(\tilde{y}).P \longrightarrow P\{\tilde{v}/\tilde{y}\}$$

As we have seen in Sect. 1.2, despite the similarities with the join calculus, this semantics does not possess the important locality property for communications on channel $x$ and, in fact, cannot be implemented without global synchronization. Term-based operational semantics may mask such implementation concerns, because by essence they can only describe global computation steps.

In this section, we address this issue by exhibiting a computational model for the join calculus, called the *reflexive chemical abstract machine* (RCHAM), which can be refined into an efficient implementation. Later, we will also use the RCHAM and its extensions to explicitly describe distributed computations. Our model addresses issues 1 and 2 directly, and resorts to structural (actually, denotational) equivalence for issues 3–5, which are too implementation-dependent to be described convincingly in a high-level model: issue 3 would require a model of thread scheduling, and issue 5 would require a model of the data structures used to organize threads; without 3 and 5, issue 4 is meaningless. However, we will show that the structural properties of the RCHAM ensure that issues 3–5 can be properly resolved by an actual implementation.

The state of the RCHAM tracks the various threads that execute a join calculus program. As is apparent from the discussion of 1–5, the RCHAM should contain two kinds of (virtual) threads:

– process threads that create new channels and end by sending a message; they will be represented by join calculus processes $P$.
– definition threads that monitor queued messages and trigger reaction rules; they will be represented by join calculus definitions $D$.

We do not specify the data structures used to organize those terms; instead, we just let the RCHAM state consist of a pair of multisets, one for definition threads, one for process threads.

**Definition 1 (Chemical Solutions).** *A chemical solution $\mathcal{S}$ is a pair $\mathcal{D} \vdash \mathcal{P}$ of a multiset $\mathcal{D} = \{\!|D_1, \ldots, D_m|\!\}$ of join calculus definitions, and a multiset $\mathcal{P} = \{\!|P_1, \ldots, P_n|\!\}$ of join calculus processes.*

| | |
|---|---|
| STR-NULL | $\vdash \mathbf{0} \rightleftharpoons \vdash$ |
| STR-PAR | $\vdash P \mid P' \rightleftharpoons \vdash P,\ P'$ |
| STR-TOP | $\top \vdash \rightleftharpoons \vdash$ |
| STR-AND | $D \wedge D' \vdash \rightleftharpoons D,\ D' \vdash$ |
| STR-DEF | $\vdash \texttt{def}\ D\ \texttt{in}\ P \rightleftharpoons D\sigma \vdash P\sigma$ |
| REACT | $J \triangleright P \vdash J\rho \rightarrow J \triangleright P \vdash P\rho$ |

Side conditions:
in STR-DEF, $\sigma$ substitutes distinct fresh names for the defined names $\mathrm{dv}(D)$;
in REACT, $\rho$ substitutes names for the formal parameters $\mathrm{rv}(J)$.

**Fig. 2.** The reflexive chemical abstract machine (RCHAM)

The intrinsic reordering of multiset elements is the only structural equivalence we will need to deal with issues 3–5. The operational semantics of the RCHAM is defined up to this reordering. Chemical solutions and the RCHAM derive their names from the close parallel between this operational semantics and the reaction rules of molecular chemistry. This chemical metaphor, first coined by Banâtre and Le Métayer [9] and applied to operational semantics by Berry and Boudol [10], can be carried out quite far:

- a message $M = x\langle v_1, \ldots, v_n\rangle$ is an *atom*, its channel name $x$ is its *valence*.
- a parallel composition $M_1 \mid \cdots \mid M_n$ of atoms is a *simple molecule*; any other process $P$ is a *complex molecule*.
- a definition rule $J \triangleright P$ is a *reaction rule* that specifies how a simple molecule may react and turn into a new, complex molecule. The rule actually specifies a reaction pattern, based solely on the valences of the reaction molecule. (And of course, in this virtual world, there is no conservation of mass, and $P$ may be arbitrarily large or small.)
- the multisets composing the RCHAM state are *chemical solutions*; multiset reordering is "Brownian motion".

The RCHAM is "reflexive" because its state contains not only a solution of molecules that can interact, but also the multiset of the rules that define those interactions; furthermore, this multiset can be dynamically extended with new rules for new valences (however, the rules for a given set of valences cannot be inspected, changed, or extended).

Computation on the RCHAM is compactly specified by the six rules given in Fig. 2. By convention, the rule for a computation step shows only the processes and definitions that are involved in the step; the rest of the solution, which remains unchanged, is implicit. For instance, Rule STR-PAR can be stated more explicitly as, for all multisets $\mathcal{D}$ and $\mathcal{P}$, and for all processes $P$ and $P'$,

$$\mathcal{D} \vdash \mathcal{P} \cup \{\!|\ P|P'\ |\!\} \rightleftharpoons \mathcal{D} \vdash \mathcal{P} \cup \{\!|\ P,\ P'\ |\!\}$$

Rule STR-DEF is a bit of an exception: its side condition formally means that $\sigma(\mathrm{dv}(D)) \cap (\mathrm{fv}(\mathcal{D}) \cup \mathrm{fv}(\mathcal{P})) = \emptyset$, where $\mathcal{D} \vdash \mathcal{P}$ is the global state of the RCHAM.

(There are several ways to make this a local operation, such as address space partitioning or random number generation, and it would be ludicrous to hard code a specific implementation in the RCHAM.)
Figure 2 defines two different kinds of computation steps:

- *reduction steps* '$\rightarrow$' describe actual "chemical" interactions, and correspond to join calculus reduction steps;
- *heating steps* '$\rightharpoonup$' describe how molecules interact with the solution itself, and correspond in part to join calculus structural equivalence. Heating is always reversible; the converse '$\rightharpoondown$' steps are called *cooling steps*; the STR-rules in Fig. 2 define both kinds of steps simultaneously, hence the '$\rightleftharpoons$' symbol.

There is not a direct correspondence between '$\rightleftharpoons$' and '$\equiv$': while scope extrusion is obviously linked to STR-DEF, commutativity-associativity of parallel composition is rather a consequence of the multiset reordering. Unlike structural equivalence, heating rules have a direct operational interpretation:

- $\overset{\text{Str-Par}}{\rightharpoonup}$ and $\overset{\text{Str-Null}}{\rightharpoonup}$ correspond to forking and ending process threads (issue 1).
- $\overset{\text{Str-Def}}{\rightharpoonup}$ corresponds to allocating a new address for a definition (issue 2), and forking a new definition thread there.
- $\overset{\text{Str-And}}{\rightharpoonup}$ and $\overset{\text{Str-Top}}{\rightharpoonup}$ correspond to entering rules in the synchronization automaton of a definition (issue 4 in part).

With one exception, cooling steps do not have a similar operational interpretation; rather, they are used to tie back the RCHAM computation to the join calculus syntax. The exception is for $\overset{\text{Str-Par}}{\rightharpoondown}$ steps that aggregate simple molecules whose names all appear in the same join pattern; there $\overset{\text{Str-Par}}{\rightharpoondown}$ steps model the queuing and sorting performed by the synchronization automaton of the definition in which that pattern appears (again, issue 4 in part). We will denote such steps by $\overset{\text{Join}}{\rightharpoondown}$.

These observations, and the connection with the direct join calculus operational semantics are supported by the following theorem (where the reflexive-transitive closure of a relation $\mathcal{R}$ is writtten $\mathcal{R}^*$, as usual).

**Theorem 2.** *Let $P, P'$ and $\mathcal{S}, \mathcal{S}'$ be join calculus processes and* RCHAM *solutions, respectively. Then*

1. $P \equiv P'$ *if and only if* $\vdash P \rightleftharpoons^* \vdash P'$
2. $P \rightarrow P'$ *if and only if* $\vdash P \rightleftharpoons^* \rightarrow \rightleftharpoons^* \vdash P'$
3. $\mathcal{S} \rightleftharpoons^* \mathcal{S}'$ *if and only if* $\mathcal{S} \rightharpoonup^* \rightharpoondown^* \mathcal{S}'$
4. $\mathcal{S} \rightleftharpoons^* \rightarrow \rightleftharpoons^* \mathcal{S}'$ *if and only if* $\mathcal{S} \rightharpoonup^* \overset{\text{Join}^*}{\rightharpoondown} \rightarrow \rightharpoondown^* \mathcal{S}'$

**Corollary 3.** *If $P_0 \rightarrow P_1 \rightarrow \cdots \rightarrow P_n$ is a join calculus computation sequence, then there exist chemical solutions $\mathcal{S}_1, \ldots, \mathcal{S}_n$ such that*

$$\vdash P_0 \rightharpoonup^* \overset{\text{Join}}{\rightharpoondown}{}^* \rightarrow \mathcal{S}_1 \rightharpoonup^* \overset{\text{Join}}{\rightharpoondown}{}^* \rightarrow \cdots \rightharpoonup^* \overset{\text{Join}}{\rightharpoondown}{}^* \rightarrow \mathcal{S}_n$$

*with $\mathcal{S}_i \rightharpoondown^* \vdash P_i$ for $1 \leq i \leq n$.*

We still have to examine issues 3–5, which we have deliberately abstracted. The RCHAM, and chemical machines in general, assumes that the atoms that interact are brought together by random motion. This is fine for theory, but a real implementation cannot be based only on chance. In our case, by Theorem 2, an RCHAM computation relies on this "magical mixing" only for $\stackrel{\text{JOIN}}{\rightarrow}$ and $\stackrel{\text{REACT}}{\rightarrow}$ steps. In both cases, we can show that no magic needs to be invoked:

- $\stackrel{\text{JOIN}}{\rightarrow}$ steps only brings together atoms that have been routed to the definition of their valence, and then only if these valences match one of the finite number of join patterns of that definition.
- $\stackrel{\text{REACT}}{\rightarrow}$ simply selects one matching in the finite set of completed matches that have been assembled at that definition.

Because synchronization decisions for a definition are always based on a finite fixed set of valences, they can be compiled into a finite state automaton; this is the compilation approach used in JoCaml—see [31] for an extensive discussion of this implementation issue.

To keep up with the chemical metaphor, definitions are very much like the *enzymes* of biochemistry: they enable reactions in a sparse solution, by providing a fixed reaction site on which reactants can assemble. It is interesting to note that the chemical machine for the pi calculus, which is in many aspects very similar to the RCHAM, fails the locality property on exactly this count: it relies solely on multiset reordering to assemble senders and receivers on a channel.

## 2 Basic Equivalences

So far, the join calculus is a calculus only by name. We have argued that it is a faithful and elegant *model* for concurrent programming. A true *calculus* implies the ability to do equational reasoning—i.e., to calculate. To achieve this we must equip the join calculus with a proper notion of "equality"; since join calculus expressions model concurrent programs, this "equality" will be a form of *program equivalence*. Unfortunately, finding the "right" equivalence for concurrent programs is a tall order:

1. Two programs $P$ and $Q$ should be equivalent only when they have exactly the same properties; in particular it should always be possible to replace one with the other in a system, without affecting the system's behavior in any visible way. This is a prerequisite, for instance, to justify the optimizations and other program transformations performed by a compiler.
2. Conversely, if $P$ and $Q$ are *not* equivalent, it should always be possible to exhibit a system for which replacing $P$ by $Q$ results in a perceivable change of behavior.
3. The equivalence should be tractable: at least, we need effective proof techniques for establishing identities, and these techniques should also be reasonably complete (from a practical, in not complexity-theoretical viewpoint).

4. The equivalence should generate a rich set of identities, otherwise there won't be much to "calculate" with. We would at least expect some identities that account for asynchrony, as well as some counterpart of the lambda calculus beta equivalence.

Unfortunately, these goals are contradictory. Taken literally, goal 1 would all but force us to use syntactic equality, which certainly fails goal 4. We must thus compromise. We give top priority to goal 4, because it wouldn't make much sense to have a "calculus" without equations. Goal 3 is our next priority, because a calculus which requires an inordinate amount of efforts to establish basic identities wouldn't be too useful. Furthermore, few interesting program equivalences can be proven from equational reasoning alone, even with a reasonable set of identities; so it is important that reasoning from first principles be tractable.

Goal 1 thus only comes in third position, which means that we must compromise on the definition of soundness: we will consider equivalences that do not preserve all observable properties, i.e., that only work at a certain level of *abstraction*. Common examples of such abstractions, for sequential programs, are observing runtime only up to a constant factor ($O(\cdot)$ complexity), not observing runtime at all (only termination), or even observing only return values (partial correctness). Obviously, we must very carefully spell out the set of properties that are preserved, for it determines how the equations of calculus (and to some extent, the calculus itself) can be used.

Even though it comes last on our priority list, we should not neglect goal 2. Because of the abstractions it involves, a correctness proof based on a formal model provides only a relative guarantee. Hence such a proof is often more useful when if *fails*, because this allows one to *find errors* in the system. Goal 2 is to make sure that all such failures can be traced to actual errors, and not to some odd technical property of the equivalence that is used. The reason goal 2 comes last is that the proof process has to be tractable in the first place for this "debugging" approach to make any practical sense[3].

The priorities we have set are not absolute, and therefore it makes sense to consider several equivalences, that strike different compromises between goals 1–4. We will study two of them in subsections 2.1 and 2.4: *may testing*, which optimizes goals 4 and 2, at the expense of goals 1 and 3, and *bisimilarity equivalence* (which we will often simplify to *bisimilarity* in the following), which sacrifices goal 2 to get a better balance between the other goals. May testing is in fact coarser than bisimilarity, so that in practice one can attempt to prove a bisimilarity, and in case of failure "degrade" to may testing to try to get a good counterexample. In sections 3 and 4 we will study three other equivalences; the complete hierarchy is summarized in Fig. 3 on page 311.

## 2.1 May Testing Equivalence

The first equivalence we consider follows rigidly from the priorities we set above: it is the coarsest equivalence that reasonably preserves observations, and it also

[3] Also, a clear successful proof will identify the features that actually make the system work, and often point out simplifications that could be made safely.

turns out to have reasonable proof techniques, which we will present in subsections 2.2 and 2.3. Moreover, may testing fulfills goal 2: when may testing equivalence fails, there exists a *finite counter-example trace.*

May testing is the equivalence that preserves all the properties that can be described in terms of a finite number of interactions (convergence in the lambda calculus [39], message exchanges in the join calculus), otherwise known as *safety properties.* This restriction may seem severe, but it follows rather directly from the choice of the syntax and semantics of the join calculus. As we noted in Sect. 1.5, we deliberately chose to abstract away the scheduling algorithm. In the absence of any hypothesis on scheduling, it is in practice impossible to decide most complexity, termination, or even progress properties. Moreover, such *liveness* properties are just abstractions of the *timing* properties which the system really needs to satisfy; and timing properties can be obtained fairly reliably by measuring the actual implementation. So, it makes practical sense for now to exclude liveness properties; but we will reconsider this decision in sections 2.4 and 3.2, using abstract scheduling assumptions.

The "testing" in may testing refers to the way safety properties are characterized in the formal definition of the may testing equivalence. We represent a safety property $\mathcal{P}$ by a *test* $T(\cdot)$, such that a process $P$ has property $\mathcal{P}$ if and only if $T(P)$ *succeeds.* Hence, $P$ and $Q$ will be equivalent if, for any test $T$, $T(P)$ succeeds iff $T(Q)$ succeeds.

To make all this formal, we need to fix a formal syntax for tests, and a formal semantics for "succeeds". We restricted ourselves to properties that can be described in terms of finite message exchanges, which can certainly be carried out by join calculus programs, or rather *contexts.* Since the join calculus contains the lambda calculus, we can boldly invoke Church's thesis and assume that a test $T(\cdot)$ can always be represented by a pair $(C[\cdot], x)$ of a join calculus *evaluation context*, and channel name $x$, which $C[\cdot]$ uses to signal success: $T(P)$ succeeds iff $C[P]$ *may* send an $x\langle\dots\rangle$ message.

**Evaluation Contexts.** Evaluation contexts are simply join calculus processes with a "hole" $[\cdot]_S$ that is not inside a definition (not *guarded*)—they are called static contexts in [35]. They are defined by the following grammar:

| | |
|---|---|
| $C[\cdot]_S ::=$ | evaluation contexts |
| $\quad [\cdot]_S$ | hole |
| $\quad \mid\; P \mid C[\cdot]_S$ | left parallel composition |
| $\quad \mid\; C[\cdot]_S \mid P$ | right parallel composition |
| $\quad \mid\; \mathtt{def}\ D\ \mathtt{in}\ C[\cdot]_S$ | process/function definition |

Formally, a context and its hole are *sorted* with a set $S$ of *captured names.* If $P$ is any process, $C[P]_S$ is the process obtained by replacing the hole in $C[\cdot]_S$ by $P$, after alpha converting bound names *not in* $S$ of $C[\cdot]_S$ that clash with $\mathrm{fv}(P)$. Provided $S$ contains enough channel names, for example all the channel names bound in $C[\cdot]_S$, or all the channel names free in $P$, this means replacing $[\cdot]_S$ by $P$ without any conversion whatsoever. We will often drop the $S$ subscript in this common case.

The structural equivalence and reduction relations are extended to contexts $C[\cdot]_S$ of the same sort $S$, with the proviso that alpha conversion of names in $S$ is not allowed. The substitution relation is similarly extended to contexts: $C[C'[\cdot]_{S'}]_S$ is a context of type $S'$.

By convention, we only allow ourselves to write a reduction $C[P]_S \to C'[P']_{S'}$ when the identity of the hole is preserved—that is, when in fact we have

$$C[P \mid [\cdot]_{S\cap S'}]_S \to C'[P' \mid [\cdot]_{S\cap S'}]_{S'}$$

Similarly, $C[P] \to C'[P']$ really means that $C[P]_S \to C'[P']_{S'}$ for some suitably large sets $S$ and $S'$.

Evaluation contexts are a special case of *program contexts* $P[\cdot]$, which are simply process terms with a (possibly guarded) hole. An equivalence relation $\mathcal{R}$ such that $Q\ \mathcal{R}\ Q'$ implies $P[Q]\ \mathcal{R}\ P[Q']$ for any program context $P[\cdot]$ is called a *congruence*; if $\mathcal{R}$ is only a preorder then it is called a *precongruence.* A congruence can be used to describe equations between subprograms. All of our equivalences are congruences for evaluation contexts, which means they can describe equations between subsystems, and most are in fact congruences (the exception only occurs for an extension of the join calculus with name testing).

**Output Observation.** The success of a test is signaled by the output of a specific message; this event can be defined syntactically.

**Definition 4 (Output predicates).** *Let $P$ be a join calculus process and $x$ be a channel name.*

- *$P \downarrow_x$ iff $P = C[x\langle\tilde{v}\rangle]_S$ for some tuple $\tilde{v}$ of names and some evaluation context $C[\cdot]_S$ that does not capture $x$—that is, such that $x \notin S$.*
- *$P \Downarrow_x$ iff $P \to^* P'$ for some $P'$ such that $P' \downarrow_x$.*

*The predicate $\downarrow_x$ tests syntactically for immediate output on $x$, and is called the* strong barb on $x$. *The* (weak) barb on $x$ *predicate $\Downarrow_x$ only tests for the possibility of output.*

The notions of barbs as minimal observations of processes were introduced by Milner and Sangiorgi [38]. The strong barb can also be defined using structural equivalence, as $P \downarrow_x$ if and only if $P \equiv \texttt{def}\ D\ \texttt{in}\ Q \mid x\langle\tilde{v}\rangle$ for some $D, Q, \tilde{v}$ such that $x \notin \mathrm{dv}(D)$.

We say that a relation $\mathcal{R}$ *preserves barbs* when, for all $x$, $P\ \mathcal{R}\ Q$ and $P \Downarrow_x$ implies $Q \Downarrow_x$. By the above, structural equivalence preserves barbs.

**May Testing.** With the preceding definitions, we can easily define may testing:

**Definition 5 (May testing preorder and equivalence).** *Let $P, Q$ be join calculus processes, and let $C[\cdot]_S$ range over evaluation contexts.*

- *$P \sqsubseteq_{\mathrm{may}} Q$ when, for any $C[\cdot]_S$ and $x$, $C[P]_S \Downarrow_x$ implies $C[Q]_S \Downarrow_x$.*
- *$P \simeq_{\mathrm{may}} Q$ when, for any $C[\cdot]_S$ and $x$, $C[P]_S \Downarrow_x$ iff $C[Q]_S \Downarrow_x$.*

*The preorder $\sqsubseteq_{\mathrm{may}}$ is called the may testing preorder, and the equivalence $\simeq_{\mathrm{may}}$ is called the may testing equivalence.*

The may testing preorder $P \sqsubseteq_{\text{may}} Q$ indicates that $P$'s behaviors are included in those of $Q$, and can thus be used to formalize "$P$ implements $Q$". Clearly, the equivalence $\simeq_{\text{may}} = \sqsubseteq_{\text{may}} \cap \sqsupseteq_{\text{may}}$ is the largest symmetric subrelation of $\sqsubseteq_{\text{may}}$.

As an easy example of may testing, we note that structural equivalence is finer than may testing equivalence: $P \equiv Q$ implies $C[P]_S \equiv C[Q]_S$, and $\equiv$ preserves barbs. By the same token, we note that we can drop the $S$ sorts in the definition of $\simeq_{\text{may}}$: $C[\cdot]_S, x$, $C'[\cdot]_S, x$ test the same property if $C[\cdot]_S \equiv C'[\cdot]_S$, so it is enough to consider contexts where no alpha conversion is needed to substitute $P$ or $Q$.

As a first non-trivial example, let us show a simple case of beta conversion:

$$\texttt{def}\ x\langle y\rangle \triangleright P\ \texttt{in}\ C[x\langle u\rangle]_u \simeq_{\text{may}} \texttt{def}\ x\langle y\rangle \triangleright P\ \texttt{in}\ C[P\{^u/_y\}]_u$$

For any test $C'[\cdot]_S, t$ we let $S' = S \cup \{x, u\}$ and define

$$C''[\cdot]_{S'} \stackrel{\text{def}}{=} C'[\texttt{def}\ x\langle y\rangle \triangleright P\ \texttt{in}\ C[[\cdot]_{S'}]_u]_S$$

then we show that $C''[x\langle u\rangle]_{S'} \Downarrow_t$ iff $C''[P\{^u/_y\}]_{S'} \Downarrow_t$. The "if" is obvious, since $C''[x\langle u\rangle]_{S'} \rightarrow C''[P\{^u/_y\}]_{S'}$. (More generally, we have $\rightarrow\ \subset\ \sqsupseteq_{\text{may}}$.) For the converse, suppose that $C''[x\langle u\rangle]_{S'} \rightarrow^* Q \downarrow_t$. If the reduction does not involve the $x\langle u\rangle$ message, then $C''[R]_{S'} \Downarrow_t$ for any $R$—including $R = P\{^u/_y\}$. Otherwise, the definition that uses $x\langle u\rangle$ can only be $x\langle y\rangle \triangleright P$, hence we have

$$C''[x\langle u\rangle]_{S'} \rightarrow^* C'''[x\langle u\rangle]_{S'} \rightarrow C'''[P\{^u/_y\}]_{S'} \rightarrow^* Q \downarrow_t$$

whence we also have $C''[P\{^u/_y\}] \rightarrow^* C'''[P\{^u/_y\}]_{S'} \Downarrow_t$.

The same proof can be carried out if $x\langle u\rangle$ appears in a general context $Q[x\langle u\rangle]$, using the notion of general context reduction from Sect. 2.3. This gives *strong* beta equivalence, for we have

$$\begin{array}{rl}
& \texttt{let}\ f(x) = E\ \texttt{in}\ Q[\texttt{let}\ z = f(u)\ \texttt{in}\ R] \\
\stackrel{\text{def}}{=} & \texttt{let}\ f(x) = E\ \texttt{in}\ Q[\texttt{def}\ \kappa\langle z\rangle \triangleright R\ \texttt{in}\ f\langle u, \kappa\rangle] \\
\simeq_{\text{may}} & \texttt{let}\ f(x) = E\ \texttt{in}\ Q[\texttt{def}\ \kappa\langle z\rangle \triangleright R\ \texttt{in}\ \texttt{let}\ v = E\{^u/_x\}\ \texttt{in}\ \kappa\langle v\rangle] \\
\simeq_{\text{may}} & \texttt{let}\ f(x) = E\ \texttt{in}\ Q[\texttt{def}\ \kappa\langle z\rangle \triangleright R\ \texttt{in}\ \texttt{let}\ v = E\{^u/_x\}\ \texttt{in}\ R\{^v/_z\}] \\
\equiv & \texttt{let}\ f(x) = E\ \texttt{in}\ Q[(\texttt{def}\ \kappa\langle z\rangle \triangleright R\ \texttt{in}\ \mathbf{0}) \mid \texttt{let}\ z = E\{^u/_x\}\ \texttt{in}\ R] \\
\simeq_{\text{may}} & \texttt{let}\ f(x) = E\ \texttt{in}\ Q[\texttt{let}\ z = E\{^u/_x\}\ \texttt{in}\ R]
\end{array}$$

since obviously $\texttt{def}\ D\ \texttt{in}\ \mathbf{0} \simeq_{\text{may}} \mathbf{0}$ for any $D$.

## 2.2 Trace Observation

We defined may testing in terms of evaluation contexts and barbs. This allowed us to stay as close as possible to our intuitive description, and exhibit compliance with goals 4 and 1. However, this style of definition does not really suit our other two goals.

In general, proving that $P \sqsubseteq_{\text{may}} Q$ can be quite intricate, because it involves reasoning about $C[P]_S \Downarrow_x$—an arbitrary long reduction in an arbitrarily large context. This double quantification may not be much of an issue for showing simple, general reduction laws such as the above, but it can quickly become unmanageable if one wants to show, say, the correctness of a given finite-state protocol. Moreover it all but precludes the use of automated model-checking tools.

If $P \sqsubseteq_{\mathrm{may}} Q$ fails, then there must be a test $C[\cdot]_S, x$ that witnesses this failure. However the existence of this $C[\cdot]_S, x$ only partly fulfills goal 2, because it illustrates the problem with the programs $P$ and $Q$ only indirectly, by the means of a third, unrelated program. Moreover, the definition of $\sqsubseteq_{\mathrm{may}}$ gives no clue for deriving this witness from a failing proof attempt.

In this section we present an alternative characterization of $\sqsubseteq_{\mathrm{may}}$ and $\simeq_{\mathrm{may}}$ that mitigates the proof problem, and largely solves the counter-example problem. This characterization formalizes the fact, stated in Sect. 2.1, that $\simeq_{\mathrm{may}}$ preserves properties based on *finite* interaction sequences. We formalize such sequences as *traces*, define the *trace-set* of a process $P$, and then show that $\sqsubseteq_{\mathrm{may}}$ corresponds to the inclusion of trace-sets, and $\simeq_{\mathrm{may}}$ to their equality.

Informally, a trace is simply an input/output sequence; however we must account for the higher-order nature of the join calculus, and this makes the definition more involved.

**Definition 6 (Traces).** *A trace $T$ is a finite sequence $J_0 \triangleright M_0, \ldots, J_n \triangleright M_n$ such that*

1. *For each element $J_i \triangleright M_i$ of the trace, $M_i$ is a single message $x_i\langle y_{i1}, \ldots, y_{il_i}\rangle$, and $J_i$ is either $\mathbf{0}$ or a join pattern.*
2. *The variables $y_{ik}$ and in $\mathrm{rv}(J_j)$ are all pairwise distinct.*
3. *Each channel name defined by $J_j$ is a $y_{ik}$ for some $i < j$ (hence, $J_0 = \mathbf{0}$).*
4. *Dually, $x_i \neq y_{jk}$ for any $j, k$, and $x_i \notin \mathrm{rv}(J_j)$ for any $j > i$.*

*We set $T_I(i) = \{y_{jk} \mid 0 \leq j < i, 1 \leq k \leq l_j\}$, so that condition 3 can be stated as $\mathrm{dv}(J_i) \subseteq T_I(i)$.*

Intuitively, to each element $J_i \triangleright M_i$ of a trace should correspond a reduction that behaves (roughly) as the join definition $J_i \triangleright M_i$: that is, the reduction should input $J_i$ and output $M_i$. The names in the $T_I(i)$ and the $\mathrm{rv}(J_i)$ are formally bound in the trace. In matching a process run, the $\mathrm{rv}(J_i)$ names should be substituted by fresh names, and the $y_{jk}$ by the arguments of the actual outputs.

**Definition 7 (Trace sets).** *A trace $T = J_0 \triangleright M_0, \ldots, J_n \triangleright M_n$ is allowed by a process $P$ (notation $P \models T$), if there is a substitution $\sigma$ that maps names in the $\mathrm{rv}(J_i)$ to distinct names not in $\mathrm{fv}(P)$, and names in the $T_I(i)$ to channel names, and a sequence $C_i[\cdot]_{S_i}$ of evaluation contexts of sort $S_i = \sigma(T_I(i))$, such that $P \equiv C_0[\mathbf{0}]_\emptyset$ and*

$$C_i[J_i\sigma]_{S_i} \rightarrow^* C_{i+1}[M_i\sigma]_{S_{i+1}}$$

*for each $i$, $0 \leq i \leq n$. Note that according to the convention we set in 2.1, this notation implies that the identity of the hole is preserved during the reduction.*

*The trace-set $\mathrm{Tr}(P)$ of $P$ is the set of all its allowed traces.*

$$\mathrm{Tr}(P) = \{T \mid P \models T\}$$

The main motivation for this rather complex set of definitions is the following result (see also [28]).

**Theorem 8 (Trace equivalence).** *For any two processes $P$ and $Q$, we have $P \sqsubseteq_{\text{may}} Q$ if and only if* $\text{Tr}(P) \subseteq \text{Tr}(Q)$, *and consequently $P \simeq_{\text{may}} Q$ if and only if* $\text{Tr}(P) = \text{Tr}(Q)$.

This theorem allows us to reach goal 2: if $P \sqsubseteq_{\text{may}} Q$ fails, then there must be some finite input/output trace that is allowed by $P$ but that is barred by $Q$. In principle, we can look for this trace by enumerating all the traces of $P$ and $Q$. This search can also be turned into a proof technique for $P \sqsubseteq_{\text{may}} Q$ that does not involve trying out arbitrary large contexts, and may be more amenable to model-checking. Note, however, that the technique still involves arbitrary long traces, and in that sense fails to meet goal 3.

As an application, let us prove the correctness of the compilation of a three-way join into two two-way joins:

$$\begin{aligned} & \textbf{def } x\langle\rangle \mid y\langle\rangle \triangleright t\langle\rangle \wedge t\langle\rangle \mid z\langle\rangle \triangleright u\langle\rangle \textbf{ in } v\langle x,y,z\rangle \\ \simeq_{\text{may}} & \textbf{ def } x\langle\rangle \mid y\langle\rangle \mid z\langle\rangle \triangleright u\langle\rangle \textbf{ in } v\langle x,y,z\rangle \end{aligned}$$

For either terms, a trace must start with $\mathbf{0} \triangleright v\langle x,y,z\rangle$, and thereafter consist of outputs of $u\langle\rangle$ after inputs of $x\langle\rangle$, $y\langle\rangle$, $z\langle\rangle$. In either case, there must be at least $n$ $x\langle\rangle$s, $y\langle\rangle$s, and $z\langle\rangle$s in $J_1,\ldots,J_n$, so both terms have exactly the same set of traces.

## 2.3 Simulation and Coinduction

While in many respects an improvement over the basic definition of $\simeq_{\text{may}}$, the trace sets do not really help with the real difficulty of $\simeq_{\text{may}}$ proofs—the quantification over arbitrary long reduction sequences that is hidden in the definition of barbs $\Downarrow_x$. Because the shape of a term changes during a reduction step, it is very hard to reason on the effect of several successive reduction steps. The kind of offhand argument we used for our first examples often turn out to be incorrect in more complex cases.

To do a rigorous equivalence proof, it is necessary to analyze reduction steps one case at a time. In many calculi this analysis is based on structural induction on the syntax, but in the join calculus this would be inappropriate because of structural equivalence. Hence we base our analysis on the triggered rule and the set of messages that match its pattern, since those are invariant under structural equivalence.

In this section we will present yet another characterization of may testing, which this time will be appropriate for step-by-step analysis. To avoid the complexity of higher-order traces, we will revert to modeling interaction with arbitrary evaluation contexts; those barely add to the overall complexity of a proof because interaction with them can be highly stylized, as Theorem 8 shows.

In order to formulate our new characterization, we turn to the technique of *coinductive definition*, which has been the power horse of most concurrent program equivalences. This simply means that we invoke Tarski's theorem to define an equivalence $\mathcal{E}$ as the greatest fixed point of a monotonic functional $\mathcal{F}$. The beauty of this definition is that it immediately gives us a generic method for proving $P \mathrel{\mathcal{E}} Q$: $P \mathrel{\mathcal{E}} Q$ iff we can find some *subfixpoint* relation $\mathcal{R}$ such that $P \mathrel{\mathcal{R}} Q$, and that for any $P', Q'$, $P' \mathrel{\mathcal{R}} Q'$ implies $P' \mathrel{\mathcal{F}(\mathcal{R})} Q'$.

To get a monotonic $\mathcal{F}$, we rely on definitions of the form "$P \mathrel{\mathcal{F}(\mathcal{R})} Q$ iff $\mathcal{P}(P, Q, \mathcal{R})$" where $\mathcal{R}$ appears only in positive $P' \mathrel{\mathcal{R}} Q'$ subformulas in $\mathcal{P}(P, Q, \mathcal{R})$. In this case a relation $\mathcal{R}$ is a subfixpoint of $\mathcal{F}$ iff $P \mathrel{\mathcal{R}} Q$ implies $\mathcal{P}(P, Q, \mathcal{R})$, a property which we will denote by $\mathcal{P}^*(\mathcal{R})$. As $\cdot^*$ distributes over conjunction, we will generally define our equivalences by a conjunction of such properties: "$\mathcal{E}$ is the coarsest relation such that $\mathcal{P}_1^*(\mathcal{E})$ and ... and $\mathcal{P}_n^*(\mathcal{E})$". In fact, we have already encountered such $\mathcal{P}_i^*$s:

1. Barb preservation: "if $P \mathrel{\mathcal{R}} Q$ then for any $x$, $P \Downarrow_x$ implies $Q \Downarrow_x$".
2. Symmetry: "if $P \mathrel{\mathcal{R}} Q$ then $Q \mathrel{\mathcal{R}} P$".
3. Precongruence for evaluation contexts:
   "if $P \mathrel{\mathcal{R}} Q$ then for any $C[\cdot]_S$, $C[P]_S \mathrel{\mathcal{R}} C[Q]_S$".

From this observation, we get our first coinductive definition of $\simeq_{\text{may}}$: it is the greatest symmetric relation that preserves barbs and is a congruence for evaluation contexts. Note that property 1 really means that $\mathcal{R}$ is contained in a fixed relation, in this case the *barb inclusion* relation $\sqsubseteq_{\Downarrow}$, defined by "$P \sqsubseteq_{\Downarrow} Q$ iff for any $x$ $P \Downarrow_x$ implies $Q \Downarrow_x$".

This first characterization of $\simeq_{\text{may}}$ merely rephrases Definition 5. To improve on this, it will prove extremely convenient to introduce diagrammatic notation. To describe a property $\mathcal{P}^*$, we lay out the relations occurring in $\mathcal{P}^*$ in a two-dimensional diagram. We indicate negatively occurring, universally-quantified relations by solid lines, and positively occurring, existentially quantified relations by dashed lines. For instance, property 3 is expressed by the diagram

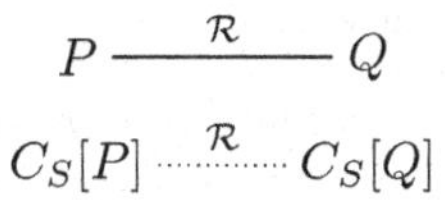

$$\begin{array}{ccc} P & \overset{\mathcal{R}}{\longrightarrow} & Q \\ C_S[P] & \overset{\mathcal{R}}{\cdots\cdots} & C_S[Q] \end{array}$$

The main property that we are interested in is commutation with the reduction relation $\rightarrow^*$, which is called *simulation*. (Simulations were introduced by Park [42] and applied to CCS by Milner [34]; see also [49].)

**Definition 9 (Simulation).** *A relation $\mathcal{R}$ between join calculus terms is a simulation if for any $P, P', Q$, if $P \rightarrow^* P'$ and $P \mathrel{\mathcal{R}} Q$, there is a term $Q'$ such that $Q \rightarrow^* Q'$ and $P' \mathrel{\mathcal{R}} Q'$. In a diagram:*

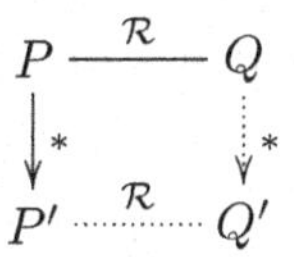

$$\begin{array}{ccc} P & \overset{\mathcal{R}}{\longrightarrow} & Q \\ \downarrow * & & \vdots * \\ P' & \overset{\mathcal{R}}{\cdots\cdots} & Q' \end{array}$$

What we call here simulation is often called the *weak simulation property* in the literature, a simulation being a relation that commutes with single-step reductions. Counting steps makes no sense in the abstract, asynchronous setting of the join calculus, so we simply drop the "weak" adjective in the rest of these notes.

Let us say that a relation $\mathcal{R}$ preserves *immediate* barbs if $P \mathrel{\mathcal{R}} Q$ and $P \downarrow_x$ implies $Q \Downarrow_x$. We can now use the simulation property to replace barb preservation by immediate barb preservation in the coinductive characterization of $\sqsubseteq_{\text{may}}$.

**Theorem 10.** *May testing preorder is a simulation, hence it is also the greatest simulation that is an evaluation context precongruence and that preserves immediate barbs.*

This is an improvement, since to consider immediate barbs it is not necessary to consider reduction steps. It would appear that we have only pushed the problem over to the simulation property, but this is not the case, as by a simple tiling argument we have

**Theorem 11.** *A relation $\mathcal{R}$ is a simulation iff*

$$\begin{array}{ccc} P & \overset{\mathcal{R}}{\longrule} & Q \\ \downarrow & & \vdots\,{*} \\ P' & \overset{\equiv\mathcal{R}}{\cdots\cdots} & Q' \end{array}$$

We consider a single step, rather than a series of steps on the left. The '$\equiv$' allows us to study reductions only up to structural equivalence. To illustrate the power of this new characterization, we establish a simple context lemma:

**Theorem 12.** *May testing preorder is a precongruence, and may-testing equivalence is a (full) congruence.*

We begin with the following lemma

**Lemma 13.** *For any (well-typed) $P$, $x$, $y$, and any tuple $\tilde{v}$ of distinct variables that matches the arity of both $x$ and $y$, we have:*

$$\texttt{def } x\langle\tilde{v}\rangle \triangleright y\langle\tilde{v}\rangle \texttt{ in } P \simeq_{\text{may}} P\{^{y}/_{x}\}$$

*Hence, both $\simeq_{\text{may}}$ and $\sqsubseteq_{\text{may}}$ are closed under substitution.*

The conclusion of lemma 13 also holds without the arity assumption, but with a more involved proof. Here, we just take a candidate relation $\mathcal{S}$ consisting of all pairs of processes structurally equivalent to $C[\texttt{def } x\langle\tilde{v}\rangle \triangleright y\langle\tilde{v}\rangle \texttt{ in } P]_S$ or $C[P\{^{y}/_{x}\}]_S$, for some $P, x, y, \tilde{v}$ satisfying the hypotheses of the lemma. Now $\mathcal{S}$ is obviously a congruence for evaluation contexts. It trivially preserves strong barbs $\downarrow_z$ in $C[\cdot]_S$ or even in $P$ if $z \neq x$, and if $P\{^{y}/_{x}\} \downarrow_y$ because $P \downarrow_x$, then $(\texttt{def } x\langle\tilde{v}\rangle \triangleright y\langle\tilde{v}\rangle \texttt{ in } P) \Downarrow_y$.

To show that $\mathcal{S}$ is a simulation, consider a reduction $C[\texttt{def } x\langle\tilde{v}\rangle \triangleright y\langle\tilde{v}\rangle \texttt{ in } P]_S \to Q$; we must have $Q \equiv C'[\texttt{def } x\langle\tilde{v}\rangle \triangleright y\langle\tilde{v}\rangle \texttt{ in } P']_{S'}$. If the rule used is

$x\langle\tilde{v}\rangle \triangleright y\langle\tilde{v}\rangle$, then $C'[P'\{^y/_x\}]_{S'} = C[P\{^y/_x\}]_S$, else $C[P\{^y/_x\}]_S \rightarrow C'[P'\{^y/_x\}]_{S'}$. Conversely, if $C[P\{^y/_x\}]_S \rightarrow Q$, and we are not in the first case above, then it can only be because the rule used matches some $y$s that have replaced $x$s. But then the $x\langle\tilde{v}\rangle \triangleright y\langle\tilde{v}\rangle$ can be used to perform these replacements, and bring us back to the first case. Thus $\mathcal{S} \subseteq \simeq_{\text{may}}$, from which we deduce lemma 13.

To establish theorem 12, we need a careful definition of a multi-holed general context. A general context $P[\cdot]_S$ of sort $S$ is a term which may contain several holes $[\cdot]_\sigma$, where $\sigma$ is a substitution with domain $S$; different holes may have different $\sigma$s. Bindings, alpha conversion, structural equivalence, and reduction are extended to general contexts, by taking $\text{fv}([\cdot]_\sigma) = \sigma(S)$. The term $P[Q]_S$ is obtained by replacing every hole $[\cdot]_\sigma$ in $P[\cdot]_S$ by $Q\sigma$, after alpha converting bound names in $P[\cdot]_S$ to avoid capturing names in $\text{fv}(Q) \setminus S$.

Consider the candidate relation

$$\mathcal{R} \stackrel{\text{def}}{=} \{(P[Q]_S, R) \mid Q \sqsubseteq_{\text{may}} Q' \text{ and } P[Q']_S \sqsubseteq_{\text{may}} R\}$$

The relation $\mathcal{R}$ is trivially closed under evaluation contexts. Let $P'[\cdot]_S$ be obtained by replacing all unguarded holes $[\cdot]_\sigma$ in $P[\cdot]_S$ with $Q\sigma$, and similarly $P''[\cdot]_S$ be obtained by replacing $[\cdot]_\sigma$ with $Q'\sigma$. Then $P'[Q']_S \sqsubseteq_{\text{may}} P''[Q']_S = P[Q']_S$ by several applications of Lemma 13, hence $P'[Q']_S \sqsubseteq_{\text{may}} R$.

If $P[Q]_S = P'[Q]_S \downarrow_x$, the $x\langle\cdots\rangle$ is in $P'[\cdot]_S$, so $P'[Q']_S \downarrow_x$, hence $R \Downarrow_x$. Similarly, any reduction step in $P'[Q]_S$ must actually take place in $P'[\cdot]_S$, i.e., it must be a $P'[Q]_S \rightarrow P'''[Q]_S$ step with $P'[\cdot]_S \rightarrow P'''[\cdot]_S$. Thus we have $P'[Q']_S \rightarrow P'''[Q']_S$, hence $R \rightarrow^* R'$ for some $R'$ such that $P'''[Q']_S \sqsubseteq_{\text{may}} R'$, hence such that $P'''[Q]_S \mathrel{\mathcal{R}} R'$. So $\mathcal{R}$ is also a simulation, hence $\mathcal{R} \subset \sqsubseteq_{\text{may}}$.

## 2.4 Bisimilarity Equivalence

Despite our success with the proofs of Lemma 13 and Theorem 12, in general the coinductive approach will not always allow us to avoid reasoning about arbitrarily long traces. This line of reasoning has only been hidden under the asymmetry of the simulation condition. This condition allows us to prove that $P \sqsubseteq_{\text{may}} Q$ with the candidate relation $\mathcal{R} = \{(P', Q) \mid P \rightarrow^* P'\}$, which is a simulation iff $P \sqsubseteq_{\text{may}} Q$. But of course, proving that $\mathcal{R}$ is a simulation is no easier than proving that $P \sqsubseteq_{\text{may}} Q$—it requires reasoning at once about all sequence $P \rightarrow^* P'$. So to really attain goal 3 we need to use a different equivalence.

There is, however, a more fundamental reason to be dissatisfied with $\simeq_{\text{may}}$: it only passes goal 1 for a very restrictive notion of soundness, by ignoring any sort of liveness properties. Thus it can label as "correct" programs that are grossly erroneous. For example, one can define in the join calculus an "internal choice" process $\bigoplus_{i \in I} P_i$ between different processes $P_i$, by

$$\texttt{def } \bigwedge_{i \in I} (\tau\langle\rangle \triangleright P_i) \texttt{ in } \tau\langle\rangle$$

Let us also write $P_1 \oplus P_2$ for $\bigoplus_{i=1}^{2} P_i$. Then we have the following for any $P$:

$$P \oplus \mathbf{0} \simeq_{\text{may}} P$$

This equation states that a program that randomly decides whether to work at all or not is equivalent to one that always works! In this example, the "error" is obvious; however, may testing similarly ignores a large class of quite subtle and malign errors called *deadlock* errors. Deadlocks occur when a subset of components of a system stop working altogether, because each is waiting for input from another before proceeding. This type of error is rather easy to commit, hard to detect by testing, and often has catastrophic consequences.

For nondeterministic sequential system, this problem is dealt with by complementing may testing with a *must* testing, which adds a "must" predicate to the barbs:

$$P \,\Box\!\!\downarrow_x \stackrel{\text{def}}{=} \text{if } P \rightarrow^* P' \not\rightarrow \text{, then } P' \downarrow_x$$

However, must testing is not very interesting for asynchronous concurrent computations, because it confuses all diverging behaviors. We refer to [28] for a detailed study of may and must testing in the join calculus.

It turns out that there is a technical solution to both of these problems, if one is willing to compromise on goal 2: simply require symmetry and simulation together.

**Definition 14.** *A* bisimulation *is a simulation $\mathcal{R}$ whose converse $\mathcal{R}^{-1}$ is also a simulation.*

*The coarsest bisimulation that respects (immediate) barbs is denoted $\dot{\approx}$.*

*The coarsest bisimulation that respects (immediate) barbs and is also a congruence for evaluation context is called* bisimilarity equivalence, *and denoted $\approx$.*

When no confusion arises, we will simply refer to $\approx$ as "bisimilarity". The definition of bisimilarity avoids dummy simulation candidates : since $\mathcal{R}^{-1}$ is also a simulation, $P \mathrel{\mathcal{R}} Q$ implies that $P$ and $Q$ must advance in lockstep, making exactly the same choices at the same time. The erroneous $P \oplus \mathbf{0} \approx P$ is avoided in a similar way. This equation can only hold if $P \rightarrow^* Q \approx \mathbf{0}$, that is, if $P$ is already a program that may not work at all.

In fact, we will show in Sect. 3.2 that under a very strong assumption of scheduling fairness, $\approx$ preserves liveness properties, so we meet goal 1 fairly well. However there are still classes of errors that we miss entirely, notably *livelocks*, i.e., situations where components careen endlessly sending useless messages to themselves, rather than producing useful output. However, we do detect livelocks where the components can *only* send useless messages to themselves, and in the cases where they *could* send useful output, randomized scheduling usually will avoid such livelocks.

Unfortunately, the previously perfect situation with respect to goals 4 and 2 is now compromised. While all the examples of Sect. 2.1 and Sect. 2.3 are actually valid for $\approx$, the three-way to two-way join compilation of Sect. 2.2 now fails to check if we add arguments to the $x$, $y$, and $z$ messages, and use several such messages with different values. The three-way join cannot emulate the decision of the two-way merger to group two $x$ and $y$ values, without deciding which $z$ value will go with them. Nonetheless the compilation is arguably correct, and does preserve all liveness properties; but $\approx$ fails, and the reasons for the failure are only technical.

## 2.5 Bisimulation Proof Techniques

The basic definition of bisimulation give only a rough idea of how to prove a bisimilarity equation. There are a number of now well-established techniques for showing bisimilarity, notably to deal with contexts and captures, and to "close" large diagrams.

First of all, let us consider the problem of quantifying over arbitrary contexts. In Sect. 4 we present an extension of the join calculus, and a new equivalence, that avoid the need to consider arbitrary evaluation contexts altogether. For the time being, let us show that they are really not much of an issue. Suppose we want to show $P \approx Q$; then we should have $(P, Q)$ in our candidate relation, as well as all terms $(C[P], C[Q])$. Now, as soon as $P$ (and $Q$) starts exchanging messages with $C[\cdot]$, $C[\cdot]$ and $P$ will become intermingled. However, if we use structural equivalence to decompose $C[\cdot]$, $P$, and $Q$, it becomes clear that the situation is not so intricate : we can take $C[\cdot] \equiv \texttt{def}\ D_C\ \texttt{in}\ (M_C \mid [\cdot])$, $P \equiv \texttt{def}\ D_P\ \texttt{in}\ M_P$, $Q \equiv \texttt{def}\ D_Q\ \texttt{in}\ M_Q$, where $M_C$, $M_P$, $M_Q$ are parallel compositions of messages, and all bound names are fresh, except that $D_C$ may define some free names of $P$ and $Q$. With those notations, we see that elements of $R$ will have the shape

$$(\texttt{def}\ D_C \wedge D_P\ \texttt{in}\ (M_C \mid M_P), \texttt{def}\ D_C \wedge D_Q\ \texttt{in}\ (M_C \mid M_Q))$$

To allow for extrusions from $P$ to $C[\cdot]$, we simply allow $D_C$ and $M_C$ to contain channel names that have been exported by $P$ and $Q$, and are thus defined in both $D_P$ and $D_Q$; this may require applying different substitutions $\sigma_P$ and $\sigma_Q$ to $D_C$ and $M_C$, to account for different names in $P$ and $Q$.

It should also be clear that in this setting, the reduction step analysis is not especially complicated by the presence of the arbitrary context. We can classify reduction steps in four categories:

1. reductions that use an unknown rule in $D_C$, with only unknown messages in $M_C$.
2. reductions that use an unknown rule in $D_C$, with some messages in $M_P$.
3. reductions that use a known rule in $D_P$, but with some unknown messages in $M_C\sigma_P$.
4. reductions that use a known rule in $D_P$, with only known messages in $M_P$.

The first two cases are easy, since a syntactically similar reduction must be performed by the right hand term. In the second case the messages in $M_P$ must be matched by messages in $M_Q$, possibly after some internal computation using known rules in $D_Q$ and other known messages in $M_Q$. Cases 3 and 4 may be harder, since $Q$ need not match the reduction precisely. In case 3, the exact number and valence of the "unknown" messages is determined by the known rule and messages, and those messages are similarly available to $Q$.

Note that cases 2, 3, and 4 correspond directly to output, input, and internal steps in a trace or labeled semantics. Hence, the extra work required for those "arbitrary contexts" amounts to two generic placeholders $D_C$ and $M_C$ in the description of the candidate bisimulation, and one extra trivial case... that is, not very much. Furthermore, we can often simplify the relation by hiding parts common to $D_P$ and $D_Q$, or $M_P$ and $M_Q$, inside $D_C$ or $M_C$, respectively. This is equivalent to the "up to context" labeled bisimulation proof technique.

There is one final wrinkle to this proof technique : to be an evaluation context congruence, a relation $\mathcal{R}$ of the shape above should contain all alpha variants of $\texttt{def}\ D_P\ \texttt{in}\ M_P$ and $\texttt{def}\ D_Q\ \texttt{in}\ M_Q$, to avoid clashes with the components of a new context $C'[\cdot]$ that is being added. This is easily handled by completing $\mathcal{R}$ with all pairs $(C[P]\rho, C[Q]\rho)$ for all injective renamings $\rho$. Reduction diagrams established for $\mathcal{R}$ also hold for the extended $\mathcal{R}$, and we can use the renamings to avoid name clashes with $C'[\cdot]$. In fact, we can further use the renamings to reserve a set of private bound names for the $D_P$ and $D_Q$ definitions.

The second technique we explore facilitates the diagram proof part, and makes it possible to meet the bisimulation requirement with a smaller relation. The general idea is to use equational reasoning to "close off" these diagrams, as we did in the proof of theorem 12. Unfortunately, the unrestricted use of $\approx$ in simulation diagrams is unsound: let $P = \texttt{def}\ x\langle\rangle \triangleright y\langle\rangle\ \texttt{in}\ x\langle\rangle$, and consider the singleton relation $\{(P, \mathbf{0})\}$. If $P \rightarrow Q$ then $Q \equiv \texttt{def}\ x\langle\rangle \triangleright y\langle\rangle\ \texttt{in}\ y\langle\rangle$, so $Q \approx P$ by the analog of lemma 13. So $\{(P, \mathbf{0})\}$ is a simulation up to $\approx$, and it also preserves immediate barbs (there are none). But $\{(P, \mathbf{0})\}$ does not preserve barbs ($P \Downarrow_y$ but $\mathbf{0} \not\Downarrow_y$), so it certainly is not a simulation.

To allow some measure of equational reasoning, we define a more restrictive notion of simulation, following [48]. This notion does not really have a valid semantic interpretation (it does step counting), but it is a convenient technical expedient that allows the use of several important equations inside simulation diagrams, the most important of which is beta reduction.

**Definition 15 (Tight simulations).** *A relation $\mathcal{R}$ is a tight simulation when*

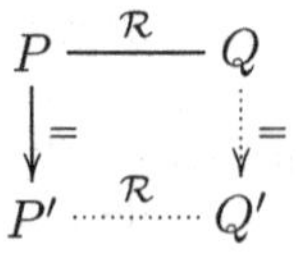

$$\begin{array}{ccc} P & \overset{\mathcal{R}}{\text{———}} & Q \\ \downarrow = & & \vdots\downarrow = \\ P' & \overset{\mathcal{R}}{\cdots\cdots} & Q' \end{array}$$

*where $P \rightarrow^= P'$ means $P \rightarrow P'$ or $P = P'$.*

**Definition 16 (Expansion).** *An* expansion *is a simulation whose converse is a tight simulation. A* compression *is the converse of an expansion. The coarsest expansion that respects the barbs is denoted $\preceq$.*

*A* tight bisimulation *is a tight simulation whose converse is a tight simulation. The coarsest tight bisimulation that respects the barbs is denoted $\asymp$.*

These technical definitions find their use with the following reformulations:

**Theorem 17 (Simulations up to).**
*A relation $\mathcal{R}$ is a tight bisimulation when*

$$\begin{array}{ccc} P & \overset{\mathcal{R}}{\longrule} & Q \\ \downarrow & & \vdots {=} \\ P' & \overset{(\asymp\cup\mathcal{R})^*}{\cdots\cdots} & Q' \end{array} \qquad\qquad \begin{array}{ccc} P & \overset{\mathcal{R}}{\longrule} & Q \\ \vdots {=} & & \downarrow \\ P' & \overset{(\asymp\cup\mathcal{R})^*}{\cdots\cdots} & Q' \end{array}$$

*A relation $\mathcal{R}$ is an expansion when*

$$\begin{array}{ccc} P & \overset{\mathcal{R}}{\longrule} & Q \\ \downarrow & & \vdots {*} \\ P' & \overset{\asymp\mathcal{R}\preceq}{\cdots\cdots} & Q' \end{array} \qquad\qquad \begin{array}{ccc} P & \overset{\mathcal{R}}{\longrule} & Q \\ \vdots {=} & & \downarrow \\ P' & \overset{(\preceq\cup\mathcal{R})^*}{\cdots\cdots} & Q' \end{array}$$

*A relation $\mathcal{R}$ is a bisimulation when*

$$\begin{array}{ccc} P & \overset{\mathcal{R}}{\longrule} & Q \\ \downarrow & & \vdots {*} \\ P' & \overset{\succeq\mathcal{R}\approx}{\cdots\cdots} & Q' \end{array} \qquad\qquad \begin{array}{ccc} P & \overset{\mathcal{R}}{\longrule} & Q \\ \vdots {*} & & \downarrow \\ P' & \overset{\approx\mathcal{R}\preceq}{\cdots\cdots} & Q' \end{array}$$

Most of the equations established with $\simeq_{\text{may}}$ are in fact valid compressions, and so can be used to close diagrams in bisimulation proofs. In particular, beta reduction is a compression.

**Theorem 18 (Beta compression).** *If $Q[\cdot]_S$ is a general context that does not capture $f$ or any names free in $E$ ($S \cap (\{f\} \cup \text{fv}(E)) = \emptyset$), then*

$$\begin{array}{l} \quad\texttt{let}\ f(\tilde{x}) = E\ \texttt{in}\ Q[\texttt{let}\ z = f(\tilde{u})\ \texttt{in}\ R]_S \\ \succeq \texttt{let}\ f(\tilde{x}) = E\ \texttt{in}\ Q[\texttt{let}\ z = E\{^{\tilde{u}}/_{\tilde{x}}\}\ \texttt{in}\ R]_S \end{array}$$

## 3 A Hierarchy of Equivalences

In this section and the next one, we continue our comparative survey of equivalences and their proof techniques. We provide useful intermediate equivalences between may-testing and bisimilarity. We give finer labeled semantics with purely coinductive proofs of equivalence. We also discuss the trade-off between different definitions of these equivalences. At the end of this section, we summarize our results as a hierarchy of equivalences ordered by inclusion.

Although we develop this hierarchy for establishing the properties of programs written in the join calculus, most of these equivalences and techniques are not specific to the join calculus. In principle, they can be applied to any calculus with a small-step reduction-based semantics, evaluation contexts, and some notion of observation. They provide a flexible framework when considering new calculi, or variants of existing calculi (see for instance [17, 4, 19]).

### 3.1 Too Many Equivalences?

In concurrency theory, there is a frightening diversity of calculi and equivalences (see, for instance, Glabbeek's classification of weak equivalences [21]). Even in our restricted setting—asynchronous concurrent programs—there are several natural choices in the definition of process equivalence, and for many of these choices there is a record of previous works that exclusively rely on each resulting equivalence.

In Sect. 2, we detailed the (largely contradictory) goals for the "right" equivalences. Before introducing useful variants, we now highlight some of the technical choices in their definitions. In order to choose the variant best adapted to the problem at hand, we need to understand the significance of such choices. For example, different styles of definition may yield the same equivalence and still provide different proof techniques. Conversely, some slight changes in a definition may in fact strongly affect the resulting equivalence and invalidate its expected properties.

**Context Closures.** As illustrated in the previous section, one may be interested in several classes of contexts. Evaluation contexts are easy to interpret in a testing scenario, but more general context-closure properties may also be useful in lemmas (e.g., beta compression). Technically, the main novelty of general contexts is that different free variables appearing under a guard may be instantiated to the same name. In the join calculus, this is inessential because *relays* from one name to another have the same effect, as expressed in Lemma 13 for may testing, but this is not the case in extensions of the join calculus considered in Sect. 4.5.

Conversely, it may be convenient to consider smaller classes of contexts to establish context closure. For instance, one may constrain the names that appear in the context, considering only contexts with a few, chosen free variables, or contexts whose local names never clash with those of the processes at hand, or contexts with a single, "flat" definition.

In the following discussion, we write $\mathcal{R}^\circ$ for the congruence of relation $\mathcal{R}$, defined as $P\ \mathcal{R}^\circ\ Q$ iff $\forall C[\cdot], C[P]\ \mathcal{R}\ C[Q]$. As our usual equivalences are all closed by application of evaluation contexts, we use plain relation symbols ($\simeq$, $\approx$,...) for them, and "dotted" relation symbols for the sibling relations defined without a context-closure requirement ($\dot{\simeq}$, $\dot{\approx}$,...).

**Primitive Observations.** The notion of basic observation is largely arbitrary. So far, we have been using the output predicates of Definition 4, given as the syntactic presence of particular messages on free names in evaluation contexts. Moreover, in our definitions of equivalences, we use a distinct predicate $\downarrow_x$ for every channel name, and we don't discriminate according to the content of message. Another, very detailed observation predicate of Sect. 2 is given by Definition 7, as one can test whether a particular execution trace is allowed by a process. Other, natural alternatives are considered below.

Fortunately, the details of observation often become irrelevant when considering relations that are (at least) closed by application of evaluation contexts. Indeed, as soon as we can use a primitive observation predicate to separate two processes, then any other "reasonable" notion of observation should be expressible using a particular context that observes it, then conveys the result of this internal observation by reducing to either of these two processes.

*Existential Predicates.* In the initial paper on barbed equivalences [38], and in most definitions of testing equivalences, a *single predicate* is used instead of an indexed family. Either there is a single observable action, often written $\omega$, or there is a single, "existential" predicate that collectively tests the presence of any message on a free name. Accordingly, for every family of predicates such as $\Downarrow_x$, we may define an existential predicate $P \Downarrow \stackrel{\text{def}}{=} \exists x.P \Downarrow_x$, and obtain existential variants for any observation-based equivalence. For instance, we let $\simeq^{\exists}_{\text{may}}$ be the largest relation closed by application of evaluation contexts that refines $P \Downarrow$. As suggested above, existential equivalences coincide with their basic equivalence when they are context-closed. For instance, one can specifically detect $\Downarrow_x$ by testing $\Downarrow$ in a context that restricts all other free names of the process being tested, and one can test for $\Downarrow$ as a the conjunction of all predicates $\Downarrow_x$, hence $\simeq^{\exists}_{\text{may}} = \simeq_{\text{may}}$. In the following, we will consider equivalences whose existential variant is much weaker.

*Transient Observations.* In the join calculus, strong barbs $\downarrow_x$ appear as messages on free names, which are names meant to be defined by the context. Due to the locality property, these messages are preserved by internal reductions, hence the strong barbs are stable: if $P \downarrow_x$ and $P \rightarrow^* P'$, then also $P' \downarrow_x$).

This is usually not the case in process calculi such as CCS or the pi calculus, where messages on free names can disappear as the result of internal communication. For instance, the reduction $\overline{x}\langle\rangle \,|\, x() \rightarrow \mathbf{0}$ erases the barb $\downarrow_x$. Transient barbs may be harder to interpret in terms of observation scenarios, and they complicate the hierarchy of equivalence [17]. However, one can enforce the permanency of barbs using a derived *committed message* predicate $P \Downarrow\!\!\Downarrow_x \stackrel{\text{def}}{=}$ if $P \rightarrow^* P'$ then $P' \downarrow_x$, instead of the predicate $\downarrow_x$ in every definition. One can also rely on the congruence property (when available) to turn transient barbs into permanent ones. In the pi calculus for instance, we let $T_x[\cdot] \stackrel{\text{def}}{=} \nu x.(x().\overline{t}\langle\rangle \,|\, [\cdot])$ and, for any process $P$ where $t$ is fresh, we have $T_x[P] \rightarrow^* \Downarrow\!\!\Downarrow_t$ iff $P \Downarrow_x$.

**Relations between Internal States.** So far, we considered a "pure" testing semantics $\simeq_{\text{may}}$ and a much finer bisimulation-based semantics $\approx$ that requires an exact correspondence between internal states. The appearance of bisimulation raises two questions:

*Can we use a coarser correspondence between internal states?* This is an important concern in our setting, because asynchronous algorithms typically use a series of local messages to simulate an atomic "distributed" state transition.

Since these messages are received independently, there is a gradual commitment to this state transition, which introduces transient states. Hence, the two processes do not advance in lockstep, and they are not bisimilar. In Sect. 3.3, we explain how we can retain some benefits of coinductive definitions in such cases.

*Should this correspondence depend on the context?* In the previous section, we defined $\approx$ all at once, as the largest $\Downarrow_x$-preserving bisimulation that is also closed by application of evaluation contexts. This style of equivalence definition was first proposed for the $\nu$-calculus in [23, 25, 24].

However, there is another, more traditional definition for CCS and for the pi calculus [38, 46, 49]. First, define the largest barbed bisimulation (written $\dot{\approx}$); then, take the largest subrelation of $\dot{\approx}$ that is closed by application of evaluation contexts (written $\dot{\approx}^\circ$). We believe that this original, two-stage definition has several drawbacks: the bare bisimulation $\dot{\approx}$ is very sensitive to the choice of observation predicates, and the correspondence between internal states may depend on the context.

The two diagrams below detail the situation: once a context has been applied on the left, the stable relation is a bisimulation, and not a congruence. Conversely, the bisimulation-and-congruence relation on the right retains the congruence property after matching reductions, and allows repeated application of contexts after reductions.

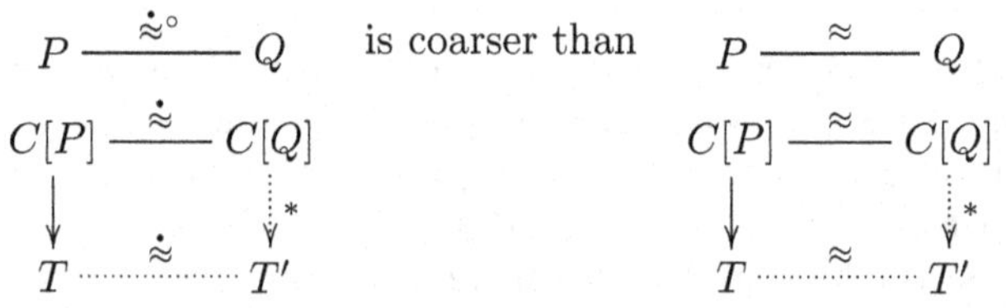

$$\begin{array}{ccc} P & \overset{\dot{\approx}^\circ}{\text{———}} & Q \\ & & \\ C[P] & \overset{\dot{\approx}}{\text{———}} & C[Q] \\ \downarrow & & \vdots * \\ T & \overset{\dot{\approx}}{\cdots\cdots} & T' \end{array} \quad \text{is coarser than} \quad \begin{array}{ccc} P & \overset{\approx}{\text{———}} & Q \\ & & \\ C[P] & \overset{\approx}{\text{———}} & C[Q] \\ \downarrow & & \vdots * \\ T & \overset{\approx}{\cdots\cdots} & T' \end{array}$$

From the two definitions, we obtain the simple inclusion $\approx \subseteq \dot{\approx}^\circ$, but the converse $\dot{\approx}^\circ \subseteq \approx$ is far from obvious: the latter inclusion holds if and only if $\dot{\approx}^\circ$ is itself a bisimulation. In Sect. 3.4, we will sketch a proof that $\dot{\approx}^\circ \subseteq \approx$ in the join calculus. Conversely, we will show that this is not the case for some simple variants of $\dot{\approx}$.

Even if the two definitions yield the same equivalence, they induce distinct proof techniques. In our experience, $\approx$ often leads to simpler proofs, because interaction with the context is more abstract: after reduction, the context may change, but remains in the class being considered in the candidate bisimulation-and-congruence.

### 3.2 Fair Testing

We are now ready to revisit our definition of testing equivalences. May testing is most useful for guaranteeing safety properties but, as illustrated by the equation $P \oplus \mathbf{0} \simeq_{\text{may}} P$, it does not actually guarantee that anything useful happens.

As we argued in subsection 2.4, for concurrent programs it is not desirable to supplement may testing with must testing in order to capture liveness properties.

We briefly considered the usual *must predicate* $\Box\downarrow_x$, but dismissed it because the predicate always failed on processes with infinite behavior (*cf.* page 296).

Instead, we use a stronger predicate that incorporates a notion of "abstract fairness". The *fair-must predicate* $\Box\Downarrow_x$ detects whether a process always retains the possibility of emitting on $x$:

$$P \,\Box\Downarrow_x \stackrel{\text{def}}{=} \text{if } P \rightarrow^* P', \text{ then } P' \rightarrow^* P'' \downarrow_x$$

Hence, $\Box\Downarrow_x$ tests for "permanent weak barbs". For all processes $P$, the test $P\,\Box\Downarrow_x$ implies $P \Downarrow_x$ and $P\,\Box\downarrow_x$. Conversely, (1) if all reductions from $P$ are deterministic, then $\Box\Downarrow_x$ and $\Downarrow_x$ coincide; (2) if there is no infinite computation, then $\Box\downarrow_x$ and $\Box\Downarrow_x$ coincide.

Much like weak barbs, fair-must predicates induces a contextual equivalence:

**Definition 19 (Fair testing equivalence).** *We have $P \sqsubseteq_{\text{may}} Q$ when, for any evaluation context $C[\cdot]$ and channel name $x$, $C[P]\,\Box\Downarrow_x$ if and only if $C[Q]\,\Box\Downarrow_x$.*

That is, fair testing is the largest congruence that respects all fair-must predicates. Similar definitions appear in [12, 40, 13]. Fair testing detects deadlocks: we have $x\langle\rangle \oplus (x\langle\rangle \oplus \mathbf{0}) \simeq_{fair} x\langle\rangle \oplus \mathbf{0}$, but $x\langle\rangle \oplus \mathbf{0} \not\simeq_{fair} x\langle\rangle$ and $x\langle\rangle \oplus \mathbf{0} \not\simeq_{fair} \mathbf{0}$.

The particular notion of fairness embedded in fair testing deserves further explanations: both may and fair-must predicates state the existence of reductions leading to a particular message, but they don't provide a reduction strategy. Nonetheless, we can interpret $P\,\Box\Downarrow_x$ as a successful observation "$P$ eventually emits the message $x\langle\rangle$". As we do so, we consider only infinite traces that emit on $x$ and we disregard any other infinite trace. Intuitively, the model is the set of barbs present on finite and infinite fair traces, for a very strong notion of fairness. For example, we have the fair testing equivalence:

$$\texttt{def}\ t\langle\rangle \triangleright x\langle\rangle \ \wedge\ t\langle\rangle \triangleright t\langle\rangle\ \texttt{in}\ t\langle\rangle \simeq_{fair} x\langle\rangle$$

where the first process provides two alternatives in the definition of $t$: either the message $x\langle\rangle$ is emitted, or the message $t\langle\rangle$ is re-emitted, which reverts the process to its initial state. It is possible to always select the second, stuttering branch of the alternative, and thus there are infinite computations that never emit $x\langle\rangle$. Nonetheless, the possibility of emitting on $x$ always remains, and any fair evaluation strategy should eventually select the first branch.

Fair testing may seem unrelated to may testing; at least, these relations are different, as can be seen using $x\langle\rangle \oplus \mathbf{0}$ and $x\langle\rangle$. Actually, fair testing is strictly finer: $\simeq_{fair} \subset \simeq_{\text{may}}$. Said otherwise, fair testing is also the largest congruence relation that refines both may- and fair-must predicates.

To prove that $\simeq_{fair}$ also preserves weak barbs $\Downarrow_x$, we use the congruence property with non-deterministic contexts of the form

$$C[\cdot] \stackrel{\text{def}}{=} \texttt{def}\ r\langle z\rangle \,|\, \mathit{once}\langle\rangle \triangleright z\langle\rangle\ \texttt{in}\ \big(\, r\langle y\rangle \,|\, \mathit{once}\langle\rangle \,|\, \texttt{def}\ x\langle\rangle \triangleright r\langle x\rangle\ \texttt{in}\ [\cdot]\,\big)$$

and establish that $P \Downarrow_x$ iff $C[P] \not\Box\Downarrow_y$. This property of fair testing also holds in CCS, in the pi calculus, and for Actors, where a similar equivalence is proposed as the main semantics [5].

As regards discriminating power, fair testing is an appealing equivalence for distributed systems: it is stronger than may-testing, detects deadlocks, but remains insensitive to termination and livelocks. Note, however, that "abstract fairness" is much stronger than the liveness properties that are typically guaranteed in implementations (*cf.* the restrictive scheduling policy in JoCaml).

Fair testing suffers from another drawback: direct proofs of equivalence are very difficult because they involve nested inductions for all quantifiers in the definition of fair-must tests in evaluation context. As we will see in the next section, the redeeming feature of fair testing is that it is coarser than bisimilarity equivalence ($\approx \subseteq \simeq_{fair}$). Thus, many equations of interest can be established in a coinductive manner, then interpreted in terms of may and fair testing scenarios. Precisely, we are going to establish an tighter characterization of fair testing in terms of *coupled simulations.*

### 3.3 Coupled Simulations

The relation between fair testing and bisimulations has been initially studied in CCS; in [12, 40] for instance, the authors introduce the notion of fair testing (actually should testing in their terminology), and remark that weak bisimulation equivalences incorporates a particular notion of fairness; they identify the problem of gradual commitment, and in general of sensitivity to the branching structure, as an undesirable property of bisimulation; finally, they establish that observational equivalence is finer than fair testing and propose a simulation-based sufficient condition to establish fair testing.

Independently, *coupled simulations* have been proposed to address similar issues [43]; this coarse simulation-based equivalence does not require an exact correspondence between the internal choices of processes, and is thus less sensitive than bisimulation to their branching structure. In our setting, we use a barbed counterpart of *weakly-coupled simulations* [44] that is not sensitive to divergence. A similar equivalence appears in the asynchronous pi calculus, where it is used to establish the correctness of the encoding of the choice operator [41].

**Definition 20.** *A pair of relations* $\leqslant, \geqslant$ *are* coupled simulations *when* $\leqslant$ *and* $\geqslant^{-1}$ *are two simulations that satisfy the coupling conditions* $\leqslant \subseteq \geqslant\leftarrow^*$ *and* $\geqslant \subseteq \rightarrow^*\leqslant$.

*A* barbed coupled-simulations relation *is an intersection* $\leqslant \cap \geqslant$ *for some pair* $\leqslant, \geqslant$ *such that* $\leqslant$ *and* $\geqslant^{-1}$ *preserve the barbs.*

*The coarsest barbed coupled-simulation relation is denoted* $\dot{\lessgtr}$. *The coarsest barbed coupled-simulation obtained from simulations that are also precongruences for evaluation contexts is called* coupled-similarity equivalence, *and denoted* $\lessgtr$.

The definition can be stated in a more readable manner using diagrams for all simulation and coupling requirements:

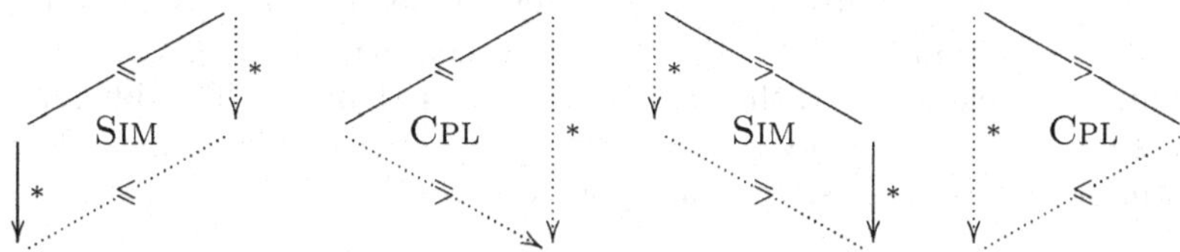


When we also have $\leqslant\ =\ \geqslant$, the coupling diagrams are trivially verified, and the coupled-simulation relation is in fact a bisimulation—in particular, we immediately obtain the inclusions $\dot{\approx} \subseteq \dot{\lesseqgtr}$ and $\approx \subseteq \lesseqgtr$.

Typically, the discrepancy between $\leqslant$ and $\geqslant$ is used to describe processes that are in a transient state, bisimilar neither to the initial state nor to any final state. For instance, using our derived internal choice operator $\oplus$, we have the diagram

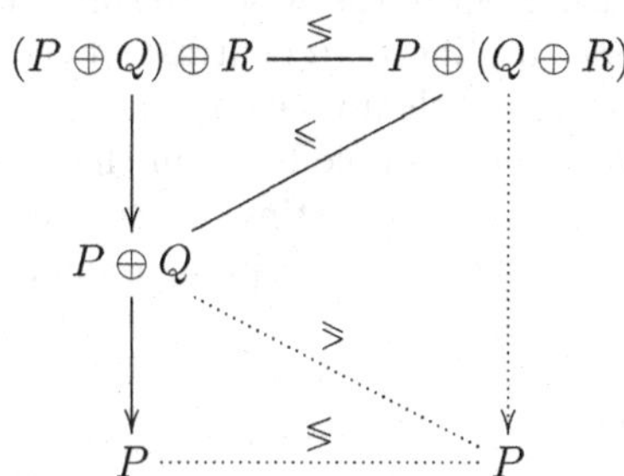


The precise relation between fair testing and coupled simulations is intriguing. These equivalences have been applied to the same problems, typically the analyses of distributed protocols where high-level atomic steps are implemented as a negotiation between distributed components, with several steps that perform a gradual commitment. Yet, their definitions are very different, and they both have their advantages: fair-testing is arguably more natural than coupled simulations, while coupled simulations can be established by coinduction.

It is not too hard to establish that barbed coupled-simulation relations also preserve fair-must barbs. The proof uses simulations in both directions, which somehow reflects the alternation of quantifiers in the definition of fair-must barbs.

**Lemma 21.** *Let $\leqslant, \geqslant$ be barbed coupled simulations. If $P \geqslant Q$ and $P \,\Box\!\Downarrow_x$, then also $Q \,\Box\!\Downarrow_x$.*

*Proof.* If $Q \rightarrow^* Q'$, these reductions can be simulated by $P \rightarrow^* P' \geqslant Q'$. Using the coupling condition, we also have $P' \rightarrow^* P'' \leqslant Q'$. By definition of $P \,\Box\!\Downarrow_x$, we have $P'' \Downarrow_x$. Finally, $\leqslant$ preserves weak barbs, and thus $Q' \Downarrow_x$.

As is the case for weak bisimulation, we can either add precongruence requirements to the definition of barbed coupled simulations and obtain a barbed coupled-simulations congruence ($\lesseqgtr$) or take the largest congruence that is contained in the largest barbed coupled-simulation relation (written $\dot{\lesseqgtr}^{\circ}$).

From these definitions and the previous lemma, we obtain the inclusions $\lessgtr \subseteq \dot{\lessgtr}^\circ \subseteq \simeq_{fair}$. Conversely, the congruence relation $\dot{\lessgtr}^\circ$ is *not* a coupled-simulation relation, and thus $\lessgtr$ is strictly finer than $\dot{\lessgtr}^\circ$. The difference appears as soon as internal choices are spawned *between* visible actions. The counter-example is especially simple in asynchronous CCS, where we have:

$$a.\overline{b} \oplus a.\overline{c} \not\lessgtr a.(\overline{b} \oplus \overline{c})$$
$$a.\overline{b} \oplus a.\overline{c} \,\dot{\lessgtr}^\circ\, a.(\overline{b} \oplus \overline{c})$$

In these processes, the outcome of the internal choice becomes visible only after communication on $a$, but the choice can be immediately performed on the left only, e.g. $a.\overline{b} \oplus a.\overline{c} \rightarrow a.\overline{b}$. If the context is applied once for all, then we know whether that context can provide a message on $a$. If this is the case, then we simulate the step above by getting that message, communicating on $a$, and reducing $\overline{b} \oplus \overline{c}$ to $\overline{b}$ on the right. Otherwise, we simulate the step by doing nothing, because both processes are inert. In contrast, if the reduction occurs on the left before the context is chosen, then we cannot simulate it on the right in a uniform manner. A similar counter-example holds in the join calculus [16].

Our next theorem relates fair testing and barbed coupled similarities; it relies on the preceding remarks, plus the surprising inclusion $\simeq_{fair} \subseteq \dot{\lessgtr}^\circ$, whose proof is detailed below.

**Theorem 22.** $\simeq_{fair} = \dot{\lessgtr}^\circ \subset \lessgtr$.

To prove $\simeq_{fair} \subseteq \dot{\lessgtr}^\circ$, we develop a semantic model of coupled simulations. We first consider a family of processes whose behavior is especially simple. We say that a process $P$ is *committed* when, for all $x$, we have $P \Downarrow_x$ iff $P \Box\Downarrow_x$. Then, no internal reduction may visibly affect $P$: let $S$ be the set of names

$$S \stackrel{\text{def}}{=} \{x \mid P \Box\Downarrow_x\} = \{x \mid P \Downarrow_x\}$$

For all $P'$ such that $P \rightarrow^* P'$, $P'$ is still committed to $S$. In a sense, $P$ has converged to $S$, which determines its outcome.

To every process $P$, we now associate the semantics $P^\flat \in \mathbb{P}(\mathbb{P}(\mathcal{N}))$ that collects these sets of names for all the committed derivatives of $P$:

$$P^\flat \stackrel{\text{def}}{=} \{S \subseteq \mathcal{N} \mid \exists P' \cdot P \rightarrow^* P' \text{ and } S = \{x \,|\, P' \Box\Downarrow_x\} = \{x \,|\, P' \Downarrow_x\}\}$$

For example, $\mathbf{0}^\flat$ is the singleton $\{\emptyset\}$ and $(x\langle\rangle \oplus y\langle\rangle)^\flat$ is the pair $\{\{x\},\{y\}\}$. As is the case for weak barbs, $P^\flat$ decreases by reduction. The predicates $\Downarrow_x$ and $\Box\Downarrow_x$ can be recovered as follows: we have $P \Downarrow_x$ if and only if $x \in \bigcup P^\flat$, and $P \Box\Downarrow_x$ if and only if $x \in \bigcap P^\flat$.

Let $\subseteq_\flat$ be the preorder defined as $P \subseteq_\flat Q \stackrel{\text{def}}{=} P^\flat \subseteq Q^\flat$. By definition of may testing and fair testing preorders, we immediately obtain ${\subseteq_\flat}^\circ \subseteq \sqsubseteq_{may}$ and ${\subseteq_\flat}^\circ \subseteq \sqsubseteq_{fair}^{-1}$. Actually, the last two preorders coincide.

**Lemma 23.** ${\subseteq_\flat}^\circ = \sqsubseteq_{fair}^{-1}$.

*Proof.* For any finite sets of names $S$ and $N$ such that $S \subseteq N$ and $t \notin N$, we define the context

$$T_S^N[\cdot] \stackrel{\text{def}}{=} \texttt{def}\ once\langle\rangle \triangleright t\langle\rangle\ \wedge\ once\langle\rangle | \prod_{x \in S} x\langle\rangle \triangleright \mathbf{0}\ \wedge \bigwedge_{x \in N \setminus S} x\langle\rangle \triangleright t\langle\rangle\ \texttt{in}\ once\langle\rangle \,|\, [\cdot]$$

and we show that $T_S^N[\cdot]$ fair-tests exactly one set of names in our semantics: for all $P$ such that $\text{fv}(P) \subseteq N$, we have $T_S^N[P]\ \Box\Downarrow_t$ if and only if $S \notin P^\flat$.

The first two clauses of the definition compete for the single message $once\langle\rangle$, hence at most one of the two may be triggered. The first clause ($once\langle\rangle \triangleright t\langle\rangle$) can be immediately triggered. The second clause can preempt this reduction only by consuming a message for each name in $S$. The third clause detects the presence of any message on a name in $N \setminus S$. The predicate $T_S^N[P]\ \Box\Downarrow_t$ holds iff all the derivatives of $P$ keep one of the two possibilities to emit the message $t\langle\rangle$, namely either don't have messages on some of the names in $S$, or can always produce a message on a name outside of $S$.

Let $P \sqsubseteq_{fair}^{-1} Q$. We let $N = \text{fv}(P) \cup \text{fv}(Q)$ to establish $P^\flat \subseteq Q^\flat$. For every set of names $S \subseteq N$, we have $S \in P^\flat$ iff $T_S^N[P]\ \not\Box\Downarrow_t$; this entails $T_S^N[Q]\ \not\Box\Downarrow_t$ and $S \in Q^\flat$. For every other set of names $S$, neither $P^\flat$ nor $Q^\flat$ may contain $S$ anyway. Thus $\sqsubseteq_{fair}^{-1} \subseteq \subseteq_\flat$, by context-closure for fair-testing $\sqsubseteq_{fair}^{-1} \subseteq {\subseteq_\flat}^\circ$, and, since the converse inclusion follows from the characterization of fair barbs given above, ${\subseteq_\flat}^\circ = \sqsubseteq_{fair}^{-1}$.

The next lemma will be used to relate $\subseteq_\flat$ to $\dot{\lessapprox}$:

**Lemma 24.** $P^\flat \neq \emptyset$

*Proof.* For every process $P$, consider the series of processes $P'_0, P'_1, \ldots, P'_n$ such that $P = P'_0 \rightarrow^* P'_1 \rightarrow^* \cdots \rightarrow^* P'_n$ and such that $\{x \mid P'_i\ \Box\Downarrow_x\}$ strictly increases with $i$. There is a least one such series $(P)$, and the length of any series is bounded by the number of names free in $P$, hence there is at least a series that is maximal for prefix-inclusion.

To conclude, we remark that $S \in P^\flat$ iff there is a maximal series of processes ending at $P'_n$ such that $S = \{x \mid P'_n\ \Box\Downarrow_x\}$.

We now establish that our semantics refines barbed coupled similarity.

**Lemma 25.** $(\subseteq_\flat, \supseteq_\flat)$ *are coupled barbed simulations, and thus* $\subseteq_\flat \cap \supseteq_\flat \subseteq \dot{\lessapprox}$.

*Proof.* We successively check that $\subseteq_\flat$ preserves the barbs, is a simulation, and meets the coupling diagram. Assume $P \subseteq_\flat Q$.

1. The barbs can be recovered from the semantics: $P \Downarrow_x$ iff $x \in \bigcup P^\flat$, and if $P \subseteq_\flat Q$ then also $x \in \bigcup Q^\flat$ and $Q \Downarrow_x$. hence $P \Downarrow_x$ implies $Q \Downarrow_x$.
2. Weak simulation trivially holds: by definition, $P^\flat$ decreases with reductions, and is stable iff $P^\flat$ is a singleton; for every reduction $P \rightarrow P'$, $P' \subseteq_\flat P \subseteq_\flat Q$, and thus reductions in $P$ are simulated by the absence of reduction in $Q$.
3. $P^\flat$ is not empty, so let $S \in P^\flat$. By hypothesis, $S \in Q^\flat$ and thus for some process $Q'_S$ we have $Q \rightarrow^* Q'_S$ and ${Q'_S}^\flat = \{S\} \subseteq P^\flat$, which provides the coupling condition from $\subseteq_\flat$ to $\supseteq_\flat$. □

By composing Lemmas 23 and 25, we obtain $\simeq_{fair} = \dot{\lessgtr}^\circ$ (Theorem 22). The proof technique associated with this characterization retains some of the structure of the purely coinductive technique for the stronger relation $\lessgtr$, so it is usually an improvement over the triple induction implied by the definition of $\simeq_{fair}$ (but not always, as was pointed out in subsection 2.4 for coinductive may-testing proofs).

### 3.4 Two Notions of Congruence

We finally discuss the relation between the equivalences $\approx$ and $\dot{\approx}^\circ$, which depend on the choice of observables. To this end, we consider bisimulations weaker than $\dot{\approx}$, obtained by considering only a finite number of observation predicates.

Let single-barbed bisimilarity $\dot{\approx}_\exists$ be the largest weak bisimulation that refines the barb $\Downarrow$, i.e. that detects the ability to send a message on any free name.

- The equivalence $\dot{\approx}_\exists$ partitions join calculus processes into three classes characterized by the predicates $\Box\Downarrow$, $\not\Downarrow$, and $\Downarrow \wedge \not\Box\Downarrow$. Hence, the congruence of single-barbed bisimilarity is just fair testing equivalence: $\dot{\approx}_\exists^\circ = \simeq_{fair}$. This characterization implies yet another proof technique for $\simeq_{fair}$, but the technique implied by Theorem 22 is usually better.
- In contrast, both $\approx_\exists$ and $\approx$ are congruences and weak bisimulations. Moreover, using the existential contexts given above, we can check that $\approx_\exists$ preserves nominal barbs $\Downarrow_x$ and that $\approx$ preserves existential barbs $\Downarrow$. This establishes $\approx_\exists = \approx$.

We thus obtain a pair of distinct "bisimulation congruences" $\dot{\approx}_\exists^\circ \neq \approx_\exists$.

While there is a big difference between one and several observation predicates, it turns out that two predicates are as good as an infinite number of them, even for the weaker notion of bisimulation congruence. In the following, we fix two nullary names $x$ and $y$, and write $\dot{\approx}_2$ for the bisimilarity that refines $\Downarrow_x$ and $\Downarrow_y$. This technical equivalence is essential to prove $\approx = \dot{\approx}^\circ$, Precisely, we are going to establish

**Theorem 26.** $\dot{\approx}_2^\circ = \approx$

Since we clearly have $\approx \subseteq \dot{\approx}^\circ \subseteq \dot{\approx}_2^\circ$, we obtain $\approx = \dot{\approx}^\circ$ as a corollary.

We first build a family of processes that are not $\dot{\approx}_2$-equivalent and retain this property by reduction. Informally, this show that there are infinitely many ways to hesitate between two messages in a branching semantics. We define an operator $\mathcal{S}(\cdot)$ that maps every finite set of processes to the set of its (strict, partial) internal sums:

$$\mathcal{S}(\mathcal{P}) \stackrel{\text{def}}{=} \{\textstyle\bigoplus_{P \in \mathcal{P}'} P \mid \mathcal{P}' \subseteq \mathcal{P} \text{ and } |\mathcal{P}'| \geq 2\}$$

**Lemma 27.** *Let $\mathcal{R}$ be a weak bisimulation and $\mathcal{P}$ be a set of processes such that, for all $P, Q \in \mathcal{P}$, the relation $P \rightarrow^* \mathcal{R}\, Q$ implies $P = Q$. Then we have:*

1. *The set $\mathcal{S}(\mathcal{P})$ retains this property.*
2. *The set $\bigcup_{n \geq 0} \mathcal{S}^n(\mathcal{P})$ that collects the iterated results of $\mathcal{S}(\cdot)$ contains only processes that are not related by $\mathcal{R}$.*

*Proof.* We first show that (0) if $P \rightarrow^* \mathcal{R}\ Q$ for some $Q \in \mathcal{S}(\mathcal{P})$, then $P \notin \mathcal{P}$. Since $Q$ has at least two summands, it must have a summand $Q' \neq P$. But then $P \rightarrow^* \mathcal{R}\ Q'$ since $\mathcal{R}$ is a bisimulation, and since $Q' \in \mathcal{P}$ we cannot have $P \in \mathcal{P}$.

We then deduce (1) of the lemma. Let $P, Q$ be two processes in $\mathcal{S}(\mathcal{P})$ such that $P \rightarrow^* \mathcal{R}\ Q$. Let $Q'$ be a summand of $Q$; we must have $P \rightarrow^* \mathcal{R}\ Q'$ since $\mathcal{R}$ is a bisimulation, and in fact $P \rightarrow P' \rightarrow^* \mathcal{R}\ Q'$ (since $Q' \in \mathcal{P}$, $Q'\ \mathcal{R}\ P$ would break (0)); but $P', Q' \in \mathcal{P}$, so $P' = Q'$ and $Q'$ is also a summand of $P$. Now we must in fact have $P\ \mathcal{R}\ Q$ since $P \rightarrow P' \rightarrow^* \mathcal{R}\ Q$ would imply $P' \in \mathcal{P}$ and thus contradict (0). Hence by symmetry any summand of $P$ is also a summand of $Q$, so $P = Q$.

To prove (2), let $P \in \mathcal{S}^n(\mathcal{P})$ and $Q \in \mathcal{S}^{n+k}(\mathcal{P})$ such that $P\ \mathcal{R}\ Q$. By induction and (1), if $k = 0$ then $P = Q$; and we must have $k = 0$, since otherwise we have $Q \rightarrow^* Q'$ for some $Q' \in \mathcal{S}^{n+1}(\mathcal{P})$, hence $P \rightarrow^* \mathcal{R}\ Q'$, which breaks (0).

As a direct consequence, the bisimilarity $\dot{\approx}_2$ separates numerous processes with a finite behavior. We build an infinite set of processes as follows:

$$\mathcal{P}_0 \stackrel{\text{def}}{=} \{\, \mathbf{0},\ x\langle\rangle,\ y\langle\rangle \,\} \qquad \mathcal{P}_{n+1} \stackrel{\text{def}}{=} \mathcal{S}(\mathcal{P}_n) \qquad \mathcal{P}_\omega \stackrel{\text{def}}{=} \bigcup_{n \geq 0} \mathcal{P}_n$$

The size of each layer $\mathcal{P}_n$ grows exponentially. Thus, $\mathcal{P}_\omega$ contains infinitely many processes that are not related by $\dot{\approx}_2$: if $P \in \mathcal{P}_n$ and $Q \in \mathcal{P}_{n+m}$, then we have $Q \rightarrow^m Q'$ for some $Q' \in \mathcal{P}_n \setminus \{P\}$, and by construction at rank $n$ this series of reduction cannot be matched by any series reductions starting from $P$.

This construction captures only processes with finite behaviors up to our bisimilarity, whereas $\dot{\approx}_2$ has many more classes than those exhibited here (e.g. classes of processes that can reach an infinite number of classes in $\mathcal{P}_\omega$).

Note that the same construction applies for single-barb bisimilarity, but quickly converges. Starting from the set $\{\mathbf{0}, x\langle\rangle\}$, we obtain a third, unrelated process $\mathbf{0} \oplus x\langle\rangle$ at rank 1, then the construction stops.

The next lemma states that a process can effectively communicate any integer to the environment by hesitating between two exclusive barbs $\Downarrow_x$ and $\Downarrow_y$, thanks to the discriminating power of bisimulation.

In the following, we rely on encodings for booleans and for integers à la Church inside the join calculus. To every integer $n \in \mathbb{N}$, we associate the representation $\mathtt{n}$; we also assume that our integers come with operations $\mathbf{is\_zero}\langle\cdot\rangle$ and $\mathbf{pred}\langle\cdot\rangle$.

To every integer, we associate a particular equivalence class of $\dot{\approx}_2$ in the hierarchy of processes $\mathcal{P}_\omega$, then we write a process that receives an integer and conveys that integer by evolving to its characteristic class. Intuitively, the context $N[\cdot]$ transforms integer-indexed barbs $int\langle\mathtt{n}\rangle$ (where $int$ is a regular name of the join calculus) into the two barbs $\Downarrow_x$ and $\Downarrow_y$.

**Lemma 28.** *There is an evaluation context $N[\cdot]$ such that, for any integers $n$ and $m$, the three following statements are equivalent:*

1. $n = m$
2. $N[int\langle\mathtt{n}\rangle] \dot{\approx}_2 N[int\langle\mathtt{m}\rangle]$
3. $N[int\langle\mathtt{n}\rangle] \rightarrow^* \dot{\approx}_2 N[int\langle\mathtt{m}\rangle]$

To establish the lemma, we program the evaluation context $N[\cdot]$ as follows, and we locate the derivatives of $N[int\langle\mathbf{n}\rangle]$ in the hierarchy of processes $(\mathcal{P}^n)_n$.

$$N[\cdot] \stackrel{\text{def}}{=} \begin{array}{l} \texttt{def}\ int\langle n\rangle | once\langle\rangle \triangleright \\ \left( \begin{array}{l} \texttt{def}\ c\langle n,x,y,z\rangle \triangleright \\ \quad \texttt{if}\ \mathbf{is\_zero}\langle\mathbf{n}\rangle\ \texttt{then}\ z\langle\rangle \\ \quad \texttt{else}\ c\langle\mathbf{pred}\langle\mathbf{n}\rangle,z,x,y\rangle \oplus c\langle\mathbf{pred}\langle\mathbf{n}\rangle,y,z,x\rangle\ \texttt{in} \\ \texttt{def}\ z\langle\rangle \triangleright \mathbf{0}\ \texttt{in} \\ c\langle n,x,y,z\rangle \oplus c\langle n,y,z,x\rangle \oplus c\langle n,z,x,y\rangle \end{array} \right) \\ \texttt{in}\ once\langle\rangle|[\cdot] \end{array}$$

In $N[\cdot]$, the name $z$ is used to encode the process $\mathbf{0}$; hence the three processes in $\mathcal{P}_0$ are made symmetric, and we can use permutations of the names $x$, $y$, and $z$ to represent them. Each integer $n$ is associated with a ternary sum of nested binary sums in the $n+1$ layer of $\mathcal{P}$: when an encoded integer is received as $int\langle\mathbf{n}\rangle$, a reduction triggers the definition of $int$ and yields the initial ternary sum; at the same time this reduction consumes the single message $once\langle\rangle$, hence the definition of $int$ becomes inert.

The next lemma uses this result to restrict the class of contexts being considered in congruence properties to contexts with at most two free (nullary) variables.

**Lemma 29.** *Let $S$ be a finite set of names. There is an evaluation context $C_2[\cdot]$ such that, for any processes $P$ and $Q$ with free variables in $S$, we have $P\dot{\approx}Q$ iff $C_2[P]\dot{\approx}_2C_2[Q]$.*

In order to establish that $\dot{\approx}_2^\circ$ is a bisimulation, we need to retain the congruence property after matching reduction steps. Since we can apply only one context before applying the bisimulation hypothesis, this single context must be able to emulate the behavior of any other context, to be selected after the reductions. We call such a context a "universal context". The details of the construction appear in [16].

The first step is to define an integer representation for every process $P$, written $[\![P]\!]$, and to build an interpreter $D_e$ that takes (1) an integer representation $[\![P]\!] \in \mathbb{N}$ and (2) the encoding of an evaluation environment $\rho$ that binds all the free names $\mathrm{fv}(P)$. The next lemma relates the source process $P$ to its interpreted representation; this result is not surprising, inasmuch as the join calculus has well enough expressive power. The lemma is established using a labeled bisimulation, as defined in Sect. 4. Some care is required to restrict the types that may appear at $P$'s interface. We omit the details of the types, the encoding, and the interpreter, and refer to [17] for the definitions and the proofs.

**Lemma 30.** *Let $\Sigma$ be a finite set of types closed by decomposition. There is a definition $D_e$ such that, for every process $P$ whose free variables can be typed in $\Sigma$ and such that $\mathrm{fv}(P) \cap \{e,\rho\} = \emptyset$, and for every environment $\rho$ such that $\forall x \in \mathrm{fv}(P), \rho([\![x]\!]) = x$, we have* $\texttt{def}\ D_e\ \texttt{in}\ e\langle[\![P]\!],\rho\rangle \approx P$.

The second step is to reduce quantification over all contexts first to quantification over all processes (using a specific context that forwards the messages),

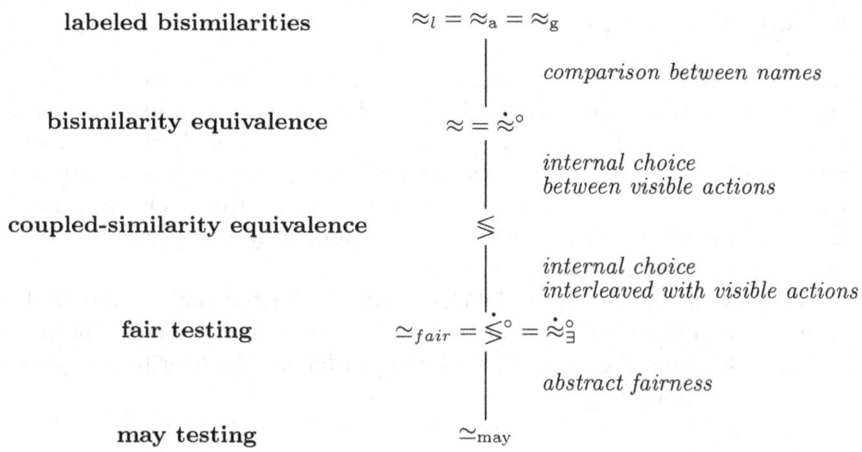


**Fig. 3.** A hierarchy of equivalences for the join calculus

then to quantification over all integers (substituting the interpreter for the process). Finally, the universal context uses internal choice to select any integer, then either manifest this choice using integer barbs, or run the interpreter on this input with an environment $\rho$ that manifests every barb using integer barbs. At each stage, the disappearance of specific integer barbs allows the bisimulation to keep track of the behavior of the context.

**Lemma 31 (Universal Context).** *Let $S$ be a finite set of names. There is an evaluation context $U_S[\cdot]$ such that, for all processes $P$ and $Q$ with* $\text{fv}(P) \cup \text{fv}(Q) \subseteq S$, *we have $U_S[P] \dot{\approx}_2 U_S[Q]$ implies $P \approx Q$*

Combining these encodings, we eventually obtain the difficult bisimulation property of $\dot{\approx}_2^\circ$, hence $\dot{\approx}_2^\circ = \approx$ and finally $\dot{\approx}^\circ = \approx$.

### 3.5 Summary: A Hierarchy of Equivalences

Anticipating on the labeled semantics in the next section, we summarize our results on equivalences in Fig. 3. Each tier in the hierarchy correspond to a notion of equivalence finer than the lower tiers. When stating and proving equational properties in a reduction-based setting, this hierarchy provides some guidance. For instance, the same proof may involve lemmas expressed as equivalences much finer (and easier to establish) than the final result. Conversely, a counter-example may be easier to exhibit at a tier lower than required.

The reader may be interested in applications of these techniques to establish more challenging equations. For detailed applications, we refer for instance to [4] for a detailed proof of the security of a distributed, cryptographic implementation of the join calculus, to [16] for a series of fully abstract encodings between variants of the join calculus, and to [19] for the correctness proof of an implementation of Ambients in JoCaml using coupled simulations.

# 4 Labeled Semantics

Labeled transition systems traditionally provide useful semantics for process calculi, by incorporating detailed knowledge of the operational semantics in their definitions and their proof techniques. Seen as auxiliary semantics for a reduction-based calculus, they offer several advantages, such as purely coinductive proofs and abstract models (e.g. synchronization trees). On the other hand, they are specific to the calculus at hand, and they may turn out to be too discriminating for asynchronous programming.

We present two variants of labeled semantics for the join calculus, and relate their notions of labeled bisimilarities to observational equivalence, thus comparing the discriminating power of contexts and labels. We refer to [18] for a more detailed presentation.

## 4.1 Open Syntax and Chemistry

In the spirit of the trace semantics given in Sect. 2.2, we introduce a refined semantics—the *open* RCHAM—that makes explicit the interactions with an abstract environment. Via these interactions, the environment can receive locally-defined names of the process when they are emitted on free names, and the environment can also emit messages on these names. We call these interactions *extrusions* and *intrusions*, respectively. To keep track of the defined names that are visible from the environment, definitions of the join calculus are marked with their extruded names when extrusions occur. In turn, intrusions are allowed only on names that are marked as extruded. The refined syntax for the join calculus has processes of the form $\mathtt{def}_S\ D \ \mathtt{in}\ P$, where $S$ is the set of names defined by $D$ and extruded to the environment. Informally, extruded names represent constants in the input interface of the process.

As a first example, consider the process $\mathtt{def}_\emptyset\ x\langle\rangle \triangleright y\langle\rangle \ \mathtt{in}\ z\langle x\rangle$. The interface contains no extruded name and two free names $y, z$. The message $z\langle x\rangle$ can be consumed by the environment, thus exporting $x$:

$$\mathtt{def}_\emptyset\ x\langle\rangle \triangleright y\langle\rangle \ \mathtt{in}\ z\langle x\rangle \xrightarrow{\{x\}\overline{z}\langle x\rangle} \mathtt{def}_{\{x\}}\ x\langle\rangle \triangleright y\langle\rangle \ \mathtt{in}\ \mathbf{0}$$

Once $x$ is known by the environment, it cannot be considered local anymore—the environment can emit on $x$—, but it is not free either—the environment cannot modify or extend its definition. A new transition is enabled:

$$\mathtt{def}_{\{x\}}\ x\langle\rangle \triangleright y\langle\rangle \ \mathtt{in}\ \mathbf{0} \xrightarrow{x\langle\rangle} \mathtt{def}_{\{x\}}\ x\langle\rangle \triangleright y\langle\rangle \ \mathtt{in}\ x\langle\rangle$$

Now the process can input more messages on $x$, and also perform the two transitions below to consume the message on $x$ and emit a message on $y$:

$$\begin{aligned}\mathtt{def}_{\{x\}}\ x\langle\rangle \triangleright y\langle\rangle \ \mathtt{in}\ x\langle\rangle \quad &\rightarrow \quad \mathtt{def}_{\{x\}}\ x\langle\rangle \triangleright y\langle\rangle \ \mathtt{in}\ y\langle\rangle \\ &\xrightarrow{\{\}\overline{y}\langle\rangle} \mathtt{def}_{\{x\}}\ x\langle\rangle \triangleright y\langle\rangle \ \mathtt{in}\ \mathbf{0}\end{aligned}$$

We now extend the RCHAM of Sect. 1.5 with extrusions, intrusions, and explicit bookkeeping of extruded names.

$$\begin{array}{llll} A, B ::= & & & \text{open processes} \\ & P & & \text{plain process} \\ & | \ \mathtt{def}_S\ D \ \mathtt{in}\ P & & \text{open definition} \\ & | \ A \,|\, B & & \text{parallel composition} \end{array}$$

**Fig. 4.** Syntax for the open join calculus

In join patterns:

$$\begin{array}{ll} \mathrm{rv}(x\langle\tilde v\rangle) \ = \{u \in \tilde v\} & \mathrm{dv}(x\langle\tilde v\rangle) \ = \{x\} \\ \mathrm{rv}(J \,|\, J') = \mathrm{rv}(J) \uplus \mathrm{rv}(J') & \mathrm{dv}(J \,|\, J') = \mathrm{dv}(J) \uplus \mathrm{dv}(J') \end{array}$$

In definitions:

$$\begin{array}{ll} \mathrm{dv}(J \triangleright P) \ \ = \mathrm{dv}(J) & \mathrm{fv}(J \triangleright P) \ \ = \mathrm{dv}(J) \cup (\mathrm{fv}(P) \backslash \mathrm{rv}(J)) \\ \mathrm{dv}(D \wedge D') = \mathrm{dv}(D) \cup \mathrm{dv}(D') & \mathrm{fv}(D \wedge D') = \mathrm{fv}(D) \cup \mathrm{fv}(D') \end{array}$$

In processes:

$$\begin{array}{ll} \mathrm{fv}(A \,|\, A') \ = (\mathrm{fv}(A) \cup \mathrm{fv}(A')) \setminus (\mathrm{xv}(A) \uplus \mathrm{xv}(A')) & \mathrm{fv}(\mathbf{0}) \ = \emptyset \\ \mathrm{xv}(A \,|\, A') \ = \mathrm{xv}(A) \uplus \mathrm{xv}(A') & \mathrm{xv}(\mathbf{0}) \ = \emptyset \\ \mathrm{fv}(\mathtt{def}_S\ D \ \mathtt{in}\, A) = (\mathrm{fv}(D) \cup \mathrm{fv}(A)) \setminus (\mathrm{dv}(D) \uplus \mathrm{xv}(A)) & \mathrm{fv}(x\langle\tilde v\rangle) = \{x, \tilde v\} \\ \mathrm{xv}(\mathtt{def}_S\ D \ \mathtt{in}\, A) = S \uplus \mathrm{xv}(A) & \mathrm{xv}(x\langle\tilde v\rangle) = \emptyset \end{array}$$

In chemical solutions:

$$\begin{array}{l} \mathrm{fv}(\mathcal{D} \vdash_S \mathcal{A}) \ = (\mathrm{fv}(\mathcal{D}) \cup \mathrm{fv}(\mathcal{A})) \setminus (\mathrm{dv}(\mathcal{D}) \uplus \mathrm{xv}(\mathcal{A})) \\ \mathrm{xv}(\mathcal{D} \vdash_S \mathcal{A}) = S \uplus \mathrm{xv}(\mathcal{A}) \end{array}$$

**Fig. 5.** Scopes in the open join calculus

**Definition 32.** Open chemical solutions, *ranged over by* $\mathcal{S}, \mathcal{T}, \ldots$, *are triples* $(\mathcal{D}, S, \mathcal{A})$, *written* $\mathcal{D} \vdash_S \mathcal{A}$, *where* $\mathcal{D}$ *is a multiset of definitions,* $S$ *is a subset of the names defined in* $\mathcal{D}$, *and* $\mathcal{A}$ *is a multiset of open processes with disjoint sets of extruded names that are not defined in* $\mathcal{D}$.

The interface of an open solution $\mathcal{S}$ consists of two disjoint sets of free names $\mathrm{fv}(\mathcal{S})$ and extruded names $\mathrm{xv}(\mathcal{S})$, defined in Fig. 5. Functions $\mathrm{dv}(\cdot)$, $\mathrm{fv}(\cdot)$, and $\mathrm{xv}(\cdot)$ are extended to multisets of terms by taking unions for all terms in the multisets.

The chemical rules for the open RCHAM are given in Fig. 6; they define families of transitions between open solutions $\rightleftharpoons$, $\rightarrow$, and $\xrightarrow{\alpha}$ where $\alpha$ ranges over labels of the form $S\overline{x}\langle\tilde v\rangle$ and $x\langle\tilde v\rangle$.

The structural rules and rule REACT are unchanged, but they now apply to open solutions. Rule STR-DEF performs the bookkeeping of exported names, and otherwise enforces a lexical scoping discipline with scope-extrusion for any name that is not exported. When applied to open solutions, these structural rules capture the intended meaning of extruded names: messages sent on extruded names can be moved inside or outside their defining process. For instance, we have the structural rearrangement

$$\vdash_S \ x\langle\tilde v\rangle \,|\, \mathtt{def}_{S'}\ D \ \mathtt{in}\ A \rightleftharpoons \vdash_S \ \mathtt{def}_{S'}\ D \ \mathtt{in}\ (x\langle\tilde v\rangle \,|\, A)$$

for any extruded name $x$, and as long as the names in $\tilde v$ are not captured by $D$ ($\{\tilde v\} \cap \mathrm{dv}(D) \subseteq S'$).

| | | | |
|---|---|---|---|
| STR-NULL | $\vdash_S \mathbf{0}$ | $\rightleftharpoons$ | $\vdash_S$ |
| STR-PAR | $\vdash_S A \mid A'$ | $\rightleftharpoons$ | $\vdash_S A, A'$ |
| STR-TOP | $\top \vdash_S$ | $\rightleftharpoons$ | $\vdash_S$ |
| STR-AND | $D \wedge D' \vdash_S$ | $\rightleftharpoons$ | $D, D' \vdash_S$ |
| STR-DEF | $\vdash_S \mathtt{def}_{S'}\ D\ \mathtt{in}\ A$ | $\rightleftharpoons$ | $D\sigma \vdash_{S \uplus S'} A\sigma$ |
| REACT | $J \triangleright P \vdash_S J\rho$ | $\rightarrow$ | $J \triangleright P \vdash_S P\rho$ |
| EXT | $\vdash_S x\langle\tilde{y}\rangle$ | $\xrightarrow{S'\overline{x}\langle\tilde{y}\rangle}$ | $\vdash_{S \cup S'}$ |
| INT | $\vdash_{S \cup \{x\}}$ | $\xrightarrow{x\langle\tilde{y}\rangle}$ | $\vdash_{S \cup \{x\}} x\langle\tilde{y}\rangle$ |

Side conditions on the reacting solution $\mathcal{S} = (\mathcal{D} \vdash_S \mathcal{A})$:
in STR-DEF, $\sigma$ substitutes distinct fresh names for $\mathrm{dv}(D) \setminus S'$;
in REACT, $\rho$ substitutes names for $\mathrm{rv}(J)$;
in EXT, the name $x$ is free, and $S' = \{\tilde{y}\} \cap (\mathrm{dv}(\mathcal{D}) \setminus S)$;
in INT, the names $\tilde{y}$ are either free, or fresh, or extruded.

**Fig. 6.** The open RCHAM

In addition, rules EXT and INT model interaction with the context. According to rule EXT, messages emitted on free names can be received by the environment; these messages export any defined name that was not previously known to the environment, thus causing the scope of its definition to be opened. This is made explicit by the set $S'$ in the label of the transition $\xrightarrow{S'\overline{x}\langle\tilde{v}\rangle}$. Names in $S'$ must be distinct from any name that appears in the interface before the transition; once these names have been extruded, they cannot be $\alpha$-converted anymore, and behave like constants. Our rule resembles the OPEN rule for restriction in the pi calculus [37], with an important constraint due to locality: messages are either emitted on free names, to be consumed by EXT, or on names defined in the open solution, to be consumed by REACT.

The rule INT enables the intrusion of messages on exported names. It can be viewed as a disciplined version of one of the two INPUT rules proposed by Honda and Tokoro for the asynchronous pi calculus, which enables the intrusion of any message [23]. The side condition of INT requires that intruded messages do not clash with local names of processes. (More implicitly, we may instead rely on the silent $\alpha$-conversion on those local names; this is the original meaning of "intrusion" in [37].)

### 4.2 Observational Equivalences on Open Terms

The notions of reduction-based equivalence defined in sections 2 and 3 are easily extended to open processes, with the same definitions and the additional requirement that related processes have the same exported names. (Indeed, it makes little sense to compare processes with incompatible interfaces such as $\mathbf{0}$ and the open deadlocked solution $\mathtt{def}_{\{y\}}\ x\langle\rangle \mid y\langle\rangle \triangleright \mathtt{in}\ \mathbf{0}$.) Context-closure properties are also easily extended to take into account open contexts. Note that, whenever we apply a context, we implicitly assume that the resulting open process is well-formed. Finally, extrusions and strong barbs are in direct correspondence—we have $A \downarrow_x$ if and only if $A \xrightarrow{S\overline{x}\langle\tilde{v}\rangle} A'$ for any $S$,$\tilde{v}$, and $A'$.

In fact, the open syntax provides a convenient notation to give selective access to some of the names defined in the processes being compared, but it does not yield any interesting new equation. Consider for instance bisimilarity equivalence on open terms:

**Lemma 33.** *For all processes $P_1$, $P_2$ and definitions $D_1$, $D_2$, let $\tilde{x}$ be a tuple of names defined in both $D_1$ and $D_2$, and let plug be a fresh name. The three following statements are equivalent:*

1. $\mathtt{def}_{\{\tilde{x}\}}\ D_1 \ \mathtt{in}\ P_1 \approx \mathtt{def}_{\{\tilde{x}\}}\ D_2 \ \mathtt{in}\ P_2$
2. $\mathtt{def}\ D_1 \ \mathtt{in}\ P_1 \,|\, plug\langle\tilde{x}\rangle \approx \mathtt{def}\ D_2 \ \mathtt{in}\ P_2 \,|\, plug\langle\tilde{x}\rangle$
3. *for all $D$ and $P$ such that* $\mathrm{fv}(\mathtt{def}\ D\ \mathtt{in}\ P) \cap (\mathrm{dv}(D_1) \cup \mathrm{dv}(D_2)) \subseteq \{\tilde{x}\}$ *and* $\mathrm{dv}(D) \cap (\mathrm{dv}(D_1) \cup \mathrm{dv}(D_2)) = \emptyset$, *we have* $\mathtt{def}\ D \wedge D_1\ \mathtt{in}\ P \,|\, P_1 \approx \mathtt{def}\ D \wedge D_2\ \mathtt{in}\ P \,|\, P_2$.

The first formulation is the most compact; it relies on open terms. Instead, the second formulation makes explicit the communication of extruded names to the environment using a message on a fresh name *plug*; the third formulation is closed by application of evaluation contexts, and is often used in direct proofs of bisimilarity equivalence (see for instance, [4]).

### 4.3 Labeled Bisimulation

By design, the open join calculus can also be equipped with the standard notion of labeled bisimilarity:

**Definition 34.** *A relation $\mathcal{R}$ on open processes is a* labeled simulation *if, whenever $A \mathcal{R} B$, we have*

1. *if $A \rightarrow A'$ then $B \rightarrow^* B'$ and $A' \mathcal{R} B'$;*
2. *if $A \xrightarrow{\alpha} A'$ then $B \rightarrow^* \xrightarrow{\alpha} \rightarrow^* B'$ and $A' \mathcal{R} B'$,*
   *for all labels $\alpha$ of shape $x\langle\tilde{v}\rangle$ or $S\overline{x}\langle\tilde{v}\rangle$ such that* $\mathrm{fv}(B) \cap S = \emptyset$.

*A relation $\mathcal{R}$ is a* labeled bisimulation *when both $\mathcal{R}$ and $\mathcal{R}^{-1}$ are labeled simulations.* Labeled bisimilarity *$\approx_l$ is the largest labeled bisimulation.*

The simulation clause for intrusions makes weak bisimulation sensitive to input interfaces: $A \approx_l B$ implies $\mathrm{xv}(A) = \mathrm{xv}(B)$. The simulation clause for extrusion does not consider labels whose set of extruded names $S$ clashes with the free names of $B$, inasmuch as these transitions can never be simulated; this standard technicality does not affect the intuitive discriminating power of bisimulation, because names in $S$ can be $\alpha$-converted before the extrusion.

As opposed to contextual equivalences, it is possible to tell whether two processes are weakly bisimilar by comparing their labeled synchronization trees, rather than reasoning on their possible contexts. For example, $x\langle u\rangle \not\approx_l x\langle v\rangle$ because each process performs an extrusion with distinct labels. Likewise, $x\langle y\rangle \not\approx_l$

$\mathtt{def}\ z\langle u\rangle \triangleright y\langle u\rangle\ \mathtt{in}\ x\langle z\rangle$ because the first process emits a free name (label $\overline{x}\langle y\rangle$) while the latter emits a local name that gets extruded (label $\{z\}\overline{x}\langle z\rangle$).

Besides, a whole range of "up to proof techniques" is available to reduce the size of the relation to exhibit when proving labeled bisimilarities [35, 38, 47, 49]. For instance, one can reason up to other bisimilarities, or up to the restriction of the input interface.

While its definition does not mention contexts, labeled bisimilarity is closed by application of any context:

**Theorem 35.** *Weak bisimilarity is a congruence.*

The proof is almost generic to mobile process calculi in the absence of external choice (see, e.g., [23, 7] for the asynchronous pi calculus); it relies on two simpler closure properties: $\approx_l$ is closed by application of evaluation contexts, and $\approx_l$ is closed by renamings. We refer to [18] for the details.

As an immediate corollary, we can place labeled bisimilarity in our hierarchy of equivalence, and justify its use as an auxiliary proof technique for observational equivalence: we have that $\approx_l$ is a reduction-based bisimulation that respects all barbs and that is closed by application of contexts, hence $\approx_l \subseteq \approx$. This inclusion is strict, as can be seen from the paradigmatic example of bisimilarity equivalence:

$$x\langle z\rangle \approx \mathtt{def}\ u\langle v\rangle \triangleright z\langle v\rangle\ \mathtt{in}\ x\langle u\rangle$$

That is, emitting a free name $z$ is the same as emitting a bound name $u$ that forwards all the messages it receives to $z$, because the extra internal move for every use of $u$ is not observable. On the contrary, labeled bisimilarity separates these two processes because their respective extrusion labels reveal that $z$ is free and $u$ is extruded. Since the contexts of the open join calculus cannot identify names in messages, more powerful contexts are required to reconcile the two semantics (see Sect. 4.5).

### 4.4 Asynchronous Bisimulation

In order to prove that two processes are bisimilar, a large candidate bisimulation can be a nuisance, as it requires the analysis of numerous transition cases. Although they are not necessarily context-closed, labeled bisimulations on open chemical solutions are typically rather large. For example, a process with an extruded name has infinitely many derivatives even if no "real" computation is ever performed. Consider the equivalence:

$$\mathtt{def}\ x\langle u\rangle \mid y\langle v\rangle \triangleright P\ \mathtt{in}\ z\langle x\rangle \approx_l \mathtt{def}\ x\langle u\rangle \mid y\langle v\rangle \triangleright Q\ \mathtt{in}\ z\langle x\rangle$$

These two processes are bisimilar because their join-pattern cannot be triggered, regardless of the messages the environment may send on $x$. Still, one is confronted with infinite models on both sides, with a distinct chemical solution for every multiset of messages that have been intruded on $x$ so far. This problem with labeled bisimulation motivates an alternative formulation of labeled equivalence.

**The Join Open** RCHAM. We modify the open RCHAM by allowing inputs only when they immediately trigger a guarded process. For example, the two processes above become inert after an extrusion $\{x\}\overline{z}\langle x\rangle$, hence trivially bisimilar. If we applied this refinement with the same labels for input as before, however, we would obtain a dubious result. The solution $x\langle\rangle \mid y\langle\rangle \mid z\langle\rangle \rhd P \vdash_{\{x,y\}} z\langle\rangle$ can progress by first inputing two messages $x\langle\rangle$ and $y\langle\rangle$, then performing a silent step that consumes these two messages together with the local message $z\langle\rangle$ already in the solution. Yet, neither $x\langle\rangle$ nor $y\langle\rangle$ alone can trigger the process $P$, and therefore this solution would become inert, too. This suggests the use of *join-inputs* on $x$ and $y$ in transitions such as

$$x\langle\rangle \mid y\langle\rangle \mid z\langle\rangle \rhd P \vdash_{\{x,y\}} z\langle\rangle \xrightarrow{x\langle\rangle \mid y\langle\rangle} x\langle\rangle \mid y\langle\rangle \mid z\langle\rangle \rhd P \vdash_{\{x,y\}} P$$

On the other hand, the solution $x\langle\rangle \mid y\langle\rangle \mid z\langle\rangle \rhd P \vdash_{\{x\}} z\langle\rangle$ is truly inert, since the environment has no access to $y$, and thus cannot trigger $P$. In this case, our refinement suppresses all input transitions.

The join open RCHAM is defined in Fig. 7 as a replacement for the intrusion rule. In contrast with rule INT of Fig. 6, the new rule REACT-INT permits the intrusion of messages only if these messages are immediately used to trigger a process. This is formalized by allowing labels $M'$ that are parallel compositions of messages. If the solution contains a complementary process $M$ such that the combination $M \mid M'$ matches the join-pattern of a reaction rule, then the transition occurs and triggers this reaction rule. As for INT, we restrict intrusions in $M'$ to messages on extruded names.

We identify intrusions in the case $M' = \mathbf{0}$ with silent steps; the rule REACT is thus omitted from the new chemical machine. Nonetheless, we maintain the distinction between internal moves and proper input moves in the discussion. In the sequel, we shall keep the symbol $\xrightarrow{\alpha}$ for the open RCHAM and use $\xrightarrow{\alpha}_{\mathrm{J}}$ for the join open RCHAM; we may drop the subscript J when no ambiguity can arise.

Each open process now has two different models: for instance, the process $\mathtt{def}_{\{x\}}\ x\langle\rangle \mid y\langle\rangle \rhd P\ \mathtt{in}\ \mathbf{0}$ has no transition in the join open RCHAM, while it has infinite series of transitions $\xrightarrow{x\langle\rangle}\xrightarrow{x\langle\rangle}\xrightarrow{x\langle\rangle}\cdots$ in the open RCHAM. A comparison between the two transition systems yields the following correspondence between their intrusions:

**Proposition 36.** *Let $A$ be an open process.*

1. *If $A \xrightarrow{x_1\langle\tilde{v}_1\rangle \mid \cdots \mid x_n\langle\tilde{v}_n\rangle}_{\mathrm{J}} B$, then $A \xrightarrow{x_1\langle\tilde{v}_1\rangle} \cdots \xrightarrow{x_n\langle\tilde{v}_n\rangle}\rightarrow B$.*
2. *If $A \mid x\langle\tilde{u}\rangle \xrightarrow{M}_{\mathrm{J}} B$ and $x \in \mathrm{xv}(A)$, then*
   *(a) either $A \xrightarrow{M}_{\mathrm{J}} A'$ with $A' \mid x\langle\tilde{u}\rangle \equiv B$;*
   *(b) or $A \xrightarrow{M \mid x\langle\tilde{u}\rangle}_{\mathrm{J}} B$.*

Accordingly, we adapt the definition of labeled bisimulation (Definition 34) to the new join open RCHAM. Consider the two processes:

$$P \stackrel{\text{def}}{=} \mathtt{def}\ x\langle\rangle \rhd a\langle\rangle \wedge a\langle\rangle \mid y\langle\rangle \rhd R\ \mathtt{in}\ z\langle x,y\rangle$$
$$Q \stackrel{\text{def}}{=} \mathtt{def}\ x\langle\rangle \mid y\langle\rangle \rhd R\ \mathtt{in}\ z\langle x,y\rangle$$

$$\text{React-Int} \qquad J \triangleright P \vdash_S M \xrightarrow{M'} J \triangleright P \vdash_S P\rho$$

Side conditions:
$\rho$ substitute names for $\mathrm{rv}(J)$, $J\rho \equiv M \mid M'$, and $\mathrm{dv}(M') \subseteq S$.

The rules Str-(Null,Par,And,Def) and Ext are the same as in Fig. 6.

**Fig. 7.** The join open RCHAM

and assume $a \notin \mathrm{fv}(R)$. With the initial open RCHAM, the processes $P$ and $Q$ are weakly bisimilar. With the new join open RCHAM and the same definition of weak bisimulation, this does not hold because $P$ can input $x\langle\rangle$ after emitting on $z$ while $Q$ cannot. But if we consider the bisimulation that uses join-input labels instead of single ones, $Q$ can input $x\langle\rangle \mid y\langle\rangle$ while $P$ cannot, and $P$ and $Q$ are still separated. It turns out that labeled bisimulation discriminates too much in the join open RCHAM.

In order to retain an asynchronous semantics, labeled bisimulation must be relaxed, so that a process may simulate a React-Int transition even if it does not immediately consume all its messages. This leads us to the following definition:

**Definition 37.** *A relation $\mathcal{R}$ is an* asynchronous simulation *if, whenever $A\ \mathcal{R}\ B$, we have*

1. *if $A \xrightarrow{S\overline{x}\langle\tilde{v}\rangle} A'$ then $B \rightarrow^* \xrightarrow{S\overline{x}\langle\tilde{v}\rangle} \rightarrow^* B'$ and $A'\ \mathcal{R}\ B'$ for all labels $S\overline{x}\langle\tilde{v}\rangle$ such that $\mathrm{fv}(B) \cap S = \emptyset$;*
2. *if $A \xrightarrow{M} A'$, then $B \mid M \rightarrow^* B'$ and $A'\ \mathcal{R}\ B'$;*
3. $\mathrm{xv}(A) = \mathrm{xv}(B)$.

*A relation $\mathcal{R}$ is an* asynchronous bisimulation *when both $\mathcal{R}$ and $\mathcal{R}^{-1}$ are asynchronous simulations.* Asynchronous bisimilarity $\approx_{\mathrm{a}}$ *is the largest asynchronous bisimulation.*

In the definition above, the usual clause for silent steps is omitted (it is subsumed by the clause for intrusions with $M = \mathbf{0}$). On the other hand, a clause explicitly requires that related solutions have the same extruded names.

Asynchronous bisimilarity and labeled bisimilarity do coincide. This validates asynchronous bisimulation as an efficient proof technique.

**Theorem 38.** $\approx_{\mathrm{a}} = \approx_l$.

To conclude our discussion on variants of labeled bisimulations, let us mention *ground bisimulation*, which is obtained by restricting the intrusions to labels that convey fresh names. As first observed in the pi calculus [23, 7, 11], asynchrony brings another interesting property as regards the number of transitions to consider: the ground variant of bisimilarities coincide with the basic one. This property also holds in the join calculus, thus providing proof techniques with, for every chemical solution, exactly one intrusion per extruded name when using labeled bisimulation, and one intrusion per "active" partial join-pattern when using asynchronous bisimulation.

## 4.5 The Discriminating Power of Name Comparison

Labeled bisimilarity is finer than (reduction-based, barbed) bisimilarity equivalence and, as in other process calculi, these two semantics coincide only if we add an operator for name comparison [25, 7]. (Alternatively, we may adapt our notion of labeled bisimilarity, as proposed by Merro and Sangiorgi [33].) In this section, we extend the syntax of the join calculus with comparisons, in the same style as [37].

$$A \stackrel{\text{def}}{=} \ldots \mid [x{=}y]\, A \qquad\qquad P \stackrel{\text{def}}{=} \ldots \mid [x{=}y]\, P$$

We also extend our chemical machines with a new reduction rule.

$$\textsc{Compare} \qquad \vdash_S [x{=}x]\, A \to \vdash A$$

A technical drawback of this extension is that renamings do not preserve bisimilarity anymore. For instance, $\mathbf{0} \approx_l [x{=}y]\, x\langle\rangle$, while after applying the renaming $\{^x/_y\}$, $\mathbf{0} \not\approx_l [x{=}x]\, x\langle\rangle$. Accordingly, labeled bisimilarity is not a congruence anymore. For instance, the context $C[\cdot] \stackrel{\text{def}}{=} \texttt{def}\ z\langle x,y\rangle \triangleright [\cdot]\ \texttt{in}\ z\langle u,u\rangle$ separates $\mathbf{0}$ and $[x{=}y]\, x\langle\rangle$. We consider equivalences that are closed only by application of evaluation contexts.

In the presence of comparisons, we still have:

**Lemma 39.** *Labeled bisimilarity is closed by application of evaluation contexts*

As regards observational equivalence, we let *bisimilarity equivalence* $\approx_{\mathsf{be}}$ be the largest barb-preserving bisimulation in the open join calculus with name comparison that is closed by application of evaluation contexts. Bisimilarity equivalence now separates $x\langle z\rangle$ from $\texttt{def}\ u\langle v\rangle \triangleright z\langle v\rangle\ \texttt{in}\ x\langle u\rangle$ by using the context $\texttt{def}\ x\langle y\rangle \triangleright [y{=}z]\, a\langle\rangle\ \texttt{in}\ [\cdot]$, and labeled bisimilarity clearly remains finer than bisimilarity equivalence. More interestingly, the converse inclusion also holds:

**Theorem 40.** *With name comparison, we have* $\approx_{\mathsf{be}} = \approx_l$.

To establish the theorem, it suffices to show that, for every label, there is an evaluation context that specifically "captures" the label. Intrusions are very easy, since it suffices to use the parallel context $x\langle\tilde{y}\rangle \,\|\, [\cdot]$. Extrusions are more delicate: for every output transition, the corresponding context receives the message, then performs name comparisons between the message content and any other free names. In contrast with output transitions, however, join calculus contexts that receive a message on a given name must define this name. Later on, our contexts silently forward any message from this name to another fresh name. Without additional care, the presence of a forwarder could be detected by name comparison, so we use instead a family of contexts that separate two aspects of a name. For every name $x \in \mathcal{N}$, we let

$$R_x[\cdot] \stackrel{\text{def}}{=} \texttt{def}\ x\langle\tilde{y}\rangle \triangleright x'\langle\tilde{y}\rangle\ \texttt{in}\ v_x\langle x\rangle \,\|\, [\cdot]$$

where the length of $\tilde{y}$ matches the arity of $x$. Assuming $x \in \mathrm{fv}(A)$, the process $R_x[A]$ uses $x'$ as a free name instead of $x$, and forwards all messages from $x$

to $x'$. An enclosing context context should still be able to discriminate whether the process sends the name $x$ or some other name. This extra capability is enabled by an auxiliary message, $v_x\langle x\rangle$, that can be received to compare $x$ to any other name. The next lemma captures the essential property of $R_x[\cdot]$:

**Lemma 41 (Accommodating the extrusions).** *For all open processes $A$ and $B$ such that $x \notin \mathrm{xv}(A) \cup \mathrm{xv}(B)$ and $x', v_x$ are not in the interface of $A$ and $B$, we have $A \approx_{\mathsf{be}} B$ if and only if $R_x[A] \approx_{\mathsf{be}} R_x[B]$.*

Informally, the contexts $R_x[\cdot]$ are the residuals of contexts that test for labels of the form $\{S\}\overline{x}\langle\tilde{y}\rangle$. Once we have a context for every label, we easily prove that $\approx_{\mathsf{be}}$ is a labeled bisimulation. Remark that the proof of the theorem would be much harder if we were using the other notion of bisimilarity equivalence (see Sect. 3.1), because we would have to characterize the whole synchronization tree at once in a single context, instead of characterizing every label in isolation. This explains why many similar results in the literature apply only to processes with image-finite transitions.

## 5 Distribution and Mobility

Although distributed programming is the main purpose of the join calculus, the distribution of resources has been kept implicit so far. As we described its semantics, we just argued that the join calculus had enough built-in locality to be implemented in a distributed, asynchronous manner.

This section gives a more explicit account of distributed programming. We extend the join calculus with *locations* and primitives for mobility. The resulting calculus allows us to express mobile agents that can move between physical sites. Agents are not only programs but core images of running processes with their communication capabilities and their internal state. Inevitably, the resulting *distributed join calculus* is a bit more complex than the core calculus of Sect. 1.

Intuitively, a location resides on a physical site, and contains a group of processes and definitions. We can move atomically a location to another site. We represent mobile agents by locations. Agents can contain mobile sub-agents represented by nested locations. Agents move as a whole with all their current sub-agents, thereby locations have a dynamic tree structure. Our calculus treats location names as first class values with lexical scopes, as is the case for channel names; the scope of every name may extend over several locations, and may be dynamically extended as the result of message passing or agent mobility. A location controls its own moves, and can move towards another location by providing the name of the target location, which would typically be communicated only to selected processes.

Since we use the distributed join calculus as the core of a programming language (as opposed to a specification language), the design for mobility is strongly influenced by implementation issues. Our definition of atomic reduction steps attempts to strike some balance between expressiveness and realistic concerns. Except for the (partial) reliable detection of physical failures, the refined operational semantics has been faithfully implemented [20, 15]. In these notes, however, we omit any specific discussion of these implementations.

## 5.1 Distributed Mobile Programming

We introduce the language with a few examples that assume the same approach to runtime distribution as in JoCaml. Execution occurs among several machines, which may dynamically join or quit the computation; the runtime support consists of several system-level processes that communicate using TCP/IP. Processes and definitions can migrate from one machine to another but, at any given point, every process and definition of the language is running at a single machine.

From an asynchronous viewpoint, and in the absence of partial failures, *locality is transparent.* Programs can be written independently of their runtime distribution, and their visible results do not depend on their localization. Indeed, it is "equivalent" to run processes $P$ and $Q$ at different machines, or to run the compound process $P \mid Q$ at a single machine. In particular, the scopes for channel names and other values do not depend on their localization: whenever a channel appears in a process, it can be used to form messages (using the name either as the address, or as the message contents) without knowing whether this channel is locally- or remotely-defined.

Of course, locality matters in some circumstances: side effects such as printing values on the local terminal depend on the current machine; besides, efficiency can be affected as message-sending over the network takes much longer than local calls; finally, the termination of some underlying runtime will affect all its local processes. For all these reasons, *locality is explicitly controlled in the language*; this locality can be adjusted using migration. In contrast, resources such as definitions and processes are not silently relocated or replicated by the system.

In JoCaml, programs being run on different machines do not initially share any channel name; therefore, they would normally not be able to interact with one another. To bootstrap a distributed computation, it is necessary to exchange a few names; this is achieved using a built-in library called the name server. Once this is done, these names can be used to communicate some more names and to build more complex communication patterns. (Formally, we bypass an explicit definition of a name server, and use instead the same free names in different locations.) The interface of the name server consists of two functions to register and look up arbitrary values in a "global table" indexed by plain strings. For instance, the process on the left below defines a local name *cos* and registers it to the name server:

| | |
|---|---|
| $\texttt{def}\ cos(x) = 1 - x^2/2\ \texttt{in}$ | $\texttt{let}\ cos = NS.lookup(\text{“}\texttt{cos}\text{”})\ \texttt{in}$ |
| $NS.register(\text{“}\texttt{cos}\text{”}, cos)$ | $print(cos(0.1)); \ldots$ |

Using the same key "cos", a remote program (such as the one on the right) can obtain the name *cos* then perform remote calls. The computation takes place on the machine that defines *cos* (in the example, the machine hosting the program on the left).

More explicitly, the program defining *cos* may define a *named location* that wraps this function definition, and may also export the location name under the key "here":

$$\begin{array}{l}\texttt{def}\ \mathit{here}[\\ \quad \mathit{cos}(x) = 1 - x^2/2\ \ :\\ \quad \mathit{NS.register}(\text{“}\texttt{cos}\text{”}, \mathit{cos}); \ldots\,]\ \texttt{in}\\ \mathit{NS.register}(\text{“}\texttt{here}\text{”}, \mathit{here}); \ldots\end{array}$$

The location definition does not affect *cos*, which can still be called locally or remotely. In addition to remote access to *cos*, another program can now obtain the location name *here*, create locally a mobile sublocation—its "agent"—and relocate this agent to *here*. This makes sense, for instance, if the agent implements processes that often call *cos*. The code on the client program may be:

$$\begin{array}{l}\texttt{def}\ f(\mathit{machine}) \triangleright\\ \quad \mathit{agent}[\\ \quad\quad \texttt{go}\ \mathit{machine};\\ \quad\quad \texttt{def}\ \mathit{cos} = \mathit{NS.lookup}(\text{“}\texttt{cos}\text{”})\ \texttt{in}\\ \quad\quad \texttt{def}\ \mathit{sum}(s, n) = \texttt{if}\ n = 0\ \texttt{then}\ s\ \texttt{else}\ \mathit{sum}(s + \mathit{cos}(n), n - 1)\ \texttt{in}\\ \quad\quad \texttt{return}\ \mathit{sum}(0, 10)\ ]\\ \mathit{print}(f(\mathit{NS.lookup}(\text{“}\texttt{here}\text{”}))); \ldots\end{array}$$

The new statement "go *location*; *P*" causes the enclosing location to migrate as a whole towards *location*'s machine before executing the following process *P*. In the program above, location *agent* migrates with its running process towards the machine that hosts *here* and *cos*, locally retrieves *cos* using the name server and runs some computation, then eventually returns a single result to *f*'s caller on the client machine.

A more complex example is an "applet server" that provides a function to create new instances of a library *at a remote location* provided by the caller. To this end, the server creates a mobile agent that wraps the instance of the library, migrates to the target location, and delivers the library interface once there. For instance, the code below implements a "one-place-buffer" library with some log mechanism:

$$\begin{array}{l}\texttt{def}\ \mathit{newOnePlaceBuffer}(\mathit{there}) \triangleright\\ \quad \texttt{def}\ \mathit{log}(s) = \mathit{print}(\text{"}\texttt{the buffer is }\text{"} + s)\ \texttt{in}\\ \quad \texttt{def}\ \mathit{applet}[\\ \quad\quad \texttt{go}\ \mathit{there};\\ \quad\quad \texttt{def}\ \mathit{put}(v) \mid \mathit{empty}\langle\rangle \triangleright \mathit{log}(\text{“}\texttt{full}\text{”}); (\mathit{full}\langle v\rangle \mid \texttt{return})\\ \quad\quad\quad \wedge\ \mathit{get}() \mid \mathit{full}\langle v\rangle \triangleright \mathit{log}(\text{“}\texttt{empty}\text{”}); (\mathit{empty}\langle\rangle \mid \texttt{return}\ v)\ \texttt{in}\\ \quad\quad \mathit{empty}\langle\rangle \mid \texttt{return}\ \mathit{put}, \mathit{get}\ \texttt{to}\ \mathit{newBuf}\ ]\ \texttt{in}\\ \quad \mathit{log}(\text{“}\texttt{created}\text{”}); \texttt{in}\\ \mathit{NS.register}(\text{“}\texttt{applet}\text{”}, \mathit{newOnePlaceBuffer}); \ldots\end{array}$$

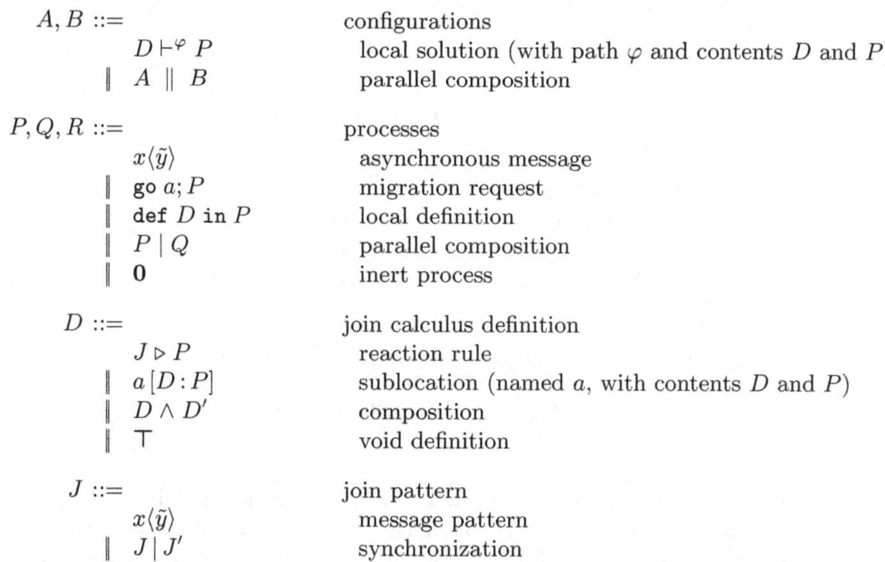

| | | |
|---|---|---|
| $A, B ::=$ | | configurations |
| | $D \vdash^{\varphi} P$ | local solution (with path $\varphi$ and contents $D$ and $P$) |
| $\|$ | $A \parallel B$ | parallel composition |
| $P, Q, R ::=$ | | processes |
| | $x\langle\tilde{y}\rangle$ | asynchronous message |
| $\|$ | $\texttt{go}\ a; P$ | migration request |
| $\|$ | $\texttt{def}\ D\ \texttt{in}\ P$ | local definition |
| $\|$ | $P \mid Q$ | parallel composition |
| $\|$ | $\mathbf{0}$ | inert process |
| $D ::=$ | | join calculus definition |
| | $J \triangleright P$ | reaction rule |
| $\|$ | $a\,[D : P]$ | sublocation (named $a$, with contents $D$ and $P$) |
| $\|$ | $D \wedge D'$ | composition |
| $\|$ | $\top$ | void definition |
| $J ::=$ | | join pattern |
| | $x\langle\tilde{y}\rangle$ | message pattern |
| $\|$ | $J \mid J'$ | synchronization |

**Fig. 8.** Syntax for the distributed join calculus

A simple applet client may be:

```
def newBuf = NS.lookup("applet") in
def here[
   def put, get = newBuf(here) in
   put(1); ...] in ...
```

In contrast with plain code mobility, the new applet can keep static access to channels located at the applet server; in our case, every call to the one-place buffer is local to the applet client, but also causes a remote log message to be sent to the applet server.

### 5.2 Computing with Locations

We now model locations and migrations as a refinement of the RCHAM. We proceed in two steps. First, we partition processes and definitions into several local chemical solutions. This flat model suffices for representing both local computation on different sites and global communication between them. Then, we introduce some more structure to account for the creation and the mobility of local solutions: we attach *location names* to solutions, and we organize them as a tree of nested locations. The refined syntax and chemical semantics appear in figures 8 and 9.

**Distributed Machines.** A distributed reflexive chemical machine (DRCHAM) is a multiset of RCHAMs. We write the global state of a DRCHAM as several *local solutions* $\mathcal{D} \vdash^{\alpha} \mathcal{P}$ connected by a commutative-associative operator $\parallel$ that

| | |
|---|---|
| COMM | $\vdash^{\alpha} x\langle\tilde{y}\rangle \parallel D \vdash^{\beta} \rightarrow \vdash^{\alpha} \parallel D \vdash^{\beta} x\langle\tilde{y}\rangle$ |
| GO | $\vdash^{\alpha a} \parallel \vdash^{\beta b} \mathsf{go}\ a; P \rightarrow \vdash^{\alpha a} \parallel \vdash^{\alpha a b} P$ |
| STR-LOC | $a[D : P] \vdash^{\alpha} \rightleftharpoons D \vdash^{\alpha a} P \parallel \vdash^{\alpha}$ |

Side conditions:
in COMM, $x \in \mathrm{dv}(D)$;
in GO, $b$ does not occur in any other path;
in STR-LOC, $a$ does not occur in any other path
and $\{D\}$, $\{P\}$ is the only content of solution $\alpha a$.

The local rules are unchanged (cf. figure 2)
distributed parallel composition $\parallel$ is associate-commutative.

**Fig. 9.** The distributed RCHAM

represents distributed composition. Each local solution is labeled by a distinct *path* $\alpha$—we will detail below the structure and the role of these paths.

Locally, every solution $\mathcal{D} \vdash^{\alpha} \mathcal{P}$ within a DRCHAM evolves as before, according to the chemical rules given for the join calculus in Fig. 2. Technically, the chemical context law is extended to enable computation in any local solution, and the side condition in STR-DEF requires that globally-fresh names be substituted for locally-defined names.

Two solutions can interact by using a new rule COMM that models global communication. This rule states that a message emitted in a given solution $\alpha$ on a channel name $x$ that is remotely defined must be forwarded to the solution $\beta$ that contains the definition of $x$. Later on, this message can be used within $\beta$ to assemble a pattern of messages and to consume it locally, using a local REACT step. This two-step decomposition of communication reflects the separation of message transport and message processing in actual implementations.

In the following, we consider only DRCHAMs where *every name is defined in at most one local solution.* This condition is preserved by the chemical semantics, and simplifies the usage of rule COMM: for every message, the rule applies at most once, and delivers the message to a unique receiving location. The actual mapping from channel names to their defining locations is static; it is maintained by the implementation. (In contrast, some recent models of distributed systems detail the explicit routing of messages in the calculus [22, 14]. From a language design viewpoint, we believe that the bookkeeping of routing information is a low-level activity that is best handled at the implementation level. At least in the distributed join calculus, the locality property makes routing information simple enough to be safely omitted from the language.)

**Remote Message Passing.** To illustrate the use of several local solutions, we model a simplistic "print spooler" that matches available printers and job requests. The spooler can be described by the rule

$$D \stackrel{\text{def}}{=} ready\langle printer\rangle | job\langle file\rangle \triangleright printer\langle file\rangle$$

We assume that there are three machines: a user machine $u$ that issues some print request, a server machine $s$ that hosts the spooler $D$, and a laser printer $p$ that registers to the spooler. We let $P$ represent the printer code. We have the series of chemical steps:

$$
\begin{array}{llll}
 & \vdash^u job\langle 1\rangle & \parallel\ D \vdash^s & \parallel\ laser\langle f\rangle \triangleright P \vdash^p ready\langle laser\rangle \\
\stackrel{\text{COMM}}{\rightarrow} & \vdash^u & \parallel\ D \vdash^s job\langle 1\rangle & \parallel\ laser\langle f\rangle \triangleright P \vdash^p ready\langle laser\rangle \\
\stackrel{\text{COMM}}{\rightarrow} & \vdash^u & \parallel\ D \vdash^s job\langle 1\rangle, ready\langle laser\rangle & \parallel\ laser\langle f\rangle \triangleright P \vdash^p \\
\stackrel{\text{REACT}}{\rightarrow} & \vdash^u & \parallel\ D \vdash^s laser\langle 1\rangle & \parallel\ laser\langle f\rangle \triangleright P \vdash^p \\
\stackrel{\text{COMM}}{\rightarrow} & \vdash^u & \parallel\ D \vdash^s & \parallel\ laser\langle f\rangle \triangleright P \vdash^p laser\langle 1\rangle
\end{array}
$$

The first step forwards the message $job\langle 1\rangle$ from the user machine $u$ to the machine that defines $job$, here the spooler $s$. Likewise, the second step forwards the message $ready\langle laser\rangle$ to the spooler. Next, synchronization occurs within the spooler between these two messages as a local reduction step. As a result, a new message on the spooler is sent to the laser printer, where it can be forwarded then processed.

From this example, we can also illustrates *global lexical scope.* To model that *laser* is initially private to the printer machine $p$, we can use a preliminary local, structural step on machine $p$:

$$\vdash^p \texttt{def}\ laser\langle f\rangle \triangleright P\ \texttt{in}\ ready\langle laser\rangle \stackrel{\text{STR-DEF}}{\rightleftharpoons} laser\langle f\rangle \triangleright P \vdash^p ready\langle laser\rangle$$

Then, the second COMM step in the series above extends the scope of *laser* to the server, which gains the ability to send messages to the printer. In contrast, the scoping rules guarantees that no other process may send such messages at this stage.

**Nested Locations.** Assuming that every location is mapped to its host machine, agent migration is naturally represented as an update of this mapping from locations to machines. For instance, a location that contains the running code of a mobile agent may migrate to the machine that hosts another location providing a particular service.

Our model of locality is *hierarchical*, locations being attached to a parent location rather than a machine. A migration request is expressed using the process $go(a); P$ where $a$ is the name of the target location and $P$ is a guarded process triggered after completing the migration. The migration is "subjective", as defined by Cardelli [14], inasmuch as it applies to the location that runs the process $go(a); P$ and its sublocations.

As regards distributed programming, there are many situations where several levels of moving resources are useful. For example, the server itself may sometimes move from one machine to another to continue the service while a machine goes down, and the termination of a machine and of all its locations can be modeled using the same mechanism as a migration. Also, some agents naturally make use of sub-agents, e.g., to spawn some parts of the computation to other machines. When a mobile agent returns to its client machine, for instance, it may contain running processes and other resources; logically, the contents of the agent should be integrated with the client: later on, if the client moves, or fails, this contents should be carried away or discarded accordingly.

From the implementer's viewpoint, the hierarchical model can be implemented as efficiently as the flat model, because each machine only has to keep track of its own local hierarchy of locations. Nonetheless, the model provides additional expressiveness to the programmer, who can assemble groups of resources that move from one machine to another as a whole. This may explain why most implementations of mobile objects provide a rich dynamic structure for controlling migration, for instance by allowing objects to be temporarily attached to one another (*cf.* [27, 26]).

Consider for instance the case of concurrent migrations: a client creates an agent to go and get some information on a server; in parallel, the server goes to another machine.

- With a flat location structure, the migration from the client to the server must be dynamically resolved to a migration to a particular machine, e.g. the machine that currently hosts the server. In the case the server moves after the arrival of the agent, the agent is left behind. That is, the mapping from locations to machines depends on the scheduling of the different migrations, and the migration to the server yields no guarantee of being on the same machine as the server.
- With a hierarchical structure, the ordering of nested migrations becomes irrelevant, and the agent is guaranteed to remain with the server as long as the agent does not explicitly request another migration, even as the server moves.

**Relating Locations to Local Chemical Solutions.** We must represent locations both as syntactic definitions (when considered as a sublocation, or in a guarded process) and as local chemical solutions (when they interact with one another). We rely on location names to relate the two structures. We assume given a countable set of location names $a, b, \ldots \in \mathcal{L}$. We also write $\alpha, \beta, ab, \alpha b, \ldots \in \mathcal{L}^*$ for finite strings of location names, or *paths*. Location names are first-class values. Much as channel names, they can be created locally, sent and received in messages, and they have a lexical scope. To introduce new locations, we extend the syntax of definitions with a new location constructor:

$$D \stackrel{\text{def}}{=} \ldots \mid a\,[D' : P]$$

where $D'$ gathers the definitions of the location, where $P$ is the code running in the location, and where $a$ is a new name for the location. As regards the scopes, $a\,[D' : P]$ *defines* the name $a$ and the names defined in $D'$.

Informally, the definition $a\,[D' : P]$ corresponds to the local solution $D' \vdash^{\beta a} P$, where $\beta$ is the path of $D$'s local solution. We say that $\vdash^{\alpha}$ is a sublocation of $\vdash^{\beta}$ when $\beta$ is a prefix of $\alpha$. In the following, DRCHAMs are multisets of solutions labeled with paths $\alpha$ that are all distinct, prefix-closed, and uniquely identified by their rightmost location name, if any. These conditions ensure that solutions ordered by the sublocation relation form a tree.

The new structural rule STR-LOC relates the two representations of locations. From left to right, the rule takes a sublocation definition and creates a running location that initially contains a single definition $D$ and a single running process $P$. From right to left, STR-LOC has a "freezing" effect on location $a$ and all its sublocations. The rule has a side condition that requires that there is no solution of the form $\vdash^{\psi a \phi}$ in the implicit chemical context for any $\psi, \phi$ in $\mathcal{L}^*$; in contrast, the definition $D$ may contain sublocations. The side condition guarantees that $D$ syntactically captures the whole subtree of sublocations in location $a$ when the rule applies. Note that the rule STR-DEF and its side condition also apply to defined location names. This guarantees that newly-defined locations are given fresh names, and also that locations that are folded back into defining processes do not leave any running sublocation behind.

In well-formed DRCHAMs, we have required that all reaction rules defining a given channel name belong to a single local solution, and that all local solutions have distinct paths. With the addition of frozen locations in solution, we also require that locations in solution all have distinct location names that do not appear in the path of any local solution. We constrain the syntax of definitions accordingly: in a well-formed definition, for all conjunctions $D \wedge D'$, we require that $\mathrm{dv}(D) \cap \mathrm{dv}(D')$ contain only port names that are not defined in a sublocation of $D$ or $D'$. For instance, the definitions $a\,[\top : \mathbf{0}] \wedge a\,[\top : \mathbf{0}]$ and $a\,[x\langle\rangle \triangleright P \wedge b\,[x\langle\rangle \triangleright Q : \mathbf{0}] : \mathbf{0}]$ are ruled out.

As an example of nested locations, we describe a series of structural rearrangements that enable some actual reduction steps. We assume that $a$ does not occur in $P_c$ or $Q$.

$$
\begin{array}{rl}
 & \vdash \texttt{def}\ c\big[x\langle u\rangle \triangleright Q \wedge a\,[D_a : P_a] : P_c\big]\ \texttt{in}\ y\langle c, x\rangle | x\langle a\rangle \\
\overset{\text{STR-DEF}}{\rightleftharpoons} & c\big[x\langle u\rangle \triangleright Q \wedge a\,[D_a : P_a] : P_c\big] \vdash y\langle c, x\rangle | x\langle a\rangle \\
\overset{\text{STR-LOC}}{\rightleftharpoons} & x\langle u\rangle \triangleright Q \wedge a\,[D_a : P_a] \vdash^{c} P_c \quad \| \quad \vdash y\langle c, x\rangle | x\langle a\rangle \\
\overset{\text{STR-DEF,PAR}}{\rightleftharpoons} & x\langle u\rangle \triangleright Q,\ a\,[D_a : P_a] \vdash^{c} P_c \quad \| \quad \vdash y\langle c, x\rangle,\ x\langle a\rangle \\
\overset{\text{STR-LOC}}{\rightleftharpoons} & D_a \vdash^{ca} P_a \quad \| \quad x\langle u\rangle \triangleright Q \vdash^{c} P_c \quad \| \quad \vdash y\langle c, x\rangle, x\langle a\rangle \\
\overset{\text{COMM}}{\rightarrow} & D_a \vdash^{ca} P_a \quad \| \quad x\langle u\rangle \triangleright Q \vdash^{c} P_c, x\langle a\rangle \quad \| \quad \vdash y\langle c, x\rangle \\
\overset{\text{REACT}}{\rightarrow} & D_a \vdash^{ca} P_a \quad \| \quad x\langle u\rangle \triangleright Q \vdash^{c} P_c, Q\{^{a}/_{u}\} \quad \| \quad \vdash y\langle c, x\rangle \\
\rightleftharpoons & \vdash \texttt{def}\ c\big[x\langle u\rangle \triangleright Q : P_c | \texttt{def}\ a\,[D_a : P_a]\ \texttt{in}\ Q\{^{a}/_{u}\}\big]\ \texttt{in}\ y\langle c, x\rangle
\end{array}
$$

Now that the bookkeeping of the location tree is handled as a special case of structural rearrangement, we can express migration as the relocation of a branch in the location tree. We extend distributed chemical semantics with a second reduction rule that operates on two chemical solutions (rule GO). Informally, location $b$ moves from its current position $\beta b$ in the tree to a new position $\alpha a b$ just under the location name $a$ passed to the migration request. The target solution $\vdash^{\alpha a}$ is identified by its name $a$. Once $b$ arrives, the guarded process $P$ is triggered. The side condition forces the preliminary application of rule STR-LOC to fold any sublocation of $a$, and thus guarantees that the branch moves as a whole.

### 5.3 Attaching Some Meaning to Locations

In the machine above, the locality structure is mostly descriptive: the distributed semantics keeps track of locality information, but the location of a particular process or definition does not affect the result of the computation, at least for the observables studied in Sect. 2. Formally, we can erase any locality information and relate the simple semantics to the distributed semantics. (Some care is required to rule out migration attempts towards one's own sublocation, which may delay or block some processes.)

To conclude, we briefly present two refined models where locality has an impact on the computation and can be partially observed.

**Partial Failure and Failure-Detection.** Our calculus can be extended with a simple "fail-stop" model of failure, in the spirit of Amadio's model for the pi calculus [8, 6], where the crash of a physical site causes the permanent failure of its processes and definitions. In the extended model, a location can *halt* with all its sublocations. The failure of a location can also be asynchronously detected at any other running location, allowing programmable error recovery.

We supplement the syntax of distributed processes with constructs for failure and asynchronous failure detection:

| | | |
|---|---|---|
| $P, Q, R ::=$ | | processes |
| | $\dots$ | *(as in Fig. 8)* |
| | $\mid$ `halt` | local failure |
| | $\mid$ `fail` $a; P$ | remote failure detection |

We also put an optional "has failed" marker $\Omega$ in front of every location name in paths, and add a side condition "the path does not contain $\Omega$" in front of every chemical reduction rule (that is, a failed location and its sublocations cannot migrate, communicate, or perform local steps). In addition, we provide two chemical rules for the new constructs:

$$\text{HALT} \qquad \vdash^{\alpha a} \texttt{halt} \rightarrow \vdash^{\alpha \Omega a}$$

$$\text{DETECT} \qquad \vdash^{\alpha a} \parallel \vdash^{\beta b} \texttt{fail}\ a; P \rightarrow \vdash^{\alpha a} \parallel \vdash^{\beta b} P$$

with side conditions: in HALT, $a$ does not occur in any other path and the marker $\Omega$ does not occur in $\alpha$; in GO, the marker $\Omega$ occurs in $\alpha$ but not in $\beta$.

Inasmuch as the only reported failures are permanent location failures, the programming model remains relatively simple[4]. For instance, the single delivery of every message is guaranteed unless the sender fails, and thus the programmer can consider larger units of failure. Besides, failure-detection provides useful

[4] In addition, timeouts are pragmatically useful, but they are trivially modeled in an asynchronous setting—they are ordinary non-deterministic reduction steps—and they do not provide any negative guarantee.

*negative information*: once a location failure is detected, no other location may interact with it, hence its task may be taken over by another location without interfering with the failed location. The model of failure is only partially supported in JoCaml (some failures may never be reported).

**Authentication and Secrecy.** Interpreting locations as security boundaries, or "principals", we have also developed a model of authentication for a variant of the join calculus [3]. In this variant, we consider only a flat and static parallel composition of locations.

As in the distributed join calculus, every name "belongs" to the single location that defines it, hence only that location can receive messages sent on that name, while other locations cannot even detect those messages. In addition, every message carries a mandatory first parameter that contains a location name, meant to be the name of the sending location, and used by the receiver to authenticate the sender. These properties are both enforced by a modified COMM rule:

$$\text{SECURE-COMM} \qquad \vdash^a x\langle c, \tilde{y}\rangle \;\;\|\;\; D_x \vdash^b \;\rightarrow\; \vdash^a \;\;\|\;\; D_x \vdash^b x\langle a, \tilde{y}\rangle$$

where $x$ is (uniquely) defined in $D_x$. Remark that the first parameter $c$ is overwritten with the correct sender identity $a$, much as in Modula 3's secure network objects [50].

These secrecy and authenticity properties provide a strong, abstract basis for reasoning on the security of distributed programs, but their semantics depends on global chemical conditions that are not necessarily met in practical implementations—when communicating with an untrusted remote machine, there is no way to check that it is running a correct implementation. This delicate implementation is actually the main issue in [3], where we show that those strong properties can be faithfully implemented using standard cryptographic primitives, with much weaker assumptions on the network. This result is expressed in terms of bisimilarity equivalences.

## Acknowledgements

These lecture notes are partly derived from previous works in collaboration with Martín Abadi, Sylvain Conchon, Cosimo Laneve, Fabrice Le Fessant, Jean-Jacques Lévy, Luc Maranget, Didier Rémy, and Alan Schmitt. We also thank our anonymous referee for his constructive comments.

## References

1. M. Abadi, C. Fournet, and G. Gonthier. Secure implementation of channel abstractions. In *Proceedings of LICS '98*, pages 105–116. IEEE, June 1998.
2. M. Abadi, C. Fournet, and G. Gonthier. Secure communications processing for distributed languages. In *Proceedings of the 1999 IEEE Symposium on Security and Privacy*, pages 74–88, May 1999.

3. M. Abadi, C. Fournet, and G. Gonthier. Authentication primitives and their compilation. In *Proceedings of POPL'00*, pages 302–315. ACM, Jan. 2000.
4. M. Abadi, C. Fournet, and G. Gonthier. Secure implementation of channel abstractions. *Information and Computation*, 2000. To appear. Manuscript available from http://research.microsoft.com/ fournet. Subsumes [1] and [2].
5. G. Agha, I. Mason, S. Smith, and C. L. Talcott. A foundation for actor computation. *Journal of Functional Programming*, 7(1):1–72, Jan. 1997.
6. R. M. Amadio. An asynchronous model of locality, failure, and process mobility. In *COORDINATION'97*, volume 1282 of *LNCS*. Springer-Verlag, 1997.
7. R. M. Amadio, I. Castellani, and D. Sangiorgi. On bisimulations for the asynchronous $\pi$-calculus. *Theoretical Computer Science*, 195(2):291–324, 1998.
8. R. M. Amadio and S. Prasad. Localities and failures. In P. Thiagarajan, editor, *Proceedings of the 14th Foundations of Software Technology and Theoretical Computer Science Conference (FST-TCS '94)*, volume 880 of *LNCS*, pages 205–216. Springer-Verlag, 1994.
9. J.-P. Banâtre and D. L. Métayer. The Gamma model and its discipline of programming. *Science of Computer Programming*, 15:55–77, 1990.
10. G. Berry and G. Boudol. The chemical abstract machine. *Theoretical Computer Science*, 96:217–248, 1992.
11. M. Boreale and D. Sangiorgi. Some congruence properties for $\pi$-calculus bisimilarities. *Theoretical Computer Science*, 198(1–2):159–176, 1998.
12. E. Brinksma, A. Rensink, and W. Vogler. Fair testing. In I. Lee and S. A. Smolka, editors, *6th International Conference on Concurrency Theory (CONCUR'95)*, volume 962 of *LNCS*, pages 313–327. Springer-Verlag, 1995.
13. E. Brinksma, A. Rensink, and W. Vogler. Applications of fair testing. In R. Gotzhein and J. Bredereke, editors, *Formal Description Techniques IX: Theory, Applications and Tools*, volume IX. Chapman and Hall, 1996.
14. L. Cardelli and A. Gordon. Mobile ambients. In *Proceedings of FoSSaCS'98*, volume 1378 of *LNCS*, pages 140–155. Springer-Verlag, 1998.
15. S. Conchon and F. Le Fessant. Jocaml: Mobile agents for objective-caml. In *ASA/MA'99*, pages 22–29. IEEE Computer Society, Oct. 1999.
16. C. Fournet. *The Join-Calculus: a Calculus for Distributed Mobile Programming.* PhD thesis, Ecole Polytechnique, Palaiseau, Nov. 1998. INRIA TU-0556. Also available from http://research.microsoft.com/ fournet.
17. C. Fournet and G. Gonthier. A hierarchy of equivalences for asynchronous calculi (extended abstract). In Larsen et al. [29], pages 844–855. Full paper available from http://research.microsoft.com/ fournet.
18. C. Fournet and C. Laneve. Bisimulations in the join-calculus. To appear in TCS, available from http://research.microsoft.com/ fournet, Oct. 2000.
19. C. Fournet, J.-J. Lévy, and A. Schmitt. An asynchronous, distributed implementation of mobile ambients. In J. van Leeuwen, O. Watanabe, M. Hagiya, P. Mosses, and T. Ito, editors, *Proceedings of IFIP TCS 2000*, volume 1872 of *LNCS*. IFIP TC1, Springer-Verlag, Aug. 2000. An extended report is available from http://research.microsoft.com/ fournet.
20. C. Fournet and L. Maranget. The join-calculus language (version 1.03 beta). Source distribution and documentation available from http://join.inria.fr/, June 1997.
21. R. Glabbeek. The linear time—branching time spectrum II; the semantics of sequential systems with silent moves (extended abstract). In E. Best, editor, *4th International Conference on Concurrency Theory (CONCUR'93)*, volume 715 of *LNCS*, pages 66–81. Springer-Verlag, 1993.

22. M. Hennessy and J. Riely. A typed language for distributed mobile processes. In *Proceedings of POPL '98*, pages 378–390. ACM, Jan. 1998.
23. K. Honda and M. Tokoro. On asynchronous communication semantics. In P. Wegner, M. Tokoro, and O. Nierstrasz, editors, *Proceedings of the ECOOP'91 Workshop on Object-Based Concurrent Computing*, volume 612 of *LNCS*, pages 21–51. Springer-Verlag, 1992.
24. K. Honda and N. Yoshida. Combinatory representation of mobile processes. In *Proceedings of POPL '94*, pages 348–360, 1994.
25. K. Honda and N. Yoshida. On reduction-based process semantics. *Theoretical Computer Science*, 152(2):437–486, 1995.
26. E. Jul. Migration of light-weight processes in emerald. *IEEE Operating Sys. Technical Committee Newsletter, Special Issue on Process Migration*, 3(1):20, 1989.
27. E. Jul, H. Levy, N. Hutchinson, and A. Black. Fine-grained mobility in the emerald system. In *Proceedings of the 11th ACM Symposium on Operating Systems Principles*, pages 62–74, November 1987.
28. C. Laneve. May and must testing in the join-calculus. Technical Report UBLCS 96-04, University of Bologna, Mar. 1996. Revised: May 1996.
29. K. Larsen, S. Skyum, and G. Winskel, editors. *Proceedings of the 25th International Colloquium on Automata, Languages and Programming (ICALP '98)*, volume 1443 of *LNCS*, Aalborg, Denmark, July 1998. Springer-Verlag.
30. F. Le Fessant. The JoCAML system prototype (beta). Software and documentation available from http://pauillac.inria.fr/jocaml, 1998.
31. F. Le Fessant and L. Maranget. Compiling join-patterns. In U. Nestmann and B. C. Pierce, editors, *HLCL '98: High-Level Concurrent Languages*, volume 16(3) of *Electronic Notes in Theoretical Computer Science*, Nice, France, Sept. 1998. Elsevier Science Publishers. To appear.
32. X. Leroy and al. The Objective CAML system 3.01. Software and documentation available from http://caml.inria.fr.
33. M. Merro and D. Sangiorgi. On asynchrony in name-passing calculi. In Larsen et al. [29], pages 856–867.
34. R. Milner. *A Calculus of Communicating Systems*, volume 92 of *LNCS*. Springer-Verlag, 1980.
35. R. Milner. *Communication and Concurrency.* Prentice Hall, New York, 1989.
36. R. Milner. *Communication and Mobile Systems: the $\pi$-Calculus.* Cambridge University Press, Cambridge, 1999.
37. R. Milner, J. Parrow, and D. Walker. A calculus of mobile processes, parts I and II. *Information and Computation*, 100:1–40 and 41–77, Sept. 1992.
38. R. Milner and D. Sangiorgi. Barbed bisimulation. In W. Kuich, editor, *Proceedings of ICALP'92*, volume 623 of *LNCS*, pages 685–695. Springer-Verlag, 1992.
39. J. H. Morris, Jr. *Lambda-Calculus Models of Programming Languages.* Ph. D. dissertation, MIT, Dec. 1968. Report No. MAC–TR–57.
40. V. Natarajan and R. Cleaveland. Divergence and fair testing. In *Proceedings of ICALP '95*, volume 944 of *LNCS*. Springer-Verlag, 1995.
41. U. Nestmann and B. C. Pierce. Decoding choice encodings. In U. Montanari and V. Sassone, editors, *7th International Conference on Concurrency Theory (CONCUR'96)*, volume 1119 of *LNCS*, pages 179–194. Springer-Verlag, Aug. 1996. Revised full version as report ERCIM-10/97-R051, 1997.
42. D. M. R. Park. *Concurrency and Automata on Infinite Sequences*, volume 104 of *LNCS*. Springer-Verlag, 1980.

43. J. Parrow and P. Sjödin. Multiway synchronization verified with coupled simulation. In R. Cleaveland, editor, *Third International Conference on Concurrency Theory (CONCUR'92)*, volume 630 of *LNCS*, pages 518–533. Springer-Verlag, 1992.
44. J. Parrow and P. Sjödin. The complete axiomatization of cs-congruence. In P. Enjalbert, E. W. Mayr, and K. W. Wagner, editors, *Proceedings of STACS'94*, volume 775 of *LNCS*, pages 557–568. Springer-Verlag, 1994.
45. B. C. Pierce and D. N. Turner. Pict: A programming language based on the pi-calculus. In G. D. Plotkin, C. Stirling, and M. Tofte, editors, *Proof, Language and Interaction: Essays in Honour of Robin Milner*. MIT Press, May 2000. ISBN 0262161885.
46. D. Sangiorgi. *Expressing Mobility in Process Algebras: First-Order and Higher-Order Paradigms.* Ph.D. thesis, University of Edinburgh, May 1993.
47. D. Sangiorgi. On the bisimulation proof method. Revised version of Technical Report ECS–LFCS–94–299, University of Edinburgh, 1994. An extended abstract appears in Proc. of MFCS'95, LNCS 969, 1994.
48. D. Sangiorgi and R. Milner. The problem of "weak bisimulation up to". In W. R. Cleaveland, editor, *Proceedings of CONCUR'92*, volume 630 of *LNCS*, pages 32–46. Springer-Verlag, 1992.
49. D. Sangiorgi and D. Walker. *The Pi-calculus: a Theory of Mobile Processes.* Cambridge University Press, July 2001. ISBN 0521781779.
50. L. van Doorn, M. Abadi, M. Burrows, and E. Wobber. Secure network objects. In *Proceedings of the 1996 IEEE Symposium on Security and Privacy*, pages 211–221, May 1996.

# An Introduction to Functional Nets

Martin Odersky

École Polytechnique Fédérale de Lausanne

**Abstract.** Functional nets combine key ideas of functional programming and Petri nets to yield a simple and general programming notation. They have their theoretical foundation in Join calculus. This paper gives an overview of functional nets as a kernel programming language, it presents an object-based version of Join calculus, and it shows how the two relate.

## Table of Contents



G. Barthe et al. (Eds.): Applied Semantics, LNCS 2395, pp. 333–377, 2002.

Over the last decades an operational view of program execution based on rewriting has become widespread. In this view, a program is seen as a term in some calculus, and program execution is modeled by stepwise rewriting of the term according to the rules of the calculus. The operational semantics still has to be complemented with a logic for program verification and a collection of laws of programming. This view is exemplified in functional programming [Bac78,Hud89], in modern theories of objects [AC96], as well as in concurrent systems based on message passing such as CSP [Hoa85], CCS [Mil80] or $\pi$-calculus [MPW92].

Ideally, the terms of a programming notation should match closely the terms of the underlying calculus, so that insights gained from the calculus can immediately be applied to the language. This aim guided the design of modern functional languages such as Scheme [ASS84], ML [Pau91], or Haskell [Bir98], based on $\lambda$-calculus, as well as concurrent languages such as Occam [Ker87], based on CSP, or Pict [PT97] and Piccola [AN00], which are based on $\pi$-calculus.

These notes give an introduction to *functional nets* which support functional, object-oriented, and concurrent programming in a simple calculus based on rewriting. Functional nets arise out of a combination of key ideas of functional programming and Petri nets [Rei85]. As in functional programming, the basic computation step in a functional net rewrites function applications to function bodies. As in Petri-Nets, a rewrite step can require the combined presence of several inputs (where in this case inputs are function applications). This fusion of ideas from two different areas results in a style of programming which is at the same time very simple and very expressive.

Functional nets have a theoretical foundation in *join calculus* [FG96,FGL+96]. They have the same relation to join calculus as classical functional programming has to $\lambda$-calculus. That is, functional nets constitute a programming method which derives much of its simplicity and elegance from close connections to a fundamental underlying calculus. $\lambda$-calculus [Chu51,Bar84] is ideally suited as a basis for functional programs, but it can support mutable state only indirectly, and nondeterminism and concurrency not at all. The pair of join calculus and functional nets has much broader applicability – functional, imperative and concurrent program constructions are supported with equal ease.

The purpose of these notes is two-fold. First, they aim to promote functional nets as an interesting programming method of wide applicability. We present a sequence of examples which show how functional nets can concisely model key constructs of functional, imperative, and concurrent programming, and how they often lead to better solutions to programming problems than conventional methods.

Second, the notes develop concepts to link our programming notation of functional nets with the underlying calculus. To scale up from a calculus to a programming language, it is essential to have a means of aggregating functions and data. We introduce *qualified definitions* as a new syntactic construct for aggregation. In the context of functional nets, qualified definitions provide more flexible control over visibility and initialization than the more conventional record- or object-constructors. They are also an excellent fit to the underlying join calculus, since they maintain the convention that every value has a name. We will present object-based join calculus, an extension of join calculus with qualified definitions. This extension comes at surprisingly low cost, in the sense that the calculus needs to be changed only minimally and all concepts carry over unchanged. By contrast, conventional record constructors would create anonymous values, which would be at odds with the name-passing nature of join.

The notation for writing examples of functional nets is derived from Funnel [AOS+00], a small language which maps directly into our object-based extension of join. An implementation of Funnel is publicly available. There are also other languages which are based in some form on join calculus, and which express the constructs of functional nets in a different way, e.g. Join [FM97] or JoCaml [Fes98]. We have chosen to develop and present a new notation since we wanted to support both functions and objects in a way which was as simple as possible.

The rest of this tutorial is structured as follows. Section 1 introduces a purely functional subset of functional nets. Section 2 presents the full formalism which supports concurrent execution. Section 3 shows how functional nets model imperative programming. Section 4 presents a collection of process synchronization techniques implemented as functional nets. Section 5 presents object-based join calculus. Section 6 explains how the high-level language is mapped to that calculus. Section 7 discusses how classes Section 8 discusses related work and concludes.

# 1 Functions and Objects

In functional programming, the fundamental execution step rewrites a function application to a function body, replacing formal parameters with actual arguments. For example, consider the usual definition of a min function

**def** min (x: Int, y: Int) = if (x < y) then x else y

and the program min (4, 3). Three rewrite steps are needed to reduce the program to its answer "3":

$$
\begin{array}{ll}
 & \mathsf{min\ (4,\ 3)} \\
\rightarrow & \mathsf{if\ (4 < 3)\ then\ 4\ else\ 3} \\
\rightarrow & \mathsf{if\ (false)\ then\ 4\ else\ 3} \\
\rightarrow & \mathsf{3}
\end{array}
$$

The first of these steps rewrites a function application, and the other two steps rewrite the built-in operator < and the built-in conditional expression. In principle, the built-ins can themselves be represented as functions, so that one can do with *only* the rewrite rule for function applications. In practice, one simply assumes appropriate reduction rules for built-ins. In the following, we let $\rightarrow$ denote single-step reduction by application of a single rewrite rule. $\twoheadrightarrow$ will denote multi-step reduction by application of 0 or more rules.

When one has nested function applications, one has a choice which application to evaluate first. We will follow a *strict* evaluation strategy which evaluates all function arguments before rewriting the application. E.g. min (4, min (3, 5)) rewrites as follows.

```
min (4, min (3, 5))  ->>  min (4, 3)  ->>  3
```

Some functional languages, such as Haskell, follow a *lazy* strategy instead, where arguments are passed unevaluated.

## 1.1 Aggregation

Functions in Funnel can be aggregated to form records. Here is an example of a record type (with several more functions left out for brevity):

```
newtype Complex = {
  def re: Float
  def im: Float
  def plus (c: Complex): Complex
}
```

This defines a new type of records containing three functions as fields, re, im, and plus. Functions re and im are parameter-less, whereas plus takes a single parameter of type Complex. A complex number can be constructed using a function like makeComplex:

```
def makeComplex (r: Float, i: Float): Complex = {
  def re = r
  def im = i
  def plus (c: Complex) = makeComplex (re + c.re, im + c.im)
}
```

Values of type complex can then be formed by calling the constructor function:

```
val one = makeComplex (1.0f, 0f)
val i   = makeComplex (0f, 1.0f)
```

Value definitions like these evaluate their right hand sides, binding it to the name given on the left-hand side. Contrast this with a parameterless function definition like

```
def oneExp = makeComplex (1.0f, 0f)
```

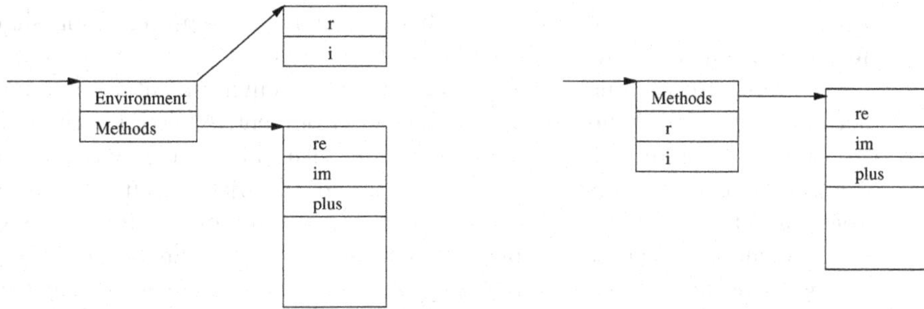


**Fig. 1.** Object Representations

This definition does not entail any evaluation itself, but each time oneExp is used the right-hand side is evaluated anew.

As usual, fields of record values are selected by an infix period. E.g. the expression one.plus (i) evaluates to the complex number $1 + i$.

### 1.2 Objects

So far, our notation was explained in terms of functions and records. Equally well, one could have used object-oriented terminology. Records are then called objects, and their fields (which are always functions in our case) are called methods. Unlike in many object-oriented programming languages, there is no need for a special syntactic form for object construction such as **new**. Instead, an object is simply defined by constructing its record of methods. The construction can be wrapped in a function itself, as was demonstrated by the case of makeComplex. Furthermore, the record methods may refer to variables bound in their environment. For instance, the methods in the record created by makeComplex refer to the parameters of makeComplex.

Looking at the situation from an implementation viewpoint, this has two consequences. First, since the created record survives the execution of the enclosing creator function, it will have to be stored in the heap rather than on the stack. Second, together with the record one needs to store the values of makeComplex's actual parameters, since these values can be accessed during evaluation of the record's methods. A good place to store these *environment variables* is as instance variables of the created heap object itself. The methods, on the other hand, need not be allocated once per call to makeComplex. Since their code is the same each time makeComplex is called, one can share their implementation among all calls to makeComplex. A record can thus be represented by a *method table* and an *environment*, as it is depicted on the left side of Figure 1. When calling a method, the environment is passed as additional parameter. This is very similar to the *closure* representation used in functional programming for first-class functions. The only difference is that a closure consists of an environment and a single function code pointer, whereas our record representation shares a single environment between all methods of a record.

One can also eliminate the indirection to the environment by making the method pointer itself the first entry of the environment. A record is then identified by just a pointer to its environment. This situation is depicted on the right of Figure 1. It corresponds exactly to the standard object layout used in many object-oriented languages. Two differences remain, however. First, fields of an environment are local to the object itself, so that they can be accessed only through a method of the record. In object-oriented terms, one would say that all instance variables are *private*[1]. Second, fields in an environment are always immutable, reflecting the purely functional nature of the language presented so far. The next sections will introduce a richer language which lets us express mutable variables. But for now we stay in the purely functional subset.

Record type definitions with **newtype** can be recursive, as is shown in the following definition of a type for lists.

```
newtype SimpleList [t] = {
   def isEmpty: Boolean
   def head: t
   def tail: SimpleList [t]
}
```

This says that a SimpleList is a record consisting of three functions. Function isEmpty returns true iff the list is empty, function head returns the first element of a (nonempty) list and function tail returns the list consisting of all elements but the first one. The definition has a type parameter 't' which represents the element type of the list. To distinguish type parameters from value parameters, we always enclose the former in square brackets [...]. Both types and functions can have type parameters.

Given a definition of lists as above, how can values of the type be defined? As in the case of makeComplex, we create constructor functions for lists. Two constructor functions are needed, depending on whether the constructed list is empty or not. The following code defines the two list constructors Nil and Cons.

```
val SimpleList = {
   def Nil [t]: SimpleList [t] = {
      def isEmpty = true
      def head = error ("Nil.head")
      def tail = error ("Nil.tail")
   }
```

[1] Actually, the term *private* does not have a standard meaning in OOP. In Simula or Smalltalk a private field can only be accessed from within methods of the same object, whereas in Java or C++ it can be accessed from any object which is a direct instance of the class which defined the field. Our scheme implements the Simula/Smalltalk meaning of the term.

```
def Cons [t] (x: t, xs: SimpleList [t]): SimpleList [t] = {
    def isEmpty = false
    def head = x
    def tail = xs
}}
```

The Nil function creates an empty list. Taking the head or tail of such a list results in an error, which is expressed here by calling the predefined error function. The Cons function creates a list consisting of a given head x and a given tail xs.

The constructors Nil and Cons are themselves methods of a record value called SimpleList. The SimpleList record value acts as a module, which provides the constructors of the list data type. Clients of the SimpleList module then construct lists using qualified names SimpleList.Nil and SimpleList.Cons. Examples:

```
def length [t] (xs: SimpleList [t]): Int =
    if (xs.isEmpty) then 0
    else 1 + length (xs.tail)

def append [t] (xs: SimpleList [t], ys: SimpleList [t]): SimpleList[t] =
    if (xs.isEmpty) then ys
    else SimpleList.Cons (xs.head, append (xs.tail, ys))
```

Note that Nil, Cons, length and append are *polymorphic* – they work for lists with arbitrary element types. The element type is represented in each case in the type parameter [t], which precedes any value parameters of the functions. When applying polymorphic functions, one can supply an actual instance type for the type parameter, as in

```
val xs: SimpleList[Int] = SimpleList.Cons [Int] (1, SimpleList.Nil [Int])
append [Int] (xs, xs)
```

But it is also possible to omit the actual type parameter, if that parameter can be inferred from the types of function's value parameters or its result type. A local type inference system [PT98,OZZ01] infers type arguments in function applications and parameter types in some local function abstractions. Unlike the Hindley/Milner type inference system [Mil78,DM82], which works by solving global equality constraint by unification, local type inference relies only on local constraint solving and type propagation. Local type inference can be extended to richer languages than Hindley/Milner but generally requires more type information in the program to be given.

### 1.3 Algebraic Datatypes

Actually, it is possible to define lists with even fewer basic methods. It would be sufficient to have a single method match which takes a *visitor* [GHJV94] record as argument. Depending on whether the list was empty or not, one of two methods of the visitor would be invoked. This structure essentially models the *algebraic data types* found in many functional languages, with the visitor taking over the role of a pattern matching case expression. Here is a new type for lists constructed along these lines:

```
newtype List[t] = {
  def match [r] (v: ListVisitor [t,r]): r
}
```

A visitor encodes the branches of a pattern matching case expression. It is represented as a record with one method for each branch. For instance, a visitor for lists would always have two methods, Nil and Cons:

```
newtype ListVisitor [t, r] = {
  def Nil: r
  def Cons (x: t, xs: List [t]): r
}
```

The intention is that the match method in List would call either the Nil method or the Cons method of its visitor argument, depending what kind of list was encountered. If the encountered list resulted from a Cons we also need to pass the arguments of the original Cons to the visitor's Cons.

Using match, one can write length and append over lists as follows:

```
def length [t] (xs: List [t]): Int = xs.match {
  def Nil = 0
  def Cons (x, xs1) = 1 + length (xs1)
}
def append [t] (xs: List[t], ys: List[t]): List[t] = xs.match {
  def Nil = ys
  def Cons (x, xs1) = List.Cons (x, append (xs1, ys))
}
```

More generally, every function over lists can be defined in terms of match. It only remains to implement this method. Clearly, its behavior will depend on whether it is called on an empty or non-empty list. Therefore, we define two list constructors Nil and Cons, with two different implementations for match. The implementations are straightforward:

```
val List = {
  def Nil [t]: List [t]                         = { def match v = v.Nil }
  def Cons [t] (x: t, xs: List[t]): List [t]    = { def match v = v.Cons (x, xs) }
}
```

In each case, match simply calls the appropriate method of its visitor argument v, passing any parameters along.

Note that the qualification with List in the visitor record in functions length and append lets us distinguish the constructor Cons, defined in List, from the visitor method Cons, which is defined locally.

### 1.4 List Methods

Actually, one could equally well define length and append as *methods* of List objects. The following example enriches the List with these and other methods.

```
newtype List [t] = {
    def match [r] (v: ListVisitor [t, r]): r

    def isEmpty: Boolean
    def head: t
    def tail: List [t]

    def length: Int
    def append (ys: List [t]): List [t]
    def filter (p: t → Boolean): List [t]
    def map [r] (f: t → r): List [r]
}
```

The constructors List.Nil and List.Cons now define in addition to match specialized implementations of all other methods in List's type:

```
val List = {
    def Nil [t]: List [t] = {
        def match (v) = v.Nil
        def isEmpty = true
        def head = error ("Nil.head")
        def tail = error ("Nil.tail")
        def length = 0
        def append (ys) = ys
        def filter (p) = Nil
        def map (f) = Nil
    }
    def Cons [t] (x: t, xs: List[t]): List [t] = {
        def match (v) = v.Cons (x, xs)
        def isEmpty = false
        def head = x
        def tail = xs
        def length = 1 + xs.length
        def append (ys) = Cons (x, xs.append (ys))
        def filter (p) = if (p (x)) then Cons (x, xs.filter (p)) else xs.filter (p)
        def map (f) = Cons (f (x), xs.map (f))
    }
}
```

## 2 Forks and Joins

The subset of the Funnel language we have seen so far was purely functional. There was no way to express a side effect or a concurrent computation of several threads. We now extend Funnel to make it into a general purpose programming language in which these concepts can be expressed. Surprisingly little new mechanism is needed for these extensions. We will concentrate in this section on basic concurrency constructs. In the next section, we will show how the same constructs also support imperative programming.

Any concurrent language needs an operator to initiate parallel computation. We introduce for this purpose the *fork* operator &. The term A & B executes its operands A and B in parallel.

A concurrent language also needs mechanisms for synchronizing threads running in parallel and for communications between them. A large number of different methods for doing this have been proposed. We use here the following simple scheme which fits very well with the functional approach we have followed so far. We admit the & operator not only in function bodies on the right hand side of a rewrite rule, but also in function headers on the left-hand side of a rewrite rule. For instance, the definition

```
def a (x: Int) & b (y: Int)  =  c (x + y) & d ()
```

would be interpreted as follows: "If there are two concurrent calls to functions a(x) and b(y), then these calls are to be replaced by two concurrent evaluations of c(x + y) and d(). As long as there is only one call to a or b this call will block until its partner in the rule is also called. An occurrence of & on the left-hand side of a definition is called a *join*, since it's effect is the joining of two previously independent threads of computation. Consequently, a left-hand side containing & symbols is also called a *join pattern.*

## 2.1 Asynchronous Channels

As a first example of join synchronization, consider an implementation of an asynchronous channel, which connects a set of producers with a set of consumers. Producers call a function put to send data to the channel while consumers call a function get to retrieve data. An implementation of a channel is realized by the following simple functional net.

```
def get: T & put (x: T) = x
```

This definition jointly defines the two functions get and put. Only put takes a parameter, and only get returns a result. We call result-returning functions like get *synchronous* , whereas functions like put are called *asynchronous.* The definition rewrites two concurrent calls to put (x) and get to the value x, which is returned to the caller of the get operation. Generally, only the first function in a join pattern can return a result, all other functions are asynchronous. Likewise, only the first operand of a fork can return a result, all other operands are asynchronous or their result is discarded.

Here is an example of a program that uses the channel abstraction.

```
def get: Int & put (x: Int) = x
def P: nil = { val x = get ; P & put (x + 1) }
P & put (1)
```

The program repeatedly reads out a number which was sent to a channel and sends back the number incremented by one. Initially, the number 1 is sent to the channel. A reduction of this program starts with the following steps (where we abbreviate the above definitions of get, put and P to **def** D).

```
     def D; P & put (1)
→    (by rewriting P to its definition)
     def D; { val x = get ; P & put (x + 1) } & put (1)
→    (by joining put (1) and get)
     def D; val x = 1 ; P & put (x + 1)
→    (by expanding the val)
     def D; P & put (1 + 1)
→    (by numeric simplification)
     def D; P & put (2)
→    (by rewriting P to its definition)
     def D; { val x = get ; P & put (x + 1) } & put (2)
→ ...
```

This program is still deterministic, in the sense that at each point only one reduction is possible. But we can change this by adding another process Q:

```
def get: Int & put (x: Int) = x
def P: nil = { val x = get ; P & put (x + 1) }
def Q: nil = { val x = get ; Q & put (x – 1) }
P & Q & put (1)
```

There are now many possible reduction sequences of this program, since either $P$ or $Q$, but not both, can react via their get operation with a previous put operation. The sequence in which the two processes execute is arbitrary, controlled only by the channel's rewrite rules. Generally, we do not assume *fairness*, so that it would be possible for P to execute infinitely often without any intervening execution of Q (or *vice versa*).

Channels can be turned into reusable abstractions by packing their operations in a record with a type parameterized with the type of messages:

```
newtype Channel [t] = {
   def get: t
   def put (x: t): nil
}
def newChannel [t]: Channel [t] = {
   def get & put (x) = x
}
```

### 2.2 Buffers

The asynchronous channel suffers from a potentially unbounded pile-up of undelivered messages if messages are produced at a higher rate than they are consumed. This problem is avoided in bounded buffers which limit the number of unconsumed messages to some given number. For instance, the following functional net implements a one-place buffer in which the number of put operations cannot exceed the number of get operations by more than one:

```
def get: T & full (x: T)      = x & empty,
    put (x: T): () & empty =  () & full (x)
```

There are two definitions which define four functions. Functions put and get are meant to be called from the producer and consumer clients of the buffer. The other two functions, full and empty, reflect the buffer's internal state, and should be called only from within the buffer.

In contrast to the situation with asynchronous channels, both get and put are now synchronous functions. The put operation returns the empty tuple () as its result. Its result type, also written (), consists of just this single value. Functions that return () are called *procedures*. The explicit () result is important since it tells us that the call to procedure put has terminated. By contrast, the put function of the asynchronous channel above does not return anything, and therefore its termination cannot be observed. Functions that do not return are called *asynchronous*. Their static return type is the empty type, written **nil**.

The "side effecting" part of the expression is full (x). Like empty, full is an asynchronous function. It's sole purpose is to enable calls to get and to pass the stored element x along.

### 2.3 Qualified Definitions

When faced with the task of turning one-place buffers into a reusable abstraction, we encounter some problems. First, not all functions of a one-place buffer should be turned into methods of a record – empty and full should remain hidden. Furthermore, before using a buffer abstraction we also need to initialize it by invoking the empty method. But empty is supposed to be internal, hence it cannot be initialized from outside! One possible solution would be to have a local definition of the four functions making up a buffer and then constructing a record with the get and put methods, which forward to the corresponding local method. But the code for this, presented below, is rather cumbersome.

```
type Buffer [t] = {
   def get: t
   def put (x: t): ()
}
def newBuffer [t]: Buffer [t] = {
   def get' & full (x: t)       = x & empty,
       put' (x: t) & empty   = () & full (x);
   { def get = get', put (x) = put' (x) } & empty
}
```

A more streamlined presentation can be obtained using *qualified definitions*. Qualified definitions mirror the qualified names used for accessing record elements. As an example, consider a re-formulation of the newBuffer function.

```
def newBuffer [t]: Buffer [t] = {
    def this.get & full (x: t)      = x & empty,
        this.put (x: t) & empty  = () & full (x);
    this & empty
}
```

The left-hand side of a definition can now contain not just simple identifiers but qualified names like this.get and this.put. In the above example the local definition thus introduces the three names this, full, and empty. this represents a record with two fields, get and put, while empty and full represent functions. Note that the naming of this is arbitrary, any other name would work equally well. Note also that empty and full are not methods of the record returned from newBuffer, so that they can be accessed only internally.

*A Note on Precedence.* We assume the following order of precedence, from strong to weak:

( ) (.)
(&)
(=)
(,)
(;)

That is, function application binds strongest, followed by parallel composition, followed by the equal sign, followed by comma, and finally followed by semicolon. Other standard operators such as +, $*$, == fall between function application and & in their usual order of precedence. When precedence risks being unclear, we'll use parentheses to disambiguate.

*A Note on Indentation.* As a syntactic convenience, we allow indentation instead of ;-separators inside blocks delimited with braces { and }. Except for the significance of indentation, braces are equivalent to parentheses. The precise rules are: (1) In a block delimited with braces a semicolon is inserted in front of any non-empty line which starts at the same indentation level as the first symbol following the opening brace, provided the symbol before the insertion point can be followed by a semicolon and the next symbol can be preceded by one. The only modification to this rule is: (2) If inserted semicolons would separate two **def** blocks, yielding **def** $D_1$ ; **def** $D_2$ say, then the two **def** blocks are instead merged into a single block, i.e. **def** $D_1$, $D_2$. (3) The top level program is treated like a block delimited with braces, i.e. indentation is significant.

With these rules, the newBuffer example can alternatively be written as follows.

```
def newBuffer [t]: Buffer [t] = {
    def this.get & full (x: t)     = x & empty
    def this.put (x: t) & empty   = () & full x
    this & empty
}
```

Rule (1) allows us to drop the semicolon after the local definition. With modification (2), one can use **def**'s in front of several defined functions which are conceptually part of a single definition. Which of the two styles is preferable is a matter of taste. Generally, the style with a single **def** works better for small definitions, whereas the style using indentation and multiple **def**'s tends to be easier to read if the individual definitions span many lines.

It is also possible to define several record names in a single definition. For instance, the following function would define a buffer with two aspects, one to be used by a consumer, the other to be used by a producer.

```
def newSplitBuffer [t] = {
    def outBuf.get & full (x: t)     = x & empty,
        inBuf.put (x: t) & empty    = () & full (x)
    (inBuf, outBuf) & empty
}
```

The newSplitBuffer function returns two names: inBuf, which names a record with the single field put, and outBuf, which also names a record with the single field get.

The identifiers which occur before a period in a join pattern always define new record names, which are defined only in the enclosing definition. It is not possible to use this form of qualified definition to add new fields to a record defined elsewhere.

We can now explain the anonymous form of record definition as an implicit qualified definition, where every defined method is prefixed with the name of the record being defined. I.e. the newChannel function given above would be regarded as syntactic sugar of the following expanded version:

```
def newChannel [t]: Channel [t] = {
    def this.get & this.put (x) = x
    this
}
```

The new interpretation gives up structured record values as a primitive language feature, replacing it by simple names. This view is a good fit with the join calculus theory underlying functional nets, since that calculus also represents every intermediate result with a name. This is further explained in Section 5.

A simple usage of the one-place buffer abstraction is illustrated in the following example.

```
def newBuffer [t]: Buffer [t] = {
   def this.get & full x        = x & empty,
       this.put (x) & empty = () & full x
   this & empty
}
val b: Buffer [Int] = newBuffer
def P (i: Int): nil = { b.put (i) ; P (i + 1) }
def Q (i: Int): nil = { val x = b.get ; Q(x + i) }
P (0) & Q (0)
```

Process P writes consecutive integers to the buffer b, which are read and summed up by process Q.

## 3 Mutable State

The mechanisms introduced so far are also sufficient to explain imperative programming, where programs manipulate a state of mutable variables. After all, a mutable variable can be easily modeled as a functional net with the following two defining equations.

```
def value: T & state (x: T)          = x & state (x),
    update (y: T) & state (x: T) = () & state (y)
```

The structure of these equations is similar to the one-place buffer in Section 2. The two synchronous functions value and update access and update the variable's current value, which is carried along as a parameter to the asynchronous function state.

The function state in the above definition appears on the left-hand sides of both equations. There is nothing strange about this. Remember that equations are rewrite rules. It is certainly possible for a function symbol to appear on the left-hand side of more than one rewrite rule, as long as all such rules form part of the same **def** block. On the other hand, it is not allowed that the same function appears several times in a single join pattern, i.e. **def** state (x) & state (y) = ... would be illegal.

Building on these definitions, we can create an abstraction for first-class mutable variables (also called a *reference cells*). The abstraction defines a type Ref [t] for reference cells and a function newRef for creating them. Here are the details.

```
newtype Ref [t] = {
   def value: t
   def update (y: t): ()
}
def newRef [t] (initial: t) = {
   def this.value & state (x: t) = x & state (x),
       this.update (y: t) & state (x: t) = () & state (y)
   this & state (initial)
}
```

As a simple usage example consider the following program which creates a reference and defines and applies an increment function for it:

```
val r: Ref [Int] = newRef (0)
def increment  =  r.update (r.value + 1)
increment
```

### 3.1 Variables

The last program shows that while it is possible to use references, it is certainly not very pleasant. To obtain a more conventional and streamlined notation we introduce the following syntactic abbreviations:

- The definition **var** x := E expands to the three definitions
  ```
  val _x  =  newRef (E)
  def x  =  _x.value
  def x_:=  =  _x.update
  ```
  The first of these creates a reference cell while the second and third definitions introduce an *accessor* function x and an *update* function x_:=. Only the last two names are visible whereas the name of the reference cell _x is meant to be inaccessible for user programs.
- Analogously, a signature **var** x: T in a record type expands to a pair of signatures for the accessor and update function.
  ```
  def x : T, x_:= : T→()
  ```
- Simple assignment expressions x := E expand to simple calls of the update function, e.g. x_:=(E).
- Qualified assignment expressions Q.x := E expand to qualified calls of the update function, e.g. Q.x_:=(E).

With these expansions one can write programs using a customary syntax for variable definition and access. For instance, the previous increment program can now be written more concisely as follows.

```
var count := 0
def increment  =  count := count + 1
increment
```

### 3.2 Loops

The second important aspect of imperative programming are its loop control structures. In principle, such structures can be written as higher-order functions, thus implementing directly their standard definitions. For instance, here is an implementation of a function for while loops:

```
def while (cond: ()→Boolean) (body: ()→()): () =
  if (cond ()) then { body () ; while (cond) (body) } else ()
```

And here is a usage example, which employs two anonymous functions for the condition and the body of the loop.

```
def exp (x: Int, y: Int) = {
    var m := 1
    var n := y
    while (|n > 0) (| m := m * x ; n := n - 1 )
    m
}
```

### 3.3 Implementation Aspects

Our presentation so far has shown that imperative programs can be seen as a special class of functional nets, and that, at least in principle, no new constructs are necessary to support them. So far, we have not yet touched on the issue of efficiency. Clearly, a literal implementation of mutable variables in terms of joins and forks would be much less efficient than a direct implementation in terms of memory cells. But nobody forces us to actually use the literal implementation. One can equally well choose an implementation of the abstract Ref type in terms of primitive memory cells. Such an implementation could no longer be represented as a functional net, but its high-level interface, as well as the programs using it, could.

Another source of inefficiency lies in the indirection entailed by reference cell objects. In many cases, it is possible to avoid the indirection by "inlining" variables at the point where they are defined. This is particularly attractive for our high-level **var** syntax since this syntax does not permit access to the variable as a first class reference, only read and write operations are permitted. Nevertheless, care must be taken because functions accessing variables can escape the environment where the variable is defined. Example:

```
def newCounter = {
    var count := 0
    def this.reset  =  count := 0,
        this.increment  =  count := count + 1,
        this.value =  count
    this
}
```

In this example, the count variable may not be stored in newCounter's stack activation record, since the record returned from newCounter still accesses count. The standard object representation of reference cells avoids the problem since we assume that objects are always stored on the heap. There exist techniques for escape analysis [PG92] which indicate whether a variable can be stored on the stack or whether it must be stored on the heap.

### 3.4 Functions and State

We now present an example which demonstrates how imperative and functional code can be combined with and substituted for each other. A often-used function over lists is foldl, which uses a given binary operator $\oplus$ and a zero value z to reduce all elements of a list to a single value:

$$\text{foldl}\ (\oplus,\ z,\ (x_1,\ ...,\ x_n))\ =\ (\ ...\ (z \oplus x_1) \oplus ...\ ) \oplus x_n\ .$$

Here's first a purely functional implementation of foldl:

```
def foldl [s,t] (f: (s,t)→s, z: s, xs: List [t]): s =
    if (xs.isEmpty) then z
    else foldl (f, f (z, xs.head), xs.tail)
```

An equivalent imperative implementation is:

```
def foldl [s,t] (f: (s,t)→s, z: s, xs: List [t]): s = {
    var acc := z
    var rest := xs
    while (| !rest.isEmpty) {
        acc := f (acc, rest.head)
        rest := rest.tail
    }
    acc
}
```

### 3.5 Stateful Objects

Objects with state arise naturally out of a combination of functional objects and variables. The newCounter function which was presented earlier provides an example. On the other hand, we can also implement stateful objects in a more direct way, by extending the implementation scheme for reference cells. An object with methods $m_1, ..., m_k$, and instance variables $x_1, ..., x_l$ with initial values $i_1, ..., i_l$ can be coded as follows.

$$\begin{array}{lcl} \textbf{def}\ \text{this}.m_1\ \&\ \text{state}\ (x_1,\ ...,\ x_l) & = & ...\ ;\ \text{state}\ (x_1^1,\ ...,\ x_l^1), \\ & \vdots & \\ \quad \text{this}.m_k\ \&\ \text{state}\ (x_1,\ ...,\ x_l) & = & ...\ ;\ \text{state}\ (x_1^k,\ ...,\ x_l^k); \\ \text{this}\ \&\ \text{state}\ (i_1,\ ...,\ i_l) & & \end{array}$$

Here, the dots after the equal signs stand for elided method bodies. The object's instance variables are represented as arguments of a state function, which is initially applied to $i_1, ..., i_l$. Each method $m_j$ consumes the current state vector of all instance variables and terminates by installing a new state in which instance variables have new values $x_1^j, ..., x_l^j$. Here is a re-formulation of counter objects using the new scheme.

```
def newCounter = {
   def this.reset & state (count: Int)  =  state (0),
       this.increment & state (count: Int)  =  state (count + 1),
       this.value & state (count: Int)  =  count & state (count)
   this
}
```

This representation technique achieves a common notion of information hiding, in that an object's instance variables cannot be accessed from outside the object. It further achieves mutual exclusion in that only one method of a given object can execute at any one time. After all, each method starts by consuming the state vector which is not re-established before the end of the method's execution. Thus, after one method commences all other method calls to the same object are blocked until the first method has terminated. In other words, objects implemented in this way are *monitors* [Han72,Hoa74].

### 3.6 Object Identity

In the object-oriented design and programming area, an object is often characterized as having "state, behavior, and identity". Our encoding of objects expresses state as a collection of applications of private asynchronous functions, and behavior as a collection of externally visible functions. But what about identity? If functional net objects had an observable identity it should be possible to define a method eq which returns true if and only if its argument is the same object as the current object. Here "sameness" has to be interpreted as "created by the same operation", structural equality is not enough. E.g., assuming that the – as yet hypothetical – eq method was added to reference objects, it should be possible to write **val** (r1, r2) = (newRef 0, newRef 0) and to have r1.eq(r1) == true and r1.eq(r2) == false.

Functional nets have no predefined operation which tests whether two names or references are the same. However, it is still possible to implement an eq method. Here's our first attempt, which still needs to be refined later.

```
newtype ObjId =
   def eq (other: ObjId): Boolean
   def testFlag: Boolean      // only for internal use
}
def newObjId: ObjId  =  {
   def this.eq (other: ObjId) & flag (x: Boolean) =
           resetFlag (other.testFlag) & flag (true)
       this.testFlag & flag (x)  =
          x & flag (x)
       resetFlag (result: Boolean) & flag (x)  =
          x & flag (false)
   this & flag (false)
}
```

$$f_1 \;\&\; \ldots \;\&\; f_m \quad = \quad g_1 \;\&\; \ldots \;\&\; g_n$$

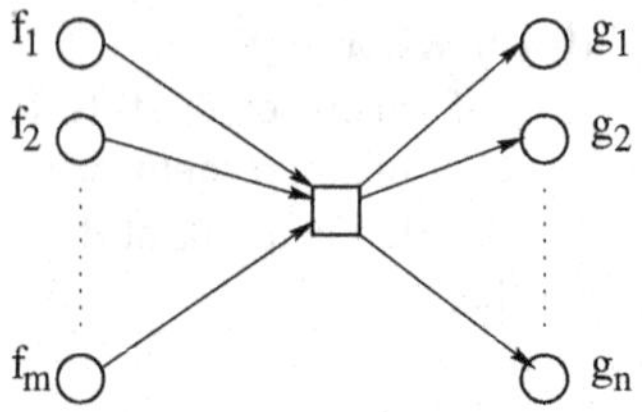

Fig. 2. Analogy to Petri nets

This defines a generator function for objects with an eq method that tests for identity. The implementation of eq relies on three helper functions, flag, testFlag, and resetFlag. Between calls to the eq method, flag false is always asserted. The trick is that the eq method asserts flag true and at the same time tests whether other.flag is true. If the current object and the other object are the same, that test will yield true. On the other hand, if the current object and the other object are different, the test will yield false, provided there is not at the same time another ongoing eq operation on object other. Hence, we have arrived at a solution of our problem, provided we can prevent overlapping eq operations on the same objects. In the next section, we will develop techniques to do so.

## 4 Concurrency

The previous sections have shown how functional nets can express sequential programs, both in functional and in imperative style. In this section, we will show their utility in expressing common patterns of concurrent program execution.

Functional nets support an resource-based view of concurrency, where calls model resources, & expresses conjunction of resources, and a definition acts as a rewrite rule which maps input sets of resources into output sets of resources. This view is very similar to the one of Petri nets [Pet62,Rei85]. In fact, there are direct analogies between the elements of Petri nets and functional nets. This is illustrated in Figure 2.

A *transition* in a Petri net corresponds to a rewrite rule in a functional net. A *place* in a Petri net corresponds to a function symbol applied to some (formal or actual) arguments. A *token* in a Petri net corresponds to some actual call during the execution of a functional net (in analogy to Petri nets, we will also call applications of asynchronous functions *tokens*). The basic execution step of a Petri net is the firing of a transition which has as a precondition that all in-going places have tokens in them. Quite similarly, the basic execution step of a functional net is a rewriting according to some rewrite rule, which has as a precondition that all function symbols of the rule's left-hand side have matching calls.

Functional nets are considerably more powerful than conventional Petri nets, however. First, function applications in a functional net can have arguments, whereas tokens in a Petri net are unstructured. Second, functions in a functional net can be higher-order, in that they can have functions as their arguments. In Petri nets, such self-referentiality is not possible. Third, definitions in a functional net can be nested inside rewrite rules, such that evolving net topologies are possible. A Petri-net, on the other hand, has a fixed connection structure.

Colored Petri nets [Jen92] let one pass parameters along the arrows connecting places with transitions. These nets are equivalent to first-order functional nets with only global definitions. They still cannot express the higher-order and evolution aspects of functional nets. Bussi and Asperti have translated join calculus ideas into standard Petri net formalisms. Their mobile Petri nets [AB96] support first-class functions and evolution, and drop at the same time the locality restrictions of join calculus and functional nets. That is, their notation separates function name introduction from rewrite rule definition, and allows a function to be defined collectively by several unrelated definitions.

In the following, we will present several well-known schemes for process synchronization and how they each can be expressed as functional nets.

### 4.1 Semaphores

*Semaphores* A common mechanism for process synchronization is a *lock* (or: *semaphore*). A lock offers two atomic actions: getLock and releaseLock. Here's the implementation of a lock as a functional net:

```
def newLock = {
   def this.getLock & this.releaseLock  =  ()
   this & this.releaseLock
}
```

It is interesting to note the similarities in the definitions of semaphores and asynchronous channels. A typical usage of a semaphore would be:

```
val s = newLock ; ...
s.getLock ; "< critical region >" ; () & s.releaseLock
```

With semaphores, we can now complete our example to define objects with identity:

```
val global = newLock
def newObjId: ObjId  =  {
   def this.testEq (other: ObjId) & flag (x: Boolean) =
           resetFlag (other.testFlag) & flag (true)
        this.testFlag & flag (x) =
           x & flag (x)
        resetFlag (result: Boolean) & flag (x)  =
           x & flag (false)
```

```
    def this.eq (other: ObjId) = {
      global.getLock ;
      val res = this.testEq (other) ;
      res & global.releaseLock
    }
    this & flag (false)
}
```

This code makes use of a global lock to serialize all calls of eq methods. This is admittedly a brute force approach to mutual exclusion, which also serializes calls to eq over disjoint pairs of objects. A more refined locking strategy is hard to come by, however. Conceptually, a critical region consists of a pair of objects which both have to be locked. A naive approach would lock first one object, then the other. But this would carry the risk of deadlocks, when two concurrent eq operations involve the same objects, but in different order.

### 4.2 Critical Regions

One problem with the previous usage pattern of semaphores is that it is easy to forget the releaseLock call, thus locking the semaphore forever. A safer solution is to pass the critical region into a higher order function which does both the getLock and releaseLock:

```
type Proc = () → ()
type Mutex = Proc → ()
def newMutex: Mutex = {
  val s = newLock
  ( region: Proc | s.getLock ; region () ; s.releaseLock )
}
```

A typical usage pattern for this would be:

```
val mutex = newMutex
...
mutex (| "< critical region >")
```

### 4.3 Synchronous Channels

A potential problem with asynchronous channels introduced in Section 2.1 is that the producer might produce data much more rapidly than the consumer consumes them. In this case, the number of pending write operations might increase indefinitely, or until memory is exhausted. The problem can be avoided by connecting producer and consumer with a synchronous channel.

In a synchronous channel, both reads and writes return and each operation blocks until the other operation is called. Synchronous channels are the fundamental communication primitive of classical $\pi$-calculus [MPW92]. They can be represented as functional nets as follows.

```
def newSyncChannel [t] = {
  def this.read & noReads              = read1 & read2,
      this.write (x: t) & noWrites     = write1 & write2 x,
      read1 & write2 (x: t)            = x & noWrites,
      write1 & read2                   = () & noReads
  this & noReads & noWrites
}
```

This implementation is more involved than the one for asynchronous channels. The added complexity stems from the fact that a synchronous channel connects two synchronous operations, yet in each join pattern there can be only one function that returns. Our solution resembles a double handshake protocol. It splits up read and write into two sub-operations each, read1, read2 and write1, write2. The sub-operations are then matched in two join patterns, in opposite senses. In one pattern it is the read sub-operation which returns whereas in the second one it is the write sub-operation. The noReads and noWrites tokens are necessary for serializing reads and writes, so that a second write operation can only start after the previous read operation is finished and vice versa.

### 4.4 Monitors

Another scheme for process communication is to use a common store made up of mutable variables, and to use mutual exclusion mechanisms to prevent multiple processes from updating the same variable at the same time. A simple mutual exclusion mechanism is the *monitor* [Han72,Hoa74]. A monitor exports a set of functions $f_1$, ..., $f_k$ while ensuring that only one of these functions can be active at any one time. At the end of Section 3 we have already seen a scheme to implement monitors by joining methods with a state vector containing all instance variables. Alternatively, we can represent instance variables as normal variables in a record's environment and use a turn "token" to achieve mutual exclusion. Here is an implementation of counters using that scheme.

```
def newSyncCounter = {
  var count := 0
  def this.reset & turn     = { count := 0 ; () & turn },
      this.increment & turn = { count := count + 1 ; () & turn },
      this.value & turn     = { val x = count ; x & turn }
  this & turn
}
```

Many monitors are more involved than this example in that a process executing in a monitor also needs to wait for conditions to be established by other processes. We can use join patterns to implement this form of waiting as well as mutual exclusion. As an example, consider the following implementation of bounded buffers.

```
def newBoundedBuffer [t] (N: Int): Buffer [t] = {
  val elems: Array [t] = newArray [t] (N)
  var in := 0; var out := 0

  def this.put (elem: t) & available & turn = {
    elems (in) := elem ; in := (in + 1) % N
    () & filled & turn
  }
  def this.get & filled & turn = {
    val elem = elems (out) ; out := (out + 1) % N
    elem & available & turn
  }
  var i := 0
  while (|i < N) {| () & available ; i := i + 1 }
  this & turn
}
```

The basic implementation of the buffer is as in [Wir83]. Buffer elements are stored in an array elems with two variables in and out keeping track of the first free and occupied position in the array. These variables are incremented modulo N, the size of the buffer. What's new here is how processes wait for their preconditions. A producer process has to wait for the buffer to become nonfull, while a consumer process has to wait for the buffer to become nonempty. Our implementation mirrors each filled slot in the buffer with a filled token. Each unfilled slot in the buffer is mirrored with an available token. Thus, the total number of filled and available tokens always equals N, the number of elements in the buffer. Initially, all slots are free, so we create N available tokens. Each subsequent put operation removes an available token and creates a filled token, while each get operation does the opposite; it removes a filled token and creates an available token. Mutual exclusion of the get and put operations is ensured by the standard turn token technique.

### 4.5 Signals

Instead of join patterns, languages such as Modula-2 or Java use *signals* to let processes executing in monitor wait for preconditions. The implementation of such signals as functional nets is a bit subtle. On the surface, a signal is quite similar to a semaphore. Like a semaphore, a signal also offers two operations, which are now called send and wait. The wait operation of a signal corresponds to the getLock operation of a semaphore in that it waits until there is a call to send and then returns. A send operation of a signal on the other hand will unblock a pre-existing wait but does nothing at all if no call to wait exists. Unlike the releaseLock operation of a semaphore, a send will not interact with a wait that is issued later. Hence, in the execution sequence releaseLock ; getLock the getLock operation will always succeed, whereas in the sequence send ; wait the wait will always block since the previous send got lost. A first attempt to implement signals as functional nets could be:

```
newtype Signal = {
    def wait: ()
    def send: nil
}
def newSignal: Signal = {
    def this.wait & this.send  =  (),
        this.send              =  nil
    this
}
```

The hope is that if there are calls to both send and wait, the wait operation will return with () whereas a send alone will reduce to process **nil**, which does nothing at all.

This implementation of signals would work if join patterns were always tried in sequence, with earlier join patterns taking precedence over later ones. Unfortunately, there's nothing that stops an implementation of functional nets from always immediately reducing a send operation to **nil**, such that a wait might block even after subsequent send's. Hence, our first attempt to implement signals fails.

It is still possible to formulate signals as functional nets. Here's one way to do it:

```
def newSignal: Signal = {
    def this.send & inactive  =  inactive,
        this.wait & inactive  =  wait1,
        wait1: () & this.send =  () & inactive
    this & inactive
}
```

The solution makes use of a token, inactive, which signals that there are no active waits. A send in inactive state simply leaves the state inactive. A wait in inactive state suppresses inactive state and continues with the blocking operation wait1. Finally, a wait1 and a send return () to the wait1 and re-establish inactive state.

The second implementation of signals "feels" more deterministic than the first one, but its correctness is not easy to establish. Indeed, if one compares actual reduction sequences one finds that every reduction sequence of send's and wait's possible in the first implementation is also possible in the second and *vice versa*. The problem is that even with the second formulation of signals a processor might never reduce an incoming wait to a wait1. For instance, it might be busy doing other things indefinitely. Therefore, send's might still overtake wait's and get lost. So have we gained nothing by refining the implementation of signals? Not quite. The second formulation still has the following property, which is generally good enough for reactive systems: Say some process in a reactive system issues a wait on some signal and at some later time all processes of that system block. If at some later time some process is triggered by an external event and, once resumed, issues a send on the same signal then the wait (or some other wait on the same signal) is guaranteed to be able to proceed.

We now reformulate the bounded buffer example to closely match conventional implementations, making use of our signal abstraction. This implementation provides an explanation of the interaction between monitors and signals, which is also quite subtle. Here is the code:

```
def newBoundedBuffer [t] (N: Int): Buffer [t] = {
  val elems: Array [t] = newArray [t] (N)
  var in := 0; var out := 0; var n := 0

  val nonFull: Signal = newSignal
  val nonEmpty: Signal = newSignal

  def this.put (elem: t) & turn  =  {
    n := n + 1
    while (|n > N) {| waitUntil (nonFull) }
    elems (in) := elem ; in := (in + 1) % N
    () & turn & (if (n ≤ 0) then nonEmpty.send)
  }

  def this.get & turn  =  {
    n := n - 1
    while (|n < 0) {| waitUntil (nonEmpty) }
    val elem = elems (out) ; out := (out + 1) % N
    elem & turn & (if (n ≥ N) then nonFull.send)
  }

  def waitUntil (s: Signal): () = ( s.wait & turn ; reEnter )
  def reEnter: () & turn = ()

  this & turn
}
```

The correct interaction of signals with monitors, hidden in languages which define Monitors as primitive constructs, requires some effort to model explicitly. When waiting for a signal, a process has to re-issue the turn token, to let other processes enter the monitor. On the other hand, once a process wakes up, it has to re-consume the turn token to make sure that it executes under mutual exclusion. The re-issue and re-consumption of the turn token is done in functions waitUntil and reEnter. Because a process might block waiting for its turn after being woken up by a send, it is not guaranteed that the awaited condition will still be established when the process finally resumes. Hence, the awaited condition needs to be tested repeatedly in a while loop. This style of monitors has been discussed together with other alternatives by Hoare [Hoa74].

Monitor languages often permit a process executing in a monitor to re-enter the monitor by calling one of its methods. This behavior is not modelled in our implementation. If a monitor method called itself recursively, or called another method of the same monitor, the call would block indefinitely waiting for a turn token. In our model such situations would have to be addressed explicitly, for instance by providing a second version of the method which was not guarded by a turn token.

The last implementation of bounded buffers is more complicated than the first. But one might still prefer it because of efficiency considerations. After all, the implementation in terms of signals uses fewer tokens than the first implementation, because it sends a signal only when a processes is waiting for it. This does not invalidate our initial implementation, however, which remains attractive as a concise and executable design.

### 4.6 Readers and Writers

A more complex form of synchronization distinguishes between *readers* which access a common resource without modifying it and *writers* which can both access and modify it. To synchronize readers and writers we need to implement operations startRead, startWrite, endRead, endWrite, such that:

- there can be multiple concurrent readers,
- there can only be one writer at one time,
- pending write requests have priority over pending read requests, but don't preempt ongoing read operations.

This form of access control is common in databases. It can be implemented using traditional synchronization mechanisms such as semaphores, but this is far from trivial. We arrive at a functional net solution to the problem in two steps.

The initial solution is given at the top of Figure 3. We make use of two auxiliary tokens. The token readers n keeps track in its argument n of the number of *ongoing* reads, while writers n keeps track in n of the number of *pending* writes. A startRead operation requires that there are no pending writes to proceed, i.e. writers 0 must be asserted. In that case, startRead continues with startRead1, which reasserts writers 0, increments the number of ongoing readers, and returns to its caller. By contrast, a startWrite operation immediately increments the number of pending writes. It then continues with startWrite1, which waits for the number of readers to be 0 and then returns. Note the almost-symmetry between startRead and startWrite, where the different order of actions reflects the different priorities of readers and writers.

This solution is simple enough to trust its correctness. But the present formulation is not yet valid Funnel because we have made use of numeric arguments in join patterns. For instance readers 0 expresses the condition that the number of readers is zero. We arrive at an equivalent formulation in Funnel through factorization. A function such as readers which represents a condition is split into several sub-functions which together partition the condition into its cases of interest. In our case we should have a token noReaders which expresses the fact that there are no ongoing reads as well as a token readers n, where n is now required to be positive. Similarly, writers n is now augmented by a case noWriters.

**Initial solution:**

```
        def this.startRead   & writers (0)  =  startRead1,
                startRead1   & readers (n)  =  () & writers (0) & readers (n+1),
            this.startWrite  & writers (n)  =  startWrite1 & writers (n+1),
                startWrite1  & readers (0)  =  (),

            this.endRead     & readers (n)  =  readers (n–1),
            this.endWrite    & writers (n)  =  writers (n–1) & readers (0)

        this & readers (0) & writers (0)
    }
```

**After factorization:**

```
    def newReadersWriters = {
        def this.startRead  & noWriters   =  startRead1,
                startRead1  & noReaders   =  () & noWriters & readers (1),
                startRead1  & readers (n) =  () & noWriters & readers (n+1),

            this.startWrite & noWriters   =  startWrite1 & writers (1),
            this.startWrite & writers (n) =  startWrite1 & writers (n+1),
                startWrite1 & noReaders   =  (),

            this.endRead    & readers (n) =  if (n == 1) then noReaders
                                             else readers (n–1),
            this.endWrite   & writers (n) =  noReaders &
                                             if (n == 1) then noWriters
                                             else writers (n–1)

        this & noReaders & noWriters
    }
```

**Fig. 3.** Readers/writers synchronization

After splitting and introducing the necessary case distinctions, one obtains the functional net listed at the bottom of Figure 3.

## 5 Foundations: The Join Calculus

Functional nets have their formal basis in join calculus [FG96]. We present *object-based join calculus* which is a variant of the original calculus. The calculus is developed in two stages. In the first stage, we study a sequential subset comprising functions and objects. This subset can be taken as the formal basis of purely functional programs of the kind we presented in Section 1. The calculus is equivalent to (call-by-value) $\lambda$-calculus [Plo75] with a record construct, but takes the opposite position on naming functions. Where $\lambda$-calculus knows only anonymous functions, functional join calculus insists that every function have a name. Furthermore, it also insists that every intermediate result be named. As such it is quite similar to common forms of intermediate code found in compilers for functional languages.

**Syntax:**

| | | | |
|---|---|---|---|
| **Names** | $x, y, z$ | | |
| **Qualified names** | $X, Y, Z$ | $=$ | $x \mid X.y$ |
| **Terms** | $M, N$ | $=$ | $\mathbf{def}\ D\ ;\ M \mid X(Y)$ |
| **Definitions** | $D$ | $=$ | $L = M \mid D, D \mid \epsilon$ |
| **Left-hand sides** | $L$ | $=$ | $X(y)$ |

**Structural Equivalence:**

1. $\alpha$-renaming:
$$\mathbf{def}\ D\ ;\ M \equiv \mathbf{def}\ [y/x]D\ ;\ [y/x]M \qquad \text{if } x \in \text{dn}(D), y \notin \text{fn}(D, M)$$
$$L = M \equiv [y/x]L = [y/x]M \qquad \text{if } x \in \text{dn}(L), y \notin \text{fn}(M)$$
2. $(,)$ on definitions is associative and commutative with $\epsilon$ as an identity:
$$D_1, D_2 \equiv D_2, D_1$$
$$D_1, (D_2, D_3) \equiv (D_1, D_2), D_3$$
$$D, \epsilon \equiv D$$
3. Nested definitions can be merged:
$$\mathbf{def}\ D_1\ ;\ (\mathbf{def}\ D_2\ ;\ M) \equiv \mathbf{def}\ D_1, D_2\ ;\ M \qquad \text{if dn}(D_2) \cap \text{fn}(D_1) = \emptyset$$

**Reduction:**

$$\mathbf{def}\ D, X(y) = M\ ;\ X(Z) \quad \rightarrow \quad \mathbf{def}\ D, X(y) = M\ ;\ [Z/y]M$$

**Fig. 4.** Purely functional calculus

The second stage adds fork and join operators to the constructs introduced in the first stage. The calculus developed at this stage is roughly equivalent to the original join calculus. We have dropped the polyadic functions of original join calculus in favor of the qualified definitions and names that allow us to model records and tuples. We have also simplified the syntax of original join calculus and have replaced its "heating" and "cooling" rules by structural equivalences between terms.

Both stages represent functional nets as reduction systems. There is in each case only a single rewrite rule, which is similar to the $\beta$-reduction rule of $\lambda$-calculus, thus closely matching intuitions of functional programming. By contrast, the original treatment of join calculus is based on a chemical abstract machine [BB90], a concept well established in concurrency theory. The two versions of join calculus complement each other and are (modulo some minor syntactical details) equivalent.

## 5.1 Purely Functional Calculus

Figure 4 presents the subset of join calculus which can express purely functional programs. The syntax of this calculus is quite small. The basic building blocks of terms are names, written here $x$, $y$, $z$. Names can be concatenated with periods to form qualified names, written $X$, $Y$, $Z$. A *term* $M$ is either a function application $X(Y)$ where both the function and the argument can be qualified names. Or it

$$
\begin{array}{ll}
\mathrm{dn}(X_1(y_1)\& \ldots \& X_n(y_n) = M) & = \{\mathrm{first}(X_1), \ldots, \mathrm{first}(X_n)\} \\
\mathrm{dn}(D_1, D_2) & = \mathrm{dn}(D_1) \cup \mathrm{dn}(D_2) \\
\mathrm{dn}(\epsilon) & = \emptyset \\
\mathrm{dn}(X_1(y_1)\& \ldots \& X_n(y_n)) & = \{y_1, \ldots, y_n\}
\end{array}
$$

$$
\begin{array}{ll}
\mathrm{fn}(X(Y)) & = \{\mathrm{first}(X), \mathrm{first}(Y)\} \\
\mathrm{fn}(\mathbf{def}\ D \ ;\ M) & = (\mathrm{fn}(D) \cup \mathrm{fn}(M)) \backslash \mathrm{dn}(D) \\
\mathrm{fn}(M_1 \& M_2) & = \mathrm{fn}(M_1) \cup \mathrm{fn}(M_2) \\
\mathrm{fn}(L = M) & = \mathrm{dn}(L) \cup (\mathrm{fn}(M) \backslash \mathrm{dn}(L)) \\
\mathrm{fn}(D_1, D_2) & = \mathrm{fn}(D_1) \cup \mathrm{fn}(D_2) \\
\mathrm{fn}(\epsilon) & = \emptyset
\end{array}
$$

**Fig. 5.** Local, defined, and free names

is a term with a local definition, **def** $D$ ; $M$. A *definition* $D$ is a sequence of rewrite rules of the form $L = M$, where $\epsilon$ stands for the empty sequence. The *left-hand side* $L$ of a rewrite rule is again a function application $X(y)$, where the function name can be a qualified name, but the argument must be a simple name. The right-hand side of a rewrite rule is an arbitrary term.

Given a qualified name $X$, let the *simple-name prefix* first$(X)$ be its leading simple name. I.e.

$$
\begin{array}{ll}
\mathrm{first}(x) & = x \\
\mathrm{first}(X.y) & = \mathrm{first}(X)
\end{array}
$$

The set of *defined names* dn$(D)$ of a definition $D$ of the form $X(y) = M$ consists of just the simple-name prefix of $X$, first$(X)$. The defined names dn$(L)$ of a left-hand side $L$ of the form $X(y)$ consist of just the formal parameter $\{y\}$. The *free names* fn$(M)$ of a term $M$ are all names which are not defined by or local to a definition in $M$. The free names of a definition $D$ are its defined names and any names which are free in the definition's right hand side, yet different from the local names of $D$. All names occurring in a term $M$ that are not free in $M$ are called *bound* in $M$. Figure 5 presents a formal definition of these sets for the full version of join calculus with concurrency.

To avoid unwanted name capture, where free names become bound inadvertently, we will always write terms subject to the following *hygiene condition*: We assume that the set of free and bound names of every term we write are disjoint. This can always be achieved by a suitable renaming of bound variables, according to the $\alpha$-*renaming* law. This law lets us rename local and defined names of definitions, provided that the new names do not clash with names which already exist in their scope.

The law is formalized by two equations, detailed in Figure 4. In these equations, $[y/x]$ denotes a substitution which maps $x$ to $y$. Substitutions are functions from names to identifiers which map all but a finite number of names to themselves. The results of applying a substitution to a qualified name, a term, or a definition are tabulated in Figure 6.

$$
\begin{array}{lll}
[Y/x]x & = Y & \\
[Y/x]z & = z & \textbf{if } x \neq z \\
[Y/x](X.z) & = ([Y/x]X).z & \\
[Y/x](X(Z)) & = ([Y/x]X)\ ([Y/x]Z) & \\
[Y/x](\textbf{def } D\ ;\ M) & = \textbf{def } [Y/x]D\ ;\ [Y/x]M & \textbf{if } x \notin \mathrm{dn}(D), \mathrm{first}(Y) \notin \mathrm{dn}(D) \\
[Y/x](M\ \&\ N) & = [Y/x]M\ \&\ [Y/x]N & \\
[Y/x](L = M) & = [Y/x]L = [Y/x]M & \textbf{if } x \notin \mathrm{dn}(L), \mathrm{first}(Y) \notin \mathrm{dn}(L) \\
[Y/x](D_1, D_2) & = [Y/x]D_1, [Y/x]D_2 & \\
[Y/x]\epsilon & = \epsilon &
\end{array}
$$

**Fig. 6.** Substitution

Some care is required in the definition of permissible renamings. For instance, consider the expression:

**def** this.f(k) = k(this) ; g(this)

Here the name this can be consistently renamed. For instance, the following expression would be considered equivalent to the previous one:

**def** that.f(k) = k(that) ; g(that)

On the other hand, the qualified function symbol f cannot be renamed without changing the meaning of the expression. For instance, renaming f to e would yield:

**def** this.e(k) = k(this) ; g(this)

This is clearly different from the expression we started with. The new expression passes a record with an e field to the function g, whereas the previous expressions passed a record with an f field.

Besides $\alpha$-renaming there are also other equalities that identify terms. All equalities together are detailed in Figure 4. The first set of laws states that the $(,)$-connective for definitions is associative and commutative, with identity $\epsilon$. In other words, sequences of definitions can be regarded as multi-sets. The second law states that nested definitions may be merged, provided this does not lead to name clashes. *Structural equivalence* $\equiv$ is the smallest relation which includes $\alpha$-renaming and these laws and which is reflexive, transitive, and compatible (i.e. closed under formation of contexts). Terms that are related by $\equiv$ are identified with each other.

The inclusion of multi-sets of definitions in the syntax is essentially for convenience, as one can translate every program with definitions consisting of multiple rewrite rules to a program that uses just one rewrite rule for each definition [FG96]. The convenience is great enough to warrant a syntax extension because the encoding is rather heavy.

Execution of terms in our calculus is defined by rewriting. Figure 4 defines a single rewrite rule, which is analogous to $\beta$-reduction in $\lambda$-calculus. The rule states that if there is an application $X(Z)$ which matches a definition of $X$, say $X(y) = M$, then we can rewrite the application to the definition's right hand side $M$, after replacing the formal parameter $y$ by the actual argument $Z$.

All functions in purely functional join have a single argument. However, it is possible to encode multiple argument functions using records. For instance, the two argument function

$$\textbf{def}\ \mathsf{f\ (x,\ y) = x + y}$$

can be expressed as

$$\textbf{def}\ \mathsf{f\ (xy)} = \{\ \textbf{val}\ \mathsf{x = xy.x}\ ;\ \textbf{val}\ \mathsf{y = xy.y}\ ;\ \mathsf{x + y}\ \}$$

This makes use of a value definition with a qualified name on its right hand side. Such value definitions can themselves be encoded as follows.

$$\textbf{val}\ x = Y\ ;\ M = \textbf{def}\ k(x) = M\ ;\ k(Y)$$

where $k$ is a fresh function name. Value definitions with more complicated right-hand sides can also be encoded using a continuation passing transform. This is further explained in Section 6.

We also admit functions which take an empty tuple of arguments, taking **def** $f() = M$ to be equivalent to **def** $f(x) = M$ for some $x \notin \text{fn}(M)$.

As an example of functional reduction, consider the reduction of a forwarding function:

$$\textbf{def}\ \mathsf{f(x) = g(x)\ ;\ f(y)} \quad \rightarrow \quad \textbf{def}\ \mathsf{f(x) = g(x)\ ;\ g(y)}$$

A slightly more complex example is the reduction of a call to an evaluation function, which takes two arguments and applies one to the other:

$$\textbf{def}\ \mathsf{apply(f,x) = f(x)\ ;\ apply(print,\ 1)} \quad \rightarrow \quad \textbf{def}\ \mathsf{apply(f,x) = f(x)\ ;\ print(1)}$$

## 5.2 Full Calculus with Concurrency

Figure 7 presents the full version of object-based join calculus with concurrency. It needs only one syntactic extension compared to the purely functional subset: the & operator is now introduced as *fork* operator on terms and as a *join* operator on left-hand sides.

The notion of structural equivalence is now richer than in the purely functional subset. Besides $\alpha$-renaming and the laws concerning definitions, there are two other sets of laws which identify terms. First, the fork operator is assumed to be associative and commutative. Second, we have a *scope extrusion* law, which states that the scope of a local definition may be extended dynamically over other operands of a parallel composition, provided this does not lead to clashes between names bound by the definition and free names of the terms that are brought in scope.

| | | | |
|---|---|---|---|
| **Names** | $x, y, z$ | | |
| **Qualified names** | $X, Y, Z$ | $=$ | $x \mid X.y$ |
| **Terms** | $M, N$ | $=$ | $\mathbf{def}\ D\ ;\ M \mid X(Y) \mid M \ \&\ N$ |
| **Definitions** | $D$ | $=$ | $L = M \mid D, D \mid \epsilon$ |
| **Left-hand sides** | $L$ | $=$ | $X(y) \mid L \ \&\ L$ |

**Structural Equivalence:** As in Figure 4, plus

4. (&) on terms is associative and commutative:
$$M_1 \ \&\ M_2 \equiv M_2 \ \&\ M_1$$
$$M_1 \ \&\ (M_2 \ \&\ M_3) \equiv (M_1 \ \&\ M_2) \ \&\ M_3$$
5. Scope extrusion:
$$(\mathbf{def}\ D\ ;\ M) \ \&\ N \equiv \mathbf{def}\ D\ ;\ (M \ \&\ N) \qquad \text{if } \mathrm{dn}(D) \cap \mathrm{fn}(N) = \emptyset.$$

**Reduction:**

$$\begin{array}{ll} & \mathbf{def}\ D, X_1(y_1) \ \&\ \ldots \ \&\ X_n(y_n) = M\ ;\ X_1(Z_1) \ \&\ \ldots \ \&\ X_n(Z_n) \ \&\ N \\ \rightarrow & \mathbf{def}\ D, X_1(y_1) \ \&\ \ldots \ \&\ X_n(y_n) = M\ ;\ [Z_1/x_1, \ldots, Z_n/x_n]M \ \&\ N \end{array}$$

**Fig. 7.** Full Calculus with Concurrency

There is still just one reduction rule, and this rule is essentially the same as in the functional subset. The major difference is that now a rewrite step may involve sets of function applications, which are composed in parallel.

The new laws of structural equivalence are necessary to bring parallel subterms which are "far apart" next to each other, so that they can match the join pattern of left-hand side. For instance, in the following example of semaphore synchronization two transformations with structural equivalences are necessary before rewrite steps can be performed.

```
  def getLock(k) & releaseLock() = k();
  releaseLock() & (def k'() = f() & g(); getLock(k'))
≡ (by commutativity of &)
  def getLock(k) & releaseLock() = k();
  (def k'() = f() & g(); getLock(k')) & releaseLock()
≡ (by scope extrusion)
  def getLock(k) & releaseLock() = k();
  def k'() = f() & g(); getLock(k') & releaseLock()
→ def getLock(k) & releaseLock() = k(); def k'() = f() & g(); k'()
→ def getLock(k) & releaseLock() = k(); def k'() = f() & g(); f() & g()
```

As an example of reduction of a program with objects and concurrency, consider the Funnel program at the top of Figure 8. The program defines an asynchronous channel using function newChannel and then reads and writes that channel.

This program is not yet in the form mandated by join calculus since it uses a synchronous function and a **val** definition. We can map this program into join calculus by adding continuation functions which make control flow for function

*Funnel Program.*

```
def newChannel = ( def this.read & this.write(x) = x ; this );
val chan = newChannel;
chan.read & chan.write(1)
```

*Join Calculus Program and Its Reduction.*

```
    def newChannel(k1) = (def this.read(k2) & this.write(x) = k2(x); k1(this));
    def k3(chan) = chan.read(k0) & chan.write(1);
    newChannel(k3)
→
    def newChannel(k1) = (def this.read(k2) & this.write(x) = k2(x); k1(this));
    def k3(chan) = chan.read(k0) & chan.write(1);
    def this'.read(k2') & this'.write(x') = k2'(x');
    k3(this')
→
    def newChannel(k1) = (def this.read(k2) & this.write(x) = k2(x); k1(this));
    def k3(chan) = chan.read(k0) & chan.write(1);
    def this'.read(k2') & this'.write(x') = k2'(x');
    this'.read(k0) & this'.write(1);
→
    def newChannel(k1) = (def this.read(k2) & this.write(x) = k2(x); k1(this));
    def k3(chan) = chan.read(k0) & chan.write(1);
    def this'.read(k2') & this'.write(x') = k2'(x');
    k0(1)
```

**Fig. 8.** Reduction involving an asynchronous channel object

returns and value definitions explicit. The second half of Figure 8 shows how this program is coded in object-based join calculus and how it is reduced. Schemes which map from our programming notation to join calculus are further discussed in the next section.

## 6 Syntactic Abbreviations

Even the extended calculus discussed in the last section is a lot smaller than the Funnel programming notation we have used in the preceding sections. This section fills the gap, by showing how Funnel constructs which are not directly supported in object-based join calculus can be mapped into equivalent constructs which are supported.

*Direct Style.* An important difference between Funnel and join calculus is that Funnel has synchronous functions and **val** definitions which bind the results of synchronous function applications. To see the simplifications afforded by these additions, it suffices to compare the Funnel program of Figure 8 with its join calculus counterpart. The join calculus version is much more cluttered because of the occurrence of the continuations $k_i$. Programs which make use of synchronous functions and value definitions are said to be in *direct style*, whereas programs that don't are said to be in *continuation passing style.* Join calculus supports only continuation passing style. To translate direct style programs into join calculus, we need a *continuation passing transform.* This transformation gives each synchronous function an additional argument which represents a continuation function, to which the result of the synchronous function is then passed.

The source language of the continuation passing transform is object-based join calculus extended with result expressions $X$ and value definitions **val** $x = M\ ;\ N$.

For the sake of the following explanation, we assume different alphabets for synchronous and asynchronous functions. We let $X^s$ range over qualified names whose final selector is a synchronous function, whereas $X^a$ ranges over qualified names whose final selector is an asynchronous function. In practice, we can distinguish between synchronous and asynchronous functions also by means of a type system, so that different alphabets are not required.

Our continuation passing transform for terms is expressed as a function $[[M]]_k$ which takes a term $M$ in the source language and a name $k$ representing a continuation as arguments, mapping these to a term in object-based join calculus. It makes use of a helper function which maps a definition in the source language to one in object-based join calculus. The transforms are defined as follows.

$$
\begin{array}{lcl}
[[\ \mathbf{val}\ \mathsf{x} = \mathsf{M}\ ;\ \mathsf{N}\ ]]\mathsf{k} & = & \mathbf{def}\ \mathsf{k'(x)} = [[\ \mathsf{N}\ ]]\mathsf{k}\ ;\ [[\ \mathsf{M}\ ]]\mathsf{k'} \\
[[\ \mathsf{X}\ ]]\mathsf{k} & = & \mathsf{k(X)} \\
[[\ \mathsf{X}^s\mathsf{(Y)}\ ]]\mathsf{k} & = & \mathsf{X}^s\mathsf{(Y, k)} \\
[[\ \mathsf{X}^a\mathsf{(Y)}\ ]]\mathsf{k} & = & \mathsf{X}^a\mathsf{(Y)} \\
[[\ \mathsf{M}\ \&\ \mathsf{N}\ ]]\mathsf{k} & = & [[\ \mathsf{M}\ ]]\mathsf{k}\ \&\ [[\ \mathsf{N}\ ]]\bot \\
[[\ \mathbf{def}\ \mathsf{D}\ ;\ \mathsf{M}\ ]]\mathsf{k} & = & \mathbf{def}\ [[\ \mathsf{D}\ ]]\ ;\ [[\ \mathsf{M}\ ]]\mathsf{k} \\
 & & \\
[[\ \mathsf{L} = \mathsf{M}\ ]] & = & [[\ \mathsf{L}\ ]]\mathsf{k'} = [[\ \mathsf{M}\ ]]\mathsf{k'} \\
[[\ \mathsf{D, D'}\ ]] & = & [[\ \mathsf{D}\ ]],\ [[\ \mathsf{D'}\ ]] \\
[[\ \epsilon\ ]] & = & \epsilon
\end{array}
$$

Here, the k' in the first equations for terms and definitions represent fresh continuation names. $\bot$ represents an error continuation. We can guarantee with a type system that $\bot$ continuations are never called. Note that the transform for rewrite rules $L = M$ applies the transform for terms to the pattern $L$. This is well-defined since the syntax of patterns is contained in the syntax of terms.

The original paper on join [FG96] defines a different contination passing transform. That transform allows several functions in a join pattern to carry results. Consequently, in the body of a function it has to be specified to which of the functions of a left hand side a result should be returned to. The advantage of this approach is that it simplifies the implementation of rendevouz situations like the synchronous channel of Section 4. The disadvantage is a more complex construct for function returns.

*Structured Terms.* In Funnel, the function part and arguments of a function application can be arbitrary terms, whereas join calculus admits only identifiers.

Terms as function arguments can be expanded out by introducing names for intermediate results.

M(N) ⇒ **val** x = M; **val** y = N; x y

The resulting expression can be mapped into join calculus by applying the continuation passing transform. The same principle is also applied in other situations where structured terms appear yet only identifiers are supported. E.g. a term $M$ used as function result can be expanded to

**val** x = M ; x

We assume here that names in the expanded term which are not present in the original source term are fresh.

*Sequencing.* Funnel supports sequencing of expressions. A sequential composition $M$ ; $N$ is simply regarded as a shorthand for a value definition, the expansion being as follows:

M ; N ⇒ **val** x = M; N

*Primitive Data Types.* Funnel supports boolean values and conditional expressions of the form if (M) then $N_1$ else $N_2$. These can be expanded using the visitor technique of Section 1. For instance, here are the expansions for the boolean values true and false and the conditional expression:

```
true                   ⇒ ( def match v = v.true )
false                  ⇒ ( def match v = v.false )
if (M) then T else F⇒  M.match ( def true = T, false = F )
```

This is essentially the Church encoding for booleans in λ-calculus. The only difference is that we use records where the encoding into λ-calculus uses λ-abstractions. Analogous techniques can be employed to encode other primitive types such as integers or characters.

# 7 Classes and Inheritance

The language constructs discussed previously cover the essential aspects of object-based, concurrent languages. We now extend this to concepts of class-based languages with inheritance. The class design we cover here is loosely based on Java's [GJSB00]. As we have done with other concepts before, we treat classes as derived constructs, which are defined in terms of the class-less base language.

## 7.1 Simple Class Definitions

A class C introduces a type (of objects) C and a "module" with the same name. The module contains constructor function for the objects described by the class.

In our model, a module is simply a record value, which has the constructor function as a member.

Following Palsberg and Schwarzbach [PS94] and [BOW98], we consider a set of classes that describe linked lists. as a running example for the material on classes. We start with a simple class for linked lists, which are not meant to be refined further. This is expressed by the **final** modifier in the class definition.

```
final class LL (x: Int) = {
    private var next: LL
    def isEmpty: Boolean = x == -1
    def elem: Int = if (this.isEmpty) then x else error();
    def getNext: LL = next
    def setNext(n: LL) = { next := n }
}
```

Linked lists have visible method isEmpty, elem, getNext and next. They also have a private field next which is can be accessed only locally.

The class above would translate to a type LL for linked-list objects, as well as a record value LL which contains a constructor for such objects.

```
newtype LL = {
    def isEmpty: Boolean
    def elem: Int
    def getNext: LL
    def setNext(n: LL): ()
}
let LL = {
    def newInstance (x: Int) = {
        var next: LL
        def isEmpty: Boolean = x == -1
        def elem: Int = if (this.isEmpty) then x else error();
        def getNext: LL = next
        def setNext(n: LL) = { next := n }
    }
}
```

The object type and the class module can be systematically derived from a class definition. Assume we have a class definition

**final class** $C(\tilde{x} : \tilde{T}) = \{ \ldots \}$

Then the object-type is a record which contains bindings for every member of the class, except those members that have been marked with a **private** modifier. The corresponding module contains a single function newInstance, which takes the class parameters $C(\tilde{x} : \tilde{T})$ as parameters and the class body as body, with all **private** modifiers removed. That is, $C$ has the outline:

```
let C = {
    def newInstance (x̃ : T̃): C = { ... }
}
```

Note that this translation gives **private** members a weaker status than they have in Java or C++. In those languages, a private field of an object can be accessed from other objects of the same class. In our translation, a private field does not form part of the object type, so that it can only be accessed from the object in which it is defined. It would be possible to adapt our translation so that it more accurately reflects the standard meaning of **private** in C++ and Java. Essentially, the modified translation would use an abstract type for **private** members the implementation of which is known only within the containing class. While possible, this translation would share the shortcomings of the standard meaning of **private** in the area of scalability. For that reason, and because it is possible to emulate hiding via abstract types in user programs, we stick here with the "lexical closure" interpretation of **private**.

## 7.2 Static Class Members

Java allows class members to be marked **static**, to indicate that these members should exist once-per-class rather than once-per object. This is easily modelled by including such members as additional fields of a class module. As an example, assume we want to define an empty list in class LL:

```
final class LL (x: Int) = {
    static let empty = LL.newInstance (-1)
    ...
}
```

Then empty becomes another field of the LL record. The type LL and the newInstance function remain as they were before.

```
let LL = {
    let empty = LL.newInstance (-1)
    def newInstance (x: Int) = {
        ...
    }
}
```

Note that by convention static members are defined before the newInstance function. Hence, they can refer to newInstance only indirectly, by selecting the module value itself.

## 7.3 Inheritance

So far, we considered a class exclusively as an object creator. We now extend this point of view by taking inheritance into account. A class can now serve as an inherited template that defines part of the behavior of objects belonging to subclasses. As an example, consider again class LL with an extension LLSub. LLSub objects are like LL objects, but the "emptiness" of a list object is determined by an additional class parameter empty instead of being encoded by the special value -1.

```
class LL(x: Int) = {
    private var next: LL
    def isEmpty: Boolean = x == -1
    def elem: Int = if (this.isEmpty) then x else error()
    def getNext: LL = next
    def setNext(n: LL) = { next := n }
}
class LLSub(x: Int, empty: Boolean) = LL(x) with {
    def isEmpty = empty
}
```

These definitions make LLSub a subtype of LL. The definition of LLSub is based on the definition of LL. Instead of repeating the definition of members of LL in LLSub, we "inherit" those members using the prefix LL(x) **with** to the class body.

Following standard approaches, we express inheritance as *delegation*. The principle is that inherited methods are forwarded to methods of an object of the inherited class, the so-called delegate. As is customary, we use the name super for this object. Care is required with self references. We would expect the self reference this to refer to the inheriting object, not the delegate, so that overriding works: When calling this.isEmpty(...) in the LL delegate of a LLSub object, it should be the redefined version of isEmpty in LLSub that is called, not the original version of isEmpty as defined in LL. We achieve this by introducing a new object constructor function, newSuper, which takes the identity of the object being constructed as parameter.

Hence, a class definition **class** C = { ... } would give rise to a function

```
def newSuper (this: C): C { ... }
```

in module C. An inheriting class D would invoke this newSuper function to create a delegate object and forward all inherited functions to it.

```
val super = C.newSuper (this)
import super
```

The construct **import** E makes available all fields of the record E in with any qualification. If the term E is of a record type with fields $x_1$, ..., $x_n$, this term is equivalent to

$$\textbf{val}\ e = E\ ;\ \textbf{val}\ x_1 = e.x_1,\ \ldots,\ x_n = e.x_n.$$

for some fresh identifier e. To create a new C object, we need to invoke C.newSuper with the created object as parameter. Hence, C.newInstance becomes:

```
def newInstance = {
  val this = newSuper (this); this
}
```

The described technique implements objects via recursive records [Car84,Red88], which is one of the two standard encoding schemes (the other is based on existential types [PT93]). Care is required in forming the right fixed point for this, since a pure call-by-value interpretation would lead to non-termination. We solve this in Funnel by evaluating recursive definitions like the one above in a lazy fashion. We first establish an as yet unfilled object for this, then pass this object to newSuper. When newSuper returns, all fields of the this object are overwritten with the corresponding fields of newSuper's result. During evaluation of newSuper it is quite legal to refer to this, for instance to pass it as an argument to another function. However, any attempt to dereference this will lead to a run-time error signalling a cyclic definition.

To return to our running example, here is the new translation of class LL:

```
newtype LL = {
  def isEmpty: Boolean
  def elem: Int
  def getNext: LL
  def setNext(n: LL): ()
}
let LL = {
  def newSuper (this: LL, x: Int): LL = {
    var next: LL
    def isEmpty: Boolean = x == -1
    def elem: Int = if (this.isEmpty) then x else error()
    def getNext = next
    def setNext(n: LL) = { next := n }
  }
  def newInstance (x: Int): LL = { val this: LL = newSuper(this, x); this }
}
```

The translation of class LLSub shows the implementation of inheritance via delegation.

```
newtype LLSub = LL with {}
let LLSub = {
  def newSuper (this: LLSub, x: Int, empty: Boolean): LLSub = {
    val super = LL.newSuper (this, x)
    import super
    def isEmpty: Boolean = empty
  }
  def newInstance (x: Int, empty: Boolean): LLSub = {
    val this: LLSub = newSuper(this, x, empty); this
  }
}
```

### 7.4 Abstract Methods

Assume now that we do not want to give an implementation of isEmpty at all, and instead want to defer such an implementation to subclasses. This can be expressed by an abstract method:

```
class LLAbs(x: Int) = {
    private var next: LL
    def getNext: LL = next
    def setNext(n: LL) = { next := n }
    abstract def isEmpty
    def elem = if (this.isEmpty) then x else error();
}
```

How should abstract methods be formalized? So far, the newSuper function returned a value of the same type as was passed into the function in the this parameter. With abstract methods, this changes. An abstract method still needs to be included in the type of the self reference, since it may be invoked as a method of this. However, it clearly cannot form part of the record defined by newSuper, since no definition is given. We model this by defining a new type named Trait in the class module. The Trait type collects all functions defined by that class. The object type is then composed of the trait type together with bindings for all abstract methods. Here are the details:

```
newtype LL = LL.Trait with {
    def isEmpty
}
let LL = {
    type Trait = {
        def elem: Int
        def getNext: LL
        def setNext(n: LL): ()
    }
    def newSuper (this: LL, x: Int): Trait = {
        var next: LL
        def getNext = next
        def setNext(n: LL) = { next := n }
        def elem = if (this.isEmpty) then x else error();
    }
}
```

Note that there is no newInstance function, which reflects the rule that no instances of classes with abstract members can be created. newInstance could not be defined anyway, since its fixed-point would not be type-correct. In

```
val this: LL = newSuper (this, x)
```

the left-hand-side this has type LL, but the right-hand side's type is LL.Trait, which is not a subtype of LL.

## 8 Conclusion and Related Work

The first five sections of this paper have shown how a large variety of program constructs can be modelled as functional nets. The next two sections have shown how functional nets themselves can be expressed in join calculus. Taken together, these steps constitute a reductionistic approach, where a large body of notations and patterns of programs is to be distilled into a minimal kernel. The reduction to essentials is useful since it helps clarify the meaning of derived program constructs and the interactions between them.

Ever since the inception of Lisp [MAE+69] and Landin's ISWIM [Lan66], functional programming has pioneered the idea of developing programming languages from calculi. Since then, there has been an extremely large body of work which aims to emulate the FP approach in a more general setting. One strand of work has devised extensions of lambda calculus with state [FH92,SF93,SRI91,ORH93,AS98] or non-determinism and concurrency [Bou89,dP95,Bou97]. Another strand of work has been designed concurrent functional languages [GMP89,Rep91,AMST97] based on some other operational semantics. Landin's program has also been repeated in the concurrent programming field, for instance with Occam and CSP [Hoa85], Pict [PT97] and $\pi$-calculus [MPW92], or Oz and its kernel [SHW95].

Our approach is closest to the work on join calculus [FG96,FGL+96,FM97, Fes98]. Largely, functional nets as described here constitute a simplification and streamlining of the original treatment of join, with object-based join calculus and qualified definitions being the main innovation. These notes are an adaptation and extension of two previous papers [Ode00a,Ode00b].

## Acknowledgements

Matthias Zenger and Christoph Zenger have designed several of the examples. I thank them and also Philippe Altherr and Michel Schinz for having suggested numerous improvements to the paper.

## References

[AB96] Andrea Asperti and Nadia Bussi. Mobile petri nets. Technical Report UBLCS-96-10, University of Bolognia, May 1996.

[AC96] Martin Abadi and Luca Cardelli. *A Theory of Objects*. Monographs in Computer Science. Springer Verlag, 1996.

[AMST97] Gul Agha, Ian A. Mason, Scott F. Smith, and Carolyn L. Talcott. A foundation for actor computation. *Journal of Functional Programming*, 7(1):1–69, 1997.

[AN00] Franz Achermann and Oscar Nierstrasz. Applications = components + scripts – a tour of Piccola. In *Software Architectures and Component Technology*. Kluwer, 2000.

[AOS+00] Philippe Altherr, Martin Odersky, Michel Schinz, Matthias Zenger, and Christoph Zenger. Funnel distribution. available from `http://lampwww.epfl.ch/funnel`, July 2000.

[AS98] Zena Ariola and Amr Sabry. Correctness of monadic state: An imperative call-by-need calculus. In *Proc. 25th ACM Symposium on Principles of Programming Languages*, pages 62–74, 1998.

[ASS84] Harold Abelson, Gerald Jay Sussman, and Julie Sussman. *The Structure and Interpretation of Computer Programs.* MIT Press, Cambridge, Massachusetts, 1984.

[Bac78] John W. Backus. Can programming be liberated from the von neumann style? *Communications of the ACM*, 21:613–641, 1978.

[Bar84] Hendrik P. Barendregt. *The Lambda Calculus: its Syntax and Semantics*, volume 103 of *Studies in Logic and the Foundations of Mathematics.* North-Holland, Amsterdam, revised edition, 1984.

[BB90] Gérard Berry and Gérard Boudol. The chemical abstract machine. In *Proc. 17th ACM Symposium on Principles of Programming Languages*, pages 81–94, January 1990.

[Bir98] Richard Bird. *Introduction to Functional Programming using Haskell.* Prentice Hall, 1998. 2nd edition.

[Bou89] Gérard Boudol. Towards a lambda-calculus for concurrent and communicating systems. In J. Díaz and F. Orejas, editors, *Proceedings TAPSOFT '1989*, pages 149–161, New York, March 1989. Springer-Verlag. Lecture Notes in Computer Science 351.

[Bou97] Gérard Boudol. The pi-calculus in direct style. In *Proc. 24th ACM Symposium on Principles of Programming Languages*, pages 228–241, 1997.

[BOW98] Kim B. Bruce, Martin Odersky, and Philip Wadler. A staticalle safe alternative to virtual types. In *Proc. 5th International Workshop on Foundations of Object-Oriented Languages, San Diego.*, January 1998.

[Car84] Luca Cardelli. A semantics of multiple inheritance. In Gilles Kahn, David B. MacQueen, and Gordon D. Plotkin, editors, *Semantics of Data Types*, pages 51–67. Springer-Verlag, June 1984. Lecture Notes in Computer Science 173.

[Chu51] Alonzo Church. *The Calculi of Lambda-Conversion*, volume 6 of *Annals of Mathematics Studies.* Princeton University Press, second edition, 1951.

[DM82] Luis Damas and Robin Milner. Principal type schemes for functional programs. In *Proc. 9th ACM Symposium on Principles of Programming Languages*, pages 207–211, January 1982.

[dP95] Ugo de'Liguoro and Adolfo Piperno. Non deterministic extensions of untyped $\lambda$-calculus. *Information and Computation*, 122(2):149–177, 1 November 1995.

[Fes98] Fabrice Le Fessant. *The JoCaml reference manual.* INRIA Rocquencourt, 1998. Available from `http://join.inria.fr`.

[FG96] Cédric Fournet and Georges Gonthier. The reflexive chemical abstract machine and the join-calculus. In *Proc. 23rd ACM Symposium on Principles of Programming Languages*, pages 372–385, January 1996.

[FGL+96] Cédric Fournet, Georges Gonthier, Jean-Jacques Lévy, Luc Maranget, and Didier Rémy. A calculus of mobile agents. In *7th International Conference on Concurrency Theory (CONCUR'96)*, pages 406–421, Pisa, Italy, August 26-29 1996. Springer-Verlag. LNCS 1119.

[FH92] Matthias Felleisen and Robert Hieb. The revised report on the syntactic theories of sequential control and state. *Theoretical Computer Science*, 103:235–271, 1992.

[FM97] Cédric Fournet and Luc Maranget. *The Join-Calculus Language.* INRIA Rocquencourt, 1997. Available from `http://join.inria.fr`.

[GHJV94] Erich Gamma, Richard Helm, Ralph Johnson, and John Vlissides. *Design Patterns : Elements of Reusable Object-Oriented Software.* Addison-Wesley, 1994.

[GJSB00] James Gosling, Bill Joy, Guy Steele, and Gilad Bracha. *The Java Language Specification, Second Edition.* Java Series, Sun Microsystems, 2000. ISBN 0-201-31008-2.

[GMP89] Alessandro Giacalone, Prateek Mishra, and Sanjiva Prasad. Facile: A symmetric integration of concurrent and functional programming. *International Journal of Parallel Programming*, 18(2):121–160, April 1989.

[Han72] Per Brinch Hansen. Structured multiprogramming. *Communications of the ACM*, 15(7):574–578, July 1972.

[Hoa85] C. A. R. Hoare. *Communicating Sequential Processes.* Prentice-Hall, Englewood Cliffs, New Jersey, 1985.

[Hoa74] C.A.R. Hoare. Monitors: An operating system structuring concept. *Communications of the ACM*, 12(10), October 74.

[Hud89] Paul Hudak. Conception, evolution, and application of functional programming languages. *ACM Computing Surveys*, 21(3):359–411, 1989.

[Jen92] K. Jensen. *Coloured Petri Nets. Basic Concepts.* EATCS Monographs on Theoretical Computer Science. Springer Verlag, 1992.

[Ker87] Jon Kerridge. *Occam programming: a practical approach.* Blackwell Scientific, 1987.

[Lan66] Peter J. Landin. The next 700 programming languages. *Communications of the ACM*, 9:157–166, March 1966.

[MAE+69] John McCarthy, Paul W. Abrahams, D. J. Edwards, T. P. Hart, and I. L. Levin. *Lisp 1.5 Programmer's Manual.* MIT Press, 1969.

[Mil78] Robin Milner. A theory of type polymorphism in programming. *Journal of Computer and System Sciences*, 17:348–375, Dec 1978.

[Mil80] Robin Milner. *A Calculus of Communicating Systems*, volume 92 of *Lecture Notes in Computer Science.* Springer-Verlag, New York, 1980.

[MPW92] Robin Milner, Joachim Parrow, and David Walker. A calculus of mobile processes. *Information and Computation*, 100:1–77, 1992.

[Ode00a] Martin Odersky. Functional nets. In *Proc. European Symposium on Programming*, number 1782 in LNCS, pages 1–25. Springer Verlag, March 2000.

[Ode00b] Martin Odersky. Programming with functional nets. Technical Report 2000/331, Departement d'Informatique, EPFL, March 2000.

[ORH93] Martin Odersky, Dan Rabin, and Paul Hudak. Call-by-name, assignment, and the lambda calculus. In *Proc. 20th ACM Symposium on Principles of Programming Languages*, pages 43–56, January 1993.

[OZZ01] Martin Odersky, Matthias Zenger, and Christoph Zenger. Colored local type inference. In *Proc. ACM Symposium on Principles of Programming Languages*, 2001.

[Pau91] L. C. Paulson. *ML for the Working Programmer.* Cambridge University Press, 1991. ISBN 0-521-39022-2.

[Pet62] C.A. Petri. Kommunikation mit Automaten. Schriften des IIM 2, Institut für Instrumentelle Mathematik, Bonn, 1962. English translation: Technical Report RADC-TR-65-377, Vol. 1, Suppl. 1, Applied Data Research, Princeton, New Jersey, Contract AF 30 (602)-3324, 1966.

[PG92] Young Gil Park and Benjamin Goldberg. Escape analysis on lists. In *Proceedings of the ACM SIGPLAN '92 Conference on Programming Language Design and Implementation, San Francisco, California*, pages 116–127. ACM Press, June 1992.

[Plo75] Gordon D. Plotkin. Call-by-name, call-by-value, and the λ-calculus. *Theoretical Computer Science*, 1:125–159, 1975.

[PS94] Jens Palsberg and Michael I. Schwartzbach. *Object-Oriented Type-Systems.* John Wiley, 1994.

[PT93] Benjamin C. Pierce and David N. Turner. Object-oriented programming without recursive types. In *Conference Record of the Twentieth Annual ACM SIGPLAN-SIGACT Symposium on Principles of Programming Languages, Charleston, South Carolina, January 10–13, 1993*, pages 299–312. ACM Press, January 1993.

[PT97] Benjamin C. Pierce and David N. Turner. Pict: A programming language based on the pi-calculus. Technical Report CSCI 476, Computer Science Department, Indiana University, 1997.

[PT98] Benjamin C. Pierce and David N. Turner. Local type inference. In *Proc. 25th ACM Symposium on Principles of Programming Languages*, 1998.

[Red88] Uday Reddy. Objects as closures: Abstract semantics of object-oriented languages. In *Proceedings of the 1988 ACM Conference on Lisp and Functional Programming*, pages 289–297, July 1988.

[Rei85] W. Reisig. *Petri Nets*, volume 4 of *EATCS Monographs on Theoretical Computer Science.* Springer-Verlag, 1985.

[Rep91] John H. Reppy. CML: A higher-order concurrent language. In *Proc. ACM SIGPLAN Conf. on Programming Language Design and Implementation*, pages 293–305, June 1991.

[SF93] Amr Sabry and John Field. Reasoning about explicit and implicit representations of state. In *SIPL '93 ACM SIGPLAN Workshop on State in Programming Languages, Copenhagen, Denmark*, pages 17–30, June 1993. Yale University Research Report YALEU/DCS/RR-968.

[SHW95] Gert Smolka, Martin Henz, and Jörg Würtz. Object-oriented concurrent constraint programming in Oz. In P. van Hentenryck and V. Saraswat, editors, *Principles and Practice of Constraint Programming*, chapter 2, pages 29–48. The MIT Press, 1995.

[SRI91] Vipin Swarup, Uday S. Reddy, and Evan Ireland. Assignments for applicative languages. In John Hughes, editor, *Functional Programming Languages and Computer Architecture*, pages 192–214. Springer-Verlag, August 1991. Lecture Notes in Computer Science 523.

[Wir83] Niklaus Wirth. *Programming in Modula-2.* Springer Verlag, 2nd edition, 1983.

# Operational Semantics and Program Equivalence

Andrew M. Pitts

Cambridge University Computer Laboratory
Cambridge CB2 3QG, UK
Andrew.Pitts@cl.cam.ac.uk

**Abstract.** This tutorial paper discusses a particular style of operational semantics that enables one to give a 'syntax-directed' inductive definition of termination which is very useful for reasoning about operational equivalence of programs. We restrict attention to contextual equivalence of expressions in the ML family of programming languages, concentrating on functions involving local state. A brief tour of structural operational semantics culminates in a structural definition of termination via an abstract machine using 'frame stacks'. Applications of this to reasoning about contextual equivalence are given.

## Table of Contents



## 1 Introduction

The various approaches to giving meanings to programming languages fall broadly into three categories: denotational, axiomatic and operational. In a denotational semantics the meaning of programs is defined abstractly using elements of some suitable mathematical structure; in an axiomatic semantics, meaning is

G. Barthe et al. (Eds.): Applied Semantics, LNCS 2395, pp. 378–412, 2002.

defined via some logic of program properties; and in an operational semantics it is defined by specifying the behaviour of programs during execution. Operational semantics used to be regarded as less useful than the other two approaches for many purposes, because it tends to be quite concrete, with important general properties of a programming language obscured by a low-level description of how program execution takes place. The situation changed with the development of a *structural* approach to operational semantics initiated by Plotkin, Milner, Kahn, and others. Structural operational semantics is now widely used for specifying and reasoning about the semantics of programs.

In this tutorial paper I will concentrate upon the use of structural operational semantics for reasoning about program properties. More specifically, I will look at operationally-based proof techniques for *contextual equivalence* of programs (or fragments of programs) in the ML language—or rather, in a core language with function and reference types that is common to the various languages in the ML family, such as Standard ML [9] and Caml [5][1]. ML is a *functional* programming language because it treats functions as values on a par with more concrete forms of data: functions can be passed as arguments, can be returned as the result of computation, can be recursively defined, and so on. It is also a *procedural* language because it permits the use of references (or 'cells', or 'locations') for storing values: references can be declared locally in functions and then created dynamically and their contents read and updated as function applications are evaluated. Although this mix of (call-by-value) higher order functions with local, dynamically allocated state is conveniently expressive, there are many subtle properties of such functions up to contextual equivalence. The traditional methods of denotational semantics do not capture these subtleties very well—domain-based models either tend to be far from 'fully abstract', or very complicated, or both. Consequently a sort of 'back to basics' movement has arisen that attempts to develop theories of program equivalence for high-level languages based directly on operational semantics (see [11] for some of the literature).

There are several different styles of structural operational semantics (which I will briefly survey). However, I will try to show that one particular and possibly unfamiliar approach to structural operational semantics using a 'frame stack' formalism—derived from the approach of Wright and Felleisen [18] and used in the redefinition of ML by Harper and Stone [6]—provides a more convenient basis for developing properties of contextual equivalence of programs than does the evaluation (or 'natural', or 'big-step') semantics used in the official definition of Standard ML [9].

*Further Reading.* Most of the examples and technical results in this paper to do with operational properties of ML functions with local references are covered in more detail in the paper [15] written jointly with Ian Stark. More recent work on this topic includes the use of labelled transition systems and bisimulations by Jeffrey and Rathke [7]; and the use by Aboul-Hosn and Hannan of static restric-

[1] I will use the concrete syntax of Caml.

tions on local state in functions to give a more tractable theory of equivalence [1]. The use of logical relations based on abstract machine semantics to analyse other programming language features, such as polymorphism, is developed in [13, 14, 3]; see also [2] and [6].

*Exercises.* Some exercises are given in Appendix B.

*Notation.* A list of the notations used in this paper is given in Appendix C.

*Acknowledgement.* I am grateful to members of the audience of the lectures on which this paper is based for their lively feedback; and to an anonymous referee of the original version of this paper, whose detailed comments helped to improve the presentation.

## 2 Functions with Local State

Consider the following two Caml expressions $p$ and $m$:

$$p \triangleq \texttt{let } a \texttt{ = ref 0 in} \quad (1)$$
$$\texttt{fun(}x \texttt{ : int) -> (}a \texttt{ := !}a \texttt{ + } x \texttt{ ; !}a\texttt{)}$$

$$m \triangleq \texttt{let } b \texttt{ = ref 0 in} \quad (2)$$
$$\texttt{fun(}y \texttt{ : int) -> (}b \texttt{ := !}b \texttt{ - } y \texttt{ ; 0 - !}b\texttt{)}$$

I claim that these Caml expressions (of type `int -> int`) are semantically equivalent, in the sense that we can use them interchangeably in any place in an ML program that expects an expression of type `int -> int` without affecting the overall behaviour of the program. Such notions of equivalence of programs go by the name of *contextual equivalence*. Here is an informal definition of this notion, that holds good for any particular kind of programming language:

> Two phrases of a programming language are *contextually equivalent* if any occurrences of the first phrase in a complete program can be replaced by the second phrase without affecting the observable results of executing the program.

This kind of program equivalence is also known as *operational*, or *observational* equivalence. To be more precise about it we have to define, for the programming language that concerns us, what we mean by a 'complete program' and by the 'observable results' of executing it. In fact different choices can be made for these notions, leading to possibly different notions of contextual equivalence for the same programming language. We postpone more precise definitions until the next section. First, let us work with this informal definition and explore some of the subtleties of mixing ML's functional and 'stateful' features.

The intuitive reason why the expressions $p$ and $m$ are contextually equivalent is that the property

> 'the contents of $b$ is the negative of the contents of $a$'

is an invariant that is true throughout the life-time of the two expressions: it is true when they are first evaluated to get functions of type `int -> int` (because `-!`$a$ = `-0` = `0` = `!`$b$ at that point); and whenever those functions are applied to an argument, although there are side-effects on the contents of $a$ and $b$, the truth of the property remains invariant. Moreover, because the property holds, the values returned by the two functions (the contents of $a$ in one case and the negative of the contents of $b$ in the other case) are equal. So even though the contents of $a$ and $b$ may be different, since the only way we can use ML programs to observe properties of these locations is via applications of the functions created by evaluating $p$ and $m$, we will never detect a difference between these two expressions.

That is the intuitive justification for the contextual equivalence of the expressions $p$ and $m$. But it depends on assertions like

> 'the only way we can use ML programs to observe properties of these locations [the ones declared locally in the expressions] is via applications of the functions created by evaluating $p$ and $m$'

whose validity is not immediately obvious. To rub home the point, let us look at another example.

```
f ≜ let a = ref 0 in                                      (3)
    let b = ref 0 in
    fun(x : int ref) -> if x == a then b else a

g ≜ let c = ref 0 in                                      (4)
    let d = ref 0 in
    fun(y : int ref) -> if y == d then d else c
```

Are these Caml expressions (of type `int ref -> int ref`) contextually equivalent? We might be led to think that they are equivalent, via the following informal reasoning, similar to that above. If we apply $f$ to an argument $\ell$, because we can always rename the bound identifiers $a$ and $b$ without changing the meaning of $f$ [2], it seems that $\ell$ can never be equal to $a$ and hence $f\,\ell$ is contextually equivalent to the private location `let a = ref 0 in a`. Similarly $g\,\ell$ should be contextually equivalent to the private location `let c = ref 0 in c`. But `let a = ref 0 in a` and `let c = ref 0 in c`, being $\alpha$-convertible, are contextually equivalent. So $f$ and $g$ give contextually equivalent results when applied to any argument. If ML function expressions satisfied the usual extensionality principle for mathematical functions (see Fig. 1), then we could conclude that $f$ and $g$ are contextually equivalent.

The presence of dynamically created state in ML function expressions can cause them to not satisfy extensionality up to contextual equivalence. In particular the function expressions $f$ and $g$ defined in equations (3) and (4) are

[2] As we might hope, $\alpha$-*convertible* expressions, i.e. ones differing only up to the names of their bound identifiers, turn out to be contextually equivalent.

'*Two functions* (defined on the same set of arguments) *are equal if they give equal results for each possible argument.*'

- True of mathematical functions (e.g. in set theory).
- False for ML function expressions in general.
- True for ML function expressions in canonical form (i.e. lambda abstractions), if we take 'equal' to mean contextually equivalent.
- True for pure functional programming languages (see [11]).
- True for languages with Algol-like block-structured local state (see [12]).

**Fig. 1.** Function Extensionality Principle

not contextually equivalent. To see this consider the following Caml interaction, where we observe a difference between the two expressions[3].

```
# let f = let a = ref 0 in let b = ref 0 in
          fun(x : int ref) -> if x == a then b else a ;;
val f : int ref -> int ref = <fun>
# let g = let c = ref 0 in
          let d = ref 0 in
          fun(y : int ref) -> if y == d then d else c ;;
val g : int ref -> int ref = <fun>
# let t = fun(h : int ref -> int ref) ->
          let z = ref 0 in h (h z) == h z ;;
val t : (int ref -> int ref) -> bool = <fun>
# t f ;;
- : bool = false
# t g ;;
- : bool = true
```

Thus the expression

$$t \triangleq \texttt{fun(}h \texttt{ : int ref -> int ref) ->} \\ \texttt{let } z \texttt{ = ref 0 in } h\,(h\ z) \texttt{ == } h\ z \tag{5}$$

has the property that $t\,f$ evaluates to `false` whereas $t\,g$ evaluates to `true`. (Why? If you are not familiar with the way ML expressions evaluate, read Sect. A.3 and then try Exercise B.1.) Thus $f$ and $g$ are not contextually equivalent expressions.

This example illustrates the fact that proving contextual *in*equivalence of two expressions is quite straightforward in principle—one just has to devise a suitable program that can use the expressions and give a different observable result with each. Much harder is the task of proving that expressions *are* contextually equivalent, since it appears that one has to consider all possible ways a program can use the expressions. For example, once we have given a proper

[3] I used the Objective Caml ⟨`www.ocaml.org`⟩ version 3.0 interpreter.

ML *evaluation relation* $\boxed{s, e \Rightarrow v, s'}$ where $\begin{cases} s = \text{initial } \textit{state} \\ e = \text{closed } \textit{expression} \text{ to be evaluated} \\ v = \text{resulting closed } \textit{canonical form} \\ s' = \text{final state} \end{cases}$

is inductively generated by rules *following the structure* of $e$; for example:

$$\frac{s, e_1 \Rightarrow v_1, s' \qquad s', e_2[v_1/x] \Rightarrow v_2, s''}{s, \texttt{let}\ x\ \texttt{=}\ e_1\ \texttt{in}\ e_2 \Rightarrow v_2, s''}$$

(See Sect. A.3 for the full definition.)
Specifying semantics via such an evaluation relation is also known as *big-step* (anon), *natural* (Kahn [8]), or *relational* (Milner) semantics.

**Fig. 2.** ML Evaluation Relation (simplified, environment-free form)

definition of the notion of contextual equivalence, how do we give a rigorous proof that the expression in equation (1) is contextually equivalent to that in equation (2)? The rest of this paper introduces some methods for carrying out such proofs.

## 3 Contextual Equivalence

I hope the examples in Sect. 2, despite their artificiality, indicate that ML's combination of

recursively defined, higher order, call-by-value functions
+
statically scoped, dynamically created, mutable state

makes reasoning about properties of contextual equivalence of ML expressions very complicated. In fact even quite simple, general properties of contextual equivalence (such as the suitably restricted form of functional extensionality mentioned in Fig. 1) are hard to establish directly. To explain why, we need to look at the precise definition of ML contextual equivalence. To do that, I have to recall the form of operational semantics used in the Definition of Standard ML [9]: see Fig. 2. The fragment of ML we will work with is given in Sects A.1 and A.2. The full set of rules inductively defining the evaluation relation for this fragment of ML is given in Sect. A.3. In fact this is a simplified form of the evaluation relation actually used in the Definition of Standard ML. The latter has an *environment* component binding free identifiers to semantic values, whereas we will get by with this simpler form, in which the environment has been 'substituted in'. (Full ML also needs various auxiliary relations, for example to deal with exception-handling, but that will not concern us here.) One advantage of this 'substituted in' formulation is that the results of evaluation do not have to be specified as a separate syntactic category of 'semantic values', but rather are a subset of all the expressions, namely the ones in *canonical form* (see Sect. A.3); this simplifies the statement of some properties of the operational semantics (such as the Type Soundness Theorem A.1). A minor side-effect of this 'substituted in' formulation is that the names of *storage locations*[4], $\ell$ (drawn from a fixed, countably infinite set *Loc*), can occur in expressions explicitly—rather than implicitly via value identifiers bound to locations in the environment. Since we only consider locations for storing integers (see Fig. 6 in Sect. 5), we can take a memory *state* to be a finite function from the set *Loc* of names of storage locations to the set $\mathbb{Z}$ of integers.

Turning now to the definition of contextual equivalence, recall from Sect. 2 that we have to make precise two things:

- what constitutes a program
- what results of program execution we observe.

ML only evaluates expressions after they have been type-checked. So we take a *program* to be a well-typed expression with no free value identifiers: see Fig. 3. The rules inductively defining the type assignment relation for our fragment of ML are given in Sect. A.4. The *Type Soundness* Theorem A.1 in that section recalls an important relationship between typing and evaluation that we will use without comment from now on. (See Exercise B.2.)

---

ML *type assignment relation* $\boxed{\Gamma \vdash e : ty}$ where $\begin{cases} \Gamma = \textit{typing context} \\ e = \textit{expression} \text{ to be typed} \\ ty = \textit{type} \end{cases}$

is inductively generated by axioms and rules *following the structure* of e; for example:

$$\frac{\Gamma \vdash e_1 : ty_1 \quad \Gamma[x \mapsto ty_1] \vdash e_2 : ty_2 \quad x \notin dom(\Gamma)}{\Gamma \vdash (\mathtt{let}\ x\ \mathtt{=}\ e_1\ \mathtt{in}\ e_2) : ty_2}$$

(See Sect. A.4 for the full definition.)

The set of ML *programs* of type *ty* $\boxed{\mathrm{Prog}_{ty}}$ is defined to be $\{\, e \mid \emptyset \vdash e : ty \,\}$.

---

**Fig. 3.** ML programs are typed

The final ingredient needed for the definition of contextual equivalence is to specify which results of program execution we observe. In Sect. 2, I used the Objective Caml interpreter to observe a difference between the two expressions defined in equations (3) and (4). From this point of view, two results of evaluation, $v, s$ and $v', s'$ say, are observationally equal if $obs(v, s) = obs(v', s')$, where *obs* is the function recursively defined by

[4] or addresses, as the authors of [9] call them.

$$\left.\begin{aligned} obs(\mathtt{c}, s) &= \mathtt{c}, \quad \text{if } \mathtt{c} = \mathtt{true}, \mathtt{false}, \mathtt{n}, \mathtt{()} \\ obs(v_1 \mathtt{\ ,\ } v_2, s) &= obs(v_1, s) \mathtt{\ ,\ } obs(v_2, s) \\ obs(\mathtt{fun(}x \mathtt{\ :\ } ty\mathtt{)\ ->\ } e, s) &= \mathtt{<fun>} \\ obs(\mathtt{fun\ } f \mathtt{\ =\ (}x \mathtt{\ :\ } ty\mathtt{)\ ->\ } e, s) &= \mathtt{<fun>} \\ obs(\ell, s) &= \mathtt{\{contents=n\}}, \quad \text{if } (\ell \mapsto \mathtt{n}) \in s \end{aligned}\right\} \tag{6}$$

and which maps to a set of result expressions $\mathtt{r}$ given by

$$\begin{aligned} \mathtt{r} ::= {} & \mathtt{true} \\ & \mathtt{false} \\ & \mathtt{n} && (\mathtt{n} \in \mathbb{Z}) \\ & \mathtt{()} \\ & \mathtt{r\ ,\ r} \\ & \mathtt{<fun>} \\ & \mathtt{\{contents=n\}} && (\mathtt{n} \in \mathbb{Z}). \end{aligned}$$

But what if I had used a different interpreter—would it affect the notion of contextual equivalence? Probably not. Evidence for this is given by the fact that we can replace *obs* by a *constant function* and still get the same notion of contextual equivalence (see Exercise B.3). In other words, rather than observing particular things about the final results of evaluation, we can just as well observe the fact that there *is* some final result at all, i.e. observe *termination* of evaluation. This gives us the following definition of contextual equivalence.

**Definition 3.1 (Contextual preorder/equivalence).** Given $e_1, e_2 \in \mathrm{Prog}_{ty}$, define

$$\begin{aligned} e_1 =_{\mathrm{ctx}} e_2 : ty &\triangleq e_1 \leq_{\mathrm{ctx}} e_2 : ty \;\;\&\;\; e_2 \leq_{\mathrm{ctx}} e_1 : ty \\ e_1 \leq_{\mathrm{ctx}} e_2 : ty &\triangleq \forall x, e, ty', s\,((x : ty \vdash e : ty') \;\;\&\;\; s, e[e_1/x]\Downarrow \;\supset\; s, e[e_2/x]\Downarrow) \end{aligned}$$

where $s, e\Downarrow$ indicates *termination*:

$$s, e\Downarrow \;\triangleq\; \exists v, s'(s, e \Rightarrow v, s').$$

**Remark 3.2 (Contexts).** The program equivalence of Definition 3.1 is 'contextual' because it examines the termination properties of programs $e[e_i/x]$ that contain occurrences of the expressions $e_i$ being equated. If we replace $e_i$ by a place-holder '$-$' (usually called a *hole*), then we get $e[-/x]$, which is an example of what is usually called a (program) context. The programs $e_i$ are *closed* expressions; for contextual equivalence of *open* expressions (ones possibly containing free identifiers) we would need to consider more general forms of context than $e[-/x]$, namely ones in which the hole can occur within the scope of a binder, such as $\mathtt{fun(}y \mathtt{\ :\ } ty\mathtt{)\ ->\ } -$. For simplicity, I have restricted attention to contextual equivalence of closed expressions, where we can use expressions with a free identifier in place of such general contexts without affecting $=_{\mathrm{ctx}}$.

Definition 3.1 is difficult to work with directly when it comes to reasoning about programs up to contextual equivalence. One problem is the quantification over all contexts $e[-/x]$. Thus to prove a property of $e_1$ up to contextual equivalence, it is not good enough just to know how $e_1$ evaluates—we have to prove termination properties for all uses $e[e_1/x]$ of it in a context $e[-/x]$. But in fact there is a more fundamental problem: *the definition of* $\Downarrow$ *is not syntax-directed.* For example, from the definition of the ML evaluation relation, we know that

$$s, \texttt{let}\ x\ \texttt{=}\ e_1\ \texttt{in}\ e_2 \Downarrow$$

holds if

$$s', e_2[v_1/x] \Downarrow$$

where $s, e_1 \Rightarrow v_1, s'$; however, $e_2[v_1/x]$ is not built from subphrases of the original phrase $\texttt{let}\ x\ \texttt{=}\ e_1\ \texttt{in}\ e_2$.

Thus at first sight it seems that one cannot expect to prove properties involving termination (and in particular, properties of contextual equivalence) by induction on the structure of expressions. Indeed, in the literature one finds more complicated forms of induction used (involving measures of the size of contexts and the length of terminating sequences of reductions), often in combination with non-obvious strengthenings of induction hypotheses. However, we will see that it is possible to reformulate the operational semantics of ML to get a structurally inductive definition of termination that facilitates inductive reasoning about contextual equivalence, $=_{\mathrm{ctx}}$. To achieve that, we need to review the original approach to *structural operational semantics* of Plotkin [17] and subsequent refinements of it.

## 4 Structural Operational Semantics

The inductively defined ML evaluation relation (Fig. 2 and Sect. A.3) is an example of the S*tructural approach to* O*perational* S*emantics* (SOS) popularised by Plotkin [17]. SOS more closely reflects our intuitive understanding of various language constructs than did previous approaches to operational semantics using abstract machines, which tended to pull apart the syntax of those constructs and build non-intuitive auxiliary data structures. The word ‘structural’ refers to the fact that the rules of SOS inductive definitions are syntax-directed, i.e. follow the abstract, tree structure of the syntax. For example, the structure of the ML expression $e$ determines what are the possible rules that can be used to deduce $s, e \Rightarrow v, s'$ from other valid instances of the ML evaluation relation. This is of great help when it comes to using an induction principle to prove properties of the inductively defined relation.

The SOS in [17] is formulated in terms of a *transition relation* (also known as a ‘reduction’, or ‘small-step’ relation). An appropriate transition relation for the fragment of ML we are considering takes the form of a binary relation between (state, expression)-pairs

$$(s\ , e) \to (s'\ , e')$$

that is inductively generated by rules following the structure of $e$. See Sect. A.5 for the complete definition. Theorem A.2 in that section sums up the relationship between the transition and evaluation relations.

The rules inductively defining such transition relations usually divide into two kinds: ones giving the basic steps of *reduction*, such as

$$\frac{v \text{ a canonical form}}{(s\ ,\ \texttt{let}\ x\ \texttt{=}\ v\ \texttt{in}\ e) \to (s\ ,\ e[v/x])}$$

and ones for *simplification steps* that say how reductions may be performed within a context, such as

$$\frac{(s\ ,\ e_1) \to (s'\ ,\ e_1')}{(s\ ,\ \texttt{let}\ x\ \texttt{=}\ e_1\ \texttt{in}\ e_2) \to (s'\ ,\ \texttt{let}\ x\ \texttt{=}\ e_1'\ \texttt{in}\ e_2)}\ .$$

The latter can be more succinctly specified using the notion of *evaluation context* [18], as follows.

**Lemma 4.1 (Felleisen-style presentation of $\to$).** *$(s\ ,\ e) \to (s'\ ,\ e')$ holds if and only if $e = \mathcal{E}[r]$ and $e' = \mathcal{E}[r']$ for some* evaluation context *$\mathcal{E}$ and* basic reduction *$(s\ ,\ r) \to (s'\ ,\ r')$, where:*

- evaluation contexts *are expression contexts (i.e. syntax trees of expressions with one leaf replaced by a placeholder, or hole, denoted by $[-]$) that want to evaluate their hole; for the fragment of ML we are using, the evaluation contexts are given by*

$$\begin{aligned} \mathcal{E} ::= {} & [-] && && (7)\\ & \texttt{if}\ \mathcal{E}\ \texttt{then}\ e\ \texttt{else}\ e \\ & \mathcal{E}\ \texttt{op}\ e && \text{for op} \in \{\texttt{=},\texttt{+},\texttt{-},\texttt{:=},\texttt{==},\texttt{;},\texttt{,}\} \\ & v\ \texttt{op}\ \mathcal{E} && \text{for op} \in \{\texttt{=},\texttt{+},\texttt{-},\texttt{:=},\texttt{==},\texttt{,}\} \\ & \texttt{op}\ \mathcal{E} && \text{for op} \in \{\texttt{!},\texttt{ref},\texttt{fst},\texttt{snd}\} \\ & \mathcal{E}\ e \\ & v\ \mathcal{E} \\ & \texttt{let}\ x\ \texttt{=}\ \mathcal{E}\ \texttt{in}\ e \end{aligned}$$

  *where e ranges over closed expressions (Sect. A.2) and v over closed expressions in canonical form (Sect. A.3);*
- basic reductions *$(s\ ,\ r) \to (s'\ ,\ r')$ are the axioms in the Plotkin-style inductive definition of $\to$ (see Sect. A.5);*
- *$\mathcal{E}[r]$ denotes the expression resulting from replacing the 'hole' $[-]$ in $\mathcal{E}$ by the expression $r$.* □

The validity of Lemma 4.1 depends upon the fact (proof omitted) that every closed expression not in canonical form is uniquely of the form $\mathcal{E}[r]$ for some evaluation context $\mathcal{E}$ and some *redex* $r$, i.e. some expression appearing on the left-hand side of one of the basic reductions. So if we have a configuration $(s\ ,\ e)$ with $e$ not in canonical form, then $e$ is of the form $\mathcal{E}[r]$, there is a basic reduction $(s\ ,\ r) \to (s'\ ,\ r')$ and we make the next step of transition from $(s\ ,\ e)$ by replacing $r$ by its corresponding *reduct* $r'$ at the same time changing the state from $s$ to $s'$.

Transitions $\boxed{\langle s\ ,\mathcal{F}s\ ,e\rangle \rightarrow \langle s'\ ,\mathcal{F}s'\ ,e'\rangle}$ where $\begin{cases} s, s' = \text{states} \\ \mathcal{F}s, \mathcal{F}s' = \textit{frame stacks} \\ e, e' = \text{closed expressions} \end{cases}$

are *defined by cases* (i.e. no induction), according to the structure of $e$ and (then) $\mathcal{F}s$. For example:

$$\langle s\ ,\mathcal{F}s\ ,\mathtt{let}\ x\ \mathtt{=}\ e_1\ \mathtt{in}\ e_2\rangle \rightarrow \langle s\ ,\mathcal{F}s \circ (\mathtt{let}\ x\ \mathtt{=}\ [-]\ \mathtt{in}\ e_2)\ ,e_1\rangle$$
$$\langle s\ ,\mathcal{F}s \circ (\mathtt{let}\ x\ \mathtt{=}\ [-]\ \mathtt{in}\ e)\ ,v\rangle \rightarrow \langle s\ ,\mathcal{F}s\ ,e[v/x]\rangle$$

(See Sect. A.6 for the full definition.)
*Initial* configurations of the abstract machine take the form $\langle s\ ,\mathcal{I}d\ ,e\rangle$ and *terminal* configurations take the form $\langle s\ ,\mathcal{I}d\ ,v\rangle$, where $\mathcal{I}d$ is the empty frame stack and $v$ is a closed canonical form.

**Fig. 4.** An ML abstract machine

We can decompose any evaluation context into a nested composition of basic evaluation contexts, or so-called *evaluation frames.* In this way we arrive at a more elementary transition relation for ML—more elementary because the transition steps are defined by case analysis rather than by induction. This is shown in Fig. 4 and defined in detail in Sect. A.6 (see also [6] for a large-scale example of this style of SOS). The nested compositions of evaluation frames are usually called *frame stacks.* For the fragment of ML we are considering, they are given by:

$$\begin{array}{lll} \mathcal{F}s ::= & \mathcal{I}d & \text{empty} \\ & \mathcal{F}s \circ \mathcal{F} & \text{non-empty} \end{array}$$

and the evaluation frames $\mathcal{F}$ by:

$$\begin{array}{lll} \mathcal{F} ::= & \mathtt{if}\ [-]\ \mathtt{then}\ e\ \mathtt{else}\ e & \\ & [-]\ \mathtt{op}\ e & \text{for } \mathtt{op} \in \{\mathtt{=}, \mathtt{+}, \mathtt{-}, \mathtt{:=}, \mathtt{==}, \mathtt{;}, \mathtt{,}\} \\ & v\ \mathtt{op}\ [-] & \text{for } \mathtt{op} \in \{\mathtt{=}, \mathtt{+}, \mathtt{-}, \mathtt{:=}, \mathtt{==}, \mathtt{,}\} \\ & \mathtt{op}\ [-] & \text{for } \mathtt{op} \in \{\mathtt{!}, \mathtt{ref}\ , \mathtt{fst}\ , \mathtt{snd}\ \} \\ & [-]\ e & \\ & v\ [-] & \\ & \mathtt{let}\ x\ \mathtt{=}\ [-]\ \mathtt{in}\ e\ . & \end{array}$$

(Just as not all expressions are well-typed, not all of the evaluation stacks in the above grammar are well typed. Typing for frame stacks is defined in Sect. 5.)

The relationship between the abstract machine steps and the evaluation relation of ML is summed up by Theorem A.3 in Sect. A.6. In particular we can express termination of evaluation in terms of termination of the abstract machine:

$$s, e \Downarrow\ \equiv\ \exists s', v\,(\langle s\ ,\mathcal{I}d\ ,e\rangle \rightarrow^* \langle s'\ ,\mathcal{I}d\ ,v\rangle)\,.$$

What one gains from the formulation of ML's operational semantics in terms of this abstract machine is the following simple, but key, observation.

*The termination relation of the abstract machine*

$$\searrow \triangleq \{ \langle s , \mathcal{F}s , e\rangle \mid \exists s', v\,(\langle s , \mathcal{F}s , e\rangle \to^* \langle s' , \mathcal{I}d , v\rangle) \}$$

*has a direct, inductive definition following the structure of* $e$ *and* $\mathcal{F}s$*:* see Sect. A.7.

We have thus achieved the aim of reformulating the structural operational semantics of ML to get a structurally inductive characterisation of termination. Before outlining what can be done with this, it is perhaps helpful to contemplate the picture in Fig. 5, summing up the relationship between $\Downarrow$ and $\searrow$.

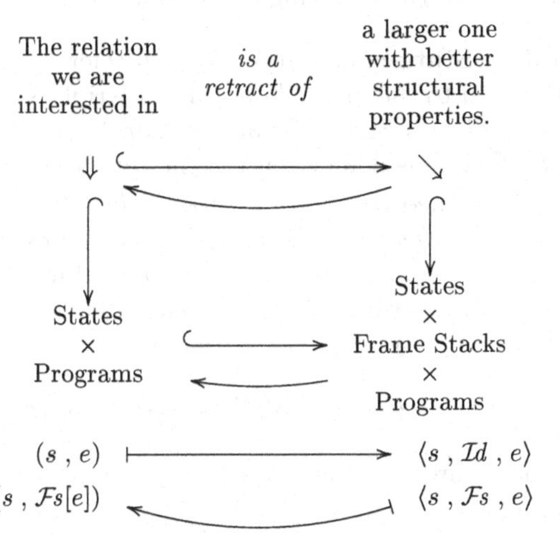


**Fig. 5.** The relationship between $\Downarrow$ and $\searrow$

## 5 Applications of the Abstract Machine Semantics

Recall the two ML expressions $p$ and $m$ defined by equations (1) and (2). In Sect. 2 it was claimed that they are contextually equivalent and some informal justification for this claim was given there. Now we can sketch how to turn that informal justification into a proper method of proof that uses a certain kind of binary 'logical relation' between ML expressions whose definition and properties depend on the abstract machine semantics of the previous section. Full details and several more examples of the use of this method can be found in [15][5]. The logical relation provides a method for proving contextual preorders

[5] In that work the logical relation is given in a symmetrical form that characterises contextual *equivalence*; here we use a one-sided version, a logical 'simulation' relation that characterises the contextual *preorder* (see Definition 3.1).

and equivalences that formalises intuitive uses of *invariant properties of local state*: given some binary relation between states, logically related expressions have the property that the change of state produced by evaluating them sends related states to related states (and produces logically related final values). This is made precise by property (I) in Theorem 5.2 below. One complication of ML compared with block-structured languages like Algol, is that local state is dynamically allocated: given an evaluation $s, e \Rightarrow v, s'$, the finite set $dom(s')$ of locations on which the final state $s'$ is defined contains $dom(s)$, but may also contain other locations, ones that have been allocated during evaluation. Thus in formulating the notion of evaluation-invariant state-relations we have to take into account how the state on freshly allocated locations should be related. We accomplish this with the following definition.

**Definition 5.1 (State-relations).** We will refer to finite sets of locations as *worlds* (with a nod to the 'possible worlds' of Kripke semantics) and write them as $w, w_1, w_2, \ldots$ The set $\mathrm{St}(w)$ of *states in world* $w$ is defined to be the set $\mathbb{Z}^w$ of integer-valued functions defined on $w$. The set $\mathrm{Prog}_{ty}(w)$ of *programs in world* $w$ of type $ty$ is defined to be $\{ e \in \mathrm{Prog}_{ty} \mid loc(e) \subseteq w \}$. The set $\mathrm{Rel}(w_1, w_2)$ of *state-relations* between worlds $w_1$ and $w_2$ is defined to be the set of all non-empty[6] subsets of $\mathrm{St}(w_1) \times \mathrm{St}(w_2)$. Given two state-relations $r \in \mathrm{Rel}(w_1, w_2)$ and $r' \in \mathrm{Rel}(w_1', w_2')$ with $w_1 \cap w_1' = \emptyset$ and $w_2 \cap w_2' = \emptyset$, their *smash product* $r \otimes r' \in \mathrm{Rel}(w_1 \cup w_1', w_2 \cup w_2')$ is

$$r \otimes r' \triangleq \{ (s_1 s_1', s_2 s_2') \mid (s_1, s_2) \in r \ \& \ (s_1', s_2') \in r' \}$$

where if $s$ and $s'$ are states, then $ss'$ is the state with $dom(ss') = dom(s) \cup dom(s')$ and for all $\ell \in dom(ss')$

$$(ss')(\ell) = \begin{cases} s'(\ell) \text{ if } \ell \in dom(s') \\ s(\ell) \ \text{ if } \ell \in dom(s) - dom(s'). \end{cases}$$

We say that a state relation $r' \in \mathrm{Rel}(w_1', w_2')$ *extends* a state relation $r \in \mathrm{Rel}(w_1, w_2)$, and write

$$r' \rhd r$$

if $r' = r \otimes r''$ for some $r''$ (so in particular $w_i \subseteq w_i'$ for $i = 1, 2$). (See Exercise B.5 for an alternative characterisation of the extension relation $\rhd$.)

**Theorem 5.2 ('Logical' simulation relation between ML programs, parameterised by state-relations).** *For each state-relation* $r \in \mathrm{Rel}(w_1, w_2)$ *we can define a relation*

$$e_1 \leq_r e_2 : ty \qquad (e_1 \in \mathrm{Prog}_{ty}(w_1), e_2 \in \mathrm{Prog}_{ty}(w_2))$$

*(for each type ty), with the following properties:*

6 This non-emptiness condition is a technical convenience which, among other things, simplifies the definition of the logical relation (Definition 5.4) at ground types.

(I) ***The simulation property of*** $\leq_r$***:*** *to prove* $e_1 \leq_r e_2 : ty$*, it suffices to show that whenever*

$$(s_1, s_2) \in r \quad \text{and} \quad s_1, e_1 \Rightarrow v_1, s_1'$$

*then there exists* $r' \rhd r$ *and* $v_2, s_2'$ *such that*

$$s_2, e_2 \Rightarrow v_2, s_2', \quad v_1 \leq_{r'} v_2 : ty \quad \text{and} \quad (s_1', s_2') \in r' \ .$$

(II) ***The extensionality properties of*** $\leq_r$ ***on canonical forms:***
  (i) *For* $ty \in \{\mathtt{bool}, \mathtt{int}, \mathtt{unit}\}$*,* $v_1 \leq_r v_2 : ty$ *if and only if* $v_1 = v_2$*.*
  (ii) $v_1 \leq_r v_2 : \mathtt{int\,ref}$ *if and only if* $!v_1 \leq_r !v_2 : \mathtt{int}$ *and for all* $\mathtt{n} \in \mathbb{Z}$*,* $(v_1 := \mathtt{n}) \leq_r (v_2 := \mathtt{n}) : \mathtt{unit}$*.*
  (iii) $v_1 \leq_r v_2 : ty_1 * ty_2$ *if and only if* $\mathtt{fst}\ v_1 \leq_r \mathtt{fst}\ v_2 : ty_1$ *and* $\mathtt{snd}\ v_1 \leq_r \mathtt{snd}\ v_2 : ty_2$*.*
  (iv) $v_1 \leq_r v_2 : ty_1 \texttt{ -> } ty_2$ *if and only if for all* $r' \rhd r$ *and all* $v_1', v_2'$

$$v_1' \leq_{r'} v_2' : ty_1 \supset v_1\, v_1' \leq_{r'} v_2\, v_2' : ty_2 .$$

*(The last property is characteristic of (Kripke) logical relations [16, 10].)*

(III) ***The relationship between*** $\leq_r$ ***and contextual equivalence:*** *for all types* $ty$*, finite sets* $w$ *of locations, and programs* $e_1, e_2 \in \mathrm{Prog}_{ty}(w)$

$$e_1 \leq_{\mathrm{ctx}} e_2 : ty \quad \mathit{iff} \quad e_1 \leq_{id_w} e_2 : ty$$

*where* $id_w \in \mathrm{Rel}(w, w)$ *is the* identity *state-relation for* $w$*:*

$$id_w \triangleq \{\ (s, s) \mid s \in \mathrm{St}(w)\ \} .$$

*Hence* $e_1$ *and* $e_2$ *are contextually equivalent if and only if both* $e_1 \leq_{id_w} e_2 : ty$ *and* $e_2 \leq_{id_w} e_1 : ty$*.* □

We have two problems to discuss. First, why does the family of relations

$$- \leq_r - : ty \qquad (r \in \mathrm{Rel}(w_1, w_2),\ w_1, w_2 \text{ finite subsets of } Loc,\ ty \text{ a type})$$

exist with the properties claimed in Theorem 5.2? Secondly, how do we use it to prove contextual equivalences like $p =_{\mathrm{ctx}} m : \mathtt{int} \texttt{->} \mathtt{int}$ from Sect. 2? We address the second problem first. It is only when we get round to the first problem that we will see why the abstract machine semantics of the previous section is so useful.

**Proof of the Contextual Equivalence of** $p$ **and** $m$**.** Consider the programs defined by equations (1) and (2). To prove $p =_{\mathrm{ctx}} m : \mathtt{int} \texttt{ -> } \mathtt{int}$, we have to show $p \leq_{\mathrm{ctx}} m : \mathtt{int} \texttt{ -> } \mathtt{int}$ and $m \leq_{\mathrm{ctx}} p : \mathtt{int} \texttt{ -> } \mathtt{int}$. We give the proof of the first contextual preorder; the argument for the second one is similar. Since $p, m \in \mathrm{Prog}_{\mathtt{int->int}}(\emptyset)$, by Theorem 5.2(III), to prove $p \leq_{\mathrm{ctx}} m : \mathtt{int} \texttt{ -> } \mathtt{int}$ it suffices to prove $p \leq_{id_\emptyset} m : \mathtt{int} \texttt{ -> } \mathtt{int}$. We do that by appealing to the simulation property of $\leq_{id_\emptyset}$ given by Theorem 5.2(I). Note that $\mathrm{St}(\emptyset)$ contains only one element, namely the empty state $\emptyset$; hence the identity state-relation $id_\emptyset$ just contains the pair $(\emptyset, \emptyset)$ and we have to check the simulation property holds for this pair of states. So suppose

$$\emptyset, p \Rightarrow v, s.$$

It follows from the syntax-directed nature of the rules for evaluation in Sect. A.3 that $v$ and $s$ are uniquely determined up to the name of a freshly created location, call it $\ell_1$:

$$v = \texttt{fun(}x \texttt{ : int) -> } \ell_1 \texttt{ := !}\ell_1 \texttt{ + } x \texttt{ ; !}\ell_1 \quad \text{and} \quad s = \{\ell_1 \mapsto \texttt{0}\}.$$

Choosing another new location $\ell_2$, define

$$r \triangleq \{ (s_1, s_2) \mid s_1(\ell_1) = -s_2(\ell_2) \} \in \mathrm{Rel}(\{\ell_1\}, \{\ell_2\}).$$

Clearly $r \rhd id_\emptyset$ holds. Also the evaluation $\emptyset, m \Rightarrow v', s'$ holds with

$$v' = \texttt{fun(}y \texttt{ : int) -> } \ell_2 \texttt{ := !}\ell_2 \texttt{ - } y \texttt{ ; 0 - !}\ell_2 \quad \text{and} \quad s' = \{\ell_2 \mapsto \texttt{0}\}.$$

We certainly have $(s, s') \in r$, since $0 = -0$. So we just have to check that $v \leq_r v' : \texttt{int -> int}$. To do that we appeal to Theorem 5.2(II)(iv) and show for all $r' \rhd r$ and all $\texttt{n} \leq_{r'} \texttt{n}' : \texttt{int}$ that $v\,\texttt{n} \leq_{r'} v'\,\texttt{n}' : \texttt{int}$. By Theorem 5.2(II)(i), this amounts to showing

$$v\,\texttt{n} \leq_{r'} v'\,\texttt{n} : \texttt{int}, \quad \text{for all } \texttt{n} \in \mathbb{Z}. \tag{8}$$

We do this by once again appealing to the simulation property Theorem 5.2(I): given any $(s_1, s_2) \in r'$, since $r' \rhd r$ we have $(s_1 \restriction_{\{\ell_1\}}, s_2 \restriction_{\{\ell_2\}}) \in r$ and hence $s_1(\ell_1) = -s(\ell_2) = \texttt{k}$, say. Then

$$s_1, v\,\texttt{n} \Rightarrow \texttt{n}', s_1[\ell_1 \mapsto \texttt{n}'] \quad \text{and} \quad s_2, v'\,\texttt{n} \Rightarrow \texttt{n}', s_1[\ell_2 \mapsto -\texttt{n}']$$

with $\texttt{n}' = \texttt{k} + \texttt{n}$. From the definition of $r' \rhd r$ in Definition 5.1 it follows that $(s_1[\ell_1 \mapsto \texttt{n}'], s_1[\ell_2 \mapsto -\texttt{n}']) \in r'$; and $\texttt{n}' \leq_{r'} \texttt{n}' : \texttt{int}$ by Theorem 5.2(II)(i). So the simulation property does indeed imply equation (8) and hence we do have $v \leq_r v' : \texttt{int -> int}$, as required. □

**Existence of the Logical Simulation Relation.** We turn now to the problem of why the logical simulation relation described in Theorem 5.2 exists. Why can't we just take the simulation property (I) of the theorem as the *definition* of $- \leq_r - : ty$ at non-canonical expressions in terms of the logical simulation relation restricted to canonical expressions?—for then we could give a definition of the latter by induction on the structure of the type $ty$, using the extensionality properties in (II). The answer is that it seems impossible to connect such a version of $- \leq_r - : ty$ with contextual equivalence as in property (III) of the theorem, defeating the purpose of introducing these relations in the first place. The reason for this lies in the fact that we are dealing with a fragment of ML with *recursively defined* functions $\texttt{fun}\ f\ \texttt{=}\ \texttt{(}x\ \texttt{:}\ ty\texttt{)}\ \texttt{->}\ e$ (and hence which is a Turing-powerful programming language, i.e. which can express all partial recursive functions from numbers to numbers)[7]. It turns out that each such recursively defined function is the least upper bound with respect to $\leq_{\mathrm{ctx}}$ of its finite unfoldings:

$$(\texttt{fun}\ f\ \texttt{=}\ \texttt{(}x\ \texttt{:}\ ty\texttt{)}\ \texttt{->}\ e) \leq_{\mathrm{ctx}} g : ty\ \texttt{->}\ ty' \ \equiv\ \forall n \geq 0\,(f_n \leq_{\mathrm{ctx}} g : ty\ \texttt{->}\ ty') \quad (9)$$

where the expressions $f_n$ are the 'finite unfoldings' of $\texttt{fun}\ f\ \texttt{=}\ \texttt{(}x\ \texttt{:}\ ty\texttt{)}\ \texttt{->}\ e$, defined as follows:

$$\left.\begin{array}{r}f_0 \triangleq \texttt{fun}\ f\ \texttt{=}\ \texttt{(}x\ \texttt{:}\ ty\texttt{)}\ \texttt{->}\ f\ x\\ f_{n+1} \triangleq \texttt{fun(}x\ \texttt{:}\ ty\texttt{)}\ \texttt{->}\ e[f_n/f]\end{array}\right\} \quad (10)$$

The least upper bound property in equation (9) follows immediately from the definition of $\leq_{\mathrm{ctx}}$ and the following 'Unwinding Theorem'.

**Theorem 5.3 (An unwinding theorem).** *Given*

$$f : ty\ \texttt{->}\ ty', x : ty \vdash e : ty'$$

*for each $n \geq 0$ define $f_n \in \mathrm{Prog}_{ty\texttt{->}ty'}$ as in equation (10). Then for all*

$$f : ty\ \texttt{->}\ ty' \vdash e' : ty''$$

*and all states $s$, it is the case that*

$$s, e'[(\texttt{fun}\ f\ \texttt{=}\ \texttt{(}x\ \texttt{:}\ ty\texttt{)}\ \texttt{->}\ e)/f]\Downarrow \quad \equiv \quad \exists n \geq 0\,(s, e'[f_n/f]\Downarrow)\ .$$

□

*Proof.* We can use the structurally inductive characterisation of termination afforded by Theorem A.4 to reduce the proof to a series of simple (if tedious) inductions. Writing $f_\omega$ for $\texttt{fun}\ f\ \texttt{=}\ \texttt{(}x\ \texttt{:}\ ty\texttt{)}\ \texttt{->}\ e$, first show that

$$\langle s\ ,\ \mathcal{F}s[f_n/f]\ ,\ e'[f_n/f]\rangle\searrow \quad \supset \quad \langle s\ ,\ \mathcal{F}s[f_\omega/f]\ ,\ e'[f_\omega/f]\rangle\searrow$$

holds for all $s$, $\mathcal{F}s$, $e'$ and $n$, by induction on the derivation of $\langle s\ ,\ \mathcal{F}s[f_n/f]\ ,\ e'[f_f/f]\rangle\searrow$ from the rules in Sect. A.7. Conversely, show for that

$$\langle s\ ,\ \mathcal{F}s[f_\omega/f]\ ,\ e'[f_\omega/f]\rangle\searrow \quad \supset \quad \exists n \geq 0(\langle s\ ,\ \mathcal{F}s[f_n/f]\ ,\ e'[f_n/f]\rangle\searrow)$$

holds all $s$, $\mathcal{F}s$ and $e'$, by induction on the derivation of $\langle s\ ,\ \mathcal{F}s[f_\omega/f]\ ,\ e'[f_\omega/f]\rangle\searrow$. Doing this requires proving a sublemma to the effect that

$$\langle s\ ,\ \mathcal{F}s[f_n/f]\ ,\ e'[f_n/f]\rangle\searrow \quad \supset \quad \langle s\ ,\ \mathcal{F}s[f_{n+1}/f]\ ,\ e'[f_{n+1}/f]\rangle\searrow$$

which is done by induction on $n$, with the base case $n = 0$ proved by induction on the derivation of $\langle s\ ,\ \mathcal{F}s[f_0/f]\ ,\ e'[f_0/f]\rangle\searrow$. The unwinding theorem follows from these results by taking $\mathcal{F}s = \mathcal{I}d$ and applying Theorem A.4. □

[7] Compared with either Caml or Standard ML, $\texttt{fun}\ f\ \texttt{=}\ \texttt{(}x\ \texttt{:}\ ty\texttt{)}\ \texttt{->}\ e$ is a non-standard canonical form; it is equivalent to the Caml expression $\texttt{let rec}\ f\ \texttt{= (fun(}x\ \texttt{:}\ ty\texttt{)}\ \texttt{->}\ e\texttt{) in}\ f$—see Sect. A.2.

If the logical relation $\leq_{id_w}$ is to coincide with $\leq_{\mathrm{ctx}}$ as in Theorem 5.2(III), it must have a property like (9). More generally, each $\leq_r$ should have a syntactic version of the 'admissibility' property that crops up in domain theory:

$$e'[(\mathtt{fun}\ f\ \mathtt{=}\ (x : ty)\ \mathtt{->}\ e)/f] \leq_r g{:}ty \equiv \forall n \geq 0\,(e'[f_n/f] \leq_r g{:}ty_1\mathtt{->}ty_2). \quad (11)$$

The problem with trying to use the simulation property of Theorem 5.2(I) as a definition of $\leq_r$ is that the existential quantification over extensions $r' \rhd r$ occurring in it makes it unlikely that equation (11) could be proved for that definition (although I do not have a specific counter-example to hand).

One can get round these difficulties by defining the logical simulation relation between expressions, $\leq_r$, in terms of a similar, auxiliary relation between frame stacks, $\mathrm{Stack}_{ty}(r)$; this in turn is defined using an auxiliary relation between canonical forms, $\mathrm{Val}_{ty}(r)$, that builds in the extensionality properties of Theorem 5.2(II). Since only well-typed expressions are considered, before giving the definitions of these auxiliary relations we need to define typing for (closed) frame stacks. We write $\vdash \mathcal{F}s : ty \multimap ty'$ to indicate that $\mathcal{F}s$ is a well-typed, closed frame stack taking an argument of type $ty$ and returning a result of type $ty'$. This relation is inductively defined by the rules

$$\frac{}{\vdash \mathcal{I}d : ty \multimap ty} \qquad \frac{\begin{array}{l}\vdash \mathcal{F}s : ty' \multimap ty'' \\ x \notin fv(\mathcal{F}) \\ [x \mapsto ty] \vdash \mathcal{F}[x] : ty'\end{array}}{\vdash \mathcal{F}s \circ \mathcal{F} : ty \multimap ty''}$$

The set of *well-typed frame stacks taking an argument of type ty and only involving locations in the world w* is defined to be

$$\mathrm{Stack}_{ty}(w) \triangleq \{\, \mathcal{F}s \mid \exists ty'(\vdash \mathcal{F}s : ty \multimap ty')\,\}. \quad (12)$$

**Definition 5.4 (A logical simulation relation).** For all worlds $w_1, w_2$, state-relations $r \in \mathrm{Rel}(w_1, w_2)$ and types $ty$, we define binary relations between programs, frame stacks and canonical forms:

$$\begin{aligned} \leq_r &\subseteq \mathrm{Prog}_{ty}(w_1) \times \mathrm{Prog}_{ty}(w_2) \\ \mathrm{Stack}_{ty}(r) &\subseteq \mathrm{Stack}_{ty}(w_1) \times \mathrm{Stack}_{ty}(w_2) \\ \mathrm{Val}_{ty}(r) &\subseteq \mathrm{Val}_{ty}(w_1) \times \mathrm{Val}_{ty}(w_2). \end{aligned}$$

The relations between programs are defined in terms of those between frame stacks:

$$\begin{aligned} &e_1 \leq_r e_2 : ty \triangleq \\ &\quad \forall r' \rhd r, \forall (s_1', s_2') \in r', \forall (\mathcal{F}s_1, \mathcal{F}s_2) \in \mathrm{Stack}_{ty}(r') \\ &\qquad (\langle s_1' \,,\, \mathcal{F}s_1 \,,\, e_1 \rangle{\searrow} \supset \langle s_2' \,,\, \mathcal{F}s_2 \,,\, e_2 \rangle{\searrow}). \end{aligned} \quad (13)$$

The relations between frame stacks are defined in terms of those between canonical forms:

$$\begin{aligned} &(\mathcal{F}s_1, \mathcal{F}s_2) \in \mathrm{Stack}_{ty}(r) \triangleq \\ &\quad \forall r' \rhd r, \forall (s_1', s_2') \in r', \forall (v_1, v_2) \in \mathrm{Val}_{ty}(r') \\ &\qquad (\langle s_1' \,,\, \mathcal{F}s_1 \,,\, v_1 \rangle{\searrow} \supset \langle s_2' \,,\, \mathcal{F}s_2 \,,\, v_2 \rangle{\searrow}). \end{aligned} \quad (14)$$

The relations between canonical forms are defined by induction on the structure of the type $ty$, for all $w_1$, $w_2$ and $r$ simultaneously:

$$
\begin{aligned}
(v_1, v_2) \in \mathrm{Val}_{\texttt{bool}}(r) &\equiv v_1 = v_2 && (15)\\
(v_1, v_2) \in \mathrm{Val}_{\texttt{int}}(r) &\equiv v_1 = v_2 && (16)\\
((), ()) \in \mathrm{Val}_{\texttt{unit}}(r) & && (17)\\
(v_1, v_2) \in \mathrm{Val}_{\texttt{int ref}}(r) &\equiv \; !v_1 \leq_r \, !v_2 : \texttt{int} \;\; \& && (18)\\
& \quad \forall \mathtt{n} \in \mathbb{Z}((v_1 := \mathtt{n}) \leq_r (v_2 := \mathtt{n}) : \texttt{unit}) &&\\
(v_1, v_2) \in \mathrm{Val}_{ty_1 * ty_2}(r) &\equiv \texttt{fst}\ v_1 \leq_r \texttt{fst}\ v_2 : ty_1 \;\; \& && (19)\\
& \quad \texttt{snd}\ v_1 \leq_r \texttt{snd}\ v_2 : ty_2 &&\\
(v_1, v_2) \in \mathrm{Val}_{ty_1 \texttt{->} ty_2}(r) &\equiv \forall r' \rhd r, \forall v_1', \forall v_2' && (20)\\
& \quad (v_1' \leq_{r'} v_2' : ty_1 \supset v_1\, v_1' \leq_{r'} v_2\, v_2' : ty_2). &&
\end{aligned}
$$

We extend the logical relation to open expressions via closing substitutions (of canonical forms for value identifiers). Thus given $\Gamma \vdash e : ty$ and $\Gamma \vdash e' : ty$ where $\Gamma = [x_1 \mapsto ty_1, \ldots, x_n \mapsto ty_n]$ say, and given $r \in \mathrm{Rel}(w_1, w_2)$ with $loc(e_i) \subseteq w_i$ for $i = 1, 2$, we define

$$\Gamma \vdash e \leq_r e' : ty \qquad (21)$$

to mean that for all extensions $r' \rhd r$ and all related canonical forms $(v_i, v_i') \in \mathrm{Val}_{ty_i}(r')$ $(i = 1..n)$, it is the case that $e[\vec{v}/\vec{x}] \leq_{r'} e'[\vec{v}'/\vec{x}] : ty$ holds.

**Proof of Theorem 5.2 (sketch).** The proof that the relations $\leq_r$ of Definition 5.4 have all the properties required by Theorem 5.2 is quite involved. The details can be found in Sects 4 and 5 of [15]. Here is a guide to finding one's way through those details.

For part (I) of the theorem we use the following connection between evaluation and the structurally inductive termination relation (a generalisation of Theorem A.4):

$$\langle s\,,\, \mathcal{F}s\,,\, e\rangle\searrow \;\; \equiv \;\; \exists s', v\ (s, e \Rightarrow v, s' \;\&\; \langle s'\,,\, \mathcal{F}s\,,\, v\rangle\searrow)\ .$$

This, together with definitions (13) and (14), yield property (I) as in the proof of [15, Proposition 5.1].

Part (II) of the theorem follows from definitions (15)–(20) once we know that the restriction of the relation $- \leq_r - : ty$ to canonical forms coincides with $\mathrm{Val}_{ty}(r)(-,-)$; this is proved in [15, Lemma 4.4].

For part (III) of the theorem we have to establish the so-called "fundamental property" of the logical relation, namely that its extension to open expressions as in (21) is preserved by all the expression-forming constructs of the language. For example

$$
\begin{aligned}
&\text{if } \Gamma[f \mapsto ty_1 \texttt{ -> } ty_2][x \mapsto ty_1] \vdash e \leq_r e' : ty_2 && (22)\\
&\text{then } \Gamma \vdash (\texttt{fun } f \texttt{ = (} x \texttt{ : } ty_1\texttt{) -> } e) \leq_r &&\\
&\qquad\qquad (\texttt{fun } f \texttt{ = (} x \texttt{ : } ty_1\texttt{) -> } e') : ty_1 \texttt{ -> } ty_2\ . &&
\end{aligned}
$$

This property and similar ones for each of the other expression-forming constructs are proved in [15, Proposition 4.8]. In particular, the proof of (22) makes use of the Unwinding Theorem 5.3 to establish $\Gamma \vdash (\texttt{fun}\ f\ \texttt{=}\ (x : ty_1)\ \texttt{->}\ e) \leq_r (\texttt{fun}\ f\ \texttt{=}\ (x : ty_1)\ \texttt{->}\ e') : ty_1\ \texttt{->}\ ty_2$ from the fact (proved by induction on $n$) that $\Gamma \vdash f_n \leq_r f'_n : ty_1\ \texttt{->}\ ty_2$ holds for the finite approximations $f_n$, $f'_n$ defined as in (10).

One immediate consequence of this fundamental property of the logical relation is that $\leq_{id_w}$ is a reflexive relation. Also, it is not hard to see that if two expressions are logically related and we change one of them up to the contextual preorder, we still have logically related expressions. Thus if $e_1 \leq_{\text{ctx}} e_2 : ty$, since we have $e_1 \leq_{id_w} e_1 : ty$, we also have $e_1 \leq_{id_w} e_2 : ty$. This is one half of property (III). The other half also follows from the fundamental property. For if $e_1 \leq_{id_w} e_2 : ty$, then for any context $x : ty \vdash e : ty'$ (where without loss of generality we assume $loc(e) \subseteq w$), the fundamental property implies that $e[e_1/x] \leq_{id_w} e[e_2/x] : ty'$ holds. So if $s, e[e_1/x] \Downarrow$, then by Theorem A.4 $\langle s\ ,\ \mathcal{I}d\ ,\ e[e_1/x]\rangle\searrow$. Using the easily verified fact that $(\mathcal{I}d, \mathcal{I}d) \in \text{Stack}_{ty}(id_w)$, it follows from $e[e_1/x] \leq_{id_w} e[e_2/x] : ty'$ and definition (13) that $\langle s\ ,\ \mathcal{I}d\ ,\ e[e_2/x]\rangle\searrow$ and hence that $s, e[e_2/x] \Downarrow$. Since this holds for all contexts $e$, we conclude that $e_1 \leq_{id_w} e_2 : ty$ does indeed imply that $e_1 \leq_{\text{ctx}} e_2 : ty$. □

**Open Problems.** The definition of $\leq_r$, with its interplay between expression-relations and frame stack-relations, was introduced to get round the difficulty of establishing the necessary fundamental properties of the logical relation (and hence property (III) of Theorem 5.2) in the presence of recursively defined functions. Note that these difficulties have to be tackled even if the particular examples of contextual equivalence we are interested in do not involve such functions (as in fact was the case in this paper). This reflects the unfortunate non-local aspect of the definition of contextual equivalence: even if the expressions we are interested in do not involve a particular language construct, we have to consider their behaviour in all contexts and the context may make use of the construct. Thus adding recursive functions complicates reasoning about non-recursive functions with local state. What other features of ML might cause trouble? I have listed some important ones in Fig. 6. There is some reason to think we could reason about the contextual equivalence of ML *structures* and *functors* using the logical relations methods outlined here: see the results about existential types in [13]. The other features—recursive mutable data, references to values of arbitrary type, and object-oriented features—are more problematic. One difficulty is that the definition of the logical relation (Definition 5.4) proceeds by induction on the structure of types. In the presence of recursive types one has to use some other approach in order to avoid a circular definition; here syntactic versions of the construction of recursively defined domains [4] may be of assistance. A more subtle problem is that some of our definitions (for example the notion of extension of state-relations in Definition 5.1) exploit the fact that we restricted attention to memory states with a very simple, 'flat' structure; many of the features listed in Fig. 6 cause memory states to have a complicated, recursive structure that blocks the use of some of the definitions as they stand.

Can the method of proving contextual equivalences outlined here be extended to larger fragments of ML with:

- structures and signatures (abstract data types)
- functions with local references to values of arbitrary types (and ditto for exception packets)
- recursively defined, mutable data structures
- OCaml-style objects and classes?

Are there other forms of logical relation, useful for proving contextual equivalences?

**Fig. 6.** Some things we do not yet know how to do

Finally, it should be pointed out that the simulation property of the logical relation in Theorem 5.2(I) is only a sufficient, but not a necessary condition for $e_1 \leq_{\mathrm{ctx}} e_2 : ty$ to hold. For example

$$awk \triangleq \texttt{let } a \texttt{ = ref 0 in} \\ \texttt{fun(}f : \texttt{unit -> unit) -> (}a \texttt{ := 1 ; } f \texttt{ () ; !}a\texttt{)} \tag{23}$$

satisfies $awk =_{\mathrm{ctx}}$ (fun($g$ : unit -> unit) -> $g$ () ; 1) : (unit -> unit) -> int, but it is not possible to use Theorem 5.2 to prove it; see Example 5.9 of [15], which discusses this example.

## 6 Conclusion

We have described a method for proving contextual equivalence of ML functions involving local state, based on a certain kind of logical relation parameterised by state-relations. Theorem 5.2 summarises the properties of this logical relation that are needed for applications. However, the construction of a suitable logical relation is complicated by the presence of recursive definitions in ML. We got around this complication by using a reformulation of the structural operational semantics of ML in terms of frame stacks. This reformulation provides a structurally inductive characterisation of termination of ML evaluation that is not only used in the definition of the logical relation, but also provides a very useful tool for proving general properties of evaluation, like the Unwinding Theorem 5.3.

## A Appendix: A Fragment of ML

### A.1 Types

| | | |
|---|---|---|
| $ty$ ::= | bool | booleans |
| | int | integers |
| | unit | unit |
| | int ref | integer storage locations |
| | $ty$ * $ty$ | pairs |
| | $ty$ -> $ty$ | functions |

### A.2 Expressions

| | |
|---|---|
| $e$ ::= $x$, $f$ | value identifiers ($x, f \in Var$) |
| `true` | boolean constants |
| `false` | |
| `if` $e$ `then` $e$ `else` $e$ | conditional |
| `n` | integer constants ($\mathtt{n} \in \mathbb{Z}$) |
| $e$ `=` $e$ | integer equality |
| $e$ `+` $e$ | addition |
| $e$ `-` $e$ | subtraction |
| `()` | unit value |
| `!`$e$ | look-up |
| $e$ `:=` $e$ | assignment |
| `ref` $e$ | storage creation |
| $e$ `==` $e$ | location equality |
| $e$ `;` $e$ | sequence |
| $e$ `,` $e$ | pair |
| `fst` $e$ | first projection |
| `snd` $e$ | second projection |
| `fun(`$x$ `:` $ty$`) ->` $e$ | function abstraction |
| `fun` $f$ `= (`$x$ `:` $ty$`) ->` $e$ | recursively defined function |
| $e\,e$ | function application |
| `let` $x$ `=` $e$ `in` $e$ | local definition |
| $\ell$ | storage locations ($\ell \in Loc$) |

**Notes.**

1. The concrete syntax of expressions is like that of Caml rather than Standard ML (not that there are any very great differences between the two languages for the fragment we are using).
2. As well as having a canonical form for function abstractions, it simplifies the presentation of the operational semantics to have a separate canonical form `fun` $f$ `= (`$x$ `:` $ty$`) ->` $e$ for recursively defined functions. In Caml this could be written as

   `let rec` $f$ `= (fun(`$x$ `:` $ty$`) ->` $e$`) in` $f$.

3. *Var* and *Loc* are some fixed, countably infinite sets (disjoint from each other, and disjoint from the set of integers, $\mathbb{Z} = \{\ldots, -2, -1, 0, 1, 2, \ldots\}$).
4. What we call *storage locations* are called *addresses* in [9]. They do not occur explicitly in the ML expressions written by users, but rather, occur implicitly via environments binding value identifiers to addresses (and to other kinds of semantic value). We will use a formulation of ML's operational semantics that does without environments, at the minor expense of having to consider an extended set of expressions, in which names of storage locations can occur explicitly.

5. We write *loc*(*e*) for the finite subset of *Loc* consisting of all storage locations occurring in the expression *e*.
6. We write *fv*(*e*) for the finite subset of *Var* consisting of all value identifiers occurring freely in the expression *e*. This finite set is defined by induction on the structure of *e*. The only interesting clauses are for the syntax-forming operations that are binders:

$$\begin{aligned} fv(\texttt{fun(}x\ \texttt{:}\ ty\texttt{)}\ \texttt{->}\ e) &\triangleq fv(e) - \{x\} \\ fv(\texttt{fun}\ f\ \texttt{=}\ \texttt{(}x\ \texttt{:}\ ty\texttt{)}\ \texttt{->}\ e) &\triangleq fv(e) - \{f, x\} \\ fv(\texttt{let}\ x\ \texttt{=}\ e_1\ \texttt{in}\ e_2) &\triangleq fv(e_1) \cup (fv(e_2) - \{x\}). \end{aligned}$$

## A.3 Evaluation Relation

This is of the form

$$s, e \Rightarrow v, s'$$

where

- *e* is a *closed* expression (i.e. *fv*(*e*) is empty)
- *v* is a closed *canonical form*, which by definition is a closed expression in the subset of expressions generated by the grammar

$$\begin{aligned} v ::= {} & x, f \\ & \texttt{true} \\ & \texttt{false} \\ & \texttt{n} \\ & \texttt{()} \\ & v\ \texttt{,}\ v \\ & \texttt{fun(}x\ \texttt{:}\ ty\texttt{)}\ \texttt{->}\ e \\ & \texttt{fun}\ f\ \texttt{=}\ \texttt{(}x\ \texttt{:}\ ty\texttt{)}\ \texttt{->}\ e \\ & \ell \end{aligned}$$

- $s, s'$ are *states*, which by definition are finite functions from *Loc* to $\mathbb{Z}$
- $loc(e) \subseteq dom(s)$ and $loc(v) \subseteq dom(s')$.

The evaluation relation is inductively defined by the following rules. (The notation $e[e_1/x]$ used in some of the rules indicates the substitution of $e_1$ for all free occurrences of $x$ in $e$; similarly, $e[e_1/x_1, e_2/x_2, \ldots]$ indicates simultaneous substitution; in this paper we will only need to consider the substitution of *closed* expressions, so I omit a discussion of avoiding capture of free identifiers by binders during substitution. The notation $s[\ell \mapsto \texttt{n}]$ used in some of the rules denotes the state mapping $\ell$ to $\texttt{n}$ and otherwise acting like $s$.)

*Canonical forms:*

$$\frac{v \text{ in canonical form}}{s, v \Rightarrow v, s}$$

*Conditional:*

$$\frac{s, e \Rightarrow \mathtt{true}, s' \quad s', e_1 \Rightarrow v, s''}{s, \mathtt{if}\ e\ \mathtt{then}\ e_1\ \mathtt{else}\ e_2 \Rightarrow v, s''} \qquad \frac{s, e \Rightarrow \mathtt{false}, s' \quad s', e_2 \Rightarrow v, s''}{s, \mathtt{if}\ e\ \mathtt{then}\ e_1\ \mathtt{else}\ e_2 \Rightarrow v, s''}$$

*Integer equality:*

$$\frac{s, e_1 \Rightarrow \mathtt{n}, s' \quad s', e_2 \Rightarrow \mathtt{n}, s''}{s, e_1 \mathtt{=} e_2 \Rightarrow \mathtt{true}, s''} \qquad \frac{s, e_1 \Rightarrow \mathtt{n}_1, s' \quad s', e_2 \Rightarrow \mathtt{n}_2, s'' \quad \mathtt{n}_1 \neq \mathtt{n}_2}{s, e_1 \mathtt{=} e_2 \Rightarrow \mathtt{false}, s''}$$

*Arithmetic:*

$$\frac{s, e_1 \Rightarrow \mathtt{n}_1, s' \quad s', e_2 \Rightarrow \mathtt{n}_2, s'' \quad \mathtt{op} \in \{\mathtt{+}, \mathtt{-}\} \quad \mathtt{n} \text{ is the result of combining } \mathtt{n}_1 \text{ and } \mathtt{n}_2 \text{ according to } \mathtt{op}}{s, e_1\ \mathtt{op}\ e_2 \Rightarrow \mathtt{n}, s''}$$

*Look-up:*

$$\frac{s, e \Rightarrow \ell, s' \quad (\ell \mapsto \mathtt{n}) \in s'}{s, \mathtt{!}e \Rightarrow \mathtt{n}, s'}$$

*Assignment:*

$$\frac{s, e_1 \Rightarrow \ell, s' \quad s', e_2 \Rightarrow \mathtt{n}, s''}{s, e_1 \mathtt{:=} e_2 \Rightarrow \mathtt{()}, s''[\ell \mapsto \mathtt{n}]}$$

*Storage creation:*

$$\frac{s, e \Rightarrow \mathtt{n}, s' \quad \ell \notin dom(s')}{s, \mathtt{ref}\ e \Rightarrow \ell, s'[\ell \mapsto \mathtt{n}]}$$

*Location equality:*

$$\frac{s, e_1 \Rightarrow \ell, s' \quad s', e_2 \Rightarrow \ell, s''}{s, e_1 \mathtt{==} e_2 \Rightarrow \mathtt{true}, s''} \qquad \frac{s, e_1 \Rightarrow \ell_1, s' \quad s', e_2 \Rightarrow \ell_2, s'' \quad \ell_1 \neq \ell_2}{s, e_1 \mathtt{==} e_2 \Rightarrow \mathtt{false}, s''}$$

*Sequence:*

$$\frac{s, e_1 \Rightarrow v_1, s' \qquad s', e_2 \Rightarrow v_2, s''}{s, e_1 \texttt{ ; } e_2 \Rightarrow v_2, s''}$$

*Pair:*

$$\frac{s, e_1 \Rightarrow v_1, s' \qquad s', e_2 \Rightarrow v_2, s''}{s, (e_1 \texttt{ , } e_2) \Rightarrow (v_1 \texttt{ , } v_2), s''}$$

*Projections:*

$$\frac{s, e \Rightarrow (v_1 \texttt{ , } v_2), s'}{s, \texttt{fst } e \Rightarrow v_1, s'} \qquad \frac{s, e \Rightarrow (v_1 \texttt{ , } v_2), s'}{s, \texttt{snd } e \Rightarrow v_2, s'}$$

*Function application:*

$$\frac{s, e_1 \Rightarrow v_1, s' \qquad s', e_2 \Rightarrow v_2, s'' \qquad v_1 = \texttt{fun(}x \texttt{ : } ty\texttt{) -> } e \qquad s'', e[v_2/x] \Rightarrow v_3, s'''}{s, e_1\, e_2 \Rightarrow v_3, s'''}$$

$$\frac{s, e_1 \Rightarrow v_1, s' \qquad s', e_2 \Rightarrow v_2, s'' \qquad v_1 = \texttt{fun } f \texttt{ = (}x \texttt{ : } ty\texttt{) -> } e \qquad s'', e[v_1/f, v_2/x] \Rightarrow v_3, s'''}{s, e_1\, e_2 \Rightarrow v_3, s'''}$$

*Local definition:*

$$\frac{s, e_1 \Rightarrow v_1, s' \qquad s', e_2[v_1/x] \Rightarrow v_2, s''}{s, \texttt{let } x \texttt{ = } e_1 \texttt{ in } e_2 \Rightarrow v_2, s''}$$

## A.4 Type Assignment Relation

This is of the form

$$\Gamma \vdash e : ty$$

where

- the *typing context* $\Gamma$ is a function from a finite set $dom(\Gamma)$ of variables to types
- $e$ is an expression
- $ty$ is a type.

It is inductively generated by the following rules. (The notation $\Gamma[x \mapsto ty]$ used in some of the rules indicates the typing context mapping $x$ to $ty$ and otherwise acting like $\Gamma$.)

*Value identifiers:*

$$\frac{\boldsymbol{x} \in dom(\Gamma) \quad \Gamma(\boldsymbol{x}) = ty}{\Gamma \vdash \boldsymbol{x} : ty}$$

*Boolean constants:*

$$\frac{\mathtt{b} \in \{\mathtt{true}, \mathtt{false}\}}{\Gamma \vdash \mathtt{b} : \mathtt{bool}}$$

*Conditional:*

$$\frac{\Gamma \vdash e : \mathtt{bool} \quad \Gamma \vdash e_1 : ty \quad \Gamma \vdash e_2 : ty}{\Gamma \vdash (\mathtt{if}\ e\ \mathtt{then}\ e_1\ \mathtt{else}\ e_2) : ty}$$

*Integer constants:*

$$\frac{\mathtt{n} \in \mathbb{Z}}{\Gamma \vdash \mathtt{n} : \mathtt{int}}$$

*Integer equality:*

$$\frac{\Gamma \vdash e_1 : \mathtt{int} \quad \Gamma \vdash e_2 : \mathtt{int}}{\Gamma \vdash (e_1 \mathtt{=} e_2) : \mathtt{bool}}$$

*Arithmetic:*

$$\frac{\Gamma \vdash e_1 : \mathtt{int} \quad \Gamma \vdash e_2 : \mathtt{int} \quad \mathtt{op} \in \{\mathtt{+}, \mathtt{-}\}}{\Gamma \vdash (e_1\ \mathtt{op}\ e_2) : \mathtt{int}}$$

*Unit value:*

$$\frac{}{\Gamma \vdash \mathtt{()} : \mathtt{unit}}$$

*Look-up:*

$$\frac{\Gamma \vdash e : \mathtt{int\ ref}}{\Gamma \vdash \mathtt{!}e : \mathtt{int}}$$

*Assignment:*

$$\frac{\Gamma \vdash e_1 : \mathtt{int\ ref} \quad \Gamma \vdash e_2 : \mathtt{int}}{\Gamma \vdash (e_1 \mathtt{:=} e_2) : \mathtt{unit}}$$

*Storage creation:*

$$\frac{\Gamma \vdash e : \mathtt{int}}{\Gamma \vdash \mathtt{ref}\ e : \mathtt{int\,ref}}$$

*Location equality:*

$$\frac{\begin{array}{l}\Gamma \vdash e_1 : \mathtt{int\,ref}\\ \Gamma \vdash e_2 : \mathtt{int\,ref}\end{array}}{\Gamma \vdash (e_1 \mathtt{==} e_2) : \mathtt{bool}}$$

*Sequence:*

$$\frac{\begin{array}{l}\Gamma \vdash e_1 : ty_1\\ \Gamma \vdash e_2 : ty_2\end{array}}{\Gamma \vdash (e_1\ ;\ e_2) : ty_2}$$

*Pair:*

$$\frac{\begin{array}{l}\Gamma \vdash e_1 : ty_1\\ \Gamma \vdash e_2 : ty_2\end{array}}{\Gamma \vdash e_1\ ,\ e_2 : ty_1 * ty_2}$$

*Projections:*

$$\frac{\Gamma \vdash e : ty_1 * ty_2}{\Gamma \vdash \mathtt{fst}\ e : ty_1} \qquad \frac{\Gamma \vdash e : ty_1 * ty_2}{\Gamma \vdash \mathtt{snd}\ e : ty_2}$$

*Function abstraction:*

$$\frac{\begin{array}{l}\Gamma[x \mapsto ty_1] \vdash e : ty_2\\ x \notin dom(\Gamma\end{array}}{\Gamma \vdash (\mathtt{fun(}x\ \mathtt{:}\ ty_1\mathtt{)}\ \mathtt{->}\ e) : ty_1\ \mathtt{->}\ ty_2}$$

*Recursively defined function:*

$$\frac{\begin{array}{l}\Gamma[f \mapsto ty_1\ \mathtt{->}\ ty_2][x \mapsto ty_1] \vdash e : ty_2\\ f, x \notin dom(\Gamma)\\ f \neq x\end{array}}{\Gamma \vdash (\mathtt{fun}\ f\ \mathtt{=}\ \mathtt{(}x\ \mathtt{:}\ ty_1\mathtt{)}\ \mathtt{->}\ e) : ty_1\ \mathtt{->}\ ty_2}$$

*Function application:*

$$\frac{\begin{array}{l}\Gamma \vdash e_1 : ty_2\ \mathtt{->}\ ty_1\\ \Gamma \vdash e_2 : ty_2\end{array}}{\Gamma \vdash e_1\, e_2 : ty_1}$$

*Local definition:*

$$\frac{\Gamma \vdash e_1 : ty_1 \quad \Gamma[x \mapsto ty_1] \vdash e_2 : ty_2 \quad x \notin dom(\Gamma)}{\Gamma \vdash (\mathtt{let}\ x\ \mathtt{=}\ e_1\ \mathtt{in}\ e_2) : ty_2}$$

*Storage locations:*

$$\frac{\ell \in Loc}{\Gamma \vdash \ell : \mathtt{int\,ref}}$$

**Theorem A.1 (Type soundness).**

$$(e, s \Rightarrow v, s') \ \&\ (\emptyset \vdash e : ty) \supset (\emptyset \vdash v : ty).$$

□

## A.5 Transition Relation

This is of the form

$$(s\ ,\ e) \to (s'\ ,\ e')$$

where $e, e'$ are closed expressions and $s, s'$ are memory states with $loc(e) \subseteq dom(s)$ and $loc(e') \subseteq dom(s')$. The transition relation is inductively defined by the following rules.

*Basic reductions:*

$$\frac{}{(s\ ,\ \mathtt{if\ true\ then}\ e_1\ \mathtt{else}\ e_2) \to (s\ ,\ e_1)}$$

$$\frac{}{(s\ ,\ \mathtt{if\ false\ then}\ e_1\ \mathtt{else}\ e_2) \to (s\ ,\ e_2)}$$

$$\frac{}{(s\ ,\ \mathtt{n} = \mathtt{n}) \to (s\ ,\ \mathtt{true})} \qquad \frac{\mathtt{n}_1 \neq \mathtt{n}_2}{(s\ ,\ \mathtt{n}_1 = \mathtt{n}_2) \to (s\ ,\ \mathtt{false})}$$

$$\frac{\mathtt{op} \in \{\mathtt{+},\mathtt{-}\} \quad \mathtt{n} \text{ is the result of combining } \mathtt{n}_1 \text{ and } \mathtt{n}_2 \text{ according to } \mathtt{op}}{(s\ ,\ \mathtt{n}_1\ \mathtt{op}\ \mathtt{n}_2) \to (s\ ,\ \mathtt{n})}$$

$$\frac{(\ell \mapsto \mathtt{n}) \in s}{(s\ ,\ !\ell) \to (s\ ,\ \mathtt{n})}$$

$$\frac{}{(s\ ,\ \ell := \mathtt{n}) \to (s[\ell \mapsto \mathtt{n}]\ ,\ ())}$$

$$\frac{\ell \notin dom(s)}{(s\ ,\ \mathtt{ref\ n}) \to (s[\ell \mapsto \mathtt{n}]\ ,\ \ell)}$$

$$\frac{}{(s\ ,\ \ell \,\texttt{==}\, \ell) \to (s\ ,\ \texttt{true})} \qquad \frac{\ell_1 \neq \ell_2}{(s\ ,\ \ell_1 \,\texttt{==}\, \ell_2) \to (s\ ,\ \texttt{false})}$$

$$\frac{v \text{ a canonical form}}{(s\ ,\ (v\ ;\ e)) \to (s\ ,\ e)}$$

$$\frac{v_1, v_2 \text{ canonical forms}}{(s\ ,\ \texttt{fst}\ (v_1\ ,\ v_2)) \to (s\ ,\ v_1)} \qquad \frac{v_1, v_2 \text{ canonical forms}}{(s\ ,\ \texttt{snd}\ (v_1\ ,\ v_2)) \to (s\ ,\ v_1)}$$

$$\frac{\begin{array}{l} v_1 = \texttt{fun(}x\ \texttt{:}\ ty\texttt{)}\ \texttt{->}\ e \\ v_2 \text{ a canonical form}\end{array}}{(s\ ,\ v_1\, v_2) \to (s\ ,\ e[v_2/x])} \qquad \frac{\begin{array}{l} v_1 = \texttt{fun}\ f\ \texttt{=}\ \texttt{(}x\ \texttt{:}\ ty\texttt{)}\ \texttt{->}\ e \\ v_2 \text{ a canonical form}\end{array}}{(s\ ,\ v_1\, v_2) \to (s\ ,\ e[v_1/f, v_2/x])}$$

$$\frac{v \text{ a canonical form}}{(s\ ,\ \texttt{let}\ x\ \texttt{=}\ v\ \texttt{in}\ e) \to (s\ ,\ e[v/x])}$$

*Simplification steps:*

$$\frac{(s\ ,\ e) \to (s'\ ,\ e')}{(s\ ,\ \texttt{if}\ e\ \texttt{then}\ e_1\ \texttt{else}\ e_2) \to (s'\ ,\ \texttt{if}\ e'\ \texttt{then}\ e_1\ \texttt{else}\ e_2)}$$

$$\frac{\begin{array}{l}(s\ ,\ e_1) \to (s'\ ,\ e_1') \\ \mathsf{op} \in \{\texttt{=}, \texttt{+}, \texttt{-}, \texttt{:=}, \texttt{==}, \texttt{;}, \texttt{,}\}\end{array}}{(s\ ,\ e_1\ \mathsf{op}\ e_2) \to (s'\ ,\ e_1'\ \mathsf{op}\ e_2)} \qquad \frac{\begin{array}{l}(s\ ,\ e) \to (s'\ ,\ e') \\ v \text{ a canonical form} \\ \mathsf{op} \in \{\texttt{=}, \texttt{+}, \texttt{-}, \texttt{:=}, \texttt{==}, \texttt{,}\}\end{array}}{(s\ ,\ v\ \mathsf{op}\ e) \to (s'\ ,\ v\ \mathsf{op}\ e')}$$

$$\frac{\begin{array}{l}(s\ ,\ e_1) \to (s'\ ,\ e_1') \\ \mathsf{op} \in \{\texttt{!}, \texttt{ref}\ , \texttt{fst}\ , \texttt{snd}\ \}\end{array}}{(s\ ,\ \mathsf{op}\, e) \to (s'\ ,\ \mathsf{op}\, e')}$$

$$\frac{(s\ ,\ e_1) \to (s'\ ,\ e_1')}{(s\ ,\ e_1\, e_2) \to (s'\ ,\ e_1'\, e_2)} \qquad \frac{\begin{array}{l}(s\ ,\ e) \to (s'\ ,\ e') \\ v \text{ a canonical form}\end{array}}{(s\ ,\ v\, e) \to (s'\ ,\ v\, e')}$$

$$\frac{(s\ ,\ e_1) \to (s'\ ,\ e_1')}{(s\ ,\ \texttt{let}\ x\ \texttt{=}\ e_1\ \texttt{in}\ e_2) \to (s'\ ,\ \texttt{let}\ x\ \texttt{=}\ e_1'\ \texttt{in}\ e_2)}$$

**Theorem A.2 (The relationship between evaluation and transition).**

$$(s, e \Rightarrow v, s') \quad \equiv \quad (s\ ,\ e) \to^* (s'\ ,\ v)$$

*where* $\to^*$ *is the reflexive-transitive closure of* $\to$. □

## A.6 An Abstract Machine

The configurations of the machine take the form $\langle s\ ,\ \mathcal{F}s\ ,\ e\rangle$ where $s$ is a state (cf. Sect. A.3), $e$ is a closed expression (cf. Sect. A.2) and $\mathcal{F}s$ is a closed frame stack. The *frame stacks* are given by:

$$\begin{array}{lll} \mathcal{F}s ::= & \mathcal{I}d & \text{empty} \\ & \mathcal{F}s \circ \mathcal{F} & \text{non-empty} \end{array}$$

where $\mathcal{F}$ is an *evaluation frame*:

$$\begin{array}{lll} \mathcal{F} ::= & \texttt{if}\ [-]\ \texttt{then}\ e\ \texttt{else}\ e & \\ & [-]\ \texttt{op}\ e & \text{for op} \in \{\texttt{=},\texttt{+},\texttt{-},\texttt{:=},\texttt{==},\texttt{;},\texttt{,}\} \\ & v\ \texttt{op}\ [-] & \text{for op} \in \{\texttt{=},\texttt{+},\texttt{-},\texttt{:=},\texttt{==},\texttt{,}\} \\ & \texttt{op}\ [-] & \text{for op} \in \{\texttt{!},\texttt{ref},\texttt{fst},\texttt{snd}\} \\ & [-]\ e & \\ & v\ [-] & \\ & \texttt{let}\ x\ \texttt{=}\ [-]\ \texttt{in}\ e & \end{array}$$

(where $e$ ranges over expressions and $v$ over expressions in canonical form). The set $fv(\mathcal{F}s)$ of free value identifiers of a frame stack $\mathcal{F}s$ are all those value identifiers occurring freely in its constituent expressions; $\mathcal{F}s$ is *closed* if $fv(\mathcal{F}s)$ is empty.

The transitions of the abstract machine, $\langle s\ ,\ \mathcal{F}s\ ,\ e\rangle \to \langle s'\ ,\ \mathcal{F}s'\ ,\ e'\rangle$, are defined by case analysis of, firstly, the structure of $e$ and then the structure of $\mathcal{F}s$:

*Case $e = v$ is in canonical form:*

$\langle s\ ,\ \mathcal{F}s \circ (\texttt{if}\ [-]\ \texttt{then}\ e_1\ \texttt{else}\ e_2)\ ,\ v\rangle \to \langle s\ ,\ \mathcal{F}s\ ,\ e_1\rangle$, if $v = \texttt{true}$
$\langle s\ ,\ \mathcal{F}s \circ (\texttt{if}\ [-]\ \texttt{then}\ e_1\ \texttt{else}\ e_2)\ ,\ v\rangle \to \langle s\ ,\ \mathcal{F}s\ ,\ e_2\rangle$, if $v = \texttt{false}$
$\langle s\ ,\ \mathcal{F}s \circ ([-]\ \texttt{op}\ e)\ ,\ v\rangle \to \langle s\ ,\ \mathcal{F}s \circ (v\ \texttt{op}\ [-])\ ,\ e\rangle$, for op $\in \{\texttt{=},\texttt{+},\texttt{-},\texttt{:=},\texttt{==},\texttt{,}\}$
$\langle s\ ,\ \mathcal{F}s \circ (v'\ \texttt{op}\ [-])\ ,\ v\rangle \to \langle s\ ,\ \mathcal{F}s\ ,\ v''\rangle$,
if $v''$ is the result of combining $v'$ and $v$ according to op $\in \{\texttt{=},\texttt{+},\texttt{-},\texttt{==},\texttt{,}\}$
$\langle s\ ,\ \mathcal{F}s \circ (\ell\ \texttt{:=}\ [-])\ ,\ v\rangle \to \langle s[\ell \mapsto \texttt{n}]\ ,\ \mathcal{F}s\ ,\ \texttt{()}\rangle$, if $v = \texttt{n}$
$\langle s\ ,\ \mathcal{F}s \circ (\texttt{!}[-])\ ,\ v\rangle \to \langle s\ ,\ \mathcal{F}s\ ,\ \texttt{n}\rangle$, if $v = \ell$ and $(\ell \mapsto \texttt{n}) \in dom(s)$
$\langle s\ ,\ \mathcal{F}s \circ (\texttt{ref}\ [-])\ ,\ v\rangle \to \langle s[\ell \mapsto \texttt{n}]\ ,\ \mathcal{F}s\ ,\ \ell\rangle$, if $v = \texttt{n}$ and $\ell \notin dom(s)$
$\langle s\ ,\ \mathcal{F}s \circ ([-]\ \texttt{;}\ e)\ ,\ v\rangle \to \langle s\ ,\ \mathcal{F}s\ ,\ e\rangle$
$\langle s\ ,\ \mathcal{F}s \circ (\texttt{fst}\ [-])\ ,\ v\rangle \to \langle s\ ,\ \mathcal{F}s\ ,\ v_1\rangle$, if $v = (v_1\ \texttt{,}\ v_2)$
$\langle s\ ,\ \mathcal{F}s \circ (\texttt{snd}\ [-])\ ,\ v\rangle \to \langle s\ ,\ \mathcal{F}s\ ,\ v_2\rangle$, if $v = (v_1\ \texttt{,}\ v_2)$
$\langle s\ ,\ \mathcal{F}s \circ ([-]\ e)\ ,\ v\rangle \to \langle s\ ,\ \mathcal{F}s \circ (v\ [-])\ ,\ e\rangle$
$\langle s\ ,\ \mathcal{F}s \circ (v'\ [-])\ ,\ v\rangle \to \langle s\ ,\ \mathcal{F}s\ ,\ e[v/x]\rangle$, if $v' = \texttt{fun(}x\ \texttt{:}\ ty\texttt{)}\ \texttt{->}\ e$
$\langle s\ ,\ \mathcal{F}s \circ (v'\ [-])\ ,\ v\rangle \to \langle s\ ,\ \mathcal{F}s\ ,\ e[v'/f, v/x]\rangle$, if $v' = \texttt{fun}\ f\ \texttt{=}\ \texttt{(}x\ \texttt{:}\ ty\texttt{)}\ \texttt{->}\ e$
$\langle s\ ,\ \mathcal{F}s \circ (\texttt{let}\ x\ \texttt{=}\ [-]\ \texttt{in}\ e)\ ,\ v\rangle \to \langle s\ ,\ \mathcal{F}s\ ,\ e[v/x]\rangle$

*Case $e$ is not in canonical form:*

$\langle s\ ,\ \mathcal{F}s\ ,\ \texttt{if}\ e\ \texttt{then}\ e_1\ \texttt{else}\ e_2\rangle \to \langle s\ ,\ \mathcal{F}s \circ (\texttt{if}\ [-]\ \texttt{then}\ e_1\ \texttt{else}\ e_2)\ ,\ e\rangle$
$\langle s\ ,\ \mathcal{F}s\ ,\ e_1\ \texttt{op}\ e_2\rangle \to \langle s\ ,\ \mathcal{F}s \circ ([-]\ \texttt{op}\ e_2)\ ,\ e_1\rangle$, for op $\in \{\texttt{=},\texttt{+},\texttt{-},\texttt{:=},\texttt{==},\texttt{;},\texttt{,}\}$
$\langle s\ ,\ \mathcal{F}s\ ,\ \texttt{op}\ e\rangle \to \langle s\ ,\ \mathcal{F}s \circ (\texttt{op}\ [-])\ ,\ e\rangle$, for op $\in \{\texttt{!},\texttt{ref},\texttt{fst},\texttt{snd}\}$
$\langle s\ ,\ \mathcal{F}s\ ,\ e_1\ e_2\rangle \to \langle s\ ,\ \mathcal{F}s \circ ([-]\ e_2)\ ,\ e_1\rangle$
$\langle s\ ,\ \mathcal{F}s\ ,\ \texttt{let}\ x\ \texttt{=}\ e_1\ \texttt{in}\ e_2\rangle \to \langle s\ ,\ \mathcal{F}s \circ (\texttt{let}\ x\ \texttt{=}\ [-]\ \texttt{in}\ e_2)\ ,\ e_1\rangle$

**Theorem A.3 (The relationship between evaluation and the abstract machine).**

$$\langle s\ ,\ \mathcal{F}s\ ,\ e\rangle \to^* \langle s'\ ,\ \mathcal{I}d\ ,\ v\rangle \quad \equiv \quad (s, \mathcal{F}s[e] \Rightarrow v, s')$$

*where the application $\mathcal{F}s[e]$ of a frame stack $\mathcal{F}s$ to an expression $e$ is defined by induction on the length of $\mathcal{F}s$ as follows:*

$$\begin{cases} \mathcal{I}d[e] \triangleq e \\ (\mathcal{F}s \circ \mathcal{F})[e] \triangleq \mathcal{F}s[\mathcal{F}[e]] \end{cases}$$

*(each evaluation frame $\mathcal{F}$ is an evaluation context containing a hole $[-]$ that can be replaced by $e$ to obtain an expression $\mathcal{F}[e]$).* □

## A.7 A Structurally Inductive Termination Relation

This is of the form

$$\langle s\ ,\ \mathcal{F}s\ ,\ e\rangle\searrow$$

where $s$ is a memory state, $\mathcal{F}s$ a frame stack and $e$ a closed expression. It is inductively defined by the following rules.

$$\frac{v \text{ a canonical form}}{\langle s\ ,\ \mathcal{I}d\ ,\ v\rangle\searrow}$$

$$\frac{\langle s\ ,\ \mathcal{F}s\ ,\ e_1\rangle\searrow \qquad v = \texttt{true}}{\langle s\ ,\ \mathcal{F}s \circ (\texttt{if}\ [-]\ \texttt{then}\ e_1\ \texttt{else}\ e_2)\ ,\ v\rangle\searrow}$$

$$\frac{\langle s\ ,\ \mathcal{F}s\ ,\ e_2\rangle\searrow \qquad v = \texttt{false}}{\langle s\ ,\ \mathcal{F}s \circ (\texttt{if}\ [-]\ \texttt{then}\ e_1\ \texttt{else}\ e_2)\ ,\ v\rangle\searrow}$$

$$\frac{\langle s\ ,\ \mathcal{F}s \circ (v\ \texttt{op}\ [-])\ ,\ e\rangle\searrow \qquad \texttt{op} \in \{\texttt{=}, \texttt{+}, \texttt{-}, \texttt{:=}, \texttt{==}, \texttt{,}\}}{\langle s\ ,\ \mathcal{F}s \circ ([-]\ \texttt{op}\ e)\ ,\ v\rangle\searrow}$$

$$\frac{\langle s\ ,\ \mathcal{F}s\ ,\ v''\rangle\searrow \qquad \texttt{op} \in \{\texttt{=}, \texttt{+}, \texttt{-}, \texttt{:=}, \texttt{==}, \texttt{,}\} \qquad v'' \text{ is result of combining } v' \text{ and } v \text{ according to } \texttt{op}}{\langle s\ ,\ \mathcal{F}s \circ (v'\ \texttt{op}\ [-])\ ,\ v\rangle\searrow}$$

$$\frac{\langle s[\ell \mapsto \texttt{n}]\ ,\ \mathcal{F}s\ ,\ \texttt{()}\rangle\searrow \qquad v = \texttt{n}}{\langle s\ ,\ \mathcal{F}s \circ (\ell\ \texttt{:=}\ [-])\ ,\ v\rangle\searrow}$$

$$\frac{\begin{array}{l}\langle s\,,\,\mathcal{F}s\,,\,\mathtt{n}\rangle\searrow\\ v=\ell\\ (\ell\mapsto\mathtt{n})\in dom(s)\end{array}}{\langle s\,,\,\mathcal{F}s\circ(\mathtt{!}[-])\,,\,v\rangle\searrow}$$

$$\frac{\begin{array}{l}\langle s[\ell\mapsto\mathtt{n}]\,,\,\mathcal{F}s\,,\,\ell\rangle\searrow\\ v=\mathtt{n}\\ \ell\notin dom(s)\end{array}}{\langle s\,,\,\mathcal{F}s\circ(\mathtt{ref}\ [-])\,,\,v\rangle\searrow}$$

$$\frac{\langle s\,,\,\mathcal{F}s\,,\,e\rangle\searrow}{\langle s\,,\,\mathcal{F}s\circ([-]\ ;\ e)\,,\,v\rangle\searrow}$$

$$\frac{\begin{array}{l}\langle s\,,\,\mathcal{F}s\,,\,v_1\rangle\searrow\\ v=(v_1\ \mathtt{,}\ v_2)\end{array}}{\langle s\,,\,\mathcal{F}s\circ(\mathtt{fst}\ [-])\,,\,v\rangle\searrow}\qquad\frac{\begin{array}{l}\langle s\,,\,\mathcal{F}s\,,\,v_2\rangle\searrow\\ v=(v_1\ \mathtt{,}\ v_2)\end{array}}{\langle s\,,\,\mathcal{F}s\circ(\mathtt{snd}\ [-])\,,\,v\rangle\searrow}$$

$$\frac{\langle s\,,\,\mathcal{F}s\circ(v\,[-])\,,\,e\rangle\searrow}{\langle s\,,\,\mathcal{F}s\circ([-]\,e)\,,\,v\rangle\searrow}$$

$$\frac{\begin{array}{l}\langle s\,,\,\mathcal{F}s\,,\,e[v/x]\rangle\searrow\\ v'=\mathtt{fun(}x\ \mathtt{:}\ ty\mathtt{)\ ->}\ e\end{array}}{\langle s\,,\,\mathcal{F}s\circ(v'\,[-])\,,\,v\rangle\searrow}\qquad\frac{\begin{array}{l}\langle s\,,\,\mathcal{F}s\,,\,e[v'/f,v/x]\rangle\searrow\\ v'=\mathtt{fun}\ f\ \mathtt{=\ (}x\ \mathtt{:}\ ty\mathtt{)\ ->}\ e\end{array}}{\langle s\,,\,\mathcal{F}s\circ(v'\,[-])\,,\,v\rangle\searrow}$$

$$\frac{\langle s\,,\,\mathcal{F}s\,,\,e[v/x]\rangle\searrow}{\langle s\,,\,\mathcal{F}s\circ(\mathtt{let}\ x\ \mathtt{=}\ [-]\ \mathtt{in}\ e)\,,\,v\rangle\searrow}$$

$$\frac{\langle s\,,\,\mathcal{F}s\circ(\mathtt{if}\ [-]\ \mathtt{then}\ e_1\ \mathtt{else}\ e_2)\,,\,e\rangle\searrow}{\langle s\,,\,\mathcal{F}s\,,\,\mathtt{if}\ e\ \mathtt{then}\ e_1\ \mathtt{else}\ e_2\rangle\searrow}$$

$$\frac{\begin{array}{l}\langle s\,,\,\mathcal{F}s\circ([-]\ \mathsf{op}\ e_2)\,,\,e_1\rangle\searrow\\ \mathsf{op}\in\{\mathtt{=},\mathtt{+},\mathtt{-},\mathtt{:=},\mathtt{==},\mathtt{,}\}\end{array}}{\langle s\,,\,\mathcal{F}s\,,\,e_1\ \mathsf{op}\ e_2\rangle\searrow}$$

$$\frac{\begin{array}{l}\langle s\,,\,\mathcal{F}s\circ(\mathsf{op}\,[-])\,,\,e\rangle\searrow\\ \mathsf{op}\in\{\mathtt{!},\mathtt{ref}\ ,\mathtt{fst}\ ,\mathtt{snd}\ \}\end{array}}{\langle s\,,\,\mathcal{F}s\,,\,\mathsf{op}\,e\rangle\searrow}$$

$$\frac{\langle s\,,\,\mathcal{F}s\circ([-]\,e_2)\,,\,e_1\rangle\searrow}{\langle s\,,\,\mathcal{F}s\,,\,e_1\,e_2\rangle\searrow}$$

Comparing the abstract machine steps in Sect. A.6 with the above rules it is not hard to see that we have:

**Theorem A.4.**

$$\langle s\,,\mathcal{F}s\,,e\rangle\searrow \quad\equiv\quad \exists s',v\;(\langle s\,,\mathcal{F}s\,,e\rangle \to^* \langle s'\,,\mathcal{I}d\,,v\rangle)\;.$$

*Hence by Theorem A.3,* $s,e\Downarrow$ *holds if and only if* $\langle s\,,\mathcal{I}d\,,e\rangle\searrow$ *does.* □

# B Exercises

**Exercise B.1.** Let $f$, $g$ and $t$ be defined as in equations (3), (4) and (5). Use the rules in Sect. A.3 to prove that

$$\emptyset, t\,f \Rightarrow \texttt{false}, s \quad\text{and}\quad \emptyset, t\,g \Rightarrow \texttt{true}, s$$

hold for some state $s$. (Here $\emptyset$ denotes the *empty state*, whose domain of definition is $dom(\emptyset) = \emptyset$, the empty set of locations.)

**Exercise B.2.** Prove the type soundness property of evaluation stated in Theorem A.1. Use induction on the derivation of the evaluation $e, s \Rightarrow v, s'$. You will first need to prove the following substitution property of the type assignment relation:

$$\Gamma \vdash e : ty \;\;\&\;\; \Gamma[x \mapsto ty] \vdash e' : ty' \;\supset\; \Gamma \vdash e'[e/x] : ty'.$$

**Exercise B.3.** Given $e_1, e_2 \in \mathrm{Prog}_{ty}$, define $e_1 \leq_{obs} e_2 : ty$ to mean that for all $x : ty \vdash e : ty'$ and all states $s$

$$s, e[e_1/x] \Rightarrow v_1, s_1 \;\supset\; \exists v_2, s_2\,.\,(s, e[e_2/x] \Rightarrow v_2, s_2) \;\;\&\;\; obs(v_1, s_1) = obs(v_2, s_2)$$

where the function $obs$ is defined in equation (2). Prove that $e_1 \leq_{obs} e_2 : ty$ holds if and only if $e_1 \leq_{\mathrm{ctx}} e_2 : ty$ does.

**Exercise B.4.** Prove Theorem A.2 relating the evaluation and transition relations of ML. First prove

$$(s\,,e) \to (s'\,,e') \;\supset\; \forall v, s''.\,(s', e' \Rightarrow v, s'') \;\supset\; (s, e \Rightarrow v, s'')$$

by induction on the derivation of $(s\,,e) \to (s'\,,e')$; deduce that if $(s\,,e) \to^* (s'\,,v)$, then $s, e \Rightarrow v, s'$. Prove the converse by induction on the derivation of $s, e \Rightarrow v, s'$.

**Exercise B.5.** Given $r \in \mathrm{Rel}(w_1, w_2)$ and $r' \in \mathrm{Rel}(w_1', w_2')$ with $w_1' \supseteq w_1$ and $w_2' \supseteq w_2$, show that $r' \rhd r$ (Definition 5.1) holds if and only if for all $(s_1', s_2') \in r'$

$$(s_1'{\restriction_{w_1}}, s_2'{\restriction_{w_2}}) \in r \;\;\&\;\; \forall (s_1, s_2) \in r\,.\,(s_1' s_1, s_2' s_2) \in r'.$$

(Here $s{\restriction_w}$ denotes the restriction of the function $s$ to $w$; and $s's$ is the state determined by the states $s'$ and $s$ as in Definition 5.1.)

**Exercise B.6.** Use the Unwinding Theorem 5.3 to prove the property of $\leq_{\mathrm{ctx}}$ stated in equation (9).

**Exercise B.7.** Suppose $f \in \mathrm{Prog}_{\texttt{int->int}}$ is a closed expression with $loc(f) = \emptyset$ and such that for all $\mathtt{n} \in \mathbb{Z}$ it is the case that $\emptyset, f\,\mathtt{n} \Downarrow$ holds. Show that $f =_{\mathrm{ctx}} memo\_f : \texttt{int -> int}$ where

```
memo_f ≜ let a = ref 0 in
         let r = ref (f 0) in
         fun(x : int) -> (if x = !a then ()
                                     else (a := x ; r := f x)) ; !r.
```

(See [15, Example 5.7], if you get stuck.)

## C List of Notation

| | |
|---|---|
| $\&$ | logical conjunction. |
| $\supset$ | logical implication. |
| $\equiv$ | logical bi-implication. |
| $=_{\mathrm{ctx}}$ | contextual equivalence—see Definition 3.1. |
| $\leq_{\mathrm{ctx}}$ | contextual preorder—see Definition 3.1. |
| $\leq_r$ | logical simulation relation—see Theorem 5.2 and Definition 5.4. |
| $\rhd$ | extension relation between state-relations—see Definition 5.1. |
| $dom(f)$ | the domain of definition of a partial function $f$. |
| $e[e_1/x]$ | expression resulting from the substitution of expression $e_1$ for all free occurrences of $x$ in expression $e$. |
| $e[e_1/x_1, \ldots, e_n/x_n]$ | expression resulting from the simultaneous substitution of expression $e_i$ for all free occurrences of $x_i$ in expression $e$ (for $i = 1, \ldots, n$). |
| $\mathcal{E}$ | an evaluation context—see equation (7) in Sect. 4. |
| $\mathcal{E}[e]$ | the expression resulting from replacing the 'hole' $[-]$ in an evaluation context $\mathcal{E}$ by the expression $e$. |
| $\mathcal{F}$ | an evaluation frame, special case of an evaluation context—see Sect. A.6. |
| $\mathcal{F}[e]$ | the expression resulting from replacing the 'hole' $[-]$ in an evaluation frame $\mathcal{F}$ by the expression $e$. |
| $\mathcal{F}s$ | a frame stack—see Sect. A.6. |
| $\mathcal{F}s[e]$ | the expression resulting from applying the frame stack $\mathcal{F}s$ to the expression $e$—see Theorem A.3. |
| $\vdash \mathcal{F}s : ty \multimap ty'$ | type assignment relation for frame stacks—see (12). |
| $f[x \mapsto y]$ | a partial function mapping $x$ to $y$ and otherwise acting like the partial function$f$. |

| | |
|---|---|
| $fv(e)$ | finite set of free value identifiers of an expression $e$. |
| $id_w$ | identity state-relation at world $w$—see Theorem 5.2(III). |
| $\Gamma \vdash e : ty$ | type assignment relation—see Sect. A.4. |
| $Loc$ | the fixed set of names of storage locations. |
| $loc(e)$ | finite set of storage locations occurring in the expression $e$. |
| $\emptyset$ | the empty set; the empty partial function; the empty state; the empty typing context. |
| $\mathrm{Prog}_{ty}$ | the set of closed expressions of type $ty$—see Definition 5.1. |
| $\mathrm{Prog}_{ty}(w)$ | the set of closed expressions of type $ty$ with locations in the finite set $w$. |
| $\mathrm{Rel}(w_1, w_2)$ | the set of binary relations between states in $\mathrm{St}(w_1)$ and in $\mathrm{St}(w_1)$. |
| $s, e \Rightarrow v, s'$ | evaluation relation—see Sect. A.3. |
| $s, e \Downarrow$ | termination relation derived from the evaluation relation $\Rightarrow$—see Definition 3.1. |
| $(s\ ,\ e) \to (s'\ ,\ e')$ | transition relation—see Sect. A.5. |
| $\langle s\ ,\ \mathcal{F}s\ ,\ e\rangle \to \langle s'\ ,\ \mathcal{F}s'\ ,\ e'\rangle$ | transition of the abstract machine—see Sect. A.6. |
| $\langle s\ ,\ \mathcal{F}s\ ,\ e\rangle\searrow$ | structurally inductive termination relation—see Sect. A.7. |
| $\mathrm{St}(w)$ | the set of memory states defined on a finite set $w$ of locations (i.e. $\mathbb{Z}^w$, the set of functions from $w$ to $\mathbb{Z}$). |
| $\mathrm{Stack}_{ty}(w)$ | the set of closed frame stacks taking an argument of type $ty$ and with locations in a finite set $w$ of locations—see (12). |
| $\mathrm{Val}_{ty}(w)$ | the set of canonical forms of type $ty$ with locations in a finite set $w$ of locations—see Sect. A.3. |
| $w$ | a finite subset of $Loc$, regarded as a 'world'. |
| $\mathbb{Z}$ | the set of integers, $\{\ldots, -2, -1, 0, 1, 2, \ldots\}$. |

## References


1. K. Aboul-Hosn and J. Hannan. Program equivalence with private state. Preprint., January 2002.
2. P. N. Benton and A. J. Kennedy. Monads, effects and transformations. In A. D. Gordon and A. M. Pitts, editors, *HOOTS '99 Higher Order Operational Techniques in Semantics, Paris, France, September 1999*, volume 26 of *Electronic Notes in Theoretical Computer Science*. Elsevier, 1999.

3. G. M. Bierman, A. M. Pitts, and C. V. Russo. Operational properties of Lily, a polymorphic linear lambda calculus with recursion. In *Fourth International Workshop on Higher Order Operational Techniques in Semantics, Montréal*, volume 41 of *Electronic Notes in Theoretical Computer Science*. Elsevier, September 2000.
4. L. Birkedal and R. Harper. Relational interpretation of recursive types in an operational setting (Summary). In M. Abadi and T. Ito, editors, *Theoretical Aspects of Computer Software, Third International Symposium, TACS'97, Sendai, Japan, September 23 - 26, 1997, Proceedings*, volume 1281 of *Lecture Notes in Computer Science*. Springer-Verlag, Berlin, 1997.
5. G. Cousineau and M. Mauny. *The Functional Approach to Programming*. Cambridge University Press, 1998.
6. R. Harper and C. Stone. An interpretation of Standard ML in type theory. Technical Report CMU–CS–97–147, Carnegie Mellon University, Pittsburgh, PA, 1997.
7. A. Jeffrey and J. Rathke. Towards a theory of bisimulation for local names. In *14th Annual Symposium on Logic in Computer Science*, pages 56–66. IEEE Computer Society Press, Washington, 1999.
8. G. Kahn. Natural semantics. Rapport de Recherche 601, INRIA, Sophia-Antipolis, France, 1987.
9. R. Milner, M. Tofte, R. Harper, and D. MacQueen. *The Definition of Standard ML (Revised)*. MIT Press, 1997.
10. P. W. O'Hearn and J. G. Riecke. Kripke logical relations and PCF. *Information and Computation*, 120:107–116, 1995.
11. A. M. Pitts. Operationally-based theories of program equivalence. In P. Dybjer and A. M. Pitts, editors, *Semantics and Logics of Computation*, Publications of the Newton Institute, pages 241–298. Cambridge University Press, 1997.
12. A. M. Pitts. Reasoning about local variables with operationally-based logical relations. In P. W. O'Hearn and R. D. Tennent, editors, *Algol-Like Languages*, volume 2, chapter 17, pages 173–193. Birkhauser, 1997. First appeared in *Proceedings 11th Annual IEEE Symposium on Logic in Computer Science*, Brunswick, NJ, July 1996, pp 152–163.
13. A. M. Pitts. Existential types: Logical relations and operational equivalence. In K. G. Larsen, S. Skyum, and G. Winskel, editors, *Automata, Languages and Programming, 25th International Colloquium, ICALP'98, Aalborg, Denmark, July 1998, Proceedings*, volume 1443 of *Lecture Notes in Computer Science*, pages 309–326. Springer-Verlag, Berlin, 1998.
14. A. M. Pitts. Parametric polymorphism and operational equivalence. *Mathematical Structures in Computer Science*, 10:321–359, 2000.
15. A. M. Pitts and I. D. B. Stark. Operational reasoning for functions with local state. In A. D. Gordon and A. M. Pitts, editors, *Higher Order Operational Techniques in Semantics*, Publications of the Newton Institute, pages 227–273. Cambridge University Press, 1998.
16. G. D. Plotkin. Lambda-definability and logical relations. Memorandum SAI-RM-4, School of Artificial Intelligence, University of Edinburgh, 1973.
17. G. D. Plotkin. A structural approach to operational semantics. Technical Report DAIMI FN-19, Aarhus University, 1981.
18. A. K. Wright and M. Felleisen. A syntactic approach to type soundness. *Information and Computation*, 115:38–94, 1994.

# Using, Understanding, and Unraveling the OCaml Language
## *From Practice to Theory and Vice Versa*

Didier Rémy

INRIA-Rocquencourt
`http://cristal.inria.fr/~remy`

**Abstract.** These course notes are addressed to a wide audience of people interested in modern programming languages in general, ML-like languages in particular, or simply in OCaml, whether they are programmers or language designers, beginners or knowledgeable readers —little prerequiresite is actually assumed.

They provide a formal description of the operational semantics (evaluation) and statics semantics (type checking) of core ML and of several extensions starting from small variations on the core language to end up with the OCaml language —one of the most popular incarnation of ML— including its object-oriented layer.

The tight connection between theory and practice is a constant goal: formal definitions are often accompanied by OCaml programs: an interpreter for the operational semantics and an algorithm for type reconstruction are included. Conversely, some practical programming situations taken from modular or object-oriented programming patterns are considered, compared with one another, and explained in terms of type-checking problems.

Many exercises with different level of difficulties are proposed all along the way, so that the reader can continuously checks his understanding and trains his skills manipulating the new concepts; soon, he will feel invited to select more advanced exercises and pursue the exploration deeper so as to reach a stage where he can be left on his own.

G. Barthe et al. (Eds.): Applied Semantics, LNCS 2395, pp. 413–536, 2002.

# Table of Contents

**Fig. 1. Road map**

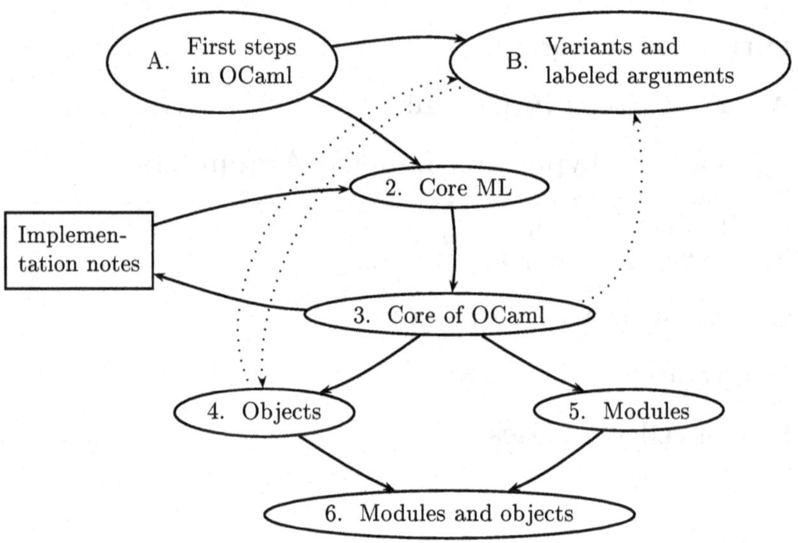


**Legend of arrows (from $A$ to $B$)**

⟶ $A$ strongly depends on $B$

⋯➤ Some part of $A$ weakly depends on some part of $B$

**Legend of nodes**

- Oval nodes are physical units.
- Rectangular nodes are cross-section topics.

# Introduction

OCaml is a language of the ML family that inherits a lot from several decades of research in type theory, language design, and implementation of functional languages. Moreover, the language is quite mature, its compiler produces efficient code and comes with a large set of general purpose as well as domain-specific libraries. Thus, OCaml is well-suited for teaching and academic projects, and is simultaneously used in the industry, in particular in several high-tech software companies.

This document is a multi-dimensional presentation of the OCaml language that combines an informal and intuitive approach to the language with a rigorous definition and a formal semantics of a large subset of the language, including ML. All along this presentation, we explain the underlying design principles, highlight the numerous interactions between various facets of the language, and emphasize the close relationship between theory and practice.

Indeed, theory and practice should often cross their paths. Sometimes, the theory is deliberately weakened to keep the practice simple. Conversely, several related features may suggest a generalization and be merged, leading to a more expressive and regular design. We hope that the reader will follow us in this attempt of putting a little theory into practice or, conversely, of rebuilding bits of theory from practical examples and intuitions. However, we maintain that the underlying mathematics should always remain simple.

The introspection of OCaml is made even more meaningful by the fact that the language is boot-strapped, that is, its compilation chain is written in OCaml itself, and only parts of the runtime are written in C. Hence, some of the implementation notes, in particular those on typechecking, could be scaled up to be actually very close to the typechecker of OCaml itself.

The material presented here is divided into three categories. On the practical side, the course contains a short presentation of OCaml. Although this presentation is not at all exhaustive and certainly not a reference manual for the language, it is a self-contained introduction to the language: all facets of the language are covered; however, most of the details are omitted. A sample of programming exercises with different levels of difficulty have been included, and for most of them, solutions can be found in Appendix C. The knowledge and the practice of at least one dialect of ML may help getting the most from the other aspects. This is not mandatory though, and beginners can learn their first steps in OCaml by starting with Appendix A. Conversely, advanced OCaml programmers can learn from the inlined OCaml implementations of some of the algorithms. Implementation notes can always be skipped, at least in a first reading when the core of OCaml is not mastered yet —other parts never depend on them. However, we left implementation notes as well as some more advanced exercises inlined in the text to emphasize the closeness of the implementation to the formalization. Moreover, this permits to people who already know the

OCaml language, to read all material continuously, making it altogether a more advanced course.

On the theoretical side —the mathematics remain rather elementary, we give a formal definition of a large subset of the OCaml language, including its dynamic and static semantics, and soundness results relating them. The proofs, however, are omitted. We also describe type inference in detail. Indeed, this is one of the most specific facets of ML.

A lot of the material actually lies in between theory and practice: we put an emphasis on the design principles, the modularity of the language constructs (their presentation is often incremental), as well as their dependencies. Some constructions that are theoretically independent end up being complementary in practice, so that one can hardly go without the other: it is often their combination that provides both flexibility and expressive power.

The document is organized in four parts (see the road maps in figure 1). Each of the first three parts addresses a different layer of OCaml: the core language (sections 2 and 3), objects and classes (Section 4), and modules (Section 5); the last part (Section 6) focuses on the combination of objects and modules, and discusses a few perspectives. The style of presentation is different for each part. While the introduction of the core language is more formal and more complete, the emphasis is put on typechecking for the section on objects and classes, the presentation of the modules system remains informal, and the last part is mostly based on examples. This is a deliberate choice, due to the limited space, but also based on the relative importance of the different parts and interest of their formalization. We then refer to other works for a more formal presentation or simply for further reading, both at the end of each section for rather technical references, and at the end of the manuscript, Page 503 for a more general overview of related work.

This document is thus addressed to a wide audience. With several entry points, it can be read in parts or following different directions (see the road maps in figure 1). People interested in the semantics of programming languages may read sections 2 and 3 only. Conversely, people interested in the object-oriented layer of OCaml may skip these sections and start at Section 4. Beginners or people interested mostly in learning the programming language may start with appendix A, then grab examples and exercises in the first sections, and end with the sections on objects and modules; they can always come back to the first sections after mastering programming in OCaml, and attack the implementation of a typechecker as a project, either following or ignoring the relevant implementation notes.

*Programming languages* are rigorous but incomplete approximations of the language of mathematics. General purpose languages are Turing complete. That is, they allow to write all algorithms. (Thus, termination and many other useful properties of programs are undecidable.) However, programming languages are not all equivalent, since they differ by their ability to describe certain kinds of algorithms succinctly. This leads to an —endless?— research for new programming structures that are more expressive and allow shorter and safer descriptions of algorithms. Of course, expressiveness is not the ultimate goal. In particular, the safety of program execution should not be given up for expressiveness. We usually limit ourselves to a relatively small subset of programs that are well-typed and guaranteed to run safely. We also search for a small set of simple, essential, and orthogonal constructs.

*Learning programming languages* Learning a programming language is a combination of understanding the language constructs and practicing. Certainly, a programming language should have a clear semantics, whether it is given formally, *i.e.* using mathematical notation, as for Standard ML [49], or informally, using words, as for OCaml. Understanding the semantics and design principles, is a prerequisite to good programming habits, but good programming is also the result of practicing. Thus, using the manual, the tutorials, and on-line helps is normal practice. One may quickly learn all functions of the core library, but even fluent programmers may sometimes have to check specifications of some standard-library functions that are not so frequently used.

Copying (good) examples may save time at any stage of programming. This includes cut and paste from solutions to exercises, especially at the beginning. Sharing experience with others may also be helpful: the first problems you face are likely to be "Frequently Asked Questions" and the libraries you miss may already be available electronically in the "OCaml hump". For books on ML see "Further reading", Page 503.

*A brief history of OCaml* The current definition and implementation of the OCaml language is the result of continuous and still ongoing research over the last two decades. The OCaml language belongs to the ML family. The language ML was invented in 1975 by Robin Milner to serve as a "meta-language", *i.e.* a control language or a scripting language, for programming proof-search strategies in the LCF proof assistant. The language quickly appeared to be a full-fledged programming language. The first implementations of ML were realized around 1981 in Lisp. Soon, several dialects of ML appeared: Standard ML at Edinburgh, Caml at INRIA, Standard ML of New-Jersey, Lazy ML developed at Chalmers, or Haskell at Glasgow. The two last dialects slightly differ from the previous ones by relying on a lazy evaluation strategy (they are called lazy languages) while all others have a strict evaluation strategy (and are called strict languages). Traditional languages, such as C, Pascal, Ada are also strict languages. Standard ML and Caml are relatively close to one another. The main differences are their implementations and their superficial —sometimes annoying— syntactic differences. Another minor difference is their module systems. However, SML does not have an object layer.

Continuing the history of Caml, Xavier Leroy and Damien Doligez designed a new implementation in 1990 called Caml-Light, freeing the previous implementation from too many experimental high-level features, and more importantly, from the old Le_Lisp back-end.

The addition of a native-code compiler and a powerful module system in 1995 and of the object and class layer in 1996 made OCaml a very mature and attractive programming language. The language is still under development: for instance, in 2000, labeled and optional arguments on the one hand and anonymous variants on the other hand were added to the language by Jacques Garrigue.

In the last decade, other dialects of ML have also evolved independently. Hereafter, we use the name ML to refer to features of the core language that are common to most dialects and we speak of OCaml, mostly in the examples, to refer to this particular implementation. Most of the examples, except those with object and classes, could easily be translated to Standard ML. However, only few of them could be straightforwardly translated to Haskell, mainly because of both languages have different evaluation strategy, but also due to many other differences in their designs.

*Resemblances and differences in a few key words* All dialects of ML are functional. That is, functions are taken seriously. In particular, they are first-class values: they can be arguments to other functions and returned as results. All dialects of ML are also strongly typed. This implies that well-typed programs cannot go wrong. By this, we mean that assuming no compiler bugs, programs will never execute erroneous access to memory nor other kind of abnormal execution step and programs that do not loop will always terminate normally. Of course, this does not ensure that the program executes what the programmer had in mind!

Another common property to all dialects of ML is type inference, that is, types of expressions are optional and are inferred by the system. As most modern languages, ML has automatic memory management, as well.

Additionally, the language OCaml is not purely functional: imperative programming with mutable values and side effects is also possible. OCaml is also object-oriented (aside from prototype designs, OCaml is still the only object-oriented dialect of ML). OCaml also features a powerful module system inspired by the one of Standard ML.

**Acknowledgments** Many thanks to Jacques Garrigue, Xavier Leroy, and Brian Rogoff for their careful reading of parts of the notes.

# Section 2

# Core ML

We first present a few examples, insisting on the functional aspect of the language. Then, we formalize an extremely small subset of the language, which, surprisingly, contains in itself the essence of ML. Last, we show how to derive other constructs remaining in core ML whenever possible, or making small extensions when necessary.

## 2.1 Discovering Core ML

Core ML is a small *functional* language. This means that functions are taken seriously, *e.g.* they can be passed as arguments to other functions or returned as results. We also say that functions are *first-class* values.

In principle, the notion of a function relates as closely as possible to the one that can be found in mathematics. However, there are also important differences, because objects manipulated by programs are always countable (and finite in practice). In fact, core ML is based on the lambda-calculus, which has been invented by Church to model computation.

Syntactically, expressions of the lambda-calculus (written with letter $a$) are of three possible forms: variables $x$, which are given as elements of a countable set, functions $\lambda x.a$, or applications $a_1\ a_2$. In addition, core ML has a distinguished construction $\mathbf{let}\ x = a_1\ \mathbf{in}\ a_2$ used to bind an expression $a_1$ to a variable $x$ within an expression $a_2$ (this construction is also used to introduce polymorphism, as we will see below). Furthermore, the language ML comes with primitive values, such as integers, floats, strings, *etc.* (written with letter $c$) and functions over these values.

Finally, a program is composed of a sequence of sentences that can optionally be separated by double semi-colon "`;;`". A sentence is a single expression or the binding, written $\mathbf{let}\ x = a$, of an expression $a$ to a variable $x$.

In normal mode, programs can be written in one or more files, separately compiled, and linked together to form an executable machine code (see Section 5.1.1). However, in the core language, we may assume that all sentences are written in a single file; furthermore, we may replace `;;` by `in` turning the sequence of sentences into a single expression. The language OCaml also offers an interactive loop in which sentences entered by the user are compiled and executed immediately; then, their results are printed on the terminal.

*Note We use the interactive mode to illustrate most of the examples. The input sentences are closed with a double semi-colons "`;;`". The output of the interpreter is only displayed when useful. Then, it appears in a smaller font and preceded by a* *double vertical bar "‖". Error messages may sometimes be verbose, thus we won't always display them in full. Instead, we use "✗" to mark an input sentence that will be rejected by the compiler. Some larger examples, called* implementation notes, *are delimited by horizontal braces as illustrated right below:*

**Implementation notes, file README**

*Implementation notes are delimited as this one. They contain explanations in English (not in OCaml comments) and several OCaml phrases.*

```
let readme = "lisez-moi";;
```

*All phrases of a note belong to the same file (this one belong to* README*) and are meant to be compiled (rather than interpreted).*

As an example, here are a couple of phrases evaluated in the interactive loop.

```
print_string "Hello\n";;
```

```
‖ Hello
‖ - : unit = ()
```

```
let pi = 4.0 *. atan 1.0;;
```

```
‖ val pi : float = 3.141593
```

```
let square x = x *. x;;
```

```
‖ val square : float -> float = <fun>
```

The execution of the first phrase prints the string "Hello\n" to the terminal. The system indicates that the result of the evaluation is of type `unit`. The evaluation of the second phrase binds the intermediate result of the evaluation of the expression `4.0 * atan 1.0`, that is the float `3.14...`, to the variable `pi`. This execution does not produce any output; the system only prints the type information and the value that is bound to `pi`. The last phrase defines a function that takes a parameter `x` and returns the product of `x` and itself. Because of the type of the binary primitive operation `*.`, which is `float -> float -> float`, the system infers that both `x` and the the result `square x` must be of type `float`. A mismatch between types, which often reveals a programmer's error, is detected and reported:

```
✗ square "pi";;
```

```
‖ Characters 7-11:
‖ This expression has type string but is here used with type float
```

Function definitions may be recursive, provided this is requested explicitly, using the keyword `rec`:

```
let rec fib n = if n < 2 then 1 else fib(n-1) + fib(n-2);;
```

```
‖ val fib : int -> int = <fun>
```

```
fib 10;;
```

```
‖ - : int = 89
```

Functions can be passed to other functions as argument, or received as results, leading to higher-functions also called *functionals*. For instance, the composition of two functions can be defined exactly as in mathematics:

```
let compose f g = fun x -> f (g x);;
```

```
val compose : ('a -> 'b) -> ('c -> 'a) -> 'c -> 'b = <fun>
```

The best illustration OCaml of the power of functions might be the function "power" itself!

```
let rec power f n =
  if n <= 0 then (fun x -> x) else compose f (power f (n-1));;
```

```
val power : ('a -> 'a) -> int -> 'a -> 'a = <fun>
```

Here, the expression `(fun x -> x)` is the anonymous identity function. Extending the parallel with mathematics, we may define the derivative of an arbitrary function `f`. Since we use numerical rather than formal computation, the derivative is parameterized by the increment step `dx`:

```
let derivative dx f = function x -> (f(x +. dx) -. f(x)) /. dx;;
```

```
val derivative : float -> (float -> float) -> float -> float = <fun>
```

Then, the third derivative `sin'''` of the sinus function can be obtained by computing the cubic power of the derivative function and applying it to the sinus function. Last, we calculate its value for the real `pi`.

```
let sin''' = (power (derivative 1e-5) 3) sin in sin''' pi;;
```

```
- : float = 0.999999
```

This capability of functions to manipulate other functions as one would do in mathematics is almost unlimited... modulo the running time and the rounding errors.

## 2.2 The Syntax of Core ML

Before continuing with more features of OCaml, let us see how a very simple subset of the language can be formalized.

In general, when giving a formal presentation of a language, we tend to keep the number of constructs small by factoring similar constructs as much as possible and explaining derived constructs by means of simple translations, such as syntactic sugar.

For instance, in the core language, we can omit phrases. That is, we transform sequences of bindings such as **let** $x_1 = a_1;;$ **let** $x_2 = a_2;; a$ into expressions of the form **let** $x_1 = a_1$ **in let** $x_2 = a_2$ **in** $a$. Similarly, numbers, strings, but also lists, pairs, *etc.* as well as operations on those values can all be treated as constants and applications of constants to values.

Formally, we assume a collection of constants $c \in \mathcal{C}$ that are partitioned into constructors $C \in \mathcal{C}^+$ and primitives $f \in \mathcal{C}^-$. Constants also come with an arity, that is, we assume a mapping *arity* from $\mathcal{C}$ to $I\!N$. For instance, integers and booleans are constructors of arity 0, pair is a constructor of arity 2, arithmetic operations, such as $+$ or $\times$ are primitives of arity 2, and `not` is a primitive of arity 1. Intuitively, constructors are passive: they may take arguments, but should ignore their shape and simply build up larger values with their arguments embedded. On the opposite, primitives are active: they may examine the shape of their arguments, operate on inner embedded values, and transform them. This difference between constants and primitives will appear more clearly below, when we define their semantics. In summary, the syntax of expressions is given below:

$$a ::= \underbrace{x \mid \lambda x.a \mid a\ a}_{\lambda\text{-}calculus} \mid c \mid \textbf{let}\ x = a\ \textbf{in}\ a \qquad c ::= \underbrace{C}_{constructors} \mid \overbrace{f}^{primitives}$$

**Implementation notes, file syntax.ml**

Expressions can be represented in OCaml by their abstract-syntax trees, which are elements of the following data-type expr:

```
type name = Name of string | Int of int;;
type constant = { name : name; constr : bool; arity : int}
type var = string
type expr =
  | Var of var
  | Const of constant
  | Fun of var * expr
  | App of expr * expr
  | Let of var * expr * expr;;
```

For convenience, we define auxiliary functions to build constants.

```
let plus = Const {name = Name "+"; arity = 2; constr = false}
let times = Const {name = Name "*"; arity = 2; constr = false}
let int n = Const {name = Int n; arity = 0; constr = true};;
```

Here is a sample program.

```
let e =
  App (Fun ("x", App (App (times, Var "x"), Var "x")),
       App (Fun ("x", App (App (plus, Var "x"), int 1)),
            int 2));;
```

Of course, a full implementation should also provide a lexer and a parser, so that the expression e could be entered using the concrete syntax $(\lambda x.x * x)\ ((\lambda x.x + 1)\ 2)$ and be automatically transformed into the abstract syntax tree above.

## 2.3 The Dynamic Semantics of Core ML

Giving the syntax of a programming language is a prerequisite to the definition of the language, but does not define the language itself. The syntax of a language describes the set of sentences that are well-formed expressions and programs that are acceptable inputs. However, the syntax of the language does not determine how these expressions are to be computed, nor what they *mean*. For that purpose, we need to define the *semantics* of the language.

(As a counter example, if one uses a sample of programs only as a pool of inputs to experiment with some pretty printing tool, it does not make sense to talk about the semantics of these programs.)

There are two main approaches to defining the semantics of programming languages: the simplest, more intuitive way is to give an *operational semantics*, which amounts to describing the computation process. It relates programs —as syntactic objects— between one another, closely following the evaluation steps. Usually, this models rather fairly the evaluation of programs on real computers. This level of description is both appropriate and convenient to prove properties about the evaluation, such as confluence or type soundness. However, it also contains many low-level details that makes other kinds of properties harder to prove. This approach is somehow too concrete —it is sometimes said to be "too syntactic". In particular, it does not explain well what programs really are.

The alternative is to give a *denotational semantics* of programs. This amounts to building a mathematical structure whose objects, called *domains*, are used to represent the meanings of programs: every program is then mapped to one of these objects. The denotational semantics is much more abstract. In principle, it should not use any reference to the syntax of programs, not even to their evaluation process. However, it is often difficult to build the mathematical domains that are used as the meanings of programs. In return, this semantics may allow to prove difficult properties in an extremely concise way.

The denotational and operational approaches to semantics are actually complementary. Hereafter, we only consider operational semantics, because we will focus on the evaluation process and its correctness.

In general, operational semantics relates programs to answers describing the result of their evaluation. Values are the subset of answers expected from *normal* evaluations.

A particular case of operational semantics is called a *reduction* semantics. Here, answers are a subset of programs and the semantic relation is defined as the transitive closure of a small-step internal binary relation (called reduction) between programs.

The latter is often called *small*-step style of operational semantics, sometimes also called Structural Operational Semantics [59]. The former is *big-step* style, sometimes also called Natural Semantics [37].

### 2.3.1 Reduction semantics

The call-by-value reduction semantics for ML is defined as follows: values are either functions, constructed values, or partially applied constants; a constructed value is a constructor applied to as many values as the arity of the constructor; a partially applied constant is either a primitive or a constructor applied to fewer values than the arity of the constant. This is summarized below, writing $v$ for values:

$$v ::= \lambda x.a \mid \underbrace{C^n\, v_1 \ldots v_n}_{\text{Constructed values}} \mid \underbrace{c^n\, v_1 \ldots v_k}_{\text{Partially applied constants}} \qquad k < n$$

In fact, a partially applied constant $c^n\ v_1 \ldots v_k$ behaves as the function $\lambda x_{k+1}. \ldots \lambda x_n.c^k\ v_1 \ldots\ v_k\ x_{k+1}\ \ldots\ x_n$, with $k < n$. Indeed, it is a value.

**Implementation notes, file `reduce.ml`**

Since values are subsets of programs, they can be characterized by a predicate `evaluated` defined on expressions:

```
let rec evaluated = function
    Fun (_,_) -> true
  | u -> partial_application 0 u
and partial_application n = function
    Const c -> (c.constr || c.arity > n)
  | App (u, v) -> (evaluated v && partial_application (n+1) u)
  | _ -> false;;
```

The small-step reduction is defined by a set of *redexes* and is closed by congruence with respect to *evaluations contexts.*

Redexes describe the reduction at the place where it occurs; they are the heart of the reduction semantics:

$$(\lambda x.a)\ v \longrightarrow a[v/x] \qquad (\beta_v)$$
$$\textbf{let } x = v \textbf{ in } a \longrightarrow a[v/x] \qquad (Let_v)$$
$$f^n\ v_1\ \ldots v_n \longrightarrow a \qquad (f^n\ v_1\ \ldots v_n, a) \in \delta_f$$

Redexes of the latter form, which describe how to reduce primitives, are also called *delta rules.* We write $\delta$ for the union $\bigcup_{f \in \mathcal{C}^-}(\delta_f)$. For instance, the rule $(\delta_+)$ is the relation $\{(\overline{p}+\overline{q}, \overline{p+q}) \mid p, q \in I\!N\}$ where $\overline{n}$ is the constant representing the integer $n$.

**Implementation notes, file `reduce.ml`**

Redexes are partial functions from programs to programs. Hence, they can be represented as OCaml functions, raising an exception `Reduce` when there are applied to values outside of their domain. The $\delta$-rules can be implemented straightforwardly.

```
exception Reduce;;
let delta_bin_arith op code = function
  | App (App (Const { name = Name _; arity = 2} as c,
               Const { name = Int x }), Const { name = Int y })
    when c = op -> int (code x y)
  | _ -> raise Reduce;;
let delta_plus = delta_bin_arith plus ( + );;
let delta_times = delta_bin_arith times ( * );;
let delta_rules = [ delta_plus; delta_times ];;
```

The union of partial function (with priority on the right) is

```
let union f g a = try g a with Reduce -> f a;;
```

The $\delta$-reduction is thus:

```
let delta =
  List.fold_right union delta_rules (fun _ -> raise Reduce);;
```

To implement ($\beta_v$), we first need an auxiliary function that substitutes a variable for a value in a term. Since the expression to be substituted will always be a value, hence closed, we do not have to perform $\alpha$-conversion to avoid variable capture.

```
let rec subst x v a =
  assert (evaluated v);
  match a with
  | Var y ->
     if x = y then v else a
  | Fun (y, a') ->
     if x = y then a else Fun (y, subst x v a')
  | App (a', a'') ->
     App (subst x v a', subst x v a'')
  | Let (y, a', a'') ->
     if x = y then Let (y, subst x v a', a'')
     else Let (y, subst x v a', subst x v a'')
  | Const c -> Const c;;
```

Then beta is straightforward:

```
let beta = function
  | App (Fun (x,a), v) when evaluated v -> subst x v a
  | Let (x, v, a) when evaluated v -> subst x v a
  | _ -> raise Reduce;;
```

Finally, top reduction is

```
let top_reduce = union beta delta;;
```

---

The evaluation contexts $E$ describe the occurrences inside programs where the reduction may actually occur. In general, a (one-hole) *context* is an expression with a hole —which can be seen as a distinguished constant, written $[\cdot]$— occurring exactly once. For instance, $\lambda x.x\ [\cdot]$ is a context. Evaluation contexts are contexts where the hole can only occur at some admissible positions that often described by a grammar. For ML, the (call-by-value) evaluation contexts are:

$$E ::= [\cdot] \mid E\ a \mid v\ E \mid \textbf{let}\ x = E\ \textbf{in}\ a$$

We write $E[a]$ the term obtained by filling the expression $a$ in the evaluation context $E$ (or in other words by replacing the constant $[\cdot]$ by the expression $a$).

Finally, the small-step reduction is the closure of redexes by the congruence rule:

$$\text{if } a \longrightarrow a' \text{ then } E[a] \longrightarrow E[a'].$$

The evaluation relation is then the transitive closure $\stackrel{\star}{\longrightarrow}$ of the small step reduction $\longrightarrow$. Note that values are irreducible, indeed.

**Implementation notes, file `reduce.ml`**

There are several ways to treat evaluation contexts in practice. The most standard solution is not to represent them, *i.e.* to represent them as evaluation contexts of the host language, using its run-time stack. Typically, an evaluator would be defined as follows:

```
let eval_top_reduce a = try eval (top_reduce a) with Reduce -> a;;
let rec eval = function
  | App (a1, a2) ->
      let v1 = eval a1 in
      let v2 = eval a2 in
      eval_top_reduce (App (v1, v2))
  | Let (x, a1, a2) ->
      let v1 = eval a1 in
      eval_top_reduce (Let (x, v1, a2))
  | a -> eval_top_reduce a;;
```

The function `eval` visits the tree top-down. On the descent it evaluates all subterms that are not values in the order prescribed by the evaluation contexts; before ascent, it replaces subtrees bu their evaluated forms. If this succeeds it recursively evaluates the reduct; otherwise, it simply returns the resulting expression.

This algorithm is efficient, since the input term is scanned only once, from the root to the leaves, and reduced from the leaves to the root. However, this is optimized implementation is not a straightforward implementation of the reduction semantics.

If efficiency is not an issue, the step-by-step reduction can be recovered by s slight change to this algorithm, stopping reduction after each step.

```
let rec one_step = function
  | App (a1, a2) when not (evaluated a1) ->
      App (one_step a1, a2)
  | App (a1, a2) when not (evaluated a2) ->
      App (a1, one_step a2)
  | Let (x, a1, a2) when not (evaluated a1) ->
      Let (x, one_step a1, a2)
  | a -> top_reduce a;;
```

Here, contexts are still implicit, and the redex is immediately filled back into the evaluation context. However, the `one_step` function can easily be decomposed into three operations: `find_redex` that returns an evaluation context and a term, the reduction per say, and the reconstruction of the result by fill the reducts back into the evaluation context. The simplest representation of contexts is to view them as functions form terms to terms as follows:

```
type context = expr -> expr;;
let hole : context = fun t -> t;;
let appL a t = App (t, a)
let appR a t = App (a, t)
let letL x a t = Let (x, t, a)
let ( ** ) e1 (e0, a0) = (fun a -> e1 (e0 a)), a0;;
```

Then, the following function split a term into a pair of an evaluation context and a term.

```
let rec find_redex : expr -> context * expr = function
  | App (a1, a2) when not (evaluated a1) ->
      appL a2 ** find_redex a1
  | App (a1, a2) when not (evaluated a2) ->
      appR a1 ** find_redex a2
  | Let (x, a1, a2) when not (evaluated a1) ->
      letL x a2 ** find_redex a1
  | a -> hole, a;;
```

Finally, it the one-step reduction rewrites the term as a pair $E[a]$ of an evaluation context $E$ and a term $t$, apply top reduces the term $a$ to $a'$, and returns $E[a]$, exactly as the formal specification.

```
let one_step a = let c, t = find_redex a in c (top_reduce t);;
```

The reduction function is obtain from the one-step reduction by iterating the process until no more reduction applies.

```
let rec eval a = try eval (one_step a) with Reduce -> a ;;
```

This implementation of reduction closely follows the formal definition. Of course, it is less efficient the direct implementation. Exercise 1 presents yet another solution that combines small step reduction with an efficient implementation.

*Remark 2.3.1.* The following rule could be taken as an alternative for $(Let_v)$.

$$\textbf{let } x = v \textbf{ in } a \longrightarrow (\lambda x.a)\ v$$

Observe that the right hand side can then be reduced to $a[v/x]$ by $(\beta_v)$. We chose the direct form, because in ML, the intermediate form would not necessarily be well-typed.

*Example 2.3.1.* The expression $(\lambda x.(x * x))\ ((\lambda x.(x + 1))\ 2)$ is reduced to the value 9 as follows (we underline the sub-term to be reduced):

$$\begin{array}{llr} & (\lambda x.(x * x))\ \underline{((\lambda x.(x + 1)))\ 2)} & \\ \longrightarrow & (\lambda x.(x * x))\ \underline{(2 + 1)} & (\beta_v) \\ \longrightarrow & \underline{(\lambda x.(x * x))\ 3} & (\delta_+) \\ \longrightarrow & \underline{(3 * 3)} & (\beta_v) \\ \longrightarrow & 9 & (\delta_*) \end{array}$$

We can check this example by running it through the evaluator:

```
eval e;;
```

```
- : expr = Const {name=Int 9; constr=true; arity=0}
```

**Exercise 1 ((**) Representing evaluation contexts)** *Above, evaluation context were left implicit, using the runtime stack, or functions from terms to terms. This exercise proposes an explicit representation of evaluation contexts as a data structure, so that can be explored by pattern matching.*

*However, contexts are represented upside-down so that they can be held by their hole so as to provide an efficient data structure for exploring and transforming terms. This follows Huet's notion of zippers [32]. (Zippers are a systematic and efficient way of representing every step while walking along a tree. Informally, the zipper is closed when at the top of the tree; walking down the tree will open up the top of the zipper, turning the top of the tree into backward-pointers so that the tree can be rebuilt when walking back up, after some of the subtrees might have been changed.)*

*From the formal definition*

$$E ::= [\cdot] \mid E\ a \mid v\ E \mid \mathbf{let}\ x = E\ \mathbf{in}\ a$$

*we deduce the following OCaml definition:*

```
type context =
  | Top
  | AppL of context * expr
  | AppR of value * context
  | LetL of string * context * expr
and value = expr
```

*Values are a subset of expressions. However, the invariant cannot be captured directly by the type system. For simplicity, we identify values with expressions. A more secure implementation could use another type to represent values.*

*Note that the type context is linear, in the sense that constructors have at more one context subterm. This leads to two opposition representation of contexts. The naive representation of context* $\mathbf{let}\ x = [\cdot]\ a_2\ \mathbf{in}\ a3$ *is* `LetL (x, AppL (Top, a2)), a3)`. *However, we shall represent them upside-down by the term* `AppL (LetL (x, Top, a3), a2)`, *following the idea of zippers —this justifies our choice of* `Top` *rather than* `Hole` *for the empty context. This should read "a* context where the hole is below the left branch of an application node whose right branch is $a_3$ and which is itself (the left branch of) a binding of $x$ whose body is $a_2$ and which is itself at the top".

*A term* $a_0$ *can usually be decomposed as a one hole context* $E[a]$ *where* $E$ *is in many ways if we do not impose that* $a$ *is a redex. For instance, taking* $(a_1\ a_2)\ a_3$, *allows the following decompositions*

$$[\cdot][\mathbf{let}\ x = a_1\ a_2\ \mathbf{in}\ a_3] \qquad (\mathbf{let}\ x = [\cdot]\ \mathbf{in}\ a_3)[a_1\ a_2] \qquad (\mathbf{let}\ x = [\cdot]\ a_2\ \mathbf{in}\ a_3)[a_1]$$

$$(\mathbf{let}\ x = a_1\ [\cdot]\ \mathbf{in}\ a_3)[a_2]$$

*(The last decomposition is only allowed if* $a_1$ *is a value.) These decompositions are them described by the following OCaml expressions, composed of a pair whose left-hand side is the context, and whose right-hand side is the term to be placed in the hole:*

```
Hole,                            Let (x, App (a1, a2), a3))
LetL (x, Hole,           a3),    App (a1, a2)
AppL (LetL (Hole, a2),   a3),    a1
AppR (LetL (Hole, a1),   a3),    a2
```

*We can represent these term graphically:*

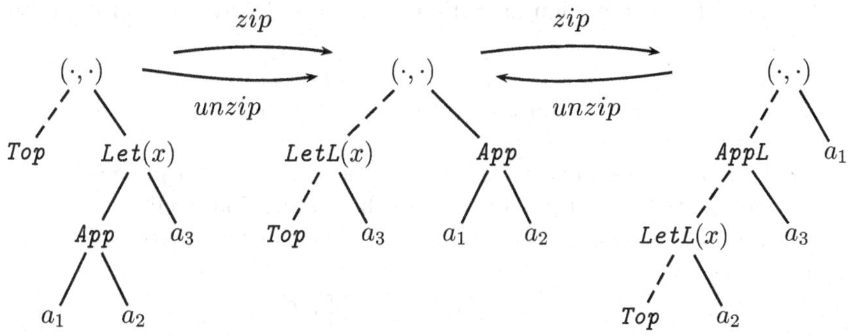


*As shown in the graph, the different decompositions can be obtained by zipping (push some of the term structure inside the context) or unzipping (popping the structure from the context back to the term). This allows a simple change of focus, and efficient exploration and transformation of the region (both up the context and down the term) at the junction.*

*Give a program* `fill` *of type* `context * expr -> expr` *that takes a pair* $(E, a)$ *of an evaluation context and an expression and returns the expression* $E[a]$ *obtained by filling the context with the expression.* Answer

*Define a function* `down` *of type* `context * expr -> context * expr` *that given a pair* $(E, a)$ *searches for a sub-context* $E'$ *of* $E$ *in evaluation position (and the residual term* $a'$ *at that position); it raises an exception* $Value$ *if* $a$ *is already a value (actually for convenience, the exception could carry the functional degree of this value,* i.e. *the number of arguments this value can be applied to while still remaining a value).* Answer

*Starting with* $(Top, a)$ *allows to find the first position* $(E_0, a_0)$ *where reduction may occur, transforming* $a_0$ *into* $a_0'$*. However, after reduction, one wish to find the next evaluation position* $(E_n, a_n)$ *given* $(E_{n-1}, a_{n-1}')$ *and knowing that* $E_{n-1}$ *was an evaluation context.*

*Define a function* `next` *that behaves as* `down`*, except that* $E'$*, may not be a sub-context of* $E$*, but also obtained by re-folding* $(E, a)$ *as much as necessary.* Answer

*Finally, define the one-step reduction, and check the evaluation steps of the program* `e` *given above and recover the function* `reduce` *of type* `expr -> expr` *that reduces an expression to a value.* Answer

*Write a pretty printer for expressions and contexts, and use it to trace evaluation steps, automatically.* Answer □

### 2.3.2 Properties of the reduction

The strategy we gave is *call-by-value*: the rule $(\beta_v)$ only applies when the argument of the application has been reduced to value. Another simple reduction strategy is *call-by-name*. Here, applications are reduced before the arguments. To obtain a call-by-name strategy, rules $(\beta_v)$ and $(Let_v)$ need to be replaced by more general versions that allows the arguments to be arbitrary expressions (in this case, the substitution operation must carefully avoid variable capture).

$$
\begin{aligned}
(\lambda x.a)\ a' &\longrightarrow a[a'/x] && (\beta_n)\\
\textbf{let } x = a' \textbf{ in } a &\longrightarrow a[a'/x] && (Let_n)
\end{aligned}
$$

Simultaneously, we must restrict evaluation contexts to prevent reductions of the arguments before the reduction of the application itself; actually, it suffices to remove $v\ E$ and $\textbf{let } x = E \textbf{ in } a$ from evaluations contexts.

$$E_n ::= [\cdot] \mid E_n\ a$$

There is, however, a slight difficulty: the above definition of evaluation contexts does not work for constants, since $\delta$-rules expect their arguments to be reduced. If all primitives are strict in their arguments, their arguments could still be evaluated first, then we can add the following evaluations contexts:

$$E_n ::= \ldots \mid (f^n\ v_1\ \ldots v_{k-1}\ E_k\ a_{k+1}\ \ldots a_n)$$

However, in a call-by-name semantics, one may wish to have constants such as `fst` that only forces the evaluation of the top-structure of the terms. This is is slightly more difficult to model.

*Example 2.3.2.* The call-by-name reduction of the example 2.3.1 where all primitives are strict is as follows:

$$
\begin{aligned}
& \underline{(\lambda x.x * x)\ ((\lambda x.(x+1))\ 2)} && \\
\longrightarrow\ & \underline{((\lambda x.(x+1))\ 2)} * ((\lambda x.(x+1))\ 2) && (\beta_n)\\
\longrightarrow\ & \underline{(2+1)} * ((\lambda x.(x+1))\ 2) && (\beta_n)\\
\longrightarrow\ & 3 * \underline{((\lambda x.(x+1))\ 2)} && (\delta_+)\\
\longrightarrow\ & 3 * \underline{(2+1)} && (\beta_n)\\
\longrightarrow\ & \underline{3 * 3} && (\delta_+)\\
\longrightarrow\ & 9 && (\delta_*)
\end{aligned}
$$

As illustrated in this example, call-by-name may duplicate some computations. As a result, it is not often used in programming languages. Instead, Haskell and other lazy languages use a *call-by-need* or *lazy* evaluation strategy: as with call-by-name, arguments are not evaluated prior to applications, and, as with call-by-value, the evaluation is shared between all uses of the same argument. However, call-by-need semantics are slightly more complicated to formalize than call-by-value and call-by-name, because of the formalization of sharing. They are quite simple to implement though, using a reference to ensure sharing and closures to delay evaluations until they are really needed. Then, the closure contained in the reference is evaluated and the result is stored in the reference for further uses of the argument.

*Classifying evaluations of programs* Remark that the call-by-value evaluation that we have defined is deterministic by construction. According to the definition of the evaluation contexts, there is at most one evaluation context $E$ such that $a$ is of the form $E[a']$. So, if the evaluation of a program $a$ reaches program $a\dagger$, then there is a unique sequence $a = a_0 \longrightarrow a_1 \longrightarrow \ldots a_n = a\dagger$. Reduction may become non-deterministic by a simple change in the definition of evaluation contexts. (For instance, taking all possible contexts as evaluations context would allow the reduction to occur anywhere.)

Moreover, reduction may be left non-deterministic on purpose; this is usually done to ease compiler optimizations, but at the expense of semantic ambiguities that the programmer must then carefully avoid. That is, when the order of evaluation does matter, the programmer has to use a construction that enforces the evaluation in the right order.

In OCaml, for instance, the relation is non-deterministic: the order of evaluation of an application is not specified, *i.e.* the evaluation contexts are:

$$\underbrace{E ::= [\cdot] \mid E\ a \mid a\ \underset{\Uparrow}{E} \mid \textbf{let } x = E \textbf{ in } a}_{\text{Evaluation is possible even if } a \text{ is not reduced}}$$

When the reduction is not deterministic, the result of evaluation may still be deterministic if the reduction is *Church-Rosser*. A reduction relation has the Church-Rosser property, if for any expression $a$ that reduces both to $a'$ or $a''$ (following different branches) there exists an expression $a'''$ such that both $a'$ and $a''$ can in turn be reduced to $a'''$. (However, if the language has side effects, Church Rosser property will very unlikely be satisfied).

For the (deterministic) call-by-value semantics of ML, the evaluation of a program $a$ can follow one of the following patterns:

$$a \longrightarrow a_1 \longrightarrow \ldots \begin{cases} a_n \equiv v & \text{normal evaluation} \\ a_n \not\longrightarrow \wedge\ a_n \not\equiv v & \text{run-time error} \\ a_n \longrightarrow \ldots & \text{loop} \end{cases}$$

Normal evaluation terminates, and the result is a value. Erroneous evaluation also terminates, but the result is an expression that is not a value. This models the situation when the evaluator would abort in the middle of the evaluation of a program. Last, evaluation may also proceed forever.

The type system will prevent run-time errors. That is, evaluation of well-typed programs will never get "stuck". However, the type system will not prevent programs from looping. Indeed, for a general purpose language to be interesting, it must be Turing complete, and as a result the termination problem for admissible programs cannot be decidable. Moreover, some non-terminating programs are in fact quite useful. For example, an operating system is a program that should run forever, and one is usually unhappy when it terminates —by accident.

**Implementation notes**

In the evaluator, errors can be observed as being irreducible programs that are not values. For instance, we can check that e evaluates to a value, while $(\lambda x.y)\ 1$ does not reduce to a value.

```
evaluated (eval e);;
evaluated (eval (App (Fun ("x", Var "y"), int 1)));;
```

Conversely, termination cannot be observed. (One can only suspect non-termination.)

### 2.3.3 Big-step operational semantics

The advantage of the reduction semantics is its conciseness and modularity. However, one drawback of is its limitation to cases where values are a subset of programs. In some cases, it is simpler to let values differ from programs. In such cases, the reduction semantics does not make sense, and one must relates programs to answers in a simple "big" step.

A typical example of use of big-step semantics is when programs are evaluated in an environment $e$ that binds variables (*e.g.* free variables occurring in the term to be evaluated) to values. Hence the evaluation relation is a triple $\rho \Vdash a \Rightarrow r$ that should be read "In the evaluation environment $e$ the program $a$ evaluates to the answer $r$."

Values are partially applied constants, totally applied constructors as before, or closures. A closure is a pair written $\langle \lambda x.a, e\rangle$ of a function and an environment (in which the function should be executed). Finally, answers are values or plus a distinguished answer `error`.

$$
\begin{aligned}
\rho &::= \emptyset \mid \rho, x \mapsto v \\
v &::= \langle \lambda x.a, \rho\rangle \mid \underbrace{C^n\ v_1 \ldots v_n}_{\text{Constructed values}} \mid \underbrace{c^n\ v_1 \ldots v_k}_{\text{Partially applied constants}} \qquad k < n \\
r &::= v \mid \texttt{error}
\end{aligned}
$$

The big-step evaluation relation (natural semantics) is often described via inference rules.

An inference rule written $\dfrac{P_1 \quad \ldots \quad P_n}{C}$ is composed of premises $P_1, \ldots P_n$ and a conclusion $C$ and should be read as the implication: $P_1 \wedge \ldots P_n \Longrightarrow C$; the set of premises may be empty, in which case the inference rule is an axiom $C$.

The inference rules for the big-step operational semantics of Core ML are described in figure 2. For simplicity, we give only the rules for constants of arity 1. As for the reduction, we assume given an evaluation relation for primitives.

Rules can be classified into 3 categories:

- Proper evaluation rules: *e.g.* Eval-Fun, Eval-App, describe the evaluation process itself.
- Error rules: *e.g.* Eval-App-Error describe ill-formed computations.
- Error propagation rules: Eval-App-Left, Eval-App-Right describe the propagation of errors.

**Fig. 2.** Big step reduction rules for Core ML

EVAL-CONST
$$\frac{\rho \Vdash a \Rightarrow v}{\rho \Vdash C^1\ a \Rightarrow C^1\ v}$$

EVAL-CONST-ERROR
$$\frac{\rho \Vdash a \Rightarrow \texttt{error}}{\rho \Vdash c\, a \Rightarrow c\ \texttt{error}}$$

EVAL-PRIM
$$\frac{\rho \Vdash a \Rightarrow v \qquad f^1\ v \longrightarrow v'}{\rho \Vdash f^1\ a \Rightarrow v'}$$

EVAL-PRIM-ERROR
$$\frac{\rho \Vdash a \Rightarrow v \qquad f^1\ v \not\longrightarrow v'}{\rho \Vdash f^1\ a \Rightarrow \texttt{error}}$$

EVAL-VAR
$$\frac{z \in dom\,(\rho)}{\rho \Vdash z \Rightarrow \rho(v)}$$

EVAL-FUN
$$\frac{}{e \vdash \lambda x.a \Rightarrow \langle \lambda x.a, \rho \rangle}$$

EVAL-APP
$$\frac{\rho \vdash a \Rightarrow \langle \lambda x.a_0, \rho_0 \rangle \qquad \rho \vdash a' \Rightarrow v \qquad \rho_0, x \mapsto v \vdash a_0 : v'}{\rho \vdash a\ a' \Rightarrow v'}$$

EVAL-APP-ERROR
$$\frac{\rho \vdash a \Rightarrow C_1\ v_1}{\rho \vdash a\ a' \Rightarrow \texttt{error}}$$

EVAL-APP-ERROR-LEFT
$$\frac{\rho \vdash a \Rightarrow \texttt{error}}{\rho \vdash a\ a' \Rightarrow \texttt{error}}$$

EVAL-APP-ERROR-RIGHT
$$\frac{\rho \vdash a \Rightarrow \langle \lambda x.a_0, \rho_0 \rangle \qquad \rho \vdash a' \Rightarrow \texttt{error}}{\rho \vdash a\ a' \Rightarrow \texttt{error}}$$

Note that error propagation rules play an important role, since they define the evaluation strategy. For instance, the combination of rules EVAL-APP-ERROR-LEFT and EVAL-APP-ERROR-RIGHT states that the function must be evaluated before the argument in an application. Thus, the burden of writing error rules cannot be avoided. As a result, the big-step operation semantics is much more verbose than the small-step one. In fact, big-step style fails to share common patterns: for instance, the reduction of the evaluation of the arguments of constants and of the arguments of functions are similar, but they must be duplicated because the intermediate state $v_1\ v_2$ is not well-formed —it is not yet value, but no more an expression!

Another problem with the big-step operational semantics is that it cannot describe properties of diverging programs, for which there is not $v$ such that $\rho \Vdash a \Rightarrow v$. Furthermore, this situation is not a characteristic of diverging programs, since it could result from missing error rules.

The usual solution is to complement the evaluation relation by a diverging predicate $\rho \Vdash a \Uparrow$.

**Implementation notes**

The big-step evaluation semantics suggests another more direct implementation of an interpreter.

```
type env = (string * value) list
and value =
  | Closure of expr * env
  (* the boolean indicates whether it is a constructor, the integer is
     the arity *)
  | Constant of constant * value list

type answer = Error | Value of value;;
let delta c l =
  match c.name with
  | "+", u::v:: _  -> u + v
  | "−", u::v:: _  -> u − v
  | _ -> raise Error

let rec eval env = function
  | Var x -> assoc x env
  | Const c -> Constant (c, [])
  | Fun (_, _) as a -> Closure (a, env)
  | App (a1, a2) ->
      begin match eval env a1, eval env a2 with
      | Constant (c, l), v ->
          let k = List.length in
          if if c.arity > k then raise Error
          else if c.arity < k then Constant (c, v::l)
          else if c.constr then Constant (c, v::l)
          else eval env (delta c (v::l))
      | _, _ -> Error
      end ;;
```

While the big-step semantics is less interesting (because less precise) than the small-steps semantics in theory, its implementation is intuitive, simple and lead to very efficient code.

This seems to be a counter-example of practice meeting theory, but actually it is not: the big-step implementation could also be seen as efficient implementation of the small-step semantics obtained by (very aggressive) program transformations.

Also, the non modularity of the big-step semantics remains a serious drawback in practice. In conclusion, although the most commonly preferred the big-step semantics is not always the best choice in practice.

## 2.4 The Static Semantics of Core ML

We start with the less expressive but simpler static semantics called *simple types*. We present the typing rules, explain type inference, unification, and only then we shall introduce polymorphism. We close this section with a discussion about recursion.

### 2.4.1 Types and programs

Expressions of Core ML are untyped —they do not mention types. However, as we have seen, some expressions do not make sense. These are expressions that after a finite number of reduction steps would be stuck, *i.e.* irreducible while not being a value. This happens, for instance when a constant of arity 0, say integer 2, is applied, say to 1. To prevent this situation from happening one must rule out not only stuck programs, but also all programs reducing to stuck programs, that is a large class of programs. Since deciding whether a program could get stuck during evaluation is equivalent to evaluation itself, which is undecidable, to be safe, one must accept to also rule out other programs that would behave correctly.

**Exercise 2 ((*) Progress in lambda-calculus)** *Show that, in the absence of constants, programs of Core ML without free variables (*i.e. *lambda-calculus) are never stuck.* □

Types are a powerful tool to classify programs such that well-typed programs cannot get stuck during evaluations. Intuitively, types abstract over from the internal behavior of expressions, remembering only the shape (types) of other expression (integers, booleans, functions from integers to integers, etc.), that can be passed to them as arguments or returned as results.

We assume given a denumerable set of type symbols $g \in \mathcal{G}$. Each symbol should be given with a fixed arity. We write $g^n$ to mean that $g$ is of arity $n$, but we often leave the arity implicit. The set of types is defined by the following grammar.

$$\tau ::= \alpha \mid g^n(\tau_1, \ldots \tau_n)$$

**Fig. 3.** Summary of types, typing environments and judgments

| | |
|---|---|
| Types | $\tau ::= \alpha \mid \tau \to \tau \mid g^n(\tau_1, \ldots \tau_n)$ |
| Typing environments | $A ::= \emptyset \mid A, z : \tau$ <br> $z ::= x \mid c$ |
| Typing judgments | $A \vdash a : \tau$ |

**Fig. 4.** Typing rules for simple types

Var-Const
$$\frac{z \in dom\,(A)}{A \vdash x : A(z)}$$

Fun
$$\frac{A, x : \tau \vdash a : \tau'}{A \vdash \lambda x.a : \tau \to \tau'}$$

App
$$\frac{A \vdash a : \tau' \to \tau \qquad A \vdash a' : \tau'}{A \vdash a\ a' : \tau}$$

Indeed, functional types, *i.e.* the type of functions play a crucial role. Thus, we assume that there is a distinguished type symbol of arity 2, the right arrow "$\to$" in $\mathcal{G}$; we also write $\tau \to \tau'$ for $\to(\tau, \tau')$. We write $ftv(\tau)$ the set of type variables occurring in $\tau$.

Types of programs are given under typing assumptions, also called *typing environments*, which are partial mappings from program variables and constants to types. We use letter $z$ for either a variable $x$ or a constant $c$. We write $\emptyset$ for the empty typing environment and $A, x : \tau$ for the function that behaves as $A$ except for $x$ that is mapped to $\tau$ (whether or not $x$ is in the domain of $A$). We also assume given an environment $A_0$ that assigns types to constants. The typing of programs is represented by a ternary relation, written $A \vdash a : \tau$ and called *typing judgments*, between type environments $A$, programs $a$, and types $\tau$. We summarize all these definitions (expanding the arrow types) in figure 3.

Typing judgments are defined as the smallest relation satisfying the inference rules of figure 4. (See 2.3.3 for an introduction to inference rules)

Closed programs are typed the initial environment $A_0$. Of course, we must assume that the type assumptions for constants are consistent with their arities. This is the following asumption.

**Assumption 0 (Initial environment)** *The initial type environment $A_0$ has the set of constants for domain, and respects arities. That is, for any $C^n \in dom\,(A_0)$ then $A_0(C^n)$ is of the form $\tau_1 \to \ldots \tau_n \to \tau_0$.*

Type soundness asserts that well-typed programs cannot go wrong. This actually results from two stronger properties, that (1) reduction preserves typings, and (2) well-typed programs that are not values can be further reduced. Of course, those results can be only proved if the types of constants and their semantics (*i.e.* their associated delta-rules) are chosen accordingly.

To formalize soundness properties it is convenient to define a relation $\sqsubseteq$ on programs to mean the preservation of typings:

$$(a \sqsubseteq a') \iff \forall(A, \tau)(A \vdash a : \tau \Longrightarrow A \vdash a' : \tau)$$

The relation $\sqsubseteq$ relates the set of typings of two programs programs, regardless of their dynamic properties.

The preservation of typings can then be stated as $\sqsubseteq$ being a smaller relation than reduction. Of course, we must make the following assumptions enforcing consistency between the types of constants and their semantics:

**Assumption 1 (Subject reduction for constants)** *The $\delta$-reduction preserves typings,* i.e., $(\delta) \subseteq (\sqsubseteq)$.

**Theorem 2.4.1 (Subject reduction).** *Reduction preserves typings*

**Assumption 2 (Progress for constants)** *The $\delta$-reduction is well-defined. If $A_0 \vdash f^n\ v_1\ \ldots v_n : \tau$, then $f^n\ v_1\ \ldots v_n \in dom\,(\delta)_f$*

**Theorem 2.4.2 (Progress).** *Programs that are well-typed in the initial environment are either values or can be further reduced.*

*Remark 2.4.1.* We have omitted the Let-nodes from expressions. With simple types, we can use the syntactic sugar **let** $x = a_1$ **in** $a_2 \triangleq (\lambda x.a_2)\ a_1$. Hence, we could derived the following typing rule, so as to type those nodes directly:

$$\text{LET-MONO}\quad \frac{A \vdash a_1 : \tau_1 \qquad A, x : \tau_1 \vdash a_2 : \tau_2}{A \vdash \textbf{let } x = a_1 \textbf{ in } a_2 : \tau}$$

### 2.4.2 Type inference

We have seen that well-typed terms cannot get stuck, but can we check whether a given term is well-typed? This is the role of type inference. Moreover, type inference will characterize all types that can be assigned to a well-typed term.

The problem of type inference is: *given a type environment $A$, a term $a$, and a type $\tau$, find all substitutions $\theta$ such that $\theta(A) \vdash a : \theta(\tau)$.* A solution $\theta$ is a principal solution of a problem $\mathcal{P}$ if all other solutions are instances of $\theta$, *i.e.* are of the form $\theta' \circ \theta$ for some substitution $\theta'$.

**Theorem 2.4.3 (principal types).** *The ML type inference problem admits principal solutions. That is, any solvable type-inference problem admits a principal solution.*

Moreover, there exists an algorithm that, given any type-inference problem, either succeeds and returns a principal solution or fails if there is no solution.

Usually, the initial type environment $A_0$ is closed, *i.e.* it has no free type variables. Hence, finding a principal type for a closed program $a$ in the initial type environment is the same problem as finding a principal solution to the type inference problem $(A, a, \alpha)$.

**Fig. 5.** Simplification of type inference problems

I-VAR-FAIL
$$\frac{A \triangleright x : \tau}{\bot} \quad \text{if } x \notin dom\,(A)$$

I-VAR
$$\frac{A \triangleright x : \tau}{A(x) \doteq \tau} \quad \text{if } x \in dom\,(A)$$

I-FUN
$$\frac{A \triangleright \lambda x.a : \tau}{\exists \alpha_1, \alpha_2. (A, x : \alpha_1 \triangleright a : \alpha_2 \wedge \tau \doteq \alpha_1 \to \alpha_2)} \quad \alpha_1, \alpha_2 \notin ftv(\tau) \cup ftv(A)$$

I-APP
$$\frac{A \triangleright a_1\, a_2 : \tau}{\exists \alpha. (A \triangleright a_1 : \alpha \to \tau \wedge A \triangleright a_2 : \alpha)} \quad \alpha \notin ftv(\tau) \cup ftv(A)$$

*Remark 2.4.2.* There is a variation to the type inference problem called *typing inference: given a term a, find the smallest type environment A and the smallest type $\tau$ such that $A \vdash a : \tau$.* ML does not have principal typings.

In the rest of this section, we show how to compute principal solutions to type inference problems. We first introduce a notation $A \triangleright a : \tau$ for type inference problems. Note that $A \triangleright a : \tau$ does not mean $A \vdash a : \tau$. The former is a (notation for a) triple while the latter is the assertion that some property holds for this triple. A substitution $\theta$ is a solution to the type inference problem $A \triangleright a : \tau$ if $\theta(A) \vdash a : \theta(\tau)$. A key property of type inference problems is that their set of solutions are closed by instantiation (*i.e.* left-composition with an arbitrary substitution). This results from a similar property for typing judgments: if $A \vdash a : \tau$, then $\theta(A) \vdash a : \theta(\tau)$ for any substitution $\theta$.

This property allows to treat type inference problems as *constraint problems*, which are a generalization of *unification problems*. The constraint problems of interest here, written with letter $U$, are of one the following form.

$$U ::= \underbrace{A \triangleright a : \tau}_{\text{typing problem}} \mid \underbrace{\tau_1 \doteq \ldots \tau_n}_{\text{multi-equation}} \mid U \wedge U \mid \exists \bar{\alpha}. U \mid \bot \mid \top$$

The two first cases are type inference problems and multi-equations (unification problems); the other forms are conjunctions of constraint problems, and the existential quantification problem. For convenience, we also introduce a trivial problem $\top$ and an unsolvable problem $\bot$, although these are definable.

It is convenient to identify constraint problems modulo the following equivalences, which obviously preserve the sets of solutions: the symbol $\wedge$ is commutative and associative. The constraint problem $\bot$ is absorbing and $\top$ is neutral for $\wedge$, that is $U \wedge \bot = \bot$ and $U \wedge \top = \top$. We also treat $\exists \alpha. U$ modulo renaming of bound variables, and extrusion of quantifiers; that is, if $\alpha$ is not free in $U$ then $\exists \alpha'. U = \exists \alpha. U[\alpha/\alpha']$ and $U \wedge \exists \alpha. U' = \exists \alpha. (U \wedge U')$.

Type inference can be implemented by a system of rewriting rules that reduces any type inference problem to a unification problem (a constraint problem that does not constraint any type inference problem). In turns, type inference problems can then be resolved using standard algorithms (and also given by rewriting rules on unificands). Rewriting rules on unificands are written either $U \longrightarrow U'$ (or $\dfrac{U}{U'}\rightsquigarrow$) and should be read "$U$ rewrites to $U'$". Each rule should preserve the set of solutions, so as to be sound and complete.

The rules for type inference are given in figure 5. Applied in any order, they reduce any typing problem to a unification problem. (Indeed, every rule decomposes a type inference problem to smaller ones, where the size is measured by the height of the program expression.)

For Let-bindings, we can either treat them as syntactic sugar and the rule Let-Sugar or use the simplification rule derived from the rule Let-Mono:

Let-Sugar
$$\frac{A \triangleright \textbf{let } x = a_1 \textbf{ in } a_2 : \tau}{A \triangleright (\lambda x.a_2)\ a_1 : \tau}\rightsquigarrow$$

Let-Mono
$$\frac{A \triangleright \textbf{let } x = a_1 \textbf{ in } a_2 : \tau}{\exists \alpha.\,(A \triangleright a_1 : \alpha \wedge A, x : \alpha \triangleright a_2 : \tau)}\rightsquigarrow$$

**Implementation notes, file `infer.ml`**

Since they are infinitely many constants (they contain integers), we represent the initial environment as a function that maps constants to types. It raises the exception `Free` when the requested constant does not exist.

We slightly differ from the formal presentation, by splitting bindings for constants (here represented by the global function `type_of_const`) and binding for variables (the only one remaining in type environments).

```
exception Undefined_constant of string
let type_of_const c =
  let int3 = tarrow tint (tarrow tint tint) in
  match c.name with
  | Int _ -> tint
  | Name ("+" | "*") -> int3
  | Name n -> raise (Undefined_constant n);;

exception Free_variable of var
let type_of_var tenv x =
  try List.assoc x tenv
  with Not_found -> raise (Free_variable x)
let extend tenv (x, t) = (x, t)::tenv;;
```

Type inference uses the function `unify` defined below to solved unification problems.

```
let rec infer tenv a t =
  match a with
  | Const c -> funify (type_of_const c) t
  | Var x -> funify (type_of_var tenv x) t

  | Fun (x, a) ->
      let tv1 = tvar() and tv2 = tvar() in
```

```
        infer (extend tenv (x, tv1)) a tv2;
        funify t (tarrow tv1 tv2)

    | App (a1, a2) ->
        let tv = tvar() in
        infer tenv a1 (tarrow tv t);
        infer tenv a2 tv

    | Let (x, a1, a2) ->
        let tv = tvar() in
        infer tenv a1 tv;
        infer (extend tenv (x, tv)) a2 t;;

  let type_of a = let tv = tvar() in infer [] a tv; tv;;
```

As an example:

```
  type_of e;;
```

### 2.4.3 Unification for simple types

Normal forms for unification problems are $\bot$, $\top$, or $\exists \overline{\alpha}. U$ where each $U$ is a conjunction of multi-equations and each multi-equation contains at most one non-variable term. (Such multi-equations are of the form $\alpha_1 \doteq \ldots \alpha_n \doteq \tau$ or $\overline{\alpha} \doteq \tau$ for short.) Most-general solutions can be obtained straightforwardly from normal forms (that are not $\bot$).

The first step is to rearrange multi-equations of $U$ into the conjunction $\overline{\alpha}_1 \doteq \tau_1 \wedge \ldots \overline{\alpha}_n \doteq \tau_n$ such that a variable of $\overline{\alpha}_j$ never occurs in $\tau_i$ for $i \leq j$. (Remark, that since $U$ is in normal form, hence completely merged, variables $\overline{\alpha}_1, \ldots \overline{\alpha}_n$ are all distinct.) If no such ordering can be found, then there is a cycle and the problem has no solution. Otherwise, the composition $(\overline{\alpha}_1 \mapsto \tau_1) \circ \ldots (\overline{\alpha}_n \mapsto \tau_n)$ is a principal solution.

For instance, the unification problem $(g_1 \to \alpha_1) \to \alpha_1 \doteq \alpha_2 \to g_2$ can be reduced to the equivalent problem $\alpha_1 \doteq g_2 \wedge \alpha_2 \doteq (g_1 \to \alpha_1)$, which is in a solved form. Then, $\{\alpha_1 \mapsto g_2, \alpha_2 \mapsto (g_1 \to g_2)\}$ is a most general solution.

The rules for unification are standard and described in figure 6. Each rule preserves the set of solutions. This set of rules implements the maximum sharing so as to avoid duplication of computations. Auxiliary variables are used for sharing: the rule GENERALIZE allows to replace any occurrence of a subterm $\tau$ by a variable $\alpha$ and an additional equation $\alpha \doteq \tau$. If it were applied alone, rule GENERALIZE would reduce any unification problem into one that only contains small terms, *i.e.* terms of size one.

In order to obtain maximum sharing, non-variable terms should never be copied. Hence, rule DECOMPOSE requires that one of the two terms to be decomposed is a small term—which is the one used to preserve sharing. In case neither one is a small term, rule GENERALIZE can always be applied, so that

**Fig. 6.** Unification rules for simple types

MERGE
$$\frac{\alpha \doteq e_1 \wedge \alpha \doteq e_2}{\alpha \doteq e_1 \doteq e_2}\rightsquigarrow$$

DECOMPOSE
$$\frac{g(\alpha_i^{i\in I}) \doteq g(\tau_i^{i\in I}) \doteq e}{g(\alpha_i^{i\in I}) \doteq e \wedge \bigwedge^{i\in I} (\alpha_i \doteq \tau_i)}\rightsquigarrow$$

FAIL if $g_1 \neq g_2$
$$\frac{g_1(\overline{\tau}_1) \doteq g_2(\overline{\tau}_2) \doteq e}{\bot}\rightsquigarrow$$

GENERALIZE if $\tau_0 \notin \mathcal{V}$ and $\alpha \notin ftv(g(\overline{\alpha}, \tau_0, \overline{\tau}')) \cup ftv(e)$
$$\frac{g(\overline{\tau}, \tau_0, \overline{\tau}') \doteq e}{\exists \alpha. \left(g(\overline{\tau}, \alpha, \overline{\tau}') \doteq e \wedge \alpha \doteq \tau_0\right)}\rightsquigarrow$$

TRIVIAL
$$\frac{\alpha \doteq \alpha \doteq e}{\alpha \doteq e}\rightsquigarrow$$

CYCLE
if $\alpha_{i+1} \in ftv(e_i), \alpha_1 \in \tau, \tau \in e_n \setminus \mathcal{V}$
$$\bigwedge_{i=1}^{n} (\alpha_i \doteq e_i) \longrightarrow \bot$$

eventually one of them will become a small term. Relaxing this constraint in the DECOMPOSE rule would still preserve the set of solutions, but it could result in unnecessarily duplication of terms.

Each of these rules except (the side condition of) the CYCLE rule have a constant cost. Thus, to be efficient, checking that the CYCLE rule does not apply should preferably be postponed to the end. Indeed, this can then be done efficiently, once for all, in linear time on the size of the whole system of equations.

Note that rules for solving unificands can be applied in any order. They will always produce the same result, and more or less as efficiently. However, in case of failure, the algorithm should also help the user and report intelligible type-error messages. Typically, the last typing problem that was simplified will be reported together with an unsolvable subset of the remaining unification problem. Therefore, error messages completely depend on the order in which type inference and unification problems are reduced. This is actually an important matter in practice and one should pick a strategy that will make error report more pertinent. However, there does not seem to be an agreement on a best strategy, so far.

**Implementation notes, file `unify.ml`**

Before we describe unification itself, we must consider the representation of types and unificands carefully. As we shall see below, the two definitions are interleaved: unificands are pointers between types, and types can be represented by short types (of height at most 1) whose leaves are variables constrained to be equal to some other types.

More precisely, a multi-equation in canonical form $\alpha_1 \doteq \alpha_2 \doteq \ldots \tau$ can be represented as a chain of indirections $\alpha_1 \mapsto \alpha_2 \mapsto \ldots \tau$, where $\mapsto$ means "has the same canonical element as" and is implemented by a link (a pointer); the last term of the chain —a variable or a non-variable type— is the canonical element of all the elements of the chain. Of course, it is usually chosen arbitrarily. Conversely, a type $\tau$ can be represented by a variable $\alpha$ and an equation $\alpha \doteq \tau$, *i.e.* an indirection $\alpha \mapsto \tau$.

A possible implementation for types in OCaml is:

```
type type_symbol = Tarrow | Tint
type texp = { mutable texp : node; mutable mark : int }
and node = Desc of desc | Link of texp
and desc = Tvar of int | Tcon of type_symbol * texp list;;
```

The field mark of type texp is used to mark nodes during recursive visits.

Variables are automatically created with different identities. This avoid dealing with extrusion of existential variables. We also number variables with integers, but just to simplify debugging (and reading) of type expressions.

```
let count = ref 0
let tvar() = incr count; ref (Desc (Tvar !count));;
```

A conjunction of constraint problems can be inlined in the graph representation of types. For instance, $\alpha_1 \doteq \alpha_2 \to \alpha_2 \wedge \alpha_2 \doteq \tau$ can be represented as the graph $\alpha_1 \mapsto (\alpha_2 \to \alpha_2)$ where $\alpha_2 \mapsto \tau$.

Non-canonical constraint problems do not need to be represented explicitly, because they are reduced immediately to canonical unificands (*i.e.* they are implicitly represented in the control flow), or if non-solvable, an exception will be raised.

We define auxiliary functions that build types, allocate markers, cut off chains of indirections (function repr), and access the representation of a type (function desc).

```
let texp d = { texp = Desc d; mark = 0 };;
let count = ref 0
let tvar() = incr count; texp (Tvar !count);;
let tint = texp (Tcon (Tint, []))
let tarrow t1 t2 = texp (Tcon (Tarrow, [t1; t2]));;
let last_mark = ref 0
let marker() = incr last_mark; !last_mark;;

let rec repr t =
  match t.texp with
    Link u -> let v = repr u in t.texp <- Link v; v
  | Desc _ -> t

let desc t =
  match (repr t).texp with
    Link u -> assert false
  | Desc d -> d;;
```

We can now consider the implementation of unification itself. Remember that a type $\tau$ is represented by an equation $\alpha \doteq \tau$, and conversely, only decomposed multi-equations are represented, concretely; other multi-equations are represented abstractly in the control stack.

Let us consider the unification of two terms $(\alpha_1 \doteq \tau_1)$ and $(\alpha_2 \doteq \tau_2)$. If $\alpha_1$ and $\alpha_2$ are identical, then so must be $\tau_1$ and $\tau_2$ and and the to equations, so the problem is already in solved form. Otherwise, let us consider the multi-equation $e$ equal to $\alpha_1 \doteq \alpha_2 \doteq \tau_1 \doteq \tau_2$. If $\tau_1$ is a variable then $e$ is effectively built by linking $\tau_1$ to $\tau_2$, and conversely if $\tau_2$ is a variable. In this case $e$ is fully decomposed, and the unification completed. Otherwise, $e$ is equivalent by rule Decompose to the conjunction of $(\alpha_1 \doteq \alpha_2 \doteq \tau_2)$ and the equations $e_i$'s resulting from the decomposition of $\tau_1 \doteq \tau_2$. The former is implemented by a link from $\alpha_1$ to $\alpha_2$. The later is implemented by recursive calls to the function `unify`. In case $\tau_1$ and $\tau_2$ are incompatible, then unification fails (rule FAIL).

```
exception Unify of texp * texp
exception Arity of texp * texp

let link t1 t2 = (repr t1).texp <- Link t2
let rec unify t1 t2 =
  let t1 = repr t1 and t2 = repr t2 in
  if t1 == t2 then () else
  match desc t1, desc t2 with
  | Tvar _, _ ->
     link t1 t2
  | _, Tvar _ ->
     link t2 t1
  | Tcon (g1, l1), Tcon (g2, l2) when g1 = g2 ->
     link t1 t2;
     List.iter2 unify l1 l2
  | _, _ -> raise (Unify (t1,t2)) ;;
```

This does not check for cycles, which we do separately at the end.

```
exception Cycle of texp list;;
let acyclic t =
  let visiting = marker() and visited = marker() in
  let cycles = ref [] in
  let rec visit t =
    let t = repr t in
    if t.mark > visiting then ()
    else if t.mark = visiting then cycles := t :: !cycles
    else
      begin
        t.mark <- visiting;
        begin match desc t with
      |   Tvar _ -> ()
      |   Tcon (g, l) -> List.iter visit l
        end;
        t.mark <- visited;
      end in
  visit t;
```

```
    if ! cycles <> [] then raise (Cycle !cycles);;
  let funify t1 t2 = unify t1 t2; acyclic t1;;
```

For instance, the following unification problems has only recursive solutions, which is detected by `cycle`;

```
  let x = tvar() in funify x (tarrow x x);;
```

```
  Uncaught exception:
  Cycle [{texp= Desc ...; mark=...}; ...].
```

**Exercise 3 ((*) Printer for acyclic types)** *Write a simple pretty printer for acyclic types (using variable numbers to generate variable names).* Answer □

### 2.4.4 Polymorphism

So far, we have only considered simple types, which do not allow any form of polymorphism. This is often bothersome, since a function such as the identity $\lambda x.x$ of type $\alpha \rightarrow \alpha$ should intuitively be applicable to any value. Indeed, binding the function to a name $f$, one could expect to be able to reuse it several times, and with different types, as in **let** $f = \lambda x.x$ **in** $f(\lambda x.(x + f\ 1))$. However, this expression does not typecheck, since while any type $\tau$ can be chosen for $\alpha$ only one choice can be made for the whole program.

One of the most interesting features of ML is its simple yet expressive form of polymorphism. ML allows type scheme to be assigned to let-bound variables that are the carrier of ML polymorphism.

A type scheme is a pair written $\forall \overline{\alpha}.\tau$ of a set of variables $\overline{\alpha}$ and a type $\tau$. We identify $\tau$ with the empty type scheme $\forall.\tau$. We use the letter $\sigma$ to represent type schemes. An instance of a type scheme $\forall \overline{\alpha}.\tau$ is a type of the form $\tau[\overline{\tau}'/\overline{\alpha}]$ obtained by a simultaneous substitution in $\tau$ of all quantified variables $\overline{\alpha}$ by simple types $\overline{\tau}'$ in $\tau$. (Note that the notation $\tau[\overline{\alpha}/\overline{\tau}']$ is an abbreviation for $(\overline{\alpha} \mapsto \overline{\tau}')(\tau)$.)

Intuitively, a type scheme represents the set of all its instances. We write $ftv(\forall \overline{\alpha}.\tau)$ for the set of free types variables of $\forall \overline{\alpha}.\tau$, that is, $ftv(\tau) \setminus \overline{\alpha}$. We also lift the definition of free type variables to typings environments, by taking the free type variables of its co-domain:

$$ftv(A) = \bigcup_{z \in dom\,(A)} ftv(A(z))$$

**Implementation notes, file `type-scheme.ml`**

The representation of type schemes is straightforward (although other representations are possible).

```
  type scheme = texp list * texp;;
```

**Exercise 4 ((*) Free type variables for recursive types)** *Implement the function* `ftv_type` *that computes $ftv(\tau)$ for types (as a slight modification to the function* `acyclic`*).* Answer

*Write a (simple version of a) function* `type_instance` *taking type scheme $\sigma$ as argument and returning a type instance of $\sigma$ obtained by renaming and stripping off the bound variables of $\sigma$ (you may assume that $\sigma$ is acyclic here).* Answer

*Even if the input is acyclic, it is actually a graph, and may contain some sharing. It would thus be more efficient to preserve existing sharing during the copying. Write such a version.* Answer □

So as to enable polymorphism, we introduce polymorphic bindings $z : \sigma$ in typing contexts. Since we can see a type $\tau$ as trivial type scheme $\forall\emptyset.\,\tau$, we can assumes that all bindings are of the form $z : \sigma$. Thus, we change rule VAR to:

$$\text{VAR-CONST}\quad \frac{A(z) = \forall\bar{\alpha}.\,\tau}{A \vdash z : \tau[\bar{\tau}'/\bar{\alpha}]}$$

Accordingly, the initial environment $A_0$ may now contain type schemes rather that simple types. Polymorphism is also introduced in the environment by the rule for bindings, which should be revised as follows:

$$\text{LET}\quad \frac{A \vdash a : \tau \qquad A, x : \forall(ftv(\tau) \setminus ftv(A)).\,\tau \vdash a' : \tau'}{A \vdash \mathbf{let}\ x = a\ \mathbf{in}\ a' : \tau'}$$

That is, the type $\tau$ found for the expression $a$ bound to $x$ must be generalized "as much as possible", that is, with respect to all variables appearing in $\tau$ but not in the context $A$, before being used for the type of variable $x$ in the expression $a'$.

Conversely, the rule for abstraction remains unchanged: $\lambda$-bound variables remain monomorphic.

In summary, the set of typing rules of ML is composed of rules FUN, APP from figure 4 plus rules VAR-CONST and LET from above.

**Theorem 2.4.4.** *Subject reduction and progress hold for ML.*

Type inference can also be extended to handle ML polymorphism. Replacing types by type schemes in typing contexts of inference problems does not present any difficulty. Then, the two rewriting I-FUN, I-APP do not need to be changed. The rewriting rule I-VAR can be easily be adjusted as follows, so as to constrain the type of a variable to be an instance of its declared type-scheme:

$$\frac{\begin{array}{l}\text{I-VAR}\\ \quad \text{if } \forall\alpha.\,\tau' = A(x)\\ \quad \text{and } \overline{\alpha} \cap ftv(\tau) = \emptyset\\ \quad A \triangleright x : \tau\end{array}}{\exists\alpha.\,\tau \doteq \tau'} \rightsquigarrow$$

The LET rule requires a little more attention because there is a dependency between the left and right premises. One solution is to force the resolution of the typing problem related to the bound expression to a canonical form before simplifying the unificand.

$$\frac{\begin{array}{l}\text{I-LET}\\ \quad \text{if } \alpha \notin ftv(A),\ A \triangleright a_1 : \alpha \rightsquigarrow \exists\overline{\beta}.\,U\\ \quad \text{and } U solved,\ U \neq \bot\\ \quad A \triangleright \mathbf{let}\ x = a_1\ \mathbf{in}\ a_2 : \tau_2\end{array}}{A, x : \forall\alpha, \overline{\beta}.\,\hat{U}(\alpha) \vdash a_2 : \tau_2} \rightsquigarrow$$

where $\hat{U}(\alpha)$ is a principal solution of $U$.

**Implementation notes, file `poly.ml`**

The implementation of type inference with ML polymorphism is a straightforward modification of type inference with simple types, once we have the auxiliary functions. We have already defined `type_instance` to be used for the implementation of the rule VAR-CONST. We also need a function `generalizable` to compute generalizable variables $ftv(t) \setminus ftv(A)$ from a type environment $A$ and a type $\tau$. The obvious implementation would compute $ftv(\tau)$ and $ftv(A)$ separately, then compute their set-difference. Although this could be easily implemented in linear type, we get a more efficient (and simpler) implementation by performing the whole operation simultaneously.

**Exercise 5 ((**) Generalizable variables)** *Generalize the implementation of* `ftv_type` *so as to obtain a direct implementation of* `generalizable` *variables.*
Answer □

A naive computation of generalizable variables will visit both the type and the environment. However, the environment may be large while all free variables of the type may be bound in the most recent part of the type environment (which also include the case when the type is ground). The computation of generalizable variables can be improved by first computing free variables of the type first and maintaining an upper bound of the number of free variables while visiting the environment, so that this visit can be interrupted as soon as all variables of $t$ are already found to be bound in $A$.

A more significant improvement would be to maintained in the structure of `tenv` the list of free variables that are not already free on the left. Yet, it is possible to implement the computation of generalizable variables without ever visiting `A` by maintaining a current level of freshness. The level is incremented when entering a let-binding and decremented on exiting; it is automatically assigned to every allocated variable; then generalizable variables are those that are still of fresh level after the weakening of levels due to unifications.

Finally, here is the type inference algorithm reviewed to take polymorphism into account:

```
let type_of_const c =
  let int3 = tarrow tint (tarrow tint tint) in
  match c.name with
  | Int _ -> [], tint
  | Name ("+" | "*") -> [], int3
  | Name n -> raise (Undefined_constant n);;

let rec infer tenv a t =
  match a with
  | Const c -> unify (type_instance (type_of_const c)) t
  | Var x -> unify (type_instance (type_of_var tenv x)) t

  | Fun (x, a) ->
     let tv1 = tvar() and tv2 = tvar() in
     infer (extend tenv (x, ([], tv1))) a tv2;
     unify t (tarrow tv1 tv2)

  | App (a1, a2) ->
     let tv = tvar() in
     infer tenv a1 (tarrow tv t);
     infer tenv a2 tv

  | Let (x, a1, a2) ->
     let tv = tvar() in
     infer tenv a1 tv;
     let s = generalizable tenv tv, tv in
     infer (extend tenv (x, s)) a2 t;;
let type_of a = let tv = tvar() in infer [] a tv; tv;;
```

## 2.5 Recursion

So as to be Turing-complete, ML should allow a form of recursion. This is provided by the **let rec** $f = \lambda x.a_1$ **in** $a_2$ form, which allows $f$ to appear in $\lambda x.a_1$, recursively. The recursive expression $\lambda x.a_1$ is restricted to functions because, in a call-by-value strategy, it is not well-defined for arbitrary expressions.

### 2.5.1 Fix-point combinator

Rather than adding a new construct into the language, we can take advantage of the parameterization of the definition of the language by a set of primitives to introduce recursion by a new primitive `fix` of arity 2 and the following type:

$$\texttt{fix} : \forall \alpha_1, \alpha_2. ((\alpha_1 \rightarrow \alpha_2) \rightarrow \alpha_1 \rightarrow \alpha_2) \rightarrow \alpha_1 \rightarrow \alpha_2$$

The semantics of `fix` is given then by its $\delta$-rule:

$$\texttt{fix}\ f\ v \longrightarrow f\ (\texttt{fix}\ f)\ v \qquad (\delta_{fix})$$

Since `fix` is of arity 2, the expression ($\texttt{fix}\ f$) appearing on the right hand side of the rule ($\delta_{fix}$) is a value and its evaluation is frozen until it appears in an application evaluation context. Thus, the evaluation must continue with the reduction of the external application of $f$. It is important that `fix` be of arity 2, so that `fix` computes the fix-point *lazily*. Otherwise, if `fix` were of arity 1 and came with the following $\delta$-rule,

$$\texttt{fix}\ f \longrightarrow f\ (\texttt{fix}\ f)$$

the evaluation of $\texttt{fix}\ f\ v$ would fall into an infinite loop (the active part is underlined):

$$\underline{\texttt{fix}\ f}\ v \longrightarrow f\ (\underline{\texttt{fix}\ f})\ v \longrightarrow f\ (f\ (\underline{\texttt{fix}\ f}))\ v \longrightarrow ...$$

For convenience, we may use **let rec** $f = \lambda x.a_1$ **in** $a_2$ as syntactic sugar for **let** $f = \texttt{fix}\,(\lambda f.\lambda x.a_1)$ **in** $a_2$.

*Remark 2.5.1.* The constant `fix` behaves exactly as the (untyped) expression

$$\lambda f'.(\lambda f.\lambda x.f'\ (f\ f)\ x)\ (\lambda f.\lambda x.f'\ (f\ f)\ x)$$

However, this expression is not typable in ML (without recursive types).

**Exercise 6 ((*) Non typability of fix-point)** *Check that the definition of* `fix` *given above is not typable in ML.* Answer □

**Exercise 7 ((*) Using the fix point combinator)** *Define the factorial function using* `fix` *and let-binding (instead of let-rec-bindings).* Answer □

**Exercise 8 ((**) Type soundness of the fix-point combinator)** *Check that the hypotheses 1 and 2 are satisfied for the fix-point combinator* `fix`. □

*Mutually recursive definitions* The language OCaml allows mutually recursive definitions. For example,

$$\textbf{let rec}\ f_1 = \lambda x.a_1\ \textbf{and}\ f_2 = \lambda x.a_2\ \textbf{in}\ a$$

where $f$ and $f'$ can appear in both $a$ and $a'$. This can be seen as an abbreviation for

$$\begin{array}{l}
\textbf{let rec}\ f_1' = \lambda f_2.\lambda x.\ \textbf{let}\ f_1 = f_1'\ f_2\ \textbf{in} \\
\qquad\qquad\qquad\qquad\qquad a_1 \\
\textbf{in} \\
\textbf{let rec}\ f_2' = \quad \lambda x.\ \textbf{let}\ f_2 = f_2'\ \textbf{in} \\
\qquad\qquad\qquad\qquad\ \ \textbf{let}\ f_1 = f_1'\ f_2\ \textbf{in} \\
\qquad\qquad\qquad\qquad\qquad a_2 \\
\textbf{in} \\
a
\end{array}$$

This can be easily generalize to

$$\textbf{let rec } f_1 = \lambda x.a_1 \textbf{ and } \ldots f_n \lambda x.a_n \textbf{ in } a$$

**Exercise 9 ((*) Multiple recursive definitions)** *Can you translate the case for three recursive functions?*

$$\textbf{let rec } f_1 = \lambda x.a_1 \textbf{ and } f_2 = \lambda x.a_2 \textbf{ and } f_3 = \lambda x.a_3 \textbf{ in } a$$

Answer □

*Recursion and polymorphism* Since, the expression **let rec** $f = \lambda x.a$ **in** $a'$ is understood as **let** $f =$ `fix` $(\lambda f.\lambda x.a)$ **in** $a'$, the function $f$ is not polymorphic while typechecking the body $\lambda x.a$, since this occurs in the context $\lambda f.[\cdot]$ where $f$ is $\lambda$-bound. Conversely, $f$ may be be in $a'$ (if the type of $f$ allows) since those occurrences are *Let*-bound.

Polymorphic recursion refers to system that would allow $f$ to be polymorphic in $a'$ as well. Without restriction, type inference in these systems is not decidable. [28,73].

### 2.5.2 Recursive types

By default, the ML type system does not allows recursive types (but it allows recursive datatype definitions —see Section 3.1.3). However, allowing recursive types is a simple extension. Indeed, OCaml uses this extension to assign recursive types to objects. The important properties of the type systems, including subject reduction and the existence of principal types, are preserved by this extension.

Indeed, type inference relies on unification, which naturally works on graphs, *i.e.* possibly introducing cycles, which are later rejected. To make the type inference algorithm work with recursive types, it suffices to remove the occur check rule in the unification algorithm. Indeed, one must then be careful when manipulating and printing types, as they can be recursive.

As shown in exercise 8, page 450, the fix point combinator is not typable in ML without recursive types. Unsurprisingly, if recursive types are allows, the call-by-value fix-point combinator `fix` is definable in the language.

**Exercise 10 ((*) Fix-point with recursive types)** *Check that* `fix` *is typable with recursive types.* Answer
*Use let-binding to write a shorter equivalent version of* `fix`*.* Answer □

**Exercise 11 ((**) Printing recursive types)** *Write a more sophisticated version of the function* `print_type` *that can handle recursive types (for instance, they can be printed as in OCaml, using* `as` *to alias types).* Answer □

See also section 4.2.1 for uses of recursive types in object types.

Recursive types are thus rather easy to incorporate into the language. They are quite powerful —they can type the fix-point— and also useful and sometimes required, as is the case for object types. However, recursive types are sometimes too powerful since they will often hide programmers' errors. In particular, it will detect some common forms of errors, such as missing or extra arguments very late (see exercise below for a hint). For this reason, the default in the OCaml system is to reject recursive types that do not involve an object type constructor in the recursion. However, for purpose of expressiveness or experimentation, the user can explicitly require unrestricted recursive types using the option `-rectypes` at his own risk of late detection of some from of errors —but the system remains safe, of course!

**Exercise 12 ((**) Lambda-calculus with recursive types)** *Check that in the absence of constants all closed programs are typable with recursive types.*

Answer □

### 2.5.3 Type inference *v.s.* type checking

ML programs are untyped. Type inference finds most general types for programs. It would in fact be easy to instrument type inference, so that it simultaneously annotate every subterm with its type (and let-bounds with type schemes), thus transforming an untyped term into type terms.

Indeed, type terms are more informative than untyped terms, but they can still be ill-typed. Fortunately, it is usually easier to check typed terms than untyped terms for well-typedness. In particular, type checking does not need to "guess" types, hence it does not need first-order unification.

Both type inference and type checking are verifying well-typedness of programs with respect to a given type system. However, type inference assumes that terms are untyped, while type checking assumes that terms are typed. This does not mean that type checking is simpler than type inference. For instance, some type checking problems are undecidable [57]. Type checking and type inference could also be of the same level of difficulty, if type annotations are not sufficient. However, in general, type annotations may be enriched with more information so that type checking becomes easier. On the opposite, there is no other flexibility but the expressiveness of the type system to adjust the difficulty of type inference.

The approach of ML, which consists in starting with untyped terms, and later infer types is usually called *a la Curry*, and the other approach where types are present in terms from the beginning and only checked is called *a la Church*.

In general, type inference is preferred by programmers who are relieved from the burden of writing down all type annotations. However, explicit types are not just annotations to make type verification simpler, but also a useful tool in structuring programs: they play a role for documentation, enables modular programming and increase security. For instance, in ML, the module system on top of Core ML is explicitly typed.

Moreover, the difference between type inference and type checking is not always so obvious. Indeed, all nodes of the language carry implicit type information. For instance, there is no real difference between 1 and $1 : int$. Furthermore, some explicit type annotations can also be hidden behind new constants... as we shall do below.

## Further Reading

Reference books on the lambda calculus, which is at the core of ML are [6,29]. Both include a discussion of the simply-typed lambda calculus. The reference article describing the ML polymorphism and its type inference algorithm, called W, is [16]. However, Mini-ML [14] is more often used as a starting point to further extensions. This also includes a description of type-inference. An efficient implementation of this algorithm is described in [61]. Of course, many other presentations can be found in the literature, sometimes with extensions.

Basic references on unification are [47,31]. A good survey that also introduces the notion of existential unificands that we used in our presentation is [38].

# Section 3

# The Core of OCaml

Many features of OCaml (and of other dialects of ML) can actually be formalized on top of core ML, either by selecting a particular choice of primitives, by encoding, or by a small extension.

## 3.1 Data Types and Pattern Matching

The OCaml language contains primitive datatypes such as integers, floats, strings, arrays, etc. and operations over them. New datatypes can also be defined using a combinations of named records or variants and later be explored using pattern matching — a powerful mechanism that combines several projections and case analysis in a single construction.

### 3.1.1 Examples in OCaml

For instance, the type of play cards can be defined as follows:

```
type card = Card of regular | Joker
and regular = { suit : card_suit; name : card_name; }
and card_suit = Heart | Club | Spade | Diamond
and card_name =  Ace | King | Queen | Jack | Simple of int;;
```

This declaration actually defines four different data types. The type `card` of cards is a variant type with two cases. `Joker` is a special card. Other cards are of the form `Card v` where `v` is an element of the type `regular`. In turn `regular` is the type of records with two fields `suit` and `name` of respective types `card_suit` and `card_name`, which are themselves variant types.

Cards can be created directly, using the variant tags and labels as constructors:

```
let club_jack = Card { name = Jack; suit = Club; };;
```

```
val club_jack : card = Card {suit=Club; name=Jack}
```

Of course, cards can also be created via functions:

```
let card n s = Card {name = n; suit = s}
let king s = card King s;;
```

```
val card : name -> suit -> card = <fun>
val king : suit -> card = <fun>
```

Functions can be used to shorten notations, but also as a means of enforcing invariants.

The language OCaml, like all dialects of ML, also offers a convenient mechanism to explore and de-structure values of data-types by pattern matching, also known as case analysis. For instance, we could define the value of a card as follows:

```
let value c =
  match c with
  | Joker -> 0
  | Card {name = Ace} -> 14
  | Card {name = King} -> 13
  | Card {name = Queen} -> 12
  | Card {name = Jack} -> 11
  | Card {name = Simple k} -> k;;
```

The function `value` explores the shape of the card given as argument, by doing case analysis on the outermost constructors, and whenever necessary, pursuing the analysis on the inner values of the data-structure. Cases are explored in a top-down fashion: when a branch fails, the analysis resumes with the next possible branch. However, the analysis stops as soon as the branch is successful; then, its right hand side is evaluated and returned as result.

**Exercise 13 ((**) Matching Cards)** *We say that a set of cards is compatible if it does not contain two regular cards of different values. The goal is to find hands with four compatible cards. Write a function* `find_compatible` *that given a hand (given as an unordered list of cards) returns a list of solutions. Each solution should be a compatible set of cards (represented as an unordered list of cards) of size greater or equal to four, and two different solutions should be incompatible.* Answer □

Data types may also be parametric, that is, some of their constructors may take arguments of arbitrary types. In this case, the type of these arguments must be shown as an argument to the type (symbol) of the data-structure. For instance, OCaml pre-defines the option type as follows:

```
type 'a option = Some of 'a | None
```

The option type can be used to get inject values $v$ of type `'a` into `Some`($v$) of type `'a option` with an extra value `None`. (For historical reason, the type argument `'a` is postfix in `'a option`.)

### 3.1.2 Formalization of superficial pattern matching

Superficial pattern matching (*i.e.* testing only the top constructor) can easily be formalized in core ML by the declaration of new type constructors, new constructors, and new constants. For the sake of simplicity, we assume that all datatype definitions are given beforehand. That is, we parameterize the language by a set of type definitions. We also consider the case of a single datatype definition, but the generalization to several definitions is easy.

Let us consider the following definition, prior to any expression:

$$\texttt{type}\ g(\overline{\alpha}) = C_1^g\ \texttt{of}\ \tau_i \mid \ldots C_n^g\ \texttt{of}\ \tau_n$$

where free variables of $\tau_i$ are all taken among $\overline{\alpha}$. (We use the standard prefix notation in the formalization, as opposed to OCaml postfix notation.)

This amounts to introducing a new type symbol $g_f$ of arity given by the length of $\overline{\alpha}$, $n$ unary constructors $C^g_1, \dots C^g_n$, and a primitive $f^g$ of arity $n+1$ with the following $\delta$-rule:

$$f^g\ (C^g_k\ \ v)\ v_1\ \dots v_k\ \dots v_n \longrightarrow v_k\ v \qquad (\delta_g)$$

The typing environment must also be extended with the following type assumptions:

$$\begin{array}{ll} C^g_i & : \forall \overline{\alpha}.\, \tau_i \to g(\overline{\alpha}) \\ f^g & : \forall \overline{\alpha}, \beta.\, g(\overline{\alpha}) \to (\tau_1 \to \beta) \to \dots (\tau_n \to \beta) \to \beta \end{array}$$

Finally, it is convenient to add the *syntactic sugar*

$$\mathtt{match}\ a\ \mathtt{with}\ C^g_1\ (x) \Rightarrow a_1 \dots \mid C^g_n\ (x) \Rightarrow a_n$$

for

$$f^g\ a\ (\lambda x.a_1) \dots (\lambda x.a_n)$$

**Exercise 14 ((***) Type soundness for data-types)** *Check that the hypotheses 1 and 2 are valid.* □

**Exercise 15 ((**) Data-type definitions)** *What happens if a free variable of $\tau_i$ is not one of the $\overline{\alpha}$'s? And conversely, if one of the $\overline{\alpha}$'s does not appear in any of the $\tau_i$'s?* Answer □

**Exercise 16 ((*) Booleans as datatype definitions)** *Check that the booleans are a particular case of datatypes.* Answer □

**Exercise 17 ((***) Pairs as datatype definitions)** *Check that pairs are a particular case of a generalization of datatypes.* Answer □

### 3.1.3 Recursive datatype definitions

Note that, since we can assume that the type symbol $g$ is given first, then the types $\tau_i$ may refer to $g$. This allows, recursive types definitions such as the natural numbers in unary basis (analogous to the definition of list in OCaml!):

$$\textbf{type}\ I\!N = Zero \mid Succ\ \mathtt{of}\ I\!N$$

OCaml imposes a restriction, however, that if a datatype definition of $g(\overline{\alpha})$ is recursive, then all occurrences of $g$ should appear with exactly the same parameters $\overline{\alpha}$. This restriction preserves the decidability of the equivalence of two type definitions. That is, the problem "*Are two given datatype definitions defining isomorphic structures?*" would not be decidable anymore, if the restriction was relaxed. However, this question is not so meaningful, since datatype definitions are generative, and types (of datatypes definitions) are always compared by name. Other dialects of ML do not impose this restriction. However, the gain is not significant as long as the language does not allow polymorphic recursion, since it will not be possible to write interesting function manipulating datatypes that would not follow this restriction.

As illustrated by the following exercise, the fix-point combinator, and more generally the whole lambda-calculus, can be encoded using variant datatypes. Note that this is not surprising, since the fix point can be implemented by a $\delta$-rule, and variant datatypes have been encoded with special forms of $\delta$-rules.

Note that the encoding uses negative recursion, that is, a recursive occurrence on the left of an arrow type. It could be shown that restricting datatypes to positive recursion would preserve termination (of course, in ML without any other form of recursion).

**Exercise 18 ((**) Recursion with datatypes)** *The first goal is to encode lambda-calculus. Noting that the only forms of values in the lambda calculus are functions, and that a function take a value to eventually a value, use a datatype* `value` *to define two inverse functions* `fold` *and* `unfold` *of respective types:*

```
val fold : (value -> value) -> value = <fun>
val unfold : value -> value -> value = <fun>
```

Answer

*Propose a formal encoding* $[\![\cdot]\!]$ *of lambda-calculus into ML plus the two functions* `fold` *and* `unfold` *so that for an expression of the encode of any expression of the lambda calculus are well-typed terms.* Answer

*Finally, check that* $[\![$`fix`$]\!]$ *is well-typed.* Answer □

### 3.1.4 Type abbreviations

OCaml also allows type abbreviations declared as **type** $g(\overline{\alpha}) = \tau$. These are conceptually quite different from datatypes: note that $\tau$ is not preceded by a constructor here, and that multiple cases are not allowed. Moreover, a data type definition **type** $g(\overline{\alpha}) = C^g\ \tau$ would define a new type symbol $g$ incompatible with all others. On the opposite, the type abbreviation **type** $g(\overline{\alpha}) = \tau$ defines a new type symbol $g$ that is compatible with the top type symbol of $\tau$ since $g(\overline{\tau}')$ should be interchangeable with $\tau$ anywhere.

In fact, the simplest, formalization of abbreviations is to expand them in a preliminary phase. As long as recursive abbreviations are not allowed, this allows to replace all abbreviations by types without any abbreviations. However, this view of abbreviation raises several problem. As we have just mentioned, it does not work if abbreviations can be defined recursively. Furthermore, compact types may become very large after expansions. Take for example an abbreviation `window` that stands for a product type describing several components of windows: `title`, `body`, etc. that are themselves abbreviations for larger types.

Thus, we need another more direct presentation of abbreviations. Fortunately, our treatment of unifications with unificands is well-adapted to abbreviations: Formally, defining an abbreviation amounts to introducing a new symbol $h$ together with an axiom $h(\overline{\alpha}) = \tau$. (Note that this is an axiom and not a multi-equation here.) Unification can be parameterized by a set of abbreviation definitions $\{h(\overline{\alpha}_h) = \tau_h \mid h \in \mathcal{A}\}$ Abbreviations are then expanded during unification, but only if they would otherwise produce a clash with another symbol. This is obtained by adding the following rewriting rule for any abbreviation $h$:

$$\frac{\alpha \doteq h(\overline{\alpha}) \doteq g(\overline{\tau}) \doteq e}{\alpha \doteq \tau_h[\overline{\alpha}/\overline{\alpha}_h] \doteq g(\overline{\tau}) \doteq e} \rightsquigarrow \quad \textsc{Abbrev} \quad \text{if } g \neq h$$

Note that sharing is kept all the way, which is represented by variable $\alpha$ in both the premise and the conclusion: before expansions, several parts of the type may use the same abbreviation represented by $\alpha$, and all of these nodes will see the expansions simultaneously.

The rule Abbrev can be improved, so as to keep the abbreviation even after expansion:

$$\frac{\alpha \doteq h(\overline{\alpha}) \doteq g(\overline{\tau}) \doteq e}{\exists \alpha'. (\alpha \doteq h(\overline{\alpha}) \doteq e \wedge \alpha' \doteq \tau_h[\overline{\alpha}/\overline{\alpha}_h] \doteq g(\overline{\tau}))} \rightsquigarrow \quad \textsc{Abbrev'} \quad \text{if } g \neq h$$

The abbreviation can be recursive, in the sense that $h$ may appear in $\tau_h$ but, as for data-types, with the tuple of arguments $\overline{\alpha}$ as the one of its definition. The the occurrence of $\tau_h$ in the conclusion of rule Abbrev' must be replaced by $\tau_h[\alpha/g(\overline{\alpha})]$.

**Exercise 19 ((*) Mutually recursive definitions of abbreviations)** *Explain how to model recursive definitions of type abbreviations* **type** $h_1(\overline{\alpha}) = \tau_1$ **and** $h_2(\overline{\alpha}_2) = \tau_2$ *in terms of several single but recursive definitions of abbreviations.*

Answer □

See also Section 4.2.1 for use of abbreviations with object types.

### 3.1.5 Record types

Record type definitions can be formalized in a very similar way to variant type definitions. The definition

$$\texttt{type } g(\overline{\alpha}) = \{f_1^g : \tau_1; \ldots f_2^g : \tau_n\}$$

amounts to the introduction of a new type symbol $g$ of arity given by the length of $\overline{\alpha}$, one $n$-ary constructor $C^g$ and $n$ unary primitives $f_i^g$ with the following $\delta$-rules:

$$f_i^g\ (C^g\ v_1 \ldots v_i \ldots v_n) \longrightarrow v_i \qquad (\delta_g)$$

As for variant types, we require that all free variables of $\tau_i$ be taken among $\overline{\alpha}$. The typing assumptions for these constructors and constant are:

$$\begin{aligned} C^g &: \forall \overline{\alpha}. \tau_1 \to \ldots \tau_n \to \overline{\alpha}\ \mathrm{g} \\ f_i^g &: \forall \overline{\alpha}. g(\overline{\alpha}) \to \tau_i \end{aligned}$$

The syntactic sugar is to write $a.f_i^g$ and $\{f_1^g = a_1; \ldots f_n^g = a_n\}$ instead of $f_i^g\ a$ and $C^g\ a_1\ \ldots a_n$.

## 3.2 Mutable Storage and Side Effects

The language we have described so far is *purely functional.* That is, several evaluations of the same expression will always produce the same answer. This prevents, for instance, the implementation of a counter whose interface is a single function `next : unit -> int` that increments the counter and returns its new value. Repeated invocation of this function should return a sequence of consecutive integers —a different answer each time.

Indeed, the counter needs to memorize its state in some particular location, with read/write accesses, but before all, some information must be shared between two calls to `next`. The solution is to use mutable storage and interact with the store by so-called *side effects.*

In OCaml, the counter could be defined as follows:

```
let new_count =
 let r = ref 0 in
 let next () = r := !r+1; !r in
 next;;
```

Another, maybe more concrete, example of mutable storage is a bank account. In OCaml, record fields can be declared mutable, so that new values can be assigned to them later. Hence, a bank account could be a two-field record, its number, and its balance, where the balance is mutable.

```
type account = { number : int; mutable balance : float }
let retrieve account requested =
  let s = min account.balance requested in
  account.balance <- account.balance -. s; s;;
```

In fact, in OCaml, references are not primitive: they are special cases of mutable records. For instance, one could define:

```
type 'a ref = { mutable content : 'a }
let ref x = { content = x }
let deref r = r.content
let assign r x = r.content <- x; x
```

### 3.2.1 Formalization of the store

We choose to model single-field store cells, *i.e.* references. Multiple-field records with mutable fields can be modeled in a similar way, but the notations become heavier.

Certainly, the store cannot be modeled by just using $\delta$-rules. There should necessarily be another mechanism to produce some side effects so that repeated computations of the same expression may return different values.

The solution is to model the store, rather intuitively. For that purpose, we introduce a denumerable collection of store locations $\ell \in \mathcal{L}$. We also extend the syntax of programs with store locations and with constructions for manipulating the store:

$$a ::= \ldots \mid \ell \mid \texttt{ref}\ a \mid \texttt{deref}\ a \mid \texttt{assign}\ a\ \ a'$$

Following the intuition, the store is modeled as a global partial mapping $s$ from store locations to values. Small-step reduction should have access to the store and be able to change its content. We model this by transforming pairs $a/s$ composed of an expression and a store rather than by transforming expressions alone.

Store locations are values.

$$v ::= \ldots \mid \ell$$

The semantics of programs that do not manipulate the store is simply lifted to leave the store unchanged:

$$a/s \longrightarrow a'/s \text{ if } a \longrightarrow a'$$

Primitives operating on the store behaves as follows:

$$\begin{array}{rll} \texttt{ref}\ v/s \longrightarrow \ell/s, \ell \mapsto v & & \ell \notin dom\,(s) \\ \texttt{deref}\ \ell/s \longrightarrow s(\ell)/s & & \ell \in dom\,(s) \\ \texttt{assign}\,\ell\ \ v/s \longrightarrow v/s, \ell \mapsto v & & \ell \in dom\,(s) \end{array}$$

Hence, we must count store location among values: Additionally, we lift the context rule to value-store pairs:

$$E[a]/s \longrightarrow E[a']/s \text{ if } a/s \longrightarrow a'/s$$

*Example 3.2.1.* Here is a simple example of reduction:

$$\begin{array}{rl} & \textbf{let}\ x = \underline{\texttt{ref 1}}\ \textbf{in}\ \texttt{assign}\ x\ \ (1 + \texttt{deref}\ x)/\emptyset \\ \longrightarrow & \underline{\textbf{let}\ x = \ell\ \textbf{in}\ \texttt{assign}\ x\ \ (1 + \texttt{deref}\ x)}/\ell \mapsto 1 \\ \longrightarrow & \texttt{assign}\,\ell\ (1 + \underline{\texttt{deref}\ \ell})/\ell \mapsto 1 \\ \longrightarrow & \texttt{assign}\,\ell\ \underline{(1 + 1)}/\ell \mapsto 1 \\ \longrightarrow & \underline{\texttt{assign}\,\ell\ (2)}/\ell \mapsto 1 \\ \longrightarrow & 2/\ell \mapsto 2 \end{array}$$

*Remark 3.2.1.* Note that, we have not modeled garbage collection: new locations created during reduction by the REF rule will remain in the store forever.

An attempt to model garbage collection of unreachable locations is to use an additional rule.

$$a/s \longrightarrow a/(s \setminus \ell) \qquad \ell \notin a$$

However, this does not work for several reasons.

Firstly, the location $\ell$ may still be accessible, indirectly: starting from the expression $a$ one may reach a location $\ell'$ whose value $s(\ell')$ may still refer to $\ell$. Changing the condition to $\ell \notin a, (s \setminus \ell)$ would solve this problem but raise another one: cycles in $s$ will never be collected, even if not reachable from $a$. So, the condition should be that of the form "$\ell$ is not accessible from $a$ using store $s$". Writing, this condition formally, is the beginning of a specification of garbage collection...

Secondly, it would not be correct to apply this rule locally, to a subterm, and then lift the reduction to the whole expression by an application of the context rule. There are two solutions to this last problem: one is to define a notion of toplevel reduction to prevent local applications of garbage collection; The other one is to complicate the treatment of store so that locations can be treated locally (see [74] for more details).

In order to type programs with locations, we must extend typing environment with assumptions for the type of locations:

$$A ::= \ldots \mid A, \ell : \tau$$

Remark that store locations are not allowed to be polymorphic (see the discussion below). Hence the typing rule for using locations is simply

$$\textsc{Loc}\quad \frac{\ell : \tau \in A}{A \vdash \ell : \tau}$$

Operations on the store can be typed as the application of constants with the following type schemes in the initial environment $A_0$:

$$\begin{aligned} \texttt{ref}\ \_ &: \forall \alpha.\, \alpha \to \texttt{ref}\ \alpha \\ \texttt{deref}\ \_ &: \forall \alpha.\ \texttt{ref}\ \alpha \to \alpha \\ \texttt{assign}\ \_\ \_ &: \forall \alpha.\ \texttt{ref}\ \alpha \to \alpha \to \alpha \end{aligned}$$

(Giving specific typing rules Ref, Deref, and Assign would unnecessarily duplicate rule App into each of them)

### 3.2.2 Type soundness

We first define store typing judgments: we write $A \vdash a/s : \tau$ if there exists a store extension $A'$ of $A$ (*i.e.* outside of domain of $A$) such that $A' \vdash a : \tau$ and $A' \vdash s(\ell) : A'(\ell)$ for all $\ell \in \mathit{dom}\,(A')$. We then redefine $\sqsubseteq$ to be the inclusion of store typings.

$$(a/s \sqsubseteq a'/s') \iff \forall (A, \tau)(A \vdash a/s : \tau \Longrightarrow A \vdash a'/s' : \tau)$$

**Theorem 3.2.1 (Subject reduction).** *Store-reduction preserves store-typings.*

**Theorem 3.2.2 (Progress).** *If $A_0 \vdash a/s : \tau$, then either $a$ is a value, or $a/s$ can be further reduced.*

### 3.2.3 Store and polymorphism

Note that store locations cannot be polymorphic. Furthermore, so as to preserve subject reduction, expressions such as `ref` $v$ should not be polymorphic either, since `ref` $v$ reduces to $\ell$ where $\ell$ is a new location of the same type as the type of $v$. The simplest solution to enforce this restriction is to restrict **let** $x = a$ **in** $a'$ to the case where $a$ is a value $v$ (other cases can still be seen as syntactic sugar for $(\lambda x.a')\ a$.) Since `ref` $a$ is not a value —it is an application— it then cannot be polymorphic. Replacing $a$ by a value $v$ does not make any difference, since `ref` is not a constructor but a primitive. Of course, this solution is not optimal, *i.e.* there are safe cases that are rejected. All other solutions that have been explored end up to be too complicated, and also restrictive. This solution, known as "value-only polymorphism" is unambiguously the best compromise between simplicity and expressiveness.

To show how subject reduction could fail with polymorphic references, consider the following counter-example.

```
✗ let id = ref (fun x -> x) in (id := succ; !id true);;
```

If "id" had a polymorphic type $\forall\alpha.\tau$, it would be possible to assign to `id` a function of the less general type, *e.g.* the type `int -> int` of `succ`, and then to read the reference with another incompatible less general type `bool -> bool`; however, the new content of `id`, which is the function `succ`, does not have type `bool -> bool`.

Another solution would be to ensure that values assigned to `id` have a type scheme at least as general as the type of the location. However, ML cannot force expressions to have polymorphic types.

**Exercise 20 ((**) Recursion with references)** *Show that the fix point combinator* `fix` *can be defined using references alone (*i.e. *using without recursive bindings, recursive types* etc.*).* Answer □

### 3.2.4 Multiple-field mutable records

In OCaml references cells are just a particular case of records with mutable fields. To model those, one should introduce locations with several fields as well. The does not raise problem in principle but makes the notations significantly heavier.

## 3.3 Exceptions

Exceptions are another imperative construct. As for references, the semantics of exceptions cannot be given only by introducing new primitives and $\delta$-rules.

We extend the syntax of core ML with:

$$a ::= \ldots \mid \texttt{try}\ a\ \texttt{with}\ x \Rightarrow a \mid \texttt{raise}\ a$$

We extend the evaluation contexts, so as to allow evaluation of exceptions and exception handlers.

$$E :: \ldots \mid \texttt{try}\ E\ \texttt{with}\ x \Rightarrow a \mid \texttt{raise}\ E$$

Finally, we add the following redex rules:

$$\begin{array}{rlr} \texttt{try}\ v\ \texttt{with}\ x \Rightarrow a & \longrightarrow v & (Try) \\ \texttt{try}\ E'[\texttt{raise}\ v]\ \texttt{with}\ x \Rightarrow a & \longrightarrow \textbf{let}\ x = v\ \textbf{in}\ a & (Raise) \end{array}$$

with the side condition for the RAISE rule that the evaluation context $E'$ does not contain any node of the form (try _ with _ ⇒ _). More precisely, such evaluation contexts can be defined by the grammar:

$$E' ::= [\cdot] \mid E'\ a \mid v\ E' \mid \texttt{raise}\ E'$$

Informally, the RAISE rule says that if the evaluation of $a$ raises an exception with a value $v$, then the evaluation should continue at the first enclosing handler by applying the right hand-side of the handler value $v$. Conversely, is the evaluation of $a$ returns a value, then the TRY rule simply removes the handler.

The typechecking of exceptions raises similar problems to the typechecking of references: if an exception could be assigned a polymorphic type $\sigma$, then it could be raised with an instance $\tau_1$ of $\sigma$ and handled with the asumption that it has type $\tau_2$ —another instance of $\sigma$. This could lead to a type error if $\tau_1$ and $\tau_2$ are incompatible. To avoid this situation, we assume given a particular closed type $\tau_0$ to be taken for the type of exceptions. The typing rules are:

RAISE
$$\frac{A \vdash a : \tau_0}{A \vdash \texttt{raise}\ a : \alpha}$$

TRY
$$\frac{A \vdash a_1 : \tau \qquad A, x : \tau_0 \vdash a_2 : \tau}{A \vdash \texttt{try}\ a_1\ \texttt{with}\ x \Rightarrow a_2 : \tau}$$

**Exercise 21 ((**) Type soundness of exceptions)** *Show the correctness of this extension.* □

**Exercise 22 ((**) Recursion with exceptions)** *Can the fix-point combinator be defined with exceptions?*

Answer □

## Further Reading

We have only formalized a few of the ingredients of a real language. Moreover, we abstracted over many details. For instance, we assumed given the full program, so that type declaration could be moved ahead of all expressions.

Despite many superficial differences, Standard ML is actually very close to OCaml. Standard ML has also been formalized, but in much more details [49,48]. This is a rather different task: the lower level and finer grain exposition, which is mandatory for a specification document, may unfortunately obscure the principles and the underlying simplicity behind ML.

Among many extensions that have been proposed to ML, a few of them would have deserved more attention, because there are expressive, yet simple to formalize, and in essence very close to ML.

Records as datatype definitions have the inconvenience that they must always be declared prior to their use. Worse, they do not allow to define a function that could access some particular field uniformly in any record containing at least this field. This problem, known as polymorphic record access, has been proposed several solutions [63,55,33,35], all of which relying more or less directly on the powerful idea of row variables [71]. Some of these solutions simultaneously allow to extend records on a given field uniformly, *i.e.* regardless of the other fields. This operation, known as polymorphic record extension, is quite expressive. However, extensible records cannot be typed as easily or compiled as efficiently as simple records.

Dually, variant allows building values of an open sum type by tagging with labels without any prior definition of all possible cases. Actually, OCaml was recently extended with such variants [23]

Datatypes can also be used to embed existential or universal types into ML [39,62,51,24].

# Section 4

# The Object Layer

We first introduce objects and classes, informally. Then, we present the core of the object layer, leaving out some of the details. Last, we show a few advanced uses of objects.

## 4.1 Discovering Objects and Classes

In this section, we start with a series of very basic examples, and present the key features common to all object oriented languages; then we introduce polymorphism, which play an important role in OCaml.

*Object, classes, and types.* There is a clear distinction to be emphasized between objects, classes, and types. *Objects* are values which are returned by evaluation and that can be sent as arguments to functions. Objects only differ from other values by the way to interact with them, that is to send them messages, or in other words, to invoke their methods.

Classes are not objects, but definitions for building objects. Classes can themselves be built from scratch or from other classes by inheritance. Objects are usually created from classes by instantiation (with the `new` construct) but can also be created from other objects by *cloning* or *overriding*.

Neither classes nor objects are types. Object have object types, which are regular types, similar to but different from arrow or product types. Classes also have types. However, class types are not regular types, as much as classes are not regular expressions, but expressions of a small class language.

Classes may be in an inheritance (sub-classing) relation, which is the case when a class inherits from another one. Object types may be in a subtyping relation. However, there is no correspondence to be made between sub-classing and subtyping, anyway.

### 4.1.1 Basic examples

A class is a model for objects. For instance, a class `counter` can be defined as follows.

```
class counter = object
  val mutable n = 0
  method incr = n <- n+1
  method get = n
end;;
```

That is, objects of the class `counter` have a mutable field `n` and two methods `incr` and `get`. The field `n` is used to record the current value of the counter and is initialized to `0`. The two methods are used to increment the counter and read its current, respectively.

As for any other declaration, the OCaml system infer a principal type for this declaration:

```
class counter :
  object
    val mutable n : int
    method get : int
    method incr : unit
  end
```

The class type inferred mimics the declaration of the class: it describes the types of each field and each method of the class.

An object is created from a class by taking an instance using the `new` construct:

```
let c = new counter;;
```

```
val c : counter = <obj>
```

Then, methods of the object can be invoked —this is actually the only form of interaction with objects.

```
c#incr; c#incr; c#get;;
```

```
- : int = 2
```

Note the use of `#` for method invocation. The expression `c.incr` would assume that `c` is a record value with an `incr` field, and thus fail here.

Fields are encapsulated, and are accessible only via methods. Two instances of the same class produce different objects with different encapsulated state. The field `n` is not at all a class-variable that would be shared between all instances. On the contrary, it is created when taking an instance of the class, independently of other objects of the same class.

```
(new counter)#get;;
```

```
- : int = 0
```

Note that the generic equality (the infix operator `=`) will always distinguish two different objects even when they are of the same class and when their fields have identical values:

```
(new counter) = (new counter);;
```

```
- : bool = false
```

Objects have their own identity and are never compared by structure.

*Classes* Classes are often used to encapsulate a piece of state with methods. However, they can also be used, without any field, just as a way of grouping related methods:

```
class out =
  object
    method char x = print_char x
```

```
    method string x = print_string x
  end;;
```

A similar class with a richer interface and a different behavior:

```
class fileout filename =
  object
    val chan = open_out filename
    method char x = output_char chan x
    method string x = output_string chan x
    method seek x = seek_out chan x
  end;;
```

This favors the so-called "programming by messages" paradigm:

```
let stdout = new out and log = new fileout "log";;
let echo_char c = stdout#char c; log#char c;;
```

Two objects may answer the same message differently, by running their own methods, *i.e.* depending on their classes.

*Inheritance* Classes are used not only to create objects, but also to create richer classes by inheritance. For instance, the `fileout` class can be enriched with a method to close the output channel:

```
class fileout' filename =
  object (self)
    inherit fileout filename
    method close = close_out chan
  end
```

It is also possible to define a class for the sole purpose of building other classes by inheritance. For instance, we may define a class of `writer` as follows:

```
class virtual writer =
  object (this)
    method virtual char : char -> unit
    method string s =
      for i = 0 to String.length s -1 do this#char s.[i] done
    method int i = this#string (string_of_int i)
  end;;
```

The class `writer` refers to other methods of the same class by sending messages to the variable `this` that will be bound dynamically to the object running the method. The class is flagged `virtual` because it refers to the method char that is not currently defined. As a result, it cannot be instantiated into an object, but only inherited. The method `char` is virtual, and it will remain virtual in subclasses until it is defined. For instance, the class `fileout` could have been defined as an extension of the class `writer`.

```
class fileout filename = object
  inherit writer
  method char x = output_char chan x
  method seek pos = seek_out pos
end
```

*Late binding* During inheritance, some methods of the parent class may be redefined. Late binding refers to the property that the most recent definition of a method will be taken from the class at the time of object creation. For instance, another more efficient definition of the class `fileout` would ignore the default definition of the method `string` for writers and use the direct, faster implementation:

```
class fileout filename = object
  inherit writer
  method char x = output_char chan x
  method string x = output_string chan x
  method seek pos = seek_out pos
end
```

Here the method `int` will call the new efficient definition of method `string` rather than the default one (as an early binding strategy would do). Late binding is an essential aspect of object orientation. However, it is also a source of difficulties.

*Type abbreviations* The definition of a class simultaneously defines a type abbreviation for the type of the objects of that class. For instance, when defining the objects `out` and `log` above, the system answers were:

```
val stdout : out = <obj>
val log : fileout = <obj>
```

Remember that the types `out` and `fileout` are only abbreviations. Object types are structural, *i.e.* one can always see their exact structure by expanding abbreviations at will:

```
(stdout : < char : char -> unit; string : string -> unit >);;
```

```
- : out = <obj>
```

(Abbreviations have stronger priority than other type expressions and are kept even after they have been expanded if possible.) On the other hand, the following type constraint fails because the type `fileout` of `log` contains an additional method `seek`.

```
(log : < char : char -> unit; string : string -> unit >);;
```

### 4.1.2 Polymorphism, subtyping, and parametric classes

*Polymorphism* play an important role in the object layer. Types of objects such as `out`, `fileout` or

```
<char : char -> unit; string: string -> unit >
```

are said to be *closed*. A closed type exhaustively enumerates the set of accessible methods of an object of this types. On the opposite, an *open* object type only specify a subset of accessible methods. For instance, consider the following function:

```
let send_char x = x#char;;
```

```
val send_char : < char : 'a; .. > -> 'a = <fun>
```

The domain of send_char is an object having at least a method char of type 'a. The ellipsis .. means that the object received as argument may also have additional methods. In fact, the ellipsis stands for an anonymous row variable, that is, the corresponding type is polymorphic (not only in 'a but also in ..). It is actually a key point that the function send_char is polymorphic, so that it can be applied to *any* object having a char method. For instance, it can be applied to both stdout or log, which are of different types:

```
let echo c = send_char stdout c; send_char log c;;
```

Of course, this would fail without polymorphism, as illustrated below:

```
(fun m -> m stdout c; m log c) send_char;;
```

*Subtyping* In most object-oriented languages, an object with a larger interface may be used in place of an object with a smaller one. This property, called *subtyping*, would then allow log to be used with type out, *e.g.* in place of stdout. This is also possible in OCaml, but the use of subtyping must be indicated explicitly. For instance, to put together stdout and log in a same homogeneous data-structure such as a list, log can be coerced to the typed stdout:

```
let channels = [stdout; (log : fileout :> out)];;
```

```
val channels : out list = [<obj>; <obj>]
```

```
let braodcast m = List.iter (fun x -> x#string m) channels;;
```

The domain of subtyping coercions may often (but not always) be omitted; this is the case here and we can simply write:

```
let channels = [stdout; (log :> out)];;
```

In fact, the need for subtyping is not too frequent in OCaml, because polymorphism can often advantageously be used instead, in particular, for polymorphic method invocation. Note that reverse coercions from a supertype to a supertype are never possible in OCaml.

*Parametric classes* Polymorphism also plays an important role in parametric classes. Parametric classes are the counterpart of polymorphic data structures such as lists, sets, *etc.* in object-oriented style. For instance, a class of stacks can be parametric in the type of its elements:

```
class ['a] stack = object
  val mutable p : 'a list = []
  method push v = p <- v :: p
  method pop =
    match p with h :: t -> p <- t; h | [] -> failwith "Empty"
end;;
```

The system infers the following polymorphic type.

```
class ['a] stack :
  object
    val mutable p : 'a list
    method pop : 'a method push : 'a -> unit
  end
```

The parameter must always be introduced explicitly (and used inside the class) when defining parametric classes. Indeed, a parametric class does not only define the code of the class, but also defines a type abbreviation for objects of this class. So this constraint is analogous to the fact that type variables free in the definition of a type abbreviation should be bound in the parameters of this abbreviation.

Parametric classes are quite useful when defining general purpose classes. For instance, the following class can be used to maintain a list of subscribers and relay messages to be sent all subscribers via the message `send`.

```
class ['a] relay = object
    val mutable l : 'a list = []
    method add x = if not (List.mem x l) then l <- x::l
    method remove x = l <- List.filter (fun y -> x <> y) l
    method send m = List.iter m l
  end;;
```

While parametric classes are polymorphic, objects of parametric classes are not. The creation of an instance of a class `new` *c* must be compared with the creation of a reference `ref` *a*. Indeed, the creation of an object may also create mutable fields, and therefore it cannot safely be polymorphic. (Even if the class types does not show any mutable fields, they might have just been hidden from a parent class.)

*The type of self* Another important feature of OCaml is its ability to precisely relate the types of two objects without knowing their exact shape. For instance, consider the library function that returns a shallow copy (a clone) of any object given as argument:

```
Oo.copy : (< .. > as 'a) -> 'a
```

Firstly, this type indicates that the argument must be an object; we can recognize the anonymous row variable "`..`", which stands for "any other methods"; secondly, it indicates that whatever the particular shape of the argument is, the result type remains exactly the same as the argument type. This type of `Oo.copy` is polymorphic, the types `fileout -> fileout`, `<gnu : int> -> <gnu : int>`, or `< > -> < >` being some example of instances. On the opposite, `int -> int` is not a correct type for `Oo.copy`.

Copying may also be internalized as a particular method of a class:

```
class copy = object (self) method copy = Oo.copy self end;;
```

```
class copy : object ('a) method copy : 'a end
```

The type `'a` of `self`, which is put in parentheses, is called *self-type*. The class type of the class `copy` indicates that the class `copy` has a method `copy` and that this method returns an object with of self-type. Moreover, this property will remain true in any subclass of `copy`, where self-type will usually become a specialized version of the the self-type of the parent class.

This is made possible by keeping self-type an open type and the class polymorphic in self-type. On the contrary, the type of the objects of a class is always closed. It is actually an instance of the self-type of its class. More generally, for any class $C$, the type of objects of a subclass of $C$ is an instance of the self-type of class $C$.

**Exercise 23 ((*) Self types)** *Explain the differences between the following two classes:*

```
class c1 = object (self) method c = Oo.copy self end
class c2 = object (self) method c = new c2 end;;
```

Answer □

**Exercise 24 ((**) Backups)** *Define a class* `backup` *with two methods* `save` *and* `restore`*, so that when inherited in an (almost) arbitrary class the method* `save` *will backup the internal state, and the method* `restore` *will return the object in its state at the last backup.* Answer □

There is a functional counterpart to the primitive `Oo.copy` that avoids the use of mutable fields. The construct `{< >}` returns a copy of self; thus, it can only be used internally, in the definition of classes. However, it has the advantage of permitting to change the values of fields while doing the copy. Below is a functional version of backups introduced in the exercise 24 (with a different interface).

```
class original =
  object (self)
    val original = None
    method copy = {< original = Some self >}
    method restore =
      match original with None -> self | Some x -> x
  end;;
```

Here, the method `copy`, which replaces the method `save` of the imperative version, returns a copy of self in which the original version has been stored *unchanged.* Remark that the field `original` does not have to be mutable.

**Exercise 25 ((***) Logarithmic Backups)** *Write a variant of either the class* `backup` *or* `original` *that keeps all intermediate backups.*

*Add a method* `clean` *that selectively remove some of the intermediate backups. For instance, keeping only versions of age* $2^0$, $2^1$, ... $2^n$. □

*Binary methods* We end this series of examples with the well-known problem of binary methods. These are methods that take as argument an object (or a value containing an object) of the same type as the type of self. Inheriting from such classes in often a problem. However, this difficulty is unnoticeable in OCaml as a result of the expressive treatment of self types and the use of polymorphism.

As an example, let us consider two players: an amateur and a professional. Let us first introduce the amateur player.

```
class amateur = object (self)
  method play x risk = if Random.int risk > 0 then x else self
end;;
```

The professional player inherits from the amateur, as one could expect. In addition, the professional player is assigned a certain level depending on his past scores. When a professional player plays against another player, he imposes himself a penalty so as to compensate for the difference of levels with his partner.

```
class professional k = object (self)
  inherit amateur as super
  method level = k
  method play x risk = super#play x (risk + self#level - x#level)
end;;
```

The class `professional` is well-typed and behaves as expected.

However, a professional player cannot be considered as an amateur player, even though he has more methods. Otherwise, a professional could play with an amateur and ask for the amateur's level, which an amateur would not like, since he does not have any level information.

This is a common pattern with binary methods: as the binary method of a class $C$ expects an argument of self-type, *i.e.* of type the type of objects of class $C$, an object of a super-class $C'$ of $C$ does not usually have is an interface rich enough to be accepted by the method of $C$.

An object of a class with a binary method has a recursive type where recursion appears at least once in a contravariant position (this actually is a more accurate, albeit technical definition of binary methods).

```
class amateur : object ('a)
  method play : 'a -> int -> 'a
end
class professional : object ('a)
  method level : int
  method play : 'a -> int -> 'a
end
```

As a result of this contravariant occurrence of recursion, the type of an object that exposes a binary method does not possess any subtype but itself. For example, `professional` is not a subtype of `amateur`, even though it has more methods. Conversely, `< level : int >` is a correct subtype for an object of the class `professional` that does not expose its binary method; thus, this type has non-trivial subtypes, such as `amateur` or `professional`.

**Exercise 26 ((**) Object-oriented strings)** *Define a class* `string` *that embeds most important operations on strings in a class.*

*Extend the previous definition with a method* `concat`. Answer □

## 4.2 Understanding Objects and Classes

In this section, we formalize the core of the object layer of OCaml. In this presentation, we make a few simplifications that slightly decrease the expressiveness of objects and classes, but retain all of their interesting facets.

One of the main restrictions is to consider fields immutable. Indeed, mutable fields are important in practice, but imperative features are rather orthogonal to object-oriented mechanisms. Imperative objects are well explained as the combination of functional objects with references: mutable fields can usually be replaced by immutable fields whose content is a reference. There is a lost though, which we will discuss below. Thus we shall still describe mutable fields, including their typechecking, but we will only describe their semantics informally.

As was already shown in the informal presentation of objects and classes, polymorphism is really a key to the expressiveness of OCaml's objects and classes. In particular, it is essential that:

- Object types are *structural* (*i.e.* they structure is transparent) and use *row variables* to allow polymorphism;
- Class types are polymorphic in the type of self to allow further refinements.

Besides increasing expressiveness, polymorphism also plays an important role for type inference: it allows to send messages to objects of unknown classes, and in particular, without having to determine the class they belong to. This is permitted by the use of structural object types and row variables. Structural types mean that the structure of types is always transparent and cannot be hidden by opaque names. (We also say that object-types have structural equality, as opposed to by-name equality of data-types.) Of course, objects are "first class" entities: they can be parameters of functions, passed as arguments or return as results.

On the contrary, classes are "second class" entities: they cannot be parameters of other expressions. Hence, only existing classes, *i.e.* of known class types can be inherited or instantiated into objects. As a result, type reconstruction for classes does not require much more machinery than type inference for components of classes, that is, roughly, than type inference for expressions of the core language.

*Syntax for objects and classes* We assume three sets $u \in \mathcal{F}$ of field names, $m \in \mathcal{M}$ of method names, and $z \in \mathcal{Z}$ of class names.

To take objects and classes into account, the syntax of the core language is extended as described in fig 7. Class bodies are either new classes, written `object B end`, or expressions of a small calculus of classes that including class variables, abstraction (over regular values —not classes), and application of classes to values.

A minor difference with OCaml is we chose to bind self in each method rather than once for all at the beginning of each class body. Methods are thus of the form $\varsigma(x)\, m$ where $x$ is a binder for self. Of course, we can always see the OCaml expression **object** $(x)\, u = a; m_1 = a_1; m_2 = a_1$ **end** as syntactic sugar for **object** $u = a; m_1 = \varsigma(x)\, a_1; m_2 = \varsigma(x)\, a_1$ **end**. Indeed, the latter is easier to manipulate formally, while the former is shorter and more readable in programs.

As suggested above, type-checking objects and classes are orthogonal, and rely on different aspects of the design. We consider them separately in two different sections.

**Fig. 7.** Syntax for objects and classes

**Expressions**

$$a ::= \ldots \mid \texttt{new}\ a \mid a\#m \mid \textbf{class}\ z = d\ \textbf{in}\ a$$

**Class expressions**

$$d ::= \underbrace{\textbf{object}\ B\ \textbf{end}}_{\text{creation}} \mid \underbrace{z \mid \lambda x.d \mid d\ a}_{\text{abstraction and instantiation}}$$

**Class bodies**

$$B ::= \emptyset \mid B\ \textbf{inherit}\ d \mid B\ \underbrace{u = a}_{\text{field}} \mid B\ \underbrace{m = \varsigma(x)\, a}_{\text{method}}$$

### 4.2.1 Type-checking objects

The successful type-checking of objects results from a careful combination of the following features: structural object types, row variables, recursive types, and type abbreviations. Structural types and row polymorphism allow polymorphic invocation of messages. The need for recursive types arise from the structural treatment of types, since object types are recursive in essence (objects often refer to themselves). Another consequence of structural types is that the types of objects tend to be very large. Indeed, they describe the types of all accessible methods, which themselves are often functions between objects with large types. Hence, a smart type abbreviation mechanism is used to keep types relatively small and their representation compact. Type abbreviations are not required in theory, but they are crucial in practice, both for smooth interaction with the user and for reasonable efficiency of type inference. Furthermore, observing that some forms of object types are never inferred allows to keep all row variables anonymous, which significantly simplifies the presentation of object types to the user.

*Object types* Intuitively, an object type is composed of the row of all visible methods with their types (for closed object types), and optionally ends with a row variable (for open object types). However, this presentation is not very modular. In particular, replacing row variables by a row would not yield a well-formed type. Instead, we define types in two steps. Assuming a countable collection of row variables $\varrho \in \mathcal{R}$, raw types and rows are described by the following grammars:

$$\tau ::= \ldots \mid \langle \rho \rangle \qquad \rho ::= 0 \mid \varrho \mid m : \tau ; \rho$$

This prohibits row variables to be used anywhere else but at the end of an object type. Still, some raw types do not make sense, and should be rejected. For instance, a row with a repeated label such as $(m : \tau; m : \tau'; \rho)$ should be rejected as ill-formed. Other types such as $\langle m : \tau; \rho \rangle \to \langle \rho \rangle$ should also be ruled out since replacing $\rho$ by $m : \tau'; \rho$ would produce an ill-formed type. Indeed, well-formedness should be preserved by well-formed substitutions. A modular criteria is to sort raw types by assigning to each row a set of labels that it should not define, and by assigning to a toplevel row $\rho$ (one appearing immediately under the type constructor $\langle\cdot\rangle$) the sort $\emptyset$.

Then, types are the set of well-sorted raw types. Furthermore, rows are considered modulo left commutation of fields. That is, $m : \tau; (m' : \tau'; \rho)$ is equal to $m' : \tau'; (m : \tau; \rho)$. For notational convenience, we assume that $(m : \_; \_)$ binds tighter to the right, so we simply write $(m : \tau; m' : \tau'; \rho)$.

*Remark 4.2.1.* Object types are actually similar to types for (non-extensible) polymorphic records: polymorphic record access corresponds to message invocation; polymorphic record extension is not needed here, since OCaml class-based objects are not extensible. Hence, some simpler kinded approach to record types can also be used [55]. (See end of Section 3, page 463 for more references on polymorphic records.)

*Message invocation* Typing message invocation can be described by the following typing rule:

$$\textsc{Message}\quad \frac{A \vdash a : \langle m : \tau; \rho\rangle}{A \vdash a\#m : \tau}$$

That is, if an expression $a$ is an object with a method $m$ of type $\tau$ and maybe other methods (captured by the row $\rho$), then the expression $a\#m$ is well-typed and has type $\tau$.

However, instead of rule Message, we prefer to treat message invocation $(a\#m)$ as the application of a primitive $(\_\#m)$ to the expression $a$. Thus, we assume that the initial environment contains the collection of assumptions $((\_.m) : \forall \alpha, \varrho. \langle m : \alpha; \varrho\rangle \to \alpha)^{m \in \mathcal{M}}$. We so take advantage of the parameterization of the language by primitives and avoid the introduction of new typing rules.

*Type inference for object types* Since we have not changed the set of expressions, the problem of type inference (for message invocation) reduces to solving unification problems, as before. However, types are now richer and include object types and rows. So type inference reduces to unification with those richer types.

The constraint that object types must be well-sorted significantly limits the application of left-commutativity equations and, as a result, solvable unification problems possess principal solutions. Furthermore, the unification algorithm for types with object-types can be obtained by a simple modification of the algorithm for simple types.

**Exercise 27 ((**) Object types)** *Check that the rewriting rules preserves the sorts.* □

**Fig. 8.** Unification for object types

Use rules of table 6 where FAIL excludes pairs composed of two symbols of the form $(m : \_; \_)$. and add the following rule:

MUTE

$$\frac{(m_1 : \alpha_1; \varrho_1) \doteq (m_2 : \alpha_2; \varrho_2) \doteq e}{\exists \varrho. (m_1 : \alpha_1; m_2 : \alpha_2; \varrho) \doteq e \wedge \varrho_1 \doteq (m_2 : \alpha_2; \varrho) \wedge \varrho_2 \doteq (m_1 : \alpha_1; \varrho)} \quad \text{if } m_1 \neq m_2 \text{ and } \alpha \notin \{\alpha_1, \alpha_2\} \cup ftv(e)$$

*Anonymous row variables* In fact, OCaml uses yet another restriction on types, which is not mandatory but quite convenient in practice, since it avoids showing row variables to the user. This restriction is global: in any unificand we forces any two rows ending with the same row variable to be equal. Such unificands can always may be written as

$$U \wedge \bigwedge^{i \in I} \left(\exists \varrho_i . \langle \overline{m_i : \tau_i}; \varrho_i \rangle \doteq e_i\right)$$

where $U$, all $\tau_i$'s and $e_i$'s do not contain any row variable. In such a case, we may abbreviate $\exists \varrho_i . \langle \overline{m_i : \tau_i}; \varrho_i \rangle \doteq e_i$ as $\langle m_i : \tau_i; 1 \rangle \doteq e$, using an anonymous row variable 1 instead of $\varrho$.

It is important to note that the property can always be preserved during simplification of unification problems.

**Exercise 28 ((**) Unification for object types)** *Give simplification rules for restricted unification problems that maintain the problem in a restricted form (using anonymous row variables).* Answer □

An alternative presentation of anonymous row variables is to use kinded types instead: The equation $\alpha \doteq \langle \overline{m : \tau}; 1 \rangle$ can be replaced by a kind constraint $\alpha :: \langle \overline{m : \tau}; 1 \rangle$ (then $\alpha \doteq \langle \overline{m : \tau}; 0 \rangle$ is also replaced by $\alpha :: \langle \overline{m : \tau}; 0 \rangle$).

*Recursive types* Object types may be recursive. Recursive types appear with classes that return self or that possess binary methods; they also often arise with the combination of objects that can call one another. Unquestionably, recursive types are important.

In fact, recursive types do not raise any problem at all. Without object types, *i.e.* in ML, types are terms of a free algebra, and unification with infinite terms for free algebras is well-known: deleting rule CYCLE from the rewriting rules of figure 6 provides a unification algorithm for recursive simple types.

However, in the presence of object types, types are no longer the terms of a free algebra, since row are considered modulo left-commutativity axioms. Usually, axioms do not mix well with recursive types (in general, pathological solutions appear, and principal unifiers may be lost.) Unrestricted left-commutativity axiom is itself problematic. Fortunately, the restriction of object types by sort constraints, which limits the use of left-commutativity, makes objects-types behave well with recursive types.

More precisely, object-types can be extended with infinite terms exactly as simple types. Furthermore, a unification algorithm for recursive object types can be obtained by removing the CYCLE rule from the rewriting rules of both figures 6 and 8.

*Remark 4.2.2.* Allowing recursive types preserves type-soundness. However, it often turns programmers' simple mistakes, such as the omission of an argument, into well-typed programs with unexpected recursive types. (All terms of the $\lambda$-calculus —without constants— are well-typed with recursive types.) Such errors may be left undetected, or only detected at a very late stage, unless the programmer carefully check the inferred types.

Recursive types may be restricted, *e.g.* such that any recursive path crosses at least an object type constructor. Such a restriction may seem arbitrary, but it is usually preferable in practice to no restriction at all.

*Type sharing* Finite types are commonly represented as trees. Recursive types, *i.e.* infinite regular trees, can be represented in several ways. The standard notation $\mu\theta.\tau$ can be used to represent the infinitely unfolded tree $\tau[\tau[\ldots/\theta]/\theta]$. Alternatively, a regular tree can also be represented as a pair $\tau \mid U$ of a term and a set of equations in canonical form. The advantage of this solution is to also represent *shared* sub-terms. For instance, the type $\alpha \to \alpha \mid \alpha \doteq \tau$ is different from the type $\tau \to \tau$ when sharing is taken into account. Sharing may be present in the source program (for instance if the user specifies type constraints;) it may also be introduced during unification. Keeping sharing increases efficiency; when displaying types, it also keeps them concise, and usually, more readable.

Moreover, type sharing is also used to keep row variables anonymous. For instance, $\langle m : \texttt{int}; \varrho\rangle \to \langle m : \texttt{int}; \varrho\rangle$, is represented as $\alpha \to \alpha$ where $\alpha \doteq \langle m : \texttt{int}; 1\rangle$. The elimination of sharing would either be incorrect or require the re-introduction of row variables.

In OCaml, type sharing is displayed using the `as` construct. A shared subterm is printed as a variable, and its equation is displayed in the tree at the leftmost outer-most occurrence of the sub-term. The last example is thus displayed as $(\langle m : \texttt{int}; 1\rangle \texttt{ as } \alpha) \to \alpha$. The previous example is simply $(\tau \texttt{ as } \alpha) \to \alpha$. The recursive type $\mu\alpha.\langle m : \texttt{int} \to \alpha\rangle$, which is represented by $\alpha$ where $\alpha \doteq \langle m : \texttt{int} \to \alpha\rangle$, is displayed as $(\langle m : \texttt{int} \to \alpha\rangle \texttt{ as } \alpha)$.

Remark that the `as` construct binds globally (while in $(\mu\alpha.\tau) \to \alpha$, the variable $\alpha$ used to name the recursive sub-term of the left branch is a free variable of the right branch).

*Type abbreviations* Although object types are structural, there are also named, so as to be short and readable. This is done using type abbreviations, generated by classes, and introduced when taking object instances.

Type abbreviations are transparent, *i.e.* they can be replaced at any time by their definitions. For instance, consider the following example

```
class c = object method m = 1 end;;
|| class c : object method m : int end
let f x = x#m in let p = new c in f p;;
```

The function f expects an argument of type $\langle m : \alpha; 1\rangle$ while p has type c. If c were a regular type symbol, the unification of those two types would fail. However, since it is an abbreviation, the unification can proceed, replacing c by its definition $\langle m : \mathtt{int}\rangle$, and finally returning the substitution $\alpha \mapsto \mathtt{int}$.

### 4.2.2 Typing classes

Typechecking classes is eased by a few design choices. First, we never need to guess types of classes, because the only form of abstraction over classes is via functors, where types must be declared. Second, the distinction between fields and methods is used to make fields never visible in objects types; they can be accessed only indirectly via method calls. Last, a key point for both simplicity and expressiveness is to type classes as if they were taking self as a parameter; thus, the type of self is an open object type that collects the minimum set of constraints required to type the body of the class. In a subclass a refined version of self-type with more constraints can then be used.

In summary, the type of a basic class is a triple $\zeta(\tau)(F; M)$ where $\tau$ is the type of self, $F$ the list of fields with their types, and $M$ the list of methods with their types. However, classes can also be parameterized by values, *i.e.* functions from values to classes. Hence, class types also contain functional class types. More precisely, they are defined by the following grammar (we use letter $\varphi$ for class types):

$$\varphi ::= \zeta(\tau)(F; M) \mid \tau \to \varphi$$

*Class bodies* Typing class bodies can first be explored on a small example. Let us consider the typing of class **object** $u = a_u; m = \varsigma(x)\, a_m$ **end** in a typing context $A$. This class defines a field $u$ and a method $m$, so it should have a class type of the form $\zeta(\tau)(u : \tau_u; m : \tau_m)$. The computation of fields of an object takes place before to the creation of the object itself. So as to prevent from accessing yet undefined fields, neither methods nor self are visible in field expressions. Hence, the expression $a_u$ is typed in context $A$. That is, we must have $A \vdash a_u : \tau_u$. On the contrary, the body of the method $m$ can see self and the field $u$, of types $\tau$ and $\tau_u$, respectively. Hence, we must have $A, x : \tau, u : \tau_u \vdash a_m : \tau_m$. Finally, we check that the type assumed for the $m$ method in the type of self is the type inferred for method $m$ in the class body. That is, *i.e.* we must have $\tau = \langle m : \tau_m; \rho\rangle$.

The treatment of the general case uses an auxiliary judgment $A \vdash B : \zeta(\tau)(F; M)$ to type the class bodies, incrementally, considering declarations from left to right. The typing rules for class bodies are given in figure 9. To start with, an empty body defines no field and no method and leaves the type of self unconstrained (rule EMPTY). A field declaration is typed in the current environment and the type of body is enriched with the new field type assumption (rule FIELD). A method declaration is typed in the current environment extended with the

**Fig. 9.** Typing rules for class bodies

EMPTY
$$\frac{}{A \vdash \emptyset : \zeta(\tau)(\emptyset;\emptyset)}$$

FIELD
$$\frac{A \vdash B : \zeta(\tau)(F;M) \qquad A \vdash a : \tau'}{A \vdash (B, u = a) : \zeta(\tau)(F \oplus u : \tau'; M)}$$

METHOD
$$\frac{A \vdash B : \zeta(\tau)(F;M) \qquad A, x : \tau, F \vdash a : \tau'}{A \vdash (B, m = \varsigma(x)\, a) : \zeta(\tau)(F; M \oplus m : \tau')}$$

INHERIT
$$\frac{A \vdash B : \zeta(\tau)(F;M) \qquad A \vdash d : \zeta(\tau)(F';M')}{A \vdash B \textbf{ inherit } d : \zeta(\tau)(F \oplus F'; M \oplus M')}$$

**Fig. 10.** Typing rules for class expressions

OBJECT
$$\frac{A \vdash B : \zeta(\tau)(F;M) \qquad \tau = \langle M; \rho\rangle}{A \vdash \textbf{object } B \textbf{ end} : \zeta(\tau)(F;M)}$$

CLASS-VAR
$$\frac{d : \forall\overline{\alpha}.\,\varphi}{A \vdash d : \varphi[\overline{\tau}/\overline{\alpha}]}$$

CLASS-FUN
$$\frac{A, x : \tau \vdash d : \varphi}{A \vdash \lambda x.d : \tau \to \varphi}$$

CLASS-APP
$$\frac{A \vdash d : \tau \to \varphi \qquad A \vdash a : \tau}{A \vdash d\, a : \varphi}$$

type assumption for self, and all type assumptions for fields; then the type of the body is enriched with the new method type assumption (rule METHOD). Last, an inheritance clause simply combines the type of fields and methods from the parent class with those of current class; it also ensures that the type of self in the parent class and in the current class are compatible. Fields or methods defined on both sides should have compatible types, which is indicated by the $\oplus$ operator, standing for compatible union.

*Class expressions* The rules for typing class expressions, described in Figure 10, are quite simple. The most important of them is the OBJECT rule for the creation of a new class: once the body is typed, it suffices to check that the type of self is compatible with the types of the methods of the class. The other rules are obvious and similar to those for variables, abstraction and application in Core ML.

Finally, we must also add the rules of Figure 11, for the two new forms of expressions. A class binding **class** $z = d$ **in** $a$ is similar to a let-binding (rule CLASS): the type of the class $d$ is generalized and assigned to the class name $z$ before typing the expression $a$. Thus, when the class $z$ is inherited in $a$, its class type is an instance of the class type of $d$. Last, the creation of objects is

**Fig. 11.** Extra typing rules for expressions

$$\textsc{Class}\quad \frac{A \vdash d : \varphi \qquad A, z : \forall(ftv(\varphi) \setminus ftv(A)).\, \varphi \vdash a : \tau}{A \vdash \textbf{class}\ z = d\ \textbf{in}\ a : \tau}$$

$$\textsc{New}\quad \frac{A \vdash d : \zeta(\tau)(F; M) \qquad \tau = \langle M; 0\rangle}{A \vdash \texttt{new}\ d : \tau}$$

typed by constraining the type of self to be exactly the type of the methods of the class (rule New). Note the difference with Object rule where the type of self may contain methods that are not yet defined in the class body. These methods would be flagged `virtual` in OCaml. Then the class itself would be virtual, which would prohibit taking any instance. Indeed, the right premise of the New rule would fail in this case. Of course, the New rule enforces that all methods that are used recursively, *i.e.* bound in present type of self, are also defined.

*Mutable fields* The extension with mutable fields is mostly orthogonal to the object-oriented aspect. This could use an operation semantics with store as in Section 3.2.

Then, methods types should also see for each a field assignment primitive $(u \leftarrow \_)$ for every field $u$ of the class. Thus the Method typing rule could be changed to

$$\textsc{Method}\quad \frac{A \vdash B : \zeta(\tau)(F; M) \qquad A, x : \tau, F, F^{\leftarrow} \vdash a : \tau'}{A \vdash (B, m = \varsigma(x)\, a) : \zeta(\tau)(F; M \oplus m : \tau')}$$

where $F^{\leftarrow}$ stands for $\{(u \leftarrow \_ : F(u) \rightarrow \texttt{unit}) \mid u \in dom\,(F)\}$.

Since now the creation of objects can extend the store, the New rule should be treated as an application, *i.e.* preventing type generalization, while with applicative objects it could be treated as a non-expansive expression and allow generalization.

*Overriding* As opposed to assignment, overriding creates a new fresh copy of the object where the value of some fields have been changed. This is an atomic operation, hence the overriding operation should take a list of pairs, each of which being a field to be updated and the new value for this field.

Hence, to formalize overriding, we assume given a collection of primitives $\{\langle u_1 = \_; \ldots; u_n = \_\rangle\}$ for all $n \in I\!N$ and all sets of fields $\{u_1, \ldots u_n\}$ of size $n$. As for assignment, rule methods should make some of these primitives visible in the body of the method, by extending the typing environment of the Method rule of Figure 9. We use the auxiliary notation $\{\langle u_1 : \tau_1; \ldots u_n : \tau_n\rangle\}^{\tau}$ for the

**Fig. 12.** Closure and consistency rules for subtyping

**Closure rules**

$$\begin{aligned}
\tau_1 \to \tau_2 \leq \tau_1' \to \tau_2' &\implies \tau_1' \leq \tau_1 \wedge \tau_2 \leq \tau_2' \\
\langle \tau \rangle \leq \langle \tau' \rangle &\implies \tau \leq \tau' \\
(m : \tau_1; \tau_2) \leq (m : \tau_1'; \tau_2') &\implies \tau_1 \leq \tau_1' \wedge \tau_2 \leq \tau_2'
\end{aligned}$$

**Consistency rules**

$$\begin{aligned}
\tau \leq \tau_1 \to \tau_2 &\implies \tau \text{ is of the shape } \tau_1' \to \tau_2' \\
\tau \leq \langle \tau_0 \rangle &\implies \tau \text{ is of the shape } \langle \tau_0' \rangle \\
\tau \leq (m : \tau_1; \tau_2) &\implies \tau \text{ is of the shape } (m : \tau_1'; \tau_2') \\
\tau \leq \mathtt{Abs} &\implies \tau = \mathtt{Abs} \\
\tau \leq \alpha &\implies \tau = \alpha
\end{aligned}$$

typing assumption

$$(\{\langle u_1 = \_; \ldots u_n = \_\rangle\} : \tau_1 \to \ldots \tau_n \to \tau)$$

and $F \star \tau$ the typing environment $\bigcup_{F' \subset F} \{\langle F' \rangle\}^\tau$. Then, the new version of the METHOD rule is:

$$\textsc{Method}\quad \frac{A \vdash B : \zeta(\tau)(F; M) \qquad A, x : \tau, F, F \star \tau \vdash a : \tau'}{A \vdash (B, m = \varsigma(x)\, a) : \zeta(\tau)(F; M \oplus m : \tau')}$$

*Subtyping* Since uses of subtyping are explicit, they do not raise any problem for type inference. In fact, subtyping coercions can be typed as applications of primitives. We assume a set of primitives $(\_ : \tau_1 :> \tau_2)$ of respective type scheme $\forall \bar{\alpha}. \tau_1 \to \tau_2$ for all pairs of types such that $\tau_1 \leq \tau_2$. Note that the types $\tau_1$ and $\tau_2$ used here are given and not inferred.

The subtyping relation $\leq$ is standard. It is structural, covariant for object types and on the right hand side of the arrow, contravariant on the left hand side of the arrow, and non-variant on other type constructors. Formally, the relation $\leq$ can be defined as the largest transitive relation on regular trees that satisfies the closure and consistency rules of figure 12:

Subtyping should not be confused with inheritance. First, the two relations are defined between elements of different sets: inheritance relates classes, while subtyping relates object types (not even class types). Second, there is no obvious correspondence between the two relations. On the one hand, as shown by examples with binary methods, if two classes are in an inheritance relation, then the types of objects of the respective classes are not necessarily in a subtyping relation. On the other hand, two classes that are implemented independently are not in an inheritance relation; however, if they implement the same interface (*e.g.* in particular if they are identical), the types of objects of these classes will be equal, hence in a subtyping relation. (The two classes will define two different abbreviations for the same type.) This can be checked on the following program:

```
class c1 = object end
```

```
class c2 = object end;;
fun x -> (x : c1 :> c2);;
```

We have c1 ≤ c2 but c1 does not inherit from c2.

**Exercise 29 (Project —type inference for objects)** *Extend the small type checker given for the core calculus to include objects and classes.* □

## 4.3 Advanced Uses of Objects

We present here a large, realistic example that illustrates many facets of objects and classes and shows the expressiveness of Objective Caml.

The topic of this example is the modular implementation of window managers. Selecting the actions to be performed (such as moving or redisplaying windows) is the managers' task. Executing those actions is the windows' task. However, it is interesting to generalize this example into a design pattern known as the *subject-observer*. This design pattern has been a challenge [10]. The observers receive information from the subjects and, in return, request actions from them. Symmetrically, the subjects execute the requested actions and communicate any useful information to their observers. Here, we chose a protocol relying on trust, in which the subject asks to be observed: thus, it can manage the list of its observers himself. However, this choice could really be inverted and a more authoritative protocol in which the master (the observer) would manage the list of its subjects could be treated in a similar way.

Unsurprisingly, we reproduce this pattern by implementing two classes modeling subjects and observers. The class `subject` that manages the list of observers must be parameterized by the type `'observer` of the objects of the class `observer`. The class `subject` implements a method `notify` to relay messages to all observers, transparently. A piece of information is represented by a procedure that takes an observer as parameter; the usage is that this procedure calls an appropriate message of the observer; the name of the message and its arguments are hidden in the procedure closure. A message is also parameterized by the sender (a subject); the method `notify` applies messages to their sender before broadcasting them, so that the receiver may call back the sender to request a new action, in return.

```
class ['observer] subject =
  object (self : 'mytype)
    val mutable observers : 'observer list = []
    method add obs = observers <- obs :: observers
    method notify (message : 'observer -> 'mytype -> unit) =
      List.iter (fun obs -> message obs self) observers
  end;;
```

The template of the observer does not provide any particular service and is reduced to an empty class:

```
class ['subject] observer = object end;;
```

To adapt the general pattern to a concrete case, one must extend, in parallel, both the `subject` class with methods implementing the actions that the observer may invoke and the `observer` class with informations that the subjects may send. For instance, the class `window` is an instance of the class `subject` that implements a method `move` and notifies all observers of its movements by calling the `moved` method of observers. Consistently, the manager inherits from the class `observer` and implements a method `moved` so as to receive and treat the corresponding notification messages sent by windows. For example, the method `moved` could simply call back the `draw` method of the window itself.

```
class ['observer] window =
  object (self : 'mytype)
    inherit ['observer] subject
    val mutable position = 0
    method move d =
      position <- position + d; self#notify (fun x -> x#moved)
    method draw = Printf.printf "[Position = %d]" position;
  end;;

class ['subject] manager =
  object
    inherit ['subject] observer
    method moved (s : 'subject) : unit = s#draw
  end;;
```

An instance of this pattern is well-typed since the manager correctly treats all messages that are send to objects of the `window` class.

```
let w = new window in w#add (new manager); w#move 1;;
```

This would not be the case if, for instance, we had forgotten to implement the `moved` method in the `manager` class.

The subject-observer pattern remains modular, even when specialized to the window-manager pattern. For example, the window-manager pattern can further be refined to notify observers when windows are resized. It suffices to add a notification method `resize` to windows and, accordingly, an decision method `resized` to managers:

```
class ['observer] large_window =
  object (self)
    inherit ['observer] window as super
    val mutable size = 1
    method resize x =
      size <- size + x; self#notify (fun x -> x#resized)
    method draw = super#draw; Printf.printf "[Size = %d]" size;
  end;;

class ['subject] big_manager =
  object
    inherit ['subject] manager as super
    method resized (s:'subject) = s#draw
  end;;
```

Actually, the pattern is quite flexible. As an illustration, we now add another kind of observer used to spy the subjects:

**Fig. 13.** Traditional inheritance

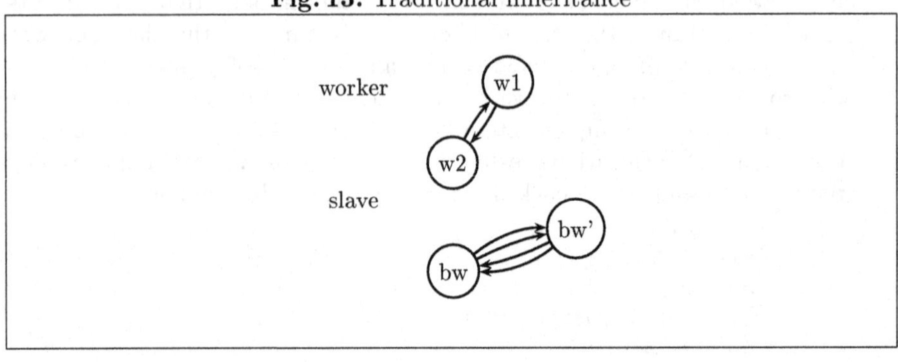


```
class ['subject] spy =
  object
    inherit ['subject] observer
    method resized (s:'subject) = print_string "<R>"
    method moved (s:'subject) = print_string "<M>"
  end;;
```

To be complete, we test this example with a short sequence of events:

```
let w = new large_window in
   w#add (new big_manager); w#add (new spy);
   w#resize 2; w#move 1;;
```

```
<R>[Position = 0][Size = 3]<M>[Position = 1][Size = 3]- : unit = ()
```

**Exercise 30 (Project —A widget toolkit)** *Implement a widget toolkit from scratch,* i.e. *using the Graphics library. For instance, starting with rectangular areas as basic widgets, containers, text area, buttons, menus, etc. can be derived objects. To continue, scroll bars, scrolling rectangles, etc. can be added.*

*The library should be design with multi-directional modularity in mind. For instance, widgets should be derived from one another as much as possible so as to ensure code sharing. Of course, the user should be able to customize library widgets. Last, the library should also be extensible by an expert.*

*In additional to the implementation of the toolkit, the project could also illustrate the use of the toolkit itself on an example.* □

The subject/observer pattern is an example of component inheritance. With simple object-oriented programming, inheritance is related to a single class. For example, figure 13 sketches a common, yet advanced situation where several objects of the same `worker` class interact intimately, for instance through binary methods. In an inherited `slave` class, the communication pattern can then be enriched with more connections between objects of the same class. This pattern can easily be implemented in OCaml, since binary methods are correctly typed in inherited classes, as shown on examples in Section 4.1.2.

**Fig. 14.** Component inheritance

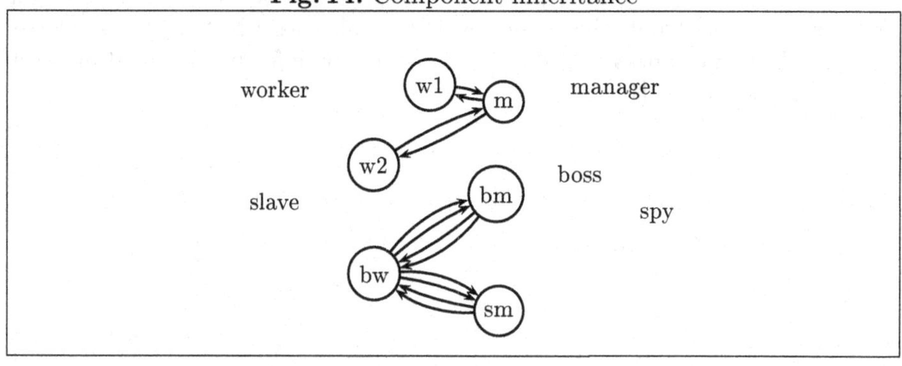


A generalization of this pattern is often used in object-oriented components. Here, the intimate connection implies several objects of related but different classes. This is sketched in figure 14 where objects of the `worker` class interact with objects of the `manager` class. What is then often difficult is to allow inheritance of the components, such that objects of the subclasses can have an enriched communication pattern and still interact safely. In the sketched example, objects of the `slave` class on the one hand and object of `boss` or `spy` classes on the other hand do interact with a richer interface.

The subject/observer is indeed an instance of this general pattern. As shown above, it can be typed successfully. Moreover, all the expected flexibility is retained, including in particular, the refinement of the communication protocol in the sub-components.

The key ingredient in this general pattern is, as for binary methods, the use of structural open object types and their parametric treatment in subclasses. Here, not only the selftype of the current class, but also the selftype the other classes recursively involved in the pattern are abstracted in each class.

## Further Reading

The addition of objects and classes to OCaml was first experimented in the language ML-ART [62] —an extension of ML with abstract types and record types— in which objects were not primitive but programmed. Despite some limitations imposed in OCaml, for sake of simplification, and on the opposite some other extensions, ML-ART can be still be seen as an introspection of OCaml object oriented features. Conversely, the reader is referred to [64,70] for a more detailed (and more technical) presentation.

Moby [20] is another experiment with objects to be mentioned because it has some ML flavor despite the fact that types are no longer inferred. However, classes are more closely integrated with the module system, including a view mechanism [66].

A short survey on the problem of binary methods is [9]. The "Subject/Observer pattern" and other solutions to it are also described in [10]. Of course, they are also many works that do not consider type inference. A good but technical reference book is [1].

# Section 5

# The Module Language

Independently of classes, Objective Caml features a powerful module system, inspired from the one of Standard ML.

The benefits of modules are numerous. They make large programs *compilable* by allowing to split them into pieces that can be separately compiled. They make large programs *understandable* by adding structure to them. More precisely, modules encourage, and sometimes force, the specification of the links (interfaces) between program components, hence they also make large programs *maintainable* and *reusable*. Additionally, by enforcing abstraction, modules usually make programs *safer*.

## 5.1 Using Modules

Compared with other languages already equipped with modules such as Modular-2, Modula-3, or Ada, the originality of the ML module system is to be a small typed functional language "on top" of the base language. The ML module system can actually be *parameterized* by the base language, which need not necessarily be ML. Thus, it could provide a language for modules other base languages.

### 5.1.1 Basic modules

Basic modules are *structures*, *i.e.* collections of phrases, written **struct** $p_1$ ... $p_n$ **end**. Phrases are those of the core language, plus definitions of sub modules **module** $X = M$ and of module types **module type** $T = S$. Our first example is an implementation of stacks.

```
module Stack =
  struct
    type 'a t = {mutable elements : 'a list }
    let create () = { elements = [] }
    let push x s = s.elements <- x :: s.elements
    let pop s =
      match s.elements with
        h:: t -> s.elements <- t; h
     | []    -> failwith "Empty stack"
  end;;
```

Components of a module are referred to using the "dot notation":

```
let s = Stack.create () in Stack.push 1 s; Stack.push 2 s; Stack.pop s;;
```

```
- : int = 2
```

Alternatively, the directive open $S$ allows to further skip the prefix and the dot, simultaneously: **struct** open $S \ldots (f\ x : t) \ldots$ **end**. A module may also be a subcomponent of another module:

```
module T =
  struct
    module R = struct let x = 0 end
    let y = R.x + 1
  end
```

The "dot notation" and open extends to and can be used in sub-modules. Note that the directive open T.R in a module Q makes all components of T.R visible to the rest of the module Q but it does not add these components to the module Q.

The system infers signatures of modules, as it infers types of values. Types of basic modules, called *signatures*, are sequences of (type) specifications, written **sig** $s_1 \ldots s_n$ **end**. The different forms of specifications are described in figure 15. For instance, the system's answer to the Stack example was:

**Fig. 15.** Specifications

| **Specification of** | **form** |
|---|---|
| values | val $x : \sigma$ |
| abstract types | type $t$ |
| manifest types | type $t = \tau$ |
| exceptions | exception $E$ |
| classes | class $z$ : object... end |
| sub-modules | module $X : S$ |
| module types | module type $T$ [ $= M$] |

```
module Stack :
  sig
    type 'a t = { mutable elements : 'a list; }
    val create : unit -> 'a t
    val push : 'a -> 'a t -> unit
    val pop : 'a t -> 'a
  end
```

An explicit signature constraint can be used to restrict the signature inferred by the system, much as type constraints restrict the types inferred for expressions. Signature constraints are written $(M : S)$ where $M$ is a module and $S$ is a signature. There is also the syntactic sugar **module** $X : S = M$ standing for **module** $X = (M : S)$.

Precisely, a signature constraint is two-fold: first, it checks that the structure complies with the signature; that is, all components specified in $S$ must be defined in $M$, with types that are at least as general; second, it makes components of $M$ that are not components of $S$ inaccessible. For instance, consider the following declaration:

```
module S : sig type t val y : t end =
  struct type t = int let x = 1 let y = x + 1 end
```

Then, both expressions `S.x` and `S.y + 1` would produce errors. The former, because x is not externally visible in `S`. The latter because the component `S.y` has the abstract type `S.t` which is not compatible with type `int`.

Signature constraints are often used to enforce type abstraction. For instance, the module `Stack` defined above exposes its representation. This allows stacks to be created directly without calling `Stack.create`.

```
Stack.pop { Stack.elements = [2; 3]};;
```

However, in another situation, the implementation of stacks might have assumed invariants that would not be verified for arbitrary elements of the representation type. To prevent such confusion, the implementation of stacks can be made abstract, forcing the creation of stacks to use the function `Stack.create` supplied especially for that purpose.

```
module Astack :
    sig
      type 'a t
      val create : unit -> 'a t
      val push : 'a -> 'a t -> unit
      val pop : 'a t -> 'a
    end = Stack;;
```

Abstraction may also be used to produce two isomorphic but incompatible views of a same structure. For instance, all currencies are represented by floats; however, all currencies are certainly not equivalent and should not be mixed. Currencies are isomorphic but disjoint structures, with respective incompatible units `Euro` and `Dollar`. This is modeled in OCaml by a signature constraint.

```
module Float =
  struct
    type t = float
    let unit = 1.0
    let plus = (+.)
    let prod = ( *. )
  end;;
```

```
module type CURRENCY =
  sig
    type t
    val unit  : t
    val plus : t -> t -> t
    val prod : float -> t -> t
  end;;
```

Remark that multiplication became an external operation on floats in the signature `CURRENCY`. Constraining the signature of `Float` to be `CURRENCY` returns another, incompatible view of `Float`. Moreover, repeating this operation returns two isomorphic structures but with incompatible types `t`.

```
module Euro = (Float : CURRENCY);;
module Dollar = (Float : CURRENCY);;
```

In `Float` the type `t` is concrete, so it can be used for "float". Conversely, it is abstract in modules `Euro` and `Dollar`. Thus, `Euro.t` and `Dollar.t` are incompatible.

```
let euro x = Euro.prod x Euro.unit;;
Euro.plus (euro 10.0) (euro 20.0);;
```

✗
```
Euro.plus (euro 50.0) Dollar.unit;;
```

Remark that there is no code duplication between Euro and Dollar.

A slight variation on this pattern can be used to provide multiple views of the same module. For instance, a module may be given a restricted interface in a given context so that certain operations (typically, the creation of values) would not be permitted.

```
module type PLUS =
  sig
    type t
    val plus : t -> t -> t
  end;;
module Plus = (Euro : PLUS)
```

```
module type PLUS_Euro =
  sig
    type t = Euro.t
    val plus : t -> t -> t
  end;;
module Plus = (Euro : PLUS_Euro)
```

On the left hand side, the type Plus.t is incompatible with Euro.t. On the right, the type t is partially abstract and compatible with Euro.t; the view Plus allows the manipulation of values that are built with the view Euro. The with notation allows the addition of type equalities in a (previously defined) signature. The expression PLUS with type t = Euro.t is an abbreviation for the signature

```
sig
  type t = Euro.t
  val plus: t -> t -> t
end
```

The with notation is a convenience to create partially abstract signatures and is often inlined:

```
module Plus = (Euro : PLUS with type t = Euro.t);;
Plus.plus Euro.unit Euro.unit;;
```

*Separate compilation* Modules are also used to facilitate separate compilation. This is obtained by matching toplevel modules and their signatures to files as follows. A compilation unit A is composed of two files:

- The implementation file a.ml is a sequence of phrases, like phrases within **struct** ... **end**.
- The interface file a.mli (optional) is a sequence of specifications, such as within sig... end.

Another compilation unit B may access A as if it were a structure, using either the dot notation A.x or the directive open A. Let us assume that the source files are: a.ml, a.mli, b.ml. That is, the interface of a B is left unconstrained. The compilations steps are summarized below:

| Command | Compiles | Creates |
|---|---|---|
| `ocamlc -c a.mli` | interface of `A` | `a.cmi` |
| `ocamlc -c a.ml` | implementation of `A` | `a.cmo` |
| `ocamlc -c b.ml` | implementation of `B` | `b.cmo` |
| `ocamlc -o myprog a.cmo b.cmo` | linking | `myprog` |

The program behaves as the following monolithic code:

```
module A : sig (* content of a.mli *) end =
  struct (* content of a.ml *) end
module B = struct (* content of b.ml *) end
```

The order of module definitions correspond to the order of `.cmo` object files on the linking command line.

### 5.1.2 Parameterized modules

A *functor*, written **functor** $(S : T) \rightarrow M$, is a function from modules to modules. The body of the functor $M$ is explicitly parameterized by the module parameter $S$ of signature $T$. The body may access the components of $S$ by using the dot notation.

```
module M = functor(X : T) ->
  struct
    type u = X.t * X.t
    let y = X.g(X.x)
  end
```

As for functions, it is not possible to access directly the body of `M`. The module `M` must first be explicitly applied to an implementation of signature `T`.

```
    module T1 = T(S1)
    module T2 = T(S2)
```

The modules `T1`, `T2` can then be used as regular structures. Note that `T1` et `T2` share their code, entirely.

## 5.2 Understanding Modules

We refer here to the literature. See the bibliography notes below for more information of the formalization of modules [27,42,43,67].

For more information on the implementation, see [44].

## 5.3 Advanced Uses of Modules

In this section, we use the running example of a bank to illustrate most features of modules and combined them together.

Let us focus on bank accounts and, in particular, the way the bank and the client may or may not create and use accounts. For security purposes, the client and the bank should obviously have different access privileges to accounts. This can be modeled by providing different views of accounts to the client and to the bank:

```
module type CLIENT =              (* client's view *)
  sig
    type t
    type currency
    val deposit : t -> currency -> currency
    val retrieve : t -> currency -> currency
  end;;

module type BANK =              (* banker's view *)
  sig
    include CLIENT
    val create : unit -> t
  end;;
```

We start with a rudimentary model of the bank: the account book is given to the client. Of course, only the bank can create the account, and to prevent the client from forging new accounts, it is given to the client, abstractly.

```
module Old_Bank (M : CURRENCY) :
    BANK with type currency = M.t =
  struct
    type currency = M.t
    type t = { mutable balance : currency }
    let zero = M.prod 0.0 M.unit and neg = M.prod (-1.0)

    let create() = { balance = zero }
    let deposit c x =
      if x > zero then c.balance <- M.plus c.balance x; c.balance
    let retrieve c x =
      if c.balance > x then deposit c (neg x) else c.balance
  end;;

module Post = Old_Bank (Euro);;
module Client :
    CLIENT with type currency = Post.currency and type t = Post.t
      =   Post;;
```

This model is fragile because all information lies in the account itself. For instance, if the client loses his account, he loses his money as well, since the bank does not keep any record. Moreover, security relies on type abstraction to be unbreakable...

However, the example already illustrates some interesting benefits of modularity: the clients and the banker have different views of the bank account. As a result an account can be created by the bank and used for deposit by both the bank and the client, but the client cannot create new accounts.

```
let my_account = Post.create ();;
Post.deposit my_account (euro 100.0);
Client.deposit my_account (euro 100.0);;
```

Moreover, several accounts can be created in different currencies, with no possibility to mix one with another, such mistakes being detected by typechecking.

```
module Citybank = Old_Bank (Dollar);;
let my_dollar_account = Citybank.create();;
```

```
Citybank.deposit my_account;;
Citybank.deposit my_dollar_account (euro 100.0);;
```

Furthermore, the implementation of the bank can be changed while preserving its interface. We use this capability to build, a more robust —yet more realistic— implementation of the bank where the account book is maintained in the bank database while the client is only given an account number.

```
module Bank (M : CURRENCY) : BANK with type currency = M.t =
  struct
    let zero = M.prod 0.0 M.unit and neg = M.prod (−1.0)
    type t = int
    type currency = M.t

    type account = { number : int; mutable balance : currency }
    (* bank database *)
    let all_accounts = Hashtbl.create 10 and last = ref 0
    let account n = Hashtbl.find all_accounts n

    let create() = let n = incr last; !last in
      Hashtbl.add all_accounts n {number = n; balance = zero}; n

    let deposit n x = let c = account n in
      if x > zero then c.balance <- M.plus c.balance x; c.balance

    let retrieve n x = let c = account n in
      if c.balance > x then (c.balance <- M.plus c.balance x; x)
      else zero
  end;;
```

Using functor application we can create several banks. As a result of generativity of function application, they will have independent and private databases, as desired.

```
module Central_Bank = Bank (Euro);;
module Banque_de_France = Bank (Euro);;
```

Furthermore, since the two modules `Old_bank` and `Bank` have the same interface, one can be used instead of the other, so as to created banks running on different models.

```
module Old_post = Old_Bank(Euro)
module Post = Bank(Euro)
module Citybank = Bank(Dollar);;
```

All banks have the same interface, however they were built. In fact, it happens to be the case that the user cannot even observe the difference between either implementation; however, this would not be true in general. Indeed, such a property can not be enforced by the typechecker.

**Exercise 31 (Polynomials with one variable)**

1. *Implement a library with operations on polynomials with one variable. The coefficients form a ring that is given as a parameter to the library.*
2. *Use the library to check, for instance, the identity* $(1+X)(1-X) = 1-X^2$.
3. *Check the equality* $(X+Y)(X-Y) = (X^2-Y^2)$ *by treating polynomials with two variables as polynomials with one variable* $X$ *and where the coefficients are the ring of the polynomials with one variable* $Y$.
4. *Write a program that reads a polynomial on the command line and evaluates it at each of the points given in* `stdin` *(one integer per line); the result should be printed in* `stdout`.

□

## Section 6

# Mixing Modules and Objects

Modules and classes play different roles. On the one hand, modules can be embedded, and parameterized by types and values. Modules also allow value and type abstraction on a large scale. On the other hand, classes provide inheritance and its late binding mechanism; they can also be parameterized by values, but on a small scale. At first, there seems to be little redundancy. Indeed, to benefit from both features simultaneously, modules and classes are often combined together.

However, both modules and classes provide means of structuring the code. Despite their resemblance at first glance, modular and object-oriented programming styles are in fact diverging: once a choice has been made to represent a structure by a module or by an object, many other choices are forced, which is sometimes bothersome.

In this section, we discusses the overlapping of features and the specificities, and show how to use them in harmony.

## 6.1 Overlapping

Many abstract datatypes can be defined using either classes or modules. A representative example is the type of stacks. Stacks have been defined as a parametric class in section 4.1.2 where operations on stacks are methods embedded into stack-objects, and as a module defining an abstract type of stacks and the associated operations in section 5.1.1. The following table summarizes the close correspondence between those two implementations.

| | class version | module version |
|---|---|---|
| The type of stacks | `'a stack` | `'a Astack.t` |
| Create a stack | `new stack` | `Astack.created ()` |
| Push $x$ on $s$ | $s$`#push` $x$ | `Astack.push` $x$ $s$ |
| Pop from $s$ | $s$`#pop` | `Astack.pop` $s$ |

More generally, all algebraic abstract types that are modifiable in place and such that all associated operations are unary (*i.e.* they take only one argument of the abstract type) can be defined as classes or as modules in almost the same way. Here, the choice between those two forms is mainly a question of programming style: some programmers prefer to see the operations of the abstract type as methods attached to values of this type, while others prefer to see them as functions outside values of the abstract type.

**Fig. 16.** Class *v.s.* Module versions of stacks

```
class ['a] stack_ext =
  object (self)
    inherit ['a] stack
    method top =
      let s = self#pop in
      self#push s; s
end;;
```

```
module StackExt =
  struct
    include Stack
    let top p =
      let s = pop p in
      push s p; s
  end;;
```

Moreover, the two alternatives are still comparable when extending the stack implementation with new operations. For instance, in both cases, a new implementation of stacks can be derived from the older one with an additional method `top` to explore the top of the stack without popping it. Both implementations, described in Figure 16, are straightforward: the class approach uses inheritance while the module approach uses the `include` construct. (The effect of `include Stack` is to rebind all components of the `Stack` structure in the substructure.)

However, the two approaches definitely differ when considering late binding, which is only possible with the class approach. For instance, redefining the implementation of `pop` would automatically benefit to the implementation of `top` (*i.e.* the method `top` would call the new definition of `pop`). This mechanism does not have any counterpart in OCaml modules.

In conclusion, if inheritance is needed, the class approach seems more appropriate, and it becomes the only possible (direct) solution if, moreover, late binding is required. Conversely, for abstract datatypes used with binary operations, such as sets with a merge operation, the module approach will be preferable, as long as inheritance is not used. Furthermore, the module approach is the only one that allows to return private data to the user, but abstractly, so as to preserve its integrity. Of course, the module system is also the basis for separate compilation.

## 6.2 Combining Modules and Classes

To benefit from the advantages of objects and modules simultaneously, an application can easily combine both aspect. Typically, modules will be used at the outer level, to provide separate compilation, inner structures, and privacy outside of the module boundaries, while classes will be components of modules, and offer extendibility, open recursion and late binding mechanisms.

We first present typical examples of such patterns, with increasing complexity and expressiveness. We conclude with a more complex —but real— example combining many features in an unusual but interesting manner.

### 6.2.1 Classes as module components

The easiest example is probably the use of modules to simply group related classes together. For instance, two classes nil and cons that are related by their usage, can be paired together in a module.

```
module Cell = struct
  exception Nil
  class ['a] nil =
    object (self : 'alist)
      method hd : 'a = raise Nil
      method tl : 'alist = raise Nil
      method null = true
    end;;
```

```
class ['a] cons h t =
  object (_ : 'alist)
    val hd = h val tl = t
    method hd : 'a = h
    method tl : 'alist = t
    method null = false
  end;;
end;;
```

Besides clarity of code, one quickly take advantage of such grouping. For instance, the nil and cons classes can be extended simultaneously (but this is not mandatory) to form an implementation of lists:

```
module List = struct
  class ['a] nil =
    object
      inherit ['a] Cell.nil
      method length = 0
    end;;
```

```
class ['a] cons h t =
  object
    inherit ['a] Cell.cons h t
    method length = 1+tl#length
  end;;
end;;
```

In turn, the module List can also be extended —but in another direction— by adding a new "constructor" append. This amounts to adding a new class with the same interface as that of the first two.

*Remark 6.2.1.* In OCaml, lists are more naturally represented by a sum data type, which moreover allows for pattern matching. However, datatypes are not extensible.

In this example, grouping could be seen as a structuring convenience, because a flattened implementation of all classes would have worked as well. However, grouping becomes mandatory for friend classes.

*Friend classes* State encapsulation in objects allows to abstract their representation by hiding all instance variables. Thus, reading and writing capabilities can be controlled by providing only the necessary methods. However, whether to expose some given part of the state is an all-or-nothing choice: either it is confined to the object or revealed to the whole world.

It is often the case that some, but not all, objects can access each other's state. A typical example (but not the only one) are objects with binary methods. A binary method of an object is called with another object of the same class as argument, so as to interact with it. In most cases, this interaction should be intimate, *e.g.* depend on the details of their representations and not only on their external interfaces. For instance, only objects having the same implementation could be allowed to interact. With objects and classes, the only way to share the representation between two different objects is to expose it to the whole world.

Modules, which provide a finer-grain abstraction mechanism, can help secure this situation, making the type of the representation abstract. Then, all friends (classes or functions) defined within the same module and sharing the same abstract view know the concrete representation.

This can be illustrated on the bank example, by turning currency into a class:

```
module type CURRENCY = sig
  type t
  class c : float ->
    object ('a)
      method v : t
      method plus : 'a -> 'a
      method prod : float -> 'a
    end
end;;
module Currency = struct
  type t = float
  class c x =
    object (_ : 'a)
      val v = x method v = v
      method plus(z:'a) = {< v = v +. z#v >}
      method prod x = {< v = x *. v >}
    end
end;;
module Euro = (Currency : CURRENCY);;
```

Then, all object of the class `Euro.c` can be combined, still hiding the currency representation.

A similar situation arises when implementing sets with a union operation, tables with a merge operation, *etc.*

### 6.2.2 Classes as pre-modules

We end this section with an example that interestingly combines some features of classes objects and modules. This example is taken from the algebraic-structure library of the formal computation system FOC [7]. The organization of such a library raises important problems: on the one hand, algebraic structures are usually described by successive refinements (a group is a monoid equipped with an additional inverse operation). The code structure should reflect this hierarchy, so that at least the code of the operations common to a structure and its derived structures can be shared. On the other hand, type abstraction is crucial in order to hide the real representations of the structure elements (for instance, to prevent from mixing integers modulo $p$ and integers modulo $q$ when $p$ is not equal to $q$). Furthermore, the library should remain extensible.

In fact, we should distinguish generic structures, which are abstract algebraic structures, from concrete structures, which are instances of algebraic structures. Generic structures can either be used to derive richer structures or be instantiated into concrete structures, but they themselves do not contain elements. On the contrary, concrete structures can be used for computing. Concrete structures can be obtained from generic ones by supplying an implementation for the basic operations. This schema is sketched in figure 17. The arrows represent the expected code sharing.

In general, as well as in this particular example, there are two kinds of expected clients of a library: experts and final users. Indeed, a good library should not only be usable, but also re-usable. Here for instance, final users of the library only need to instantiate some generic structures to concrete ones and use these to perform computation. In addition, a few experts should be able to extend the library, providing new generic structures by enriching existing ones, making them available to the final users and to other experts.

**Fig. 17.** Algebraic structures

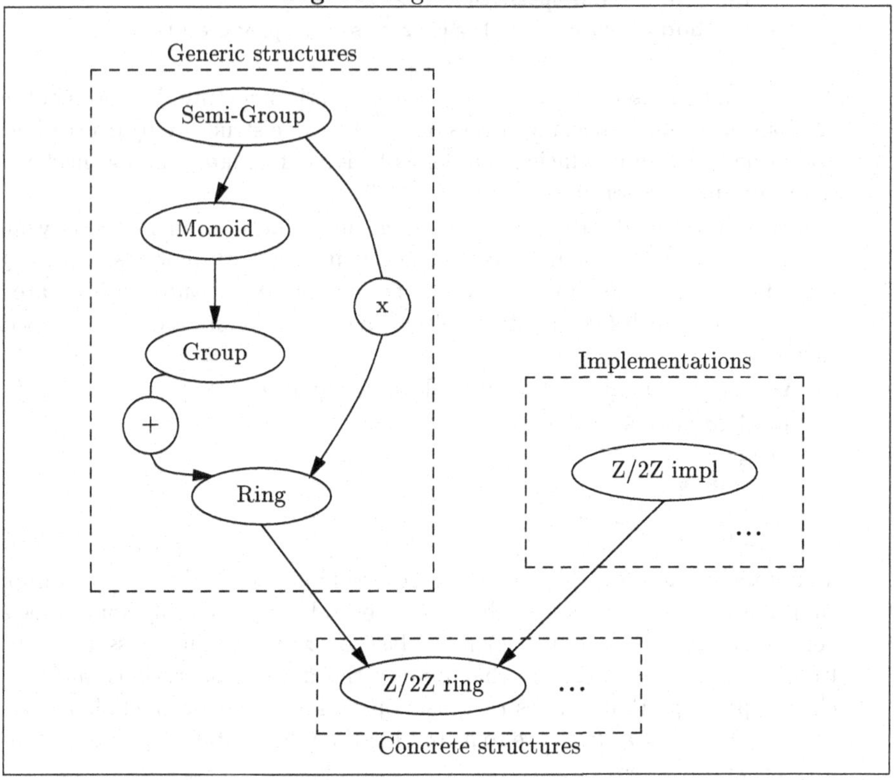

The first architecture considered in the FOC project relies on modules, exclusively; modules facilitates type abstraction, but fails to provide code sharing between derived structures. On the contrary, the second architecture represents algebraic structures by classes and its elements by objects; inheritance facilitates code sharing, but this solution fails to provide type abstraction because object representation must be exposed, mainly to binary operations.

The final architecture considered for the project mixes classes and modules to combine inheritance mechanisms of the former with type abstraction of the latter. Each algebraic structure is represented by a module with an abstract type `t` that is the representation type of algebraic structure elements (*i.e.* its "carrier"). The object `meth`, which collects all the operations, is obtained by inheriting from the virtual class that is parameterized by the carrier type and that defines the derived operations. For instance, for groups, the virtual class `['a] group` declares the basic group operations (`equal`, `zero`, `plus`, `opposite`) and defines the derived operations (`not_equal`, `minus`) once and for all:

```
class virtual ['a] group =
  object(self)
    method virtual equal: 'a -> 'a -> bool
    method not_equal x y = not (self#equal x y)
    method virtual zero: 'a
    method virtual plus: 'a -> 'a -> 'a
    method virtual opposite: 'a -> 'a
    method minus x y = self#plus x (self#opposite y)
  end;;
```

A class can be reused either to build richer generic structures by adding other operations or to build specialized versions of the same structure by overriding some operations with more efficient implementations. The late binding mechanism is then used in an essential way.

(In a more modular version of the group structure, all methods would be private, so that they can be later ignored if necessary. For instance, a group should be used as the implementation of a monoid. All private methods are made public, and as such become definitely visible, right before a concrete instance is taken.)

A group is a module with the following signature:

```
module type GROUP =
  sig
    type t
    val meth: t group
  end;;
```

To obtain a concrete structure for the group of integers modulo $p$, for example, we supply an implementation of the basic methods (and possibly some specialized versions of derived operations) in a class `z_pz_impl`. The class `z_pz` inherits from the class `[int] group` that defines the derived operations and from the class `z_pz_impl` that defines the basic operations. Last, we include an instance of this subclass in a structure so as to hide the representation of integers modulo $p$ as OCaml integers.

```
class z_pz_impl p =
  object
    method equal (x : int) y = (x = y)
    method zero = 0
    method plus x y = (x + y) mod p
    method opposite x = p - 1 - x
  end;;
class z_pz p =
  object
    inherit [int] group
    inherit z_pz_impl p
  end;;
module Z_pZ =
  functor (X: sig val p : int end) ->
   ( struct
      type t = int
      let meth = new z_pz X.p
      let inj x =
        if x >= 0 && x < X.p then x else failwith "Z_pZ.inj"
      let proj x = x
    end : sig
      type t
      val meth: t group
      val inj: int -> t
      val proj: t -> int
    end);;
```

This representation elegantly combines the strengths of modules (type abstraction) and classes (inheritance and late binding).

**Exercise 32 (Project —A small subset of the FOC library)** *As an exercise, we propose the implementation of a small prototype of the FOC library. This exercise is two-fold.*

*On the one hand, it should include more generic structures, starting with sets, and up to at least rings and polynomials.*

*On the other hand, it should improve on the model given above, by inventing a more sophisticated design pattern that is closer to the model sketched in figure 17 and that can be used in a systematic way.*

*For instance, the library could provide both an open view and the abstraction functor for each generic structure. The open view is useful for writing extensions of the library. Then, the functor can be used to produce an abstract concrete structure directly from an implementation.*

*The pattern could also be improved to allow a richer structure (*e.g.* a ring) to be acceptable in place only a substructure is required (*e.g.* an additive group).*

*The polynomials with coefficients in* $\mathbb{Z}/2\mathbb{Z}$ *offers a simple yet interesting source of examples.* □

## Further Reading

The example of the FOC system illustrates a common situation that calls for hybrid mechanisms for code structuring that would more elegantly combine the features of modules and classes. This is an active research area, where several solutions are currently explored. Let us mention in particular "mixin" modules and objects with "views". The former enrich the ML modules with inheritance and a late binding mechanism [18,4,5]. The latter provide a better object-encapsulation mechanism, in particular in the presence of binary operations and "friend" functions; views also allow to forget or rename methods more freely [66,69].

Other object-oriented languages, such as CLOS, detach methods from objects, transforming them into overloaded functions. This approach is becoming closer to traditional functional programming. Moreover, it extends rather naturally to multi-methods [13,22,8] that allow to recover the symmetry between the arguments of a same algebraic type. This approach is also more expressive, since method dispatch may depend on several arguments simultaneously rather than on a single one in a privileged position. However, this complicates abstraction of object representation. Indeed, overloading makes abstraction more difficult, since the precise knowledge of the type of arguments is required to decide what version of the method should be used.

# Further Reading

The OCaml compiler, its programming environment and its documentation are available at the Web site `http://caml.inria.fr`. The documentation includes the reference manual of the language and some tutorials.

The recent book of Chailloux, Manoury and Pagano [12] is a complete presentation of the OCaml language and of its programming environment. The book is written in French, but an English version should be soon available electronically. Other less recent books [15,72,26] use the language Caml Light, which approximatively correspond to the core OCaml language, covering neither its module system, nor objects.

For other languages of the ML family, [56] is an excellent introductory document to Standard ML and [49,48] are the reference documents for this language. For Haskell, the reference manual is [36] and [68,30] give a very progressive approach to the language.

Typechecking and semantics of core ML are formalized in several articles and book sections. A concise and self-contained presentation can also be found in [41,40, chapter 1]. A more modern formalization of the semantics, using small-step reductions, and type soundness can be found in [74]. Several introductory books to the formal semantics of programming languages [25,50,65] consider a subset of ML as an example. Last, [11] is an excellent introductory article to type systems in general.

The object and class layer of OCaml is formalized in [64]. A reference book on object calculi is [1]; this book, a little technical, formalizes the elementary mechanisms underlying object-oriented languages. Another integration of objects in a language of the ML family lead to the prototype language *Moby* described in [20]; a view mechanism for this language has been proposed in [21].

Several formalization of Standard ML and OCaml modules have been proposed. Some are based on calculi with unique names [49,46], others use type theoretical concepts [27,42]; both approaches are compared and related in [43,67].

## Beyond ML

ML is actually better characterized by its type system than by its set of features. Indeed, several generalizations of the ML type system have been proposed to increase its expressiveness while retaining its essential properties and, in particular, type inference.

Subtyping polymorphism, which is used both in popular languages such as Java and in some academic higher-order languages, has long been problematic in an ML context. (Indeed, both Java and higher-order languages share in common that types of abstractions are not inferred.) However, there has been proposals to add subtyping to ML while retaining type-inference. They are all based on a form of subtyping constraints [3,19,60] or, more generally, on typing constraints [52] and differ from one another mostly by their presentation. However, none of these works have yet been turned into a large scale real implementation. In particular, displaying types to the user is a problem that remains to be dealt with.

Other forms of polymorphism are called *ad hoc*, or *overloading* polymorphism by optimists. Overloading allows to bind several unrelated definitions to the same name in the same scope. Of course, then, for each occurrence of an overloaded name, one particular definition must be chosen. This selection process, which is called name resolution, can be done either at compile-time or at run-time, and overloading is called *static* or *dynamic*, accordingly. Name resolution for static overloading is done in combination with type-checking and is based on the type context in which the name is used. For example, static overloading is used in Standard ML for arithmetic operations and record accesses. Type information may still be used in the case of dynamic overloading, but to add, whenever necessary, run-time type information that will be used to guide the name resolution, dynamically. For example, type classes in Haskell [36] are a form of dynamic overloading where type information is carried by class dictionaries [53,34], indirectly. Extensional polymorphism [17] is a more explicit form of dynamic overloading: it allows to pattern-match on the type of expressions at run-time. This resembles to, but also differ from dynamics values [45,2].

The system $F^{\omega}_{<:}$, which features both higher-order types and subtyping, is quite expressive, hence very attractive as the core of a programming language. However, its type inference problem is not decidable [73]. A suggestion to retain its expressiveness and the convenience of implicit typing simultaneously is to provide only partial type reconstruction [58,54]. Here, the programmer must write some, but not all, type information. The goal is of course that very little type information will actually be necessary to make type reconstruction decidable. However, the difficulty remains to find a simple specification of where and when annotations are mandatory, without requiring too many obvious or annoying annotations. An opposite direction to close the gap between ML and higher-order type systems is to embed higher-order types into ML types [24]. However, this raises difficulties that are similar to partial type reconstruction.

Actually, most extensions of ML explored so far seem to fit into two categories. Either, they reduce to insignificant technical changes to core ML, sometimes after clever reformulation though, or they seem to increase the complexity in disproportion with the gain in expressiveness. Thus, the ML type system might be a stable point of equilibrium —a best compromise between expressiveness and simplicity. This certainly contributed to its (relative) success. This also raised the standards for its its successor.

# Appendix A

# First Steps in OCaml

Let us first check the "Hello world" program. Use the editor to create a file `hello.ml` containing the following single line:

```
print_string "Hello world!\n";;
```

Then, compile and execute the program as follows:

```
ocamlc -o hello hello.ml
./hello
```

```
Hello World
```

Alternatively, the same program could have been typed interactively, using the interpreter `ocaml` as a big desk calculator, as shown in the following session:

```
ocaml
```

```
        Objective Caml version 3.00

#
```

```
print_string "hello world!\n";;
```

```
hello world!
- : unit = ()
```

To end interactive sessions type `^D` (`Control D`) or call the `exit` function of type `int -> unit`:

```
exit 0;;
```

Note that the `exit` function would also terminate the execution in a compiled program. Its integer argument is the return code of the program (or of the interpreter).

**Exercise 33 ((*) Unix commands true and false)** *Write the Unix commands* `true` *et* `false` *that do nothing but return the codes* `0` *and* `1`*, respectively.*

Answer □

The interpreter can also be used in batch mode, for running scripts. The name of the file containing the code to be interpreted is passed as argument on the command line of the interpreter:

```
ocaml hello.ml
```

```
Hello World
```

Note the difference between the previous command and the following one:

```
ocaml < hello.ml
```

```
        Objective Caml version 3.00

# Hello World
```

```
- : unit = ()
#
```

The latter is a "batch" interactive session where the input commands are taken from the file `hello.ml`, while the former is a script execution, where the commands of the file are evaluated in script mode, which turns off interactive messages.

*Phrases* of the core language are summarized in the table below:

| | |
|---|---|
| – value definition | **let** $x = e$ |
| – [mutually recursive] function definition[s] | **let** [ **rec** ] $f_1\ x_1\ ... = e_1$ ... [ **and** $f_n\ x_n\ ... = e_n$] |
| – type definition[s] | **type** $q_1 = t_1$... [ **and** $q_n = t_n$ ] |
| – expression | $e$ |

Phrases (optionally) end with ";;".

```
(* That is a comment (* and this is a comment inside
   a comment *) continuing on several lines *)
```

Note that an opening comment paren "(*" will absorb everything as part of the comment until a well-balanced closing comment paren "*)" is found. Thus, if you inadvertently type the opening command, you may think that the interpreter is broken because it swallows all your input without ever sending any output but the prompt.

Use `^C` (Control-C) to interrupt the evaluation of the current phrase and return to the toplevel if you ever fall in this trap!

Typing `^C` can also be used to stop a never-ending computation. For instance, try the infinite loop

```
while true do () done;;
```

and observe that there is no answer. Then type `^C`. The input is taken into account immediately (with no trailing carriage return) and produces the following message:

```
^C
Interrupted.
```

*Expressions* are

| | |
|---|---|
| – local definition | **let** $x = e_1$ **in** $e_2$ |
| (+ mutually recursive local function definitions) | |
| – anonymous function | **fun** $x_1\ ...\ x_n$ -> $e$ |
| – function call | $f\ x_1\ ...\ x_n$ |
| – variable | $x$ ($M.x$ if $x$ is defined in $M$) |
| – constructed value | $(e_1, e_2)$ |
| including constants | 1, 'c', "aa" |
| – case analysis | **match** $e$ **with** $p_1$ -> $e_1 \ldots \mid p_n$ -> $e_n$ |
| – handling exceptions | **try** $e$ **with** $p_1$ -> $e_1 \ldots \mid p_n$ -> $e_n$ |
| – raising exceptions | **raise** $e$ |

| | |
|---|---|
| – for loop | `for` $i = e_0$ `[down]to` $e_f$ `do` $e$ `done` |
| – while loop | `while` $e_0$ `do` $e$ `done` |
| – conditional | `if` $e_1$ `then` $e_2$ `else` $e_3$ |
| – sequence | $e; e'$ |
| – parenthesis | $(e)$ or `begin` $e$ `end` |

Remark that there is no notion of instruction or procedure, since all expressions must return a value. The unit value `()` of type `unit` conveys no information: it is the unique value of its type.

The expression $e$ in `for` and `while` loops, and in sequences must be of type `unit` (otherwise, a warning message is printed).

Therefore, useless results must explicitly be thrown away. This can be achieved either by using the `ignore` primitive or an anonymous binding.

```
ignore;;
```
```
- : 'a -> unit = <fun>
```
```
ignore 1; 2;;
```
```
- : int = 2
```
```
let _ = 1 in 2;;
```
```
- : int = 2
```

(The anonymous variable `_` used in the last sentence could be replaced by any regular variable that does not appear in the body of the `let`)

*Basic types, constants, and primitives* are described in the following table.

| Type | Constants | Operations |
|---|---|---|
| unit | `()` | no operation! |
| bool | `true` `false` | `&&` `\|\|` `not` |
| char | `'a'` `'\n'` `'\097'` | `Char.code` `Char.chr` |
| int | 1 2 3 | + - * / `max_int` |
| float | 1.0 2. 3.14 6e23 | +. -. *. /. `cos` |
| string | `"a\tb\010c\n"` | `^` `s.[i]` `s.[i] <- c` |

**Polymorphic types and operations**

| | | |
|---|---|---|
| arrays | `[\| 0; 1; 2; 3 \|]` | `t.(i)` `t.(i) <- v` |
| pairs | (1, 2) | `fst` `snd` |
| tuples | (1, 2, 3, 4) | Use pattern matching! |

Infixes become prefixes when put between parentheses.

For instance, `( + )` $x_1$ $x_2$ is equivalent to $x_1$ `+` $x_2$. Here, it is good practice to leave a space between the operator and the parenthesis, so as not to fall in the usual trap: The expression "`(*)`" would not mean the product used as a prefix, but the unbalanced comment starting with the character "`)`" and waiting for its closing comment paren "`*)`" closing paren.

*Array* operations are polymorphic, but arrays are homogeneous:

```
[| 0; 1; 3 |];;
```
```
- : int array = [|0; 1; 3|]
```
```
[| true; false |];;
```
```
- : bool array = [|true; false|]
```

Array indices vary from 0 to $n - 1$ where $n$ is the array size.

Array projections are *polymorphic*: they operate on any kind of array:

```
fun x -> x.(0);;
```
```
- : 'a array -> 'a = <fun>
```
```
fun t k x -> t.(k) <- x;;
```
```
- : 'a array -> int -> 'a -> unit = <fun>
```

Arrays must always be initialized:

```
Array.create;;
```
```
- : int -> 'a -> 'a array = <fun>
```

The type of the initial element becomes the type of the array.

*Tuples* are heterogeneous; however, their arity is fixed by their type: a pair `(1, 2)` of `int * int` and a triple `(1, 2, 3)` of type `int * int * int` are incompatible.

The projections are polymorphic but are defined only for a fixed arity. For instance, `fun (x, y, z) -> y` returns the second component of any triple. There is no particular syntax for projections, and pattern matching must be used. The only exceptions are `fst` and `snd` for pairs defined in the standard library.

*Records* In OCaml, records are analogous to variants and must be declared before being used. See for example the type `regular` used for cards (Exercise 3.1, page 454). Mutable fields of records must be declared as such at the definition of the record type they belong to.

```
type 'a annotation = { name : string; mutable info : 'a};;
```
```
type 'a annotation = { name : string; mutable info : 'a; }
```
```
fun x -> x.info;;
```
```
- : 'a annotation -> 'a = <fun>
```
```
let p = { name = "John"; info = 23 };;
```
```
val p : int annotation = {name="John"; info=23}
```
```
p.info <- p.info + 1;;
```
```
- : unit = ()
```

*Command line* Arguments passed on the command line are stored in the string array `Sys.argv`, the first argument being the name of the command.

**Exercise 34 ((*) Unix command echo)** *Implement the Unix echo function.*
Answer □

The standard library `Arg` provides an interface to extract arguments from the command line.

*Input-output* A summary of primitives for manipulating channels and writing on them is given in the two tables below. See the core and standard libraries for an exhaustive list.

**Predefined channels**

`stdin : in_channel`
`stdout : out_channel`
`stderr : out_channel`

**Creating channels**

`open_out : string -> out_channel`
`open_in : string -> in_channel`
`close_out : out_channel -> unit`

**Reading on stdin**

`read_line : unit -> string`
`read_int : unit -> int`

**Writing on stdout**

`print_string : string -> unit`
`print_int : int -> unit`
`print_newline : unit -> unit`

**Exercise 35 ((**) Unix cat and grep commands)** *Implement the Unix* `cat` *command that takes a list of file names on the command line and print the contents of all files in order of appearance; if there is no file on the command line, it prints stdin.* Answer
*The Unix* `grep` *command is quite similar to* `cat` *but only list the lines matching some regular expression. Implement the command* `grep` *by a tiny small change to the program* `cat`*, thanks to the standard library* `Str`*.* Answer □

**Exercise 36 ((**) Unix wc command)** *Implement the Unix* `wc` *command that takes a list of file names on the command line and for each file count characters, words, and lines; additionally, but only if there were more than one file, it presents a global summary for the union of all files.* Answer □

# Appendix B

# Variant Types and Labeled Arguments

In this appendix we briefly present two recent features of the OCaml language and illustrate their use in combination with classes. Actually, they jointly complement objects and classes in an interesting way: first, they provide a good alternative to multiple class constructors, which OCaml does not have; second, variant types are also a lighter-weight alternative to datatype definitions and are particularly appropriate to simulate simple typecases in OCaml. Note that the need for typecases is sufficiently rare, thanks to the expressiveness of OCaml object type-system, that an indirect solution to typecases is quite acceptable.

## B.1 Variant Types

Variants are tagged unions, like ML datatypes. Thus, they allow values of different types to be mixed together in a collection by tagging them with variant labels; the values may be retrieved from the collection by inspecting their tags using pattern matching.

However, unlike datatypes, variants can be used without a preceding type declaration. Furthermore, while a datatype constructor belong to a unique datatype, a variant constructor may belong to any (open) variant.

*Quick overview* Just like sum type constructors, variant tags must be capitalized, but they must also be prefixed by the back-quote character as follows:

```
let one = `Int 1 and half = `Float 0.5;;
```

```
val one : [> `Int of int] = `Int 1
val half : [> `Float of float] = `Float 0.5
```

Here, variable `one` is bound to a variant that is an integer value tagged with `` `Int``. The `>` sign in the type ``[> `Int of int]`` means that `one` can actually be a assigned a super type. That is, values of this type can actually have another tag. However, if they have have tag `` `Int`` then they must carry integers. Thus, both `one` and `half` have compatible types and can be stored in the same collection:

```
let collection = [ one; half ];;
```

```
val collection : [> `Int of int | `Float of float] list =
  [` Int 1; `Float 0.5]
```

Now, the type of `collection` is a list of values, that can be integers tagged with `` `Int`` or floating point values tagged with `` `Float``, or values with another tag.

Values of a heterogeneous collection can be retrieved by pattern matching and then reified to their true type:

```
let float = function
  | ` Int x -> float_of_int x
  | ` Float x -> x;;
```

```
val float : [< `Int of int | `Float of float] -> float = <fun>
```

```
let total =
  List.fold_left (fun x y -> x +. float y) 0. collection ;;
```

*Implementing typecase with variant types* The language ML does not keep types at run time, hence there is no typecase construct to test the types of values at run time. The only solution available is to explicitly tag values with constructors. OCaml data types can be used for that purpose but variant types may be more convenient and more flexible here since their constructors do not have to be declared in advance, and their tagged values have all compatible types.

For instance, we consider one and two dimensional point classes and combine their objects together in a container.

```
class point1 x = object method getx = x + 0 end;;
let p1 = new point1 1;;
```

To make objects of the two classes compatible, we always tag them. However, we also keep the original object, so as to preserve direct access to the common interface.

```
let pp1 = p1, `Point1 p1;;
```

We provide testing and coercion functions for each class (these two functions could of also be merged):

```
exception Typecase;;
let is_point1 = function _, `Point1 q -> true | _ -> false;;
let to_point1 = function _, `Point1 q -> q | _ -> raise Typecase;;
```

as well as a safe (statically typed) coercion `point1`.

```
let as_point1 = function pq -> (pq :> point1 * _);;
```

Similarly, we define two-dimensional points and their auxiliary functions:

```
class point2 x y = object inherit point1 x method gety = y + 0 end;;
let p2 = new point2 2 2;;
let pp2 = (p2 :> point1), `Point2 p2;;
let is_point2 = function _, `Point2 q -> true | _ -> false;;
let to_point2 = function _, `Point2 q -> q | _ -> raise Typecase;;
let as_point2 = function pq -> (pq :> point2 * _);;
```

Finally, we check that objects of both classes can be collected together in a container.

```
let l =
  let ( @:: ) x y = (as_point1 x) :: y in
  pp1 @:: pp2 @:: [];;
```

Components that are common to all members of the collection can be accessed directly (without membership testing) using the first projection.

```
let getx p = (fst p)#getx;;
List.map getx l;;
```

Conversely, other components must accessed selectively via the second projection and using membership and conversion functions:

```
let gety p = if is_point2 p then (to_point2 p) # gety else 0;;
List.map gety l;;
```

## B.2 Labeled Arguments

In the core language, as in most languages, arguments are anonymous.

Labeled arguments are a convenient extension to the core language that allow to consistently label arguments in the declaration of functions and in their application. Labeled arguments increase safety, since argument labels are checked against their definitions. Moreover, labeled arguments also increase flexibility since they can be passed in a different order than the one of their definition. Finally, labeled arguments can be used solely for documentation purposes.

For instance, the erroneous exchange of two arguments of the same type —an error the typechecker would not catch— can be avoided by labeling the arguments with distinct labels. As an example, the module `StdLabels.String` provides a function `sub` with the following type:

```
StdLabels.String.sub;;
```

```
- : string -> pos:int -> len:int -> string = <fun>
```

This function expects three arguments: the first one is anonymous, the second and third ones are labeled `pos` and `len`, respectively. A call to this function can be written

```
String.sub "Hello" ~pos:0 ~len:4
```

or equivalently,

```
String.sub "Hello" ~len:4 ~pos:0
```

since labeled arguments can be passed to the function in a different order. Labels are (lexically) enclosed between ~ and :, so as to distinguish them from variables.

By default, standard library functions are not labeled. The module `StdLabels` redefines some modules of the standard library with labeled versions of some functions. Thus, one can include the command

```
open StdLabels;;
```

at the beginning of a file to benefit from labeled versions of the libraries. Then, `String.sub` could have been used as a short hand for `StdLabels.String.sub` in the example above.

Labeled arguments of a function are declared by labeling the arguments accordingly in the function declaration. For example, the labeled version of `substring` could have been defined as

```
let substring s ~pos:x ~length:y = String.sub s x y;;
```

Additionally, there is a possible short-cut that allows us to use the name of the label for the name of the variable. Then, both the ending : mark at the end of the label and the variable are omitted. Hence, the following definition of `substring` is equivalent to the previous one.

```
let substring s ~pos ~length = String.sub s pos length;;
```

## B.3 Optional Arguments

Labels can also be used to declare default values for some arguments.

*Quick overview* Arguments with default values are called optional arguments, and can be omitted in function calls —the corresponding default values will be used. For instance, one could have declared a function substring as follows

```
let substring ?pos:(p=0) ~length:l s = String.sub s p l;;
```

This would allow to call substring with its length argument and an anonymous string, leaving the position to its default value 0. The anonymous string parameter has been moved as the last argument, inverting the convention taken in String.sub, so as to satisfy the requirement than an optional argument must always be followed by an anonymous argument which is used to mark the end optional arguments and replace missing arguments by their default values.

*Application to class constructors* In OCaml, objects are created from classes with the new construct. This amounts to having a unique constructor of the same name as the name of the class, with the same arity as that of the class.

In object-oriented languages, it is common and often quite useful to have several ways of building objects of the same class. One common example are is to have default values for some of the parameters. Another situation is to have two (or more) equivalent representations for an object, and to be able to initialized the object using the object either way. For instance, complex points can be defined by giving either cartesian or polar coordinates.

One could think of emulating several constructors by defining different variants of the class obtained by abstraction and application of the original class, each one providing a new class constructor. However, this schema breaks modularity, since classes cannot be simultaneously refined by inheritance.

Fortunately, labeled arguments and variant types can be used together to provide the required flexibility, as it there were several constructors, but with a unique class that can be inherited.

For example, two-dimensional points can be defined as follows:

```
class point ~x:x0 ?y:(y0=0) () =
  object method getx = x0 + 0 method gety = y0 + 0 end;;
```

(The extra unit argument is used to mark the end of optional arguments.) Then, the $y$ coordinate may be left implicit, which defaults to 0.

```
let p1 = new point ~x:1 ();;
let p2 = new point ~x:1 ~y:2 ();;
```

Conversely, one could define the class so that

```
class point arg =
  let x0, y0 =
   match arg with
  | ` Cart (x,y) -> x, y
```

```
| ` Polar(r,t) -> r *. cos t, r *. sin t in
object method getx = x0 method gety = y0 end;;
```

Then, points can be build by either passing cartesian or polar coordinates

```
let p1 = new point (`Cart (1.414, 1.));;
let p2 = new point (`Polar (2., 0.52));;
```

In this case, one could also choose optional labels for convenience of notation, but at the price of some dynamic detection of ill-formed calls:

```
class point ?x ?y ?r ?t () =
  let x0, y0 =
    match x, y, r, t with
  | Some x, Some y, None, None -> x, y
  | None, None, Some r, Some t -> r *. cos t, r *. sin t
  | _, _, _, _ -> failwith "Cart and Polar coordinates can't be mixed" in
  object method getx = x0 method gety = y0 end;;
let p1 = new point ~x:2. ~y:0.52 ();;
let p2 = new point ~r:1.414 ~t:0.52 ();;
```

# Appendix C

# Answers to Exercises

## Exercise 1, page 431

```
let rec fill = function
  | Top, e as ce -> e
  | AppL (c, l), e -> fill (c, App (e, l))
  | AppR (e1, c), e2 -> fill (c, App (e1, e2))
  | LetL (x, c, e2), e1 -> fill (c, Let (x, e1, e2));;
```

```
exception Value of int;;
let rec down (c,e) =
  match e with
  | Var _ -> raise (Value (−1))
  | Const c when c.constr -> raise (Value c.arity)
  | Const c -> raise (Value (c.arity − 1))
  | Fun (_,_) -> raise (Value 0)
  | Let (x, e1, e2) -> down (LetL (x, c, e2), e1)
  | App (e1, e2) as e ->
      try down (AppL (c, e2), e1) with Value k ->
        try down (AppR (e1, c), e2) with Value _ ->
          if k > 0 then raise (Value (k−1)) else c, e;;
```

We use negative degree to represent errors (0 would work as well). In fact, the exception `Value` rather stands for irreducible.

**Exercise 1 (continued)** We first define a function that may climb up $k$ application nodes, to be used when $a$ is a value with functionality $k$.

```
let rec up k (c, e) =
  let next ce = if k > 0 then up (pred k) ce else ce in
  match c with
  | Top -> raise (Value k)
  | LetL (x, c', e2) ->
     ( c', (Let (x, e, e2)))
  | AppR (e', c') ->
      next (c', App (e',e))
  | AppL (c', e') ->
      try down (AppR (e, c'), e') with Value _ ->
        next (c', App (e, e'));;
```

Then, from the current position, we attempt to further decompose $a'$, and if it is a functional value of degree $k$, we may climb back $k$ steps; otherwise, we continue searching for a value on the right

```
let next ce = try down ce with Value k -> up k ce;;
```

```
let one_step ce = let (c', e') = next ce in (c', top_reduce e');;
let ce0 = Top, e;;
let ce1 = one_step ce0;;
let ce2 = one_step ce1;;
let ce3 = one_step ce2;;
let ce4 = one_step ce3;;
let ce5 = one_step ce4;;
```

The evaluation if the iteration of the one-step reduction until the expression is a value.

```
let eval e =
  let rec reduce ce = try reduce (one_step ce) with Value _ -> fill ce in
  reduce (down (Top, e));;
eval e;;
```

```
- : expr = Const {name=Int 9; constr=true; arity=0}
```

**Exercise 1 (continued)** We write a single function that enables to print a context alone, an expression alone, or a context and an expression to put in the hole. Actually, we print all of them as expressions but use a special constant as a hook to recognize when we reached the context.

```
let hole = Const {name = Name "[]"; arity = 0; constr = true};;
let rec expr_with expr_in_hole k out =
  let expr = expr_with expr_in_hole in
  let string x = Printf.fprintf out x in
  let paren p f =
    if k > p then string "("; f(); if k > p then string ")" in
  function
    | Var x -> string "%s" x
    | Const _ as c when c = hole ->
      string "[%a]" (expr_with hole 0) expr_in_hole
    | Const {name = Int n} -> string "%d" n
    | Const {name = Name c} -> string "%s" c
    | Fun (x,a) ->
      paren 0 (fun()-> string "fun %s -> %a" x (expr 0) a)
    | App (App (Const {name = Name ("+" | "*" as n)}, a1), a2) ->
      paren 1 (fun()->
        string "%a %s %a" (expr 0) a1 n (expr 0) a2)
    | App (a1, a2) ->
      paren 1 (fun()-> string "%a %a" (expr 1) a1 (expr 2) a2)
    | Let (x, a1, a2) ->
      paren 0 (fun()->
        string "let x = %a in %a" (expr 0) a1 (expr 0) a2);;
```

```
let print_context_expr out (c, e) =
  expr_with e 0 out (fill (c, hole))
let print_expr out e = expr_with hole 0 out e
let print_context out c = print_expr out (fill (c, hole));;
```

Then, it suffices to instrument the one_step and eval functions.

```
let eval e =
  let out = stdout in
  let print_step ce =
    let (c, e) = next ce in
    Printf.fprintf out "<-- %a\n" print_context_expr (c, e);
    let e' = top_reduce e in
    Printf.fprintf out "--> %a\n" print_context_expr (c, e');
   ( c, e') in
  let rec reduce ce =
    try reduce (print_step ce) with Value _ -> fill ce in
  Printf.fprintf out "e  =  %a\n" print_expr e;
  let e' =  reduce (down (Top, e)) in
  Printf.fprintf out "e' =  %a\n" print_expr e';
  e';;
let _ = eval e;;
```

```
e  =  (fun x -> x * x) ((fun x -> x + 1) 2)
<-- (fun x -> x * x) [(fun x -> x + 1) 2]
--> (fun x -> x * x) [2 + 1]
<-- (fun x -> x * x) [2 + 1]
--> (fun x -> x * x) [3]
<-- [(fun x -> x * x) 3]
--> [3 * 3]
<-- [3 * 3]
--> [9]
e' =  9
- : expr = Const {name=Int 9; constr=true; arity=0}
```

## Exercise 3, page 446

```
let print_type t =
  let rec print k out t =
    let string x = Printf.fprintf out x in
    let paren p f =
      if  k > p then string "("; f(); if k > p then string ")" in
    let t = repr t in
    begin match desc t with
    | Tvar n -> string "'a%d" n
    | Tcon (Tint, []) -> string "int"
    | Tcon (Tarrow, [t1; t2]) ->
        paren 0 (fun() ->
          string "%a -> %a" (print 1) t1 (print 0) t2)
    | Tcon (g, l) -> raise (Arity (t, t))
```

```
    end in
  acyclic t;
  print 0 stdout t;;
```

### Exercise 4, page 446

We can either chose an function version:

```
let ftv_type t =
  let visited = marker() in
  let rec visit ftv t =
    let t = repr t in
    if t.mark = visited then ftv
    else
      begin
        t.mark <- visited;
        match desc t with
      |   Tvar _ -> t::ftv
      |   Tcon (g, l) -> List.fold_left visit ftv l
      end in
  visit [] t;;
```

or an imperative version:

```
let ftv_type t =
  let ftv = ref [] in
  let visited = marker() in
  let rec visit t =
    let t = repr t in
    if t.mark = visited then ()
    else
      begin
        t.mark <- visited;
        match desc t with
      |   Tvar _ -> ftv := t::!ftv
      |   Tcon (g, l) -> List.iter visit l
      end in
  visit t; !ftv;;
```

```
let type_instance (q, t) =
  acyclic t;
  let copy t = let t = repr t in t, tvar() in
  let copied = List.map copy q in
  let rec visit t =
    let t = repr t in
    try List.assq t copied with Not_found ->
      begin match desc t with
    |   Tvar _ | Tcon (_, []) -> t
    |   Tcon (g, l) -> texp (Tcon (g, List.map visit l))
      end in
  visit t;;
```

**Exercise 4 (continued)** To keep sharing, every instance of a node will be kept in a table, and the mark of the old node will be equal (modulo a translation) to the index of the corresponding node in the table. Since we do not know at the beginning the size of the table. we write a library of extensible arrays.

```
module Iarray =
  struct
    type 'a t = { mutable t : 'a array; v : 'a }
    let create k v = { t = Array.create (max k 3) v; v = v }
    let get a i =
      if Array.length a.t > i then a.t.(i) else a.v
    let set a i v =
      let n = Array.length a.t in
      if n > i then a.t.(i) <- v else
      begin
        let t = Array.create (2 * n) a.v in
        Array.blit a.t 0 t 0 n;
        a.t <- t;
        t.(i) <- v;
      end
  end;;
```

Now, we can define the instance function. The polymorphic variables are created first. Then, when we meet variables that have not been created, we know that they should be shared rather than duplicated.

```
let type_instance (q, t) =
  let table = Iarray.create 7 (tvar()) in
  let poly = marker() in
  let copy_var t =
      let t' = tvar() in let p = marker() in
      t.mark <- p; Iarray.set table (p - poly) t'; t' in
  let q' = List.map copy_var q in
  let rec visit t =
    let t = repr t in
    if t.mark > poly then Iarray.get table (t.mark -poly)
    else
      begin match desc t with
    | Tvar _ | Tcon (_, []) -> t
    | Tcon (g, l) ->
        let t' = copy_var t in
        t'.texp <- Desc (Tcon (g, List.map visit l)); t'
      end in
  visit t;;
```

### Exercise 5, page 448

The function `visit_type` visit all nodes of a type that are not marked to be `excluded` and has not yet been `visited` and applying a function `f` to each visited none.

```
let visit_type exclude visited f t = let rec visit t =
```

```
    let t = repr t in
    if t.mark = exclude || t.mark == visited then ()
    else
      begin
        t.mark <- visited; f t;
        match desc t with
      | Tvar _ -> ()
      | Tcon (g, l) -> List.iter visit l
      end in
  visit t;;
```

The generalization mark variables that are free in the environment, then list variables in the type that are noted mark as free in the environment.

```
  let generalizable tenv t0 =
    let inenv = marker() in
    let mark m t = (repr t).mark <- m in
    let visit_asumption (x, (q, t)) =
      let bound = marker() in
      List.iter (mark bound) q; visit_type bound inenv ignore t in
    List.iter visit_asumption tenv;
    let ftv = ref [] in
    let collect t = match desc t with Tvar _ -> ftv := t::!ftv | _ -> () in
    let free = marker() in
    visit_type inenv free collect t0;
   ! ftv;;
  let x = tvar();;
  generalizable [] (tarrow x x);;
```

## Exercise 6, page 450

It suffices to remark there is a subterm $f\ f$ in a context where $f$ is bound to a lambda. Hence both occurrences of $f$ must have the same type, which is not possible since the type of the right occurrence should be the domain of the (arrow) type of the other one.

## Exercise 7, page 450

```
  let fact' fact x = if x = 0 then 1 else x * fact (x-1);;
  let fact x = fix fact' x;;
```

### Exercise 9, page 451

$$
\begin{array}{l}
\textbf{let rec } f'_1 = \lambda f_2.\lambda f_3.\lambda x.\ \textbf{let } f_1 = f'_1\ f_2\ f_3 \textbf{ in} \\
\qquad\qquad\qquad\qquad\quad a_1 \\
\textbf{in} \\
\textbf{let rec } f'_2 = \qquad \lambda f_3.\lambda x.\ \textbf{let } f_2 = f'_2\ f_3 \textbf{ in} \\
\qquad\qquad\qquad\qquad\quad \textbf{let } f_1 = f'_1\ f_2\ f_3 \textbf{ in} \\
\qquad\qquad\qquad\qquad\quad a_2 \\
\textbf{in} \\
\textbf{let rec } f'_3 = \qquad\quad \lambda x.\ \textbf{let } f_3 = f'_3 \textbf{ in} \\
\qquad\qquad\qquad\qquad\quad \textbf{let } f_2 = f'_2\ f_3 \textbf{ in} \\
\qquad\qquad\qquad\qquad\quad \textbf{let } f_1 = f'_1\ f_2\ f_3 \textbf{ in} \\
\qquad\qquad\qquad\qquad\quad a_3 \\
\textbf{in} \\
a
\end{array}
$$

### Exercise 10, page 451

Let us be lazy and use `ocaml -rectypes`:

```
let fix =
 (fun f' ->
     ( fun f -> (fun x -> f' (f f) x))
     ( fun f -> (fun x -> f' (f f) x))
 );;
```

```
val fix : (('a -> 'b) -> 'a -> 'b) -> 'a -> 'b = <fun>
```

```
let fact = fix fact' in fact 5;;
```

```
- : int = 120
```

```
let fix f' = let g f x = f' (f f) x in g g;;
```

```
val fix : (('a -> 'b) -> 'a -> 'b) -> 'a -> 'b = <fun>
```

```
let fact = fix fact' in fact 5;;
```

```
- : int = 120
```

### Exercise 11, page 451

```
let print_type t =
  let cyclic = marker() in
  begin try acyclic t
  | with Cycle l -> List.iter (fun t -> (repr t).mark <- cyclic) l;
  end;
  let named = marker() in
  let rec print k out t =
    let string x = Printf.fprintf out x in
```

```
let paren p f =
  if k > p then string "("; f(); if k > p then string ")" in
let t = repr t in
if t.mark > named then string "'a%d" (t.mark - named)
else
  begin match desc t with
  | Tvar n ->
      t.mark <- marker(); string "'a%d" (t.mark - named)
  | Tcon (Tint, []) ->
      string "int"
  | Tcon (Tarrow, [t1; t2]) when t.mark = cyclic ->
      t.mark <- marker();
      string "(%a -> %a as 'a%d)"
     (  print 1) t1 (print 1) t2 (t.mark - named);
  | Tcon (Tarrow, [t1; t2]) ->
      paren 0 (fun() ->
        string "%a -> %a" (print 1) t1 (print 1) t2)
  | Tcon (g, l) -> raise (Arity (t, t))
  end in
print 0 stdout t;;
```

### Exercise 12, page 452

The only way the type-checker is by finding unbound variables, or by unification errors. The former cannot occur with closed terms. In turn, unification can failed either with occur check or with clashes when attempting to unify two terms with different top symbols. Recursive types removes occur-check. In the absence of primitive operations, types are either variables or arrow types. The only type constructor is →, so that there will never be any clash during unification.

### Exercise 13, page 455

The only difficulty comes from the `Joker` card, which can be used in place of any other card. As a result, we cannot use a notion of binary equivalence of two cards, which would not be transitive. Instead, we define an asymmetric relation `agrees_with`: for instance, the card `Joker` agrees with `King`, but not the converse. For convenience, we also define the relation `disagree_with`, which is the negation of the symmetric relation `agrees_with`.

```
let agrees_with x y =
  match x, y with
    Card u, Card v -> u.name = v.name
  | _, Joker -> true
  | Joker, Card _ -> false
let disagrees_with x y = not (agrees_with y x);;
```

We actually provide a more general solution `find_similar` that searches sets of `k` similar cards among a `hand`. This function is defined by induction. If the `hand` is empty, there is no solution. If the first element of the `hand` is a `Joker`, we search for sets of `k-1` similar elements in the rest of the `hand` and add the `Joker` in front of each set. Otherwise, the first element of `hand` is a regular card `h`: we first search for the set of all elements matching the card `h` in the rest of the hand; this set constitutes a solution if its size if at least `k`; then, we add all other solutions among the rest of the hand that disagree with `h`. Otherwise, the solutions are only those that disagree with `h`.

```
let rec find_similar k hand =
  match hand with
  | []   -> []
  | Joker :: t ->
     List.map (fun p -> Joker::p) (find_similar (k - 1) t)
  | h :: t ->
     let similar_to_h = h :: List.find_all (agrees_with h) t in
     let others =
       find_similar k (List.find_all (disagrees_with h) t) in
     if List.length similar_to_h >= k then similar_to_h :: others
     else others;;
let find_carre = find_similar 4;;
```

Here is an example of search:

```
find_carre
 [ king Spade; Joker; king Diamond; Joker; king Heart;
   king Club; card Queen Spade; card Queen Club; club_jack ];;
```

```
- : card list list =
[[ Card {suit=Spade; name=King}; Joker; Card {suit=Diamond; name=King};
   Joker; Card {suit=Heart; name=King}; Card {suit=Club; name=King}];
 [ Joker; Joker; Card {suit=Spade; name=Queen};
   Card {suit=Club; name=Queen}]]
```

### Exercise 15, page 456

It would still be correct if $\tau_i$ contains a variable that does not belong to $\overline{\alpha}$, since this variable would not be generalized in the types of constructors and destructors. (Of course, it would be unsafe to generalize such a variable: for instance, one could then define **type** $g$ = $C^g$ `of` $\alpha$ with $C^g$: $\forall\alpha.\alpha \rightarrow g$ and $f : \forall\alpha,\beta.g \rightarrow (\alpha \rightarrow \beta) \rightarrow \beta$ and assign any type to the expression $e \stackrel{\triangle}{=}$ `match` $C^g$ 1 `with` $C^g\ y \Rightarrow y \equiv f\ (C^g\ 1)\ (\lambda y.y)$, which reduces to the integer 1.)

Conversely, it is safe, although strange and useless, that $\overline{\alpha}$ contains superfluous variables. Consider for instance the definition **type** $g(\alpha) = C^g$ `of int`. Then $g1$ would have type $g(\alpha)$ for any type $\alpha$.

Note that the latter is allowed in OCaml, while the former is rejected.

### Exercise 16, page 456

We may use the following type definition: **type** `bool = True of unit | False of unit` and see the expression `if` $a$ `then` $a_1$ `else` $a_2$ as syntactic sugar for `match`$_{\texttt{bool}}$ $a$ `with True` $x \Rightarrow a_1$ | `False` $x \Rightarrow a_2$.

**Exercise 17, page 456**

The generalization is to allow constructors of any arity.

$$\texttt{type } g(\overline{\tau}) = C^g \texttt{ of } \overline{\tau}_i \mid \ldots C^g \texttt{ of } \overline{\tau}_n$$

This is rather easy and left as an exercise. Then, one could define:

$$\begin{array}{l} \textbf{type } (\alpha_1, \alpha_2)\ (\_ * \_) = (\_,\_) \texttt{ of } (\alpha_1,\ \alpha_2) \\ \texttt{fst} \stackrel{\triangle}{=} \lambda z.(F_* \ z\ (\lambda x.\lambda y.x)) \\ \texttt{snd} \stackrel{\triangle}{=} \lambda z.(F_* \ z\ (\lambda x.\lambda y.y)) \end{array}$$

**Exercise 18, page 457**

```
type value = Value of (value -> value);;
let fold f = Value f
let unfold (Value f) = f;;
```

**Exercise 18 (continued)**

$$\begin{array}{rl} [x] & = x \\ [\lambda x.a] & = \texttt{fold}\ (\lambda x.[a]) \\ [a_1\ a_2] & = \texttt{unfold}\ ([a_1]\ [a_2]) \end{array}$$

**Exercise 18 (continued)** Here, let us use the compiler! For sake of readability, we abbreviate fold and unfold.

```
let ( ! )  f = fold f and  ( @ ) a1 a2 = unfold a1 a2;;
let fix =
 !( fun f' ->
     !(  fun f -> !(fun x -> f' @ (f @ f) @ x))
        @ !( fun f -> !(fun x -> f' @ (f @ f) @ x))
  );;
```

**Exercise 19, page 458**

$$\begin{array}{l} \textbf{type } h_1'(\overline{\alpha}, \alpha_2) = \tau_1[\alpha_2/h_2(\overline{\alpha})] \\ \textbf{type } h_2(\overline{\alpha}) = \tau_2[h_1'(\overline{\alpha}, h_2(\overline{\alpha}))/h_1(\overline{\alpha})] \\ \textbf{type } h_1(\overline{\alpha}) = h_1'(\overline{\alpha}, h_2(\overline{\alpha})) \end{array}$$

## Exercise 20, page 462

The function `fix` should take as argument a function `f'` and return a function `f` so that `f x` is equal to `f' f x`. The solution is to store `f` in a reference `r`. We temporarily create the reference `r` with a dummy function (that is not meant to be used). Assuming that the reference will later contain the correct version of `f`, we can define `f` as `fun x -> f' !r x`. Hence, the following solution:

```
let fix f' =
  let r = ref (fun _ -> raise (Failure "fix")) in
  let f x = f' !r x in
  r := f; ! r;;
```

```
val fix : (('a -> 'b) -> 'a -> 'b) -> 'a -> 'b = <fun>
```

Note that the exception should never be raised because the content of the reference is overridden by `f` before being reference is used.

We could also use the option type to initialized the content of the reference to `None` and replace it later with `Some f`. However, would not avoid raising an exception if the value of the reference where to be `None` when being read, even though this situation should never occur dynamically in a correct implementation.

As an example, we define the factorial function:

```
let fact' fact n = if n > 0 then n * fact (n−1) else 1 in
fix fact' 6;;
```

```
- : int = 720
```

## Exercise 22, page 463

The answer is positive. The reason is that exceptions hide the types of values that they communicate, which may be recursive types.

We first to define two inverse functions `fold` and `unfold`, using the following exception to mask types of values:

```
exception Hide of ((unit -> unit) -> (unit -> unit));;

let fold f = fun (x : unit) -> (raise (Hide f); ())
let unfold f = try (f(): unit); fun x -> x with Hide y -> y;;
```

```
val fold : ((unit -> unit) -> unit -> unit) -> unit -> unit = <fun>
val unfold : (unit -> unit) -> (unit -> unit) -> unit -> unit = <fun>
```

The two functions `fold` and `unfold` are inverse coercions between type $U \to U$ and $U$ where $U$ is `unit` $\to$ `unit`: They can be used to embed any term of the untyped lambda calculus into a well-typed term, using the following well-known encoding:

$$\begin{aligned} [x] &= x \\ [\lambda x.a] &= \texttt{fold}\ (\lambda x.[a]) \\ [a_1\ a_2] &= \texttt{unfold}\ ([a_1]\ [a_2]) \end{aligned}$$

In particular, [`fix`] is well-typed.

**Exercise 23, page 471**

They differ when being inherited:

```
class cm1 = object inherit c1 method m = () end
class cm2 = object inherit c2 method m = () end;;
```

The method c of class cm2 returns an object of type c2 instead of cm2, as checked below:

```
((new cm1)#c : cm1);;
((new cm2)#c : cm2);;
```

Also, while the types c1 and c2 are equal, the type cm1 is only a subtype of cm2.

**Exercise 24, page 471**

```
class backup =
  object (self)
    val mutable backup = None
    method save = backup <- Some (Oo.copy self)
    method restore =
      match backup with None -> self | Some x -> x
  end;;
```

**Exercise 26, page 472**

The only problem is the method concat that is a pseudo-binary method. There are two possible solutions. The first is not to make it a binary method, and let the class be parametric:

```
class ['a] ostring s = object (self)
  val s = s
  method repr = s
  method concat (t:'a) = {< s = s ^ t # repr >}
end;;
```

The second, more natural solution is to make concat a binary method by making the parameter be the self-type.

```
class ostring s = object (self : 'a)
  val s = s
  method repr = s
  method concat (t:'a) = {< s = s ^ t # repr >}
end;;
```

**Exercise 28, page 476**

For sake of readability, we only describe simplified rules covering all cases.

$$\frac{\langle p : \alpha_p; q : \tau_q; 1\rangle \doteq \langle p : \tau_p; r : \tau_r; 1\rangle \doteq e}{\langle p : \alpha_p; q : \tau_q; r : \tau_r; 1\rangle \doteq e \wedge \alpha_p \doteq \tau_p} \rightsquigarrow \qquad \frac{\langle p : \tau_p; 1\rangle \doteq \langle p : \alpha_p; q : \tau_q; 0\rangle \doteq e}{\langle p : \tau_p; q : \tau_q; 0\rangle \doteq e \wedge \alpha_p \doteq \tau_p} \rightsquigarrow$$

$$\frac{\langle p : \tau_p; 0\rangle \doteq \langle p : \alpha_p; 0\rangle \doteq e}{\langle p : \alpha_p; 0\rangle \doteq e \wedge \alpha_p \doteq \tau_p} \rightsquigarrow \qquad \frac{\langle q : \tau_q; 0\rangle \doteq \langle r : \tau_r; 0\rangle \doteq e}{\bot} \rightsquigarrow$$

The generalization is obvious: the occurrences of $p : \alpha_p$, $p : \tau_p$, $q : \tau_q$, and $r : \tau_r$, can be replaced by finite mappings from labels to types $P$, $P'$, $Q$, and $R$ of disjoint domain except for $P$ and $P'$ of identical domain.

These (generalized) rules should be added to those for simple types, where rule FAIL and DECOMPOSE are not extended to the object type constructor, nor the row constructors.

**Exercise 33, page 505**

```
exit 0;;
exit 1;;
```

**Exercise 34, page 508**

```
for i = 1 to Array.length Sys.argv - 1
do print_string Sys.argv.(i); print_char ' ' done;
print_newline();;
```

**Exercise 35, page 509**

```
let echo chan =
  try while true do print_endline (input_line chan) done
  with End_of_file -> ();;

if Array.length Sys.argv <= 1 then echo stdin
else
  for i = 1 to Array.length Sys.argv - 1
  do
    let chan = open_in Sys.argv.(i) in
    echo chan;
    close_in chan
  done;;
```

```
let pattern =
  if Array.length Sys.argv < 2 then
    begin
      print_endline "Usage: grep REGEXP file1 .. file2";
      exit 1
    end
  else
    Str.regexp Sys.argv.(1);;

let process_line l =
  try let _ = Str.search_forward pattern l 0 in print_endline l
  with Not_found -> ()

let process_chan c =
  try while true do process_line (input_line c) done
  with End_of_file -> ();;

let process_file f =
  let c = open_in f in process_chan c; close_in c;;

let () =
  if Array.length Sys.argv > 2 then
    for i = 2 to Array.length Sys.argv - 1
    do process_file  Sys.argv.(i) done
  else
    process_chan stdin;;
```

## Exercise 36, page 509

```
type count = {
  mutable chars : int;
  mutable lines : int;
  mutable words : int;
};;

let new_count() = {chars = 0; lines = 0; words = 0};;
let total = new_count();;

let cumulate wc =
  total.chars <- total.chars + wc.chars;
  total.lines <- total.lines + wc.lines;
  total.words <- total.words + wc.words;;

let rec counter ic iw wc =
  let c = input_char ic in
  wc.chars <- wc.chars + 1;
  match c with
  | ' ' | '\t' ->
      if iw then wc.words <- wc.words + 1 else ();
```

```
      counter ic false wc
  | '\n' ->
      wc.lines <- wc.lines + 1;
      if iw then wc.words <- wc.words + 1 else ();
      counter ic false wc
  | c ->
      counter ic true wc;;

let count_channel ic wc =
  try counter ic false wc with
  | End_of_file -> cumulate wc; close_in ic;;

let output_results s wc =
  Printf.printf "%7d%8d%8d %s\n" wc.lines  wc.words wc.chars  s;;

let count_file file_name =
  try
    let ic = open_in file_name in
    let wc = new_count() in
    count_channel ic wc;
    output_results file_name wc;
  with Sys_error s -> print_string s; print_newline(); exit 2;;

let main () =
  let nb_files = Array.length Sys.argv - 1 in
  if nb_files > 0 then
    begin
      for i = 1 to nb_files do
        count_file Sys.argv.(i)
      done;
      if nb_files > 1 then output_results "total" total;
    end
  else
    begin
      let wc = new_count() in
      count_channel stdin wc;
      output_results "" wc;
    end;
  exit 0;;

main();;
```

## References


1. Martín Abadi and Luca Cardelli. *A theory of objects.* Springer, 1997.
2. Martín Abadi, Luca Cardelli, Benjamin C. Pierce, and Didier Rémy. Dynamic typing in polymorphic languages. *Journal of Functional Programming*, 5(1):111–130, January 1995.
3. Alexander Aiken and Edward L. Wimmers. Type inclusion constraints and type inference. In *Conference on Functional Programming Languages and Computer Architecture*, pages 31–41. ACM press, 1993.
4. Davide Ancona and Elena Zucca. A theory of mixin modules: Basic and derived operators. *Mathematical Structures in Computer Science*, 8(4):401–446, August 1998.
5. Davide Ancona and Elena Zucca. A primitive calculus for module systems. In Gopalan Nadathur, editor, *PPDP'99 - International Conference on Principles and Practice of Declarative Programming*, volume 1702 of *Lecture Notes in Computer Science*, pages 62–79. Springer-Verlag, 1999.
6. Hans P. Barendregt. *The Lambda-Calulus. Its Syntax and Semantics*, volume 103 of *Studies in Logic and The Foundations of Mathematics.* North-Holland, 1984.
7. Sylvain Boulmé, Thérèse Hardin, and Renaud Rioboo. Modules, objets et calcul formel. In *Actes des Journées Francophones des Langages Applicatifs.* INRIA, 1999.
8. François Bourdoncle and Stephan Merz. Type checking higher-order polymorphic multi-methods. In *Proceedings of the 24th ACM Conference on Principles of Programming Languages*, pages 302–315, July 1997.
9. Kim B. Bruce, Luca Cardelli, Giuseppe Castagna, the Hopkins Objects Group (Jonathan Eifrig, Scott Smith, Valery Trifonov), Gary T. Leavens, and Benjamin Pierce. On binary methods. *Theory and Practice of Object Systems*, 1(3):221–242, 1996.
10. Kim B. Bruce, Martin Odersky, and Philip Wadler. A statically safe alternative to virtual types. In *European Conference on Object-Oriented Programming (ECOOP)*, Brussels, July 1998.
11. Luca Cardelli and Peter Wegner. On understanding types, data abstraction, and polymorphism. *Computing surveys*, 17(4):471–522, 1985.
12. Emmanuel Chailloux, Pascal Manoury, and Bruno Pagano. *Développement d'applications avec Objective Caml.* O'Reilly, 2000.
13. Craig Chambers. The Cecil Language: Specification & Rationale. Technical Report 93-03-05, University of Washington, 1993.
14. Dominique Clément, Joëlle Despeyroux, Thierry Despeyroux, and Gilles Kahn. A simple applicative language: Mini-ML. In *proceedings of the conference Lisp and Functional Programming, LFP'86.* ACM Press, August 1986. Also appears as INRIA Research Report RR-529, May 1986.
15. Guy Cousineau and Michel Mauny. *Approche fonctionnelle de la programmation.* Ediscience, 1995.
16. Luis Damas and Robin Milner. Principal type-schemes for functional programs. In *ACM Symposium on Principles of Programming Languages*, pages 207–212. ACM Press, 1982.
17. Catherine Dubois, François Rouaix, and Pierre Weis. Extensional polymorphism. In *Proceedings of the 22th ACM Conference on Principles of Programming Languages*, January 1995.

18. Dominic Duggan and Constantinos Sourelis. Mixin modules. In *International Conference on Functional Programming 96*, pages 262–273. ACM Press, 1996.
19. J. Eifrig, S. Smith, and V. Trifonov. Type inference for recursively constrained types and its application to OOP. In *Mathematical Foundations of Programming Semantics*, 1995.
20. Kathleen Fisher and John Reppy. The design of a class mechanism for Moby. In *Proceedings of the ACM SIGPLAN '99 Conference on Programming Languages, design and Implementations*, pages 37–49, Atlanta, May 1999. ACM SIGPLAN, acm press.
21. Kathleen Fisher and John Reppy. Extending Moby with inheritance-based subtyping. In *Proceedings of the 14th European Conference on Object-Oriented Programming*, 2000.
22. Alexandre Frey and François Bourdoncle. The Jazz home page. Free software available at `http://www.cma.ensmp.fr/jazz/index.html`.
23. Jacques Garrigue. Programming with polymorphic variants. In *ML Workshop*, September 1998.
24. Jacques Garrigue and Didier Rémy. Extending ML with semi-explicit higher-order polymorphism. In *International Symposium on Theoretical Aspects of Computer Software*, volume 1281 of *Lecture Notes in Computer Science*, pages 20–46. Springer, September 1997.
25. Carl A. Gunter. *Semantics of Programming Languages: Structures and Techniques.* Foundations of Computing. MIT Press, 1992.
26. Thérèse Accart Hardin and Véronique Donzeau-Gouge Viguié. *Concepts et outils de programmation — Le style fonctionnel, le style impératif avec CAML et Ada.* Interéditions, 1992.
27. Robert Harper and Mark Lillibridge. A type-theoretic approach to higher-order modules with sharing. In *ACM Symposium on Principles of Programming Languages*, pages 123–137. ACM Press, 1994.
28. F. Henglein. *Polymorphic Type Inference and Semi-Unification.* PhD thesis, Courant Institute of Mathematical Sciences, New York University., 1989.
29. J. Roger Hindley and Jonathan P. Seldin. *Introduction to Combinators and λ-calculus.* Volume 1 of London Mathematical Society Student texts. Cambridge University Press, 1986.
30. Paul Hudak. *The Haskell School of Expression: Learning Functional Programming through Multimedia.* Cambridge University Press, 2000.
31. Gérard Huet. *Résolution d'équations dans les langages d'ordre* $1, 2, \ldots, \omega$. Thèse de doctorat d'état, Université Paris 7, 1976.
32. Gérard Huet. The zipper. *Journal of Functional Programming*, 7(5):549–554, 1997.
33. Lalita A. Jategaonkar and John C. Mitchell. ML with extended pattern matching and subtypes (preliminary version). In *Proceedings of the ACM Conference on Lisp and Functional Programming*, pages 198–211, Snowbird, Utah, July 1988.
34. Mark P. Jones. *Qualified Types: Theory and Practice.* Cambridge University Press, November 1994.
35. Mark P. Jones and Simon Peyton Jones. Lightweight extensible records for haskell. In *Proceedings of the 1999 Haskell Workshop*, number UU-CS-1999-28 in Technical report, 1999.
36. Simon Peyton Jones and John Hughes. Report on the programming language Haskell 98. Technical report, `http://www.haskell.org`, 1999.
37. Gilles Kahn. Natural semantics. In *Symposium on Theoretical Aspects of Computer Science*, pages 22–39, 1987.

38. Claude Kirchner and Jean-Pierre Jouannaud. Solving equations in abstract algebras: a rule-based survey of unification. Research Report 561, Université de Paris Sud, Orsay, France, April 1990.
39. Konstantin Läufer and Martin Odersky. Polymorphic type inference and abstract data types. *ACM Transactions on Programming Languages and Systems*, 16(5):1411–1430, September 1994.
40. Xavier Leroy. Polymorphic typing of an algorithmic language. Research report 1778, INRIA, 1992.
41. Xavier Leroy. *Typage polymorphe d'un langage algorithmique.* Thèse de doctorat, Université Paris 7, 1992.
42. Xavier Leroy. Applicative functors and fully transparent higher-order modules. In *ACM Symposium on Principles of Programming Languages*, pages 142–153. ACM Press, 1995.
43. Xavier Leroy. A syntactic theory of type generativity and sharing. *Journal of Functional Programming*, 6(5):667–698, 1996.
44. Xavier Leroy. A modular module system. *Journal of Functional Programming*, 10(3):269–303, 2000.
45. Xavier Leroy and Michel Mauny. Dynamics in ML. *Journal of Functional Programming*, 3(4):431–463, 1993.
46. David B. MacQueen and Mads Tofte. A semantics for higher-order functors. In D. Sannella, editor, *Programming languages and systems – ESOP '94*, volume 788 of *Lecture Notes in Computer Science*, pages 409–423. Springer-Verlag, 1994.
47. Alberto Martelli and Ugo Montanari. An efficient unification algorithm. *ACM Transactions on Programming Languages and Systems*, 4(2):258–282, 1982.
48. Robin Milner and Mads Tofte. *Commentary on Standard ML.* The MIT Press, 1991.
49. Robin Milner, Mads Tofte, Robert Harper, and David MacQueen. *The definition of Standard ML (revised).* The MIT Press, 1997.
50. John C. Mitchell. *Foundations for Programming Languages.* MIT Press, 1996.
51. Martin Odersky and Konstantin Läufer. Putting type annotations to work. In *Proceedings of the 23th ACM Conference on Principles of Programming Languages*, pages 54–67, January 1996.
52. Martin Odersky, Martin Sulzmann, and Martin Wehr. Type inference with constrained types. *TAPOS*, 5(1), 1999.
53. Martin Odersky, Philip Wadler, and Martin Wehr. A second look at overloading. In *Proc. ACM Conf. on Functional Programming and Computer Architecture*, pages 135–146, June 1995.
54. Martin Odersky, Christoph Zenger, and Matthias Zenger. Colored local type inference. In *ACM Symposium on Principles of Programming Languages*, 2001.
55. Atsushi Ohori. A polymorphic record calculus and its compilation. *ACM Transactions on Programming Languages and Systems*, 17(6):844–895, 1996.
56. Lawrence C. Paulson. *ML for the working programmer.* Cambridge University Press, 1991.
57. Benjamin C. Pierce. Bounded quantification is undecidable. *Information and Computation*, 112(1):131–165, July 1994. Also in Carl A. Gunter and John C. Mitchell, editors, *Theoretical Aspects of Object-Oriented Programming: Types, Semantics, and Language Design* (MIT Press, 1994). Summary in *ACM Symposium on Principles of Programming Languages, Albuquerque, New Mexico.*
58. Benjamin C. Pierce and David N. Turner. Local type inference. In *Proceedings of the 25th ACM Conference on Principles of Programming Languages*, 1998. Full version available as Indiana University CSCI Technical Report 493.

59. G. D. Plotkin. A Structural Approach to Operational Semantics. Technical Report DAIMI FN-19, University of Aarhus, 1981.
60. François Pottier. Simplifying subtyping constraints: a theory. To appear in *Information & Computation*, August 2000.
61. Didier Rémy. Extending ML type system with a sorted equational theory. Research Report 1766, Institut National de Recherche en Informatique et Automatisme, Rocquencourt, BP 105, 78 153 Le Chesnay Cedex, France, 1992.
62. Didier Rémy. Programming objects with ML-ART: An extension to ML with abstract and record types. In Masami Hagiya and John C. Mitchell, editors, *International Symposium on Theoretical Aspects of Computer Software*, number 789 in Lecture Notes in Computer Science, pages 321–346, Sendai, Japan, April 1994. Springer-Verlag.
63. Didier Rémy. Type inference for records in a natural extension of ML. In Carl A. Gunter and John C. Mitchell, editors, *Theoretical Aspects Of Object-Oriented Programming. Types, Semantics and Language Design.* MIT Press, 1994.
64. Didier Rémy and Jérôme Vouillon. Objective ML: An effective object-oriented extension to ML. *Theory And Practice of Object Systems*, 4(1):27–50, 1998. A preliminary version appeared in the proceedings of the 24th ACM Conference on Principles of Programming Languages, 1997.
65. John C. Reynolds. *Theories of Programming Languages.* Cambridge University Press, 1998.
66. Jon G. Riecke and Christopher A. Stone. Privacy via subsumption. *Theory and Practice of Object Systems*, 1999.
67. Claudio V. Russo. *Types for modules.* PhD thesis, University of Edinburgh, 1998.
68. Simon Thompson. *Haskell: the craft of functional programming.* Addison-Wesley, 1999.
69. Jérôme Vouillon. Combining subsumption and binary methods: An object calculus with views. In *ACM Symposium on Principles of Programming Languages.* ACM Press, 2000.
70. Jérôme Vouillon. *Conception et réalisation d'une extension du langage ML avec des objets.* Thèe de doctorat, Université Paris 7, October 2000.
71. Mitchell Wand. Complete type inference for simple objects. In D. Gries, editor, *Second Symposium on Logic In Computer Science*, pages 207–276, Ithaca, New York, June 1987. IEEE Computer Society Press.
72. Pierre Weis and Xavier Leroy. *Le langage Caml.* Dunod, 1999.
73. Joe B. Wells. Typability and type checking in system $f$ are equivalent and undecidable. *Annals of Pure and Applied Logic*, 98(1–3):111–156, 1999.
74. Andrew K. Wright and Matthias Felleisen. A syntactic approach to type soundness. *Information and Computation*, 115(1):38–94, 1994.

## List of All Exercises

### Section 2



### Section 3



### Section 4



### Section 5

**Section 6**

| | | |
|---|---|---|
| 32, *85* | | Project —A small subset of the FOC library |

**Appendix A**

| | | |
|---|---|---|
| 33, *89* | * | Unix commands true and false |
| 34, *92* | * | Unix command echo |
| 35, *93* | ** | Unix cat and grep commands |
| 36, *93* | ** | Unix wc command |

# Index